macroeconomics

MACROECONOMICS

sixth edition

RUDIGER DORNBUSCH

Department of Economics
Massachusetts Institute of Technology

STANLEY FISCHER

The World Bank
and
Department of Economics
Massachusetts Institute of Technology

McGraw-Hill, Inc.

New York   St. Louis   San Francisco   Auckland
Bogotá   Caracas   Lisbon   London   Madrid
Mexico City   Milan   Montreal   New Delhi
San Juan   Singapore   Sydney   Tokyo   Toronto

MACROECONOMICS

This book is printed on acid-free paper.

4 5 6 7 8 9 0   DOC   DOC   9 0 9 8 7 6 5 4

ISBN 0-07-017844-5

This book was set in Times Roman by Monotype
Composition Company. The editors were Scott D.
Stratford and Elaine Rosenberg; the designer was Joan
Greenfield; the production supervisor was Kathryn Porzio.
R. R. Donnelley & Sons Company was printer and binder.

Library of Congress Cataloging-in-Publication Data

Dornbusch, Rudiger.
   Macroeconomics / Rudiger Dornbusch, Stanley
   Fischer.—6th ed.
      p.   cm.
   "International edition"
   Includes indexes.
   ISBN 0-07-017844-5 (hard: acid-free paper)
   1. Macroeconomics.   I. Fischer, Stanley.
   II. Title.
HB172.5.D67   1994
339—dc20   93-20536

ABOUT THE AUTHORS

RUDIGER DORNBUSCH did his undergraduate work in Switzerland and holds a Ph.D. from the University of Chicago. He has taught at Chicago, Rochester, and since 1975 at MIT. His research is primarily in international economics, with a major macroeconomic component. His special research interests are the behavior of exchange rates, high inflation and hyperinflation, and the international debt problem. He visits and lectures extensively in Europe and in Latin America, where he takes an active interest in problems of stabilization policy, and has held visiting appointments in Brazil and Argentina. His writing includes *Open Economy Macroeconomics* and, with Stanley Fischer and Richard Schmalensee, *Economics*. His interests in public policy take him frequently to testify before Congress and to participate in international conferences. He regularly contributes newspaper editorials on current policy issues here and abroad.

STANLEY FISCHER was an undergraduate at the London School of Economics and has a Ph.D. from MIT. He taught at the University of Chicago while Rudi Dornbusch was a student there, starting a long friendship and collaboration. From 1973 to 1987 he has taught at MIT and spent several leaves at the Hebrew University in Jerusalem. From 1988–1991, on leave from MIT, he was Vice President, Development Economics and Chief Economist, The World Bank, Washington, D.C. His main research interests are in economic growth and development, inflation and stabilization, indexation, and international and macroeconomics. He has published widely in these areas and participates regularly in scholarly meetings. He is the editor of the *NBER Macroeconomics Annual*, initiated by the National Bureau of Economic Research to bridge the gap betweeen theory and policy in the macroeconomic area.

To Eliana and Rhoda

CONTENTS IN BRIEF

CONTENTS

part two **AGGREGATE DEMAND, SUPPLY, AND GROWTH** *187*

PREFACE

When we decided to write a text on macroeconomics in 1977, we had in mind bringing the important lessons of the 1970s into mainstream teaching. Inflation was as much an issue then as deep recessions, but it was not integrated into the basic texts. There was a need for a textbook that could usefully guide students and teachers over the full range of business-cycle problems, whether the issue was how to stop inflation in an overheating economy or how to meet the challenge of creating employment in a depressed economy. At the time, the inflation problem was new to textbooks, and many of the standard answers to recession economics needed upgrading.

Now, 15 years later, we are at it again. This sixth edition of *Macroeconomics* reflects three concerns: First, we have maintained the middle-of-the-road approach. Students should learn foremost what is established and useful, not what is esoteric or at best speculative. There is plenty of room to bring in new ideas, but the emphasis must be on what can be asserted with great confidence as right and to the point. Second, we have tried to reflect the changing tone and emphasis that emerges from the past decade of macroeconomic events and scholarly research. There is no reason to belittle the powerful battle that has been going on in the profession; we do give it full and substantial coverage, but as reporters and teachers, not as proponents of a school. Third, we have been merciless in forcing ourselves to cut the material in this book—by nearly 25 percent. There is an enormous amount that could be added, but the challenge for the teacher is clearly to focus on what is central, to teach a way of thinking, giving the student the framework and the references to go further if he or she wishes to do so. We are confident we have accomplished that goal.

Our book is used today not only in the United States but around the world, in many languages and far more countries, from Canada to Argentina to Australia, all over Eurupe, in India, Indonesia, and Japan, from China and Albania to Russia. Even before the Czech Republic gained independence from communism, an underground translation was secretly used in macroeconomics seminars at Charles University in Prague. There is no greater pleasure for teachers and textbook authors than to see their efforts succeed so concretely around the world.

ACKNOWLEDGMENTS

In going through six editions we have accumulated an enormous amount of intellectual debt. Students and teachers over the years have written to us to comment on their satisfaction with this book, but they also have not been shy in pointing out errors and shortcomings. If the book today is strikingly better, they all deserve much of the credit, and we want them to know of our gratitude and of our openness to further suggestions.

We have in the past acknowledged our debts to correspondents, colleagues, and students individually. There is no longer room to do that, but we have to depart from our new rule to thank Michael Chapman for his superb assistance in preparing this sixth edition.

In addition, McGraw-Hill would like to thank the reviewers of this edition. They include Professors Robert Bannon, University of California, Santa Cruz; Daniel Bergan, Northeastern Illinois University; David Finley, Colby College; Juergen Fleck, Hollins College; Edward Gamber, Lafayette College; William Gibson, University of Vermont; Rae Jean Goodman, U.S. Naval Academy; Steven Husted, University of Pittsburgh; Beth Ingram, University of Iowa; Robert Lind, Cornell University; Robert Murphy, Boston College; and John Veitch, University of Southern California.

ADDITIONAL MATERIAL

An *Instructor's Manual* and *Text Bank* to accompany the text have been prepared by Professor Juergen Fleck of Hollins College. The *Instructor's Manual* has been substantially updated and includes chapter summaries, learning objectives, solutions to the end-of-chapter problems, and many additional problems (and their solutions) to be used for class discussion, homework assignments, or examination questions. The *Test Bank* has been expanded and now includes 1000 questions.

The *Study Guide,* by Richard Startz of the University of Washington—Seattle, that accompanies the text has again been revised and brought up to date. The *Study Guide* contains a wide range of questions, starting from the very easy and progressing in each chapter to material that will challenge the more advanced student. It is a great help in studying, particularly since active learning is so important in mastering new material.

Learning can be made more active yet with the help of the software program. *PC-Macroeconomics,* developed by Professors F. Gerard Adams of the University of Pennsylvania and Eugene Kroch of Villanova University. It is available for purchase combined with the text for the first time, as well as separate from the text. The program follows the sequencing in the text and patiently builds the analytical framework by using empirical data that allow students to understand macroeconomics in a step-by-step integration of text, data, and graphics. Students can either view the analysis in a demonstration mode, choose to interact within the parameters set in the program, or change those parameters as desired. There is also a "Policy Game" that gives students meaningful experience in analyzing various policy options. *PC-Macroeconomics* uses the Lotus 1-2-3 application program (version 2.0 or higher) for IBM-PCs and most compatibles. The computer problems appear in the textbook at the end of each chapter, and are indicated by 🖫 . A new Appendix at the end of the text gives full instructions for using the software.

Good luck!

Rudiger Dornbusch
Stanley Fischer

part one

INTRODUCING THE ECONOMY: FACTS AND FIRST MODELS

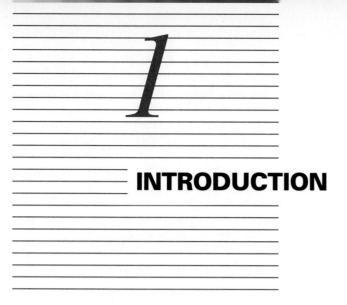

INTRODUCTION

*M*acroeconomics is concerned with the behavior of the economy as a whole—with booms and recessions, the economy's total output of goods and services and the growth of output, the rates of inflation and unemployment, the balance of payments, and exchange rates. Macroeconomics deals both with long-run economic growth and with the short-run fluctuations that constitute the business cycle.

Macroeconomics focuses on the economic behavior and policies that affect consumption and investment, the dollar and the trade balance, the determinants of changes in wages and prices, monetary and fiscal policies, the money stock, the federal budget, interest rates, and the national debt.

In brief, macroeconomics deals with the major economic issues and problems of the day. To understand these issues, we have to reduce the complicated details of the economy to manageable essentials. *Those essentials lie in the interactions among the goods, labor, and assets markets of the economy, and in the interactions among national economies whose residents trade with each other.*

In dealing with the essentials, we go beyond details of the behavior of individual economic units, such as households and firms, and the determination of prices in particular markets, which are the subject matter of microeconomics. In macroeconomics we deal with the market for goods as a whole, treating all the markets for different goods—such as the markets for agricultural products and for medical services—as a single market. Similarly, we deal with the labor market as a whole, abstracting from differences between the markets for, say, unskilled labor and doctors. We deal with the assets markets as a whole, abstracting from differences between the markets for IBM shares and for Rembrandt paintings. The benefit of the abstraction is increased understanding of the vital interactions among the goods, labor, and assets markets. Passing over the details of thousands of individual markets allows us to focus more clearly on these key markets. The cost of the abstraction is that omitted details sometimes matter.

The difference between microeconomics and macroeconomics is primarily one of emphasis and exposition. In studying price determination in a single industry, it is convenient for microeconomists to assume that prices in other industries are given. In macroeconomics, in which we study the average price level, it is for the most part sensible to ignore changes in relative prices of goods among different industries. In microeconomics, it is convenient to assume that the total income of all consumers is given and then to ask how consumers divide their spending of that income among different goods. In macroeconomics, by contrast, the aggregate level of income or spending is among the key variables to be studied.

It is only a short step from studying how the macroeconomy works to asking how to make it perform better. The fundamental questions are, *Can* the government and *should* the government intervene in the economy to improve its performance? The great macroeconomists have always enjoyed a keen interest in the application of macrotheory to policy. This was true in the case of John Maynard Keynes and is true of American leaders in the field, including the older Nobel laureate generation, such as Milton Friedman of the University of Chicago and the Hoover Institution, Franco Modigliani and Robert Solow of MIT, and James Tobin of Yale University. The younger leaders, such as Robert Barro and Martin Feldstein of Harvard University, Robert Lucas of the University of Chicago, and Robert Hall, Thomas Sargent, and John Taylor of Stanford University, despite being more—and in some cases altogether—skeptical about the wisdom of active government policies, also have strong views on policy issues.

Because macroeconomics is closely related to the economic problems of the day, it does not yield its greatest rewards to those whose primary interest is theoretical. The need for compromise between the comprehensiveness of the theory and its manageability inevitably makes macrotheory a little untidy at the edges. And the emphasis in macroeconomics is on the manageability of the theory and on its applications. This book uses macroeconomics to illuminate economic events from the great depression through the 1990s. We refer continually to real world events to elucidate the meaning and the relevance of the theoretical material.

1-1 ISSUES AND CONTROVERSIES

There are three central issues on the research agenda in macroeconomics.

- How do we explain periods of high and persistent unemployment?

  For example, in the 1930s unemployment was over 20 percent for several years, and the postwar period has also seen high unemployment rates on several occasions. In the United States, unemployment reached 10.8 percent in 1982 and came down to 6 percent only at the end of the 1980s. By 1991–1992 it again exceeded 7 percent. Several European economies, including those of the United Kingdom and France, suffered double-digit unemployment during much of the eighties and again in 1992–1993.

  Macroeconomic research focuses on persistent unemployment as a central question. There are many theories of why persistent high unemployment is possible, and we shall develop the most important in this book. There is also the policy question of what should be done about unemployment. Some say not much and advocate a hands-off policy: the government should put in place appropriate unemployment compensation schemes but ought not otherwise undertake any special policies such as tax cuts to deal with unemployment. This view may seem extraordinary to someone new to economics and even to someone who has spent a life in the field. Others argue that the government should pursue an active fiscal policy, for instance, by cutting taxes and/or raising government spending when unemployment is high so as to create demand and hence jobs. Who is right?

- How do we explain inflation?

Why did prices in the United States rise by more than 10 percent a year in 1979 and 1980 and by less than 4 percent in 1992? Why did prices in Russia rise by 20 or even 30 percent per month in 1992? And what causes hyperinflations, when prices rise by much more than 1,000 percent per year, as they did in some Latin American countries in the 1980s and in Russia in 1992? The policy issues here are how to keep inflation low; and, if it is high, how to reduce it without causing a recession. For some the answer lies in getting central bank monetary policy right; for others the issue is much wider. Who is right?

- What determines economic growth?

Why has output per person risen more or less steadily in the United States at an annual rate of 1.7 percent, doubling every 41 years? And why has output grown more rapidly in Japan than in the United States over the past century? Will the Japanese economy keep growing more rapidly than the U.S. economy when income per person reaches the U.S. level—as, by some measures, it already has? For some the answer to achieving higher growth is active government policies in the area of infrastructure and technology; for others it is a minimum of government interference that sets the best framework for growth. Who is right?[1]

The questions of whether the government *can* and *should* do something about each of these issues and *what* is best to do have been at the center of macroeconomics for a long time. These questions continue to divide the profession, and every generation develops its own debate, reinterpreting past events or experiences in various parts of the world. The three leading issues identified here certainly do not exhaust the debate. There are, for example, questions about policy in the open economy: Should governments fix exchange rates such as the $/Deutsche mark rate or should exchange rates be market-determined? For some analysts a world system of fixed rates is a critical anti-inflation check—nobody can get much out of line. For others, flexible or market-determined rates are just another place where they believe markets are more appropriate than government intervention. Interestingly, macroeconomists can be classified into

---

[1]For an immediate glance at different perspectives see Robert L. Bartley, *The Seven Fat Years. And How to Do It Again* (New York: The Free Press, 1992), and Angus Maddison, *Dynamic Forces in Capitalist Development. A Long-Run Comparative View* (New York: Oxford University Press, 1992).

two broad schools of thought. With small variations—particularly on exchange rates—adherents of the two camps have almost predictable responses to most issues of macroeconomics and macroeconomic policy design.

Schools of Thought

There have long been two main intellectual traditions in macroeconomics. One school of thought believes that markets work best if left to themselves; the other believes that government intervention can significantly improve the operation of the economy. In the 1960s, the debate on these questions involved *monetarists*, led by Milton Friedman, on one side, and *Keynesians*, including Franco Modigliani and James Tobin, on the other. In the 1970s, the debate on much the same issues brought to the fore a new group—the *new classical macroeconomists*, who by and large replaced the monetarists in keeping up the argument against using active government policies to try to improve economic performance. On the other side are third-generation Keynesians; they may not share many of the detailed beliefs of Keynesians three or four decades ago, except the belief that government policy can help the economy perform better.

THE NEW CLASSICAL SCHOOL

The new classical macroeconomics, which developed in the 1970s, remained influential in the 1980s. This school of macroeconomics, which includes among its leaders Robert Lucas, Thomas Sargent, Robert Barro, and Edward Prescott and Neil Wallace of the University of Minnesota, shares many policy views with Friedman. It sees the world as one in which individuals act rationally in their self-interest in markets that adjust rapidly to changing conditions. The government, it is claimed, is likely only to make things worse by intervening. Their approach is a challenge to traditional macroeconomics, which sees a role for useful government action in an economy that is viewed as adjusting sluggishly, with slowly responding prices, poor information, and social customs impeding the rapid clearing of markets.

The central working assumptions of the new classical school are three:[2]

- Economic agents *maximize*. Households and firms make *optimal* decisions. This means that they use all available information in reaching decisions and that those decisions are the best possible in the circumstances in which they find themselves.
- Expectations are *rational*, which means they are statistically the best predictions of the future that can be made using the available information. Indeed, the new classical school is sometimes described as the *rational expectations school*, even though rational expectations is only one part of the theoretical approach of the new classical economists.[3] Rational expectations imply that people will eventually come to understand whatever government policy is being used, and thus that it is not possible to fool most of the people all the time or even most of the time.

---

[2] See Robert Lucas, *Models of Business Cycles* (Oxford: Basil Blackwell, 1987).
[3] The rational expectations assumption is also used by many economists outside the new classical paradigm.

■ *Markets clear.* There is no reason why firms or workers would not adjust wages or prices if that would make them better off. Accordingly prices and wages adjust in order to equate supply and demand; in other words, markets clear. Market clearing is a powerful assumption, as we shall see presently.

One dramatic implication of these assumptions, which seem so reasonable individually, is that there is no possibility for *involuntary* unemployment. Any unemployed person who really wants a job will offer to cut his or her wage until the wage is low enough to attract an offer from some employer. Similarly, anyone with an excess supply of goods on the shelf will cut prices so as to sell. Flexible adjustment of wages and prices leaves all individuals *all the time* in a situation in which they work as much as they want and firms produce as much as they want.

The essence of the new classical approach is the assumption that markets are continuously in equilibrium. In particular, new classical macroeconomists regard as incomplete or unsatisfactory any theory that leaves open the possibility that private individuals could make themselves better off by trading among themselves. As Lucas put it, "there are no $50 bills lying on the sidewalk," meaning that if there were ways in which individuals could improve their material position, they would do so.

Adherents of the new classical school do not doubt that the great depression did take place, and they recognize that the measured unemployment rate occasionally reaches more than 10 percent. But they have developed explanations that try to account for high unemployment even when the new classical premises hold.

THE NEW KEYNESIANS

The new classical group remains highly influential in today's macroeconomics. But a new generation of scholars, the *new Keynesians*, mostly trained in the Keynesian tradition but moving beyond it, emerged in the 1980s. The group includes among others George Akerlof and Janet Yellen and David Romer of the University of California–Berkeley, Olivier Blanchard of MIT, Greg Mankiw and Larry Summers of Harvard, and Ben Bernanke of Princeton University. They do not believe that markets clear all the time but seek to understand and explain exactly why markets can fail.[4]

The new Keynesians argue that markets sometimes do not clear even when individuals are looking out for their own interests. Both information problems and costs of changing prices lead to some price rigidities, which help cause macroeconomic fluctuations in output and employment. For example, in the labor market, firms that cut wages not only reduce the cost of labor but are also likely to wind up with a poorer-quality labor force. Thus they will be reluctant to cut wages. If it is costly for firms to change the prices they charge and the wages they pay, the changes will be infrequent; but if all firms adjust prices and wages infrequently, the economywide level of wages and prices may not be flexible enough to avoid occasional periods of even high unemployment.

---

[4]See Gregory Mankiw and David Romer (eds.), *New Keynesian Economics* (Cambridge, Mass.: MIT Press, 1991).

Economic Controversy

There is no denying that there are conflicts of opinion and even theory between different camps. And because macroeconomics is about the real world, the differences that exist are sure to be highlighted in political and media discussions of economic policy.

It is also the case, though, that there are significant areas of agreement and that the different groups, through discussion and research, continually evolve new areas of consensus and a sharper idea of where precisely the differences lie. For instance, there is now a consensus emerging on the importance of information problems for wage and price setting and economic fluctuations. In this book we do not emphasize the debate, preferring to discuss the substantive matters, but we do indicate alternative views of an issue whenever that is relevant.

In the remainder of this chapter we present an overview of the key concepts with which macroeconomics deals.

1-2 KEY CONCEPTS

Gross Domestic Product

Gross domestic product (GDP) is the value of all final goods and services produced in the economy in a given time period (quarter or year). GDP is the basic measure of economic activity.

Three important distinctions must be made:

- *Nominal* versus *real* GDP
- *Levels* of GDP, nominal or real, versus the *growth* of GDP
- GDP versus GDP *per capita*

We now examine these distinctions. Figure 1-1 shows two measures of GDP—*nominal*, or *current dollar*, GDP and *real*, or *constant dollar*, GDP.[5] Nominal GDP measures the value of the economy's total output, at the prices prevailing in the period during which the output is produced. Real GDP measures the total output produced in any one period at the prices of some base year. Real GDP, which values the output produced in different years at the *same* prices, implies an estimate of the real or physical change in production or output between any specified years. At present, 1987 serves as the base year for real GDP measurement.

In Table 1-1, nominal GDP is equal to $6,060 billion in 1992 and $2,708 billion in 1980 (see, too, Figure 1-1). Thus nominal GDP grew at an average rate of 6.9 percent during the period 1980–1992. Real GDP was $4,980 billion in 1992 and $3,776

---

[5]Notice that the scale for GDP in Fig. 1-1 is not linear. The scale is logarithmic, which means that equal ratios are represented by equal distances. For instance, the distance from 900 to 1,800 is the same as the distance from 1,200 to 2,400, since GDP doubles in both cases. On a logarithmic scale, a variable growing at a constant rate (e.g., 4 percent per annum) is represented by a straight line.

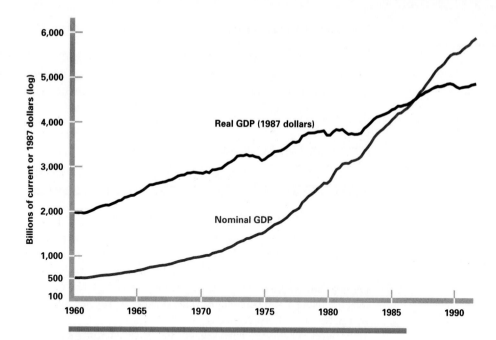

FIGURE 1-1

REAL AND NOMINAL GDP, 1960–1992. Nominal GDP measures the output of the goods and services produced in the economy in a given period, using the prices of that period. Real GDP measures the value of the output using the prices of a *given* year, in this case 1987. Nominal GDP has risen more rapidly than real GDP because prices have been rising. (SOURCE: DRI/McGraw-Hill.)

TABLE 1-1

ALTERNATIVE MEASURES OF GDP (dollars in billlions)

	nominal GDP	real GDP*	per capita real GDP*
1980	2,708	3,776	16,579
1985	4,038	4,280	17,887
1992	6,060	4,980	19,500
Growth rate per year, 1980–1992	6.9%	2.3%	1.4%

*Measured in 1987 prices.

SOURCE: DRI/McGraw-Hill.

billion in 1980, implying an average annual growth rate of real GDP of only 2.3 percent per year over the period.

Another measure of GDP looks at income *per capita*, adjusting the value of output by the size of the population. If we divide nominal GDP by population—255.4 million people in 1992—we obtain *per capita* nominal GDP, which was $23,730 per member of the population, or on average.

INFLATION AND NOMINAL GDP

Figure 1-1 shows that nominal GDP has risen much more rapidly than real GDP. The difference between the growth rates of real and nominal GDP occurs because the prices of goods have been rising, or there has been *inflation*. The inflation rate is the percentage rate of increase of the level of prices during a given period.

Real GDP grew at an average annual rate of 2.3 percent over the 12 years from 1980 to 1992, while nominal GDP grew at an average annual rate of 6.9 percent. Because real GDP is calculated holding the prices of goods constant, the difference is entirely due to inflation, or rising prices. Over the 12-year period, prices were on average rising at 4.6 percent per year. In other words, the average rate of inflation over that period was 4.6 percent per year.[6]

With 1987 as the base year for the prices at which output is valued, we observe in Figure 1-1 two implications of the distinction between nominal and real GDP. First, in 1987 the two are equal, because in the base year, current and constant dollars are the same. Second, with inflation, nominal GDP rises faster than real GDP, and therefore, after 1987, nominal GDP exceeds real GDP. The converse is, of course, true before 1987.

GROWTH AND REAL GDP

We turn next to the reasons for the growth of real GDP. The *growth rate* of the economy is the rate at which real GDP is increasing. Anytime we refer to growth or the growth rate without a qualifying word, we mean the growth rate of real GDP. On average, most economies grow by a few percentage points per year over long periods. For instance, U.S. real GDP grew at an average rate of 3.1 percent per year from 1960 to 1992. But this growth has certainly not been smooth, as Figure 1-1 confirms.

What causes real GDP to grow over time? The first reason real GDP changes is that the available amount of resources in the economy changes. The resources are conveniently split into capital and labor. The labor force, consisting of people either working or looking for work, grows over time and thus provides one source of increased production. The capital stock, including buildings and machines, likewise has been rising over time, providing another source of increased output. Increases in the availability of factors of production—the labor and capital used in the production of goods and services—thus account for part of the increase in real GDP.

The second reason for real GDP to change is that the efficiency with which

---

[6]We are calculating the inflation rate here as the difference between the growth rate of nominal GDP and the rate of inflation. This calculation is approximately correct at reasonably low rates of inflation and growth, but at higher rates of inflation, it is necessary to calculate the inflation rate directly from prices.

TABLE 1-2
PER CAPITA REAL INCOME GROWTH RATES, 1913–1990
(average annual growth rate)

country	growth rate	country	growth rate
Argentina	0.6	India	1.0
Brazil	2.4	Japan	3.5
China	2.2	Spain	2.0
France	2.1	U.K.	1.6
Ghana	0.1	U.S.	1.7

SOURCE: A. Maddison, "A Comparison of GDP Per Capita Income Levels in Developed and Developing Countries, 1700–1980," *Journal of Economic History,* March 1983, table 2, updated from 1980–1990 by the authors, from *World Tables,* 1992 (The World Bank).

factors of production work may change. These efficiency improvements are called productivity increases. Over time, the same factors of production can produce more output. These increases in the efficiency of production result from changes in knowledge, including learning by doing, as people learn through experience to perform familiar tasks better.

Table 1-2 compares growth rates of real per capita income in different countries. Studies of the sources of growth across countries and history seek to explain the reasons that a country like Brazil grew very rapidly (at least until the late 1980s), while Ghana, for example, has had very little growth. Ghana's income per person in 1980 was only 20 percent higher than in 1913, whereas Brazil's income had increased more than fivefold. Obviously, it would be well worth knowing what policies, if any, can raise a country's average growth rate over long periods of time.

Employment and Unemployment

The third source of change in real GDP is a change in the employment of the given resources available for production. Not all the capital and labor available to the economy is actually used at all times.

The *unemployment rate* is the fraction of the labor force that cannot find jobs. For example, in 1982, a reduction in the employment of labor, or a rise in unemployment, shows up in Figure 1-1 as a fall in real GDP. Indeed, in that year unemployment rose to 10.8 percent, the highest unemployment rate in the post–World War II period. More than one person out of every ten who wanted to work could not find a job. Such unemployment levels had not been experienced since the great depression of the 1930s.

Inflation, Growth, and Unemployment: The Record

Macroeconomic performance is judged by the three broad measures we have introduced: the *inflation* rate, the *growth* rate of output, and the rate of *unemployment*. News of these three variables makes the headlines because these issues affect our daily lives. They also dominate the research agenda in macroeconomics.

During periods of inflation, the prices of goods people buy are rising. Partly for this reason, inflation is unpopular, even if people's incomes rise along with the prices. Inflation is also unpopular because it is often associated with other disturbances to the economy—such as the oil price increases of the 1970s—that would make people worse off even if there were no inflation. Inflation is frequently a major political issue, as it was, for instance, in the 1980 presidential election between Jimmy Carter and Ronald Reagan, when the high rate of inflation contributed to Reagan's victory. And again, in 1988, low inflation (and high growth over several years) helped the election of George Bush. In 1992, the slow growth of the economy over the previous 4 years helped President Clinton defeat then-President Bush.

When the growth rate is high, the production of goods and services is rising, making possible an increased standard of living. With the high growth rate typically go lower unemployment and the availability of more jobs. High growth is a target and hope of most societies.

The growth rate of real GDP per person is the most important of all the macroeconomic indicators by which to judge the economy's long-run performance. Per capita GDP doubles every 35 years if it grows at 2 percent per year. In that case, each generation could look forward to a material standard of living double that of its parents. If per capita GDP grows at only 1 percent per annum, it takes 70 years to double. Over long periods, small differences in growth rates thus mount up to big differences in the standard of living that a country can achieve.

High unemployment rates are a major social problem. Jobs are difficult to find. The unemployed suffer a loss in their standard of living, personal distress, and sometimes a lifetime deterioration in their career opportunities. When unemployment reaches double-digit percentages—and even well short of that—it becomes the number-one social and political issue.

Macroeconomic Performance, 1952–1992

Table 1-3 shows that economic performance in the United States deteriorated sharply from the decade of the sixties to the seventies. Inflation and unemployment increased, and growth fell.

The table also shows the radical change in inflation performance after 1982. As the economy recovered from high unemployment in 1981–1982, the unemployment rate began to fall, growth increased, and inflation stayed low for some time. Many hoped that the economy was in for another high-growth, low-inflation decade like the sixties. Collapsing oil prices in 1985–1986 reinforced that expectation. Indeed, until 1988, when unemployment had declined to as little as 5 percent, inflation was not a major issue. But by 1989 the inflation issue was back and the fight against inflation led to the recession of 1990–1991. Even so, the long expansion period from 1982 to 1989 was more like the sixties than the seventies. By the early 1990s the issue was no longer inflation but rather how to get growing again and, most important, how to ensure continuing long-term advances in the standard of living. The fear of a declining standard of living was portrayed in *The Age of Diminished Expectations*, an influential,

TABLE 1-3
MACROECONOMIC PERFORMANCE, 1952–1992

period	inflation, % p.a.	growth, % p.a.	unemployment rate, % of the labor force
1952–1962	1.3	2.9	5.1
1962–1972	3.3	4.0	4.7
1972–1982	8.7	2.2	7.0
1982–1992	3.8	2.7	7.0

NOTE: Unemployment rate is average of rates for years shown; inflation rate is for CPI; "p.a." means per annum.

SOURCE: *Economic Report of the President, 1992,* and DRI/McGraw-Hill.

popular study of economic problems of the American economy by MIT economist Paul Krugman.[7]

As we develop macroeconomics in this book, we are looking for answers to the questions that recent macroeconomic performance raises. Why did the inflation rate rise from the fifties to the seventies and then fall rapidly? Will the growth rate return to the high levels of the sixties? Can the unemployment rate be reduced below 5 percent? And, of course, what economic policies, if any, can produce low inflation, low unemployment, and high growth all at the same time?

The Business Cycle and the Output Gap

Inflation, growth, and unemployment are related through the *business cycle*. The business cycle is the more or less regular pattern of expansion (recovery) and contraction (recession) in economic activity around the path of trend growth. At a cyclical *peak*, economic activity is high relative to trend; and at a cyclical *trough*, the low point in economic activity is reached. Inflation, growth, and unemployment all have clear cyclical patterns, as we will show below. For the moment we concentrate on measuring the behavior of output or real GDP relative to trend over the business cycle.

The black line in Figure 1-2 shows the *trend path* of real GDP. The trend path of GDP is the path GDP would take if factors of production were fully employed. Over time, real GDP changes for the two reasons we already noted. First, more resources become available: the size of the population increases, firms acquire machinery or build plants, land is improved for cultivation, the stock of knowledge increases as new goods and new methods of production are invented and introduced. This increased availability of resources allows the economy to produce more goods and services, resulting in a rising trend level of output.

But, second, factors are not *fully employed* all the time. Full employment of

[7]Paul Krugman, *The Age of Diminished Expectations* (Cambridge, Mass.: MIT Press, 1990).

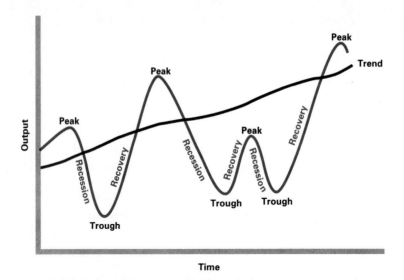

FIGURE 1-2

THE BUSINESS CYCLE. Output, or GDP, does not grow at its trend rate. Rather, it fluctuates irregularly around trend, showing business cycle patterns from trough through recovery to peak, and then from peak through recession and back to the trough. Business cycle output movements are not regular in timing or in size. Nor is the trend growth rate constant; it varies with changes in technical knowledge and the growth of supplies of factors of production.

factors of production is an economic, not a physical, concept. Physically, labor is fully employed if everyone is working 16 hours per day all year. In economic terms, there is full employment of labor when everyone who wants a job can find one within a reasonable amount of time. Because the economic definition is not precise, we typically define full employment of labor by some convention, for example, that labor is fully employed when the unemployment rate is 5.5 percent. Capital similarly is never fully employed in a physical sense; for example, office buildings or lecture rooms, which are part of the capital stock, are used only part of the day.

Output is not always at its trend level, that is, the level corresponding to (economic) full employment of the factors of production. Rather output fluctuates around the trend level. During an *expansion* (or *recovery*) the *employment* of factors of production increases, and that is a source of increased production. Output can rise above trend because people work overtime and machinery is used for several shifts. Conversely, during a *recession* unemployment increases and less output is produced than can in fact be produced with the existing resources and technology. The wavy line in Figure 1-2 shows these cyclical departures of output from trend. Deviations of output from trend are referred to as the *output gap*.

The output gap measures the gap between actual output and the output the

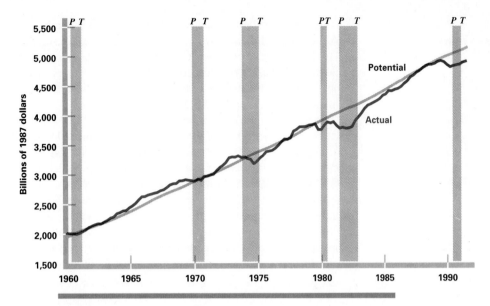

FIGURE 1-3

ACTUAL AND POTENTIAL OUTPUT, 1960–1992. Potential output is the full-employment level of output. It grows like trend output in Figure 1-2. Actual GDP fluctuates around potential, falling below during recession and rising up toward the potential level during recoveries. Shaded areas represent recessions. (Source: DRI/McGraw-Hill.)

economy could produce at full employment given the existing resources. Full-employment output is also called *potential output*.

$$\text{Output gap} \equiv \text{potential output} - \text{actual output} \qquad (1)$$

The output gap allows us to measure the size of the cyclical deviations of output from potential output or trend output (we use these terms interchangeably). Figure 1-3 shows actual and potential output for the United States. The shaded bars represent recessions, with the letters P and T denoting cyclical peaks and troughs.[8]

The figure shows that the output gap grows during a recession, such as in 1982. More resources become unemployed, and actual output falls below potential output. Conversely, during an expansion, most strikingly in the long expansion of the 1960s, the gap declines and ultimately even becomes negative. A negative gap means that there is overemployment, overtime for workers, and more than the usual rate of utilization of machinery. It is worth noting that the gap is sometimes very sizable. For example, in 1982 it amounted to as much as 10 percent.

---

[8]Dating of the business cycle is done by the National Bureau of Economic Research (NBER). The NBER is a private, nonprofit research organization based in Cambridge, Massachusetts.

Establishing the level of potential output is a difficult problem. In the 1960s it was believed that full employment corresponded to a measured rate of unemployment of 4 to 4.5 percent of the labor force. Changes in the composition of the labor force, including increases in the proportion of younger workers and female workers, who change jobs more frequently, raised the estimate of the full-employment rate of unemployment to a range around 5.5 percent in the 1980s.

There are several series for calculating potential GDP, which differ in the assumption they make about the full-employment rate of unemployment.[9] Even though there is no unique way of calculating potential output, the GDP gap still provides an important indicator of how the economy is performing and in which direction policies should try to move the economy's level of activity.

When looking at the business cycle fluctuations in Figure 1-3, one question that naturally arises is whether expansions succumb inevitably to old age, or whether they are instead brought to an end by policy mistakes. As we shall see, often a long expansion reduces unemployment too much, causes inflationary pressures, and therefore triggers policies to fight inflation—and such policies usually create recessions.

1-3 RELATIONSHIPS AMONG MACROECONOMIC VARIABLES

The preliminary look at the data presented above and our discussion of the business cycle suggest—correctly—that we should expect to find simple relationships among the major macroeconomic variables of growth, unemployment, and inflation. Such relationships do exist, as we now document.

Growth and Unemployment

We have already noted that changes in the employment of factors of production provide one of the sources of growth in real GDP. We would then expect high GDP growth to be accompanied by declining unemployment. That is indeed the case, as we observe from Figure 1-4. On the vertical axis, Figure 1-4 shows the growth rate of real output in a particular year, and on the horizontal axis the change in the unemployment rate in that year. For example, in 1984, the growth rate of output was 6.8 percent and the reduction in the unemployment rate was 2.1 percentage points. Thus we plot the point labeled 1984 in the upper left-hand region. That region corresponds to a period of expansion and falling unemployment rates.

By contrast, in the lower right-hand region, points such as those labeled 1975 and 1982 are periods of recession—low growth and rising unemployment rates. Note that even when there is some growth, as in 1981, unemployment rates may be rising. It takes growth rates above about 2.25 percent to cause unemployment rates to come down. The year 1984 stands out as having the most rapid growth and largest reduction in unemployment in 32 years.

---

[9]The estimate of potential output in Fig. 1-3 is calculated by DRI/McGraw-Hill.

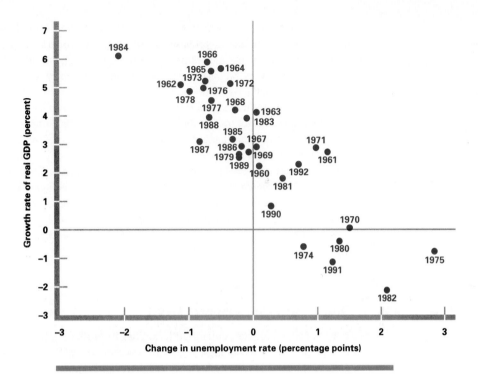

FIGURE 1-4
GROWTH AND THE CHANGE IN THE UNEMPLOYMENT RATE, 1960–1992.
High rates of growth cause the unemployment rate to fall, and low
or negative rates of growth are accompanied by increases in the
unemployment rate. The relationship shown by the scatter of the
points in this figure is summarized by *Okun's law*, which links the
growth rate to the change in the unemployment rate.

OKUN'S LAW

A relationship between real growth and changes in the unemployment rate is known
as *Okun's law*, named after its discoverer, the late Arthur Okun of the Brookings
Institution, former chairman of the Council of Economic Advisers (CEA). Okun's law
says that the unemployment rate declines when growth is above the trend rate of 2.25
percent. Specifically, for every percentage point of growth in real GDP above the trend
rate that is sustained for a year, the unemployment rate declines by one-half percentage
point. This relationship is stated in equation (2) where Δu denotes the change in the
unemployment rate, y is the growth rate of output, and 2.25 is the trend growth of output.

To show the use of the formula, suppose growth in a given year is 4.25 percent.
That would imply an unemployment rate reduction of 1.0 [= 0.5(4.25 − 2.25)]
percentage point.

$$\Delta u = -0.5(y - 2.25) \tag{2}$$

Okun's law, the status of which is somewhat exaggerated by calling it a law rather than an empirical regularity, provides a rule of thumb for translating growth rates of output into reductions in the unemployment rate. Although the rule is only approximate and will not work very precisely from year to year, it still gives a sensible translation from growth to unemployment.

Okun's law is a useful guide to policy because it allows us to ask how a particular growth target will affect the unemployment rate over time. Suppose we were in a deep recession with 9 percent unemployment. How many years would it take us to return to, say, 6 percent unemployment? The answer depends on how fast the economy grows in the recovery. One possible path for a return to 6 percent unemployment is for output to grow at 4.25 percent per year for 3 years. On this path, each year we grow at 2 percent above trend, and thus each year we take one percentage point off the unemployment rate. An alternative recovery strategy is front-loaded: growth is high at the beginning and then slows down, for example, 5.25, 4.25, and 3.25 percent growth in successive years.

Inflation and the Business Cycle

Expansionary aggregate demand policies tend to produce inflation, unless they occur when the economy is at high levels of unemployment. Protracted periods of low aggregate demand tend to reduce the inflation rate. Figure 1-5 shows one measure of inflation for the U.S. economy for the period since 1960. The inflation measure in the figure is the rate of change of the *consumer price index* (*CPI*), the cost of a given basket of goods, representing the purchases of a typical urban consumer.[10]

Figure 1-5 shows the *rate of increase* of prices. We can also look at the *level* of prices. All the inflation of the 1960s and 1970s adds up to a large increase in the price level. In the period from 1960 to 1992, the price level more than quadrupled. A typical basket of goods that cost $1 in 1960 cost $4.73 by 1992. Most of that increase in prices took place after the early 1970s.

Inflation, like unemployment, is a major macroeconomic concern. However, the costs of inflation are much less obvious than those of unemployment. In the case of unemployment, potential output is going to waste, and it is therefore clear why the reduction of unemployment is desirable. In the case of inflation, there is no obvious loss of output. As we noted previously, consumers in part dislike inflation because it is often associated with disturbances, such as the oil price shocks, that reduce their real incomes. It is also argued that inflation upsets familiar price relationships and reduces the efficiency of the price system. Whatever the reasons, policy makers have been willing to increase unemployment in an effort to reduce inflation—that is, to trade off some unemployment for less inflation.[11]

---

[10]By contrast, the measure of inflation obtained in Fig. 1-1 by comparing nominal and real GDP is the rate of change of the GDP deflator. The CPI rate of inflation is the most frequently used, and the GDP deflator is the next most popular. Chapter 2 presents more details on the different price indexes.

[11]For a very readable account of inflation, see Milton Friedman, "The Causes and Cures of Inflation," in his *Money Mischief* (New York: Harcourt Brace Jovanovich, 1992).

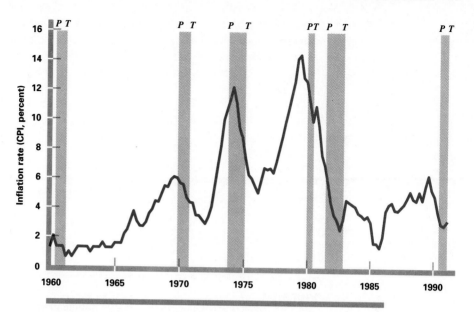

FIGURE 1-5

THE RATE OF INFLATION IN CONSUMER PRICES, 1960–1992. The inflation rate falls during and after recessions, and then—over the period shown—tends to rise later in the recovery. (SOURCE: DRI/McGraw-Hill.)

Inflation–Unemployment Tradeoffs

The *Phillips curve* describes an empirical relationship between wage and price inflation and unemployment: the higher the rate of unemployment, the lower the rate of inflation. It was made famous in the 1950s in Great Britain and has since become a cornerstone of macroeconomic discussion. Figure 1-6 presents a typical downward-sloping Phillips curve showing that high rates of unemployment are accompanied by low rates of inflation and vice versa. The curve suggests that less unemployment can always be attained by incurring more inflation and that the inflation rate can always be reduced by incurring the costs of more unemployment. In other words, the curve suggests there is a tradeoff between inflation and unemployment. As can be seen in Figure 1-7, inflation and unemployment rates in the United States appeared to fit the simple Phillips curve pattern for the 1960s.

Economic events since 1970, particularly the combination of high inflation and high unemployment in 1974 and 1981, have led to considerable skepticism about the unemployment-inflation relation shown in Figure 1-6. Figure 1-7 makes it clear that the data for the last 30 years do not fit any simple relationship of the form shown in Figure 1-6.

As we will develop in this book, the modern view is that in the short run of, say, 3 years, there is a relation between inflation and unemployment of the type shown in Figure 1-6. This *short-run Phillips curve*, however, does not remain stable. It shifts

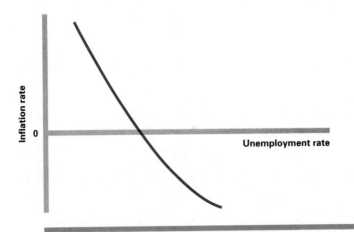

FIGURE 1-6
A PHILLIPS CURVE. The Phillips curve suggests a tradeoff between inflation and unemployment: less unemployment can always be obtained by incurring more inflation—or inflation can be reduced by allowing more unemployment.

as expectations of inflation change. In the long run, there is no tradeoff worth speaking about between inflation and unemployment. In the long run, the unemployment rate is basically independent of the long-run inflation rate.

The tradeoffs between inflation and unemployment always have to be taken into account when the government is considering whether and how it can increase growth and employment or reduce inflation.

1-4 AGGREGATE DEMAND AND SUPPLY

The key overall concepts in analyzing output, inflation, growth, and the role of policy are *aggregate demand* and *aggregate supply*. In this section we provide a brief preview of these concepts and of their interaction, with the aim of showing where we are heading.

The level of output and the price level are determined by the interaction of aggregate demand and aggregate supply. Under some conditions, employment depends only on total spending, or aggregate demand. At other times, supply limitations are an important part of the policy problem and have to receive major attention.

From the 1930s to the late 1960s, macroeconomics was very much demand-oriented. But in recent years the emphasis has shifted, and aggregate supply and *supply-side economics* have gained in importance. This shift of emphasis and interest was no doubt fostered by the slow growth and high inflation experienced by the industrialized countries in the 1970s.

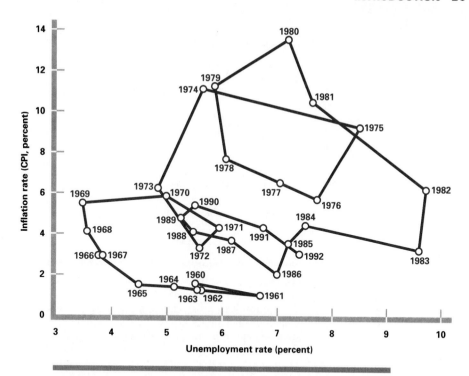

FIGURE 1-7

INFLATION AND UNEMPLOYMENT, 1960–1992. The actual history of
inflation and unemployment in the United States since 1960 shows
no simple Phillips curve relationship. There are periods, for instance,
1963–1969, 1976–1979, and 1980–1982, that fit the general shape of
the Phillips curve, but in between there are periods when both
inflation and unemployment increase or sometimes (e.g., 1984–
1986) decrease.

What are the relationships among aggregate demand and aggregate supply, output
and employment, and prices? Aggregate demand is the relationship between spending
on goods and services and the level of prices. When unemployment is high, increased
spending, or an increase in aggregate demand, will raise output and employment with
little effect on prices. Under such conditions, for example, during the great depression
of the thirties, it would certainly be appropriate to use expansionary aggregate demand
policies to increase output.

But if the economy is close to full employment, increased aggregate demand
will be reflected primarily in higher prices or inflation. The aggregate supply side of
the economy has then to be introduced. The aggregate supply curve specifies the
relationship between the amount of output firms produce and the price level. The supply
side not only enters the picture in telling us how successful demand expansions will
be in raising output and employment, but it also has a role of its own. Supply disturbances, or *supply shocks*, can reduce output and raise prices, as was the case in the

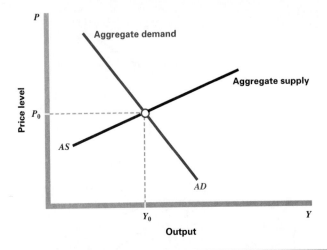

FIGURE 1-8

AGGREGATE DEMAND AND SUPPLY. The basic tools for analyzing
output, the price level, inflation, and growth are the aggregate
supply and demand curves. Shifts in either aggregate supply or
aggregate demand will cause the level of output to change—thus
affecting growth—and will also change the price level—thus
affecting inflation. Through Okun's law, changes in output are linked
to changes in the unemployment rate. For the first six chapters, we
concentrate on aggregate demand. Then in the later chapters, we
introduce the aggregate supply curve, thereby completing the
analysis.

1970s when the price of oil increased sharply. Conversely, policies that increase
productivity, and thus the level of aggregate supply at a given price level, can help
reduce inflationary pressures.

Graphical Analysis

Figure 1-8 shows aggregate demand and supply curves. The vertical axis P is the price
level, and the horizontal axis Y is the level of real output or income. Although the
curves look like the ordinary supply and demand curves of microeconomics, an understanding of the curves in the figure will not be reached until Chapters 7 and 8.

Aggregate demand is the total demand for goods and services in the economy.
It depends on the aggregate price level, as shown in Figure 1-8. The aggregate demand
curve can be shifted by monetary and fiscal policy. The aggregate supply curve shows
the price level associated with each level of output. It can, to some extent, be shifted
by fiscal policy.

Aggregate supply and demand interact to determine the price level and output
level. In Figure 1-8, P_0 is the equilibrium price level and Y_0 the equilibrium level of

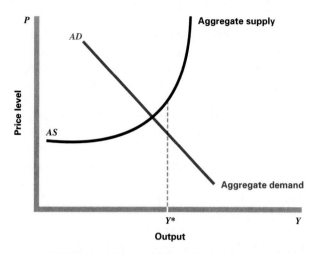

FIGURE 1-9

AGGREGATE DEMAND AND NONLINEAR AGGREGATE SUPPLY. A key fact about the aggregate supply curve is that it is not linear. At low levels of output, prices do not change much on the aggregate supply schedule, implying that more output will be supplied without much increase in prices. But as the economy gets close to full employment or potential output, further increases in output will be accompanied by increased prices.

output. If the *AD* curve in the figure shifts upward to the right, then the extent to which output and prices, respectively, are changed depends on the steepness of the aggregate supply curve.[12] If the *AS* curve is very steep, then a given increase in aggregate demand mainly causes prices to rise and has very little effect on the level of output. If the *AS* curve is flat, a given change in aggregate demand will be translated mainly into an increase in output and hardly at all into an increase in the price level.

One of the crucial points about macroeconomic adjustment is that the aggregate supply curve is not a straight line. Figure 1-9 shows that at low levels of output, below potential output *Y**, the aggregate supply curve is quite flat. When output is below potential, there is very little tendency for prices of goods and factors (wages) to fall. Conversely, for output above potential, the aggregate supply curve is steep and prices tend to rise when demand increases. The effects of changes in aggregate demand on output and prices therefore depend on the level of actual relative to potential output.

All these observations are by way of a very important warning. In Chapters 3 through 6 we focus on aggregate demand as the determinant of the level of output. We shall assume that prices are given and constant and that output is determined by the level of demand—that there are no supply limitations. We are thus talking about the very flat part of the aggregate supply curve, at levels of output below potential.

---

[12]Experiment with graphs like Fig. 1-8 to be sure you understand this fact.

The suggestion that output rises to meet the level of demand without a rise in prices leads to a very activist conception of policy. Under these circumstances, without any obvious tradeoffs, policy makers would favor very expansionary policies to raise demand and thereby cause the economy to move to a high level of employment and output. There are circumstances in which such a policy view is altogether correct. The early 1960s are a case in point. Figure 1-3 shows that in those years output was substantially below potential. There were unused resources, and the problem was a deficiency of demand. By contrast, in the late 1960s and the late 1980s the economy was operating at full employment. There was no significant GDP gap. An attempt to expand output or real GDP further would run into supply limitations and force up prices rather than the production of goods. In those circumstances, a model that assumes that output is demand-determined and that increased demand raises output and *not* prices is simply inappropriate.

Should we think that the model with fixed prices and demand-determined output is very restricted and perhaps artificial? The answer is no. There are two reasons for this. First, the circumstances under which the model is appropriate—those of high unemployment—are neither unknown nor unimportant. Unemployment and downward price rigidity are continuing features of the U.S. economy. Second, even when we come to study the interactions of aggregate supply and demand in Chapter 7 and later, we need to know how given policy actions *shift* the aggregate demand curve at a given level of prices. Thus all the material of Chapters 3 through 6 on aggregate demand plays a vital part in our understanding of the effects of monetary and fiscal policy on the price level as well as an output in circumstances in which the aggregate supply curve is upward-sloping.

What, then, is the warning of this section? It is simply that the very activist spirit of macroeconomic policy under conditions of unemployment must not cause us to overlook the existence of supply limitations and price adjustment when the economy is near full employment.

1-5 OUTLINE AND PREVIEW OF THE TEXT

We have sketched the major issues we shall discuss in the book. We now outline our approach to macroeconomics and the order in which the material will be presented. The key overall concepts, as already noted, are aggregate demand and aggregate supply. Aggregate demand is influenced by monetary policy, primarily through interest rates and expectations, and by fiscal policy. Aggregate supply is affected by fiscal policy and also by disturbances such as changes in the supply of oil.

The coverage by chapters starts in Chapter 2 with national income accounting, emphasizing data and relationships that are used repeatedly later in the book. Chapters 3 through 6 are concerned with aggregate demand. Chapters 7 through 9 introduce aggregate supply and show how aggregate supply and demand interact to determine both real GDP and the price level. Chapter 10 develops the crucial issue of long-run growth. Then in Chapters 11 through 15, we present material that clarifies and deepens the understanding of aggregate demand and of *stabilization policies*—policies designed to keep the economy closer to a path of full employment and stable prices. Chapters 16 and 17 perform a similar service for aggregate supply and the interactions of aggregate supply and demand. In Chapters 18 and 19 we discuss the relationships among budget-deficits, debt, inflation, and hyperinflation. Chapter 20 extends the discussion of Chapter 6 on the role of international trade in macroeconomics.

1-6 PREREQUISITES AND RECIPES

In concluding this introductory chapter we offer a few words on how to use this book. First, we note that there is no mathematical prerequisite beyond high school algebra. We do use equations when they appear helpful, but they are not an indispensable part of the exposition. Nevertheless, they can and should be mastered by any serious student of macroeconomics.

The technically harder chapters or sections can be skipped or dipped into. Either we present them as supplementary material, or we provide sufficient nontechnical coverage to help the reader get on without them later in the book. The reason we do present more advanced material or treatment is to afford complete and up-to-date coverage of the main ideas and techniques in macroeconomics. Even though you may not be able to grasp every point of such sections on first reading—and should not even try to—these sections should certainly be read to get the main message and an intuitive appreciation of the issues that are raised.

The main problem you will encounter will come from trying to comprehend the interaction of several markets and many variables, as the direct and feedback effects in the economy constitute a quite formidable system. How can you be certain to progress efficiently and with some ease? The most important thing is to ask questions. Ask yourself, as you follow the argument, Why is it that this or that variable should affect, say, aggregate demand? What would happen if it did not? What is the critical link?

There is no substitute whatsoever for *active learning*. Reading sticks at best for 7 weeks. Are there simple rules for active study? The best way to study is to use pencil and paper and work through the argument by drawing diagrams, experimenting with flowcharts, writing out the logic of an argument, working out the problems at the end of each chapter, and underlying key ideas. Two extremely helpful supplements to this text are the *Study Guide*, by Professor Richard Startz of the University of Washington, and a software package, *PC-Macroeconomics*, by Professor F. Gerard Adams of the University of Pennsylvania and Professor Eugene Kroch of Villanova University. The end-of-chapter problems generally include problems that use *PC-Macroeconomics*. Both contain much useful material and problems that will help in your studies. Another valuable exercise is to take issue with an argument or position, or to spell out the defense for a particular view on policy questions. Beyond that, if you get stuck, read on for half a page. If you are still stuck, go back five pages.

You should also learn to use the index. Several concepts are discussed at different levels in different chapters. If you come across an unfamiliar term or concept, check the index to see whether and where it was defined and discussed earlier in the book.

As a final word, this chapter is designed for reference purposes. You should return to it whenever you want to check where a particular problem fits or to what a particular subject is relevant. The best way to see the forest is from Chapter 1.

KEY TERMS

Monetarists	Trough
Keynesians	Recovery or expansion
New classical macroeconomists	Recession
Rational expectations	Output gap
GDP, nominal and real	Okun's law
Inflation	Phillips curve
Unemployment	Growth
Business cycle	Stabilization policies
Trend or potential output	Aggregate demand and supply
Peak	

COMPUTER EXERCISES

Using the data and the graphical tools available in Chapter 1 of *PC-Macroeconomics*, examine the relationships between the following variables:

1. *GDP* and *potential GDP* in a time series plot. Can you see the business cycle? Where are the booms and recessions? Specifically, create a time plot of real GDP (#2) and real potential GDP (#3), and write down the years in which there were booms and recessions. (Press any key when through looking at the graph; it will return you to the graphing menu.)

2. *Consumption* and *income* in time series and scatter plots. What relationship between consumption and income do you see? Specifically,
   (a) Create a time plot with real disposable personal income (#13) and real personal consumption expenditures (#4).
   (b) Create a scatter plot with real disposable personal income (#13) as the independent variable (*X*-axis variable) and real personal consumption expenditures (#4) as the dependent variable (*Y*-axis variable). For the scatter plot, have the package fit the best line to those points (answer "yes" to the question about fitting the best line). From this simple relationship, what would you conclude is the value of the *MPC*?

3. *Imports* and *GDP* in time series and scatter plots. What kind of relationship do you observe? Specifically,
   (a) Create a time plot of real GDP (#2) and real imports (#11).
   (b) Create a scatter plot with real GDP (#2) as the independent variable and real imports (#11) as the dependent variable. Is the relationship direct or inverse? What is the value of the marginal propensity to import?

4. *Unemployment change* and *GDP growth rate* scatter plot. Specifically, graph Okun's law using the following instructions:
   (a) Generate a new variable (first, #31) equal to the first difference of the unemployment rate (#25) and call it UDIFF.
   (b) Generate a new variable (second, #32) equal to the percentage change in real GDP (#2) and call it PCGDP87.
   (c) Replicate Figure 1-4 on page 17 in the text with UDIFF (#31) as the independent variable and PCGDP87 (#32) as the dependent variable. Don't bother to have the fitted line drawn.
   (d) Notice that, also on page 17, the Okun's law equation is given using UDIFF (Δu) as the *dependent* variable and PCGDP87 (y) as the independent variable. Carry out this

same exercise, this time allowing the computer to provide the best-fitting line. What is the formula you obtain?

5. *Inflation* and *unemployment* in a scatter plot. Do you see a relationship? Is there one during certain periods? Specifically, graph the Phillips curve by creating a scatter plot using the unemployment rate (#25) as the independent variable and inflation (#24) as the dependent variable. Determine whether there is a clear relationship over the entire period and/or within certin subperiods.

6. During the 1980s, the United States suffered from twin deficits—in the budget and in the balance of payments. Use the data to examine the factors that might cause these deficits. Might there be a relationship between the two deficits?

NATIONAL INCOME ACCOUNTING

M acroeconomics is ultimately concerned with the determination of the economy's total output, the price level, the level of employment, interest rates, and the other variables discussed in Chapter 1. To fully understand the determination of those variables, we have also to understand what they are and how they are measured in practice. To do so, we begin with the *national income accounts*.

The national income accounts give us regular estimates of GDP, the basic measure of the economy's performance in producing goods and services. The first part of this chapter discusses the measurement and meaning of GDP. But the national income accounts are useful also because they provide us with a conceptual framework for describing the relationships among three key macroeconomic variables: output, income, and spending. Those relationships are described in the second part of this chapter.

2-1 GROSS DOMESTIC PRODUCT AND NET DOMESTIC PRODUCT

Calculating Gross Domestic Product

GDP is the value of all final goods and services produced in the country within a given period. It includes the value of goods produced, such as houses and CDs, and the value of services, such as airplane rides and economists' lectures. The output of each of these is valued at its market price, and the values are added together to give GDP. National income accounts for the U.S. economy since 1929 are available on a systematic basis. There are several different estimates for periods before 1929. In 1992 the value of GDP in the U.S. economy was about $5,950 billion, or nearly $6 trillion.

There are a number of subtleties in the calculation of GDP.

FINAL GOODS AND VALUE ADDED

GDP is the value of *final* goods and services produced. The insistence on final goods and services is simply to make sure that we do not double-count. For example, we would not want to include the full price of an automobile in GDP and then also include as part of GDP the value of the tires that were sold to the automobile producer to put on the car. The components of the car that are sold to the manufacturers are called *intermediate* goods, and their value is not included in GDP. Similarly, the wheat that goes into bread is an intermediate good. We count only the value of the bread as part of GDP; we do not count in the value of the wheat sold to the miller and the value of the flour sold to the baker.

In practice, double counting is avoided by working with *value added*. At each stage of the manufacture of a good, only the value added to the good at that stage of manufacture is counted as part of GDP. The value of the wheat produced by the farmer is part of GDP. Then the value of the flour sold by the miller minus the cost of the wheat is the miller's value added. If we follow this process along, we will see that the sum of value added at each stage of processing will be equal to the final value of the bread sold.[1]

CURRENT OUTPUT

GDP consists of the value of output *currently produced*. It thus excludes transactions in existing commodities, such as old masters or existing houses. We count the construction of new houses as part of GDP, but we do not add trade in existing houses. We do, however, count the value of realtors' fees in the sale of existing houses as part of GDP. The realtor provides a current service in bringing buyer and seller together, and that is appropriately part of current output.

MARKET PRICES

GDP values goods at *market prices*. The market price of many goods includes indirect taxes such as the sales tax and excise taxes, and thus the market price of goods is not the same as the price the seller of the goods receives. The net price, the market price minus indirect taxes, is the *factor cost*, which is the amount received by the factors of production that manufactured the good. GDP is valued at market prices and not at factor cost. This point becomes important when we relate GDP to the incomes received by the factors of production.[2]

Valuation at market prices is a principle that is not uniformly applied, because there are some components of GDP that are difficult to value. There is no very good way of valuing the services of homemakers, or a self-administered haircut, or, for that matter, the services of the police force or the government bureaucracy. Some of these activities are simply omitted from currently measured GDP, as, for instance, homemakers' services. Government services are valued at cost, so the wages of government employees are taken to represent their contribution to GDP. There is no unifying

---

[1]How about the flour that is directly purchased by households for baking at home? It is counted as a contribution toward GDP since it represents a final sale.

[2]The value of output measured at factor cost is referred to as *national income*. On this point see Appendix 2-2 at the end of this chapter.

principle in the treatment of these awkward cases, but rather a host of conventions is used.

GDP and GNP

There is a distinction between GDP and *gross national product*, or *GNP*. GNP is the value of final goods and services produced by domestically owned factors of production within a given period. The difference between GDP and GNP arises because some of the output produced within a given country is made by factors of production owned abroad. For instance, part of U.S. GDP corresponds to the profits earned by Honda from its U.S. manufacturing operations. These profits are part of Japanese GNP, because they are the income of Japanese-owned capital. Similarly, part of French GDP corresponds to the income earned by an American working in Paris. That American's income is part of U.S. GNP though it is not part of U.S. GDP.

The difference between GDP and GNP corresponds to the *net* income earned by foreigners. When GDP exceeds GNP, residents of a given country (say Canada) are earning less abroad than foreigners are earning in that country (in this example, Canada). In the United States, GNP has exceeded GDP for the post–World War II period, by over 1 percent in the 1970s. Since 1980 the gap between U.S. GNP and GDP has narrowed almost to the vanishing point.

Until November 1991, the United States presented GNP as the basic measure of the economy's output. It switched to GDP for three reasons: that is what most other countries do, so that international comparisons became easier; GDP is easier to measure, since data on net foreign earnings are poor; and GDP is a better measure of the job-creating potential of the economy than is GNP. Since the difference between GDP and GNP is very small for the United States, the measure used in analyzing the U.S. economy makes very little difference. The difference is much larger for some other economies: for instance, Canada's GDP in 1990 was 103.7 percent of GNP; Switzerland's GDP in 1990 was 95 percent of GNP.

Gross and Net Domestic Product

Capital wears out, or *depreciates*, while it is being used to produce output. *Net domestic product* (NDP) is equal to GDP minus the *capital consumption allowance,* a measure of depreciation. NDP thus comes closer to measuring the net amount of goods produced in the country in a given period—it is the total value of production minus the value of the amount of capital used up in producing that output. Depreciation is typically about 11 percent of GDP, so that NDP is usually about 89 percent of GDP.

2-2 REAL AND NOMINAL GDP

Nominal GDP measures the value of output in a given period in the prices of that period, or, as it is sometimes put, in *current dollars*.[3] Thus 1993 nominal GDP measures

---

[3]National income account data are regularly reported in the *Survey of Current Business (SCB)*. Historical data are available in the September issue of *SCB*; in the Commerce Department's *Business Statistics*, a biennial publication; and in the annual *Economic Report of the President*.

TABLE 2-1

REAL AND NOMINAL GDP, AN ILLUSTRATION

	1987 nominal GDP	1993 nominal GDP	1993 real GDP*
Bananas	15 at $0.20 $ 3.00	20 at $0.30 $ 6.00	20 at $0.20 $ 4.00
Oranges	50 at 0.22 11.00	60 at 0.25 15.00	60 at 0.22 13.20
	$14.00	$21.00	$17.20

*Measured in 1987 prices.

the value of the goods produced in 1993 at the market prices prevailing in 1993, and 1986 nominal GNP measures the value of goods produced in 1986 at the market prices that prevailed in 1986.

Nominal GDP changes from year to year for two reasons. The first reason is that the physical output of goods changes. The second is that market prices change. As an extreme and unrealistic example, one could imagine the economy producing exactly the same output in 2 years between which all prices have doubled. Nominal GDP in the second year would be twice the nominal GDP in the first year, even though the physical output of the economy had not changed at all.

Real GDP measures changes in *physical* output in the economy between different time periods by valuing all goods produced in the two periods *at the same prices*, or in *constant dollars*. Real GDP is now measured in the national income accounts in the prices of 1987. That means that, in calculating real GDP, today's physical output is multiplied by the prices that prevailed in 1987 to obtain a measure of what today's output would have been worth had it been sold at the prices of 1987.

In Table 2-1 we present a simple example that illustrates the calculation of nominal and real GDP. The hypothetical outputs and prices of bananas and oranges in 1987 and 1993 are shown in the first two columns of Table 2-1. Nominal GDP in 1987 was $14, and nominal GDP in 1993 was $21, or an increase in nominal GDP of 50 percent. However, much of the increase in nominal GDP is purely a result of the increase in prices and does not reflect an increase in physical output. When we calculate real GDP in 1993 by valuing 1993 output at the prices of 1987, we find real GDP equal to $17.20, which is an increase of 23 percent rather than 50 percent. The 23 percent increase is a better measure of the increase in physical output of the economy than is the 50 percent increase.

We see from the table that the output of bananas rose by 33 percent from 1987 to 1993, while the output of oranges increased by 20 percent. We should thus expect our measure of the increase in real output to be somewhere between 20 and 33 percent, as it is.

Changes in nominal GDP that result from price changes do not tell us anything about the performance of the economy in producing goods and services. That is why we use real rather than nominal GDP as the basic measure for comparing output in different years. Figure 2-1 shows real GDP over the period since 1960. Note particularly that in some periods real GDP fell. That happened in the recessions of 1973–1975,

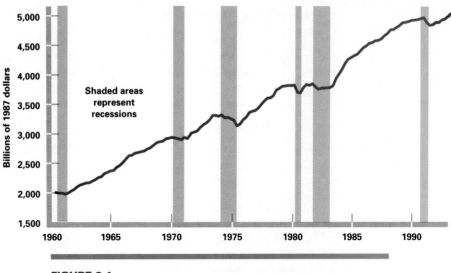

FIGURE 2-1
U.S. REAL GDP, 1960–1992. (SOURCE: DRI/McGraw-Hill.)

1980, 1981–1982, and 1990–1991. The recession periods, shaded in the figure, stand out as years of low or negative real GDP growth.

Problems of GDP Measurement

GDP data are, in practice, used not only as a measure of how much is being produced, but also as a measure of the welfare of the residents of a country. Economists and politicians talk as if an increase in real GDP means that people are better off. But GDP data are far from perfect measures of either economic output or welfare. There are, specifically, four major problems:

- Some outputs are poorly measured because they are not traded in the market. Specific examples include government services, nonmarket activities such as volunteer work, and do-it-yourself activities in the home.
- It is difficult to account correctly for improvements in the quality of goods. This has been the case particularly for computers, whose quality has improved dramatically while their price has fallen sharply. But it applies to almost all goods, such as cars, whose quality changes over time. The national income accountants attempt to adjust for improvements in quality, but the task is not easy, especially when new products and new models are being invented.
- Some activities measured as adding to real GDP in fact represent the use of resources to avoid or contain "bads" such as crime or risks to national security.

box 2-1⎯ ## GDP MEASUREMENT

Two problems of GDP measurement are the possibility that large parts of economic activity escape being counted in GDP and that the data are frequently and quite substantially revised. We take up the two problems in turn.

THE UNDERGROUND ECONOMY

By some estimates, as much as 30 percent of U.S. GDP may not be measured in the GDP accounts. Here are examples of transactions that generate goods and services that might not make it into measured GDP: working at a second job for cash, illegal gambling, working after entering the country illegally, working while collecting unemployment benefits, illegal drug dealing, working for tips that are not fully reported, selling home-grown tomatoes for cash.*

People attempt to conceal transactions that are not inherently illegal, but for which they are not complying with tax or immigration laws or other government regulations; and they conceal transactions that are themselves illegal, such as drug dealing. The U.S. national income accounts do not include the value of illegal activities in GDP as a matter of principle, so part of the underground economy would not count even if it could be measured. But many other countries and economists have no objection to including illegal activities if they can be measured.

The remaining activities in the underground economy occur mainly because people are trying to avoid losing some government benefit or avoid paying taxes, and these activities should be included in GDP.

How large is the underground economy, and how can it be measured? Estimates range widely. For the United States, conservative numbers are 3 to 4 percent of GDP, with a radical number of 33 percent of GDP. Estimates for foreign countries are similar; for instance, for Canada, estimates range from 4 to 22 percent of GDP, and for Italy, from 8 to 33 percent.

The largest estimates for the United States were based on the holdings of currency, on the argument that black-market transactions are undertaken mainly using currency. The ratio of currency holdings to bank deposits increased from less than 25 percent in 1959 to 40 percent in 1984, and it is argued that the reason is the increasing share of underground economic activity. The ratio of currency to bank deposits has fallen since 1984. Alternative estimates are based on inconsistencies in the GDP accounts, for instance, differences between total spending and total income. The Bureau of Economic Analysis, which creates the GDP accounts,

---

*A more complete list is provided in the excellent survey article by Carol S. Carson, "The Underground Economy: An Introduction," *Survey of Current Business*, May 1984; see also part II of the same article, in the July 1984 *Survey of Current Business*. There was an explosion of research on the underground economy in the mid-1980s; for a review of three books on the topic see Peter M. Gutman, *Journal of Economic Literature*, March 1983, pp. 117–120.

believes the underground economy is 3 percent of GDP or less, while the Internal Revenue Service has come up with an estimate as high as 8 percent of GDP. The evidence in favor of really large corrections, say, more than 10 percent, is weak.

What problems does the underground economy pose for GDP measurement? The main problem is that the relative importance of underground activities may have been changing. If, say, the underground economy was always equal to 10 percent of reported GDP, then measured GDP would show accurately the rate at which output *changes* over time. But if the underground economy grows relative to the measured economy, then the measured growth rate of output is below the true growth rate. It was the claim that the underground economy had been growing rapidly, and that therefore slow economic growth in the seventies was in large part a statistical illusion, that spurred research on the topic. But because of the difficulty of getting data on the underground economy, this research has not been conclusive.

GDP REVISIONS AND THE ACCURACY OF GDP ESTIMATES

There are several estimates of GDP for a given period. First to be reported is the so-called *advance* estimate for a given quarter, which appears about 3 weeks after the end of the quarter. These data are then revised a month later (the preliminary estimate) and once more a month after that (the final estimate). The data are then revised each July for the next 3 years, and thereafter a comprehensive revision of all GDP data (a so-called *benchmark* revision) is carried out every 5 years.

It is thus clear that GDP data are not, when they first appear, firm estimates; nor, for that matter, is any GDP figure for any year ever guaranteed not to change at some future date. The reason is that many of the data are not measured directly but rather are based on surveys and guesses. Considering that GDP is supposed to measure the value of *all* production of goods and services in the economy, it is not surprising that not all the data are available within a few weeks after the period of production. The data are revised as new figures come in and as the Bureau of Economic Analysis improves its data collection and estimation methods.

Data revisions may be quite large. The estimate of how fast GDP grew from one quarter to the next can sometimes change by 2 to 3 percent (at an annual rate) between the first and third estimates of GDP. But changes in the benchmark year for calculating real GDP also introduce important revisions. For example, GDP growth in the period 1977–1990 with the old (1982-based) GDP series was estimated to be 2.7 percent per year. But with the data revisions and the shift to 1987 as the base year undertaken in 1991, the growth rate for 1977–1990 is now estimated to have been only 2.5 percent per year.* ∎

---

*See *Survey of Current Business*, December 1991, which presents a discussion of the revision of GNP statistics and the adjustments to the new 1987 base year.

■ The accounts do not take environmental pollution and degradation into account. This issue is particularly important in developing countries. For instance, one study of Indonesia claims that properly accounting for environmental degradation reduces the annual growth rate of the economy in recent years by 3 percent.[4]

Attempts have been made to construct an *adjusted* GNP series that takes account of some of these difficulties, moving closer to a measure of welfare. The most comprehensive of these studies, by Robert Eisner of Northwestern University, estimates an adjusted GNP series in which the level of real GNP is about 50 percent higher than the official estimates.[5] Interestingly, while the adjusted level of GNP by far exceeds the official series, the estimated *growth rate* of real GNP over the 1946–1981 period is almost identical to the official estimate.[6]

2-3 PRICE INDEXES

The GDP Deflator

The calculation of real GDP gives us a useful measure of inflation known as *the GDP deflator*. The GDP deflator is the ratio of nominal GDP in a given year to real GDP of that year. The deflator measures the change in prices that has occurred between the base year and the current year. Using the example of Table 2-1, we can get a measure of inflation between 1987 and 1993 by comparing the value of 1993 GNP in 1993 prices and 1987 prices. The ratio of nominal to real GNP in 1993 is 1.22 (= 21/17.2). In other words, output is 22 percent higher in 1993 when it is valued using the higher prices of 1993 than valued in the lower prices of 1987. We ascribe the 22 percent increase to price increases, or inflation, over the 1987–1993 period.

Since the GDP deflator is based on a calculation involving all the goods produced in the economy, it is a widely based price index that is frequently used to measure inflation.

The Consumer and Producer Price Index

The *consumer price index* (CPI) measures the cost of buying a fixed basket of goods and services representative of the purchases of urban consumers. The CPI differs from the GDP deflator in three main ways. First, the deflator measures the prices of a much

---

[4]R. Repetto, W. Magrath, M. Wells, C. Beer, and F. Rossini, *Wasting Assets: Natural Resources in the National Income Accounts*, World Resources Institute, Washington, DC, June 1989.

[5]Eisner estimated an adjusted GNP rather than GDP series because he did his work at the time when GNP was used as the basic measure of output.

[6]Eisner presents his data in his book *The Total Incomes System of Accounts* (Chicago: University of Chicago Press, 1989). In Appendix E, he also reviews a variety of other attempts to adjust the standard accounts for major inadequacies.

TABLE 2-2

IMPORTANT PRICE INDEXES

	CPI, 1982–1984 = 100	GDP deflator, 1987 = 100
1960	29.6	26.0
1970	38.8	35.1
1980	82.4	71.7
1992	140.4	120.9
Average inflation 1960–1992	4.99%	4.92%

SOURCE: DRI/McGraw-Hill.

wider group of goods than the CPI does. CPI prices are measured by field-workers who go into shops and make phone calls to discuss the prices of the goods being sold by firms. Second, the CPI measures the cost of a given basket of goods, which is the same from year to year. The basket of goods included in the GDP deflator, however, differs from year to year, depending on what is produced in the economy in each year. When corn crops are large, corn receives a relatively large weight in the computation of the GDP deflator. By contrast, the CPI measures the cost of a fixed basket of goods that does not vary over time. Third, the CPI directly includes prices of imports, whereas the deflator includes only prices of goods *produced* in the United States.[7]

The two main indexes used to compute inflation, the GDP deflator and the CPI, accordingly differ in behavior from time to time. For example, at times when the price of imported oil rises rapidly, the CPI is likely to rise faster than the deflator.

Table 2-2 shows the CPI and the GDP deflator for the period 1960–1992. The GDP deflator expresses prices in the current year relative to 1987 prices, using quantities of the current year as weights. For the CPI, 1982–1984 is used as the base period. Although this need not be the case, the indexes change at essentially the same rate over the entire period. Both show substantial annual rates of inflation, rising prices, at an average rate of 5 percent per annum. There is no sense in which one of the indexes is "correct" while the others are not. The indexes measure changing prices of different baskets of goods.

The *producer price index* (PPI) is the third price index that is widely used. Like the CPI, this is a measure of the cost of a given basket of goods. It differs from the CPI partly in its coverage, which includes, for example, raw materials and semifinished goods. It differs, too, in that it is designed to measure prices at an early stage of the distribution system. Whereas the CPI measures prices where urban households actually do their spending—that is, at the retail level—the PPI is constructed from prices at the level of the first significant commercial transaction.

This makes the PPI a relatively flexible price index and one that generally signals

---

[7]Detailed discussion of the various price indexes can be found in the Bureau of Labor Statistics *Handbook of Methods* and in the Commerce Department's biennial *Business Statistics*.

TABLE 2-3

GDP AND COMPONENTS OF DEMAND, 1992

	$ billions	percent
Personal consumption expenditures	4,094	68.9
Gross private domestic investment	770	12.9
Government purchases of goods and services	1,115	18.8
Net exports of goods and services	− 33	− 0.6
Gross domestic product	5,946	100.0

SOURCE: *Survey of Current Business.*

changes in the general price level, or the CPI, some time before they actually materialize. For this reason the PPI and, more particularly, some of its subindexes, such as the index of "sensitive materials," serve as one of the business cycle indicators that are closely watched by policy makers.

We now return to the relationships between income and spending.

2-4 OUTLAYS AND COMPONENTS OF DEMAND

In this section we look at the demand for output and discuss the *components* of the aggregate demand for domestically produced goods and services, the different purposes for which GDP is demanded.

Total demand for domestic output is made up of four components: (1) consumption spending by households; (2) investment spending by businesses; (3) government (federal, state, and local) purchases of goods and services; and (4) foreign demand. We now look more closely at each of these components.

Consumption Spending

Table 2-3 presents a breakdown of the demand for goods and services in 1992 by components of demand. The table shows that the chief component of demand is *consumption spending* by the household sector. This includes anything from food to golf lessons, but it involves also, as we shall see in discussing investment, consumer spending on durable goods such as automobiles—spending that might be regarded as investment rather than consumption.

Figure 2-2 shows the share of consumption in GNP both in Japan and in the United States. Note that the consumption share is not constant by any means. Observe, too, that Japan consumes a far smaller share of its GNP than is the case in the United States. The rising share of consumption in the United States in the 1980s is considered one of the important reasons for poor economic performance. Higher consumption (or lower saving), as we will see in a moment, means either less investment or larger trade deficits.

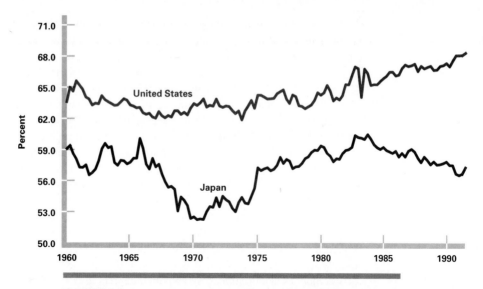

FIGURE 2-2

CONSUMPTION AS A SHARE OF GDP: THE UNITED STATES AND JAPAN, 1960–1992 (percent). (SOURCE: International Financial Statistics.)

Government Purchases

Next in importance we have *government purchases* of goods and services. This includes such items as national defense expenditures, road paving by state and local governments, and salaries of government employees.

We draw attention to the use of certain words in connection with government spending. We refer to government spending on goods and services as *purchases* of goods and services. In addition, the government makes *transfer payments*, payments that are made to people without their providing a current service in exchange. Typical transfer payments are social security benefits and unemployment benefits. We speak of *transfers plus purchases* as *government expenditure*. The federal government budget, of the order of $1,500 billion ($1.5 trillion), refers to federal government expenditure. Less than half that sum is for federal government purchases of goods and services; most of it is for transfers.

Investment Spending

Gross private domestic investment requires some definitions. First, throughout this book, *investment* means additions to the physical stock of capital. As we use the term, investment does *not* include buying a bond or purchasing stock in General Motors. Practically, investment includes housing construction, building of machinery, construction of factories and offices, and additions to a firm's inventories of goods.

If we think of investment more generally as any current activity that increases the economy's ability to produce output in the future, we would include not only physical investment but also what is known as investment in human capital. Human capital is the knowledge and ability to produce that is embodied in the labor force. Education can be regarded as investment in human capital.[8]

The classification of spending as consumption or investment is to a significant extent a matter of convention. From the economic point of view, there is little difference between a household's building up an inventory of peanut butter and a grocery store's doing the same. Nevertheless, in the national income accounts, the individual's purchase is treated as a personal consumption expenditure, whereas the store's purchase is treated as investment in the form of inventory investment. Although these borderline cases clearly exist, we can apply a simple rule of thumb: investment is associated with the business sector's adding to the physical stock of capital, including inventories.[9]

Similar issues arise in the treatment of household sector expenditures. For instance, how should we treat purchases of automobiles by households? Since automobiles usually last for several years, it would seem sensible to classify household purchases of automobiles as investment. We would then treat the *use* of automobiles as providing consumption services. (We could think of imputing a rental income to owner-occupied automobiles.) However, the convention is to treat all households' expenditures as consumption spending. This is not quite so bad as it might seem, since the accounts do separate households' purchases of *durable goods* like cars and refrigerators from their other purchases.

In passing, we note that in Table 2-3 investment is defined as "gross" and "domestic." It is gross in the sense that depreciation is not deducted. Net investment is gross investment minus depreciation. The term *domestic* means that this is investment spending by domestic residents but is not necessarily spending on goods produced within this country. It may well be an expenditure on foreign goods. Similarly, consumption and government spending may also be partly for imported goods. On the other hand, some of domestic output is sold to foreigners.

Net Exports

The item "net exports" appears in Table 2-3 to show the effects on aggregate demand for domestic output of domestic spending on foreign goods and of foreign spending on domestic goods. When foreigners purchase goods we produce, that adds to the demand for domestically produced goods. Correspondingly, that part of our spending

---

[8]In the total incomes system of accounts (TISA) referred to in footnote 6 above, the definition of investment is broadened to include investment in human capital, which means that total investment in that system is more than one-third of GNP. But in this book we mean by investment only additions to the physical capital stock.

[9]The GDP accounts record as investment *business sector* additions to the stock of capital. Some government spending, for instance, for roads or schools, also adds to the capital stock. Estimates of the capital stock owned by government are available in the *Survey of Current Business*, for instance, January 1992, pp. 136–137.

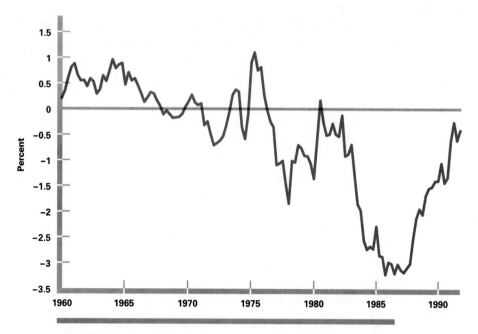

FIGURE 2-3

U.S. NET EXPORTS, 1960–1992 (percent of GDP). (Source: DRI/McGraw-Hill.)

that goes for foreign goods has to be subtracted from the demand for domestically produced goods. Accordingly, the difference between exports and imports, called *net exports*, is a component of the total demand for our goods. Net exports were negative for much of the 1980s, as shown in Figure 2-3, reflecting a high level of imports and a low level of exports; note though that net exports began to rise rapidly after 1987.

The point can be illustrated with an example. Assume that consumption spending was higher by $20 billion. How much higher would GDP be? If we assume that government and investment spending remained unchanged, we might be tempted to say that GDP would have been $20 billion higher. That is correct if all the additional spending had fallen on our goods. The other extreme, however, is the case in which all the additional spending falls on imports. In that event, consumption would be up $20 billion *and* net exports would be down $20 billion, with *no* net effect on GDP.

2-5 GDP AND PERSONAL DISPOSABLE INCOME

GDP is a measure of the output produced in the economy. Corresponding to this output is the income received by the owners of the factors of production—labor, capital, and land—that are used to produce the output. *Personal disposable income* is the level of income available for spending and saving by households in the economy. A number

FACTOR SHARES IN NATIONAL INCOME

Table 1 shows how national income is split (*factor shares*) among different types of incomes. The most striking fact in the table is the very large share of wages and salaries—compensation of employees—in national income. This accounts for 75 percent of national income. Proprietors' income is income from unincorporated businesses. Rental income of persons includes the *imputed* income of owner-occupied housing* and income from ownership of patents, royalties, and so on. The net interest category consists of interest payments by domestic businesses and the rest of the world to individuals and firms who have lent to them.

The division of national income into various classes is not very important for our macroeconomic purposes. It reflects, in part, answers to such questions as whether corporations are financed by debt or equity, whether a business is or is not incorporated, and whether the housing stock is owned by persons or corporations—which, in turn, are owned by persons.† ∎

TABLE 1
NATIONAL INCOME AND ITS DISTRIBUTION, 1992*

	$ billions	percent
National income	4,705	
Compensation of employees	3,506	74.5
Proprietors' income	396	8.4
Rental income of persons	2	0.0
Corporate profits	382	8.1
Net interest	419	8.9

*Based on data for first three quarters of 1992.
SOURCE: *Survey of Current Business.*

*GDP includes an estimate of the services homeowners receive by living in their homes. This is estimated by calculating the rent on an equivalent house. Thus the homeowner is treated as if she pays herself rent for living in her home.
†You might want to ask how Table 1 would be modified for each of the possibilities described in this sentence.

of adjustments have to be made to GDP to arrive at the level of personal disposable income; the relationship is described in some detail in Appendix 2-2, which includes a number of further definitions.

Four Adjustments

The need for these adjustments stems from four complications:

- Net income received from abroad increases individuals' disposable income.
- Most obviously, the government enters the picture in two ways: the government

collects taxes and makes transfer payments. Transfer payments are payments that do not represent compensation for current productive activities. Examples of transfers are pensions and unemployment compensation. Taxes (income taxes, Social Security taxes, excise taxes, etc.) reduce household income relative to GDP; transfer payments raise it relative to GDP.

- Business sector transitions emerge as another complication. Businesses do not distribute to households all the income they receive. To the extent that businesses retain earnings rather than paying them out to their shareholders, household income falls short of GDP. Businesses also make transfer payments (in the form of pensions) to households and thus, just as in the case of government, raise household income relative to GDP.

- Not all of GDP is available as income for households because part of output has to be set aside to maintain the economy's productive capacity, to replace depreciating capital. As noted earlier, depreciation amounts to about 11 percent of GDP in the U.S. economy.

In summary, we can write a definition of personal disposable income as follows:[10]

$$\text{Personal disposable income} \equiv \text{GDP} + \text{net factor income from abroad} \\ - \text{depreciation} - \text{retained earnings} \qquad (1)^{11} \\ + \text{transfers} - \text{taxes}$$

The Allocation of Personal Disposable Income

Personal disposable income is the amount households have available to spend or save. Table 2-4 shows how households allocate their disposable income. By far the largest outlay is for personal consumption. Most of the remainder is saved. Small amounts of personal disposable income are used to make interest payments and to make transfers to foreigners.

The U.S. personal saving rate is among the world's lowest. We shall see later why this worries some economists.

2-6 SOME IMPORTANT IDENTITIES

In this section we summarize the discussion of the preceding sections by writing down a set of national income relationships that we use extensively in Chapter 3. We introduce here some notation and conventions that we follow throughout the book.

---

[10]Throughout the book we distinguish identities from equations. Identities are statements that are *always* true because they are directly implied by definitions of variables or accounting relationships. They do not reflect any economic behavior but are extremely useful in organizing our thinking. Identities, or definitions, are shown with the sign $\equiv$, and equations with the usual equality sign $=$.

[11]Note that this definition looks at the income households actually receive. But households own the firms and therefore also own the undistributed profits of firms. Some economists argue that a more meaningful definition of household income simply cuts through the "veil" of the business sector and thus includes even undistributed profits.

TABLE 2-4

THE ALLOCATION OF PERSONAL DISPOSABLE INCOME, 1992

	$ billions	$ billions	percent of disposable income
Personal disposable income		4,429.6	100
Personal outlays		4,216.1	95.2
Personal consumption spending	4,093.9		
Interest paid by persons	112.0		
Transfers to foreigners (net)	10.2		
Personal savings		213.5	4.8

SOURCE: *Survey of Current Business.*

For analytical work in the following chapters, we simplify our analysis by making assumptions that ensure that disposable income is equal to GDP. For the most part we disregard depreciation and thus the difference between GDP and NDP as well as the difference between gross and net investment. We refer simply to investment spending. We also disregard indirect taxes and business transfer payments. With these conventions in mind, *we refer to national income and GDP interchangeably as income or output.* These simplifications have no serious consequences and are made only for convenience. Finally, and only for a brief while, we omit both the government and foreign sectors.

A Simple Economy

We denote the value of output in our simple economy, which has neither a government nor foreign trade, by Y. Consumption is denoted by C and investment spending by I. The first key identity is that between output produced and output sold. Output sold can be written in terms of the components of demand as the sum of consumption and investment spending. Accordingly, we can write the identity of output produced and output sold:

$$Y \equiv C + I \qquad (2)$$

Now, is equation (2) really an identity? Is it inevitably true that all output produced is either consumed or invested? After all, do not firms sometimes make goods that they are unable to sell? The answer to each of the questions is yes. Firms do sometimes make output that they cannot sell and that accumulates as inventories on their shelves. *However, we count the accumulation of inventories as part of investment* (as if the firms sold the goods to themselves to add to their inventories), and therefore, all output is either consumed or invested. Note that we are talking here about *actual* investment, which includes investment in inventories that firms might be very unhappy to make.

The next step is to draw up a relation among saving, consumption, and GDP. It is convenient to ignore the existence of corporations and consolidate, or add together, the entire private sector. Using this convention, we know that private sector income is Y, since the private sector receives as income the value of goods and services produced. Why? Because who else would get it? There is no government or external sector yet.

Now the private sector receives, as disposable personal income, the whole of income Y. How will that income be allocated? Part will be spent on consumption, and part will be saved. Thus we can write

$$Y \equiv S + C \tag{3}$$

where S denotes private sector saving. Identity (3) tells us that the whole of income is allocated to either consumption or saving. Next, identities (2) and (3) can be combined to read

$$C + I \equiv Y \equiv C + S \tag{4}$$

The left-hand side of identity (4) shows the components of demand, and the right-hand side shows the allocation of income. The identity emphasizes that output produced is equal to output sold. The value of output produced is equal to income received, and income received, in turn, is spent on goods or saved.

Identity (4) can be slightly reformulated to let us look at the relation between saving and investment. Subtracting consumption from each part of identity (4), we have

$$I \equiv Y - C \equiv S \tag{5}$$

Identity (5) shows that in this simple economy *investment is identically equal to saving*.

One can think of what lies behind this relationship in a variety of ways. In a very simple economy, the only way the individual can save is by undertaking an act of physical investment—for example, by storing grain or building an irrigation channel. In a slightly more sophisticated economy, one could think of investors financing their investing by borrowing from individuals who save.

However, it is important to recognize that equation (5) expresses the identity between investment and saving and that some of the investment might well be undesired inventory investment.

Reintroducing the Government and Foreign Trade

We can now reintroduce the government sector and the external sector.[12] First, for the government we denote purchases of goods and services by G and all taxes by TA. Transfers to the private sector (including interest) are denoted by TR. Net exports (exports minus imports) are denoted by NX.

---

[12]*Government* here means the federal government plus state and local governments.

We return to the identity between output produced and sold, taking account now of the additional components of demand, G and NX. Accordingly, we restate the contents of Table 2-4 by writing

$$Y \equiv C + I + G + NX \tag{6}$$

Once more we emphasize that in identity (6) we use actual investment in the identity and thus do not rule out the possibility that firms might not be content with the investment. Still, as an accounting identity, equation (6) will hold.

Next we turn to the derivation of the very important relation between output and disposable income. Now we have to recognize that part of income is spent on taxes and that the private sector receives net transfers (TR) in addition to national income. Disposable income (YD) is thus equal to income plus transfers less taxes:

$$YD \equiv Y + TR - TA \tag{7}$$

Disposable income, in turn, is allocated to consumption and saving:

$$YD \equiv C + S \tag{8}$$

Combining identities (7) and (8), we have:

$$C + S \equiv YD \equiv Y + TR - TA \tag{9}$$

or

$$C \equiv YD - S \equiv Y + TR - TA - S \tag{9a}$$

Identity (9a) states that consumption is disposable income less saving or, alternatively, that consumption is equal to income plus transfers less taxes and saving. Now we use the right-hand side of equation (9a) to substitute for C in identity (6). With some rearrangement, we obtain

$$S - I \equiv (G + TR - TA) + NX \tag{10}$$

Saving, Investment, the Government Budget, and Trade

Identity (10) cannot be overemphasized. The first set of terms on the right-hand side $(G + TR - TA)$ is the *government budget deficit*. $(G + TR)$ is equal to total government spending, consisting of government purchases of goods and services (G) plus government transfer payments (TR). TA is the amount of taxes received by the government. The difference $(G + TR - TA)$ is the excess of government spending over its receipts, or its budget deficit. The second term on the right-hand side is the excess of exports over imports, or the *net exports of goods and services*, or net exports for short.

Thus, identity (10) states that the excess of saving over investment $(S - I)$ of the private sector is equal to the government budget deficit plus the trade surplus. The

TABLE 2-5

THE BUDGET DEFICIT, TRADE, SAVING, AND INVESTMENT (billions of dollars)

saving (S)	investment (I)	budget deficit (BD)	net exports (NX)
750	750	0	0
750	600	150	0
750	650	0	100
750	770	150	−170

identity suggests—correctly—that there are important relations among the excess of private saving over investment $(S - I)$, the government budget $(G + TR - TA)$, and the external sector. For instance, if, for the private sector, saving is equal to investment, then the government's budget deficit (surplus) is reflected in an equal external deficit (surplus).

Table 2-5 shows the significance of identity (10). To fix ideas, suppose that private sector saving S is equal to $750 (billion). In the first two rows we assume that exports are equal to imports, so that the trade surplus is zero. In row 1, we assume the government budget is balanced. Investment accordingly has to equal $750 billion. In the next row we assume the government budget deficit is $150 billion. *Given the level of saving* of $750 billion and a zero trade balance, it has to be true that investment is now lower by $150 billion. Row 3 shows how this relationship is affected when there is a trade surplus.

Any sector that spends more than it receives in income has to borrow to pay for the excess spending. The private sector has three ways of disposing of its saving. It can make loans to the government, which thereby pays for the excess of its spending over the income it receives from taxes. Or the private sector can lend to foreigners, who are buying more from us than we are buying from them. They therefore are earning less from us than they need in order to pay for the goods they buy from us, and we have to lend to cover the difference. Or the private sector can lend to business firms, which use the funds for investment. In all three cases, households will be paid back later, receiving interest or dividends in addition to the amount they lent.

The last row of Table 2-5 is relevant to the change in the U.S. budget and trade deficits during the eighties. Early in the decade, the government budget deficit increased. Private saving did not increase much, and private investment did not fall. Accordingly, as a matter of arithmetic, the United States had to be importing more than it was exporting. That is what happened, as shown in Figure 2-3.

In the 1980s there was much discussion of the *twin deficits*—the budget deficit and the trade deficit. Identity (10) is helpful in seeing that budget deficits must have a counterpart: if the government spends more than it receives in revenues, then it has to borrow, either at home (private saving exceeds investment) or abroad (imports exceed exports). The identity makes it clear that budget deficits need not be matched one-for-one by negative net exports. Thus there is no inevitable one-to-one link between the two deficits. And indeed, by 1991 the next export deficit of the United States had

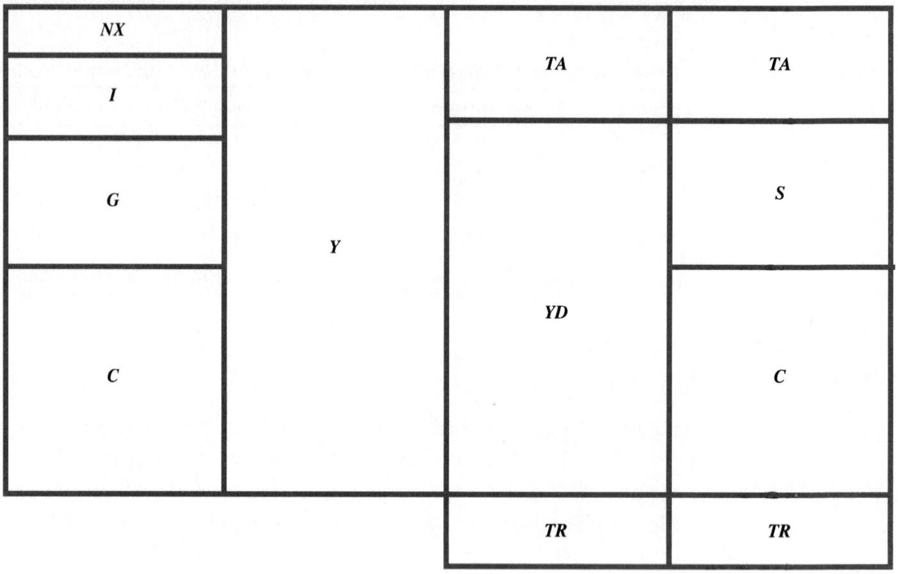

FIGURE 2-4
THE BASIC MACROECONOMIC IDENTITY:

$$C + G + I + NX \equiv Y \equiv YD + (TA - TR)$$
$$\equiv C + S + (TA - TR) \qquad (11)$$

The left-hand side is the demand for output by components; it is identically equal to output supplied. Output supplied is equal to GDP. Disposable income is equal to GDP plus transfers less taxes. Disposable income is allocated to saving and consumption.

declined to $20 billion, from its 1987 peak of $140 billion, even though the budget deficit had increased during that period.

Bringing Everything Together

In Figure 2-4 the goal is to summarize in a convenient form the different perspectives on GDP. There is first the proposition that output is equal to the components of demand, $Y = C + I + G + NX$. Second, output produced in an economy accrues as incomes to the factors of production. But because of the government sector we must also introduce taxes and transfers. Thus disposable income is equal to output plus transfers less taxes, $YD = Y + TR - TA$. Finally, disposable income is allocated to consumption and saving, $YD = Y + TR - TA = C + S$.

2-7 SUMMARY

1. Nominal gross domestic product, or GDP, is the value, measured at market prices, of the output of final goods and services produced within the country.
2. Gross national product is the value of output produced by factors of production owned by residents of the country. GNP differs from GDP both because some goods made in the country are produced by foreign-owned factors of production and because our citizens receive income from abroad, for example, if they own assets abroad.
3. Real GDP is the value of the economy's output measured in the prices of some base year. Real GDP comparisons, which are all based on the same set of prices for valuing output, provide a better measure of the change in the economy's physical output than nominal GDP comparisons, which also reflect inflation.
4. The GDP deflator is the ratio of nominal to real GDP. It provides one measure of the rise in prices from the base date at which real GDP is valued. Other frequently used price indexes are the consumer and producer price indexes.
5. Spending on GDP is divided into consumption, investment, government purchases of goods and services, and net exports. The division between consumption and investment in the national income accounts is somewhat arbitrary at the edges.
6. The excess of the private sector's saving over investment is equal to the sum of the budget deficit and net exports [equation (10)].
7. For the remainder of the book we use a simplified model for convenience. We assume away depreciation, indirect taxes, business transfer payments, and the difference between households and corporations. For this simplified model, Figure 2-4 and equation (12) review the *basic macroeconomic identity:*

$$C + G + I + NX \equiv Y \equiv YD + (TA - TR) \equiv C + S + (TA - TR) \qquad (11)$$

The left-hand side is the demand for output by components and is identically equal to GDP plus transfers less taxes. Disposable income is allocated to saving and consumption.

KEY TERMS

Final goods	Disposable personal income
Consumption	Government purchases
Market prices	Government expenditure
Gross domestic product (GDP)	Investment
Gross national product (GNP)	Depreciation
Net domestic product (NDP)	Net exports
GDP deflator	Consumer durables
Consumer price index (CPI)	Government budget deficit
Producer price index (PPI)	Twin deficits
Transfers	

PROBLEMS

1. In the text, we calculated the change in real GDP in the hypothetical economy of Table 2-1, using the prices of 1987. Calculate the change in real GDP between 1987 and 1993 using the same data, but *in the prices of 1993*. Your answer should demonstrate that the prices that are used to calculate real GDP do affect the calculated growth rate, but typically not by very much.

2. Show from national income accounting that:
   (a) An increase in taxes (while transfers remain constant) must imply a change in net exports, government purchases, or the saving-investment balance.
   (b) An increase in disposable personal income must imply an increase in consumption or an increase in saving.
   (c) An increase in both consumption and saving must imply an increase in disposable income.
   [For both (b) and (c) assume there are no interest payments by households or transfer payments to foreigners.]

3. The following is information from the national income accounts for a hypothetical country:

GDP	$6,000
Gross investment	800
Net investment	200
Consumption	4,000
Government purchases of goods and services	1,100
Government budget surplus	30

   What is
   (a) NDP?
   (b) net exports?
   (c) government taxes minus transfers?
   (d) disposable personal income?
   (e) personal saving?

4. What would happen to GDP if the government hired unemployed workers, who had been receiving amount TR in unemployment benefits, as government employees to do nothing, and now paid them TR? Explain.

5. What is the difference in the national income accounts between
   (a) A firm's buying an auto for an executive and the firm's paying the executive additional income to buy the automobile herself?
   (b) Your hiring your spouse (who takes care of the house) rather than having him or her do the work without pay?
   (c) Your deciding to buy an American car rather than a German car?

6. Explain the following terms: (a) value added, (b) inventory investment, (c) GDP deflator, (d) disposable personal income.

7. The following discussion deals with GNP, GDP, and NDP.
   (a) In 1991, U.S. GDP was $5,677.5 billion; GNP was $5,694.9 billion. Why is there a difference?
   (b) In 1991, U.S. GDP was $5,677.5 billion; NDP was $5,051.4 billion. What accounts for the difference? How typical is the 1991 difference as a fraction of GDP?

8. This question deals with price index numbers. Consider a simple economy in which only

three items are in the CPI: food, housing, and entertainment (fun). Assume in the base period, say, 1987, the household consumed the following quantities at the then prevailing prices:

	quantity	price, $ per unit	expenditure, $
Food	5	14	70
Housing	3	10	30
Fun	4	5	20
Total			120

(a) Define the consumer price index.

(b) Assume that the basket of goods that defines the CPI is as given in the table. Calculate the CPI for 1994 if the prices prevailing in 1994 are as follows: food, $30 per unit; housing, $20 per unit; and fun, $6 per unit.

*(c) Show that the change in the CPI relative to the base year is a weighted average of the individual price changes, where the weights are given by the base year expenditure shares of the various goods.

9. Use Appendix 2-2 and the following 1991 GDP data (in billions) to answer this question:
   GDP = $5,678
   GNP = $5,695
   NDP = $5,051
   Indirect taxes = $474
   Other (net) = −$1

Using Table A2-1:
   (a) What are (i) depreciation and (ii) national income?
   (b) Why are indirect taxes deducted from NDP to get national income?

10. Assume that GDP is $6,000, personal disposable income is $5,100, and the government budget deficit is $200. Consumption is $3,800, and the trade deficit is $100.
   (a) How large is saving (S)?
   (b) What is the size of investment (I)?
   (c) How large is government spending (G)?

11. Show that a country that spends more than its income must have an external deficit.

COMPUTER EXERCISES

National Income Accounts

1. Demonstrate that:
   (a) Given national income, an increase in *CCA* or indirect business taxes will increase GDP.
   (b) An increase in personal income taxes will reduce personal disposable income.
   (c) An increase in corporate profits will reduce personal income unless there is an offsetting increase in dividends.

---

*An asterisk denotes a more difficult problem.

2. Write down the equations implied by each of the four income statements. Demonstrate that a change in *I* is possible only if there are appropriate changes in *SP, RE, CCA,* or *BS.* (These concepts are defined in the module.)

3. Make a change and then consider what is necessary to keep the accounts in balance:
   (a) An increase in *G* (remember, in the short run real GDP is fixed).
   (b) An increase in *G* offset by a corresponding increase in *TP.*
   (c) A decision by consumers to increase saving.

4. Explain why the difference between national income and personal income is relatively small. How could you make it larger?

Price Indexes

1. Run the "Demo" for this section of Chapter 2. Now, in contrast to the demo, suppose the price of watches rises by 25 percent instead of falling 10 percent and the price of bread falls by 10 percent rather than rising 25 percent. What is the impact on the consumer price index? Does this result have anything to do with the share of consumer spending on food? Explain.

2. Suppose purchases of watches rise from year 0 to year 1 by 500 rather than by 200. What is the impact on the CPI? What is the impact on the GDP deflator? Why the difference?

3. Suppose the composition of consumer purchases is different all along. For example, suppose that consumers buy twice as much bread each year. What is the impact on both types of price indexes? Explain.

APPENDIX 2-1: PRICE INDEX FORMULAS

Both the PPI and CPI are price indexes that compare the current and base year cost of a basket of goods of *fixed* composition. If we denote the base year quantities of the various goods by q_0^i and their base year prices by p_0^i, the cost of the basket in the base year is $\Sigma\, p_0^i q_0^i$, where the summation (Σ) is over all the goods in the basket. The cost of a basket of the *same* quantities but at today's prices is $\Sigma\, p_t^i q_0^i$, where p_t^i is today's price. The CPI or PPI is the ratio of today's cost to the base year cost, or

$$\text{Consumer or producer price index} = \frac{\Sigma\, p_t^i q_0^i}{\Sigma\, p_0^i q_0^i} \times 100$$

This is a so-called *Laspeyres,* or *base-weighted,* price index.

The GDP deflator, by contrast, uses the weights of the *current* period to calculate the price index. Let q_t^i be the quantities of the different goods produced in the current year.

$$\text{GDP deflator} = \frac{\text{GDP measured in current prices}}{\text{GDP measured in base year prices}} = \frac{\Sigma\, p_t^i q_t^i}{\Sigma\, p_0^i q_t^i} \times 100$$

This is known as a *Paasche,* or *current-weighted,* price index.

Comparing the two formulas we see that they differ only in that q_0^i, or the base year quantities, appears in both numerator and denominator of the CPI and PPI formula, whereas q_t^i appears in the formula for the deflator. In practice, the CPI, PPI, and GDP deflator indexes differ also because they involve different collections of goods.

PROBLEM: Calculate both the Laspeyres and Paasche price indexes for the information in Table 2-1.

APPENDIX 2-2: RELATION BETWEEN GDP AND PERSONAL DISPOSABLE INCOME

This appendix sets out the steps that are needed to calculate the level of personal disposable income, starting from GDP. The necessity for these adjustments arises from five sources: the difference between GDP and GNP, reflecting net income received from abroad; depreciation; transfers; taxes and subsidies; and the presence of a business sector that retains some profits and makes some transfer payments to households.

The first step is to move from GDP to GNP, to account for net income from other countries. The second step is to move from GNP to NNP (net national product), from "gross" to "net," in order to reflect depreciation. Thus net national product, or NNP, is GNP less depreciation.

Table A2-1 summarizes the remaining steps from NNP to personal disposable income.

TABLE A2-1

GDP AND PERSONAL DISPOSABLE INCOME, 1991 (billions of dollars)

Gross domestic product			5,677.5
Plus	Net factor payments from abroad	17.5	
Equals	Gross national product		5,694.9
Less	Capital consumption allowance	626.1	
Equals	Net national product		5,068.8
Less	Indirect taxes	475.2	
	Other (net)	49.4	
Equals	National income		4,544.2
Less	Corporate profits	346.3	
	Social security contributions	528.8	
Plus	Government and business transfers to persons	771.1	
	Interest adjustment	251.1	
	Dividends	137.0	
Equals	Personal income		4,828.3
Less	Personal tax and nontax payments	618.7	
Equals	Disposable personal income		4,209.6

SOURCE: *Survey of Current Business.*

3

INCOME AND SPENDING

*O*ne of the central questions in macroeconomics is why output fluctuates around its potential level. Growth is highly uneven. In business cycle fluctuations, booms and recessions, output fluctuates relative to the trend of potential output. In the past two decades there have been four recessions, in which output declined relative to trend—even falling in some years, including 1991—and then recoveries in which output rose relative to trend.

This chapter offers a first theory of these fluctuations in real output relative to trend. The cornerstone of this model is the interdependence between output and spending: spending determines output and income, but output and income determine spending.

The *Keynesian* model of income determination we develop in this chapter is very simple and will be elaborated in later chapters. The central simplification is that we assume for the time being that prices do not change at all, and that firms are willing to sell *any* amount of output at the given level of prices. Thus the aggregate supply curve, shown in Chapter 1, is assumed to be entirely flat.

Of course, prices do in fact change. We assume for now that they are constant in order to develop the notion of *aggregate demand*. When in later chapters we relax the assumption that prices are fixed and allow them to change, we will find that the conclusions derived in this chapter are qualified, though not reversed.

We now study how the level of output is determined when the aggregate supply curve is flat. The key concept of *equilibrium output* is introduced immediately.

3-1 AGGREGATE DEMAND AND EQUILIBRIUM OUTPUT

Aggregate demand is the total amount of goods demanded in the economy. Distinguishing among goods demanded for consumption (*C*), for investment (*I*), by the government (*G*), and net exports (*NX*), aggregate demand (*AD*) is given by

$$AD = C + I + G + NX \tag{1}$$

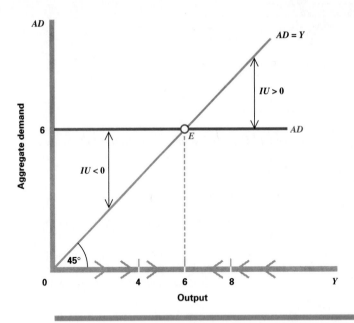

FIGURE 3-1

EQUILIBRIUM WITH CONSTANT AGGREGATE DEMAND. Aggregate
demand is shown by the *AD* line and is equal to 6 (trillion dollars).
Output is at its equilibrium level when it is equal to aggregate
demand, which equals 6. Thus the equilibrium is at point *E*, as
shown. At any other output level, inventories are changing in a way
that causes firms to change their production in a direction that
moves output toward the equilibrium level.

In general, the quantity of goods demanded, or aggregate demand, depends on the
level of income in the economy. But for now we shall assume that the amount of
goods demanded is constant, independent of the level of income.

Aggregate demand is shown in Figure 3-1 by the horizontal line *AD*. In the
diagram, aggregate demand is equal to 6 (trillion dollars). This means that the total
amount of goods demanded in the economy is $6,000 billion, independent of the level
of income. If the quantity of goods demanded is constant, independent of the level of
income, what determines the actual level of income? We have to turn to the concept
of equilibrium output.

Equilibrium Output

Output is at its *equilibrium* level when the quantity of output produced is equal to the
quantity demanded. An equilibrium situation is one which no forces are causing to
change. We now explain why output is at its equilibrium level when it is equal to
aggregate demand.

In Figure 3-1 we show the level of output on the horizontal axis. The 45° line serves as a reference line that translates any horizontal distance into an equal vertical distance. Thus, anywhere on the 45° line, labeled *AD* = *Y*, the level of aggregate demand is equal to the level of output. For instance, at point *E*, both output and aggregate demand are equal to 6 (trillion dollars).

Point *E* is therefore the point of equilibrium output, at which the quantity of output produced is exactly equal to the quantity demanded. Suppose that firms were producing some other amount, say 8 units. Then output would exceed demand. Firms would be unable to sell all they produce and would find their warehouses filling with inventories of unsold goods. They would then cut their output. This is shown by the horizontal arrow pointing left from the output level of 8. Similarly, if output were less than 6, say 4, firms would either run out of goods or be running down their inventories. They would therefore increase output, as shown by the horizontal arrow pointing to the right from the output level of 4.

Thus at point *E*, the equilibrium level of output, firms are selling as much as they produce, people are buying the amount they want to purchase, and there is no tendency for the level of output to change. At any other level of output, the pressure from increasing or declining inventories causes firms to change the level of output.

Equilibrium Output and the National Income Identity

We defined equilibrium output as that level of output at which aggregate demand for goods is equal to output:

$$AD\,(= C + I + G + NX) = Y \tag{2}$$

We now have to dispose of an unsettling issue that arises from out study of national income accounting. In Chapter 2 we defined the level of output, *Y*, as equal to ($C + I + G + NX$), without ever saying that output has to be equal to aggregate demand. That seems to mean that demand equals output at *any* level of output.

Recall that aggregate demand is the amount of goods people *want to buy*, whereas investment and consumption in the national income accounts are the amounts of the goods *actually* bought. In particular, the investment measured in the national accounts includes *involuntary*, or *unintended* (or *undesired*), inventory changes, which occur when firms find themselves selling more or fewer goods than they had planned to sell.

We thus distinguish between the actual aggregate demand measured in an accounting context and the economic concept of planned (desired, intended) aggregate demand.

In the national income accounts, *actual aggregate demand* ($C + I + G + NX$) is equal to the *actual* level of output (*Y*). If firms miscalculate the demands of households, government, and foreigners, planned aggregate demand does not equal actual aggregate demand. Suppose first that firms overestimate demand. In terms of Figure 3-1, suppose that firms decide to produce 8 units of output, expecting to be able to sell that amount. However, aggregate demand is only 6. The firms thus sell 6 units of output. But they are left with 2 (trillion), which they have to add to their inventories. In the national income accounts, additions to inventories count as investment. Of course, this is not *planned* or *desired* investment, but even so it does count as actual investment. Looking at the national income accounts of such an economy, we would see output equal to 8. However, that does not mean that 8 is the equilibrium level of output, because 2 (trillion) units of investment were undesired additions to inventories.

When aggregate demand—the amount people want to buy—is not equal to output, there is unplanned inventory investment or disinvestment. We summarize this as

$$IU = Y - AD \tag{3}$$

where *IU* is unplanned additions to inventory.

In Figure 3-1, unplanned inventory investment is shown by the vertical arrows. When output exceeds 6, there is unplanned inventory investment. When output is less than 6, there are unplanned reductions in inventories. Thus at the equilibrium level of income, 6 in Figure 3-1, and only at that level of income, aggregate demand or planned spending is equal to actual output.

The *equilibrium* level of income is the level of income (or output) at which planned spending is equal to actual output, so that there is no involuntary inventory accumulation or rundown. Output is at its equilibrium level when

$$Y = AD \tag{2a}$$

Summarizing, there are three essential notions in this section:

1. Aggregate demand determines the equilibrium level of output.
2. At equilibrium, unintended changes in inventories are zero, and consumers, the government, and foreign purchasers of our goods are all purchasing the amounts they want to purchase.
3. An adjustment process for output based on unintended inventory changes will actually move output to its equilibrium level.[1]

Note, too, that the definition of equilibrium implies that actual spending equals planned spending. In equilibrium, aggregate demand, which is planned spending, equals output. Since output identically equals income, we see also that *in equilibrium, planned spending equals income.*

3-2   THE CONSUMPTION FUNCTION AND AGGREGATE DEMAND

With the concept of equilibrium output firmly defined, we now focus on the determinants of aggregate demand, and particularly on consumption demand. For simplicity, we

[1]The adjustment process we describe raises the possibility that output will temporarily exceed its new equilibrium level during the adjustment to an increase in aggregate demand. This is the *inventory cycle*. Suppose firms desire to hold inventories which are proportional to the level of demand. When demand unexpectedly rises, inventories are depleted. In subsequent periods, the firms have to produce not only to meet the new higher level of aggregate demand, but also to restore the depleted inventories and raise them to the new higher level. While firms are rebuilding their inventories and also producing to meet the higher level of demand, their total production will exceed the new higher level of aggregate demand.

omit both the government and foreign trade, therefore setting both *G* and *NX* equal to zero.

The demand for consumption goods is not in practice constant, but rather increases with income—families with higher incomes consume more than families with lower incomes, and countries where income is higher typically have higher levels of total consumption. The relationship between consumption and income is described by the *consumption function.*

The Consumption Function

We assume that consumption demand increases with the level of income:

$$C = \overline{C} + cY \qquad \overline{C} > 0 \qquad 0 < c < 1 \tag{4}$$

This consumption function is shown by the red line in Figure 3-2. The variable $\overline{C}$, the *intercept,* represents the level of consumption when income is zero.[2] For every dollar increase in income, the level of consumption increases by \$*c*. For example, if *c* is 0.90, then for every \$1 increase in income, consumption rises by 90 cents. The *slope* of the consumption function is *c*. Along the consumption function the level of consumption rises with income. Box 3-1 shows that this relationship holds in practice.

The coefficient *c* is sufficiently important to have a special name, the *marginal propensity to consume.* The marginal propensity to consume is the increase in consumption per unit increase in income. In our case, the marginal propensity to consume is less than 1, which implies that out of a dollar increase in income, only a fraction, *c,* is spent on consumption.

Consumption and Saving

What happens to the rest of the dollar of income, the fraction $(1 - c)$, that is not spent on consumption? If it is not spent, it must be saved. Income is either spent or saved; there are no other uses to which it can be put. It follows that any theory that explains consumption is equivalently explaining the behavior of saving.

More formally, look at equation (5), which says that income that is not spent on consumption is saved, or

$$S \equiv Y - C \tag{5}$$

Equation (5) tells us that by definition *saving is equal to income minus consumption.*

---

[2]Two points need to be made about the consumption function (4). First, individuals' consumption demands are related to the amount of income they have available to spend, i.e., their disposable income (*YD*), rather than just to the level of output. However, in this section where we are ignoring the role of government and foreign trade, disposable income is equal to the level of income and output. Second, how can individuals consume anything when their income is zero? For some time, they can sell off their assets, such as stocks, bonds, and the house. Eventually, though, it would be difficult to continue to buy goods when income is zero.

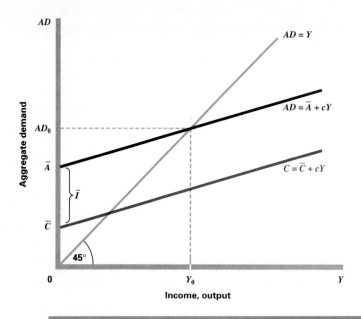

FIGURE 3-2
THE CONSUMPTION FUNCTION AND AGGREGATE DEMAND. The consumption function shows the level of consumption spending at each level of income. The intercept of the consumption function is $\bar{C}$ and its slope is the marginal propensity to consume, c. Aggregate demand is the sum of the demands for consumption and investment goods. Investment demand, I, is assumed constant and is added to consumption demand to obtain the level of aggregate demand at each level of income. The line AD shows how aggregate demand increases with income.

The consumption function in equation (4) together with equation (5), which we call the *budget constraint,* imply a saving function. The saving function relates the level of saving to the level of income. Substituting the consumption function in equation (4) into the budget constraint in equation (5) yields the saving function

$$S \equiv Y - C = Y - \bar{C} - cY = -\bar{C} + (1 - c)Y \tag{6}$$

From equation (6), we see that saving is an increasing function of the level of income because the *marginal propensity to save,* $s = 1 - c$, is positive.

In other words, saving increases as income rises. For instance, suppose the marginal propensity to consume, c, is 0.9, meaning that 90 cents out of each extra dollar of income is consumed. Then the marginal propensity to save, s, is 0.10, meaning that the remaining 10 cents of each extra dollar of income is saved.

Planned Investment and Aggregate Demand

We have now specified one component of aggregate demand, consumption demand. We must also consider the determinants of investment spending, or an *investment function.* We cut short the discussion for the present by simply assuming that planned investment spending is constant, at the level $\bar{I}$.

With government spending and net exports each assumed equal to zero, aggregate demand is the sum of consumption and investment demands:

$$
\begin{aligned}
AD &= C + \bar{I} \\
&= \overline{C} + \bar{I} + cY \qquad\qquad (7) \\
&= \overline{A} + cY
\end{aligned}
$$

The aggregate demand function (7) is shown in Figure 3-2. Part of aggregate demand, $\overline{A} = \overline{C} + \bar{I}$, is independent of the level of income, or autonomous. But *aggregate demand also depends on the level of income.* It increases with the level of income because consumption demand increases with income. The aggregate demand schedule is obtained by adding (vertically) the demands for investment and consumption at each level of income. At the income level Y_0 in Figure 3-2, the level of aggregate demand is AD_0.

Equilibrium Income and Output

The next step is to use the aggregate demand function, *AD,* in Figure 3-2 and equation (7) to determine the equilibrium levels of output and income. We do this in Figure 3-3.

Recall the basic point of this chapter: the equilibrium level of income is such that aggregate demand equals output (which in turn equals income). The 45° line, $AD = Y,$ in Figure 3-3 shows points at which output and aggregate demand are equal. Only at point *E,* and at the corresponding equilibrium levels of income and output (Y_0), does aggregate demand exactly equal output.[3] At that level of output and income, planned spending precisely matches production.

The arrows in Figure 3-3 indicate once again how the economy reaches equilibrium. At any income level below Y_0, firms find that demand exceeds output and that their inventories are declining. They therefore increase production. Conversely, for output levels above Y_0, firms find inventories piling up and therefore cut production. As the arrows show, this process leads to the output level Y_0, at which current production exactly matches planned aggregate spending and unintended inventory changes are therefore equal to zero.

THE FORMULA FOR EQUILIBRIUM OUTPUT

The determination of equilibrium output in Figure 3-3 can also be described using equation (7) and the equilibrium condition in the goods market, which is that output is equal to aggregate demand:

---

[3]We frequently use the subscript 0 to denote the equilibrium level of a variable.

box 3-1 THE CONSUMPTION-INCOME RELATIONSHIP

The consumption function of equation (4),

$$C = \overline{C} + cY$$

provides a good first description of the consumption-income relationship. Annual consumption and disposable personal income data for the United States for the years since 1959 are plotted in Figure 1. Recall from Chapter 2 that disposable personal income is the amount of income households have available for either spending or saving after paying taxes and receiving transfers.

The figure reveals a very close relationship between consumption and disposable income. The actual relationship is

$$C = 0.92YD$$

where C and YD are measured in billions of real (1987) dollars.

Note two points: first, it turns out that the constant in the consumption function, $\overline{C}$, is in practice very close to zero; we nonetheless retain $\overline{C}$ in the text, since it provides a more general form of the consumption function; second, although the relationship between consumption and disposable income is close, not all the points in Figure 1 lie exactly on the line. That means that something other than disposable income is affecting consumption in any given year. We turn our attention to those other factors determining consumption in Chapter 11. Meanwhile, it is reassuring that equation (4) is a quite accurate description of the real world's consumption-income relationship. ∎

$$Y = AD \tag{8}$$

The level of aggregate demand, AD, is specified in equation (7). Substituting for AD in equation (8), we have the equilibrium condition as

$$Y = \overline{A} + cY \tag{9}$$

Since we have Y on both sides of the equilibrium condition in equation (9), we can collect the terms and solve for the equilibrium level of income and output, denoted by Y_0:

$$Y_0 = \frac{1}{1 - c}\overline{A} \tag{10}$$

Figure 3-3 sheds light on equation (10). The position of the aggregate demand schedule is characterized by its slope, c (the marginal propensity to consume), and

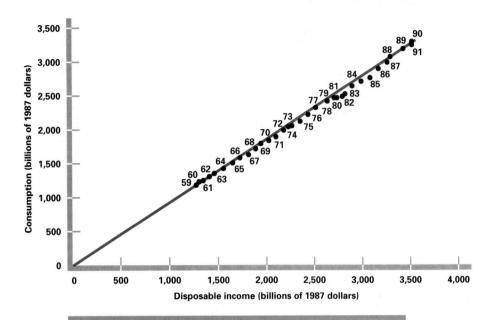

FIGURE 1

THE CONSUMPTION-INCOME RELATION, 1959–1991. There is a close relationship in practice between consumption spending and disposable income. Consumption spending rises on average by 92 cents for every extra dollar of disposable income. The colored line is the fitted regression line that summarizes the relationship shown by the points for the individual years.

intercept, $\overline{A}$ (autonomous spending). Given the intercept, a steeper aggregate demand function—as would be implied by a higher marginal propensity to consume—implies a higher level of equilibrium income. Similarly, for a given marginal propensity to consume, a higher level of autonomous spending—in terms of Figure 3-3, a larger intercept—implies a higher equilibrium level of income. These results, suggested by Figure 3-3, are easily verified using equation (10), which gives the formula for the equilibrium level of income.

Thus, the equilibrium level of output is higher the larger the marginal propensity to consume, *c,* and the higher the level of autonomous spending, $\overline{A}$.

Saving and Investment

There is a useful alternative formulation of the equilibrium condition that aggregate demand is equal to output. *In equilibrium, planned investment equals saving.* This condition applies only to an economy in which there is no government and no foreign trade.

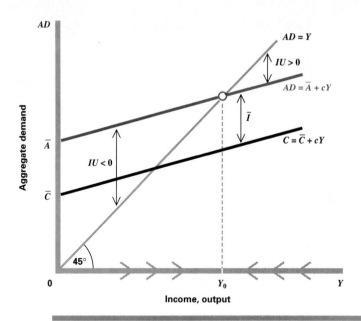

FIGURE 3-3

DETERMINATION OF EQUILIBRIUM INCOME AND OUTPUT. Output is at its equilibrium level when aggregate demand is equal to output. This occurs at point *E*, corresponding to the output (and income) level Y_0. At any higher level of output, aggregate demand is below the level of output, firms are unable to sell all they produce, and there is undesired accumulation of inventories. Firms therefore reduce output, as shown by the arrows. Similarly, at any level of output below Y_0, aggregate demand exceeds output, firms run short of goods to sell, and they therefore increase output. Only at the equilibrium output level, Y_0, are firms producing the amount that is demanded, and there is no tendency for the level of output to change.

To understand this relationship, return to Figure 3-3. The vertical distance between the aggregate demand and consumption schedules in that figure is equal to planned investment spending, $\bar{I}$. Note also that the vertical distance between the consumption schedule and the 45° line measures saving ($S = Y - C$) at each level of income.

The equilibrium level of income is found where *AD* crosses the 45° line, at *E*. Accordingly, at the equilibrium level of income—and only at that level—the two vertical distances are equal. Thus at the equilibrium level of income, saving equals (planned) investment. By contrast, above the equilibrium level of income, Y_0, saving (the distance between the 45° line and the consumption schedule) exceeds planned investment, while below Y_0, planned investment exceeds saving.

The equality between saving and investment at equilibrium is an essential characteristic of the equilibrium level of income. We can see that by starting with the basic equilibrium condition, equation (8), $Y = AD$. If we subtract consumption from both

TABLE 3-1

THE MULTIPLIER

round	increase in demand this round	increase in production this round	total increase in income
1	$\Delta \bar{A}$	$\Delta \bar{A}$	$\Delta \bar{A}$
2	$c\Delta \bar{A}$	$c\Delta \bar{A}$	$(1 + c)\Delta \bar{A}$
3	$c^2\Delta \bar{A}$	$c^2\Delta \bar{A}$	$(1 + c + c^2)\Delta \bar{A}$
4	$c^3\Delta \bar{A}$	$c^3\Delta \bar{A}$	$(1 + c + c^2 + c^3)\Delta \bar{A}$
...	...	...	...
...	...	...	...
...	...	...	$\dfrac{1}{1 - c}\Delta \bar{A}$

Y and *AD,* we realize that $Y - C$ is saving and $AD - C$ is planned investment. In symbols,

$$Y = AD$$
$$Y - C = AD - C \tag{11}$$
$$S = \bar{I}$$

Thus, the condition $S = \bar{I}$ is merely another way of stating the basic equilibrium condition.

3-3 THE MULTIPLIER

In this section we develop an answer to the following question: By how much does a $1 increase in autonomous spending raise the equilibrium level of income? There appears to be a simple answer. Since, in equilibrium, income equals aggregate demand, it would seem that a $1 increase in (autonomous) demand or spending should raise equilibrium income by $1. That answer is wrong. Let us now see why.

Suppose first that output increased by $1 to match the increased level of autonomous spending. This increase in output and income would in turn give rise to further *induced* spending as consumption rises because the level of income has risen. How much of the initial $1 increase in income would be spent on consumption? Out of an additional dollar of income, a fraction (*c*) is consumed. Assume then that production increases further to meet this induced expenditure, that is, that output and thus income increase by $(1 + c)$. That will still leave us with an excess demand, because the expansion in production and income by $(1 + c)$ will give rise to further induced spending. This story could clearly take a long time to tell. Does the process have an end?

In Table 3-1 we lay out the steps in the chain. The first round starts off with an increase in autonomous spending, $\Delta \bar{A}$. Next we allow an expansion in production to meet exactly that increase in demand. Production accordingly expands by $\Delta \overline{A}$. This increase in production gives rise to an equal increase in income and therefore, via the marginal propensity to consume, c, gives rise in the second round to induced expenditures of size $c(\Delta \overline{A})$. Assume again that production expands to meet this increase in spending. The production adjustment this time is $c\Delta \overline{A}$, and so is the increase in income. This gives rise to a third round of induced spending equal to the marginal propensity to consume times the increase in income $c(c\Delta \overline{A}) = c^2 \Delta \overline{A}$. Since the marginal propensity to consume, c, is less than 1, the term c^2 is less than c, and therefore induced expenditures in the third round are smaller than those in the second round.

If we write out the successive rounds of increased spending, starting with the initial increase in autonomous demand, we obtain

$$\begin{aligned} \Delta AD &= \Delta \overline{A} + c\Delta \overline{A} + c^2 \Delta \overline{A} + c^3 \Delta \overline{A} + \cdots \\ &= \Delta \overline{A}(1 + c + c^2 + c^3 + \cdots) \end{aligned} \tag{12}$$

For a value of $c < 1$, the successive terms in the series become progressively smaller. In fact, we are dealing with a geometric series, so the equation simplifies to

$$\Delta AD = \frac{1}{1 - c} \Delta \overline{A} = \Delta Y_0 \tag{13}$$

The cumulative change in aggregate spending is thus equal to a multiple of the increase in autonomous spending. This could also have been deduced from equation (10). The multiple $1/(1 - c)$ is called the *multiplier*.[4] The multiplier is the amount by which equilibrium output changes when autonomous aggregate demand increases by one unit.

The concept of the multiplier is sufficiently important to create new notation. The general definition of the multiplier is $\Delta Y/\Delta \overline{A}$, the change in equilibrium output when autonomous demand increases by one unit. In this specific case, omitting the government sector and foreign trade, we define the multiplier as α, where

$$\alpha \equiv \frac{1}{1 - c} \tag{14}$$

Inspection of the multiplier in equation (14) shows that the larger the marginal propensity to consume, the larger the multiplier. With a marginal propensity to consume of 0.6, the multiplier is 2.5; for a marginal propensity to consume of 0.8, the multiplier is 5. A higher marginal propensity to consume implies that a larger fraction of an additional dollar of income will be consumed, thereby causing a larger induced increase in demand.

Why focus on the multiplier? The reason is that we are developing an explanation of fluctuations in output. The multiplier suggests that output changes when autonomous

---

[4]If you are familiar with the calculus, you will realize that the multiplier is nothing other than the derivative of the equilibrium level of income, Y_0, in equation (10) with respect to autonomous spending. Use the calculus on equation (10) and later on equation (22) to check the statements in the text.

spending (including investment) changes, *and* that the change in output can be larger than the change in autonomous spending. The multiplier is the formal way of describing a commonsense idea: if the economy for some reason—for example, a loss in confidence that reduces investment spending—experiences a shock that reduces income, then people whose incomes have gone down will spend less, thereby driving equilibrium income down even further. The multiplier is therefore part of an explanation of why output fluctuates.[5]

The Multiplier in Pictures

Figure 3-4 provides a graphical interpretation of the effects of an increase in autonomous spending on the equilibrium level of income. The initial equilibrium is at point E with an income level Y_0. Now autonomous spending increases from $\overline{A}$ to $\overline{A}'$. This is represented by a parallel upward shift of the aggregate demand schedule to AD'. The upward shift means that now, at each level of income, aggregate demand is higher by an amount $\Delta\overline{A} \equiv \overline{A}' - \overline{A}$.

Aggregate demand now exceeds the initial level of output, Y_0. Consequently, inventories begin to run down. Firms will respond to the increase in demand and declining inventories by expanding production, say to income level Y'. This expansion in production gives rise to induced expenditure, increasing aggregate demand to the level A_G. At the same time, the expansion reduces the gap between aggregate demand and output to the vertical distance FG. The gap between demand and output is reduced because the marginal propensity to consume is less than 1.

Thus, with a marginal propensity to consume less than unity, a sufficient expansion in output will restore the balance between aggregate demand and output. In Figure 3-4 the new equilibrium is indicated by point E', and the corresponding level of income is Y_0'. The change in income required is therefore $\Delta Y_0 = Y_0' - Y_0$.

The magnitude of the income change required to restore equilibrium depends on two factors. The larger the increase in autonomous spending, represented in Figure 3-4 by the parallel shift in the aggregate demand schedule, the larger the income change. Furthermore, the larger the marginal propensity to consume—that is, the steeper the aggregate demand schedule—the larger the income change.

Another Derivation

Finally, there is yet another way of deriving the multiplier. Remember that in equilibrium, aggregate demand equals income or output. From one equilibrium to another, it must therefore be true that the change in income, ΔY_0, is equal to the change in aggregate demand, ΔAD:

---

[5]*Warning:* The multiplier is necessarily greater than 1 in this simplified model of income determination, but as we shall see in the discussion of "crowding out" in Chap. 4, there may be circumstances in which it is less than 1.

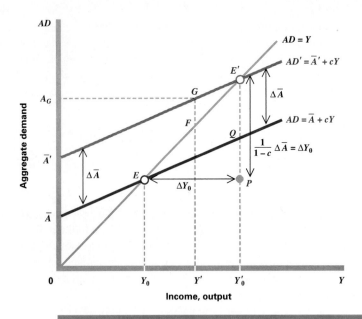

FIGURE 3-4

GRAPHICAL DERIVATION OF THE MULTIPLIER. When there is an increase in autonomous demand, the aggregate demand schedule shifts up to *AD'*. The equilibrium moves from *E* to *E'*. The increase in equilibrium output $(Y'_0 - Y_0)$, which equals distance *PE* equal to *PE'*, exceeds the increase in autonomous demand, *E'Q*. From the diagram we see that the excess is a result of the *AD* curve's having a positive slope rather than being horizontal. In other words, the multiplier exceeds 1 because consumption demand increases with output—any increase in output produces further increases in demand.

$$\Delta Y_0 = \Delta AD \tag{15}$$

Next we split the change in aggregate demand into the change in autonomous spending, $\Delta \overline{A}$, and the change in expenditure induced by the consequent change in income, that is $c \Delta Y_0$:

$$\Delta AD = \Delta \overline{A} + c \Delta Y_0 \tag{16}$$

Combining equations (15) and (16), the change in income is

$$\Delta Y_0 = \Delta \overline{A} + c \Delta Y_0 \tag{17}$$

or, collecting terms,

$$\Delta Y_0 = \frac{1}{1 - c} \Delta \overline{A} \tag{18}$$

Summary

There are three points to remember from this discussion of the multiplier.

1. An increase in autonomous spending raises the equilibrium level of income.
2. The increase in income is a multiple of the increase in autonomous spending.
3. The larger the marginal propensity to consume, the larger the multiplier arising from the relation between consumption and income.

3-4 THE GOVERNMENT SECTOR

Whenever there is a recession, people expect and demand that the government do something about it. What can the government do? The government directly affects the level of equilibrium income in two separate ways. First, government purchases of goods and services, G, are a component of aggregate demand. Second, taxes and transfers affect the relation between output and income, Y, and the *disposable income—* income available for consumption or saving—that accrues to household, YD. In this section, we show how government purchases, taxes, and transfers affect the equilibrium level of income.

The definition of aggregate demand has to be augmented to include government purchases of goods and services—purchases of military equipment and services of bureaucrats, for instance. Thus we have

$$AD \equiv C + \overline{I} + G \tag{7a}$$

Consumption will no longer depend on income, but rather on disposable income, YD. Disposable income (YD) is the net income available for spending by households after receiving transfers from and paying taxes to the government. It thus consists of income plus transfers less taxes, $Y + TR - TA$. The consumption function is now

$$C = \overline{C} + cYD = \overline{C} + c(Y + TR - TA) \tag{4a}$$

A final step is a specification of fiscal policy. Fiscal policy is the policy of the government with regard to the level of government purchases, the level of transfers, and the tax structure. We assume that the government purchases a constant amount, $\overline{G}$; that it makes a constant amount of transfers, $\overline{TR}$; and that it collects a fraction, t, of income in the form of taxes:

$$G = \overline{G} \qquad TR = \overline{TR} \qquad TA = tY \tag{19}$$

With this specification of fiscal policy, we can rewrite the consumption function, after substitution from equation (19) for *TR* and *TA* in equation (4a), as

$$C = \overline{C} + c(Y + \overline{TR} - tY) \qquad (20)$$
$$= \overline{C} + c\overline{TR} + c(1 - t)Y$$

Note in equation (20) that transfers raise autonomous consumption spending by the marginal propensity to consume out of disposable income, *c,* times the amount of transfers.[6] Income taxes, by contrast, lower consumption spending at each level of income. That reduction arises because households' consumption is related to *disposable* income rather than income itself, and income taxes reduce disposable income relative to the level of income.

While the marginal propensity to consume out of disposable income remains *c,* now the marginal propensity to consume out of income is $c(1 - t)$, where $(1 - t)$ is the fraction of income left after taxes. For example, if the marginal propensity to consume, *c,* is 0.8 and the tax rate is 0.25, then the marginal propensity to consume out of income, $c(1 - t)$, is 0.6 $[= 0.8 \times (1 - 0.25)]$.

Combining (7a), (19), and (20), we have

$$AD = (\overline{C} + c\overline{TR} + \overline{I} + \overline{G}) + c(1 - t)Y \qquad (21)$$
$$= \overline{A} + c(1 - t)Y$$

The effects of the introduction of government on the aggregate demand schedule are shown in Figure 3-5. The new aggregate demand schedule, denoted *AD'* in the figure, starts out higher than the original schedule, *AD,* but has a flatter slope. The intercept is larger because it now includes both government spending, $\overline{G}$, and the part of consumption resulting from transfer payments by the government, $c\overline{TR}$. The slope is flatter because households now have to pay part of every dollar of income in taxes and are left with only $(1 - t)$ of that dollar. Thus, as equation (21) shows, the marginal propensity to consume out of income is now $c(1 - t)$ instead of *c.*

Equilibrium Income

We are now set to study income determination when the government is included. We return to the equilibrium condition for the goods market, $Y = AD$, and, using equation (21), write the equilibrium condition as

$$Y = \overline{A} + c(1 - t)Y$$

We can solve this equation for Y_0, the equilibrium level of income, by collecting terms in Y:

---

[6]We are assuming no taxes are paid on transfers from the government. As a matter of fact, taxes are paid on some transfers, such as interest payments on the government debt, and not paid on other transfers, such as welfare benefits.

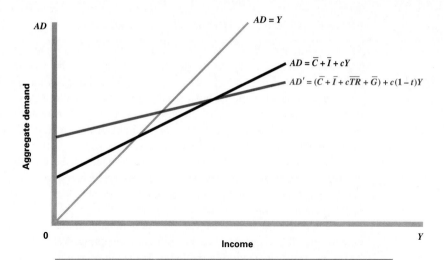

FIGURE 3-5

GOVERNMENT AND AGGREGATE DEMAND. Government affects aggregate demand through its own purchases, assumed here to be fixed at the autonomous level $\overline{G}$, through transfers $\overline{TR}$, and through taxes. Taxes are assumed to be a constant proportion, t, of income. Under these assumptions, the introduction of government shifts the intercept of the aggregate demand curve up and flattens the curve.

$$Y[1 - c(1 - t)] = \overline{A}$$

$$Y_0 = \frac{1}{1 - c(1 - t)} (\overline{C} + c\overline{TR} + \overline{I} + \overline{G}) \tag{22}$$

$$Y_0 = \frac{\overline{A}}{1 - c(1 - t)}$$

In comparing equation (22) with equation (10), we see that the government sector makes a substantial difference. It raises autonomous spending by the amount of government purchases, $\overline{G}$, and by the amount of induced spending out of net transfers, $c\overline{TR}$.

INCOME TAXES AND THE MULTIPLIER

At the same time *income taxes lower the multiplier* in equation (22). If the marginal propensity to consume is 0.8 and taxes are zero, the multiplier is 5; with the same marginal propensity to consume and a tax rate of 0.25, the multiplier is cut in half to $1/[1 - 0.8(0.75)] = 2.5$. Income taxes reduce the multiplier because they reduce the induced increase of consumption out of changes in income. Thus in Figure 3-5, the inclusion of taxes flattens the aggregate demand curve and hence reduces the multiplier.

INCOME TAXES AS AUTOMATIC STABILIZERS

The proportional income tax is one example of the important concept of *automatic stabilizers*. An automatic stabilizer is any mechanism in the economy that reduces the amount by which output changes in response to a change in autonomous demand.

One explanation of the business cycle is that it is caused by shifts in autonomous demand, especially investment. Sometimes, it is argued, investors are optimistic and investment is high—and so, therefore, is output. But sometimes they are pessimistic, and so both investment and output are low.

Swings in investment demand will have a smaller effect on output when automatic stabilizers—such as a proportional income tax, which reduces the multiplier—are in place. This means that in the presence of automatic stabilizers we should expect output to fluctuate less than it would without them.

The proportional income tax is not the only automatic stabilizer.[7] Unemployment benefits enable the unemployed to continue consuming even if they do not have a job. This means that demand falls less when someone becomes unemployed than it would if there were no benefits. This too makes the multiplier smaller and output more stable. Higher unemployment benefits and income tax rates in the post–World War II period are reasons that business cycle fluctuations have on average been less extreme since 1945 than they were earlier.

Effects of a Change in Government Purchases

We now consider the effects of changes in fiscal policy on the equilibrium level of income. In our simple model, there are three possible changes in fiscal variables: changes in government purchases, changes in transfers, and changes in the income tax.

Consider first a change in government purchases in Figure 3-6, where the initial level of income is Y_0. An increase in government purchases is a change in autonomous spending and therefore shifts the aggregate demand schedule upward by an amount equal to the increase in government purchases. At the initial level of output and income, the demand for goods exceeds output, and accordingly, firms expand production until the new equilibrium, at point E', is reached.

By how much does income expand? Recall that the change in equilibrium income will equal the change in aggregate demand, or

$$\Delta Y_0 = \Delta \overline{G} + c(1 - t)\Delta Y_0$$

where the remaining terms ($\overline{C}, \overline{TR}$, and $\overline{I}$) are constant by assumption. Thus, the change in equilibrium income is

$$\Delta Y_0 = \frac{1}{1 - c(1 - t)} \Delta \overline{G} = \alpha_G \, \Delta \overline{G} \qquad (23)$$

---

[7]Automatic stabilizers are discussed by T. Holloway, "The Economy and the Federal Budget: Guide to Automatic Stabilizers," *Survey of Current Business,* July 1984.

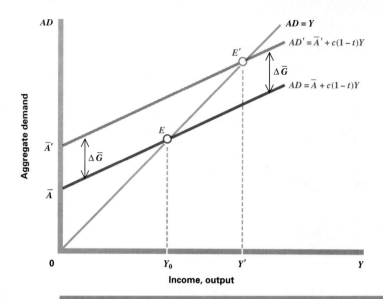

FIGURE 3-6

THE EFFECTS OF AN INCREASE IN GOVERNMENT PURCHASES. An increase in government spending shifts the aggregate demand schedule up from AD to AD'. Output rises from Y_0 to Y'. The multiplier is smaller now than it was in Figure 3-4.

where we have introduced the notation α_G to denote the multiplier in the presence of income taxes:

$$\alpha_G \equiv \frac{1}{1 - c(1 - t)} \qquad (24)$$

Thus a \$1 increase in government purchases will lead to an increase in income in excess of a dollar. With a marginal propensity to consume of $c = 0.8$ and an income tax rate of $t = 0.25$, we would have a multiplier of 2.5: a \$1 increase in government spending raises equilibrium income by \$2.50.

Effects of an Income Tax Change

Next consider the effects of a reduction in the income tax rate. This is illustrated in Figure 3-7 by an increase in the slope of the aggregate demand function, because that slope is equal to the marginal propensity to spend out of income, $c(1 - t)$. At the initial level of income, the aggregate demand for goods now exceeds output because

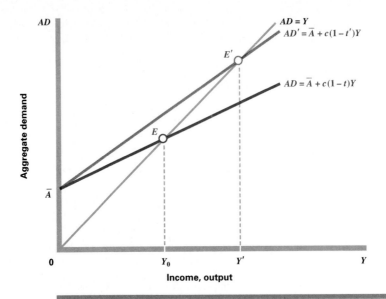

FIGURE 3-7

THE EFFECTS OF A DECREASE IN THE TAX RATE. A reduction in the income tax rate leaves the consumer with a larger proportion of every dollar of income earned. Accordingly, a larger proportion of every extra dollar of income is consumed. The aggregate demand curve swings upward, from *AD* to *AD'*. It becomes steeper because the income tax cut, in effect, acts like an increase in the propensity to consume. The equilibrium level of income rises from Y_0 to Y'.

the tax reduction causes increased consumption. The new, higher equilibrium level of income is Y'.

To calculate the change in equilibrium income, we equate the change in income to the change in aggregate demand. The change in aggregate demand has two components. The first is the change in spending at the initial level of income that arises from the tax cut. This part is equal to the marginal propensity to consume out of disposable income times the change in disposable income due to the tax cut, $cY_0\Delta t$, where the term $Y_0\Delta t$ is the initial level of income times the change in the tax rate. The second component of the change in aggregate demand is the induced spending due to higher income. This is now evaluated at the new tax rate t' and has the value of $c(1 - t')\Delta Y_0$. We can therefore write[8]

$$\Delta Y_0 = -cY_0\Delta t + c(1 - t')\Delta Y_0 \qquad (25)$$

or
$$\Delta Y_0 = -\frac{cY_0}{1 - c(1 - t')}\Delta t \qquad (26)$$

---

[8]You should check equation (26) by using equation (22) to write out Y_0 corresponding to a tax rate of t, and Y'_0 corresponding to t'. Then subtract Y_0 from Y'_0 to obtain ΔY_0 as given in equation (26).

Effects of Increased Transfer Payments

An increase in transfer payments increases autonomous demand, as can be seen in equation (21), in which autonomous demand includes the term $c\overline{TR}$. An increase in transfer payments therefore increases income by c times as much as an increase in government purchases of goods. The multiplier for transfer payments is smaller than that for government spending because part of any increase in $\overline{TR}$ is saved.

Summary

1. Government purchases and transfer payments act like increases in autonomous spending in their effects on equilibrium income.
2. A proportional income tax reduces the proportion of each extra dollar of output that is received as disposable income by consumers, and thus has the same effects on equilibrium income as a reduction in the propensity to consume.
3. A reduction in transfers lowers equilibrium output.

Implications

Since the theory we are developing implies that changes in government spending and taxes affect the level of income, it seems that fiscal policy can be used to stabilize the economy. When the economy is in a recession, or growing slowly, perhaps taxes should be cut or spending increased to get output to rise. And when the economy is booming, perhaps taxes should be increased or government spending cut to get back down to full employment. Indeed, fiscal policy is used actively to try to stabilize the economy, as in 1993, when the Clinton administration created short-term stimulus to help revive growth.

3-5 THE BUDGET

Government budget deficits are now the norm in the United States, and surpluses are nowhere in sight. But it was not always so, and it is not so now in some other countries. For most of its history the U.S. *federal* government has run surpluses in peacetime and deficits during wars. It is only in the last 20 years that peacetime deficits have become standard in the United States.[9] An example of a country where the budget is in surplus is Japan, where over the period 1987–1992, the budget surplus averaged 2 percent of GDP.

The budget deficit on which the media and politicians focus is the federal budget deficit, which in fiscal year 1992 was \$314 billion, or 5.4 percent of GDP.[10] "Government" in the national income accounts consists of all levels of government—federal,

---

[9]See the graph of the federal budget deficit since 1946 in the end papers. We deal with the budget in more detail in later chapters.

[10]The fiscal year starts on October 1 of the previous year.

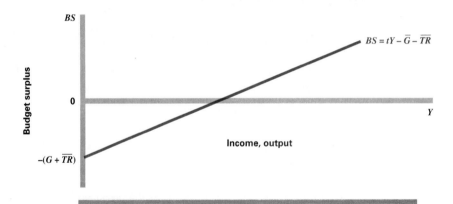

FIGURE 3-8

THE BUDGET SURPLUS. The budget surplus, or deficit, depends in part on the level of income. Given the tax rate, *t*, and $\overline{G}$ and $\overline{TR}$, the budget surplus will be high if income is high—because then the government takes in a lot of taxes. But if the level of income is low, there will be a budget deficit because government tax receipts are small.

state, and local. The state and local governments tend to run small (less than 1 percent of GDP) surpluses in boom years and small deficits in recession years.

Why the concern over the budget deficit? The fear is that the government's borrowing makes it difficult for private firms to borrow and invest, and thus slows the economy's growth. Full understanding has to wait until later chapters, but we start now, dealing with the government budget, its effects on output, and the effects of output on the budget.

The first important concept is the *budget surplus,* denoted by *BS*. The budget surplus is the excess of the government's revenues, consisting of taxes, over its total expenditures, consisting of purchases of goods and services and transfer payments.

$$BS \equiv TA - \overline{G} - \overline{TR} \tag{27}$$

A negative budget surplus, an excess of expenditure over taxes, is a *budget deficit.*

Substituting in equation (27) the assumption of a proportional income tax that yields tax revenues $TA = tY$ gives us

$$BS = tY - \overline{G} - \overline{TR} \tag{27a}$$

In Figure 3-8 we plot the budget surplus as a function of the level of income for given $\overline{G}$, $\overline{TR}$, and income tax rate, *t*. At low levels of income, the budget is in deficit (the surplus is negative) because government spending, $\overline{G} + \overline{TR}$, exceeds income tax collection. For high levels of income, by contrast, the budget shows a surplus, since income tax collection exceeds expenditures in the form of government purchases and transfers.

Figure 3-8 shows that the budget deficit depends not only on the government's policy choices, reflected in the tax rate (t), purchases ($\overline{G}$), and transfers ($\overline{TR}$), but also on anything else that shifts the level of income. Suppose there is an increase in investment demand that increases the level of output. Then the budget deficit will fall or the surplus will increase because tax revenues have risen. But the government has done nothing that changed the deficit.

We should therefore not be surprised to see budget deficits in recessions. Those are periods when the government's tax receipts are low. And in practice, transfer payments, through unemployment benefits, also increase in recessions, even though we are taking $\overline{TR}$ as autonomous in our model.

The Effects of Government Purchases and Tax Changes on the Budget Surplus

Next we show how changes in fiscal policy affect the budget. In particular, we want to find out whether an increase in government purchases must reduce the budget surplus. At first sight, this appears obvious, because increased government purchases, from equation (27), are reflected in a reduced surplus or increased deficit. On further thought, however, the increased government purchases will cause an increase (multiplied) in income and, therefore, increased income tax collection. This raises the interesting possibility that tax collection might increase by more than government purchases.

A brief calculation shows that the first guess is right—increased government purchases reduce the budget surplus. From equation (23) we see that the change in income due to increased government purchases is equal to $\Delta Y_0 \equiv \alpha_G \Delta G$. A fraction of that increase in income is collected in the form of taxes, so that tax revenue increases by $t\alpha_G \Delta G$. The change in the budget surplus, using equation (24) to substitute for α, is therefore

$$
\begin{aligned}
\Delta BS &= \Delta TA - \Delta \overline{G} \\
&= t\alpha_G \Delta \overline{G} - \Delta \overline{G} \\
&= \left[\frac{t}{1 - c(1 - t)} - 1 \right] \Delta \overline{G} \\
&= -\frac{(1 - c)(1 - t)}{1 - c(1 - t)} \Delta \overline{G}
\end{aligned}
\tag{28}
$$

which is unambiguously negative.

We have, therefore, shown that an increase in government purchases will reduce the budget surplus, although in this model by considerably less than the increase in purchases. For instance, for $c = 0.8$ and $t = 0.25$, a \$1 increase in government purchases will create a \$0.375 reduction in the surplus.

In the same way, we can consider the effects of an increase in the tax rate on the budget surplus. We know that the increase in the tax rate will reduce the level of income. It might thus appear that an increase in the tax rate, keeping the level of government spending constant, could reduce the budget surplus. In fact, an increase in the tax rate increases the budget surplus, despite the reduction in income that it causes, as you are asked to show in problem 7 at the end of this chapter.[11]

We signal here another interesting result known as the *balanced budget multiplier.* Suppose government spending and taxes are raised in amounts such that in the new equilibrium the budget is unchanged. By how much will output rise? The answer is that for this special experiment the multiplier is equal to 1—output rises by exactly the increase in government spending and no more. You are asked to demonstrate this result in problem 12.

3-6 THE FULL-EMPLOYMENT BUDGET SURPLUS

A final topic to be treated here is the concept of the *full-employment budget surplus.*[12] Recall that increases in taxes add to the surplus and that increases in government expenditures reduce the surplus. Increases in taxes have been shown to reduce the level of income; and increases in government purchases and transfers, to increase the level of income. It thus seems that the budget surplus is a convenient, simple measure of the overall effects of fiscal policy on the economy. For instance, when the budget is in deficit, we would say that fiscal policy is expansionary, tending to increase GNP.

However, the budget surplus by itself suffers from a serious defect as a measure of the direction of fiscal policy. The defect is that the surplus can change because of changes in autonomous private spending—as can be seen in Figure 3-8. Thus, an increase in the budget deficit does not necessarily mean that the government has changed its policy in an attempt to increase the level of income.

Since we frequently want to measure the way in which fiscal policy is being used to affect the level of income, we require some measure of policy that is independent of the particular position of the business cycle—boom or recession—in which we may find ourselves. Such a measure is provided by the *full-employment surplus,* which we denote by BS^*. The full-employment budget surplus measures the budget surplus at the full-employment level of income or at potential output. Using Y^* to denote the full-employment level of income, we can write

$$BS^* = tY^* - \overline{G} - \overline{TR} \qquad (29)$$

There are other names for the full-employment surplus, among them the *cyclically adjusted surplus* (or deficit), the *high-employment surplus,* the *standardized employment surplus,* and the *structural surplus.* The new names all refer to the same concept as

[11]The theory that tax rate cuts would increase government revenue (or tax rate increases reduce government revenue) is associated with Arthur Laffer, formerly at the University of Chicago and University of Southern California. Laffer's argument, however, did not depend on the aggregate demand effects of tax cuts but, rather, on the possibility that a tax cut would lead people to work more. This is a strand in supply-side economics, which we examine in Chapter 19.

[12]The concept has a long history; it was first used by E. Cary Brown, "Fiscal Policy in the Thirties: A Reappraisal," *American Economic Review,* December 1956.

the full-employment surplus, but they avoid implying that there is a unique level of full-employment output that the economy has not yet reached. They suggest, reasonably, that the concept is merely a convenient measuring rod that fixes a given level of employment as the reference point.

To see the difference between the actual and the full-employment budgets, we subtract the actual budget in equation (27a) from equation (29) to obtain

$$BS^* - BS = t(Y^* - Y) \qquad (30)$$

The only difference arises from income tax collection.[13] Specifically, if output is below full employment, the full-employment surplus exceeds the actual surplus. Conversely, if actual output exceeds full-employment (or potential) output, the full-employment surplus is less than the actual surplus. The difference between the actual and the full-employment budget is the *cyclical* component of the budget. In a recession the cyclical component tends to show a deficit and in a boom there may even be a surplus.

Table 3-2 reports the actual budget deficit and the full-employment deficit, as well as the unemployment rate, over the period 1980–1992. It is clear that whenever

TABLE 3-2

THE FEDERAL BUDGET DEFICIT AND UNEMPLOYMENT, 1980–1992

	BUDGET DEFICIT, PERCENT OF GDP		unemployment rate, percent
	actual	full-employment	
1980	2.2	1.0	7.2
1981	1.9	0.3	7.6
1982	4.3	1.2	9.7
1983	5.2	2.5	9.6
1984	4.4	3.0	7.5
1985	4.5	3.2	7.2
1986	4.7	3.4	7.0
1987	3.4	2.2	6.2
1988	2.8	2.0	5.5
1989	2.4	1.6	5.3
1990	3.0	1.9	5.5
1991	3.5	1.7	6.8
1992	5.0	3.6	7.4

SOURCE: DRI/McGraw-Hill.

---

[13]In practice, transfer payments, such as welfare and unemployment benefits, are also affected by the state of the economy, so that *TR* also depends on the level of income. But the major cause of differences between the actual surplus and the full-employment surplus is taxes. Automatic movements in taxes caused by a change in income are about five times the size of automatic movements in spending. (See T. M. Holloway and J. C. Wakefield, "Sources of Change in the Federal Government Deficit, 1970–86," *Survey of Current Business,* May 1985.)

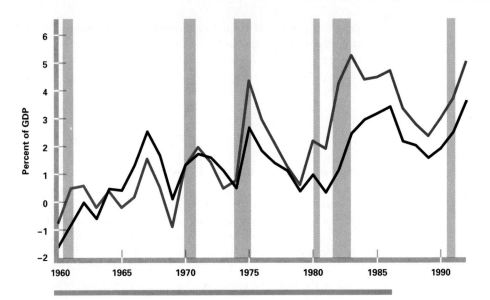

FIGURE 3-9
THE FULL-EMPLOYMENT AND ACTUAL BUDGET DEFICITS, 1960–1991
(percent of GDP) (SOURCE: DRI/McGraw-Hill.)

the unemployment rate is high, as in the 1980–1982 and 1990–1991 recessions, the cyclical component of the budget shows a large deficit. By contrast, when the economy is at full employment, as in 1988, the cyclical component of the deficit is zero.

We next look at the full-employment budget deficit shown in Figure 3-9. Public concern about the deficit mounted in the 1980s. For many economists, the behavior of the deficit during the high-unemployment years 1982 and 1983 was not especially worrisome. The actual budget is usually in deficit during recessions. But the shift toward deficit of the full-employment budget was regarded as an entirely different matter.

Two final words of warning. First, there is no certainty as to the true full-employment level of output. Various assumptions about the level of unemployment that corresponds to full employment are possible. The usual assumptions now are that full employment means an unemployment rate of about 5.0 to 5.5 percent, although when the actual unemployment rate was higher there were some estimates as high as 7 percent. Estimates of the full-employment deficit or surplus will differ, depending on the assumptions made about the economy at full employment.

Second, the high-employment surplus is not a perfect measure of the thrust of fiscal policy. There are several reasons for this: a change in spending with a matching increase in taxes, leaving the deficit unchanged, will raise income; expectations about future fiscal policy changes can affect current income; and in general, because fiscal policy involves the setting of a number of variables—the tax rate, transfers, and government purchases—it is difficult to describe the thrust of fiscal policy perfectly by a single number. But the high-employment surplus is nevertheless a useful guide to the direction of fiscal policy.[14]

3-7 SUMMARY

1. Output is at its equilibrium level when the aggregate demand for goods is equal to the level of output.
2. Aggregate demand consists of planned spending by households on consumption, by firms on investment goods, by government on its purchases of goods and services, and net exports.
3. When output is at its equilibrium level, there are no unintended changes in inventories and all economic units are making precisely the purchases they had planned to. An adjustment process for the level of output based on the accumulation or rundown of inventories leads the economy to the equilibrium output level.
4. The level of aggregate demand is itself affected by the level of output (equal to the level of income) because consumption demand depends on the level of income.
5. The consumption function relates consumption spending to income. Consumption rises with income. Income that is not consumed is saved, so that the saving function can be derived from the consumption function.
6. The multiplier is the amount by which a $1 change in autonomous spending changes the equilibrium level of output. The greater the propensity to consume, the higher the multiplier.
7. Government purchases and government transfer payments act like increases in autonomous spending in their effects on the equilibrium level of income. A proportional income tax has the same effect on the equilibrium level of income as a reduction in the propensity to consume. A proportional income tax thus reduces the multiplier.
8. The budget surplus is the excess of government receipts over expenditures. When the government is spending more than it receives, the budget is in deficit. The size of the budget surplus (deficit) is affected by the government's fiscal policy variables—government purchases, transfer payments, and tax rates.
9. The actual budget surplus is also affected by changes in tax collection and transfers resulting from movements in the level of income that occur as a result of changes in private autonomous spending. The full-employment (high-employment) budget surplus is used as a measure of the active use of fiscal policy. The full-employment surplus measures the budget surplus that would exist if output were at its potential (full-employment) level.

---

[14]For further discussion of the full-employment deficit and alternative measures of fiscal policy, see Congressional Budget Office, *The Economic Outlook,* February 1984, Appendix B; Darrel Cohen, "A Comparison of Fiscal Measures Using Reduced Form Techniques," Board of Governors of the Federal Reserve System, 1989; Olivier Blanchard et al., "The Sustainability of Fiscal Policy: New Answers to an Old Question," *OECD Economic Studies,* Autumn 1990. Early each year the Congressional Budget Office publishes *The Economic and Budget Outlook,* which contains an analysis of current fiscal policy and estimates of the full-employment budget.

10. A final caveat: All the results derived in this chapter assume that prices are fixed. We will see later how price adjustment dampens the output response to price changes.

KEY TERMS

Aggregate demand	Marginal propensity to save
Equilibrium output	Multiplier
Unintended (undesired) inventory accumulation	Automatic stabilizer
	Budget surplus
Planned aggregate demand	Budget deficit
Consumption function	Balanced budget multiplier
Marginal propensity to consume	Full-employment (high-employment) surplus

PROBLEMS

1. Here we investigate a particular example of the model studied in Sections 3-2 and 3-3 with no government. Suppose the consumption function is given by $C = 100 + 0.8Y$, while investment is given by $I = 50$.
   (a) What is the equilibrium level of income in this case?
   (b) What is the level of saving in equilibrium?
   (c) If, for some reason, output were at the level of 800, what would the level of involuntary inventory accumulation be?
   (d) If I were to rise to 100 (we discuss what determines I in later chapters), what would the effect be on equilibrium income?
   (e) What is the value of the multiplier, α, here?
   (f) Draw a diagram indicating the equilibria in both 1a and 1d.

2. Suppose consumption behavior were to change in problem 1 so that $C = 100 + 0.9Y$, while I remained at 50.
   (a) Would you expect the equilibrium level of income to be higher or lower than in 1a? Calculate the new equilibrium level, Y', to verify this.
   (b) Now suppose investment increases to $I = 100$, just as in 1d. What is the new equilibrium income?
   (c) Does this change in investment spending have more or less of an effect on Y than in problem 1? Why?
   (d) Draw a diagram indicating the change in equilibrium income in this case.

3. We showed in the text that the equilibrium condition $Y = AD$ is equivalent to the $S = I$, or saving = investment, condition. Starting from $S = I$ and the saving function, derive the equilibrium level of income, as in equation (10).

4. (a) Using the relationship between the marginal propensity to consume, c, and the marginal propensity to save, s, write equation (14) for the multiplier in terms of s rather than c.
   (b) Does the formula you derived in 4(a) apply also when the government enters the picture and the multiplier is given in equation (24)? Explain.

5. This problem relates to the so-called paradox of thrift. Suppose that $I = I_0$ and that $C = \bar{C} + cY$.

(a) Draw a diagram where income is measured on the horizontal axis and investment and saving on the vertical axis.

(b) What is the saving function, that is, the function that shows how saving is related to income?

(c) Draw the investment function which is flat. Explain why the intersection of the saving and investment function gives us the equilibrium level of output.

(d) Suppose individuals want to save more at every level of income. Show, using a figure like Figure 3-4, how the saving function is shifted.

(e) What effect does the increased desire to save have on the new equilibrium level of saving? Explain the paradox.

6. Now let us look at a model that is an example of the one presented in Sections 3-4 and 3-5; that is, it includes government purchases, taxes, and transfers. It has the same features as the one in problems 1 and 2 except that it also has a government. Thus, suppose consumption is given by $C = 100 + 0.8YD$ and that $I = 50$, while fiscal policy is summarized by $G = 200$, $TR = 62.5$, and $t = 0.25$.

(a) What is the equilibrium level of income in this more complete model?

(b) What is the value of the new multiplier, α_G? Why is this less than the multiplier in problem 1(e)?

7. Using the same model as in problem 5, determine the following:

(a) What is the value of the budget surplus, BS, when $I = 50$?

(b) What is BS when I increases to 100?

(c) What accounts for the change in BS between 7b and 7a?

(d) Assuming that the full-employment level of income, Y^*, is 1,200, what is the full-employment budget surplus BS^* when $I = 50$? 100? (Be careful.)

(e) What is BS^* if $I = 50$ and $G = 250$, with Y^* still equal to 1,200?

(f) Explain why we use BS^* rather than simply BS to measure the direction of fiscal policy.

8. Suppose we expand our model to take account of the fact that transfer payments, TR, do depend on the level of income, Y. When income is high, transfer payments such as unemployment benefits will fall. Conversely, when income is low, unemployment is high and so are unemployment benefits. We can incorporate this into our model by writing transfers as $TR = \overline{TR} - bY$, $b > 0$. Remember that equilibrium income is derived as the solution to $Y_0 = C + I + G = cYD + I + G$, where $YD = Y + TR - TA$ is disposable income.

(a) Derive the expression for Y_0 in this case, just as equation (22) was derived in the text.

(b) What is the new multiplier?

(c) Why is the new multiplier less than the standard one, α_G?

(d) How does the change in the multiplier relate to the concept of automatic stabilizers?

9. Now we look at the role taxes play in determining equilibrium income. Suppose we have an economy of the type in Sections 3-4 and 3-5, described by the following functions:

$$C = 50 + 0.8YD$$
$$\bar{I} = 70$$
$$\overline{G} = 200$$
$$\overline{TR} = 100$$
$$t = 0.20$$

(a) Calculate the equilibrium level of income and the multiplier in this model.

(b) Calculate also the budget surplus, *BS*.

(c) Suppose that *t* increases to 0.25. What is the new equilibrium income? The new multiplier?

(d) Calculate the change in the budget surplus. Would you expect the change in the surplus to be more or less if $c = 0.9$ rather than 0.8?

(e) Can you explain why the multiplier is 1 when $t = 1$?

10. Suppose the economy is operating at equilibrium, with $Y_0 = 1,000$. If the government undertakes a fiscal change so that the tax rate, *t*, increases by 0.05 and government spending increases by 50, will the budget surplus go up or down? Why?

11. Suppose Congress decides to reduce transfer payments (such as welfare) but to increase government purchases of goods and services by an equal amount. That is, it undertakes a change in fiscal policy such that $\Delta G = -\Delta TR$.

(a) Would you expect equilibrium income to rise or fall as a result of this change? Why? Check your answer with the following example: Suppose that initially, $c = 0.8$, $t = 0.25$, and $Y_0 = 600$. Now let $\Delta G = 10$ and $\Delta TR = -10$.

(b) Find the change in equilibrium income, ΔY_0.

(c) What is the change in the budget surplus, ΔBS? Why has *BS* changed?

*12. *The Balanced Budget Multiplier.* The balanced budget multiplier states that an increase in government spending combined with an increase in taxes such that the budget surplus is unchanged will raise output by exactly the increase in government spending. (Equivalently, the multiplier for a balanced budget change in government spending is one.) We now ask you to demonstrate that result. To start, note that since $BS = TA - TR - G$, and *TR* does not change, it has to be that $\Delta BS = \Delta TA - \Delta G = 0$, so that

$$\Delta TA = \Delta G \tag{P1}$$

Note also that the change in output, ΔY, has to be equal to the change in aggregate demand, ΔAD, and that the change in aggregate demand results from changes in government spending and in consumption:

$$\begin{aligned}
\Delta Y = \Delta AD &= \Delta G + \Delta C \\
&= \Delta G + c\Delta YD \tag{P2} \\
&= \Delta G + c(\Delta Y - \Delta TA)
\end{aligned}$$

Using equation (P1) and the last line of equation (P2), you should be able to get the balanced budget multiplier result.

(*Note:* If you can do calculus, you may want to try to derive the result using the calculus. To do so you will have to impose the constraint that the change in government spending is equal to the change in tax receipts.)

*13. Suppose the aggregate demand function is as in the accompanying figure. Notice that at Y_0 the slope of the aggregate demand curve is greater than 1. (This would happen if $c > 1$.) Complete this picture as is done in Figure 3-3 to include the arrows indicating adjustment when $Y \neq Y_0$ and show what *IU* is for $Y < Y_0$ and $Y > Y_0$. What is happening in this example, and how does it differ fundamentally from Figure 3-3?

---

*An asterisk denotes a more difficult problem.

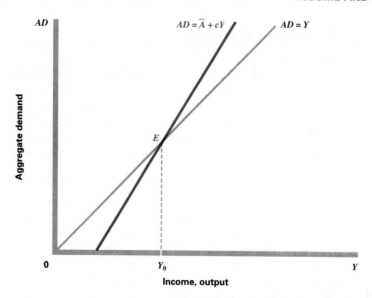

*14. This problem anticipates our discussion of the open economy in Chapter 6. It is hard, and only the ambitious student should try it. You are asked to derive some of the results that will be shown there. We start with the assumption that foreign demand for our goods is given and equal to X. Our demand for foreign goods, or imports, denoted Q, is a linear function of income.

$$\text{Exports} = \bar{X} \qquad \text{Imports} = Q = \bar{Q} + mY$$

where m is the *marginal propensity to import*.

(a) The trade balance, or net exports, NX, is defined as the excess of exports over imports. Write an algebraic expression for the trade balance and show in a diagram net exports as a function of the level of income. (Put Y on the horizontal axis.)

(b) Show the effect of a change in income on the trade balance, using your diagram. Show also the effect of a change in exports on the trade balance, given income.

(c) The equilibrium condition in the goods market is that aggregate demand for *our* goods be equal to supply. Aggregate demand for our goods includes exports but excludes imports. Thus we have

$$Y = C + \bar{I} + NX$$

where we have added net exports (exports less imports) to investment and consumption. Using the expression for net exports developed in 14a and the consumption function $C = cY$, derive the equilibrium level of income, Y_0.

(d) On the basis of your expression for the equilibrium level of income in 14c, what is the effect of a change in exports, X, on equilibrium income? Interpret your result and discuss the multiplier in an open economy.

(e) Using your results in 14a and 14d, show the effect of an increase in exports on the trade balance.

📁 COMPUTER EXERCISES

1. By running some examples, illustrate the relationship between the multiplier and the *MPC*. Specifically, provide the values of the multiplier when the *MPC* takes on the values 0.75, 0.8, 0.85, 0.9, and 0.95.

2. Suppose that the economy is operating below full employment. Government authorities wish to achieve a target Y of 275. What policy changes in expenditures or taxes achieve the target? Which method produces the smallest budget surplus? Specifically, determine the $\Delta \overline{G}$ and $\Delta \overline{TR}$ that will get the level of output to 275. Before doing it by trial and error, can you calculate the required changes based on the information given in the problem? If so, do it, then verify your answer by carrying out the simulation with your calculated changes.

3. Show that the multiplier effect of an increase in government spending is different from that associated with an increase in transfer payments or a reduction in taxes. Why? Specifically, run two exercises, the first with $\Delta \overline{G} = 10$ and the second with $\Delta \overline{TR} = 10$. What are the values of the respective multipliers ($\Delta Y/10$), and why (intuitively) are they different in this way? (Again, you can do this by hand first.)

4. What is the multiplier for an increase in government spending that is paid for by an equal increase in taxes? (Note that here you must simulate the tax increase by *reducing* $\Delta \overline{TR}$.) Specifically, in the same exercise set $\Delta \overline{G} = 10$ and $\Delta \overline{TR} = -7$; and noting that the new equilibrium gives a net tax increase of 10 ($\Delta T = \Delta \overline{G} = 10$), determine the multiplier for the joint change.

5. For a given change in the marginal tax rate (t), what is the change in government spending required to attain the former equilibrium? Specifically, change t from 0.30 to 0.35 and determine the $\Delta \overline{G}$ that will restore $Y = 250$. (*Hint:* After changing t and solving the model, use the new multiplier and the necessary ΔY to compute $\Delta \overline{G}$).

6. Suppose consumers decide to save more. What happens? Why can't you increase the total amount of *total* saving? Make sure to use *total saving, which is equal to personal (or private) saving plus the budget surplus* (i.e., public saving): Total saving = $(YD - C) + (T - G) = S + BS$ ... where $T = TA - TR$ (i.e., net taxes). Specifically, use $\Delta \overline{C} = -5$ (a drop in the intercept of the consumption function but a rise in the intercept of saving function). What happens to the level of total saving (i.e., in the new equilibrium compared to the initial equilibrium)? Why? You may also want to try the following alternative exercise: go back to the initial $\overline{C}$, but reduce the *MPC* (parameter c) from 0.85 to 0.80—equivalent to raising the *MPS*. Does the same phenomenon occur?

MONEY, INTEREST, AND INCOME

*T*he stock of money, interest rates, and the Federal Reserve seemingly have no place in the model of income determination developed so far. But money plays an important role in the economy. Interest rates are a significant determinant of aggregate spending, and the Federal Reserve, which controls money growth and interest rates, is the first institution to be blamed when the economy gets into trouble. For instance, the blame for the 1990–1991 recession is often placed on the Federal Reserve's tight money policies in 1989, and the length of the recession is blamed on the Fed's failure to cut interest rates sharply enough during 1991.

This chapter introduces money and monetary policy and builds an explicit framework of analysis in which to study the interaction of goods and assets markets. This new framework leads to an understanding of the determination of interest rates and of their role in the business cycle. Figure 4-1 shows the interest rate on Treasury bills. The interest rate on Treasury bills represents the payment, per dollar per year, that someone who lends to the U.S. government receives. Thus, an interest rate of 5 percent means that someone who lends $100 to the government for 1 year will receive 5 percent, or $5, in interest. Figure 4-1 immediately suggests some questions: What factors cause the interest rate to increase, as occurred, for example, in 1980–1981? Why were interest rates lower in 1992 than at any time for the past 20 years? Equally important, what difference do changes in interest rates make to output and employment?

The model we introduce in this chapter, the *IS-LM model*, is the core of modern macroeconomics. It maintains the spirit and, indeed, many details of the model of the previous chapter. The model is broadened, though, by introducing the interest rate as an additional determinant of aggregate demand. In Chapter 3, autonomous spending and fiscal policy were the chief determinants of aggregate demand. Now we add the interest rate and argue that a reduction in the interest rate raises aggregate demand. This seems to be a minor extension which can readily be handled in the context of Chapter 3. This is not entirely correct, because we have to ask what determines the interest rate. That question extends our model to include the markets for financial assets

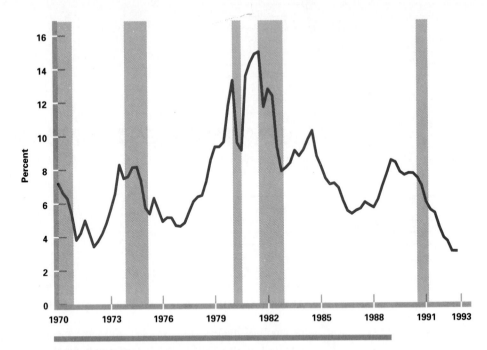

FIGURE 4-1
THE INTEREST RATE ON TREASURY BILLS, 1970–1992 (percent per year).
(SOURCE: DRI/McGraw-Hill.)

and forces us to study the interaction of goods and assets markets. Interest rates and income are jointly determined by equilibrium in the goods and assets markets.

What is the payoff for that complication? The introduction of assets markets and interest rates serves three important purposes:

1. The extension shows how monetary policy works.
2. The analysis qualifies the conclusions of Chapter 3. Consider Figure 4-2, which lays out the logical structure of the model. Thus far we looked at the box called "goods market." By adding the assets markets, we provide a fuller analysis of the effect of fiscal policy, and we introduce monetary policy. We shall see, for instance, that an expansionary fiscal policy generally raises interest rates, thereby dampening its expansionary impact. Indeed, under certain conditions, the increase in interest rates may be sufficient to offset *fully* the expansionary effects of fiscal policy. Clearly, such an extreme possibility is an important qualification to our study of fiscal policy in Chapter 3.
3. Even if the interest rate changes just mentioned only dampen (rather than offset fully) the expansionary effects of fiscal policy, they have an important side effect. The *composition* of aggregate demand between investment and consumption spending depends on the interest rate. Higher interest rates dampen aggregate demand mainly by reducing investment. Thus, an expansionary fiscal policy tends

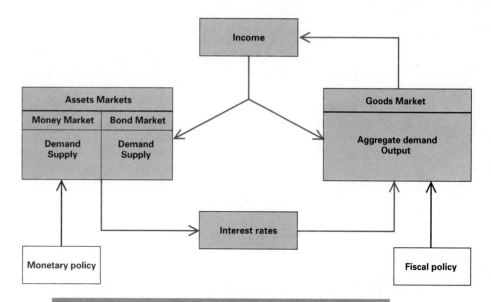

FIGURE 4-2

THE STRUCTURE OF THE *IS-LM* MODEL. The *IS-LM* model emphasizes the interaction between the goods and assets markets. The model of Chapter 3 looks at income determination by arguing that income affects spending, which in turn determines output and income. Now we add the effects of interest rates on spending, and thus income, and the dependence of assets markets on income. Higher income raises money demand and thus interest rates. Higher interest rates lower spending and thus income. Spending, interest rates, and income are determined jointly by equilibrium in the goods *and* assets markets.

to raise consumption through the multiplier but tends to reduce investment because it increases interest rates. Because the rate of investment affects the growth of the economy, this side effect of fiscal expansion is a sensitive and important issue in policy making.

These three reasons justify the more complicated model we study in this chapter. The extended model also helps us understand how the financial markets work.

Outline of the Chapter

We use Figure 4-2 once more to lay out the structure of this chapter. We start in Section 4-1 with a discussion of the link between interest rates and aggregate demand. Here we use the model of Chapter 3 directly, augmented to include the interest rate as a determinant of aggregate demand. We derive a key relationship—the *IS* curve—

that shows combinations of interest rates and levels of income for which the goods markets clear. In Section 4-2, we turn to the assets markets and in particular to the money market. We show that the demand for money depends on interest rates and income and that there are combinations of interest rates and income levels—the *LM* curve—for which the money market clears.[1] In Section 4-3, we combine the two schedules to study the joint determination of interest rates and income. Section 4-4 lays out the adjustment process toward equilibrium. In Section 4-5, which is optional, we formally present the full *IS-LM* model.

The *IS-LM* model continues to be used more than half a century after its introduction because it provides a simple and appropriate framework for analyzing the effects of monetary and fiscal policy on the demand for output and on interest rates. We reserve policy applications of the model for Chapter 5, not because models and their applications should be kept apart (on the contrary, they should not) but only to avoid making this chapter too long.

4-1 THE GOODS MARKET AND THE *IS* CURVE

In this section we derive a *goods market equilibrium schedule*, the *IS* curve. The *IS* curve (or schedule) shows combinations of interest rates and levels of output such that planned spending equals income. The goods market equilibrium schedule is an extension of income determination with a 45°-line diagram. Now investment is no longer fully exogenous but is also determined by the interest rate.

In Chapter 3, Equation (22), we derived an expression for equilibrium income:

$$Y_0 = \frac{\overline{A}}{1 - \overline{c}} \tag{1}$$

where we define $c(1 - t)$ as $\overline{c}$. Equilibrium income in this simple Keynesian model has two determinants: autonomous spending (A) and the propensity to consume out of income ($\overline{c}$). Autonomous spending includes government spending, investment spending, and autonomous consumption spending. The propensity to consume out of income, as seen from equation (1), depends on the propensity to consume out of disposable income (c) and on the fraction of a dollar of income retained after taxes ($1 - t$). The higher the level of autonomous spending and the higher the propensity to consume, the higher the equilibrium level of income.

Investment and the Interest Rate

Thus far, investment spending (I) has been treated as *entirely* exogenous—some number like $800 billion, determined outside the model of income determination. Now, as we

---

[1] The terms *IS* and *LM* are shorthand representations, respectively, of the relationships investment (*I*) equals saving (*S*)—goods market equilibrium—and money demand (*L*) equals money supply (*M*), or money market equilibrium. The classic article that introduced this model is J. R. Hicks, "Mr. Keynes and the Classics: A Suggested Interpretation," *Econometrica*, 1937, pp. 147–159.

make our macromodel more complete by introducing interest rates as a part of the model, investment spending, too, becomes endogenous. The desired or planned rate of investment is lower the higher the interest rate.

A simple argument shows why. Investment is spending on additions to a firm's capital, such as machines, or buildings. Typically firms borrow to purchase investment goods. The higher the interest rate for such borrowing, the lower the profits firms can expect to make by borrowing to buy new machines or buildings, and therefore the less they will be willing to borrow and invest. Conversely, firms will want to borrow and invest more when interest rates are lower.

The Investment Demand Schedule

We specify an investment spending function of the form[2]

$$I = \bar{I} - bi \qquad b > 0 \tag{2}$$

where i is the rate of interest and b measures the interest response of investment. $\bar{I}$ now denotes autonomous investment spending, that is, investment spending that is independent of both income and the rate of interest.[3] Equation (2) states that the lower the interest rate, the higher is planned investment, with the coefficient b measuring the responsiveness of investment spending to the interest rate.

Figure 4-3 shows the investment schedule of equation (2). The schedule shows for each level of the interest rate the amount that firms plan to spend on investment. The schedule is negatively sloped to reflect the assumption that a reduction in the interest rate increases the profitability of additions to the capital stock and therefore leads to a larger rate of planned investment spending.

The position of the investment schedule is determined by the slope—the term b in equation (2)—and by the level of autonomous investment spending, $\bar{I}$. If investment is highly responsive to the interest rate, a small decline in interest rates will lead to a large increase in investment, so that the schedule is almost flat. Conversely, if investment responds little to interest rates, the schedule will be more nearly vertical. Changes in autonomous investment spending, $\bar{I}$, shift the investment schedule. An increase in $\bar{I}$ means that at each level of the interest rate, firms plan to invest at a higher rate. This would be shown by a rightward shift of the investment schedule.

---

[2] Here and in other places in the book, we specify linear (straight-line) versions of behavioral functions. We use the linear form to simplify both the algebra and the diagrams. The linearity assumption is not misleading so long as we confine ourselves to talking about small changes in the economy. You should often draw nonlinear versions of our diagrams to be sure you can work with them.

[3] In Chap. 3, investment spending was defined as autonomous with respect to income. Now that the interest rate appears in the model, we have to extend the definition of autonomous to mean independent of *both* the interest rate and income. To conserve notation, we continue to use $\bar{I}$ to denote autonomous investment, but we recognize that the definition has broadened.

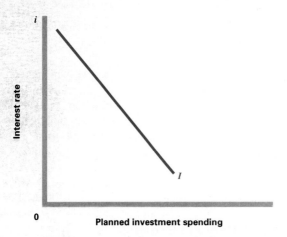

FIGURE 4-3
THE INVESTMENT SCHEDULE. The investment schedule shows the
planned level of investment spending at each rate of interest.
Because higher interest rates reduce the profitability of additions to
the capital stock, higher interest rates imply lower planned rates of
investment spending. Changes in autonomous investment shift the
investment schedule.

The Interest Rate and Aggregate Demand: The *IS* Curve

We now modify the aggregate demand function of Chapter 3 to reflect the new planned
investment spending schedule. Aggregate demand still consists of the demand for
consumption, investment, and government spending on goods and services, only now
investment spending depends on the interest rate. We have

$$AD \equiv C + I + G$$
$$= c\overline{TR} + c(1 - t)Y + \overline{I} - bi + \overline{G} \qquad (3)$$
$$= \overline{A} + \overline{c}Y - bi$$

where

$$\overline{A} \equiv c\overline{TR} + \overline{I} + \overline{G} \qquad (4)$$

From equation (3) we see that an increase in the interest rate reduces aggregate demand
for a given level of income because a higher interest rate reduces investment spending.
Note that the term $\overline{A}$, which is the part of aggregate demand unaffected by either the
level of income or the interest rate, does include part of investment spending, namely,
$\overline{I}$. As noted earlier, $\overline{I}$ is the *autonomous* component of investment spending, which is
independent of the interest rate (and income).

At any given level of the interest rate, we can still proceed as in Chapter 3 to

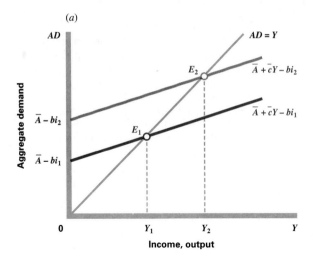

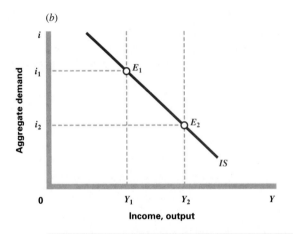

FIGURE 4-4

DERIVATION OF THE *IS* CURVE. At an interest rate i_1, equilibrium in the goods market is at point E_1 in the upper panel with an income level Y_1. In the lower panel this is recorded as point E_1, also. A fall in the interest rate to i_2 raises aggregate demand, increasing the level of spending at each income level. The new equilibrium income level is Y_2. In the lower panel, point E_2 records the new equilibrium in the goods market corresponding to an interest rate i_2.

determine the equilibrium level of income and output. As the interest rate changes, however, the equilibrium level of income changes. We derive the *IS* curve using Figure 4-4.

For a given level of the interest rate, say, i_1, the last term of equation (3) is a constant (bi_1), and we can, in Figure 4-4*a*, draw the aggregate demand function of

Chapter 3, this time with an intercept $\overline{A} - bi_1$. The equilibrium level of income obtained in the usual manner is Y_1 at point E_1. Since that equilibrium level of income was derived for a given level of the interest rate (i_1), we plot that pair (i_1, Y_1) in the bottom panel as point E_1. We now have one point, E_1, on the *IS* curve.

Consider next a lower interest rate, i_2. Investment spending is higher when the interest rate falls. In terms of Figure 4-4a, that implies an upward shift of the aggregate demand schedule. The curve shifts upward because the intercept, $\overline{A} - bi$, has increased. Given the increase in aggregate demand, the equilibrium shifts to point E_2, with an associated income level Y_2. At point E_2, in the bottom panel, we record the fact that interest rate i_2 implies the equilibrium level of income Y_2—equilibrium in the sense that the goods market is in equilibrium (or that the goods market *clears*). Point E_2 is another point on the *IS* curve.

We can apply the same procedure to all conceivable levels of the interest rate and thereby generate all the points that make up the *IS* curve. They have in common the property that they represent combinations of interest rates and income (output) at which the goods market clears. That is why the *IS* curve is called the *goods market equilibrium schedule*.

Figure 4-4 shows that the *IS* curve is negatively sloped, reflecting the increase in aggregate demand associated with a reduction in the interest rate. We can also derive the *IS* curve by using the goods market equilibrium condition, that income equals planned spending, or

$$Y = AD = \overline{A} + \overline{c}Y - bi \tag{5}$$

which can be simplified to

$$Y = \alpha_G(\overline{A} - bi) \qquad \alpha_G = \frac{1}{1 - \overline{c}} \tag{6}$$

where α_G is the multiplier of Chapter 3. Equation (6) should be compared with (1) at the beginning of this chapter. Note from equation (6) that a higher interest rate implies a lower level of equilibrium income for a given $\overline{A}$, as Figure 4-4 shows.

The construction of the *IS* curve is quite straightforward and may even be deceptively simple. We can gain further understanding of the economics of the *IS* curve by asking and answering the following questions:

- What determines the slope of the *IS* curve?

- What determines the position of the *IS* curve, given its slope, and what causes the curve to shift?

- What happens when the interest rate and income are at levels such that we are not on the *IS* curve?

The Slope of the *IS* Curve

We have already noted that the *IS* curve is negatively sloped because a higher level of the interest rate reduces investment spending, thereby reducing aggregate demand

and thus the equilibrium level of income. The steepness of the curve depends on how sensitive investment spending is to changes in the interest rate and also on the multiplier, α_G, in equation (6).

Suppose that investment spending is very sensitive to the interest rate, so that b in equation (6) is large. Then, in terms of Figure 4-4, a given change in the interest rate produces a large change in aggregate demand, and thus shifts the aggregate demand curve in Figure 4-4a up by a large amount. A large shift in the aggregate demand schedule produces a correspondingly large change in the equilibrium level of income. If a given change in the interest rate produces a large change in income, the *IS* curve is very flat. This is the case if investment is very sensitive to the interest rate, that is, if b is large. Correspondingly, with b small and investment spending not very sensitive to the interest rate, the *IS* curve is relatively steep.

THE ROLE OF THE MULTIPLIER

Consider next the effects of the multiplier, α_G, on the steepness of the *IS* curve. Figure 4-5 shows aggregate demand curves corresponding to different multipliers. The coefficient $\bar{c}$ on the darker aggregate demand curves is smaller than the corresponding coefficient $\bar{c}'$ on the lighter aggregate demand curves. The multiplier is accordingly larger on the lighter aggregate demand curves. The initial levels of income, Y_1 and Y_1', correspond to the interest rate i_1 on the lower pair of dark and light aggregate demand curves, respectively.

A given reduction in the interest rate, to i_2, raises the intercept of the aggregate demand curves by the same vertical distance, as shown in Figure 4-5a. However, the implied change in income is very different. For the lighter curve, income rises to Y_2', while it rises only to Y_2 on the darker line. The change in equilibrium income corresponding to a given change in the interest rate is accordingly larger as the aggregate demand curve is steeper; that is, the larger the multiplier, the greater the rise in income. As we see from the lower figure, the larger the multiplier, the flatter the *IS* curve. Equivalently, the larger the multiplier, the larger the change in income produced by a given change in the interest rate.

We have thus seen that the smaller the sensitivity of investment spending to the interest rate and the smaller the multiplier, the steeper the *IS* curve. This conclusion is confirmed using equation (6). We can turn equation (6) around to express the interest rate as a function of the level of income:

$$i = \frac{\overline{A}}{b} - \frac{Y}{\alpha_G b} \tag{6a}$$

Thus, for a given change in Y, the associated change in i will be larger in size as b is smaller and as α_G is smaller.

Given that the slope of the *IS* curve depends on the multiplier, fiscal policy can affect that slope. The multiplier, α_G, is affected by the tax rate: an increase in the tax rate reduces the multiplier. Accordingly, the higher the tax rate, the steeper is the *IS* curve.[4]

---

[4]In problem 3 we ask you to relate this fact to the discussion of automatic stabilizers in Chap. 3.

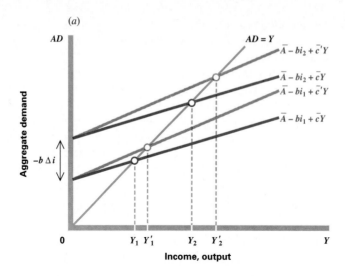

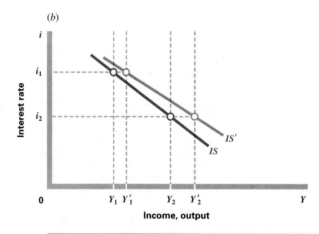

FIGURE 4-5
EFFECTS OF THE MULTIPLIER ON THE STEEPNESS OF THE *IS* CURVE. The diagram shows that corresponding to a higher marginal propensity to spend, and hence a steeper aggregate demand schedule, there is a flatter *IS* schedule.

The Position of the *IS* Curve

Figure 4-6 shows two different *IS* curves, the lighter one of which lies to the right and above the darker *IS* curve. What might cause the *IS* curve to be at *IS'* rather than at *IS*? The answer is, An increase in the level of autonomous spending.

In Figure 4-6*a* we show an initial aggregate demand curve drawn for a level of autonomous spending $\overline{A}$ and for an interest rate i_1. Corresponding to the initial aggregate

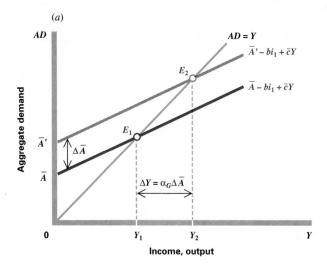

(a)

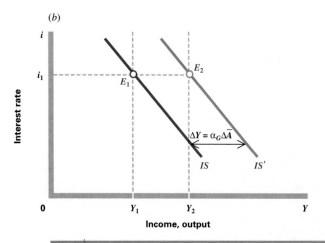

(b)

FIGURE 4-6

A SHIFT IN THE *IS* CURVE CAUSED BY A CHANGE IN AUTONOMOUS
SPENDING. An increase in aggregate demand due to higher
autonomous spending shifts the aggregate demand curve in part (*a*)
up, raising the equilibrium level of output at interest rate i_1. The *IS*
schedule in part (*b*) shifts. At each level of the interest rate,
equilibrium income is now higher. The horizontal shift of the *IS*
schedule is equal to the multiplier times the increase in autonomous
spending.

demand curve is the point E_1 on the *IS* curve in Figure 4-6*b*. Now, at the same interest rate, let the level of autonomous spending increase to $\overline{A}'$. The increase in autonomous spending increases the equilibrium level of income at the interest rate i_1. The point E_2 in Figure 4-6*b* is thus a point on the new goods market equilibrium schedule *IS'*. Since E_1 was an arbitrary point on the initial *IS* curve, we can perform the exercise for all levels of the interest rate and thereby generate the new curve, *IS'*. Thus, an increase in autonomous spending shifts the *IS* curve out to the right.

By how much does the curve shift? The change in income as a result of the change in autonomous spending can be seen from the top panel to be just the multiplier times the change in autonomous spending. That means that the *IS* curve is shifted horizontally by a distance equal to the multiplier times the change in autonomous spending, as in the lower panel.

The level of autonomous spending from equation (4) is

$$\overline{A} \equiv c\overline{TR} + \overline{I} + \overline{G}$$

Accordingly, an increase in government purchases or transfer payments will shift the *IS* curve out to the right, with the extent of the shift depending on the size of the multiplier. A reduction in transfer payments or in government purchases shifts the *IS* curve to the left.

Positions off the *IS* Curve

We gain understanding of the meaning of the *IS* curve by considering points off it. Figure 4-7 reproduces Figure 4-4*b*, along with two additional points—the *dis*equilibrium points E_3 and E_4. Consider the question of what is true for points off the schedule, such as E_3 and E_4. At point E_3 we have the same level of income, Y_1, as at E_1, but the interest rate is lower. Therefore the demand for investment is higher than at E_1, and the demand for goods is higher than at E_1. This means the demand for goods must exceed the level of output, and so there is an *excess demand for goods*. Similarly, at point E_4, the interest rate is higher than at E_2, the demand for goods is lower than at E_2, and there is an *excess supply of goods*.

This discussion shows that points above and to the right of the *IS* curve—points like E_4—are points of excess supply of goods. This is indicated by *ESG* (excess supply of goods) in Figure 4-7. Points below and to the left of the *IS* curve are points of excess demand for goods (*EDG*). At a point like E_3, the interest rate is too low and aggregate demand is therefore too high relative to output.

Summary

Here are the major points about the *IS* curve:

1. The *IS* curve is the schedule of combinations of the interest rate and level of income such that the goods market is in equilibrium.
2. The *IS* curve is negatively sloped because an increase in the interest rate reduces

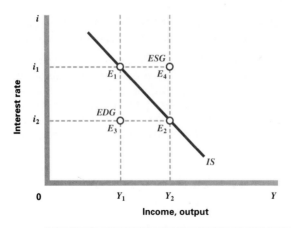

FIGURE 4-7
EXCESS SUPPLY (*ESG*) AND DEMAND (*EDG*) IN THE GOODS MARKET.
Points above and to the right of the *IS* schedule correspond to an
excess supply of goods, and points below and to the left to an
excess demand for goods. At a point such as E_4, interest rates are
higher than at E_2 on the *IS* curve. At the higher interest rates,
investment spending is too low, and thus output exceeds planned
spending and there is an excess supply of goods.

planned investment spending and therefore reduces aggregate demand, thus reducing the equilibrium level of income.

3. The smaller the multiplier and the less sensitive investment spending is to changes
   in the interest rate, the steeper the *IS* curve.
4. The *IS* curve is shifted by changes in autonomous spending. An increase in
   autonomous spending, including an increase in government purchases, shifts the
   IS curve out to the right.
5. At points to the right of the curve, there is excess supply in the goods market;
   at points to the left of the curve, there is excess demand for goods.

Now we turn to the assets markets.

4-2 THE ASSETS MARKETS AND THE *LM* CURVE

The assets markets are the markets in which money, bonds, stocks, houses, and other
forms of wealth are traded. Up to this point in the book, we have ignored the role of
these markets in affecting the level of income, and it is now time to remedy the omission.

There is a large variety of assets, and a tremendous volume of trading occurs
every day in the assets markets. We describe the most important of the assets that can
be owned in the United States in Box 4-1. But we shall simplify matters by grouping

box 4-1

ASSETS AND ASSET RETURNS

Assets fall into two broad categories, financial assets and tangible assets. A further subdivision identifies four main asset categories in the economy: money; other interest-bearing assets (credit market instruments or bonds for short); equities, or stocks; and tangible, or real, assets. Table 1 shows the main categories of assets held by U.S. households in 1991. These asset holdings are reported by the Federal Reserve in its publication *Balance Sheets for the US Economy*. We now comment briefly on each category.

MONEY AND OTHER DEPOSITS

The money stock proper consists of assets that can be immediately used for making payments. Money includes currency (notes and coins) and also deposits on which checks can be written. At the end of 1991, currency and checkable deposits (a measure of money called $M1$) amounted to $898 billion.* A broader measure of money (called $M2$) includes in addition to checkable deposits at banks also money market mutual funds and other deposits such as savings accounts. This measure of money was $3,440 billion at the end of 1991.

From the 1930s until the mid-1970s, no interest was paid on checkable deposits. During that period, people held checkable deposits purely for the convenience. Now interest is paid on checkable deposits. Thus they are now held partly because they pay interest but also because they offer a convenient way of making payments.

BONDS

A bond is a promise by a borrower to pay the lender a certain amount (the principal) at a specified date (the maturity date of the bond) and to pay a given amount of interest per year in the meantime. Thus we might have a bond, issued by the U.S. Treasury, that pays $10,000 on June 1, 2005, and until that time pays 7 percent interest ($700) per year. Bonds are issued by many types of borrowers—governments, municipalities, and corporations. The interest rates on bonds issued by different borrowers reflect the differing risks of default. Default occurs when a borrower is unable to meet the commitment to pay interest or principal. Corporations sometimes default, and during the great depression of the 1930s, so did some cities. In the late 1970s there was fear that New York City would default; in the 1980s there was fear that many foreign governments would do so; and in the early 1990s there was a fear that some major U.S. corporations would default.

A *perpetuity* is a bond which promises to pay interest forever, but not to repay the principal on the bond. The British government has issued perpetuities, called in their case *Consols*, since the nineteenth century. Anyone who owns a Consol has a right to receive a given number of pounds each year, but the government is not committed to repurchasing the bond. It is out there, in the hands of the public, forever.

---

*If you use Table 1 and calculate 2.4 percent of $24,291 billion, you will figure out that U.S. *households'* currency and checkable deposits at the end of 1991 amounted to $583 billion. The difference between $898 billion and $583 billion represents holdings of $M1$ by businesses, government agencies, and foreigners.

TABLE 1

HOUSEHOLD ASSET HOLDINGS IN 1991 (percent of total household assets)

Total household assets ($ billion)	24,291
Financial assets	62.5
Checkable deposits and currency	2.4
Other deposits	11.5
Credit market instruments (bonds)	8.2
Equities	
Corporate	12.6
Noncorporate	10.6
Life insurance and pension fund reserves	16.0
Other financial assets	1.2
Tangible assets	37.5

By the end of 1991, individuals in the United States held a total of $1,995 billion in the form of bonds. Nearly $840 billion consisted of government bonds held by individuals. Households held relatively small amounts of corporate bonds—under $180 billion.

EQUITIES OR STOCKS

Equities or stocks are claims to a share of the profits of an enterprise. For example, a share in IBM entitles the owner to a share of the profits of that corporation. The shareholder, or stockholder, receives the return on equity in two forms. Most firms pay regular *dividends*, which means that stockholders receive a certain amount for each share they own. Firms may also decide not to distribute profits to the stockholders but rather retain the profits and reinvest them by adding to the firms' stocks of machines and structures. When this occurs, the shares become more valuable since they now represent claims on the profits from a larger capital stock. Therefore, the price of the stock in the market will rise, and stockholders can make *capital gains*. A capital gain is an increase, per period of time, in the price of an asset. Of course, when the outlook for a corporation turns sour, stock prices can fall and stockholders can incur capital losses.

Thus the return on stocks, or the yield to a holder of a stock, is equal to the dividend (as a percentage of price) plus the capital gain.

Suppose we look at 1992 and 1993 and consider the yield on a stock in an imaginary company, BioMiracles, Inc. In 1992 the stock traded for $15. In 1993, the stock pays a dividend of $0.75 and the stock price increases to $16.50. What is the yield on the stock? The yield per year is equal to 15.0 percent, which is the dividend as a percentage of the initial price [5 percent = (0.75/15) × 100] plus 10.0 percent, which is the $1.50 capital gain as a percentage of the initial price.

At the end of 1991, the value of equity held by households in the United States was $5,636 billion. Nearly half of this equity was in noncorporate businesses.

REAL ASSETS

Real assets, or tangible assets, are the machines, land, and structures owned by corporations and the consumer durables (cars, washing machines, stereos, etc.) and residences owned by households. These assets carry a return that differs from one asset to another. Owner-occupied residences provide a return to owners who enjoy living in them and not paying monthly rent; the machines a firm owns contribute to producing output and thus making profits. The assets are called *real* to distinguish them from *financial* assets (money, stocks, bonds). The total value of tangible assets at the end of 1991 was $9.1 trillion, or over $35,400 per person.

The value of equities and bonds held by individuals cannot be added to the total tangible wealth in the economy to get the total wealth of individuals. The reason is that the equities and bonds individuals hold are claims on the part of tangible wealth that is held by corporations. The equity share gives an individual a part ownership in the factory and machinery.

In macroeconomics, to make things manageable, we lump assets into two categories. On one side we have money, with the specific characteristic that it is the only asset that serves as a means of payment. On the other side we have all other assets. Because money offers the convenience of being a means of payment, it carries a lower return than other assets, but that differential depends on the relative supplies of assets. As we see in this chapter, when the Fed reduces the money stock and increases the supply of other assets (we say "bonds"), the yield on other assets increases.

The appendix to Chapter 12 develops the relationship between interest rates and asset prices or present values. The appendix can be read independently of Chapter 12, and the interested student can study that material now. ■

---

all available assets into two groups, *money* and *interest-bearing assets*.[5] Thus we proceed as if there are only two assets, money and all others. It will be useful to think of the other assets as marketable claims to future income, such as *bonds*.

A bond is a promise to pay to its holder certain agreed-upon amounts of money at specified dates in the future. For example, a borrower sells a bond in exchange for a given amount of money today, say $100, and promises to pay a fixed amount, say $6, each year to the person who owns the bond, and to repay the full $100 (the principal) after some fixed period of time, such as 3 years. In this example, the interest rate is 6 percent, for that is the percentage of the amount borrowed that the borrower pays each year.

---

[5] We assume in this section that certain assets, such as the capital that firms use in production, are not traded. That too is a simplification. A more complete treatment of the assets markets would allow for the trading of capital and would introduce a relative price for the capital operated by firms. This treatment is usually reserved for advanced graduate courses. For such a treatment of the assets markets, see James Tobin, "A General Equilibrium Approach to Monetary Theory," *Journal of Money, Credit and Banking*, February 1969, pp. 15–29.

The Wealth Constraint

At any given time, an individual has to decide how to allocate his or her financial wealth between alternative types of assets. The more bonds held, the more interest received on total financial wealth. The more money held, the more likely the individual is to have money available when he or she wants to make a purchase. The person who has $1,000 in financial wealth has to decide whether to hold, say, $900 in bonds and $100 in money, or rather, $500 in each type of asset, or even $1,000 in money and none in bonds. Decisions on the form in which to hold assets are *portfolio decisions*.

The example makes it clear that the portfolio decisions on how much money to hold and on how many bonds to hold are really the same decision. Given the level of financial wealth, the individual who has decided how many bonds to hold has implicitly also decided how much money to hold. There is a *wealth budget constraint* which states that the sum of the individual's demand for money and demand for bonds has to add up to that person's total financial wealth.

Real and Nominal Money Demand

At this stage we have to reinforce the crucial distinction between *real* and *nominal* variables. The nominal demand for money is the individual's demand for a given number of dollars. Similarly, the nominal demand for bonds is the demand for a given number of dollars' worth of bonds. The real demand for money is the demand for money expressed in terms of the number of units of goods that money will buy; it is equal to the nominal demand for money divided by the price level. If the nominal demand for money is $100 and the price level is $2 per good—meaning that the representative basket of goods costs $2—then the real demand for money is 50 goods. If the price level later doubles to $4 per good and the demand for nominal money likewise doubles to $200, the real demand for money is unchanged at 50 goods.

Real money balances—real balances for short—are the quantity of nominal money divided by the price level. The real demand for money is called the *demand for real balances*. Similarly, real bond holdings are the nominal quantity of bonds divided by the price level.

The wealth budget constraint in the assets markets states that the demand for real balances, which we denote L, plus the demand for real bond holdings, which we denote DB, must add up to the real financial wealth of the individual. Real financial wealth is, of course, simply nominal wealth, WN, divided by the price level, P:

$$L + DB \equiv \frac{WN}{P} \tag{7}$$

Note, again, that the wealth budget constraint implies, given an individual's real wealth, that a decision to hold more real balances is also a decision to hold less real wealth in the form of bonds. This implication allows us to discuss assets markets entirely in terms of the money market. Why? Because, given real wealth, when the money market is in equilibrium, the bond market will turn out also to be in equilibrium. We now show why that should be.

The total amount of real financial wealth in the economy consists of existing real money balances and real bonds. Thus, total real financial wealth is equal to

$$\frac{WN}{P} \equiv \frac{M}{P} + SB \tag{8}$$

where M is the stock of nominal money balances and SB is the real value of the supply of bonds. Total real financial wealth consists of real balances and real bonds. The distinction between equations (7) and (8) is that equation (7) is a constraint on the amount of assets individuals wish to hold, whereas equation (8) is merely an accounting relationship that tells us how much financial wealth there is in the economy. There is no implication in the accounting relationship in equation (8) that individuals are necessarily happy to hold the amounts of money and bonds that actually exist in the economy.

Now substitute equation (7) into equation (8) and rearrange terms to obtain

$$\left(L - \frac{M}{P} \right) + (DB - SB) \equiv 0 \tag{9}$$

Let us see what equation (9) implies. Suppose that the demand for real balances, L, is equal to the existing stock of real balances, $\overline{M}/P$. Then the first term in parentheses in equation (9) is equal to zero, and therefore the second term in parentheses must also be zero. Thus, if the demand for real money balances is equal to the real money supply, the demand for real bonds, DB, must be equal to the supply of real bonds, SB.

Stating the same proposition in terms of "markets," we can say the following: The *wealth budget constraint* implies that when the money market is in equilibrium ($L = \overline{M}/P$), the bond market, too, is in equilibrium ($DB = SB$). Similarly, when there is excess demand in the money market, so that $L > \overline{M}/P$, there is an excess supply of bonds, that is, $DB < SB$. We can therefore fully discuss the assets markets by concentrating our attention on the money market.

The Demand for Money

We turn now to the money market and initially concentrate on the demand for real balances.[6] The demand for money is a demand for *real* balances because people hold money for what it will buy. The higher the price level, the more nominal balances a person has to hold to be able to purchase a given quantity of goods. If the price level doubles, then an individual has to hold twice as many nominal balances in order to be able to buy the same amount of goods.

The demand for real balances depends on the level of real income and the interest rate. It depends on the level of real income because individuals hold money to pay for their purchases, which, in turn, depend on income. The demand for money depends

---

[6]The demand for money is studied in depth in Chap. 13; here we present the arguments underlying the demand for money only briefly.

also on the cost of holding money. The cost of holding money is the interest that is forgone by holding money rather than other assets. The higher the interest rate, the more costly it is to hold money and, accordingly, the less cash will be held at each level of income.[7] Individuals can economize on their holdings of cash when the interest rate rises by being more careful in managing their money and by making transfers from money to bonds whenever their money holdings become large. If the interest rate is 1 percent, then there is very little benefit from holding bonds rather than money. However, when the interest rate is 10 percent, then it is worth some effort not to hold more money than is needed to finance day-to-day transactions.

On these simple grounds, then, the demand for real balances increases with the level of real income and decreases with the interest rate. The demand for real balances is accordingly written[8]

$$L = kY - hi \qquad k, h > 0 \tag{10}$$

The parameters k and h reflect the sensitivity of the demand for real balances to the level of income and the interest rate, respectively. A \$5 increase in real income raises money demand by $5k$ real dollars. An increase in the interest rate by one percentage point reduces real money demand by h real dollars.

The demand function for real balances, equation (10), implies that for a given level of income, the quantity demanded is a decreasing function of the rate of interest. Such a demand curve is shown in Figure 4-8 for a level of income Y_1. The higher the level of income, the larger is the demand for real balances, and therefore the further to the right the demand curve. The demand curve for a higher level of real income, Y_2, is also shown in Figure 4-8.

The Supply of Money, Money Market Equilibrium, and the *LM* Curve

To study equilibrium in the money market, we have to say how the supply of money is determined. The nominal quantity of money, M, is controlled by the Federal Reserve System (Fed), and we take it as given at the level $\overline{M}$. We assume the price level is constant at the level $\overline{P}$, so that the real money supply is at the level $\overline{M}/\overline{P}$.[9]

In Figure 4-9, we show combinations of interest rates and income levels such that the demand for real balances exactly matches the available supply. Starting with the level of income, Y_1, the corresponding demand curve for real balances, L_1, is shown in Figure 4-9b. It is drawn, as in Figure 4-8, as a decreasing function of the interest

---

[7] Some types of money, including most bank deposits, earn interest, but at a lower rate than bonds. But several sizable parts of money holding—including currency—earn no interest, so that overall, money earns less interest than other assets and the analysis of this chapter is applicable.

[8] Once again, we use a linear equation to describe a relationship. You should experiment with an alternative form, for example, $L = kY + h'/i$, where k and h' are positive. How would the equivalent of Fig. 4-8 look for this demand function?

[9] Since, for the present, we are holding constant the money supply and price level, we denote that by a bar.

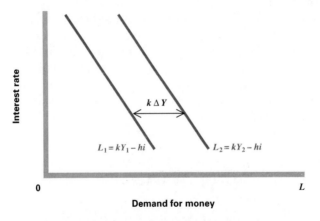

FIGURE 4-8
THE DEMAND FOR REAL BALANCES AS A FUNCTION OF THE INTEREST
RATE AND REAL INCOME. The demand for real balances is drawn as a
function of the rate of interest. The higher the rate of interest, the
lower the quantity of real balances demanded, given the level of
income. An increase in income raises the demand for money. This is
shown by a rightward shift of the money demand schedule.

rate. The existing supply of real balances, $\overline{M/P}$, is shown by the vertical line, since it is given and therefore is independent of the interest rate. At interest rate i_1 the demand for real balances equals the supply. Therefore, point E_1 is an equilibrium point in the money market. That point is recorded in Figure 4-9a as a point on the *money market equilibrium schedule*, or the *LM* curve.

Consider next the effect of an increase in income to Y_2. In Figure 4-9b, the higher level of income causes the demand for real balances to be higher at each level of the interest rate, and so the demand curve for real balances shifts up and to the right, to L_2. The interest rate increases to i_2 to maintain equilibrium in the money market at that higher level of income. Accordingly, the new equilibrium point is E_2. In Figure 4-9a, we record point E_2 as a point of equilibrium in the money market. Performing the same exercise for all income levels, we generate a series of points that can be linked to give us the *LM* schedule.

The *LM* schedule, or money market equilibrium schedule, shows all combinations of interest rates and levels of income such that the demand for real balances is equal to the supply. Along the *LM* schedule, the money market is in equilibrium.

The *LM* curve is positively sloped. An increase in the interest rate reduces the demand for real balances. To maintain the demand for real balances equal to the fixed supply, the level of income has to rise. Accordingly, money market equilibrium implies that an increase in the interest rate is accompanied by an increase in the level of income.

The *LM* curve can be obtained directly by combining the demand curve for real balances, equation (10), and the fixed supply of real balances. For the money market to be in equilibrium, demand has to equal supply, or

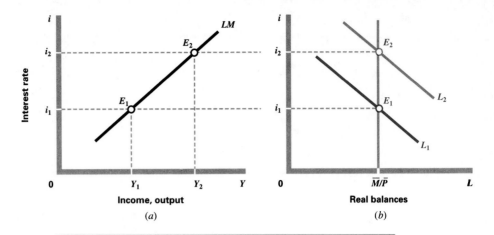

FIGURE 4-9
DERIVATION OF THE *LM* CURVE. The right-hand panel shows the money market. The supply of real balances is the vertical line $\overline{M}/\overline{P}$. The nominal money supply $\overline{M}$ is fixed by the Fed, and the price level $\overline{P}$ is assumed given. Demand for money curves L_1 and L_2 corresponds to different levels of income. When the income level is Y_1, L_1 applies, and the equilibrium interest rate is i_1. This gives point E_1 on the *LM* schedule in part (*a*). At income level Y_2, greater than Y_1, the equilibrium interest rate is i_2, yielding point E_2 on the *LM* curve.

$$\frac{\overline{M}}{\overline{P}} = kY - hi \tag{11}$$

Solving for the interest rate:

$$i = \frac{1}{h}\left(kY - \frac{\overline{M}}{\overline{P}}\right) \tag{11a}$$

The relationship (11*a*) is the *LM* curve.

Next we ask the same questions about the properties of the *LM* schedule that we asked about the *IS* curve.

The Slope of the *LM* Curve

The greater the responsiveness of the demand for money to income, as measured by k, and the lower the responsiveness of the demand for money to the interest rate, h, the steeper the *LM* curve will be. This point can be established by experimenting with Figure 4-9. It can also be confirmed by examining equation (11*a*), where a given

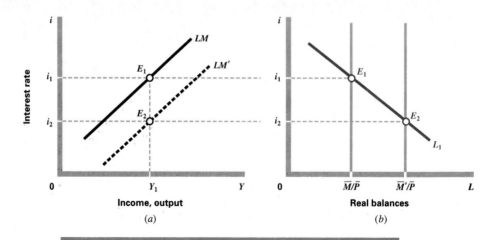

FIGURE 4-10

AN INCREASE IN THE SUPPLY OF MONEY FROM $\overline{M}$ TO $\overline{M}'$ SHIFTS THE *LM* CURVE TO THE RIGHT. An increase in the stock of real balances shifts the supply schedule in the right panel from $\overline{M}/\overline{P}$ to $\overline{M}'/\overline{P}$. At the initial income level Y_1, the equilibrium interest rate in the money market falls to i_2. In the left panel we show point E_2 as one point on the new *LM* schedule, corresponding to the higher money stock. Thus an increase in the real money stock shifts the *LM* schedule down and to the right.

change in income, ΔY, has a larger effect on the interest rate, i, the larger is k and the smaller is h. If the demand for money is relatively insensitive to the interest rate, so that h is close to zero, the *LM* curve is nearly vertical. If the demand for money is very sensitive to the interest rate, so that h is large, then the *LM* curve is close to horizontal. In that case, a small change in the interest rate must be accompanied by a large change in the level of income in order to maintain money market equilibrium.

The Position of the *LM* Curve

The real money supply is held constant along the *LM* curve. It follows that a change in the real money supply will shift the *LM* curve. In Figure 4-10, we show the effect of an increase in the real money supply. In Figure 4-10*b*, we draw the demand for real money balances for a level of income Y_1. With the initial real money supply, $\overline{M}/\overline{P}$, the equilibrium is at point E_1, with an interest rate i_1. The corresponding point on the *LM* schedule is E_1.

Now the real money supply increases to $\overline{M}'/P$, which we represent by a rightward shift of the money supply schedule. To restore money market equilibrium at the income level Y_1, the interest rate has to decline to i_2. The new equilibrium is therefore at point E_2. This implies that in Figure 4-10*a*, the *LM* schedule shifts to the right and down to *LM'*. At each level of income the equilibrium interest rate has to be lower to induce

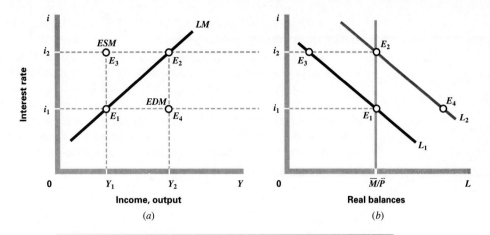

FIGURE 4-11

EXCESS DEMAND (*EDM*) AND SUPPLY (*ESM*) OF MONEY. Points above and to the left of the *LM* schedule correspond to an excess supply of real balances; points below and to the right, to an excess demand for real balances. Starting at point E_1 in the left panel, an increase in income takes us to E_4. At E_4 in the right panel, there is an excess demand for money—and thus at E_4 in the left panel there is an excess demand for money. By a similar argument, we can start at E_2 and move to E_3, at which the level of income is lower. This creates an excess supply of money.

people to hold the larger real quantity of money. Alternatively, at each level of the interest rate the level of income has to be higher so as to raise the transactions demand for money and thereby absorb the higher real money supply. These points can be noted, too, from inspection of the money market equilibrium condition in equation (11).

Positions off the *LM* Curve

Next we consider points off the *LM* schedule in order to characterize them as situations of excess demand or excess supply of money. For that purpose, look at Figure 4-11, which reproduces Figure 4-9 but adds the disequilibrium points E_3 and E_4. Look first at point E_1, where the money market is in equilibrium. Next assume an increase in the level of income to Y_2. This will raise the demand for real balances and shift the demand curve to L_2. At the initial interest rate, the demand for real balances would be indicated by point E_4 in Figure 4-11b, and we would have an excess demand for money—an excess of demand over supply—equal to the distance E_1E_4. Accordingly, point E_4 in Figure 4-11a is a point of excess demand for money: the interest rate is too low and/ or the level of income too high for the money market to clear. Consider, next, point E_3 in Figure 4-11b. Here we have the initial level of income Y_1, but an interest rate that is too high to yield money market equilibrium. Accordingly, we have an excess supply of money equal to the distance E_3E_2. Point E_3 in Figure 4-11a therefore corresponds to an excess supply of money.

More generally, any point to the right and below the *LM* schedule is a point of excess demand for money, and any point to the left and above the *LM* curve is a point of excess supply. This is shown by the *EDM* and *ESM* notations in Figure 4-11a.

Recall also from the wealth budget constraint, equation (9), that when there is an excess supply of money, there is automatically an excess demand for bonds. Thus a position like E_3 in Figure 4-11a is one of an excess demand for bonds—which is not surprising, given that the interest rate at E_3 is well above the level E_1 at which the bond and money markets clear.

Summary

The following are the major points about the *LM* curve:

1. The *LM* curve is the schedule of combinations of interest rates and levels of income such that the money market is in equilibrium.
2. When the money market is in equilibrium, so is the bond market. The *LM* curve therefore is also the schedule of combinations of interest rates and levels of income such that the bond market is in equilibrium.
3. The *LM* curve is positively sloped. Given the fixed money supply, an increase in the level of income, which increases the quantity of money demanded, has to be accompanied by an increase in the interest rate. This reduces the quantity of money demanded and thereby maintains money market equilibrium.
4. The *LM* curve is shifted by changes in the money supply. An increase in the money supply shifts the *LM* curve to the right.
5. At points to the right of the *LM* curve, there is an excess demand for money, and at points to its left, there is an excess supply of money.

We are now ready to discuss the joint equilibrium of the goods and assets markets. That is to say, we can now discuss how output and interest rates are determined.

4-3 EQUILIBRIUM IN THE GOODS AND ASSETS MARKETS

The *IS* and *LM* schedules summarize the conditions that have to be satisfied in order for the goods and money markets, respectively, to be in equilibrium. The task now is to determine how these markets are brought into *simultaneous* equilibrium. For simultaneous equilibrium, interest rates and income levels have to be such that *both* the goods market *and* the money market are in equilibrium. That condition is satisfied at point E in Figure 4-12. The equilibrium interest rate is therefore i_0 and the equilibrium level of income is Y_0, given the exogenous variables, in particular the real money supply and fiscal policy.[10] At point E, both the goods market and the assets markets are in equilibrium.

---

[10] In general, exogenous variables are those whose values are not determined within the system being studied.

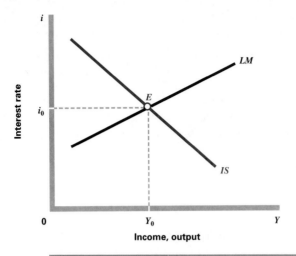

FIGURE 4-12

GOODS AND ASSETS MARKET EQUILIBRIUM. Goods and assets markets
clear at point *E*. Interest rates and income levels are such that the
public holds the existing stock of money and planned spending
equals output.

Figure 4-12 summarizes our analysis: the interest rate and the level of output
are determined by the interaction of the assets (*LM*) and goods (*IS*) markets.

It is worth stepping back now to review our assumptions and the meaning of the
equilibrium at *E*. The major assumption is that the price level is constant and that firms
are willing to supply whatever amount of output is demanded at that price level. Thus,
we assume the level of output Y_0 in Figure 4-12 will be willingly supplied by firms at
the price level $\overline{P}$. We repeat that this assumption is one that is temporarily needed for
the development of the analysis; it will be dropped in Chapter 7 when we begin to
study the determinants of the price level.

At point *E* in Figure 4-12, the economy is in equilibrium, given the price level,
because both the goods and money markets are in equilibrium. The demand for goods
is equal to the level of output on the *IS* curve. And on the *LM* curve, the demand for
money is equal to the supply of money. That also means the supply of bonds is equal
to the demand for bonds, as the discussion of the wealth budget constraint showed.
Accordingly, at point *E*, firms are producing their planned amount of output (there is
no unintended inventory accumulation or rundown), and individuals have the portfolio
compositions they desire.

Changes in the Equilibrium Levels of Income and the Interest Rate

The equilibrium levels of income and the interest rate change when either the *IS* or
the *LM* curve shifts. Figure 4-13, for example, shows the effects of an increase in the

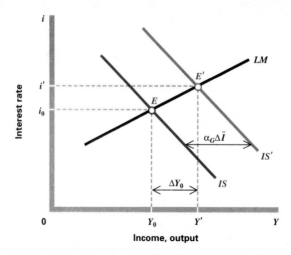

FIGURE 4-13
EFFECTS OF AN INCREASE IN AUTONOMOUS SPENDNG ON INCOME AND
THE INTEREST RATE. An increase in autonomous spending shifts the
IS schedule out and to the right. Income increases, and the
equilibrium income level rises. The increase in income is less than is
given by the simple multiplier α_G. This is because interest rates
increase and dampen investment spending.

rate of autonomous investment on the equilibrium levels of income and the interest
rate. Such an increase raises autonomous spending, $\bar{A}$, and therefore shifts the *IS* curve
to the right. That results in a rise in the level of income and an increase in the interest
rate at point E'.

Recall that an increase in autonomous investment spending, $\Delta \bar{I}$, shifts the *IS*
curve to the right by the amount $\alpha_G \Delta \bar{I}$, as we show in Figure 4-13. In Chapter 3,
where we dealt only with the goods market, we would have argued that $\alpha_G \Delta \bar{I}$ would
be the change in the level of income resulting from the change of $\Delta \bar{I}$ in autonomous
spending. But it can be seen in Figure 4-13 that the change in income here is only
ΔY_0, which is clearly less than the shift in the *IS* curve, $\alpha_G \Delta \bar{I}$.

What explains the fact that the increase in income is smaller than the increase
in autonomous spending, $\Delta \bar{I}$, times the multiplier, α_G? Diagrammatically, it is clear
that the explanation is the slope of the *LM* curve. If the *LM* curve were horizontal,
there would be no difference between the extent of the horizontal shift of the *IS* curve
and the change in income. If the *LM* curve were horizontal, then the interest rate would
not change when the *IS* curve shifts.

But what is the economics of what is happening? The increase in autonomous
spending does tend to increase the level of income. But an increase in income increases
the demand for money. With the supply of money fixed, the interest rate has to rise
to ensure that the demand for money stays equal to the fixed supply. When the interest
rate rises, investment spending is reduced because investment is negatively related to

the interest rate. Accordingly, the equilibrium change in income is less than the horizontal shift of the *IS* curve, $\alpha_G \Delta \bar{I}$.

We have now provided an example of the use of the *IS-LM* apparatus. That apparatus is very useful for studying the effects of monetary and fiscal policy on income and the interest rate, and we so use it in Chapter 5. Before we do so, however, we discuss how the economy moves from one equilibrium, such as *E*, to another, such as *E'*.

4-4 ADJUSTMENT TOWARD EQUILIBRIUM

Suppose that the economy were initially at a point like *E* in Figure 4-13 and that one of the curves then shifted, so that the new equilibrium was at a point like *E'*. How would that new equilibrium actually be reached? The adjustment would involve changes in both the interest rate and the level of income. To study how they move over time, we make two assumptions:

1. Output increases whenever there is an excess demand for goods and declines whenever there is an excess supply of goods. This assumption reflects the adjustment of firms to undesired rundown and accumulation of inventories.
2. The interest rate rises whenever there is an excess demand for money and falls whenever there is an excess supply of money. This adjustment occurs because an excess demand for money implies an excess supply of other assets (bonds). In attempting to acquire more money, people try to sell off bonds and thereby cause bond prices to fall or their yields (interest rates) to rise.

A detailed discussion of the relationship between the price of a bond and its yield is presented in the appendix to Chapter 12. Here we give only a brief explanation. For simplicity, consider a bond that promises to pay the holder of the bond $5 per year forever. The $5 is known as the bond *coupon*, and a bond that promises to pay a given amount to the holder of the bond forever is known as a *perpetuity*. If the yield available on other assets is 5 percent, the perpetuity will sell for $100 because at that price it, too, yields 5 percent ($= \$5/\$100$). Now suppose that the yield on other assets rises to 10 percent. Then the price of the perpetuity will drop to $50 because only at that price does the perpetuity yield 10 percent; that is, the $5 per year interest on a bond costing $50 gives its owners a 10 percent yield on their $50. This example makes it clear that *the price of a bond and its yield are inversely related, given the coupon.*

In point 2 above we assumed that an excess demand for money causes asset holders to attempt to sell off their bonds, thereby causing bond prices to fall and their yields to rise. Conversely, when there is an excess supply of money, people attempt to use their money to buy up other assets, raising the prices of the other assets and lowering their yields.

In Figure 4-14 we apply the analysis to study the adjustment of the economy. Four regions are represented, and they are characterized in Table 4-1. We know from Figure 4-11 that there is an excess supply of money above the *LM* curve, and hence we show *ESM* in regions I and II in Table 4-1. Similarly, we know from Figure 4-7 that there is an excess demand for goods below the *IS* curve. Hence, we show *EDG*

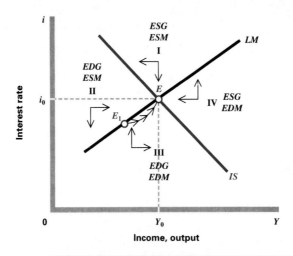

FIGURE 4-14
DISEQUILIBRIUM AND DYNAMICS IN THE GOODS AND MONEY MARKETS.
Income and interest rates adjust to the disequilibrium in goods
markets and assets markets. Specifically, interest rates fall when
there is an excess supply of money and rise when there is an
excess demand. Income rises when aggregate demand for goods
exceeds output and falls when aggregate demand is less than
output. The system converges over time to the equilibrium at *E*.

TABLE 4-1
DISEQUILIBRIUM AND ADJUSTMENT

	GOODS MARKET		MONEY MARKET	
region	disequilibrium	adjustment: output	disequilibrium	adjustment: interest rate
I	*ESG*	Falls	*ESM*	Falls
II	*EDG*	Rises	*ESM*	Falls
III	*EDG*	Rises	*EDM*	Rises
IV	*ESG*	Falls	*EDM*	Rises

for regions II and III in Table 4-1. You should be able to explain the remaining entries of Table 4-1.

The adjustment directions specified in assumptions 1 and 2 above are represented by arrows. Thus, for example, in region IV we have an excess demand for money, which causes interest rates to rise as other assets are sold off for money and their prices decline. The rising interest rates are represented by the upward-pointing arrow.

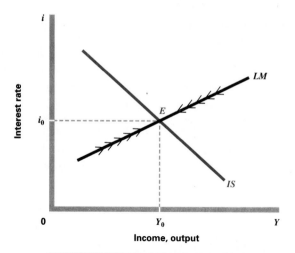

FIGURE 4-15

ADJUSTMENT TO EQUILIBRIUM WHEN THE MONEY MARKET ADJUSTS
QUICKLY. If the money market adjusts very rapidly, then the
economy is always in monetary equilibrium. In the diagram this
corresponds to always being on the *LM* schedule. When there is
excess demand for goods, output and interest rates are rising, and
when there is excess supply of goods, output and interest rates are
falling.

There is also an excess supply of goods in region IV and, accordingly, involuntary
inventory accumulation, to which firms respond by reducing output. Declining output
is indicated by the leftward-pointing arrow. The adjustments shown by the arrows will
lead ultimately, perhaps in a cyclical manner, to the equilibrium point E. For example,
starting at E_1 we show the economy moving to E, with income and the interest rate
increasing along the *adjustment path* indicated.

Rapid Asset Market Adjustment

For many purposes it is useful to restrict the dynamics by the reasonable assumption
that the money market adjusts very quickly and the goods market adjusts relatively
slowly. Since the money market can adjust merely through the buying and selling of
bonds, the interest rate adjusts rapidly and the money market effectively is always in
equilibrium. Such an assumption implies that we are always on the *LM* curve; any
departure from the equilibrium in the money market is almost instantaneously eliminated
by an appropriate change in the interest rate. In disequilibrium, we therefore move
along the *LM* curve, as is shown in Figure 4-15.

The goods market adjusts relatively slowly because firms have to change their
production schedules, which takes time. For points below the *IS* curve, we move up

along the *LM* schedule with rising income and interest rates, and for points above the *IS* schedule, we move down along the *LM* schedule with falling output and interest rates until point *E* is reached. The adjustment process is *stable* in that the economy does move to the equilibrium position at *E*.

The adjustment process shown in Figure 4-15 is very similar to that of Chapter 3. To the right of the *IS* curve, there is an excess supply of goods, and firms are therefore accumulating inventories. They cut production in response to their inventory buildup, and the economy moves down the *LM* curve. The difference between the adjustment process here and in Chapter 3 is the following: here, when there is an excess supply of goods and as the economy moves toward the equilibrium level of income, with a falling interest rate, desired investment spending actually rises.

4-5 A FORMAL TREATMENT OF THE *IS-LM* MODEL

Our exposition so far has been verbal and graphical. We now round off the analysis with a more formal treatment of the *IS-LM* model.

Equilibrium Income and the Interest Rate

The intersection of the *IS* and *LM* schedules determines equilibrium income and the equilibrium interest rate. We now derive expressions for these equilibrium values by using the equations of the *IS* and *LM* schedules. Recall from earlier in the chapter:

IS schedule:
$$Y = \alpha_G(\overline{A} - bi) \tag{6}$$

and the equation describing money market equilibrium as

LM schedule:
$$i = \frac{1}{h}\left(kY - \frac{\overline{M}}{P}\right) \tag{11a}$$

The intersection of the *IS* and *LM* schedules in the diagrams corresponds to a situation in which both the *IS* and *LM* equations hold—the *same* interest rate and income levels assure equilibrium in *both* the goods and the money market. In terms of the equations, this means we can substitute the interest rate from the *LM* equation (11a) into the *IS* equation (6):

$$Y = \alpha_G\left[\overline{A} - \frac{b}{h}\left(kY - \frac{\overline{M}}{P}\right)\right]$$

Collecting terms and solving for the equilibrium level of income, we obtain

$$Y_0 = \gamma\overline{A} + \gamma\frac{b}{h}\frac{\overline{M}}{P} \tag{12}$$

where $\gamma = \alpha_G/(1 + k\alpha_G b/h)$. Equation (12) shows that the equilibrium level of income depends on two exogenous variables: autonomous spending, $\overline{A}$, including fiscal policy parameters (I, G, TR); and the real money stock, $\overline{M}/P$. Equilibrium income is higher the higher the level of autonomous spending, $\overline{A}$, and the higher the stock of real balances.

The equilibrium rate of interest, i_0, is obtained by substituting the equilibrium income level, Y_0, from equation (12) into the equation of the *LM* schedule (11*a*):

$$i_0 = \frac{k}{h}\gamma\overline{A} - \frac{1}{h + kb\alpha_G}\frac{\overline{M}}{P} \tag{13}$$

Equation (13) shows that the equilibrium interest rate depends on the parameters of fiscal policy captured in the multiplier and the term $\overline{A}$ and on the real money stock. A higher real money stock implies a lower equilibrium interest rate.

For policy questions we are interested in the precise relation between changes in fiscal policy or changes in the real money stock and the resulting changes in equilibrium income. *Monetary* and *fiscal policy multipliers* provide the relevant information.

The Fiscal Policy Multiplier

The fiscal policy multiplier shows how much an increase in government spending changes the equilibrium level of income, holding the real money supply constant. Examine equation (12) and consider the effect of an increase in government spending on income. The increase in government spending, $\Delta\overline{G}$, is a change in autonomous spending, so that $\Delta\overline{A} = \Delta\overline{G}$. The effect of the change in $\overline{G}$ is given by

$$\frac{\Delta Y_0}{\Delta\overline{G}} = \gamma \qquad \gamma = \frac{\alpha_G}{1 + k\alpha_G\dfrac{b}{h}} \tag{14}$$

The expression γ is the fiscal or government spending multiplier once interest rate adjustment is taken into account. Consider how this multiplier, γ, differs from the simpler expression α_G that applied under constant interest rates. Inspection shows that γ is less than α_G since $1/(1 + k\alpha_G b/h)$ is a fraction. This represents the dampening effect of increased interest rates associated with a fiscal expansion in the *IS-LM* model.

We note that the expression in equation (14) is almost zero if h is very small and will be equal to α_G if h approaches infinity. This corresponds, respectively, to vertical and horizontal *LM* schedules. Similarly, a large value of either b or k serves to reduce the effect of government spending on income. Why? A high value of k implies a large increase in money demand as income rises and hence a large increase in interest rates required to maintain money market equilibrium. In combination with a high b, this implies a large reduction in private aggregate demand.

The Monetary Policy Multiplier

The monetary policy multiplier shows how much an increase in the real money supply increases the equilibrium level of income, keeping fiscal policy unchanged. Using equation (12) to examine the effects of an increase in the real money supply on income, we have

$$\frac{\Delta Y_0}{\Delta (\overline{M/P})} = \frac{b}{h}\gamma \tag{15}$$

The smaller h and k and the larger b and α_G, the more expansionary the effect of an increase in real balances on the equilibrium level of income. Large b and α_G correspond to a very flat *IS* schedule.

4-6   SUMMARY

1. The *IS-LM* model presented in this chapter is the basic model of aggregate demand that incorporates the assets markets as well as the goods market. It lays particular stress on the channels through which monetary and fiscal policy affect the economy.
2. The *IS* curve shows combinations of interest rates and levels of income such that the goods market is in equilibrium. Increases in the interest rate reduce aggregate demand by reducing investment spending. Thus at higher interest rates, the level of income at which the goods market is in equilibrium is lower—the *IS* curve slopes downward.
3. The demand for money is a demand for *real* balances. The demand for real balances increases with income and decreases with the interest rate, the cost of holding money rather than other assets. With an exogenously fixed supply of real balances, the *LM* curve, representing money market equilibrium, is upward-sloping. Because of the wealth constraint, equilibrium of the money market implies equilibrium of the remaining assets markets—summarized here under the catchall phrase "bond market."
4. The interest rate and level of output are jointly determined by the simultaneous equilibrium of the goods and money markets. This occurs at the point of intersection of the *IS* and *LM* curves.
5. Assuming that output is increased when there is an excess demand for goods and that the interest rate rises when there is an excess demand for money, the economy does move toward the new equilibrium when one of the curves shifts. Typically we think of the assets markets as clearing rapidly so that, in response to a disturbance, the economy tends to move along the *LM* curve to the new equilibrium.
6. The more formal analysis of Section 4-5 shows precisely how changes in monetary and fiscal policy affect the economy, through the *multipliers* of monetary and fiscal policy.
7. *A final warning*: We are assuming here that any level of output that is demanded can be produced by firms at the constant price level. Price level behavior, including inflation, is discussed in substantially more detail first in Chapters 7–9 and then in Chapter 16. Those chapters build on the analysis of the *IS-LM* model.

KEY TERMS

IS curve	Portfolio decisions
LM curve	Real balances (real money balances)
IS-LM model	Wealth budget constraint
Bond	Monetary policy multiplier
Money	Fiscal policy multiplier

PROBLEMS

1. The following equations describe an economy. (Think of *C, I, G*, etc., as being measured in billions and *i* as a percentage; a 5 percent interest rate implies $i = 5$.)

$$C = 0.8(1 - t)Y \tag{P1}$$

$$t = 0.25 \tag{P2}$$

$$I = 900 - 50i \tag{P3}$$

$$\overline{G} = 800 \tag{P4}$$

$$L = 0.25Y - 62.5i \tag{P5}$$

$$\overline{M/P} = 500 \tag{P6}$$

(a) What is the equation that describes the *IS* curve?
(b) What is the general definition of the *IS* curve?
(c) What is the equation that describes the *LM* curve?
(d) What is the general definition of the *LM* curve?
(e) What are the equilibrium levels of income and the interest rate?
(f) Describe in words the conditions that are satisfied at the intersection of the *IS* and *LM* curves, and explain why this is an equilibrium.

2. Continue with the same equations.
(a) What is the value of α_G, which corresponds to the simple multiplier (with taxes) of Chapter 3?
(b) By how much does an increase in government spending of $\Delta \overline{G}$ increase the level of income in this model, which includes the assets markets?
(c) By how much does a change in government spending of $\Delta \overline{G}$ affect the equilibrium interest rate?
(d) Explain the difference between your answers to 2a and 2b.

3. (a) Explain in words how and why the multiplier α_G and the interest sensitivity of aggregate demand affect the slope of the *IS* curve.
(b) Explain why the slope of the *IS* curve is a factor in determining the working of monetary policy.

4. Explain in words how and why the income and interest sensitivities of the demand for real balances affect the slope of the *LM* curve.

5. (a) Why does a horizontal *LM* curve imply that fiscal policy has the same effects on the economy as we derived in Chapter 3?
(b) What is happening in this case in terms of Figure 4-2?
(c) Under what circumstances might the *LM* curve be horizontal?

6. It is possible that the interest rate might affect consumption spending. An increase in the interest rate could, in principle, lead to increases in saving and therefore a reduction in consumption, given the level of income. Suppose that consumption were in fact reduced by an increase in the interest rate. How would the *IS* curve be affected?

7. Suppose that the money supply, instead of being constant, increased (slightly) with the interest rate.
   (a) How would this change affect the construction of the *LM* curve?
   (b) Could you see any reason why the Fed might follow a policy of increasing the money supply along with the interest rate?

8. (a) How does an increase in the tax rate affect the *IS* curve?
   (b) How does the increase affect the equilibrium level of income?
   (c) How does the increase affect the equilibrium interest rate?

9. Draw a graph of how *i* and *Y* respond over time (i.e., use time as the horizontal axis) to an increase in the money supply. You may assume that the money market adjusts much more rapidly than the goods market.

10. (a) Show that a given change in the money stock has a larger effect on output the less interest sensitive the demand for money. (You can answer using either graphs or the formal analysis of Section 4-5.)
    (b) How does the response of the interest rate to a change in the money stock depend on the interest sensitivity of money demand?

11. In 1991 the Treasury bill rate decreased from 6.3 percent in January to 4.1 percent in December. The economy fell deeper into recession during this period (i.e., *Y* was declining). Can you explain this pattern of declining output and declining interest rates using the *IS-LM* model? (*Hint*: Ask which curve has to shift in what direction to produce the income and interest rate pattern of 1991.) Can you think of any change that would have caused the *IS* or *LM* curve to shift in the way implied by your answer to the question?

COMPUTER EXERCISES

1. By increasing government purchases by 20, determine
   (a) The change in output and calculate the value of the (new) spending multiplier (which now includes endogenous investment).
   (b) The amount of investment that has been crowded out.
   (c) The effect on the budget surplus.

2. Raise the interest sensitivity of investment and determine what happens to the effectiveness of fiscal policy. Specifically,
   (a) Return to the BASE solution, then change *b* from 12 to 15 and solve. What is the current *Y*?
   (b) With *b* now at 15, increase government purchases by 20. What is the current *Y*?
   (c) Compare the current output levels in (a) and (b) to determine the change in *Y* resulting from a change in government purchases. What is that change in *Y*? How does it compare with the change in exercise 1 above? Why do you get this result?
   (d) From your results above, calculate the value of the (new) spending multiplier when $b = 15$.

3. Return to the BASE solution, then increase the money supply by 20. After comparing the base and current solutions, what type(s) of spending change? Why?

4. Raise the interest sensitivity of investment and determine what happens to the effectiveness of monetary policy. Specifically,

(a) Return to the BASE solution, then change b from 12 to 15 and solve. What is the current Y? (This should agree with 2a above.)

(b) With b now at 15, increase the money supply by 20. What is the current Y?

(c) Compare the current output levels in (a) and (b) to determine the change in Y resulting from a change in money supply. What is that change in Y? How does it compare with the change in 3 above?

(d) From your results above, state what happens to the effectiveness of monetary policy if the interest sensitivity of investment rises.

MONETARY AND FISCAL POLICY

*I*n the fall of 1991, the United States seemed headed for a double-dip recession, as the economic recovery that many had thought was well under way showed signs of running out of steam. Figure 5-1 shows how the economy went into recession in the third quarter of 1990, seemed to be emerging from it in the second quarter of 1991, although growth picked up only in late 1992.

The fear of a double-dip recession pushed politicians and policy makers into extensive debate and some action. The Fed cut interest rates sharply: the average Treasury bill rate in the first quarter of 1992 was only 3.9 percent, well below the 6.0 percent of a year earlier, as can also be seen in Figure 5-1. And the Congress began discussing a fiscal package that would help the recovery by cutting taxes and increasing government spending. In his State of the Union Address in January 1993, the President proposed his own set of stimulatory fiscal changes. Before the President and the Congress could agree on a fiscal package, the data for the first quarter of 1993 came out and the recovery seemed once more to be back on track—although, to be sure, this appeared to be one of the least rapid recoveries in history.

In this chapter we use the *IS-LM* model developed in Chapter 4 to show how monetary and fiscal policy work. These are the two main macroeconomic policy tools the government can call on to try to keep the economy growing at a reasonable rate, with low inflation. They are the policy tools the government uses to try to shorten recessions, as in 1991, and to prevent booms from getting out of hand. As Figure 4-2 shows, fiscal policy has its initial impact in the goods market, and monetary policy has its initial impact mainly in the assets markets. But because the goods and assets markets are closely interconnected, both monetary and fiscal policies have effects on both the level of output and interest rates.

5-1 MONETARY POLICY

In Chapter 4, we showed how an increase in the quantity of money affects the economy, increasing the level of output by reducing interest rates. The Federal Reserve System, a quasi-independent part of the government, is responsible for monetary policy.

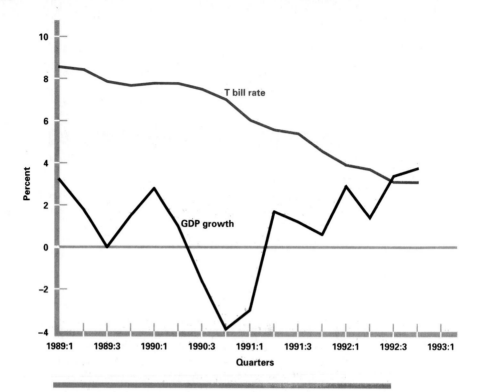

FIGURE 5-1
THE 1990–1992 RECESSION. The recession began in the third quarter of
1990 and seemed to be ending in the second quarter of 1991. Then
at the end of 1991, the recovery weakened, and a double-dip
recession looked possible. The Fed kept cutting interest rates as it
attempted to get the recovery back on track.

The Fed conducts monetary policy mainly through *open market operations*, which
we study in more detail in Chapter 14. In an open market operation, the Federal Reserve
buys bonds in exchange for money, thus increasing the stock of money, or it sells
bonds in exchange for money paid by the purchasers of the bonds, thus reducing the
money stock.

We take here the case of an open market purchase of bonds. The Fed pays for
the bonds it buys with money *that it can create*. One can usefully think of the Fed as
printing money with which to buy bonds, even though that is not strictly accurate.
When the Fed buys bonds, it reduces the quantity of bonds available in the market
and thereby tends to increase their price, or lower their yield—only at a lower interest
rate will the public be prepared to hold a smaller fraction of its wealth in the form of
bonds and a larger fraction in the form of money.

Figure 5-2 shows graphically how an open market purchase works. The initial
equilibrium at point E is on the initial LM schedule that corresponds to a real money
supply, $\overline{M}/P$. Consider next an open market purchase by the Fed. This increases the

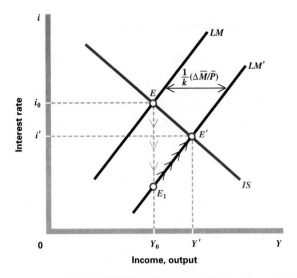

FIGURE 5-2
MONETARY POLICY. An increase in the real money stock shifts the *LM* schedule to the right. The asset markets adjust immediately, and interest rates decline between points *E* and E_1. The lower interest rates stimulate investment, and spending and income rise until a new equilibrium is reached at point *E'*. Once all adjustments have taken place, a rise in the real money stock raises equilibrium income and lowers equilibrium interest rates.

nominal quantity of money and, given the price level, the real quantity of money. As a consequence, the *LM* schedule will shift to *LM'*. Therefore, the new equilibrium will be at point *E'* with a lower interest rate and a higher level of income. The equilibrium level of income rises because the open market purchase reduces the interest rate and thereby increases investment spending.

By experimenting with Figure 5-2, you can show that the steeper the *LM* schedule, the larger the change in income. If money demand is very sensitive to the interest rate, then a given change in the money stock can be absorbed in the assets markets with only a small change in the interest rate. The effects of an open market purchase on investment spending would then be small. By contrast, if the demand for money is not very sensitive to the interest rate, a given change in the money supply will cause a large change in the interest rate and have a big effect on investment demand. Similarly, if the demand for money is very sensitive to income, a given increase in the money stock can be absorbed with a relatively small change in income and the monetary multiplier will be smaller.[1]

---

[1]The precise expression for the monetary policy multiplier is given in equation (15) in Chap. 4. If you have worked through the optional Sec. 4-5, you should use that equation to confirm the statements in this paragraph.

Consider next the adjustment process to the monetary expansion. At the initial equilibrium point, E, the increase in the money supply creates an excess supply of money to which the public adjusts by trying to buy other assets. In the process, asset prices increase and yields decline. By our assumption that the assets markets adjust rapidly, we move immediately to point E_1, where the money market clears, and where the public is willing to hold the larger real quantity of money because the interest rate has declined sufficiently. At point E_1, however, there is an excess demand for goods. The decline in the interest rate, given the initial income level Y_0, has raised aggregate demand and is causing inventories to run down. In response, output expands and we start moving up the LM' schedule. Why does the interest rate rise in the adjustment process? Because the increase in output raises the demand for money and the bigger demand for money has to be checked by higher interest rates.

Thus the increase in the money stock first causes interest rates to fall as the public adjusts its portfolio and then—through lower interest rates—increases aggregate demand.

The Transmission Mechanism

Two steps in the *transmission mechanism*—the process by which changes in monetary policy affect aggregate demand—are essential. The first is that an increase in real balances generates a *portfolio disequilibrium*, that is, at the prevailing interest rate and level of income, people are holding more money than they want. This causes portfolio holders to attempt to reduce their money holdings by buying other assets, thereby changing asset prices and yields. In other words, the change in the money supply changes interest rates. The second stage of the transmission process occurs when the change in interest rates affects aggregate demand.

These two stages of the transmission process appear in almost every analysis of the effects of changes in the money supply on the economy. The details of the analysis will often differ—some analyses will have more than two assets and more than one interest rate; some will include an influence of interest rates on other categories of demand, in particular consumption and spending by local government.[2]

Table 5-1 summarizes the stages in the transmission mechanism. There are two critical links between the change in real balances and the ultimate effect on income. First, the change in real balances, by bringing about portfolio disequilibrium, must lead to a change in interest rates. Second, that change in interest rates must change aggregate demand. Through these two linkages, changes in the real money stock affect the level of output in the economy. But that outcome immediately implies the following: if portfolio imbalances do not lead to significant changes in interest rates—for whatever reason—or if spending does not respond to changes in interest rates, the link between

---

[2]Some analyses also include a mechanism by which changes in real balances have a direct effect on aggregate demand through the real balance effect. The argument is that wealth affects consumption demand (as we shall see in Chap. 11) and that an increase in real balances increases wealth and therefore consumption demand. The real balance effect is not very important empirically, because the relevant real balances are only a small part of wealth. The classic work on the topic is Don Patinkin, *Money, Interest, and Prices*, 2nd ed. (New York: Harper and Row, 1965).

TABLE 5-1
THE TRANSMISSION MECHANISM

(1)	(2)	(3)	(4)
Change in real money supply	Portfolio adjustments lead to a change in asset prices and interest rates	Spending adjusts to the change in interest rates	Output adjusts to the change in aggregate demand

money and output does not exist. We refer to the responsiveness of aggregate demand—rather than investment spending—to the interest rate because consumption demand may also respond to the interest rate. Higher interest rates may lead to more saving and less consumption at a given level of income. Empirically, it has been difficult to isolate such an interest rate effect on consumption. We now study these linkages in more detail.

The Liquidity Trap

In discussing the effects of monetary policy on the economy, two extreme cases have received much attention. The first is the *liquidity trap*, a situation in which the public is prepared, at a given interest rate, to hold whatever amount of money is supplied. This implies that the *LM* curve is horizontal and that changes in the quantity of money do not shift it. In that case, monetary policy carried out through open market operations has no effect on either the interest rate or level of income. In the liquidity trap, monetary policy is powerless to affect the interest rate.

There is a liquidity trap at a zero interest rate. At a zero interest rate, the public would not want to hold any bonds, since money, which also pays zero interest, has the advantage of being usable in transactions. Accordingly, if the interest rate ever, for some reason, were zero, increases in the quantity of money could not induce anyone to shift into bonds and thereby reduce the interest rate on bonds below zero. An increase in the money supply in this case would have no effect on the interest rate or income— the economy would be in a liquidity trap where monetary policy does not work.

The possibility of a liquidity trap at low positive (rather than zero) interest rates is a notion that grew out of the theories of the great English economist John Maynard Keynes. Keynes himself did state, though, that he was not aware of there ever having been such a situation, nor are we today, 60 years later.[3]

Banks' Reluctance to Lend?

In 1991 a different possibility arose to suggest that sometimes monetary policy actions by the Fed might have only a very limited impact on the economy. In step (3) in Table

---

[3] J. M. Keynes, *The General Theory of Employment, Interest and Money* (New York: Macmillan, 1936), p. 207.

5-1, investment spending should increase in response to lower interest rates. Firms that plan to increase their investment spending typically borrow from banks to finance their spending. However, in 1991, as interest rates declined, banks were reluctant to increase their lending.

The underlying reason was that many banks had made bad loans at the end of the 1980s, especially to finance real estate deals. When the real estate market collapsed in 1990 and 1991, banks faced the prospect that a significant portion of their existing borrowers could not repay in full. Not surprisingly, they showed little enthusiasm to lend more to new, perhaps risky, borrowers. Rather, they preferred to lend to the government, by buying its securities such as Treasury bills. Lending to the U.S. government is as safe as any loan can be, because the U.S. government always pays its debts.

If banks will not lend to firms, then an important part of the transmission mechanism between a Fed open market purchase and an increase in aggregate demand and output is put out of action. Careful study suggested that banks were lending less to private firms than usual for this stage of the business cycle.[4] However, many argued that further open market operations, leading to further cuts in interest rates, would get the economy moving again. That is, they were arguing that if a given dose of Fed medicine had less effect on bank lending than usual, then the dose should be increased. They appear to have been right, and by 1992, bank lending was picking up.

The Classical Case

The polar opposite of the horizontal *LM* curve—which implies that monetary policy cannot affect the level of income—is the vertical *LM* curve. The *LM* curve is vertical when the demand for money is entirely unresponsive to the interest rate.

Recall from Chapter 4 [equation (11)] that the *LM* curve is described by

$$\frac{\overline{M}}{\overline{P}} = kY - hi \tag{1}$$

If h is zero, then corresponding to a given real money supply, $\overline{M}/\overline{P}$, there is a unique level of income, which implies that the *LM* curve is vertical at that level of income. (Sneak a look ahead at Figure 5-4.)

The vertical *LM* curve is called the *classical case*. Rewriting equation (1), with h set equal to zero, and with $\overline{P}$ moved to the right-hand side, we obtain

$$\overline{M} = k\overline{P}Y \tag{2}$$

We see that the classical case implies that nominal GDP, $P \times Y$, depends only on the quantity of money. This is the classical *quantity theory of money*, which argues that the level of nominal income is determined solely by the quantity of money.

---

[4]See, for example, Ben Bernanke and Cara Lown, "The Credit Crunch," *Brookings Papers on Economic Activity*, 1991, 2.

When the *LM* curve is vertical, a given change in the quantity of money has a maximal effect on the level of income. Check this by moving a vertical *LM* curve to the right and comparing the resultant change in income with the change produced by a similar horizontal shift of a nonvertical *LM* curve.

By drawing a vertical *LM* curve, you can also see that shifts in the *IS* curve do not affect the level of income when the *LM* curve is vertical. *Thus when the LM curve is vertical, monetary policy has a maximal effect on the level of income, and fiscal policy has no effect on income.* The vertical *LM* curve, implying the comparative effectiveness of monetary over fiscal policy, is sometimes associated with the view that "only money matters" for the determination of output. Since the *LM* curve is vertical only when the demand for money does not depend on the interest rate, the interest sensitivity of the demand for money turns out to be an important issue in determining the effectiveness of alternative policies. The evidence, to be reviewed in Chapter 13, is that the interest rate does affect the demand for money.

5-2 FISCAL POLICY AND CROWDING OUT

This section shows how changes in fiscal policy shift the *IS* curve, the curve that describes equilibrium in the goods market. Recall that the *IS* curve slopes downward because a decrease in the interest rate increases investment spending, thereby increasing aggregate demand and the level of output at which the goods market is in equilibrium. Recall also that changes in fiscal policy shift the *IS* curve. Specifically, a fiscal expansion shifts the *IS* curve to the right.

The equation of the *IS* curve, derived in Chapter 4, is repeated here for convenience:

$$Y = \alpha_G(\overline{A} - bi) \qquad \alpha_G = \frac{1}{1 - c(1 - t)} \tag{3}$$

Note that $\overline{G}$, the level of government spending, is a component of autonomous spending, $\overline{A}$, in equation (3). The income tax rate, t, is part of the multiplier. Thus both government spending and the tax rate affect the *IS* schedule.

An Increase in Government Spending

Figure 5-3 show that a fiscal expansion raises equilibrium income and the interest rate. At unchanged interest rates, higher levels of government spending increase the level of aggregate demand. To meet the increased demand for goods, output must rise as shown by a shift in the *IS* schedule. At each level of the interest rate, equilibrium income must rise by α_G times the increase in government spending. For example, if government spending rises by 100 and the multiplier is 2, then equilibrium income must increase by 200 at each level of the interest rate. Thus the *IS* schedule shifts to the right by 200.

If the economy is initially in equilibrium at point *E* and government spending rises by 100, we would move to point *E″* *if the interest rate stayed constant. At E″*

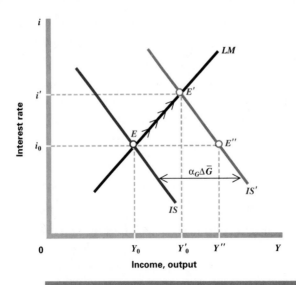

FIGURE 5-3

EFFECTS OF AN INCREASE IN GOVERNMENT SPENDING. An increase in government spending raises aggregate demand at each level of the interest rate and thus shifts the *IS* schedule to the right, to *IS'*. At point *E* there is now an excess demand for goods. Output rises, and with it the interest rate, because the income expansion raises money demand. The new equilibrium is at point *E'*. The increase in income ($Y'_0 - Y_0$) is less than the amount indicated by the simple multiplier ($Y'' - Y_0$) because higher interest rates crowd out some investment spending.

the goods market is in equilibrium in that planned spending equals output. But the assets market is no longer in equilibrium. Income has increased, and therefore the quantity of money demanded is higher. Because there is an excess demand for real balances, the interest rate rises. Firms' planned investment spending declines at higher interest rates, and thus aggregate demand falls off.

What is the complete adjustment, taking into account the expansionary effect of higher government spending and the dampening effects of the higher interest rate on private spending? Figure 5-3 shows that only at point *E'* do *both* the goods and assets markets clear. Only at point *E'* is planned spending equal to income and, at the same time, the quantity of real balances demanded equal to the given real money stock. Point *E'* is therefore the new equilibrium point.

The Dynamics of Adjustment

We continue to assume that the money market clears quickly and continuously, while output adjusts only slowly. This implies that as government spending increases, we stay initially at point E, since there is no disturbance in the money market. The excess demand for goods, however, leads firms to increase output, and that increase in output and income raises the demand for money. The resulting excess demand for money, in turn, causes interest rates to be bid up, and we proceed up along the LM curve with rising output and rising interest rates, until we reach the new equilibrium at point E'.

Crowding Out

Comparing E' to the initial equilibrium at E, we see that increased government spending raises both income and the interest rate. But another important comparison is between points E' and E'', the equilibrium in the goods market at unchanged interest rates. Point E'' corresponds to the equilibrium we studied in Chapter 3, when we neglected the impact of interest rates on the economy. In comparing E'' and E' it becomes clear that the adjustment of interest rates and their impact on aggregate demand dampen the expansionary effect of increased government spending. Income, instead of increasing to the level Y'', rises only to Y_0'.

The reason that income rises only to Y_0' rather than to Y'' is that the rise in the interest rate from i_0 to i' reduces the level of investment spending. We say that the increase in government spending *crowds out* investment spending. Crowding out occurs when expansionary fiscal policy causes interest rates to rise, thereby reducing private spending, particularly investment.

What factors determine how much crowding out takes place? In other words, what determines the extent to which interest rate adjustments dampen the output expansion induced by increased government spending? By drawing for yourself different IS and LM schedules you will be able to show the following:

- Income increases more, and interest rates increase less, the flatter the LM schedule.
- Income increases less, and interest rates increase less, the flatter the IS schedule.
- Income and interest rates increase more the larger the multiplier, α_G, and thus the larger the horizontal shift of the IS schedule.

In each case the extent of crowding out is greater the more the interest rate increases when government spending rises.

To illustrate these conclusions, we turn to the two extreme cases we discussed in connection with monetary policy, the liquidity trap and the classical case.

The Liquidity Trap

If the economy is in the liquidity trap, so that the LM curve is horizontal, an increase in government spending has its full multiplier effect on the equilibrium level of income. There is no change in the interest rate associated with the change in government spending, and thus no investment spending is cut off. There is therefore no dampening of the effects of increased government spending on income.

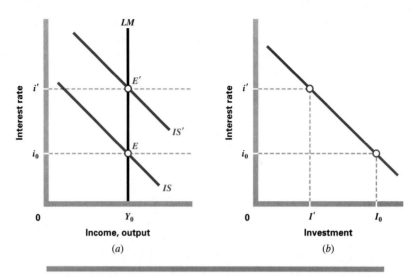

FIGURE 5-4

FULL CROWDING OUT. With a vertical *LM* schedule, a fiscal expansion, shifting out the *IS* schedule, raises interest rates, not income. Government spending displaces, or crowds out, private spending, one for one.

You should draw your own *IS-LM* diagrams to confirm that if the *LM* curve is horizontal, monetary policy has no impact on the equilibrium of the economy and fiscal policy has a maximal effect. Less dramatically, if the demand for money is very sensitive to the interest rate, so that the *LM* curve is almost horizontal, fiscal policy changes have a relatively large effect on output, while monetary policy changes have little effect on the equilibrium level of output.

The Classical Case and Crowding Out

If the *LM* curve is vertical, then an increase in government spending has *no* effect on the equilibrium level of income and only increases the interest rate. This case, already noted when we discussed monetary policy, is shown in Figure 5-4*a*, where an increase in government spending shifts the *IS* curve to *IS'* but has no effect on income. If the demand for money is not related to the interest rate, as a vertical *LM* curve implies, then there is a unique level of income at which the money market is in equilibrium.

Thus, with a vertical *LM* curve, an increase in government spending cannot change the equilibrium level of income and only raises the equilibrium interest rate. But if government spending is higher and output is unchanged, there must be an offsetting reduction in private spending. In this case, the increase in interest rates crowds out an amount of private (particularly investment) spending equal to the increase in government spending. Thus there is full crowding out if the *LM* curve is vertical.[5]

In Figure 5-4 we show the crowding out in panel (*b*), where the investment schedule of Figure 4-3 is drawn. The fiscal expansion raises the equilibrium interest rate from i_0 to i' in panel (*a*). In panel (*b*), as a consequence, investment spending declines from the level I_0 to I'.

Is Crowding Out Likely?

How seriously must we take the possibility of crowding out? Here three points must be made. The first point is also an important warning. So far we are assuming an economy with prices given, in which output is below the full-employment level. In these conditions, when fiscal expansion increases demand, firms can increase the level of output by hiring more workers. But when we talk about fully employed economies in later chapters, crowding out becomes a much more realistic possibility because firms cannot then increase output. In such conditions an increase in demand will lead to an increase in the price level rather than an increase in output.

Second, however, in an economy with unemployed resources there will *not* be full crowding out because the *LM* schedule is not, in fact, vertical. A fiscal expansion will raise interest rates, but income will also rise. Crowding out is therefore a matter of degree. The increase in aggregate demand raises income, and with the rise in income, the level of saving rises. This expansion in saving, in turn, makes it possible to finance a larger budget deficit without *completely* displacing private spending.

We can look at this proposition with the help of equation (4), which relates savings to investment as described in Chapter 3:[6]

$$S = I + (G + TR - TA) \qquad (4)$$

Here the term $G + TR - TA$ is the budget deficit. Now from equation (4) an increase in the deficit, given saving, must lower investment. In simple terms, when the deficit rises, the government has to borrow to pay for its excess spending. That borrowing uses part of households' saving, leaving less available for firms to borrow to finance their investment spending. But if saving rises with a government spending increase because income rises, then there need not be a one-for-one decline in investment. In an economy with unemployment, crowding out is incomplete because the increased demand for goods raises real income and output; saving rises and interest rates do not rise so much (because of interest-responsive money demand) that they choke off investment.

---

[5]Note that in principle consumption spending could be reduced by an increase in the interest rate, so that both investment and consumption would be crowded out. Further, as we will see in Chap. 6, fiscal expansion can also crowd out net exports.

[6]In equation (4), we leave out the role of trade. The full identity, which we use in Chap. 6, is $S = I + (G + TR - TA) + NX$, where NX stands for net exports, or net foreign lending.

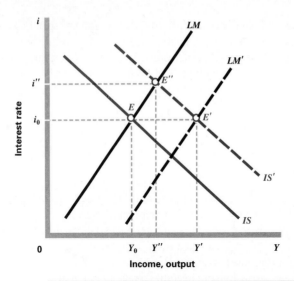

FIGURE 5-5

MONETARY ACCOMMODATION OF FISCAL EXPANSION. A fiscal expansion shifts the *IS* curve to *IS'* and moves the equilibrium of the economy from *E* to *E''*. Because the higher level of income has increased the quantity of money demanded, the interest rate rises from i_0 to i'', thereby crowding out investment spending. But the Fed can accommodate the fiscal expansion, creating more money and shifting the *LM* curve to *LM'* and the equilibrium of the economy to *E'*. The interest rate remains at level i_0, and the level of output rises to *Y'*.

The third point is that with unemployment, and thus a possibility for output to expand, interest rates need not rise at all when government spending rises, and there need not be any crowding out. This is true because the monetary authorities can *accommodate* the fiscal expansion by an increase in the money supply. Monetary policy is *accommodating* when, in the course of a fiscal expansion, the money supply is increased in order to prevent interest rates from increasing. Monetary accommodation is also referred to as *monetizing budget deficits*, meaning that the Federal Reserve prints money to buy the bonds with which the government pays for its deficit. When the Fed accommodates a fiscal expansion, both the *IS* and *LM* schedules shift to the right, as in Figure 5-5. Output will clearly increase, but interest rates need not rise. Accordingly, there need not be any adverse effects on investment.

5-3 THE COMPOSITION OF OUTPUT AND THE POLICY MIX

Table 5-2 summarizes our analysis of the effects of expansionary monetary and fiscal policy on output and the interest rate, provided the economy is not in a liquidity trap

TABLE 5-2
SUMMARY: POLICY EFFECTS ON INCOME AND INTEREST RATES

policy	equilibrium income	equilibrium interest rate
Monetary expansion	+	−
Fiscal expansion	+	+

or in the classical case. Since the liquidity trap and the classical case represent, at best, extremes useful for expositional purposes, it is apparent that policy makers can in practice use either monetary or fiscal policy to affect the level of income.

What difference does it make whether monetary or fiscal policy is used to control output? The choice between monetary and fiscal policy as tools of stabilization policy is an important and controversial topic. One basis for decision is the flexibility and speed with which these policies can be implemented and take effect.

Here we do not discuss speed and flexibility, but rather look at what these policies do to the components of aggregate demand, that is, to investment, consumption, and government spending, respectively. In that respect, there is a sharp difference between monetary and fiscal policy.[7] Monetary policy operates by stimulating interest-responsive components of aggregate demand, primarily investment spending. There is strong evidence that the earliest effect of monetary policy is on residential construction.

Fiscal policy, by contrast, operates in a manner that depends on precisely what goods the government buys or what taxes and transfers it changes. Here we might be talking of government purchases of goods and services such as defense spending, or a reduction in the corporate profits tax, sales taxes, or Social Security contributions. Each policy affects the level of aggregate demand and causes an expansion in output, but the composition of the increase in output depends on the specific policy. An increase in government spending raises consumption spending along with government purchases. An income tax cut has a direct effect on consumption spending. An investment subsidy, discussed next, increases investment spending. All expansionary fiscal policies will raise the interest rate if the quantity of money is unchanged.

An Investment Subsidy

Both an income tax cut and an increase in government spending raise the interest rate and reduce investment spending. However, it is possible for the government to raise investment spending through an *investment subsidy*, shown in Figure 5-6. In the United States, the government has sometimes subsidized investment through the *investment tax credit*, whereby a firm's tax payments are reduced when it increases its investment spending. For instance, President Clinton proposed an investment tax credit in his 1993 fiscal package.

---

[7]The two types of policy differ also in their impact on exports, as we shall see in Chap. 6.

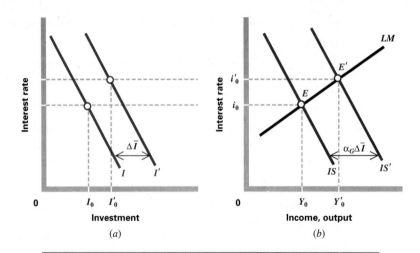

FIGURE 5-6

AN INVESTMENT SUBSIDY. An investment subsidy shifts the investment schedule in panel (*a*) at each interest rate out and to the right. The increase in planned investment shows in panel (*b*) as a shift of the *IS* curve. Equilibrium income rises to Y'_0, and the interest rate increases to i'_0. At the higher interest rate, investment is still higher, I'_0, than it was initially. Thus an investment subsidy raises interest rates, income, and investment.

When the government subsidizes investment, it essentially pays part of the cost of each firm's investment. An investment subsidy shifts the investment schedule in Figure 5-6*a*. At each interest rate, firms now plan to invest more. With investment spending higher, aggregate demand increases.

In panel (*b*), the *IS* schedule shifts by the amount of the multiplier times the increase in autonomous investment brought about by the subsidy. The new equilibrium is at point E', where goods and money markets are again in balance. But note now that although interest rates have risen, we see, in panel (*a*), that investment is higher. Investment is at the level I'_0, up from I_0. The interest rate increase dampens but does not reverse the impact of the investment subsidy. Here is an example in which both consumption, induced by higher income, and investment rise as a consequence of expansionary fiscal policy.

Table 5-3 summarizes the impacts of different types of fiscal policy on the composition of output, as well as on output and the interest rate.

The Policy Mix

In Figure 5-7 we show the policy problem of reaching full-employment output, Y^*, for an economy that is initially at point E with unemployment. Should we choose a fiscal expansion, moving to point E_1 with higher income and higher interest rates? Or

TABLE 5-3

ALTERNATIVE FISCAL POLICIES

	interest rate	consumption	investment	GDP
Income tax cut	+	+	−	+
Government spending	+	+	−	+
Investment subsidy	+	+	+	+

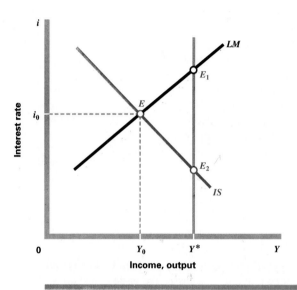

FIGURE 5-7

EXPANSIONARY POLICIES AND THE COMPOSITION OF OUTPUT. In an economy with output Y_0 below the full-employment level, Y^*, there is a choice of using monetary or fiscal expansion to move to full employment. Monetary expansion would move the *LM* curve to the right, putting the equilibrium at E_2. Fiscal expansion shifts the *IS* curve, putting the new equilibrium at E_1. The expansionary monetary policy reduces the interest rate, while the expansionary fiscal policy raises it. The lower interest rate in the case of monetary policy means that investment is higher at E_2 than at E_1 (except if the *IS* curve was shifted by an investment subsidy).

should we choose a monetary expansion, leading to full employment with lower interest rates at point E_2? Or should we pick a policy mix of fiscal expansion and accommodating monetary policy, leading to an intermediate position?

Once we recognize that all the policies raise output but differ significantly in their impact on different sectors of the economy, we open up a problem of political economy. Given the decision to expand aggregate demand, who should get the primary benefit? Should the expansion take place through a decline in interest rates and increased investment spending, or should it take place through a cut in taxes and increased personal spending, or should it take the form of an increase in the size of government?

Questions of speed and predictability of policies apart, the issues have been settled by political preferences. Conservatives will argue for a tax cut anytime. They will favor stabilization policies that cut taxes in a recession and cut government spending in a boom. Over time, given enough cycles, the government sector becomes very small, as a conservative would want it to be. The counterpart view belongs to those who believe that there is a broad scope for government spending on education, the environment, job training, infrastructure, and the like, and who, accordingly, favor expansionary policies in the form of increased government spending and higher taxes to curb a boom. Growth-minded people and the construction lobby argue for expansionary policies that operate through low interest rates or investment subsidies.

The recognition that monetary and fiscal policy changes have different effects on the composition of output is important. It suggests that policy makers can choose a *policy mix*—a combination of monetary and fiscal policies—that will not only get the economy to full employment but also make a contribution to solving other policy problems. We now discuss the policy mix in action.

5-4   THE POLICY MIX IN ACTION

In this section we review the U.S. monetary-fiscal policy mix of the 1980s, the economic debate over how to deal with the U.S. recession in 1990 and 1991, and the policy decisions made in Germany in the early 1990s as the country struggled with the macroeconomic consequences of the unification of East and West Germany.

This section not only discusses the issue of the policy mix in the real world, but also introduces the problem of inflation. Systematic study of inflation begins in Chapter 7, when we introduce aggregate supply and drop the assumption that the price level is fixed.

For now, we need to know that policies that reduce aggregate demand, such as reducing the growth rate of money or government spending, tend to reduce the inflation rate along with the level of output. An expansionary policy increases inflation together with the level of output. Recall also that inflation is unpopular, and that governments will generally try to reduce the inflation rate after it has risen.

The 1980s Recession and Recovery

Economic policy in the United States in the early 1980s departed radically from the policies of the previous two decades. First, tight money was implemented at the end of 1979 to fight an inflation rate that had reached record peacetime levels; then, in 1981, an expansionary fiscal policy was put in place as President Reagan's program of tax cuts and increased defense spending began.

Figure 5-8 shows the unemployment, inflation, and interest rates between 1972 and 1992. In 1973 the United States and the rest of the world were hit by the first oil

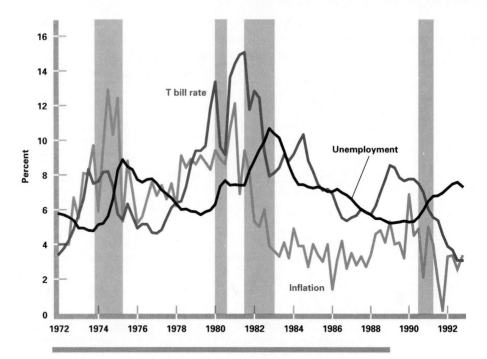

FIGURE 5-8
INFLATION, UNEMPLOYMENT, AND THE INTEREST RATE, 1972–1992.

shock, in which the oil-exporting countries raised the price of oil fourfold. The oil price increase raised other prices and, in the United States, helped create inflation and also a recession in which unemployment increased to the then post–World War II record rate of 8.9 percent. The recession ended in 1975. Economic policy under the Carter administration (1977–1981) was generally expansionary; by 1979 unemployment was below 6 percent and thus close to the full-employment level. Inflation increased with the expansionary policies of the period, and then in 1979 the inflation rate jumped as the second oil shock hit and the price of oil doubled.

The rising inflation was extremely unpopular, and it was clear that some policy changes had to be made. In October 1979 the Fed acted, turning monetary policy in a highly restrictive direction. The monetary squeeze was tightened in the first half of 1980, at which point the economy went into a minirecession. After a brief recovery, 1982 brought the deepest recession since the great depression.

The reason for the sharp decline in activity was tight money. Because inflation was still above 10 percent and the money stock was growing at only 5.1 percent in 1981, the real money supply was falling. Interest rates continued to climb (Table 5-4). Not surprisingly, investment, especially construction, collapsed. The economy was dragged into a deep recession with a trough in December 1982.

Table 5-4 also shows the second component of the early 1980s policy mix: the full-employment deficit increased rapidly from 1981 to 1984. The 1981 tax bill cut

TABLE 5-4

THE 1982 RECESSION AND THE RECOVERY (percent)

	1980	1981	1982	1983	1984
Nominal interest rate*	11.5	14.0	10.7	8.6	9.6
Real interest rate†	2.0	4.0	4.5	4.5	5.2
Full-employment deficit	0.4	0.0	1.1	2.1	3.0
Unemployment rate	7.0	7.5	9.5	9.5	7.4
GDP gap	6.4	7.1	11.6	10.4	6.2
Inflation‡	9.5	10.0	6.2	4.1	4.4

*Three-month Treasury bill rate.

†Three-month Treasury bill rate less inflation rate of the GDP deflator.

‡GDP deflator.

SOURCE: DRI/McGraw-Hill.

tax rates for individuals, with the cuts coming into effect over the next 3 years, and increased investment subsidies for corporations. The full-employment deficits in those years are the largest in peacetime U.S. history.

With a policy mix of easy fiscal and tight monetary policy, the analysis of Figure 5-7 tells us to expect a rise in the interest rate. With investment subsidies increased, Figure 5-6 tells us to look for the possibility that investment increases along with the interest rate.

The first element—a rise in the interest rate—indeed occurred. That may be a surprise if you look only at the treasury bill rate in Box 5-1. But when there is inflation, the correct interest rate to consider is not the *nominal* rate but the *real* rate. The real interest rate is the nominal (stated) rate of interest minus the rate of inflation. Over the period 1981–1984 the *real* interest rate increased sharply even as the *nominal* rate declined. The real cost of borrowing went up, although the nominal cost went down. Investment spending responded to both the increased interest rates and the recession, falling 13 percent between 1981 and 1982, and the investment subsidies and prospects of recovery, increasing 49 percent between 1982 and 1984.

The unemployment rate peaked at 10.8 percent in the last quarter of 1982 and then steadily declined under the impact of the huge fiscal expansion. Further fiscal expansion in 1984 and 1985 pushed the recovery of the economy forward, and the expansion continued throughout the 1980s.

The Recession of 1990–1991

The policy mix in the early 1980s featured highly expansionary fiscal policy and tight money. The tight money succeeded in reducing the inflation of the late 1970s and very early 1980s, at the expense of a serious recession. Expansionary fiscal policy then drove a recovery during which real interest rates increased sharply.

The recovery and expansion continued through the 1980s. By the end of 1988, the economy was close to full employment, and the inflation rate was nearing 5 percent. Fearing a continuing increase in inflation, the Fed tightened monetary policy, sharply raising the Treasury bill rate throughout 1988 and into 1989. By early 1989, the unemployment rate touched its low for the decade, 5.0 percent.

The Fed kept nominal interest rates high—though declining—through 1989 (Figure 5-8), and for a while it seemed to have put just the right amount of pressure on the brakes. The growth of real GNP slowed through 1989, inflation declined a bit, and unemployment slowly rose.

But by the middle of 1990, it was clear that the economy was heading for a recession. The recession was later determined to have begun in July 1990.[8] By the time it ended, this was the longest peacetime expansion on record—91 months—although the expansion of the 1960s, at 105 months, was longer.

The recession started before the Iraqi invasion of Kuwait in August. The price of oil jumped when Iraq invaded, and for a time the Fed was faced with the quandary of deciding whether to keep monetary policy tight by holding interest rates up in order to fight inflation, or pursuing an expansionary policy in order to fight the recession. It compromised, letting interest rates fall slowly, but not much. The oil price rise turned out to be short-lived, and by the end of the year it was clear that the recession was the big problem.[9]

It was also clear that it was up to the Fed to fight the recession, because fiscal policy was immobilized. Why? First, the budget deficit (see Table 5-5) was already large, and expected to rise, and no one was enthusiastic about increasing it. And second, for the political economy reasons we mentioned earlier, the Republican administration and the Democratic Congress fundamentally disagreed on the type of fiscal policy changes that should be made.

From the end of 1990, the Fed began to cut interest rates aggressively. The economy showed signs of recovering in the second quarter of 1991 but faltered in the fourth quarter of 1991 (Table 5-5). The political and economic talk turned to the possibility of a double-dip recession.

The Fed, fearing that the Congress and the President would agree on a fiscal policy change that would raise the budget deficit even more, cut the interest rate very sharply at the end of 1991, pushing it lower than it had been since 1972.

By the end of 1992, a recovery, very moderate by past standards, had begun. And the Fed's aggressive action had probably helped prevent an expansionary fiscal policy change. Nonetheless, with the benefit of hindsight, it is clear that the Fed should have moved much more rapidly to cut interest rates during the early part of 1991. Of course, there is a bias in the way we evaluate policy makers. The Fed played an active part in helping keep the expansion going as long as it did during the 1980s, but we focus on the recession. The Fed rarely receives credit for doing things right but certainly gets the blame for its mistakes.

---

[8]The dates of peaks and troughs in the business cycle are determined *after the fact* by a committee of economists at the National Bureau of Economic Research in Cambridge, Massachusetts. See Robert E. Hall, "The Business Cycle Dating Process," *The NBER Reporter*, Winter 1991/92, and Victor Zarnovitz, *Business Cycles: Theory, History, Indicators and Forecasting* (Chicago: University of Chicago Press, 1991).

[9]Stephen McNees, "The 1990–91 Recession in Historical Perspective," *New England Economic Review* (Federal Reserve Bank of Boston), January/February 1992, presents comparative data on this and earlier recessions.

box 5-1 **NOMINAL AND REAL INTEREST RATES**

In a world without inflation, changes in nominal interest rates can be used to judge changes in the cost of loans for firms or households. But when there is inflation, we need to make the crucial distinction between *nominal* interest rates and *real* interest rates. Investment decisions depend on inflation-adjusted or real interest rates. The real interest rate is the nominal (stated) rate of interest minus the rate of inflation.

To understand the distinction between real and nominal interest rates, realize that when prices are rising, when there is inflation, borrowers pay back in dollars that have lost value compared with the dollars they borrowed. If prices are rising 10 percent and we can borrow at 6 percent, then we can take the dollars we borrow, buy goods or invest, sell the goods a year later for 10 percent more dollars than we paid (because prices have risen 10 percent in the meantime), and pay back only the 6 percent interest. We would be ahead by 4 percent. In this case the real cost of borrowing is negative even though we are paying 6 percent nominal interest. To calculate the *real* cost of borrowing, deduct the inflation rate from the interest rate.

Let i continue to denote the nominal interest rate; π, the rate of inflation; and r, the (realized or actual) real interest rate. Our definition of the real interest rate then is

$$r = i - \pi$$

Figure 1 shows the rate of inflation of the GDP deflator and the Treasury bill rate. Note that in 1976–1978 the interest rate was almost equal to the rate of inflation so that real interest rates were zero or even negative. But in the 1980s real interest rates turned sharply positive. In 1981–1982 real interest rates reached a record level of more than 8 percent, causing a sharp recession. ∎

The German Policy Mix, 1990–1992

When East and West Germany were united in 1990, the West German government accepted the obligation to attempt to raise living standards in the eastern part of Germany rapidly. This required an immediate increase in government spending, in East German infrastructure, and in transfer payments to the residents of the former East Germany.

For political reasons, the German government did not want to raise taxes much. In effect, the government decided to run a loose fiscal policy, reflected in the increase in the budget deficit, seen in Table 5-6. If aggregate demand and inflation were to be kept in check, it was up to the German central bank, the Bundesbank.

The Bundesbank is widely regarded as the most anti-inflationary of all central banks, and it was certainly not going to accommodate the increase in government spending. Accordingly, it kept money tight and allowed interest rates in Germany to rise to levels that had not been seen in that country since the early 1980s. While the German nominal interest rate of 9.2 percent in 1991 does not look especially high, it

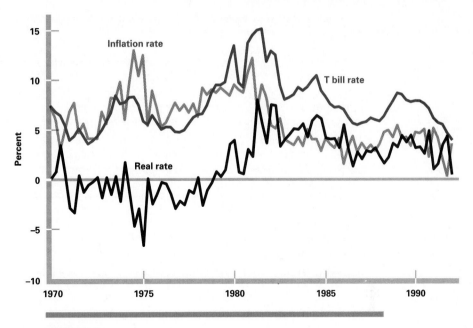

FIGURE 1

INTEREST RATES AND INFLATION, 1970–1992. (SOURCE: DRI/McGraw-Hill.)

is worth noting that the real interest rate in Germany in 1991 was well above that in the United States.[10]

The Bundesbank kept money tight through 1992, all the time criticizing the government's loose fiscal policy and the inflation that it had unleashed. In many countries, the German inflation rate in 1991 and 1992, under 5 percent, would be regarded as a miracle of low inflation. But in Germany, where low inflation is part of the national consensus, inflation at that rate is a matter for real concern.

The German policy mix of the early 1990s is like that of the United States in the early 1980s—easy fiscal policy and tight monetary policy. The consequences are also similar—high interest rates and a deficit in the current account of the balance of payments. In the next chapter we add international trade to our basic model. We will see there that the inclusion of foreign trade modifies but does not fundamentally alter

---

[10]In the problem set, we ask you to calculate the real interest rates in Germany and the United States in 1991. This can be done using Tables 5-5 and 5-6.

TABLE 5-5
THE 1990–1991 RECESSION (percent)

	1990		1991				1992
	3	4	1	2	3	4	1
GDP growth	−1.6	−3.9	−3.0	1.7	1.2	0.6	2.7
Inflation rate*	4.7	3.9	5.3	3.5	2.4	2.4	3.1
Unemployment rate	5.6	6.0	6.5	6.8	6.8	7.0	7.2
Treasury bill rate	7.5	7.0	6.0	5.6	5.4	4.5	3.9
Budget deficit/GDP	2.6	3.5	2.6	3.7	3.7	4.2	4.9
Full-employment deficit/GDP†	0.0	0.5	1.0	1.8	1.8	2.4	3.0

Dates are by quarter.

*GDP deflator.

†Calculated by DRI/McGraw-Hill.

SOURCE: DRI/McGraw-Hill.

TABLE 5-6
MACROECONOMIC CONSEQUENCES OF GERMAN UNIFICATION

	1989	1990	1991	1992
GDP growth	3.8	4.5	0.9	1.8
Inflation rate (GDP deflator)	2.6	3.4	5.1	5.3
Budget deficit/GDP	0.2	−1.7	−2.8	−3.2
Nominal interest rate	7.1	8.5	9.2	9.2

SOURCE: International Monetary Fund.

the analysis of the impacts of monetary and fiscal policy on the economy. We will also see that the combination of tight monetary and easy fiscal policy tends to produce a deficit in the balance of payments.

5-5 SUMMARY

1. Monetary policy affects the economy in the first instance by changing the interest rate, and then by affecting aggregate demand. An increase in the money supply reduces the interest rate and increases investment spending and aggregate demand, thus increasing equilibrium output.

2. There are two extreme cases in the operation of monetary policy. In the classical case the demand for real balances is independent of the rate of interest. In that case monetary policy is highly effective. The other extreme is the liquidity trap,

the case in which the public is willing to hold *any* amount of real balances at the going interest rate. In that case changes in the supply of real balances have no impact on interest rates and therefore do not affect aggregate demand and output.

3. Taking into account the effects of fiscal policy on the interest rate modifies the multiplier results of Chapter 3. Fiscal expansion, except in extreme circumstances, still leads to an income expansion. However, the rise in interest rates that comes about through the increase in money demand caused by higher income dampens the expansion.

4. Fiscal policy is more effective the smaller are the induced changes in interest rates and the smaller is the response of investment to these interest rate changes.

5. The two extreme cases, the liquidity trap and the classical case, are useful to show what determines the magnitude of monetary and fiscal policy multipliers. In the liquidity trap, monetary policy has no effect on the economy, whereas fiscal policy has its full multiplier effect on output and no effect on interest rates. In the classical case, changes in the money stock change income. But fiscal policy has no effect on income—it affects only the interest rate. In this case there is complete crowding out of private spending by government spending.

6. A fiscal expansion, because it leads to higher interest rates, displaces or crowds out some private investment. The extent of crowding out is an important issue in assessing the usefulness and desirability of fiscal policy as a tool of stabilization policy.

7. The question of the monetary-fiscal policy mix arises because expansionary monetary policy reduces the interest rate while expansionary fiscal policy increases the interest rate. Accordingly, expansionary fiscal policy increases output while reducing the level of investment; expansionary monetary policy increases output and the level of investment.

8. Governments have to choose the mix in accordance with their objectives for economic growth, or increasing consumption, or from the viewpoint of their beliefs about the desirable size of the government.

9. The real interest rate is the nominal rate minus the inflation rate.

KEY TERMS

Open market operation	Monetary-fiscal policy mix
Liquidity trap	Monetary accommodation
Classical case	Monetizing budget deficits
Crowding out	Investment subsidy
Composition of output	Real interest rate

PROBLEMS

1. In the text we describe the effect of an open market purchase by the Fed.
   (a) Define an open market sale by the Fed.
   (b) Show the impact of an open market sale on the interest rate and output. Show both the immediate and the longer-term impacts.

2. The economy is at full employment. Now the government wants to change the composition of demand toward investment and away from consumption without, however, allowing aggregate demand to go beyond full employment. What is the required policy mix? Use the *IS-LM* diagram to show your policy proposal.

3. Discuss the role of the parameters α_G, h, b, and k in the transmission mechanism linking an increase in government spending to the resulting change in equilibrium income. In developing the analysis use the following table:

(1)	(2)	(3)
Increase in $\bar{G}$ raises aggregate demand and output.	The increase in income raises money demand and hence interest rates.	The increase in interest rates reduces investment spending and hence dampens output expansion.

4. Suppose the government cuts income taxes. Show in the *IS-LM* model the impact of the tax cut under two assumptions: one, the government keeps interest rates constant through an accommodating monetary policy; two, the money stock remains unchanged. Explain the difference in results.

5. Discuss the circumstances under which the monetary and fiscal policy multipliers are each, in turn, equal to zero. Explain in words why this can happen and how likely you think this is.

6. Consider two alternative programs for contraction. One is the removal of an investment subsidy; the other is a rise in income tax rates. Use the *IS-LM* model and the investment schedule, as shown in Figure 5-6, to discuss the impact of these alternative policies on income, interest rates, and investment.

*7. Suppose the parameters k and α_G are 0.5 and 2, respectively. Assume there is an increase of $1 billion in government spending. By how much must the real money stock be increased to hold interest rates constant? (You will have to go back to the end of Chapter 4 to answer this question.)

8. In Figure 5-7 the economy can move to full employment by an expansion in either money or the full-employment deficit. Which policy leads to E_1 and which to E_2? How would you expect the choice to be made? Who would most strongly favor moving to E_1? to E_2? What policy would correspond to "balanced growth"?

9. "We can have the GNP path we want equally well with a tight fiscal policy and an easier monetary policy, or the reverse, within fairly broad limits. The real basis for choice lies in many subsidiary targets, besides real GNP and inflation, that are differentially affected by fiscal and monetary policies." What are some of the subsidiary targets referred to in the quote? How would they be affected by alternative policy combinations?

10. Calculate the average real interest rate in the United States in 1991, and in Germany, using Tables 5-5 and 5-6. What impact do you expect the difference to have on investment rates in the two countries?

11. As of the middle of 1992, many observers believed that the short-term interest rate in the United States would rise as the economy recovered from the recession. The Treasury bill rate in the middle of 1992 was below 4 percent as a result of expansionary monetary policy. How has the interest rate changed since then? Use a diagram like Figure 5-3 to explain these recent changes.

💾 COMPUTER EXERCISES

1. Congress is considering a tax cut to stimulate GDP. You work for the chairman of the Federal Reserve Board, who says he is worried about crowding out and asks you to determine what change in the money supply would be required to accommodate the tax cut. Specifically, suppose that the tax cut was to occur as an increase in the intercept (e.g., a credit to each family), which can be characterized by an increase in transfers of 20.
   (a) What change in (direction and value of) the money supply will accommodate the tax reduction (i.e., would neutralize the crowding out effect . . . approximately)?
   (b) Based on this accommodative monetary policy [the combination of fiscal and monetary policies you arrived at in (a)], what will be the effects on (i) output, (ii) the interest rate, (iii) consumption, (iv) the budget surplus (or deficit)? Give both the directions and the amounts of change.

2. One tax cut plan calls for an accompanying reduction in military spending, so as not to affect the budget deficit. Return to the BASE solution, then, once again, raise transfer payments by 20. Then
   (a) Determine the approximate magnitude of the drop in government purchases that must take place in order to leave the budget surplus unchanged.
   (b) Determine the overall effect on output of this combined change in transfers and government purchases. What name is given to this type of joint policy?

3. By choosing new values for the parameters below and by viewing the respective graphs, convince yourself that each of the following leads to a flatter *IS* curve:
   (i) More interest sensitivity of investment (larger b).
   (ii) Higher marginal propensity to consume (larger c).
   (iii) Reduced marginal tax rate (lower t).

   In problem 2 of Chapter 4, you demonstrated the implications of the first (larger b) on the effectiveness of fiscal policy. Pick either one of the next two (larger c or lower t) and determine whether it yields similar implications about the effectiveness of fiscal policy:
   (a) Raise c from 0.85 to 0.9, and find the current Y.
   (b) Increase government purchases by 20 and find the current Y.
   (c) Using (a) and (b), calculate the change in output resulting from an increase in government purchases of 20, when the *MPC* is 0.9 rather than 0.85.
   (d) Compare your answer in (c) to problem 1 of Chapter 4 to determine whether the effectiveness of fiscal policy on output rises or falls.
   (e) Does the existence of a flatter *IS* curve always imply less effectiveness of fiscal policy? Why or why not?

4. There is a drop in consumer confidence ($\bar{C}$ drops by 5).
   (a) What would the Fed have to do if it wanted to eliminate the resulting recession (both direction and magnitude of $\bar{M}$?)
   (b) What would be the ultimate effects on (i) the interest rate, (ii) investment, (iii) consumption, (iv) the budget surplus (or deficit)?

INTERNATIONAL LINKAGES

A s the twentieth century draws to a close, national economies are becoming more closely interrelated, and the notion that we are moving toward a global economy becomes increasingly accepted. Economic influences from abroad already have a powerful effect on the U.S. economy. And U.S. economic policies have even more substantial effects on foreign economies.

Whether the U.S. economy grows or moves into recession makes a big difference to Mexico and even to Japan, and whether other industrial countries shift to fiscal stimulus or stringency makes a difference to the U.S. economy. A tightening of U.S. monetary policy that raises interest rates not only affects interest rates worldwide, but also changes the value of the dollar relative to other currencies, and thus affects U.S. competitiveness and worldwide trade and GNP.

In this chapter we present the key linkages among *open* economies—economies that trade with others—and introduce some first pieces of analysis. We present more detail on international aspects of macroeconomics in Chapter 20.

Any economy is linked to the rest of the world through two broad channels: *trade* (in goods and services) and *finance*. The *trade* linkage means that some of a country's production is exported to foreign countries, while some goods that are consumed or invested at home are produced abroad and imported. In the 1980s, U.S. exports of goods and services amounted to 8.8 percent of GNP, while imports were equal to 10.6 percent of GNP. By comparison with other countries the United States engages in relatively little international trade—it is a relatively closed economy. For the Netherlands, at the other extreme—a very open economy—imports and exports each amount to about 60 percent of GNP.

The trade linkages are nonetheless important for the United States. Spending on imports escapes from the circular flow of income, in the sense that part of the income spent by U.S. residents is not spent on domestically produced goods; by contrast, exports appear as an increase in the demand for domestically produced goods. Thus the basic *IS-LM* model of income determination must be amended to include international effects.

In addition, the prices of U.S. goods relative to those of our competitors have direct impacts on demand, output, and employment. A decline in the dollar prices of our competitors, relative to the prices at which U.S. firms sell, shifts demand away from U.S. goods toward goods produced abroad. Our imports rise and exports fall. This is precisely what happened in the United States between 1980 and 1985, when the value of the dollar increased to record levels relative to foreign currencies, imports became cheap, and foreigners found U.S. goods very expensive. Conversely, when the value of the dollar declines relative to other currencies, U.S.-produced goods become relatively cheaper, demand here and abroad shifts toward our goods, exports rise, and imports decline.

There are also strong international links in the area of *finance*. U.S. residents, whether households, banks, or corporations, can hold U.S. assets such as Treasury bills or corporate bonds, or they can hold assets in foreign countries, say in Canada or in Germany. Most U.S. households, in fact, hold almost exclusively U.S. assets, but that is certainly not true for banks and large corporations. Portfolio managers shop around the world for the most attractive yields, and they may well conclude that German government bonds, yen bonds issued by the Japanese government, or Swiss bonds offer a better yield—all things considered—than U.S. bonds.

As international investors shift their assets around the world, they link asset markets here and abroad, and thereby affect income, exchange rates, and the ability of monetary policy to influence interest rates. We show in this chapter how the *IS-LM* analysis has to be modified to take international trade and finance linkages into account. The first step is to discuss exchange rates and the balance of payments.

6-1 THE BALANCE OF PAYMENTS AND EXCHANGE RATES

The *balance of payments* is the record of the transactions of the residents of a country with the rest of the world. There are two main accounts in the balance of payments: the current account and the capital account. Table 6-1 shows recent data for the United States.

The *current account* records trade in goods and services, as well as transfer payments. Services include freight, royalty payments, and interest payments. Services also include *net investment income,* the interest and profits on our assets abroad less the income foreigners earn on assets they own in the United States. Transfer payments consist of remittances, gifts, and grants. The *trade balance* simply records trade in goods. Adding trade in services and net transfers, we arrive at the current account balance.

The simple rule for balance of payments accounting is that any transaction that gives rise to a payment by a country's residents is a deficit item in that country's balance of payments. Thus, imports of cars, gifts to foreigners, a purchase of land in Spain, or making a deposit in a bank in Switzerland—all are deficit items. Examples of surplus items, by contrast, would be U.S. sales of airplanes abroad, payments by foreigners for U.S. licenses to use American technology, pensions from abroad received by U.S. residents, and foreign purchases of U.S. assets.

The current account is in *surplus* if exports exceed imports plus net transfers to foreigners, that is, if receipts from trade in goods and services and transfers exceed payments on this account.

TABLE 6-1

THE UNITED STATES BALANCE OF PAYMENTS (billions of dollars)

	1989	1990	1991
Current account	−106	−92	−9
Trade balance	−116	−108	−74
Capital account			
Net private capital*	121	59	−21
Balance of payments	15	−33	−30

*Including statistical discrepancy.

Source: *Federal Reserve Bulletin.*

The *capital account* records purchases and sales of assets, such as stocks, bonds, and land. There is a capital account surplus—also called a net capital inflow—when our receipts from the sale of stocks, bonds, land, bank deposits, and other assets exceed our payments for our own purchases of foreign assets.

External Accounts Must Balance

The central point of international payments is very simple: individuals and firms have to pay for what they buy abroad. If a person spends more than his income, his deficit needs to be financed by selling assets or by borrowing. Similarly, if a country runs a deficit[1] in its current account, spending more abroad than it receives from sales to the rest of the world, the deficit needs to be financed by selling assets or by borrowing abroad. These sales of assets or borrowing imply that the country is running a capital account surplus. Thus, any current account deficit is of necessity *financed* by an offsetting capital inflow.

$$\text{Current account deficit} + \text{net capital inflow} = 0 \tag{1}$$

Equation (1) makes a drastic point: if a country has no assets to sell, if it has no foreign currency reserves to use up, and if nobody will lend to it, then the country *has* to achieve balance in its current account, however painful and difficult that may be. For example, Russia today wants foreign loans to import more than its exports. Unless it receives loans, the Russian current account will be balanced.

It is often useful to split the capital account into two separate parts: (1) the transactions of the country's private sector and (2) official reserve transactions, which correspond to the central bank's activities. A current account deficit can be financed by private residents selling off assets abroad, or borrowing abroad. Alternatively, or

---

[1]It is only shorthand to say that "a country runs a deficit"; the full statement is that the residents of the country, taken together, run a deficit.

as well, a current account deficit can be financed by the government, which runs down its reserves of foreign exchange,[2] selling foreign currency in the foreign exchange market. Conversely, when there is a surplus the private sector may use the foreign exchange revenues it receives to pay off debt or buy assets abroad; alternatively, the central bank can buy the (net) foreign currency earned by the private sector, and add it to its reserves of foreign currency.

The increase in official reserves is also called the overall *balance of payments surplus*. We can summarize the discussion in the following statement:[3]

Balance of payments surplus = increase in official exchange reserves   (1*a*)

= current account surplus + private net capital inflow

If both the current account and the private capital account are in deficit, then the overall balance of payments is in deficit, that is, the central bank is losing reserves. When one account is in surplus and the other is in deficit to precisely the same extent, the overall balance of payments is zero—neither in surplus nor in deficit.[4]

As Table 6-1 shows, the U.S. current account was in deficit in all three years 1989–1991 (as it has been since 1982). But, whereas in 1989 capital inflows more than financed the current account deficit, in 1991 there was both a deficit on current account and a net capital outflow, or private capital account deficit. Accordingly, while the United States was accumulating reserves in 1989, it was running them down by selling foreign exchange in 1991.

Fixed Exchange Rates

We focus now on how central banks, through their official transactions, *finance,* or provide the means of paying for, balance of payments surpluses and deficits. At this point we distinguish between fixed and floating exchange rate systems.

In a *fixed exchange rate system,* foreign central banks stand ready to buy and sell their currencies at a fixed price in terms of some other currency. The major countries had fixed exchange rates against one another from the end of World War II until 1973.

In Germany, for example, the central bank, the Bundesbank, would buy or sell any amount of dollars in the 1960s at 4 deutsche marks (DM) per U.S. dollar. The French central bank, the Banque de France, stood ready to buy or sell any amount of dollars at 4.90 French francs (FF) per U.S. dollar. The fact that the central banks were prepared to buy or sell *any* amount of dollars at these fixed prices or exchange rates

---

[2] All governments hold some amounts of foreign currency or other foreign assets. These are the country's official reserves.

[3] The term "net private capital flows" is not entirely correct. Included here are also official capital flows unrelated to the exchange market operations. For example, the purchase of a new U.S. embassy building in Kiev would be an official capital account transaction, which would be put into the category "net private capital flows." For our purposes the broad distinctions are enough.

[4] Balance of payments data are poor. Changes in official reserves are generally accurately reported, trade flow data are reasonably good, data on service flows are poor, and capital flow data are extremely poor. For example, in 1990, there was a statistical discrepancy of $64 billion (the largest on record) in the U.S. balance of payments data, larger than reported net private capital movements.

means that market prices would indeed be equal to the fixed rates. Why? Because nobody who wanted to buy U.S. dollars would pay more than 4.90 francs per dollar when francs could be purchased at that price from the Banque de France. Conversely, nobody would part with dollars in exchange for francs for less than 4.90 francs per dollar if the Banque de France, through the commercial banking system, was prepared to buy dollars at that price.

INTERVENTION

Foreign central banks hold *reserves*—inventories of dollars and gold that they can sell for dollars—to sell when they want to or have to intervene in the foreign exchange market. *Intervention* is the buying or selling of foreign exchange by the central bank.

What determines the amount of intervention that a central bank has to do in a fixed exchange rate system? We already have the answer to that question. The balance of payments measures the amount of foreign exchange intervention needed from the central banks. For example, if the United States were running a deficit in the balance of payments vis-à-vis Germany, so that the demand for marks in exchange for dollars exceeded the supply of marks in exchange for dollars from Germans, the Bundesbank would buy the excess dollars, paying for them with marks.[5]

Fixed exchange rates thus operate like any other price support scheme, such as those in agricultural markets. Given market demand and supply, the price fixer has to make up the excess demand or take up the excess supply. In order to be able to ensure that the price (exchange rate) stays fixed, it is obviously necessary to hold an inventory of foreign currencies, or foreign exchange, that can be provided in exchange for the domestic currency.

So long as the central bank has the necessary reserves, it can continue to intervene in the foreign exchange markets to keep the exchange rate constant. However, if a country persistently runs deficits in the balance of payments, the central bank eventually will run out of reserves of foreign exchange and will be unable to continue its intervention.

Before that point is reached, the central bank is likely to decide that it can no longer maintain the exchange rate, and it will then devalue the currency. In 1967, for instance, the British devalued the pound from $2.80 per pound to $2.40 per pound. That meant it became cheaper for Americans and other foreigners to buy British pounds, and the devaluation thus affected the balance of payments by making British goods relatively cheaper.

Since 1979, several European countries have tried to keep their exchange rates constant against each other's in the *European Monetary System.* This is discussed in Box 6-1.

---

[5] Which central bank in fact intervenes in the foreign exchange market in the fixed rate system? If there was an excess supply of dollars and an excess demand for marks, either the Bundesbank could buy dollars in exchange for marks or the Fed could sell marks in exchange for dollars. In practice, during the fixed rate period, each foreign central bank undertook to *peg* (fix) its exchange rate vis-à-vis the dollar, and most foreign exchange intervention was undertaken by the foreign central banks. The Fed was nonetheless involved in the management of the exchange rate system since it frequently made dollar loans to foreign central banks that were in danger of running out of dollars.

box 6-1

THE EMS: FIXED EXCHANGE RATES, WITH LIMITED FLEXIBILITY

Since 1979, several European countries, including Germany, France, and Italy, have kept their mutual exchange rates essentially fixed, within the *European Monetary System*, or EMS for short.* The EMS rules allow limited flexibility of exchange rates, within a narrow band around a centrally agreed exchange rate, or *parity*. Figure 1 shows the bands for the italian lira, which originally was allowed a 6 percent band around its parity, and which since 1990 has narrowed its band to 2.5 percent. In September 1992, this policy broke down.

The combination of fixed central parity with a band allowing some flexibility is known as a *target zone* regime. In a target zone regime the central bank is committed to keeping the exchange rate from moving outside specified upper and lower limits. Within the target zone the rate is allowed to be determined by market forces.

In the first decade of the EMS, the central exchange rates were occasionally reset or realigned as differences in inflation rates among EMS members led to changes in competitiveness that made it impossible for the central banks to keep exchange rates within the bands. For instance, the figure shows that Italy realigned in 1985 and 1987. By the late 1980s, there were very few changes in parities, and EMS member central banks and governments increased their commitment to maintaining the parities. However, in 1992, several countries had to change their exchange rates within the EMS, and Britain shifted back to a floating rate.

While rates within the EMS operate according to a target zone system, the exchange rates of all the members fluctuate against the currencies of nonmember countries. Thus the DM (and the French franc, Italian lira, Dutch guilder, etc.) are fully flexible against the dollar and yen, even though flexibility against EMS member currencies is limited.

The EMS prevented exchange rate fluctuations within Europe during the 1980s, a time when there were massive swings in other exchange rates, for instance, the dollar–DM rate. In 1992, though, the system came under the pressure of German unification, as German interest rates increased and speculators attached weaker currencies such as the British pound, the Italian lira, and the Spanish peseta.

In 1992, European governments agreed to move toward *European Monetary Union* (EMU), the creation of a single currency for countries that enter the EMU. It is possible, though unlikely, that by the year 2000 the DM, French franc, lira, British pound, and other famous currencies will have disappeared to be replaced by the ECU (European currency unit).

The EMU is very controversial. German citizens are happy with the DM and don't know why they should give it up. The English value the eight centuries of history of the pound sterling, and argue that it should not be cut prematurely short. Economists worry that the adjustment difficulties experienced in Europe in 1992

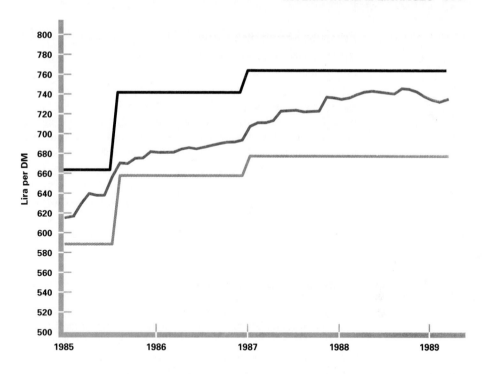

are only a sample of the problems that would arise if there were no chance of changing exchange rates. Most likely, EMU will start with a single currency among Germany, France, and the Benelux countries, and others will join later.

Even the name ECU is controversial. The *Ecu* is an old French coin, and the French prefer the new currency be spelled Ecu. The Germans want ECU, or some other neutral name.

Why move to a single currency? The motivation is both political and economic. Politically, supporters of European unity see the introduction of a European money as another step on the road to a unified (Western) Europe. Economically, the use of a single currency reduces all the costs of changing money and operating in different currencies in different countries. The question is whether these benefits outweigh the costs of the loss of flexibility in adjusting to economic shocks caused by the loss of national currencies.

---

*See Daniel Gros and Niels Thygesen, *European Monetary Integration* (London: St. Martin's Press, 1992); and Horst Ungerer et al., *The European Monetary System: Development and Perspectives,* International Monetary Fund, Occasional Paper No. 73 (Washington, D.C., 1990).

Flexible Exchange Rates

Under fixed exchange rates, the central banks have to provide whatever amounts of foreign currency are needed to finance payments imbalances. In a *flexible rate system,* by contrast, the central banks allow the exchange rate to adjust to equate the supply and demand for foreign currency. If the exchange rate of the dollar against the mark were 65 cents per mark and German exports to the United States increased, thus increasing the demand for marks by Americans, the Bundesbank could simply stand aside and let the exchange rate adjust. In this particular case, the exchange rate could move from 65 cents per mark to a level such as 67 cents per mark, making German goods more expensive in terms of dollars and thus reducing the demand for them by Americans. We shall later in this chapter examine the way in which changes in exchange rates under floating rates affect the balance of payments. The terms *flexible rates* and *floating rates* are used interchangeably.

Floating, Clean and Dirty

In a system of *clean floating,* central banks stand aside completely and allow exchange rates to be freely determined in the foreign exchange markets. Since the central banks do not intervene in the foreign exchange markets in such a system, official reserve transactions are, accordingly, zero. That means the balance of payments is zero in a system of clean floating: the exchange rate adjusts to make the current and capital accounts sum to zero.

In practice, the flexible rate system, in effect since 1973, has not been one of clean floating. Instead, the system has been one of *managed,* or *dirty, floating.* Under managed floating, central banks intervene to buy and sell foreign currencies in attempts to influence exchange rates. Official reserve transactions are, accordingly, not equal to zero under managed floating. The reasons for this central bank intervention under floating rates are discussed in Chapter 20.

Terminology

Exchange rate language can be very confusing. In particular, the terms *depreciation* and *appreciation* and *devaluation* and *revaluation* recur in any discussion of international trade and finance.

Figure 6-1 shows the dollar–deutsche mark (DM) exchange rate since 1958. We use the figure to clarify some points of terminology. The vertical axis shows the exchange rate measured as DM per $U.S. First note that we show two subperiods, the fixed rate period lasting through the 1960s until 1972 and the flexible rate regime. During the fixed rate period the dollar price of the DM remained constant for lengthy periods. It was constant, or pegged, at a constant level by the Bundesbank except for two DM revaluations in 1960 and 1970.

A *devaluation* takes place when the price of foreign currencies under a fixed rate regime is increased by official action. A devaluation thus means that foreigners pay less for the devalued currency or that residents of the devaluing country pay more for foreign currencies. The opposite of a devaluation is a *revaluation.*

FIGURE 6-1
THE DOLLAR–DEUTSCHE MARK EXCHANGE RATE, 1958–1992. (Source: DRI/
McGraw-Hill.)

Changes in the price of foreign exchange under flexible exchange rates are
referred to as *currency depreciation* or *appreciation*. A currency *depreciates* when,
under floating rates, it becomes less expensive in terms of foreign currencies. For
instance, if the exchange rate of the pound sterling changes from $1.80 per pound to
$1.75 per pound, the pound is depreciating against the dollar. By contrast, the currency
appreciates when it becomes more expensive in terms of foreign money.

For example, in Figure 6-1 we see that in 1979–1985 the DM was depreciating,
meaning that it took more and more DM to buy a dollar. By contrast, in 1985–1988
the DM was appreciating. Although the terms devaluation/revaluation and depreciation/
appreciation are used in fixed and flexible rate regimes, respectively, there is no
economic difference. These terms describe the direction in which an exchange rate
moves.

Summary

1. The balance of payments accounts are a record of the transactions of the economy
   with other economies. The capital account describes transactions in assets, while
   the current account covers transactions in goods and services, and transfers.

TABLE 6-2
NOMINAL AND REAL EXCHANGE RATES FOR THE
U.S. DOLLAR

	$/yen	$/DM	EFFECTIVE RATE INDEX, 1980:1 = 100 nominal	real
1976	0.00337	0.35	91	92
1980	0.00441	0.55	101	101
1985	0.00419	0.34	72	77
1990	0.00691	0.62	106	108
1992	0.00790	0.64	118	102

SOURCE: DRI/McGraw-Hill.

2. Any payment to foreigners is a deficit item in the balance of payments. Any payment from foreigners is a surplus item. The balance of payments deficit (or surplus) is the sum of the deficits (or surpluses) on current and capital accounts.
3. Under fixed exchange rates, central banks stand ready to meet all demands for foreign currencies at a fixed price in terms of the domestic currency. They *finance* the excess demands for, or supplies of, foreign currency (i.e., the balance of payments deficits or surpluses, respectively) at the pegged (fixed) exchange rate by running down, or adding to, their reserves of foreign currency.
4. Under flexible exchange rates, the demands for and supplies of foreign currency are equated through movements in exchange rates. Under clean floating, there is no central bank intervention and the balance of payments is zero. But central banks sometimes intervene in a floating rate system, engaging in so-called dirty floating.

6-2 EXCHANGE RATE MEASURES AND THE U.S. DOLLAR

Since 1973 the U.S. dollar has floated, more or less freely. Although there has been intervention for most of that period—except in the early 1980s—the dollar exchange rate has fluctuated substantially.

Table 6-2 shows several measures of exchange rates. The first two columns give the conventional measure, that is, the price of the foreign currency in terms of the dollar. For example, 1 DM cost 34 cents in 1985. These are also called *bilateral nominal* exchange rates. They are bilateral in the sense that they are exchange rates for one currency against another, and they are nominal because they specify the exchange rate in nominal terms, as so many dollars or cents per DM or per yen.

Often we want to characterize the movement of the dollar relative to all other currencies in a single number rather than by looking at the separate exchange rates for the DM, the yen, the French franc, and so on. That is, we want an *index* for the

FIGURE 6-2

THE U.S. REAL AND NOMINAL EXCHANGE RATES, 1976–1992 (1980 = 100).
(SOURCE: DRI/McGraw-Hill.)

exchange rate against other currencies, just as we use a price index to show how the prices of goods in general have changed.

The third and fourth columns in Table 6-2 present indexes of the *multilateral or effective exchange rate.* The effective or multilateral rate represents the price of a representative basket of foreign currencies, each weighted by its importance to the United States in international trade. Thus the yen receives a large weight, as does the Canadian dollar, because large shares of our trade are with Japan and Canada. By contrast, Germany, France, and Italy receive much smaller weights.

Figure 6-2 shows the effective dollar index with a base of 1980 = 100. The effective exchange rate index shows the very large appreciation of the dollar relative to the currencies of our trading partners in the 1980s—more than 40 percent between 1980 and 1985—followed by a subsequent depreciation.

The effective exchange rate index measures the average nominal exchange rate. But to know whether our goods are becoming relatively cheaper or more expensive than foreign goods, we also have to take into account what happened to prices here and abroad. To do so, we look at the *real effective exchange rate,* or simply the *real exchange rate.*

The real exchange rate is the ratio of foreign to domestic prices, measured in the same currency. It measures a country's competitiveness in international trade. The real exchange rate is defined as

$$\text{Real exchange rate} = R = \frac{eP_f}{P} \tag{2}$$

where P and P_f are the price levels here and abroad, respectively, and e is the dollar price of foreign exchange. Note that since P_f represents foreign prices, for example, prices measured in DM, and the exchange rate is measured as so many dollars per DM, the numerator expresses prices abroad measured in dollars; with the domestic price level, measured in this case in dollars, in the denominator, the real exchange rate expresses prices abroad relative to those at home.

A rise in the real exchange rate, or a real depreciation, means that goods abroad have become more expensive relative to goods at home. Other things equal, this implies that people—both at home and abroad—are likely to switch some of their spending to goods produced at home. This is often described as an increase in the competitiveness of our products. Conversely a decline in R, or a real appreciation, means that our goods have become relatively more expensive, or that we have lost competitiveness.

Figure 6-2 shows, in addition to the nominal effective exchange rate, the U.S. real exchange rate for the 1970s and 1980s. The measure reported here shows the dollar prices of our trading partners for manufactures relative to our own prices for manufactures, eP_f/P. There were very large losses in U.S. competitiveness in the 1980–1985 period, but then the dollar started depreciating, and by 1992 it had reached a far more favorable level of competitiveness than in the mid-1980s. Note also how closely the nominal and real effective exchange rates move together. The reason is that the inflation rates of our major trading partners were similar to those of the United States, so that the big changes in the real exchange rate were caused by movements in the nominal exchange rate rather than inflation differences.

6-3 TRADE IN GOODS, MARKET EQUILIBRIUM, AND THE BALANCE OF TRADE

With the basic concepts of international trade and finance in hand, we can now study the effects of trade in goods on the level of income and the effects of various disturbances on both income and the trade balance—which, in this section, we use as shorthand for the current account. We do not include the capital account at this stage, so that for the present the current account and the balance of payments are the same.

In this section we fit foreign trade into the *IS-LM* framework. We assume that the price level is given and that output that is demanded will be supplied. It is both conceptually and technically easy to relax the fixed price assumption, and we shall do so in Chapter 20. But because it is important to be clear on how the introduction of trade modifies the analysis of aggregate demand, we start from the familiar and basic level of the *IS-LM* model.

Domestic Spending and Spending on Domestic Goods

In an open economy, part of domestic output is sold to foreigners (exports), and part of spending by domestic residents falls on foreign goods (imports). We have to modify the *IS* curve accordingly.

The most important change is that domestic spending no longer determines domestic output. Instead, *spending on domestic goods* determines domestic output. Some spending by domestic residents falls on imports, for instance, purchases of imported beer. Demand for domestic goods, by contrast, includes exports, or foreign demand, along with part of spending by domestic residents.

The effect of external transactions on the demand for domestic output was examined in Chapter 2. Recall the definitions:

$$\text{Spending by domestic residents} = A = C + I + G \tag{3}$$

$$\text{Spending on domestic goods} = A + NX = (C + I + G) + (X - Q) \tag{4}$$

$$= (C + I + G) + NX$$

where X is the level of exports, Q is imports, and NX is the trade (goods and services) surplus. The definition of spending by domestic residents ($C + I + G$) remains that of the earlier chapters. Spending on domestic goods is total spending by domestic residents *less* their spending on imports *plus* foreign demand, or exports. Since exports minus imports is the trade surplus, or net exports (NX), spending on domestic goods is spending by domestic residents plus the trade surplus.

With this clarification we can return to our model of income determination. We will assume that domestic spending depends on the interest rate and income, so that we can write

$$A = A(Y, i) \tag{5}$$

Net Exports

Net exports, or the excess of exports over imports, depend on our income, which affects import spending; on foreign income, Y_f, which affects foreign demand for our exports; and on the real exchange rate, R, defined previously. A rise in R or a real depreciation improves our trade balance as demand shifts from goods produced abroad to those produced at home:[6]

$$NX = X(Y_f, R) - Q(Y, R) = NX(Y, Y_f, R) \tag{6}$$

We can immediately state three important results:

- A rise in foreign income, other things being equal, improves the home country's trade balance and therefore raises aggregate demand.

---

[6]Note two points about net exports in equation (6). First, we measure net exports in terms of domestic output. To do so we must measure imports (Q) in terms of their value in our currency. Second, we *assume* that a real appreciation worsens the trade balance and a real depreciation (a rise in R) improves the trade balance. This is a matter of assumption since there are opposing effects of changes in volume and in price. We return to this point in Chap. 20.

- A real depreciation by the home country improves the trade balance and therefore increases aggregate demand.

- A rise in home income raises import spending and hence worsens the trade balance.

Goods Market Equilibrium

The increase in import demand caused by a one dollar increase in income is called the *marginal propensity to import.* The marginal propensity to import measures the fraction of an extra dollar of income spent on imports. The fact that part of income will be spent on imports (rather than being spent on domestic goods) implies that the *IS* curve will be steeper than it would be in a closed economy. For a given reduction in interest rates it takes a smaller increase in output and income to restore goods market equilibrium.

The open economy *IS* curve includes net exports as a component of aggregate demand. Therefore, the level of competitiveness, as measured by the real exchange rate R, affects the *IS* curve. A real depreciation increases the demand for domestic goods, shifting the *IS* curve out and to the right. Likewise, an increase in foreign income and with it an increase in foreign spending on our goods will increase net exports or demand for our goods. Thus, we write

IS curve: $$Y = A(Y, i) + NX(Y, Y_f, R) \qquad (7)$$

Since the equilibrium level of income will now depend on both foreign income and the real exchange rate, we will have to ask how disturbances in foreign income, or real exchange rate changes, affect the equilibrium level of income.

Figure 6-3 shows the effect of a rise in foreign income. The higher foreign spending on our goods raises demand and hence, at unchanged interest rates, requires an increase in output. This is shown by the rightward shift of the *IS* schedule. The full effect of an increase in foreign demand thus is an increase in interest rates and an increase in domestic output and employment. It is easy to go through the opposite change. A weakening of foreign economies reduces their imports and hence pulls down domestic demand. Equilibrium income at home would fall, as would our interest rates.

Figure 6-3 can also help explain the effect of a real depreciation. As we saw, a real depreciation raises net exports at each level of income and hence shifts the *IS* schedule up and to the right. A real depreciation therefore leads to a rise in our equilibrium income.

Table 6-3 summarizes the effects of different disturbances on the equilibrium levels of income and net exports. Each of these examples can be worked out using the *IS* schedule in conjunction with the net export schedule.

Repercussion Effects

In an interdependent world, our policy changes affect other countries as well as ourselves, and then feed back on our economy. When we increase government spending,

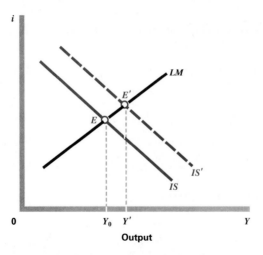

FIGURE 6-3

THE EFFECT OF A RISE IN FOREIGN INCOME. A rise in foreign income shifts the *IS* schedule out and to the right, from *IS* to *IS'*. Equilibrium income rises from *E* to *E'*.

TABLE 6-3

EFFECTS OF DISTURBANCE ON INCOME AND NET EXPORTS

	increase in home spending	increase in foreign income	real depreciation
Income	+	+	+
Net exports	−	+	+

our income rises; part of the increase in income will be spent on imports, which means that income will rise abroad, too. The increase in foreign income will then raise foreign demand for our goods, which in turn adds to the domestic income expansion brought about by higher government spending, and so on.

These *repercussion effects* can be important in practice. When the United States expands, it tends, like a locomotive, to pull the rest of the world into an expansion. Likewise, when the rest of the world expands we share in that expansion because the market for our exports expands.

Repercussion effects also arise in response to exchange rate changes. In Table 6-4 we show empirical estimates of the impact of changes in real exchange rates on U.S. real GNP. The table reports the effect of a 10 percent dollar depreciation against all other industrialized-country currencies. The U.S. level of output expands strongly; abroad, by contrast, real GNP falls. The reason is that the increase in U.S. net exports raises income at home while lowering demand and output abroad.

TABLE 6-4

EFFECTS OF A 10% DOLLAR DEPRECIATION
(percent change in real GNP)

impact on	year 1	year 3
U.S.	0.3	1.1
Non-U.S. OECD	− 1.4	− 4.8

SOURCE: Ralph Bryant et al., *Empirical Macroe-conomics for Interdependent Economies,* vol. 2 (Washington, D.C.: The Brookings Institution, 1988), p. 224.

Note that whereas an expansionary fiscal policy increases both our GDP and that of other countries, a depreciation of the exchange rate increases our income while reducing foreign incomes.

6-4 CAPITAL MOBILITY

One of the striking facts about the international economy is the high degree of integration, or linkage, among financial, or capital, markets—the markets in which bonds and stocks are traded. In most industrial countries today there are no restrictions on holding assets abroad. U.S. residents, or residents in Germany or the United Kingdom, can hold their wealth either at home or abroad. They therefore search around the world for the highest return (adjusted for risk), thereby linking yields in capital markets in different countries. For example, if rates in New York rose relative to those in Canada, investors would turn to lending in New York, while borrowers would turn to Toronto. With lending up in New York and borrowing up in Toronto, yields would quickly fall into line.

In the simplest world, in which exchange rates are fixed forever, taxes are the same everywhere, and foreign asset holders never face political risks (nationalization, restrictions on transfer of assets, default risk by foreign governments), we would expect all asset holders to pick the asset that has the highest return. That would force asset returns into strict equality everywhere in the world capital markets because no country could borrow for less.

In reality, though, none of these three conditions exists. There are tax differences among countries; exchange rates can change, perhaps significantly, and thus affect the payoff in dollars of a foreign investment; and finally, countries sometimes put up obstacles to capital outflows, or they could simply find themselves unable to pay. These are among the reasons interest rates are not equal across countries.

However, interest rate differentials among major industrialized countries, adjusted to eliminate the risk of exchange rate changes, are quite small in practice. Consider the case of the United States and Canada. Once interest rates are measured on a "covered" basis, so that the exchange risk is eliminated, they should be exactly the same.[7] In fact the differential is very small, averaging less than 0.5 percent, a result primarily of tax differences. We take this evidence to support the view that capital is very highly mobile across borders, as we assume henceforth.

Our working assumption from now on is that capital is *perfectly* mobile. Capital is perfectly mobile internationally when investors can purchase assets in any country they choose, quickly, with low transactions costs, and in unlimited accounts. When capital is perfectly mobile, asset holders are willing and able to move large amounts of funds across borders in search of the highest return or lowest borrowing cost.

The high degree of capital market integration implies that any one country's interest rates cannot get too far out of line without bringing about capital flows that tend to restore yields to the world level. To return to the previous example, if Canadian yields fell relative to U.S. yields, there would be a capital outflow from Canada because lenders would take their funds out of Canada and borrowers would try to raise funds in Canada. From the point of view of the balance of payments, this implies that a relative decline in interest rates—a decline in our rates relative to those abroad—will worsen the balance of payments because of the capital outflow resulting from lending abroad by U.S. residents.

The recognition that interest rates affect capital flows and the balance of payments has important implications for stabilization policy. First, because monetary and fiscal policies affect interest rates, the policies have an effect on the capital account and therefore on the balance of payments. The effects of monetary and fiscal policies on the balance of payments are *not* limited to the trade balance effects discussed earlier but extend to the capital account. The second implication is that the way in which monetary and fiscal policies work in affecting the domestic economy and the balance of payments changes when there are international capital flows.

The Balance of Payments and Capital Flows

We introduce the role of capital flows within a framework in which we assume that the home country faces a given price of imports and a given export demand. In addition, we assume that the world rate of interest, i_f (i.e., the rate of interest in foreign capital markets), is given. Moreover, with perfect capital mobility, capital flows into the home country at an unlimited rate if our interest rate is above that abroad (from now on, until further notice, we assume that exchange risk is absent). Conversely, if our rate is below that abroad, capital outflows will be unlimited.

Next we look at the balance of payments. The balance of payments surplus, *BP,* is equal to the trade surplus, *NX,* plus the capital account surplus, *CF:*

$$BP = NX(Y, Y_f, R) + CF(i - i_f) \qquad (8)$$

In equation (8) we have shown the trade balance as a function of domestic and foreign income and the real exchange rate, and the capital account as depending on

---

[7]Cover, or protection, against the risk of exchange rate changes can be obtained by buying a futures contract, which promises (of course, at a cost) to pay a given amount of one currency in exchange for a specified amount of another currency at a given future date. There are in practice simpler ways of obtaining foreign exchange risk cover, but the essential mechanism is the same.

the *interest differential.*[8] An increase in income worsens the trade balance, and an increase in the interest rate above the world level pulls in capital from abroad, and thus improves the capital account. It follows that when income increases, even the tiniest increase in interest rates is enough to maintain an overall balance of payments equilibrium. The trade deficit would be financed by a capital inflow.

Policy Dilemmas: Internal and External Balance

The potential for capital flows to finance a current account deficit is extremely important. Countries frequently face policy dilemmas, in which a policy designed to deal with one problem worsens another problem. In particular, there is sometimes a conflict between the goals of *external* and *internal balance.*

External balance exists when the balance of payments is close to balance. Otherwise the central bank is either losing reserves—which it cannot keep on doing—or gaining reserves, which it does not want to do forever.[9] Internal balance exists when output is at the full-employment level. In addition, countries want to maintain *internal balance,* or full employment.

In Figure 6-4 we show the schedule $BP = 0$, derived from equation (8), along which we have balance of payments equilibrium. Our key assumption—perfect capital mobility—is reflected in the shape of the pictured schedule. Only at a level of interest rates equal to that of rates abroad can we have external balance; if domestic interest rates are higher, there is a vast capital account and overall surplus, and if they are below foreign rates, there is an unlimited deficit.

Thus $BP = 0$ must be flat at the level of world interest rates. Points above the $BP = 0$ schedule correspond to a surplus, and points below to a deficit. We have also drawn, in Figure 6-4, the full-employment output level, Y^*. Point E is the only point at which both internal and external balance are achieved. Point E_1, for example, corresponds to a case of unemployment and a balance of payments deficit. Point E_2, by contrast, is a case of deficit and overemployment.

We can talk about policy dilemmas in terms of points in the four quadrants of Figure 6-4. For instance, at point E_1, there is a deficit in the balance of payments as well as unemployment. An expansionary monetary policy would deal with the unemployment problem but would worsen the balance of payments, thus apparently presenting a dilemma for the policy maker. The presence of interest-sensitive capital flows suggests the solution to the dilemma: if the country can find a way of raising the interest rate, it would obtain financing for the trade deficit.

This means that both monetary and fiscal policy would have to be used to achieve external and internal balance simultaneously. Each point in Figure 6-4 can be viewed

---

[8]When capital mobility is perfect, the domestic and foreign interest rates cannot get out of line, so in equilibrium we will find that $i = i_f$; however, we show the capital flows equation with i potentially not equal to i_f in order to demonstrate the forces at work—including potentially massive capital flows—that produce equilibrium.

[9]However, some governments (for example, Taiwan) do seem to want to have very large current account surpluses in order to be able to run capital account deficits that allow them to buy large amounts of foreign assets.

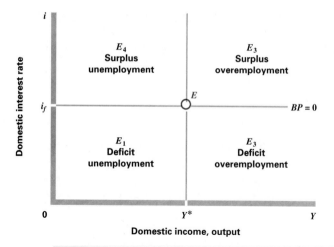

FIGURE 6-4

INTERNAL AND EXTERNAL BALANCE UNDER FIXED EXCHANGE RATES. Full employment is obtained at an output level Y^*. The internal balance schedule is therefore the vertical line at Y^*. Along $BP = 0$ the balance of payments is in equilibrium. Points above the BP schedule correspond to surpluses, and points below to deficits in the balance of payments. With perfect capital mobility the balance of payments can be in equilibrium only when home interest rates equal those abroad. Thus $BP = 0$ is flat at the level of world interest rates.

as an intersection of an *IS* and an *LM* curve. Each curve has to be shifted, but how? How the adjustment takes place depends critically on the exchange rate regime.

6-5 THE MUNDELL-FLEMING MODEL: PERFECT CAPITAL MOBILITY UNDER FIXED EXCHANGE RATES

We are now ready to extend the analysis of output determination to the open economy with perfect capital mobility. In this section we assume the exchange rate is fixed. In the next section we consider output determination with flexible exchange rates.

The analysis extending the standard *IS-LM* model to the open economy under perfect capital mobility has a special name, the *Mundell-Fleming model*. Robert Mundell, now a professor at Columbia University, and the late Marcus Fleming, who was a researcher at the International Monetary Fund, developed this analysis in the 1960s, well before flexible exchange rates came into operation.[10] Although later research has refined their analysis, the initial Mundell-Fleming formulation shown here remains

---

[10]Mundell's work on international macroeconomics has been extraordinarily important. The adventurous student should certainly consult his two books: *International Economics* (New York: Macmillan, 1967) and *Monetary Theory* (Pacific Palisades, Calif.: Goodyear, 1971). A more recent discussion can be found in Jacob Frenkel and Michael Mussa, "Asset Markets, Exchange Rates and the Balance of Payments," in R.W.

TABLE 6-5

PAYMENTS IMBALANCES, INTERVENTION, AND THE MONEY SUPPLY WITH FIXED EXCHANGE RATES AND PERFECT CAPITAL MOBILITY

1. Tightening of money
2. Increased interest rates
3. Capital inflow, payments surplus
4. Pressure for currency appreciation
5. Intervention by selling home money and buying foreign money
6. Monetary expansion due to intervention lowers interest rate
7. Back to initial interest rates, money stock, and payments balance

essentially intact as a way of understanding how policies work under high capital mobility.

Under perfect capital mobility the slightest interest differential provokes infinite capital flows. It follows that with perfect capital mobility, central banks cannot conduct an independent monetary policy under fixed exchange rates. To see why, suppose a country wishes to raise interest rates. It tightens monetary policy, and interest rates rise. Immediately, portfolio holders worldwide shift their wealth to take advantage of the new rate. As a result of the huge capital inflow the balance of payments shows a gigantic surplus; foreigners try to buy domestic assets, tending to cause the exchange rate to appreciate, and forcing the central bank to intervene to hold the exchange rate constant. It buys the foreign money, in exchange for domestic money. This intervention causes the home money stock to increase. As a result the initial monetary contraction is reversed. The process comes to an end when home interest rates have been pushed back down to the initial level.

The conclusion is: *Under fixed exchange rates and perfect capital mobility, a country cannot pursue an independent monetary policy. Interest rates cannot move out of line with those prevailing in the world market. Any attempt at independent monetary policy leads to capital flows and a need to intervene until interest rates are back in line with those in the world market.*

Table 6-5 shows the steps in the argument. The commitment to a fixed rate involves step 5. With the exchange rate tending to appreciate because foreigners are trying to buy the domestic currency, the central bank has to provide the domestic currency. Just as in an open market operation the central bank buys and sells bonds for money, so in intervention in the foreign exchange market the monetary authority buys and sells foreign money (yen, DM, or Canadian dollars) for domestic money. Thus the money supply is linked to the balance of payments. Surpluses imply *automatic* monetary expansion; deficits imply monetary contraction.

Jones and P. Kenen (eds.), *Handbook of International Economics,* vol. 2 (Amsterdam: North Holland, 1985). Empirical results in line with the Mundell-Fleming model can be found in R. Bryant et al. (eds.), *Empirical Macroeconomics for Interdependent Economies* (Washington, D.C.: The Brookings Institution, 1988) and Pete Richardson, "The Structure and Simulation Properties of the OECD's Interlink Model," *OECD Economic Studies,* no. 10, Spring 1988.

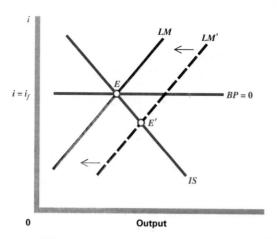

FIGURE 6-5

MONETARY EXPANSION UNDER FIXED RATES AND PERFECT CAPITAL MOBILITY. Under perfect capital mobility the balance of payments can be in equilibrium only at the interest rate $i = i_f$. At even slightly higher rates there are massive capital inflows; at lower rates there are capital outflows. A monetary expansion that cuts interest rates to point E' causes downward pressure on the exchange rate. The monetary authorities must intervene, selling foreign exchange and buying domestic money until the *LM* schedule has shifted back to its initial position.

Monetary Expansion

It is worthwhile looking at this point in terms of the open economy *IS-LM* model. In Figure 6-5 we show the *IS* and *LM* schedules as well as the $BP = 0$ schedule, which now, because of perfect capital mobility, is a horizontal line. Only at a level of interest rates equal to those abroad, $i = i_f$, can the country have payments balance. At any other interest rate, capital flows are so massive that the balance of payments cannot be in equilibrium, and the central bank has to intervene to maintain the exchange rate. This intervention shifts the *LM* schedule.

Consider specifically a monetary expansion that starts from point E. The *LM* schedule shifts down and to the right, and the economy moves to point E'. But at E' there is a large payments deficit and hence pressure for the exchange rate to depreciate. The central bank must intervene, selling foreign money and receiving domestic money in exchange. The supply of domestic money therefore declines. As a result, the *LM* schedule shifts back up and to the left. The process continues until the initial equilibrium at E is restored.

Indeed, with perfect capital mobility the economy never even gets to point E'. The response of capital flows is so large and rapid that the central bank is forced to reverse the initial expansion of the money stock as soon as it attempts it. Conversely, any attempt to contract the money stock would immediately lead to vast reserve losses, forcing an expansion of the money stock and a return to the initial equilibrium.

Fiscal Expansion

Fiscal expansion under fixed exchange rates with perfect capital mobility is, by contrast, extremely effective. We describe the effects in terms of the *IS-LM* model, but we do not draw the diagram, leaving that for one of the end-of-chapter problems.

With the money supply initially unchanged, a fiscal expansion moves the *IS* curve up and to the right, tending to increase both the interest rate and the level of output. The higher interest rate sets off a capital inflow that would lead the exchange rate to appreciate. To maintain the exchange rate, the central bank has to expand the money supply, thus increasing income further. Equilibrium is restored when the money supply has increased enough to drive the interest rate back to its original level, $i = i_f$. In this case, with an endogenous money supply, the interest rate is effectively fixed, and the simple Keynesian multiplier of Chapter 3 applies for a fiscal expansion.

The Endogenous Money Stock

Although the assumption of perfect capital mobility is extreme, it is a useful benchmark case that in the end is not too far from reality. The essential point is that *the commitment to maintain a fixed exchange rate makes the money stock endogenous* because the central bank has to provide the foreign exchange or domestic money that is demanded at the fixed exchange rate. Thus even when capital mobility is less than perfect, the central bank has only limited ability to change the money supply without having to worry about maintaining the exchange rate.

Box 6-2 describes the effects of the fiscal expansion set off by German unification, and the consequences for Germany's neighbors whose exchange rates were fixed against the deutsche mark.

6-6 PERFECT CAPITAL MOBILITY AND FLEXIBLE EXCHANGE RATES

In this section we use the Mundell-Fleming model to explore how monetary and fiscal policy works in an economy that has fully flexible exchange rates and perfect capital mobility. We assume in this section that domestic prices are fixed, even though the exchange rate is flexible. In Chapter 20 we examine how flexible exchange rates work when domestic prices are flexible.[11]

Under fully flexible exchange rates the central bank does not intervene in the market for foreign exchange. The exchange rate must adjust to clear the market so that the demand for and supply of foreign exchange balance. Without central bank intervention, therefore, the balance of payments must be equal to zero.

Under fully flexible exchange rates the absence of intervention implies a zero balance of payments. Any current account deficit must be financed by private capital

---

[11] The reason it is not misleading to examine the behavior of a system with flexible exchange rates and fixed domestic prices is that in practice most changes in nominal exchange rates in economies with relatively low inflation rates are in fact changes in the real exchange rate, as can be seen in Fig. 6-2. The analysis of this section would not apply in cases in which the nominal exchange rate changes and domestic prices rise in the same proportion so that the real exchange rate is unchanged.

box 6-2 **GERMAN UNIFICATION AND EXTERNAL PROBLEMS**

In the fall of 1989 the Berlin wall came down and the unification of West and East Germany was soon under way. The West German government undertook a massive fiscal expansion in East Germany. The fiscal program included large-scale investment in East Germany's infrastructure, investment in industry, and an extensive income support program for the unemployed and for those working in loss-making firms.

The large fiscal expansion helped moderate the economic collapse in East Germany. But it came at the expense of a big budget deficit. The expansionary fiscal policy brought with it a deterioration of the current account, higher interest rates, and an appreciation of the deutsche mark (see Figure 6-1), as the Mundell-Fleming model predicts.

Whereas West Germany had been a net lender in world markets, starting in 1991 there was a deficit in the current account. German resources were being redirected from supplying the world market to reconstructing East Germany.

TABLE 1
GERMAN UNIFICATION (percent of GNP)

	1989	1990	1991	1992*
Current account	4.8	3.1	− 1.3	− 0.7
Budget deficit	0.2	1.7	2.8	3.2
Interest rate	7.1	8.5	9.3	9.8

*Forecast.

SOURCE: IMF, *World Economic Outlook*, October 1992.

The German fiscal expansion had undesirable side effects on Germany's European trading partners, with whom Germany has a fixed exchange rate (see Box 6-1). In West Germany the economy overheated since demand from the East fell mostly on West German goods. In response to the overheating, the Bundesbank tightened monetary policy, raising interest rates sharply.

Countries like France and Italy in principle faced the choice of devaluing within the European monetary system, or else they could allow their interest rates to increase along with German interest rates. Because they valued stable exchange rates, they defended their currencies by raising interest rates to match those in Germany. Without the benefit of a fiscal expansion as had occurred in Germany, their economies slowed down sharply. Germany's trading partners kept urging the Bundesbank to cut interest rates, but the Bundesbank argued that it had to keep on fighting inflation. The episode makes the point that fixed exchange rates are hard to maintain when countries' policies go in opposite directions or when they face disturbances that are not the same for everyone. ∎

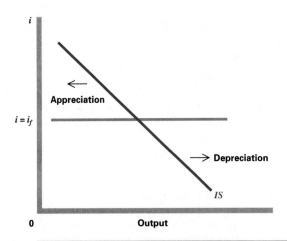

FIGURE 6-6

THE EFFECT OF EXCHANGE RATES ON AGGREGATE DEMAND. With
perfect capital mobility and flexible rates, capital flows have a
strong impact on demand. If home interest rates fall below i_f, there
are capital outflows leading to exchange depreciation, a gain in
competitiveness, and hence a rise in demand for domestic goods,
shown by the rightward shift of the *IS* schedule. Conversely, if
interest rates go above i_f, the capital inflows lead to appreciation,
loss of competitiveness, and a decline in demand for domestic
goods, shown by the leftward-shifting *IS* curve.

*inflows; a current account surplus is balanced by capital outflows. Adjustments in the
exchange rate ensure that the sum of the current and capital accounts is zero.*

A second implication of fully flexible exchange rates is that the central bank can
set the money supply at will. Since there is no obligation to intervene, there is no
longer any link between the balance of payments and the money supply.

Perfect capital mobility implies that there is only one interest rate at which the
balance of payments will balance:[12]

$$i = i_f \tag{9}$$

At any other interest rate, capital flows are so large that the balance of payments cannot
be zero. We show this in Figure 6-6 by the line $i = i_f$.

From equation (7) we remember that the real exchange rate is a determinant of
aggregate demand and therefore changes in the real exchange rate shift the *IS* schedule.
Given prices P and P_f, a depreciation makes the home country more competitive,

---

[12] Equation (9) assumes that investors do not expect the exchange rate to change. Otherwise, nominal interest
rates differ among countries by an amount that reflects expected changes in the exchange rate, in a way to
be described in Chapter 20.

improves net exports, and hence shifts the *IS* schedule to the right. Conversely, a real appreciation means our goods become relatively more expensive, and hence the trade balance worsens and demand for domestic goods declines so that the *IS* schedule shifts to the left.

The arrows in Figure 6-6 link the movement of aggregate demand to the interest rate. If the home interest rate were higher than i_f, capital inflows would cause currency appreciation. At any point above the $i = i_f$ schedule, the exchange rate is appreciating, our goods are becoming relatively more expensive, and aggregate demand is falling. Thus the *IS* schedule will be shifting to the left. Conversely, any point below the $i = i_f$ schedule corresponds to depreciation, improving competitiveness, and increasing aggregate demand. The *IS* schedule will therefore be shifting to the right. We now see how various disturbances affect output and the exchange rate.

Adjustment to a Real Disturbance

Using our model, represented by equations (7), (8), and (9), we want to know how various changes affect the level of output, the interest rate, and the exchange rate. The first change we look at is an exogenous rise in the world demand for our goods, or an increase in exports.

Starting from an initial equilibrium at point *E* in Figure 6-7, we see that the increase in foreign demand implies an excess demand for our goods. At the initial interest rate, exchange rate, and output level, demand for our goods now exceeds the available supply. For goods market equilibrium at the initial interest rate and exchange rate, we require a higher level of output. Accordingly, the *IS* schedule shifts out and to the right, to *IS'*.

Now consider for a moment point *E'*, at which the goods and money markets clear. Here output has increased to meet the increased demand. The rise in income has increased money demand and thus raised equilibrium interest rates. But point *E'* is not an equilibrium, because the balance of payments is not in equilibrium. In fact, we would not reach point *E'* at all. The tendency for the economy to move in that direction, as we now show, will bring about an exchange rate appreciation that will take us all the way back to the initial equilibrium at *E*.

The Adjustment Process

Suppose, then, that the increase in foreign demand takes place and that, in response, there is a tendency for output and income to increase. The induced increase in money demand will raise interest rates and thus will bring us out of line with international interest rates. The resulting capital inflows immediately put pressure on the exchange rate. The capital inflow causes our currency to appreciate.

The exchange appreciation means, of course, that import prices fall and domestic goods become relatively more expensive. Demand shifts away from domestic goods, and net exports decline. In terms of Figure 6-7, the appreciation implies that the *IS* schedule shifts back from *IS'* to the left. Next, we have to ask how far the exchange

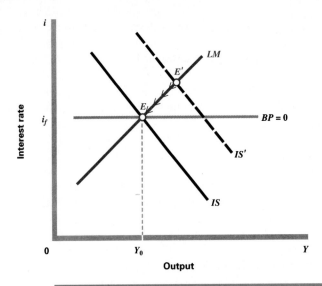

FIGURE 6-7

EFFECTS OF AN INCREASE IN THE DEMAND FOR EXPORTS. A rise in foreign demand for our goods, at the initial exchange rate and interest rate at point *E*, creates an excess demand for goods. The *IS* schedule shifts out to *IS'*, and the new goods and money market equilibrium is at point *E'*. But at *E'* our interest rate exceeds that abroad. Capital will tend to flow into our country in response to the increased interest rate, and the resulting balance of payments surplus leads to currency appreciation. The appreciation means that we become less competitive. The *IS* schedule starts shifting back as a result of the appreciation, and the process continues until the initial equilibrium at *E* is reached. In the end, increased exports (or a fiscal expansion) do not change output. They simply lead to currency appreciation and thereby to an offsetting change in net exports.

appreciation will go and to what extent it will dampen the expansionary effect of increased net exports.

The exchange rate will keep appreciating as long as our interest rate exceeds the world level. This implies that the exchange appreciation must continue until the *IS* schedule has shifted back all the way to its initial position. This adjustment is shown by the arrows along the *LM* schedule. Only when we return to point *E* will output and income have reached a level consistent with monetary equilibrium at the world rate of interest.

We have now shown that under conditions of perfect capital mobility, an expansion in exports has no lasting effect on equilibrium output. With perfect capital mobility the tendency for interest rates to rise, as a result of the increase in export demand, leads to currency appreciation and thus to a complete offset of the increase in exports. Once we return to point *E*, net exports are back to their initial level. The exchange rate has, of course, appreciated. Imports will increase as a consequence of the appreciation, and the initial expansion in exports is, in part, offset by the appreciation of our exchange rate.

Fiscal Policy

We can extend the usefulness of this analysis by recognizing that it is valid for disturbances other than an increase in exports. The same analysis applies to a fiscal expansion. A tax cut or an increase in government spending would lead to an expansion in demand in the same way as increased exports. Again, the tendency for interest rates to rise leads to appreciation and therefore to a fall in exports and increased imports. There is, accordingly, complete crowding out here. The crowding out takes place not, as in Chapter 5, because higher interest rates reduce investment, but because the exchange appreciation reduces net exports.

The important lesson here is that real disturbances to demand do not affect equilibrium output under flexible rates with perfect capital mobility. We can drive the lesson home by comparing a fiscal expansion under flexible rates with the results we derived for the fixed rate case. In the previous section, we showed that with a fixed exchange rate, fiscal expansion under conditions of capital mobility is highly effective in raising equilibrium output. For flexible rates, by contrast, a fiscal expansion does not change equilibrium output. Instead, it produces an offsetting exchange rate appreciation and a shift in the composition of domestic demand toward foreign goods and away from domestic goods.

This analysis helps in understanding developments in the U.S. economy in the early 1980s, when a fiscal expansion was accompanied by a current account deficit.

Adjustment to a Change in the Money Stock

We turn next to analysis of a change in the money stock, and show that it leads under flexible exchange rates to an increase in income and a depreciation of the exchange rate. The analysis uses Figure 6-8. We start from an initial position at point E and consider an increase in the nominal quantity of money, $\overline{M}$. Since prices are given, we have an increase in the real money stock, $\overline{M}/\overline{P}$. At E there will be an excess supply of real balances. To restore equilibrium, interest rates would have to be lower or income would have to be larger. Accordingly, the LM schedule shifts down and to the right to LM'.

We ask once again whether the economy is in equilibrium at point E'. At E', goods and money markets are in equilibrium (at the initial exchange rate), but interest rates have fallen below the world level. Capital outflows therefore put pressure on the exchange rate, leading to a depreciation. The exchange depreciation caused by the capital outflow leads import prices to increase, domestic goods become more competitive, and the demand for our output expands. The IS curve shifts out and to the right, and it continues doing so until exchange depreciation has raised demand and output to the level indicated by point E''. Only at E'' do we have goods and money market

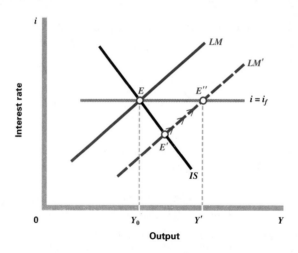

FIGURE 6-8
EFFECTS OF AN INCREASE IN THE MONEY STOCK. A monetary expansion
shifts the *LM* schedule to *LM'*. At point *E'* the goods and money
markets clear, but our interest rate is below the world level.
Therefore, capital will tend to flow out, the balance of payments
goes into deficit, and the exchange rate depreciates. The
depreciation means that we become more competitive. Net exports
rise, and therefore the *IS* curve shifts out and to the right (not
shown). The process continues until the *IS* curve reaches *E"*. Interest
rates are again at the world level, and the depreciation has led to a
higher level of income. Monetary policy thus works by increasing
net exports.

equilibrium compatible with the world rate of interest. Consequently, there is no further
tendency for exchange rates and relative prices, and hence demand, to change.[13]

We have now shown that a monetary expansion leads to an increase in output
and a depreciation of the exchange rate under flexible rates. One way of thinking about
this result is that with $\overline{P}$ fixed, an increase in $\overline{M}$ increases $\overline{M}/\overline{P}$. The demand for real
balances (L) is, from Chapter 4, equal to $L(i, Y)$. Since i cannot differ from the world
rate of interest, Y has to rise to equate the demand for money to the supply. The
exchange depreciation raises net exports, and that increase in net exports, in turn,
sustains the higher level of output and employment. One interesting implication of our
analysis, then, is the proposition that monetary expansion improves the current account
through the induced depreciation.

How do our results compare with those in a fixed exchange rate world? Under
fixed rates, the monetary authorities cannot control the nominal money stock, and an

---

[13] In the problem set at the end of this chapter we ask you to show that the current account improves between
E' and *E"*, even though the increased level of income increases imports.

TABLE 6-6

EFFECTS OF U.S. POLICY ACTIONS (percentage increase in GNP)

	fiscal expansion*	monetary expansion†
U.S.	2.7	5.3
Japan	0.4	−0.6
Germany	0.5	−0.8

*A 5 percent of GNP increase in government spending.

†A 10 percent increase in the money supply.

SOURCE: Paul Masson et al., *Multimod Mark II: A Revised and Extended Model*, International Monetary Fund, Occasional Paper No. 71, 1990, Tables 9 and 10.

attempt to expand money will merely lead to reserve losses and a reversal of the increase in the money stock. Under flexible rates, by contrast, the central bank does not intervene, and so the money stock increase is *not* reversed in the foreign exchange market. The depreciation and expansion in output actually do take place, given the assumed fixed prices. The fact that the central bank *can* control the money stock under flexible rates is a key aspect of that exchange rate system.

Table 6-6 shows estimates of the quantitative impact of U.S. fiscal and monetary expansions on GNP in the United States and abroad, under flexible exchange rates. The table reports the percentage change in GDP over the first 2 years (on average) in response to two experiments. One is a sustained increase in government spending equal to 5 percent of GDP. The other is a monetary expansion of 10 percent. Note that, as expected, U.S. GNP expands in each case. Interestingly, in line with our model, a U.S. fiscal expansion raises foreign output. By contrast, a U.S. monetary expansion reduces output abroad. The reason is that the dollar depreciates and that makes the rest of the world less competitive.

Beggar-Thy-Neighbor Policy and Competitive Depreciation

We have shown that a monetary expansion in the home country leads to exchange depreciation, an increase in net exports, and therefore an increase in output and employment. But our increased net exports correspond to a deterioration in the trade balance abroad. The domestic depreciation shifts demand from foreign goods toward domestic goods. Abroad, output and employment decline. It is for this reason that a depreciation-induced change in the trade balance has been called a *beggar-thy-neighbor policy*— it is a way of exporting unemployment or of creating domestic employment at the expense of the rest of the world.

Recognition that exchange depreciation is mainly a way of shifting demand from one country to another, rather than changing the level of world demand, is important. It implies that exchange rate adjustment can be a useful policy when countries find themselves in different stages of a business cycle—for example, one in a boom (with overemployment) and the other in a recession. In that event, a depreciation by the country experiencing a recession would shift world demand in its direction and thus work to reduce divergences from full employment in each country.

By contrast, when countries' business cycles are highly synchronized, such as in the 1930s or in the aftermath of the oil shock of 1973, exchange rate movements will not contribute much toward worldwide full employment. If total world demand is at the wrong level, exchange rate movements do not correct the level of aggregate demand but essentially affect only the allocation of a *given* world demand among countries.

Nevertheless, from the point of view of an individual country, exchange depreciation works to attract world demand and raise domestic output. If every country tried to depreciate to attract world demand, we would have *competitive depreciation* and a shifting around of world demand rather than an increase in the worldwide level of spending. And if everyone depreciated to roughly the same extent, we would end up with exchange rates about where they started. Coordinated monetary and/or fiscal policies rather than depreciations are needed to increase demand and output in each country when worldwide aggregate demand is at the wrong level.

6-7 SUMMARY

1. The balance of payments accounts are a record of the international transactions of the economy. The current account records trade in goods and services as well as transfer payments. The capital account records purchases and sales of assets. Any transaction that gives rise to a payment by a U.S. resident is a deficit item for the United States.
2. The overall balance of payments surplus is the sum of the current and capital accounts surpluses. If the overall balance is in deficit, we have to make more payments to foreigners than they make to us. The foreign currency for making these payments is supplied by central banks.
3. Under fixed exchange rates, the central bank holds constant the price of foreign currencies in terms of the domestic currency. It does this by buying and selling foreign exchange at the fixed exchange rate. It has to keep reserves of foreign currency for that purpose.
4. Under floating or flexible exchange rates, the exchange rate may change from moment to moment. In a system of clean floating, the exchange rate is determined by supply and demand without central bank intervention. Under dirty floating, the central bank intervenes by buying and selling foreign exchange in an attempt to influence the exchange rate.
5. The introduction of trade in goods means that some of the demand for our output comes from abroad and that some spending by our residents is on foreign goods. The demand for our goods depends on the real exchange rate as well as the levels of income at home and abroad. A real depreciation or increase in foreign income increases net exports and shifts the *IS* curve out to the right. There is equilibrium in the goods market when the demand for domestically produced goods is equal to the output of those goods.
6. The introduction of capital flows points to the effects of monetary and fiscal

TABLE 6-7

THE EFFECTS OF MONETARY AND FISCAL POLICY UNDER PERFECT CAPITAL MOBILITY

fixed rates	flexible rates
MONETARY EXPANSION	
No output change; reserve losses equal to money increase	Output expansion; trade balance improves; exchange depreciation
FISCAL EXPANSION	
Output expansion; trade balance worsens	No output change; reduced net exports; exchange appreciation

policy on the balance of payments through interest rate effects on capital flows. An increase in the domestic interest rate relative to the world interest rate leads to a capital inflow that can finance a current account deficit.

7. When capital mobility is perfect, interest rates in the home country cannot diverge from those abroad. This has major implications for the effects of monetary and fiscal policy under fixed and floating exchange rates. These effects are summarized in Table 6-7.

8. Under fixed exchange rates and perfect capital mobility, monetary policy is powerless to affect output. Any attempt to reduce the domestic interest rate by increasing the money stock would lead to a huge outflow of capital, tending to cause a depreciation which the central bank would then have to offset by buying domestic money in exchange for foreign money. This reduces the domestic money stock until it returns to its original level. Under fixed exchange rates with capital mobility, the central bank cannot run an independent monetary policy.

9. Fiscal policy is highly effective under fixed exchange rates with complete capital mobility. A fiscal expansion tends to raise the interest rate, thereby leading the central bank to increase the money stock to maintain the exchange rate constant, reinforcing the expansionary fiscal effect.

10. Under floating rates, monetary policy is highly effective and fiscal policy is ineffective in changing output. A monetary expansion leads to depreciation, increased exports, and increased output. Fiscal expansion, however, causes an appreciation and completely crowds out net exports.

11. If an economy with floating rates finds itself with unemployment, the central bank can intervene to depreciate the exchange rate and increase net exports and thus aggregate demand. Such policies are known as beggar-thy-neighbor policies because the increase in demand for domestic output comes at the expense of demand for foreign output.

KEY TERMS

Exchange rate
Current account

Nominal and real exchange rate
Depreciation

Capital account

Balance of payments

Fixed exchange rate

Floating exchange rate

Clean floating

Intervention

Dirty floating

Appreciation

Repercussion effects

Capital mobility

Internal and external balance

Mundell-Fleming model

Beggar-thy-neighbor policy

PROBLEMS

1. This problem formalizes some of the questions about income and trade balance determination in the open economy. (Before doing it, read the appendix to this chapter.) We assume, as a simplification, that the interest rate is given and equal to $i = i_0$, and also that the real exchange rate is constant. We assume aggregate spending by domestic residents is

$$A = \bar{A} + cY - bi$$

and net exports, NX, are given by

$$NX = X - Q$$

Import spending is given by

$$Q = \bar{Q} + mY$$

where $\bar{Q}$ is autonomous import spending. Exports are given and are equal to

$$X = \bar{X}$$

(a) What is the total demand for domestic goods? The balance of trade?

(b) What is the equilibrium level of income?

(c) What is the balance of trade at that equilibrium level of income?

(d) What is the effect of an increase in exports on the equilibrium level of income? What is the multiplier?

(e) What is the effect of increased exports on the trade balance?

2. Suppose that, in problem 1,

$$\bar{A} = 400 \qquad c = 0.8 \qquad b = 30 \qquad i_0 = 5 \text{ (percent)} \qquad \bar{Q} = 0 \qquad m = 0.2 \qquad X = 250$$

(a) Calculate the equilibrium level of income.

(b) Calculate the balance of trade.

(c) Calculate the open economy multiplier, that is, the effect of an increase in $\bar{A}$ on equilibrium output. (To answer this question, you may want to use the appendix to this chapter.)

(d) Assume there is a reduction in export demand of $\Delta X = 1$ (billion). By how much does income change? By how much does the trade balance worsen?

(e) How much does a one percentage point increase in the interest rate (from 5 percent to 6 percent) improve the trade balance? Explain why the trade balance improves when the interest rate rises.

(f) What policies can the country pursue to offset the impact of reduced exports on domestic income and employment as well as the trade balance?

3. It is sometimes said that a central bank is a necessary condition for a balance of payments deficit. What is the explanation for this argument?

4. Consider a country that is in a position of full employment and balanced trade. The exchange rate is fixed and capital is not mobile. Which of the following types of disturbance can be remedied with standard aggregate demand tools of stabilization? Indicate in each case the impact on external and internal balance as well as the appropriate policy response.
   (a) A loss of export markets
   (b) A reduction in saving and a corresponding increase in demand for domestic goods
   (c) An increase in government spending
   (d) A shift in demand from imports to domestic goods
   (e) A reduction in imports with a corresponding increase in saving.

5. (a) Use the formula $1/(m + s)$ for the foreign trade multiplier (see the appendix) to discuss the impact on the trade balance of an increase in autonomous domestic spending.
   (b) Comment on the proposition that the more open the economy, the smaller the domestic income expansion.

6. This question is concerned with the repercussion effects of a domestic expansion once we recognize that, as a consequence, output abroad will expand. Suppose that at home there is an increase in autonomous spending $\Delta\bar{A}$ that falls entirely on domestic goods. (Assume constant interest rates throughout this problem.)
   (a) What is the resulting effect on income, disregarding repercussion effects? What is the impact on our imports? Denote the increase in imports by ΔQ.
   (b) Using the result for the increase in imports, we now ask what happens abroad. Our increase in imports appears to foreign countries as an increase in their exports and therefore as an increase in demand for their goods. In response, their output expands. Assuming the foreign marginal propensity to save is s^* and the foreign propensity to import is m^*, by how much will a foreign country's income expand as a result of an increase in its exports?
   (c) Now combine the pieces by writing the familiar equation for equilibrium in the domestic goods market: change in supply, ΔY, equals the total change in demand, $\Delta\bar{A} + \Delta X - m\Delta Y + (1 - s)\Delta Y$, or

$$\Delta Y = \frac{\Delta\bar{A} + \Delta X}{s + m}$$

   Noting that our increase in exports, ΔX, is equal to foreigners' increase in imports, we can replace ΔX with the answer to 6b to obtain a general expression for the multiplier with repercussions.
   (d) Substitute your answer to 6b in the formula for the change in our exports, $\Delta X = m^*\Delta Y^*$.
   (e) Calculate the complete change in our income, including repercussion effects. Now compare your result with the case in which repercussion effects are omitted. What difference do repercussion effects make? Is our income expansion larger or smaller with repercussion effects?
   (f) Consider the trade balance effect of a domestic expansion with and without repercussion effects. Is the trade deficit larger or smaller once repercussion effects are taken into account?

7. Assume that capital is perfectly mobile, the price level is fixed, and the exchange rate is flexible. Now let the government increase purchases. Explain first why the equilibrium levels

of output and the interest rate are unaffected. Then show whether the current account improves or worsens as a result of the increased government purchases of goods and services.

8. Assume that there is perfect mobility of capital. How does the imposition of a tariff affect the exchange rate, output, and the current account? (*Hint:* Given the exchange rate, the tariff reduces our demand for imports.)

9. Explain how and why monetary policy retains its effectiveness when there is perfect mobility of capital.

10. Show graphically how fiscal policy works with capital mobility and fixed exchange rates.

11. Was U.S. policy from 1980 to 1985 consistent with a beggar-thy-neighbor approach to trade policy?

12. In 1990–1992 Finland fell into serious difficulties. The collapse of exports to the Soviet Union and a dramatic fall in the prices of pulp and paper—an important export item—led to both a recession and a current account deficit. What adjustment policies would you recommend for such a case?

COMPUTER EXERCISES

For these exercises you will need to construct a table with five columns and ten rows. Each column, (a) through (e), is for each of the five following simulations:

(a) BASE solution (simply write the values in from the base solution before any simulation is carried out).
(b) Increase exports by 10.
(c) Increase government purchases by 10.
(d) Increase transfer payments by 11.75.
(e) Increase the money supply by 15.

Each row, 1 through 10, is for each of following ten variables whose values you will enter on the basis of each of the five simulations:

1. Output (Y)	5. Budget surplus (BS)	8. Balance of payments (BP)
2. Interest rate (i)	6. Government purchases (G)	9. Net exports (NX)
3. Investment rate (I)	7. Net taxes (T)	10. Net capital flows (CF)
4. Consumption (C)		

Remember to reset to the BASE solution before each successive simulation.

Based on the information from your table of simulations, provide a *very brief* response to each of the following questions. [Note that output (Y) should be the same in columns (b) through (e).]

1. Why did $\Delta \overline{TR}$ have to exceed $\Delta \overline{G}$ in order to have the same effect on output?

2. (a) What is the value of the general fiscal multiplier? Show your work.
   (b) What is the value of the monetary policy multiplier? Show your work.

3. (a) Relative to the base case, why is i higher for $\Delta \overline{X}$, $\Delta \overline{G}$, and $\Delta \overline{TR}$?
   (b) Why is the new value of i the *same* for those three changes?
   (c) Why is i lower for $\Delta \overline{M}$?

4. Why did I fall under $\Delta \overline{X}$, $\Delta \overline{G}$, and $\Delta \overline{TR}$ and rise under $\Delta \overline{M}$?

5. (a) Why did C rise under all four policies?

(b) Why did *C* rise by the *same amounts* under $\Delta\overline{X}$, $\Delta\overline{G}$, and $\Delta\overline{M}$?
(c) Why did *C* rise by *more* under $\Delta\overline{TR}$?

6. (a) Why did *BS* rise under $\Delta\overline{X}$ and $\Delta\overline{M}$?
(b) Why did *BS* rise by the *same amount* under $\Delta\overline{X}$ and $\Delta\overline{M}$?
(c) Why did *BS* fall under $\Delta\overline{G}$ and $\Delta\overline{TR}$?
(d) Why did *BS* fall by *different amounts* under $\Delta\overline{G}$ and $\Delta\overline{TR}$?

7. (a) Why did *NX* rise under $\Delta\overline{X}$?
(b) Why did *NX* fall (slightly) under $\Delta\overline{G}$, $\Delta\overline{TR}$, and $\Delta\overline{M}$?
(c) Why did *NX* fall by the *same amount* under $\Delta\overline{G}$, $\Delta\overline{TR}$, and $\Delta\overline{M}$?

8. (a) Why did *CF* rise under $\Delta\overline{X}$, $\Delta\overline{G}$, and $\Delta\overline{TR}$?
(b) Why did *CF* rise by the *same amount* under $\Delta\overline{X}$, $\Delta\overline{G}$, and $\Delta\overline{TR}$?
(c) Why did *CF* fall under $\Delta\overline{M}$?

9. Assume that the base case output (585.3) is the full-employment level of output.
(a) Under $\Delta\overline{G} = 10$, can a subsequent change in transfers restore both internal and external balance? If so, how large must the change be? If not, why not?
(b) Under $\Delta\overline{X} = 10$, can a subsequent change in transfers restore both internal and external balance? If so, how large must the change be? If not, why not?

APPENDIX: THE OPEN ECONOMY *IS-LM* MODEL

We start by assuming a simple form for the net export equation:

$$NX = X - mY + vR \qquad R = eP_f/P \qquad (A1)$$

where *X* is a constant representing all other influences including the role of foreign income. Note that because the coefficient of the real exchange rate, *v*, is positive, a real depreciation or a rise in *R* improves the trade balance. The larger *v* is, the more responsive is the trade balance to the real exchange rate. Note, too, the influence of home income on the trade balance: a rise in income raises imports and hence worsens the trade balance. The coefficient *m* denotes the marginal propensity to import. It indicates the rise in imports per dollar increase in income.

With this formulation, equilibrium in the goods market becomes

IS curve: $$Y = \overline{A} + NX = \overline{A} + cY - bi + \overline{X} - mY + vR \qquad (A2)$$

or $$Y = \frac{\overline{A} - bi + \overline{X} + vR}{1 - c + m} \qquad (A2a)$$

Now note that the marginal propensity to consume, *c*, plus the marginal propensity to save, *s*, must be equal to unity: $1 = c + s$. Hence, substituting $1 - c = s$ into equation (A2a), we have

$$Y = \frac{\overline{A} - bi + \overline{X} + vR}{s + m} \qquad (A2b)$$

We refer to the term $1/(s + m)$ as the simple open economy multiplier. It indicates the impact on home income, given interest rates, foreign income, and the real exchange rate, of an increase in domestic autonomous spending, $\Delta\overline{A}$. Equation (A2b) also shows the impact of real depreciation on home income: a rise in the real exchange rate, *R*, raises home income by $v/(s + m)$. The rise is larger the more responsive the trade balance is to the real exchange rate and the larger the simple open economy multiplier.

Consider next how the open economy model works under flexible exchange rates and perfect capital mobility. We simply add the *LM* schedule and the assumption $i = i_f$:

$$\frac{\overline{M}}{\overline{P}} = kY - hi_f \tag{A3}$$

In equation (A3) we have already made the substitution $i = i_f$.

Thus we can determine from equation (A3) that the equilibrium level of income is

$$Y = \frac{1}{k}\left(\frac{\overline{M}}{\overline{P}} + hi_f\right) \tag{A4}$$

The home real money supply and the world interest rate thus determine the equilibrium level of income. The exchange rate adjusts to clear the goods market. Equating equations (A2b) and (A4) allows us to solve for the equilibrium real exchange rate:

$$R = \frac{s + m}{kv}\frac{\overline{M}}{\overline{P}} + \frac{[(s + m)h + kb]i_f}{kv} = \frac{\overline{A} + \overline{X}}{v} \tag{A5}$$

Thus a fiscal expansion or a rise in $\overline{M}$ leads to real appreciation, while a monetary expansion leads to real depreciation.

DATA APPENDIX

In the following table, exports and imports in billions of constant 1982 dollars are given by *EX*87 and *IM*87 and in billions of current dollars by *EX* and *IM*. The current account, *CA*, is in billions of current dollars. The real exchange rate (*R*) is an index, with 1987 = 100.

	EX87	IM87	EX	IM	CA	R
1959	73.775	95.600	20.650	22.325	−2.280	NA
1960	88.475	96.125	25.275	22.850	2.820	NA
1961	89.825	95.350	26.050	22.700	3.820	NA
1962	95.025	105.500	27.425	24.950	3.380	NA
1963	101.800	107.650	29.425	26.150	4.400	NA
1964	115.425	112.900	33.600	28.100	6.820	NA
1965	118.075	124.450	35.375	31.525	5.410	NA
1966	125.725	143.675	38.950	37.050	3.030	NA
1967	130.025	153.750	41.350	39.900	2.590	NA
1968	140.225	177.700	45.300	46.550	0.590	NA
1969	147.750	189.250	49.250	50.500	0.420	NA
1970	161.275	196.425	56.975	55.750	2.330	NA
1971	161.900	207.800	59.325	62.350	−1.450	NA
1972	173.725	230.250	66.225	74.225	−5.780	NA
1973	210.325	244.400	91.750	91.175	7.070	NA

	EX87	IM87	EX	IM	CA	R
1974	234.350	238.425	124.300	127.475	1.940	NA
1975	232.875	209.775	136.300	122.725	18.060	100.5
1976	243.400	249.725	148.850	151.150	4.180	95.9
1977	246.850	274.675	158.750	182.450	− 14.490	98.1
1978	270.200	300.075	186.150	212.275	− 15.400	105.8
1979	293.550	304.100	228.900	252.700	0.200	104.9
1980	320.550	289.875	279.200	293.900	1.200	104.5
1981	326.125	304.125	303.025	317.675	7.260	93.0
1982	296.725	304.100	282.600	303.200	− 5.860	85.1
1983	285.950	342.050	276.700	328.100	− 40.180	82.9
1984	305.725	427.700	302.400	405.100	− 98.990	78.5
1985	309.250	454.625	302.050	417.600	− 122.250	76.9
1986	329.575	484.675	319.200	451.700	− 145.420	91.4
1987	364.050	507.050	363.975	507.050	− 160.200	100.0
1988	421.650	525.675	444.175	552.200	− 126.370	105.2
1989	471.775	545.425	508.000	587.725	− 101.200	101.1
1990	509.975	561.800	557.000	625.900	− 90.460	104.5
1991	539.400	561.225	598.175	620.000	− 3.690	102.7
1992	571.475	614.625	634.325	667.050	− 57.9	102.0

SOURCE: DRI/McGraw-Hill and International Monetary Fund.

part two

AGGREGATE DEMAND, SUPPLY, AND GROWTH

AGGREGATE DEMAND AND SUPPLY: AN INTRODUCTION

W hy does a government permit recessions to continue, when they can be cured simply by expansionary monetary or fiscal policy? A large part of the answer is that expansionary aggregate demand policies increase inflation—so that a government considering whether to increase demand has to weigh the costs of higher inflation against the benefits of higher output and lower unemployment.

Thus far, we have not looked at inflation; our analysis has assumed that the price level is fixed. We studied the impacts of changes in the money supply, or of taxes, or of government spending, assuming that whatever amount of goods was demanded would be supplied, *at the existing price level.* But, of course, inflation is one of the major concerns of citizens, policy makers, and macroeconomists.

The time has therefore come to bring the price level and the inflation rate—the rate of change of the price level—into the center of our analysis. Figure 7-1 shows the model of *aggregate demand and supply* that we use to study the joint determination of the price level and the level of output. The aggregate demand curve, *AD*, which is downward-sloping, is derived from the *IS-LM* model. We show why it slopes downward and what causes it to shift. The aggregate supply curve, *AS*, will also be introduced in this chapter and developed further in Chapter 8. The intersection of the *AD* and *AS* schedules at *E* determines the equilibrium level of output, Y_0, and the equilibrium price level, P_0. Shifts in either schedule cause the price level and the level of output to change.

The aggregate demand-supply model is the basic macroeconomic model for studying output and price level determination. In both macroeconomics and microeconomics, demand and suply curves are the essential tools for studying output and price determination. But the aggregate demand and supply curves are not as simple as the microeconomic demand and supply curves—there is more going on in the background of the aggregate curves.

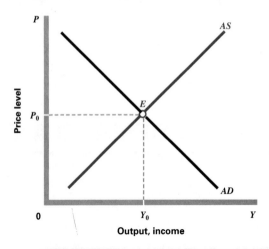

FIGURE 7-1

AGGREGATE SUPPLY AND DEMAND. The diagram shows the complete model of aggregate demand and supply that is used to explain the joint determination of the levels of output and prices. The aggregate demand curve, *AD*, is based on the *IS-LM* model studied in earlier chapters. The aggregate supply curve, *AS*, is developed in this chapter and Chapter 8. Their intersection at point *E* determines the level of output, Y_0, and the price level, P_0.

7-1 INTRODUCING AGGREGATE DEMAND AND SUPPLY

Before we go deeply into the factors underlying the aggregate demand and supply curves, we show how the curves will be used. Suppose that the Fed increases the money supply. What effects will that have on the price level and output? In particular, does an increase in the money supply cause the price level to rise, thus producing inflation? Or does the level of output rise, as it did in the analysis of earlier chapters? Or do both output and the price level rise?

Figure 7-2 shows that an increase in the money supply shifts the aggregate demand curve, *AD*, to the right, to *AD'*. (We see later in this chapter why that should be so.) The shift of the aggregate demand curve moves the equilibrium of the economy from *E* to *E'*. The price level rises from P_0 to P', and the level of output from Y_0 to Y'. Thus an increase in the money stock causes both the level of output and the price level to rise.

Figure 7-2 shows that the amount by which the price level rises depends on the slope of the aggregate supply curve and the extent to which the aggregate demand curve shifts. We now look more deeply into the aggregate demand and supply curves.

7-2 THE AGGREGATE DEMAND CURVE

The *aggregate demand curve* shows the combinations of the price level and level of output at which the goods and assets markets are simultaneously in equilibrium. At

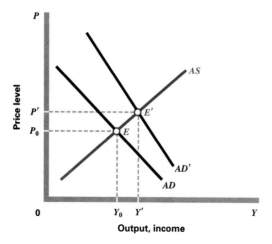

FIGURE 7-2

THE EFFECTS OF AN INCREASE IN THE NOMINAL MONEY STOCK. An increase in the money stock shifts the aggregate demand curve from *AD* to *AD'*. The equilibrium moves from *E* to *E'*, resulting in higher levels of both prices and output. Thus an increase in the money stock results in part in higher prices rather than entirely in higher output.

any point on the aggregate demand curve, for instance, point *B* in Figure 7-3, we see that for the given price level, P_0, the level of output at which the goods and assets markets are in equilibrium is Y_0.

We can already give a preliminary explanation of why the aggregate demand curve slopes downward. Suppose that the goods and assets markets are in equilibrium at a level of output like Y_0 with given price level P_0. Now suppose the price level falls. With a given nominal stock of money, a fall in the price level creates an increase in the quantity of *real balances.* This reduces interest rates, increases investment demand, and therefore increases aggregate spending. Accordingly, when the price level falls, the equilibrium level of spending rises; therefore the *AD* curve slopes down.

We now go into detail. At any given price level, we use the *IS-LM* model to determine the level of output at which the goods and assets markets are in equilibrium. In the top panel of Figure 7-4 we show the *IS-LM* model. The position of the *IS* curve depends on fiscal policy. The *LM* schedule is drawn for a given nominal money stock, $\overline{M}$, and a given price level, P_0, and thus for a given real money stock $\overline{M}/P_0$. The equilibrium interest rate is i_0, and the equilibrium level of output is Y_0.[1]

---

[1]We derive the aggregate demand curve here using diagrams; students who prefer equations can start instead from the formal presentation in Box 7-1. Note also that, strictly speaking, the aggregate demand curve should be drawn as a hyperbola and not a straight line. We show it as a straight line for convenience.

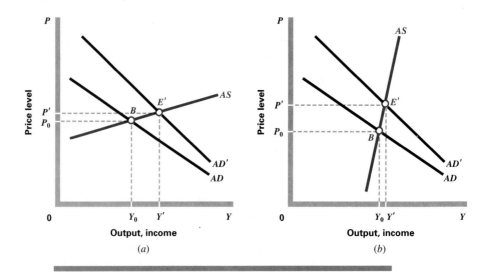

FIGURE 7-3

AGGREGATE DEMAND AND SUPPLY CURVES DEFINED. At any point on the aggregate demand curve, both the goods and assets markets are in equilibrium. This is the equilibrium given by the intersection of the *IS* and *LM* curves, as described in Chapter 4. For instance, with price level P_0, the level of output at which both goods and assets markets are in equilibrium is Y_0. The aggregate supply curve, *AS*, describes the relation between the price level and the amount of output firms wish to supply. For instance, at price level P_0, firms want to supply output Y_0.

A Change in the Price Level

Consider the effect of a fall in the price level from P_0 to P'. This reduction in the price level increases the real money stock from $\overline{M}/P_0$ to $\overline{M}/P'$. To clear the money market with an increased real money stock, either interest rates must fall, so that the public holds more cash balances, or output must rise, thus increasing the transactions demand for money.

In the top panel of Figure 7-4, the *LM* curve shifts downward and to the right, to *LM'*. The new equilibrium is shown at point E', where once again both the money market clears—because we are on the *LM* curve—and the goods market clears—because we are on the *IS* curve. The new equilibrium level of output is Y', corresponding to the lower price level P'. Thus a reduction in the price level, *given the nominal quantity of money*, results in an increase in equilibrium and spending.

The derivation of the *AD* schedule can be seen in the lower panel of Figure 7-4. The economy is initially in equilibrium at points E in both panels. The equilibrium interest rate is i_0, the level of output is Y_0, and the corresponding price level is P_0. Now the price level drops to P'. In the upper panel, the equilibrium moves to E' as a result of the shift of the *LM* curve to *LM'*. Corresponding to point E' in the upper panel is point E' in the lower panel, at price level P' and the level of income and output Y'.

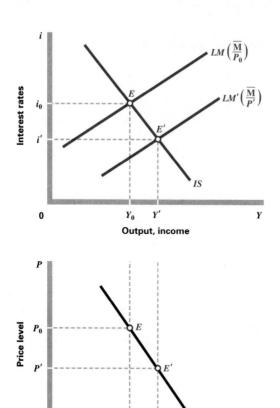

FIGURE 7-4

DERIVATION OF THE AGGREGATE DEMAND SCHEDULE. The upper panel
shows the *IS* schedule and the initial *LM* schedule drawn for the real
money stock, $\overline{M}'/P_0$. Equilibrium is at point *E*. In the lower panel we
record that at a price level P_0 the equilibrium level of income and
spending is Y_0. This is shown by point *E*. At a lower level of prices,
say, *P'*, the real money stock is $\overline{M}/P'$, and therefore the *LM* schedule
shifts to *LM'*. Equilibrium income now is at *Y'*. Again, in the lower
panel we show at point *E'* the combination of the price level, *P'*,
and the corresponding equilibrium level of income and spending,
Y'. Considering different levels of prices and connecting the
resulting points such as *E* and *E'*, we derive the aggregate demand
schedule, *AD*. The schedule shows the equilibrium level of spending
at each level of prices, given the nominal money stock and fiscal
policy.

box 7-1

*FORMAL PRESENTATION OF AGGREGATE DEMAND

In Chapter 5 we showed that equilibrium income is determined by the intersection of the *IS-LM* curves, *given* the level of prices and money. We also demonstrated that the equilibrium level of income in the *IS-LM* model can be written as

$$Y = \gamma \overline{A} + \beta \frac{\overline{M}}{P} \qquad (B1)$$

The terms

$$\gamma = \frac{\overline{\alpha}h}{h + k\overline{\alpha}b} \qquad \beta = \gamma \frac{b}{h}$$

are constants that depend on all the parameters. These multipliers represent a convenient shorthand notation for all the channels through which the impact of changes in autonomous spending or real balances affect equilibrium income. We remember that γ is interpreted as the government spending multiplier when interest rates are endogenous. The coefficient β is the multiplier for changes in the *real* money stock.

Thus both E and E' in the lower panel are points on the *AD* schedule. We could now consider all possible price levels and the corresponding levels of real balances. For each level of real balances there is a different *LM* curve in the upper panel. Corresponding to each *LM* curve is an equilibrium level of income, which would be recorded in the lower panel at the price level that results in the *LM* curve in the upper panel. Connecting all these points gives us a downward-sloping aggregate demand curve, *AD*, as shown in Figure 7-4.

The *AD* curve is downward-sloped because there is a definite relation between equilibrium spending and the price level: the higher the price level, the lower are real balances and hence the lower the equilibrium level of spending and output. Box 7-1 sets out the derivation of the aggregate demand curve more formally.

Note also from Figure 7-4 that the interest rate changes as we move down the *AD* curve. The interest rate i' at E' is lower than the interest rate i_0 at E. That is, the interest rate declines along with the price level as we move down and to the right along the *AD* curve.

The Slope of the *AD* Curve

The slope of the *AD* curve reflects the extent to which a change in real balances changes the equilibrium level of spending, taking both assets and goods markets into account.

The key point in understanding the *AD* curve is to recognize that it is nothing more than the intersections of *IS-LM* curves for different price levels—which is how we derived it in Figure 7-4. Accordingly, equation (B1) is the equation that identifies the *AD* schedule. Equation (B1) shows the equilibrium output level associated with each level of prices, *given* exogenous spending, $\bar{A}$, and the *nominal* quantity of money, $\bar{M}$. We can focus more explicitly on the price level by simply solving equation (B1) for the price level. Rearranging the terms of the resulting equation we have

$$P = \beta \, \frac{\overline{M}}{Y - \gamma\overline{A}} \tag{B2}$$

In this convenient form we immediately recognize that the *AD* schedule is drawn for a given level of nominal money and exogenous spending $\bar{A}$. We also note that, given output and exogenous spending, prices are proportionate to the money stock. Thus changes in $\overline{M}$ translate into equiproportionate changes in *P*. We return to this point later in discussing monetarism.

This handy formula for the *AD* schedule makes it easier to consider the factors that determine the position of the *AD* curve. You will also recognize that (B2) implies that the *AD* curve is not actually a straight line but rather a hyperbola. ■

---

*The asterisk denotes a more difficult section.

AD curve. What is the effect of a change in real balances due to lower prices, given nominal money? In Chapters 4 and 5 we showed the following results using the *IS-LM* schedules:

- An increase in real balances leads to a larger increase in equilibrium income and spending, the smaller the interest responsiveness of money demand and the higher the interest responsiveness of investment demand.

- An increase in real balances leads to a larger increase in equilibrium income and spending, the larger the multiplier and the smaller the income response of money demand.

Because the slope of the *AD* curve is determined by the effect of a change in real balances on equilibrium spending and output, the same factors that determine the effects of a change in the stock of money on equilibrium output and spending also determine the slope of the *AD* curve. If a given change in real balances has a large impact on equilibrium spending, then the *AD* curve will be very flat—because a small change in the price level creates a large change in equilibrium spending. But if a given change in real balances has a small effect on equilibrium spending and output, then the *AD* curve will be steep; in that case it takes a large change in the price level to create a small change in spending and output.

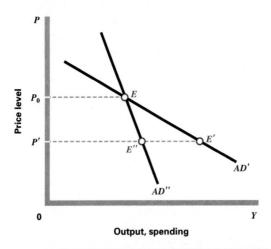

FIGURE 7-5

THE SLOPE OF THE *AD* SCHEDULE. The diagram shows two possible *AD* schedules. Along *AD"* a change in prices from P_0 to P' has a smaller effect on spending than along *AD'*. The former corresponds to the case in which changes in real balances have little impact on equilibrium income and spending; the latter, to the case in which real balance changes exert significant effects.

Accordingly, we see that

1. The *AD* curve is flatter (*a*) the smaller the interest responsiveness of the demand for money and (*b*) the larger the interest responsiveness of investment demand.
2. The *AD* curve is flatter (*a*) the larger the multiplier and (*b*) the smaller the income responsiveness of the demand for money.

To fix ideas further, it is useful to think for a moment about the *AD* schedule in terms of the extreme classical and liquidity trap cases. In the classical case, in which money demand is entirely unresponsive to interest rates and the *LM* curve is vertical, changes in real balances have a big effect on income and spending. In Figure 7-5 that case corresponds to a very flat *AD* schedule, such as *AD'*, as we should expect based on point 1*a* above. Conversely, in the liquidity trap case, where the public is willing to hold any amount of real balances at unchanged interest rates, a fall in prices and a rise in the real money stock have very little effect on income and spending.[2] In Figure

---

[2]The reason a reduction in prices increases output at all in this case is the *real balance effect*: with lower prices, the value of real balances held by the public is higher, their wealth is accordingly higher, and therefore their consumption spending and output are higher. The real balance effect is central to monetary theory as developed in the classical treatise by Don Patinkin, *Money, Interest, and Prices*, 2nd ed. (New York: Harper and Row, 1965).

7-5 that would correspond to an almost vertical *AD* curve, as suggested again by point 1*a* above. A vertical *AD* curve means that the planned level of spending is unresponsive to the price level.

You should now experiment with alternative *IS* and *LM* schedules to see how the effects of a change in the price level depend on the slopes of the *IS* and *LM* curves and the factors underlying those slopes. In doing so you will confirm the points summarized above and implied by the equations in Box 7-1. In problem 3 at the end of the chapter, we ask you to demonstrate some of these links.

7-3 AGGREGATE DEMAND POLICIES

In Figure 7-2 we showed that an increase in the quantity of money shifts the aggregate demand curve. Both fiscal and monetary policy changes shift the *AD* curve, and we now show why and how that happens, starting with a fiscal expansion.

In the upper panel of Figure 7-6 the initial *LM* and *IS* schedules correspond to a given nominal quantity of money and the price level P_0. Equilibrium is obtained at point *E*, and there is a corresponding point on the *AD* schedule in the lower panel.

Now the government increases its spending, say on infrastructure. As a consequence, the *IS* schedule shifts outward and to the right. At the initial price level there is a new equilibrium at point *E'* with higher interest rates and a higher level of income and spending. Thus at the initial level of prices, P_0, equilibrium income and spending are now higher. We show this by plotting point *E'* in the lower panel. Point *E'* is a point on the new aggregate demand curve *AD'*, reflecting the effect of higher government spending.

Of course, we could have started with any other point on the original *AD* curve, and we would then have shown in the lower panel how the rise in government spending leads to a higher equilibrium level of output at each price level. In that way we would trace out the entire *AD'* schedule, which lies to the right of *AD*.

In fact, we can say more: at each level of prices, and hence of real balances, the *AD* schedule shifts to the right by an amount indicated by the fiscal policy multiplier.[3] A fiscal expansion leads to a higher level of income and spending, the larger the interest responsiveness of money demand, the smaller the interest responsiveness of aggregate demand, and the larger the marginal propensity to consume.

Thus if the fiscal policy multiplier was, for example, 1.5, then a $1 (billion) increase in government spending would increase equilibrium income and spending by $1.5 (billion), at the given price level. In response to any change in government spending, the *AD* schedule would shift to the right by 1.5 times the increase in $\overline{G}$.

The Effect of a Monetary Expansion on the *AD* Curve

An increase in the nominal money stock implies a higher real money stock at each level of prices. In the assets markets interest rates decline to induce the public to hold

---

[3]In Chap. 5 and Box 7-1 we show that the fiscal policy multiplier is given by the expression $\gamma = h\overline{\alpha}/(h + kb\overline{\alpha})$, where h is the interest responsiveness of money demand, $\overline{\alpha}$ the simple Keynesian multiplier, k the income response of money demand, and b the interest response of investment demand.

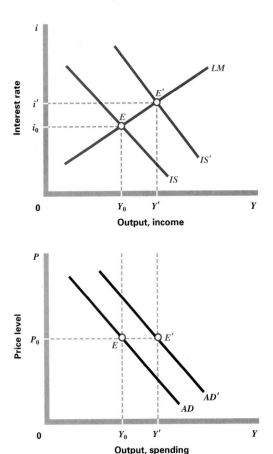

FIGURE 7-6

THE EFFECT OF A FISCAL EXPANSION ON THE *AD* SCHEDULE. A fiscal expansion, such as an increase in government spending, shifts the *IS* curve in the upper panel to *IS'*. At any given price level, such as P_0, the equilibrium in the upper panel shifts to *E'*, with higher level of output *Y'* and higher interest rate *i'*. Point *E'* in the lower panel is on the new aggregate demand schedule, *AD'*, corresponding to price level P_0. We could similarly trace the effect of increased government spending on the equilibrium level of output and spending in the lower panel for every price level, and thus show that the *AD* curve shifts out to *AD'* when fiscal policy is expansionary.

higher real balances. The decline in interest rates, in turn, stimulates aggregate demand and thus raises the equilibrium level of income and spending. In Figure 7-7 we show that an increase in the nominal money stock shifts the *AD* schedule up and to the right.

A simple and important conclusion emerges when we ask how the *AD* curve shifts when the money stock changes. Here we consider the *upward* shift of the schedule.

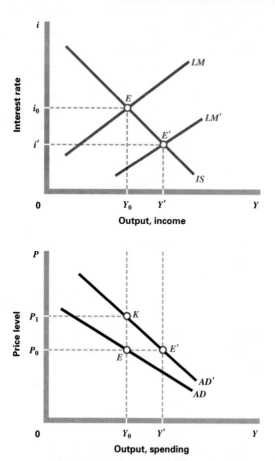

FIGURE 7-7

THE EFFECTS OF AN INCREASE IN THE MONEY STOCK ON THE *AD*
SCHEDULE. An increase in the money stock shifts the *LM* curve to
LM' in the upper panel. The equilibrium level of income rises from
Y_0 to Y' at the initial price level, P_0. Correspondingly, the *AD* curve
moves out to the right, to *AD'*, with point E' in the lower panel
corresponding to E' in the upper panel. The *AD* curve shifts up in
exactly the same proportion as the increase in the money stock. For
instance, at point *K* the price level, P_1, is higher than P_0 in the same
proportion that the money supply has risen. Real balances at *K* and
AD' are therefore the same as at *E* on *AD*.

Recall that what matters for equilibrium income and spending is the *real* money supply,
$\overline{M}/P$. If an increase in nominal money is matched by an equiproportionate increase in
prices, $\overline{M}/P$ is unchanged, and hence interest rates, aggregate demand, and equilibrium
income and spending will remain unchanged. This gives us the clue to the vertical
shift of the *AD* schedule.

*An increase in the nominal money stock shifts the AD schedule up exactly in
proportion to the increase in nominal money.* Thus if, starting at point *E* in the lower

panel of Figure 7-7, we have a 10 percent increase in $\overline{M}$, real spending will be unchanged only if prices also rise by 10 percent, thus leaving real balances unchanged. Therefore the *AD* schedule shifts upward by 10 percent. At point *K* in Figure 7-7, *real* balances are the same as at *E*, and therefore interest rates and equilibrium income and spending are the same as at *E*.

We have now completed the derivation of the aggregate demand schedule. Important points to recall are that the *AD* schedule is shifted to the right both by increases in the money stock and by expansionary fiscal policy. In the remainder of this chapter we show how to use this tool to discuss the effects of monetary and fiscal policy *on both the level of output and the price level* under alternative assumptions about the supply side.

7-4   THE AGGREGATE SUPPLY CURVE

The aggregate supply curve describes, for each given price level, the quantity of output firms are willing to supply. For instance, returning to Figure 7-3, at point *E*, with price level P_0, firms are willing to supply output equal to Y_0. The amount of output firms are willing to supply depends on the prices they receive for their goods and the amounts they have to pay for labor and other factors of production. *Accordingly, the aggregate supply curve reflects conditions in the factor markets—especially the labor market—as well as the goods markets.*

We develop the aggregate supply curve in detail in Chapter 8, showing not only why it is in general positively sloped, but also that the aggregate supply curve is likely to shift from period to period. In this chapter we show how supply conditions affect the impact of aggregate demand policies by concentrating on two special cases.

The *Keynesian case* is shown in Figure 7-8a, where the aggregate supply curve is horizontal. The *Keynesian aggregate supply curve* is horizontal, indicating that firms will supply whatever amount of goods is demanded at the existing price level.

The idea underlying the Keynesian aggregate supply curve is that because there is unemployment, firms can obtain as much labor as they want at the current wage. Their average costs of production therefore are assumed not to change as their output levels change. They are accordingly willing to supply as much as is demanded at the existing price level.

The Classical Supply Curve

Figure 7-8b shows the opposite extreme, a vertical supply curve. In the *classical case*, the aggregate supply curve is vertical, indicating that the same amount of goods will be supplied whatever the price level.

The classical supply curve is based on the assumption that the labor market is always in equilibrium with full employment of the labor force. If the entire labor force is being employed, then output cannot be raised above its current level even if the price level rises. There is no more labor available to produce any extra output. Thus the aggregate supply curve will be vertical at the level of output corresponding to full employment of the labor force, Y^* in Figure 7-8b.

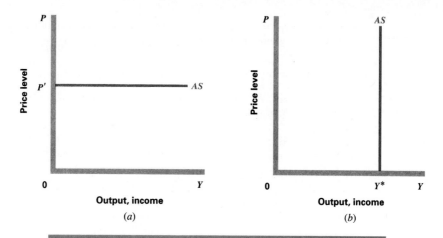

FIGURE 7-8

KEYNESIAN AND CLASSICAL SUPPLY FUNCTIONS. The Keynesian aggregate supply curve is horizontal, implying that any amount of output will be supplied at the existing price level. This is shown in panel (*a*), where the *AS* curve is horizontal at price level *P'*. The classical supply function is based on the assumption that there is always full employment of labor, and thus that output is always at the level corresponding to full employment of labor, *Y**, and *independent of the price level*. This is shown by the vertical aggregate supply curve in panel (*b*).

The labor market equilibrium underlying the vertical schedule is assumed to be maintained by speedy adjustments of the nominal wage. For example, suppose that the economy is in equilibrium and the aggregate demand curve shifts to the right. At the existing price level, the quantity of goods demanded increases. Now firms try to obtain more labor. Each firm attempts to hire more labor, offering to pay higher wages if necessary. But there is no more labor available in the economy, and so firms are unable to obtain more workers. Instead, in competing against each other for workers, they merely bid up wages. Because wages are higher, the prices the firms charge for their output will also be higher. But output will be unchanged.[4]

The classical supply curve is based on the belief that the labor market works smoothly, always maintaining full employment of the labor force. Full employment is maintained through movements in the wage. The Keynesian aggregate supply curve is instead based on the assumption that the wage does not change much or at all when there is unemployment, and thus that unemployment can continue for some time.

These two cases—the classical, representing continuing labor market equilibrium, and the Keynesian, assuming wages do not adjust—are the two extremes. In Chapter

---

[4]The adjustment described here assumes that there is a fixed supply of labor. However, *provided wages are fully flexible*, the classical supply curve applies also when labor supply increases with the real wage, as we will see at the beginning of Chap. 8.

8 we develop the theory of aggregate supply and show why the aggregate supply curve is in practice positively sloped—lying between the Keynesian and classical cases.

7-5 FISCAL AND MONETARY POLICY UNDER ALTERNATIVE SUPPLY ASSUMPTIONS

Aggregate supply and demand curves together determine the equilibrium level of income and prices in the economy. Now that we have derived the aggregate demand curve, and shown how it is shifted by policy changes, we use the aggregate demand and supply model to study the effects of monetary and fiscal policy in the two extreme supply cases—Keynesian and classical.

We should expect that the conclusions we reach in the Keynesian supply case are precisely the same as those reached in Chapters 4 and 5. In those chapters, in developing the *IS-LM* model, we assumed that whatever amount of goods was demanded would be supplied at the existing price level. And of course, as Figure 7-8a shows, the Keynesian supply curve implies that any amount of goods demanded will be supplied at the existing price level.

The Keynesian Case

In Figure 7-9 we combine the aggregate demand schedule with the Keynesian aggregate supply schedule. The initial equilibrium is at point *E*, where *AS* and *AD* intersect. At that point the goods and assets markets are in equilibrium.

Consider now a fiscal expansion. As we have already seen, increased government spending, or a cut in tax rates, shifts the *AD* schedule out and to the right from *AD* to *AD'*. The new equilibrium is at point *E'*, where output has increased. Because firms are willing to supply *any* amount of output at the level of prices P_0, there is no effect on prices. The only effect of higher government spending in Figure 7-9 is to increase output and employment. In addition, as we know from the *IS-LM* model that lies behind the *AD* schedule, the fiscal expansion will raise equilibrium interest rates.

We leave it to you to show that, in the Keynesian case, an increase in the nominal quantity of money likewise leads to an expansion in equilibrium output. With a horizontal *AS* schedule there is again no impact on prices. The magnitude of the output expansion then depends, in the Keynesian case, only on the monetary policy multiplier that determines the extent of the horizontal shift of the *AD* schedule.

Thus, as expected, all conclusions about the effects of policy changes in the Keynesian supply case are those of the simple *IS-LM* model.

The Classical Case: Fiscal Policy

In the classical case the aggregate supply schedule is vertical at the full-employment level of output. Firms will supply the level of output *Y** whatever the price level. Under this supply asssumption we obtain results very different from those reached using the Keynesian model. Now the price level is not given but rather depends on the interaction of supply and demand.

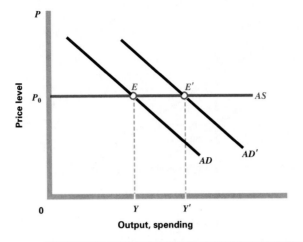

FIGURE 7-9

A FISCAL EXPANSION: THE KEYNESIAN CASE. In the Keynesian case, with output in perfectly elastic supply at a given price level, a fiscal expansion increases equilibrium income from *Y* to *Y'*. This is exactly the result already derived with the *IS-LM* model.

In Figure 7-10 we study the effect of a fiscal expansion under classical supply assumptions. The aggregate supply schedule is *AS*, with equilibrium initially at point *E*. Note that at point *E* there is full employment because, by assumption, firms supply the full-employment level of output at any level of prices.

The fiscal expansion shifts the aggregate demand schedule from *AD* to *AD'*. At the initial level of prices, P_0, spending in the economy rises to point *E'*. At price level P_0 the demand for goods has risen. But firms cannot obtain the labor to produce more output, and output supply cannot respond to the increased demand. As firms try to hire more workers, they only bid up wages and their costs of production, and therefore they charge higher prices for their output. The increase in the demand for goods therefore leads only to higher prices, and not at all to higher output.

The increase in prices reduces the real money stock and leads to an increase in interest rates and a reduction in spending. The economy moves up the *AD'* schedule until prices have risen enough, and real balances have fallen enough, to raise interest rates and reduce spending to a level consistent with full-employment output. That is the case at price level *P'*. At point *E"* aggregate demand, at the higher level of government spending, is once again equal to aggregate supply.

Crowding Out Again

Note what has happened in Figure 7-10: output is unchanged at the full-employment level, Y^*, but government spending is higher. That must mean the private sector is spending less—its spending must have fallen by precisely the amount government

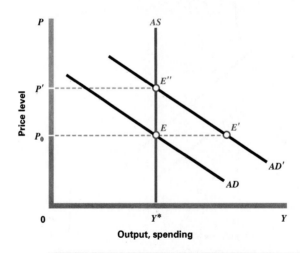

FIGURE 7-10

A FISCAL EXPANSION: THE CLASSICAL CASE. The supply of output is perfectly inelastic at the full-employment level of output, Y^*. A fiscal expansion raises equilibrium spending, at the initial price level P_0, from E to E'. But now there is excess demand because firms are unwilling to supply that much output. Prices increase, and that reduces real balances until we reach point E''. At E'' government spending is higher, but the higher price level means lower real balances, higher interest rates, and hence reduced private spending. At E'' increased government spending has crowded out an equal amount of private spending.

spending has risen. There is thus *full*, or complete, *crowding out*. Recall that crowding out occurs when an increase in government spending results in less spending by the private sector. Typically, government spending crowds out some investment. But in the case shown in Figure 7-10, with a classical supply curve, every dollar increase in real government spending is offset by a dollar reduction in private spending, so that crowding out is complete.

We thus reach the following important result: *In the classical case increased real government spending leads to full crowding out.* We now explain the mechanism through which crowding out occurs.

Figure 7-11 shows the *IS-LM* diagram, but augmented by the line Y^* at the full-employment level of output. The initial equilibrium is at point E, at which the money market clears and planned spending equals output. The fiscal expansion shifts the *IS* schedule to *IS'*. At an unchanged price level, and assuming firms were to meet the increase in demand by expanding production, we would move to point E'. But that is not possible under classical supply assumptions. Faced with an excess demand for goods, firms try to expand but in fact end up raising prices rather than output. The price increase, in turn, reduces real balances and therefore shifts the *LM* schedule up. Prices will increase until the excess demand has been eliminated. That means the *LM* schedule shifts up and to the left until we reach a new equilibrium at point E''.

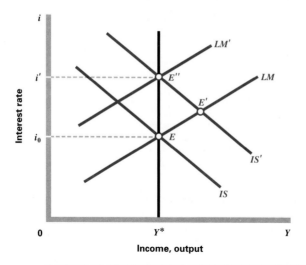

FIGURE 7-11

CROWDING OUT IN THE CLASSICAL CASE. A fiscal expansion in the classical case leads to full crowding out. The fiscal expansion shifts the *IS* schedule to *IS'*. At the initial price level the economy would move to point *E'*, but there is excess demand since firms supply only *Y**. Prices increase, shifting the *LM* schedule up and to the left until *LM'* is reached. The new equilibrium is at point *E"*, at which interest rates have risen enough to displace an amount of private spending equal to the increase in government demand.

At E'' the goods market clears at the full-employment level of output. Interest rates have increased compared with the initial equilibrium at E, thereby reducing private spending to make room for increased government purchases. Note that the money market is also in equilibrium. Output and income are the same as at point E. The higher interest rate reduces the demand for real balances, matching the decline in the real money stock.

We have now seen two mechanisms that produce full crowding out. In Chapter 5, crowding out is complete if the *LM* curve is vertical. In that case, crowding out occurs because money demand is interest-inelastic. In this chapter, full crowding out occurs because aggregate supply limits total output. In brief, in Chapter 5 crowding out is a demand phenomenon; here it is a supply phenomenon.[5]

We summarize in Table 7-1 the effects of a fiscal expansion under classical and Keynesian supply conditions. The table reinforces our understanding of the two models; in one case—the classical case—only prices adjust; in the other—Keynesian—case, only output. These cases are extremes, and we would expect that normally adjustment occurs in both output and prices.

[5]In the problem set, we ask you to explain the distinction.

TABLE 7-1

THE EFFECTS OF A FISCAL EXPANSION

aggregate supply	output	interest rate	prices
Keynesian	+	+	0
Classical	0	+	+

Monetary Expansion under Classical Conditions

Under Keynesian supply conditions, with prices given, a rise in the nominal money stock means a rise in the real money stock. Equilibrium interest rates decline as a consequence, and output rises. Consider by contrast the adjustments that occur in response to a monetary expansion when the aggregate supply curve is vertical and the price level is no longer fixed.

In Figure 7-12 we study an expansion in the nominal money stock under classical supply conditions. The initial full-employment equilibrium is at point E, where the AD and AS schedules intersect. Now the nominal money stock is increased, and accordingly, the aggregate demand schedule shifts up and to the right to AD'. If prices were fixed, the economy would move to E', the Keynesian equilibrium. But now output is in fixed supply. The increase in aggregate demand leads to an excess demand for goods. Firms that attempt to expand, by hiring more workers, bid up wages and costs. Prices increase in response, which means real balances fall back toward their initial level. In fact prices keep rising until the excess demand for goods disappears. Thus they must increase until the economy reaches point E'', where AS intersects the new aggregate demand schedule, AD'. Only when aggregate demand is again equal to full-employment supply does the goods market clear and the pressure for prices to rise disappear.

Consider now the adjustment that takes place in moving from E to E''. There is no change in output, only a change in the price level. Note, that prices rise in exactly the same proportion as the nominal quantity of money.[6] We saw that in response to an increase in nominal money the AD schedule shifts upward in the same proportion as the increase in money. Thus at point E'' the real money stock, $\overline{M}/P$, is back to its initial level. At E'' both nominal money and the price level have changed in the same proportion, leaving real money and hence interest rates and aggregate demand unchanged. We thus have an important implication of the classical model: *Under classical supply conditions an increase in nominal money raises the price level in the same proportion, but leaves interest rates and real output unchanged.*

In Table 7-2 we summarize the effects of an increase in the nominal money stock under Keynesian and classical supply conditions. Once again we look at the effects on output, prices, and interest rates. In addition we show the effect on real

---

[6]In problem 7 we ask you to use the IS and LM curves to show how the change in the money supply works. To answer the problem you could use a diagram like Figure 7-11.

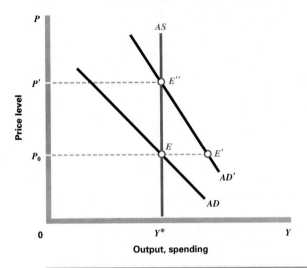

FIGURE 7-12

THE EFFECT OF A MONETARY EXPANSION UNDER CLASSICAL SUPPLY
ASSUMPTIONS. Starting from the full-employment equilibrium at
point *E*, an increase in the nominal money stock shifts the aggregate
demand schedule to *AD'*. At the initial price level there is now an
excess demand for goods. Prices increase, and thus the real money
stock declines toward its initial level. Price increases continue until
the economy reaches point *E"*. Here the *real* money stock has
returned to its initial level, and with output unchanged, interest rates
are again at their initial level. Thus a monetary expansion affects
only prices, not output or interest rates.

TABLE 7-2

THE EFFECTS OF AN INCREASE IN THE NOMINAL MONEY STOCK

aggregate supply	output	interest rate	prices	real balances
Keynesian	+	−	0	+
Classical	0	0	+	0

balances, $\overline{M}/P$. Under classical supply conditions, none of the *real* variables, such as
output, interest rates, or real balances, is affected by a change in the nominal money
stock. Only the price level changes.

Frictional Unemployment and the Natural Rate of Unemployment

Taken literally, the classical model implies that there is no unemployment. In equilibrium, everyone who wants to work is working. But there is always some unemployment.

That level of unemployment is accounted for by labor market frictions, which occur because the labor market is always in a state of flux. Some people are moving and changing jobs, other people are looking for jobs for the first time, some firms are expanding and are hiring new workers, others have lost business and have to reduce employment, firing workers.

Because it takes time for an individual to find the right new job, there will always be some *frictional* unemployment as people search for jobs. Frictional unemployment is the unemployment that exists as a result of individuals' shifting between jobs and looking for new jobs.

There is some amount of frictional unemployment associated with the full-employment level of employment, and the corresponding full-employment level of output, Y^*. That amount of unemployment is called the *natural rate*. The *natural rate of unemployment* is the rate of unemployment arising from normal labor market frictions that exist when the labor market is in equilibrium.

The natural rate, which we discuss further in Chapter 16, has been estimated at different times to be between 4 and 7 percent of the labor force in the United States. Current estimates are that the natural rate is about 5.5 percent.

The full classical (or neoclassical) theory of aggregate supply is that unemployment is always at the natural rate and output always at the full-employment level, and any unemployment is purely frictional.

7-6   THE QUANTITY THEORY AND THE NEUTRALITY OF MONEY

The classical model of supply, in combination with the *IS-LM* model describing the demand side of the economy, has extremely strong implications. Because, by assumption, output is maintained at the full-employment level by full wage and price flexibility, monetary and fiscal policy do not affect output. Fiscal policy affects interest rates and the *distribution* of spending between the government and the private sector and between consumption and investment. Monetary policy affects only the price level.

These implications about the effects of monetary policy on output are consistent with the *quantity theory of money.* The quantity theory of money in its strongest form asserts that the price level is proportional to the stock of money. In the case of the classical supply curve, an increase in the quantity of money produces, in equilibrium, a proportional increase in the price level. In this case, money is *neutral.*

The Neutrality of Money

Money is *neutral* when changes in the money stock lead only to changes in the price level, with no real variables (output, employment, and interest rates) changing. For instance, money is neutral in the second row of Table 7-2, where in response to a change in the money stock, only the price level changes, with output, interest rates, and real balances remaining unchanged.

We saw earlier that the classical supply curve has the powerful and important implication that fiscal policy cannot affect output. The neutrality of money likewise has strong policy implications. For instance, if money were neutral, there would be an easy way to reduce the inflation rate if we ever wanted to do that. All we would have to do would be to reduce the rate at which the money stock is growing.

In practice, it is very difficult to reduce inflation without producing a recession in the adjustment process. The 1979–1983 period in the United States makes the point. When a lower growth rate of money leads first to unemployment, and only later to lower inflation, as it did in the recession in 1982, then we know that money is not neutral. Changes in the quantity of money do have real effects—monetary policy affects the level of output. This means that the aggregate supply curve cannot be vertical in the short run.

The Modern Quantity Theory: Monetarism

The strict quantity theory asserts that the price level is proportional to the quantity of money. Although the quantity theory is centuries, and perhaps millennia, old, few have believed in the strict quantity theory. That is, few have believed that the price level is strictly proportional to the money stock, or that money is the *only* factor affecting the price level. Rather, quantity theorists argued and argue that increases in the money stock is, in practice, the single most important factor producing inflation.

Milton Friedman, Nobel Prize winner and the leading modern exponent of the quantity theory and the importance of money, wrote:

> Since men first began to write systematically about economic matters they have devoted special attention to the wide movements in the general level of prices that have intermittently occurred. Two alternative explanations have usually been offered. One has attributed the changes in prices to changes in the quantity of money. The other has attributed the changes in prices to war or to profiteers or to rises in wages or to some other special circumstance of the particular time and place. . . . The first explanation has generally been referred to as the quantity theory of money. . . . In its most rigid and unqualified form the quantity theory asserts strict proportionality between the quantity of what is regarded as money and the level of prices. Hardly anyone has held the theory in that form. . . . What quantity theorists have held in common is the belief that these qualifications are of secondary importance for substantial changes in either prices or the quantity of money, so that the one will not in fact occur without the other.[7]

Friedman is the recognized intellectual leader of an influential group of economists, called *monetarists*, who emphasize the role of money and monetary policy in affecting the behavior of output and prices. Leading monetarists include the late Karl Brunner of the University of Rochester, Allan Meltzer of Carnegie-Mellon University, William Poole of Brown University, Anna Schwartz of the National Bureau of Economic Research and Hunter College, and Robert Barro of Harvard University.

Modern quantity theorists disagree also with the strict quantity theory in not believing that the supply curve is vertical in the short run. Monetarists such as Friedman argue that a reduction in the money stock does in practice *first* reduce the level of output, and only later have an effect on prices.

---

[7]Milton Friedman, "Money: The Quantity Theory," in *The International Encyclopedia of the Social Sciences*, vol. 10 (London: Crowell Collier and Macmillan, Inc., 1968), pp. 432–447.

Thus Friedman and other monetarists make an important distinction between the short- and long-run effects of changes in money.[8] They argue that in the long run money is more or less neutral. Changes in the money stock, after they have worked their way through the economy, have no real effects and only change prices; the quantity theory and the neutrality of money are, from this long-run perspective, not just theoretical possibilities, but instead a reasonable description of the way the world works. But in the short run, they argue, monetary policy and changes in the money stock can and do have important real effects.[9]

7-7 SUMMARY

1. The aggregate supply and demand model is used to show the determination of the equilibrium levels of *both* output and prices.

2. The aggregate demand schedule, *AD*, shows at each price level the level of output at which the goods and assets markets are in equilibrium. This is the quantity of output demanded at each price level. Along the *AD* schedule fiscal policy is given, as is the nominal quantity of money. The *AD* schedule is derived using the *IS-LM* model.

3. Moving down and along the *AD* schedule, lower prices raise the real value of the money stock. Equilibrium interest rates fall, and that increases aggregate demand and equilibrium spending.

4. A fiscal expansion shifts the *AD* schedule outward and to the right. An increase in the nominal money stock shifts the *AD* curve up by the same proportion as the money stock increases.

5. The aggregate supply schedule, *AS*, shows at each level of prices the quantity of real output firms are willing to supply.

6. The Keynesian supply schedule is horizontal, implying that firms supply as much goods as are demanded at the existing price level. The classical supply schedule is vertical. It would apply in an economy that has full price and wage flexibility. In such a frictionless economy, employment and output are always at the full-employment level.

7. Under Keynesian supply conditions, with prices fixed, both monetary and fiscal expansion raise equilibrium output. A monetary expansion lowers interest rates, while a fiscal expansion raises them.

8. Under classical supply conditions a fiscal expansion has no effect on output. But a fiscal expansion raises prices, lowers real balances, and increases equilibrium

---

[8]For a more recent statement of the monetarist position see Milton Friedman, ''The Quantity Theory of Money,'' in *The New Palgrave Dictionary of Economics* (New York: Stockton, 1987), and ''Whither Inflation,'' *Wall Street Journal*, July 1989. See, too, the historical study written with Anna J. Schwartz, *Monetary Trends in the United States and the United Kingdom* (Chicago: University of Chicago Press, 1982), as well as William Dewald, ''Monetarism Is Dead: Long Live the Quantity Theory of Money,'' Federal Reserve Bank of St. Louis *Review*, July/August 1988.

[9]There is more to monetarism than the argument that money is the most important determinant of macroeconomic performance, but we leave the evidence on this and the other tenets of monetarism for further discussion in Chapters 13 and 17.

interest rates. That is, under classical supply conditions there is full crowding out. Private spending declines by exactly the increase in government demand.

9. A monetary expansion, under classical supply conditions, raises prices in the same proportion as the rise in nominal money. All real variables—specifically, output and interest rates—remain unchanged. When changes in the money stock have no real effects, money is said to be *neutral*.

10. The strict quantity theory of money states that prices move in proportion to the nominal money stock. Modern quantity theorists or monetarists accept the view that there is no exact link between money and prices, but they argue that changes in the money stock are, in practice, the most important single determinant of *long-run* changes in the price level.

KEY TERMS

Aggregate demand curve
Aggregate supply curve
Keynesian aggregate supply curve
Classical aggregate supply curve

Quantity theory of money
Neutrality of money
Full crowding out
Monetarism

PROBLEMS

1. (a) Explain why we need to introduce the aggregate demand and supply model.
   (b) Define the aggregate demand and supply curves.

2. Discuss, using the *IS-LM* model, what happens to interest rates as prices change along a given *AD* schedule.

3. Show graphically that the *AD* curve is steeper the larger the interest responsiveness of the demand for money and the smaller the multiplier.

4. Explain why the classical supply curve is vertical and explain the mechanisms that ensure continued full employment of labor in the classical case.

5. Suppose full-employment output increases from Y^* to $Y^{*'}$. What does the quantity theory predict will happen to the price level?

6. In goods market equilibrium in a closed economy, $S + TA - TR = I + G$. Use this equation to explain why, in the classical case, a fiscal expansion must lead to full crowding out.

7. Show, using *IS* and *LM* curves, why money is neutral in the classical supply case. (Refer to footnote 6 for hints.)

8. Suppose the government reduces the personal income tax rate from t to t'.
   (a) What is the effect on the *AD* schedule?
   (b) What is the effect on the equilibrium interest rate?
   (c) What happens to investment?

9. Suppose there is a decline in the demand for money. At each output level and interest rate the public now wants to hold lower real balances.
   (a) In the Keynesian case, what happens to equilibrium output and to prices?
   (b) In the classical case, what is the effect on output and on prices?

10. Repeat problem 9, using the quantity theory of money to explain the effect of the money demand shift on prices.

11. Suppose the government undertakes a balanced budget increase in spending. Government spending rises from G to G', and there is an accompanying increase in tax rates so that at the initial level of output the budget remains balanced.
    (a) Show the effect on the AD schedule.
    (b) Discuss the effect of the balanced budget policy on output and interest rates in the Keynesian case.
    (c) Discuss the effect in the classical case.

12. (a) Define the strict quantity theory.
    (b) Define monetarism.
    (c) What type of statistical evidence would you need to collect in order to support or refute the major argument of monetarism presented in this chapter?

13. Explain the meaning of the statement that in Chapter 5, crowding out is a demand phenomenon, whereas in the classical supply case, it is a supply-side phenomenon.

COMPUTER EXERCISES

For each of the following six exercises, carry out the proposed policy changed under the AS assumption given in that problem and determine the
    (a) Change in output.
    (b) Change in interest rate.
    (c) Change in price level.
    (d) Value of the fiscal or monetary policy multiplier (fiscal for exercises 1–3 and monetary for exercises 4–6).

Record these changes in a table whose columns are (a) through (d) above and whose rows are the six scenarios listed below:

Stimulative fiscal policy:

1. Assume that AS is flat. Increase autonomous spending $(\overline{A})$ by 20.

2. Assume that AS has intermediate slope. Again, increase $\overline{A}$ by 20.

3. Assume that AS is vertical. Again, increase $\overline{A}$ by 20.

Stimulative monetary policy:

4. Assume that AS is flat. Increase the money supply $(\overline{M})$ by 20.

5. Assume that AS has intermediate slope. Again, increase $\overline{M}$ by 20.

6. Assume that AS is vertical. Again, increase $\overline{M}$ by 20.

Other questions:

7. Which exercise (of 1 through 6 above) demonstrates the neutrality of money?

8. If the aggregate supply curve is vertical, can accommodative monetary policy affect output? Can stimulative monetary policy get rid of the crowding out effect caused by stimulative fiscal policy? Why or why not?

AGGREGATE SUPPLY: WAGES, PRICES, AND EMPLOYMENT

*I*n this chapter we develop the aggregate supply side of the economy. The aggregate supply curve is built up from the links among wages, prices, employment, and output. The model of aggregate supply we develop here makes it possible to examine the dynamic response of output and prices to changes in monetary and fiscal policy. In addition, it enables us to study how the economy adjusts to *supply shocks* such as the sudden, sharp increases in oil prices in 1973–1974, 1979–1980, and, briefly, following the Iraqi invasion of Kuwait in 1990.

Before we get down to business, some words of warning, and some of encouragement. The warning is that the theory of aggregate supply is one of the least settled areas in macroeconomics. In an idealized world, in which prices and wages adjust rapidly, the labor market would adjust rapidly to ensure full employment, and we would be in the world of the classical supply curve of Chapter 7. But in practice the labor market seems to adjust slowly to changes in aggregate demand, the unemployment rate is clearly not always at the natural level, and output does change when aggregate demand changes.

The words of encouragement are that although there is a variety of models of aggregate supply, the basic phenomenon that has to be explained—the apparent slow adjustment of output to changes in demand—is widely agreed upon. All modern models, however different their starting points, tend to reach a similar result, that in the short run the aggregate supply curve is positively sloped, but in the long run it is vertical.

8-1 WAGES, PRICES, AND OUTPUT: THE FACTS

The classical model of macroeconomics holds that the economy is *always* at full employment. Any unemployment that is observed is purely frictional—workers moving from one job to another. Moreover, because there is no nonfrictional unemployment in that model there can also be no relation between the state of the labor market and

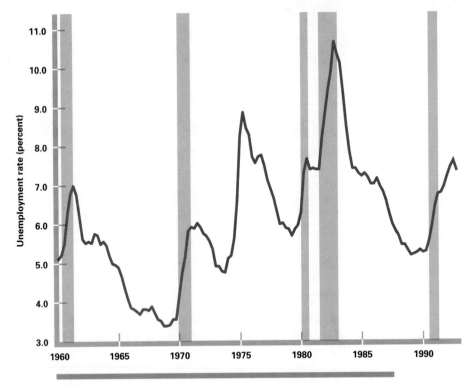

FIGURE 8-1
THE U.S. CIVILIAN UNEMPLOYMENT RATE, 1959–1992. (Source: DRI/
McGraw-Hill.)

the behavior of wages—wages are determined by productivity and the impact of money
on prices, not at all by unemployment.

Contrary to that rendition, two major facts about the labor market need to be
placed at the center of a realistic macroeconomic model. First, the rate of unemployment
fluctuates far more than is consistent with the view that all unemployment is frictional.
Figure 8-1 shows the unemployment rate for the period since 1959. It cannot be that
the 10.8 percent unemployment rate at the end of 1982 was equal to the natural rate,
much less that the 25 percent unemployment rate in 1933, in the depths of the great
depression, can have been equal to the natural rate. Thus it cannot be that the labor
market is always in equilibrium at the full-employment level of employment.

The second fact that is inconsistent with the neoclassical theory is that there
appears to be a systematic relationship between the rate of change of wages and
unemployment.

The Phillips Curve

In 1958 A. W. Phillips, then a professor at the London School of Economics, published
a comprehensive study of wage behavior in the United Kingdom for the years 1861–

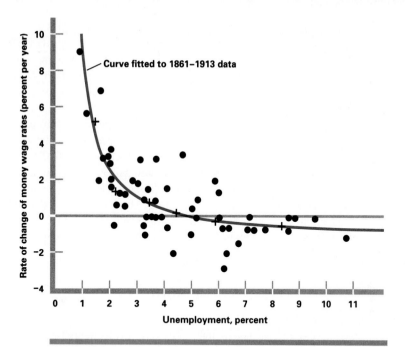

FIGURE 8-2
THE ORIGINAL PHILLIPS CURVE FOR THE UNITED KINGDOM. (SOURCE:
A. W. Phillips, ''The Relation between Unemployment and the Rate
of Change of Money Wages in the United Kingdom, 1861–1957,''
Economica, November 1958.)

1957.[1] The main finding is summarized in Figure 8-2, reproduced from his article: The
Phillips curve is an inverse relationship between the rate of unemployment and the
rate of increase in money wages. The higher the rate of unemployment, the lower is
the rate of wage inflation. In other words, there is a tradeoff between wage inflation
and unemployment.

The Phillips curve shows that the rate of wage inflation decreases with the
unemployment rate. Letting W be the wage this period and W_{-1} the wage last period,
the rate of wage inflation, g_w, is defined as

$$g_w = \frac{W - W_{-1}}{W_{-1}} \tag{1}$$

With u^* representing the natural rate of unemployment we can write the simple Phillips
curve as

$$g_w = -\epsilon(u - u^*) \tag{2}$$

---

[1] A. W. Phillips, ''The Relation between Unemployment and the Rate of Change of Money Wages in the
United Kingdom, 1861–1957,'' *Economica*, November 1958.

where ϵ measures the responsiveness of wages to unemployment. This equation states that wages are falling when the unemployment rate exceeds the natural rate, that is, when $(u > u^*)$, and rising when unemployment is below the natural rate.

The Phillips curve implies that wages and prices adjust slowly to changes in aggregate demand. Why? Suppose the economy is in equilibrium with prices stable and unemployment at the natural rate. Now there is an increase in the money stock of, say, 10 percent. Prices and wages both have to rise by 10 percent for the economy to get back to equilibrium. But the Phillips curve shows that for wages to rise by an extra 10 percent, the unemployment rate will have to fall. That will cause the rate of wage increase to go up. Wages will start rising, prices too will rise, and eventually the economy will return to the full-employment level of output and unemployment. In the meantime the increase in the money stock caused a reduction in unemployment. This point can be readily seen by rewriting equation (2), using the definition of the rate of wage inflation, in order to look at the level of wages today relative to the past level:

$$W = W_{-1}[1 - \epsilon(u - u^*)] \qquad (2a)$$

For wages to rise above their previous level, unemployment must fall below the natural rate.

Although Phillips's own curve relates the rate of increase of wages or wage inflation to unemployment, as in equation (2), the term *Phillips curve* gradually came to be used to describe either the original Phillips curve *or* a curve relating the rate of increase of *prices*—the rate of inflation—to the unemployment rate. Figure 8-3 shows inflation and unemployment data for the United States in the 1960s that appear entirely consistent with the Phillips curve.

The Policy Tradeoff

The Phillips curve rapidly became a cornerstone of macroeconomic policy analysis. It suggested that policy makers could choose different combinations of unemployment and rates of inflation. For instance, they could have low unemployment as long as they put up with high inflation—say, the situation in the late 1960s in Figure 8-3. Or they could maintain low inflation by having high unemployment, as in the early 1960s.

But that simple Phillips curve relationship has not held up well since the 1960s, either in Britain or in the United States. Figure 8-4 shows the behavior of inflation and unemployment in the United States over the entire period since 1960. The data for the 1970s and 1980s do not fit the simple Phillips curve story.

Our task now is to develop a theory of aggregate supply that will build on the insights of the original Phillips curve and also explain why inflation and unemployment rates in the 1970s and 1980s were so far from the Phillips relationship that seemed so strong in the 1960s. Evidently, there is more than just unemployment affecting the rate of change of wages and inflation.

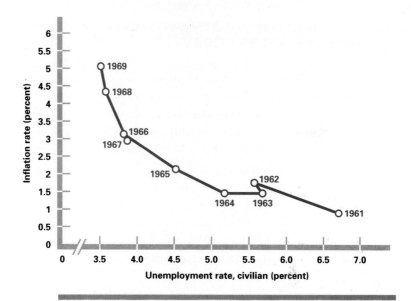

FIGURE 8-3
INFLATION AND UNEMPLOYMENT: UNITED STATES, 1961–1969. (SOURCE: DRI/McGraw-Hill.)

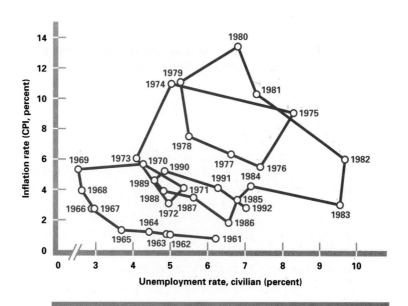

FIGURE 8-4
INFLATION AND UNEMPLOYMENT: UNITED STATES, 1961–1992. (SOURCE: DRI/McGraw-Hill.)

8-2　THE WAGE-UNEMPLOYMENT RELATIONSHIP: WHY ARE WAGES STICKY?

In the neoclassical theory of supply, wages adjust instantly to ensure that output is always at the full-employment level. But output is not always at the full-employment level, and the Phillips curve suggests that wages adjust slowly in response to changes in unemployment. The key question in the theory of aggregate supply is why the nominal wage adjusts slowly to shifts in demand, or why wages are *sticky*. Wages are sticky, or wage adjustment sluggish, when wages move slowly over time, rather than being fully and immediately flexible, so as to ensure full employment at every point in time.

To clarify the assumptions that we make about wage stickiness, we translate the Phillips curve in equation (2) into a relationship between the rate of change of wages, g_w, and the level of employment. We denote the full-employment level of employment by N^* and the actual level of employment by N. We then define the unemployment rate as the fraction of the full-employment labor force, N^*, that is not employed:[2]

$$u = \frac{N^* - N}{N^*} \tag{3}$$

Substituting equation (3) into (2), we obtain the Phillips curve relationship between the level of employment and the rate of change in wages:

$$g_w = \frac{W - W_{-1}}{W_{-1}} = \epsilon \left(\frac{N^* - N}{N^*} \right) \tag{2b}$$

or, rewriting the equation, we show the Phillips curve as a relationship between the wage this period, the wage last period, and the actual level of employment:

$$W = W_{-1} \left[1 + \epsilon \left(\frac{N - N^*}{N^*} \right) \right] \tag{4}$$

Equation (4), the wage-employment relationship, *WN*, is shown in Figure 8-5. The wage this period is equal to the wage that prevailed last period (say, last quarter), but with an adjustment for the level of employment. At full employment ($N = N^*$), this period's wage is equal to last period's. If employment is above the full-employment level, the wage increases above last period's wage. If employment is below the full-employment level, the wage this period falls below last period's wage. The extent to which the wage responds to employment depends on the parameter ϵ. If ϵ is large, unemployment has large effects on the wage, and the *WN* line is steep.

---

[2]Equation (3) implies that the unemployment rate is zero at full employment, when $N = N^*$. In fact, there is positive frictional unemployment even when the economy is at full employment. We are implicitly defining the unemployment rate in equation (3) relative to the natural rate of unemployment. Thus when u in equation (3) is positive (or negative), the actual rate of unemployment exceeds (or is less than) the natural rate. Actual unemployment can be below the natural rate because people are working overtime.

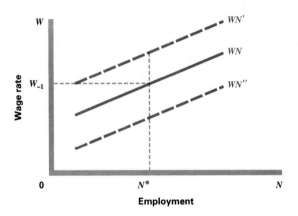

FIGURE 8-5

THE WAGE-EMPLOYMENT RELATION. Within a period, the wage increases with the level of employment, as shown by *WN*. If employment is at its neoclassical equilibrium level, N^*, the wage level in this period is equal to the wage last period. The *WN* curve shifts over time if employment differs from the full-employment level, N^*. If N exceeds N^* this period, the *WN* curve will shift upward to *WN'* next period.

The Phillips curve relationship in equation (4) also implies that the *WN* relationship shifts over time, as is also shown in Figure 8-5. If there is overemployment this period, the *WN* curve will shift upward next period to *WN'*. If there is less than full employment this period, the *WN* curve will shift downward next period to *WN''*. Thus, changes in aggregate demand that alter the rate of unemployment this period will have effects on wages in subsequent periods. In other words, the adjustment to a change in employment is dynamic, that is, it takes place over time.

Wage Stickiness

Although there are different approaches to macroeconomics, each school of thought has had to try to explain the reason there is a Phillips curve or, equivalently, the reasons for wage stickiness. The explanations are not mutually exclusive, and we shall therefore briefly mention several of the leading approaches.

IMPERFECT INFORMATION—MARKET CLEARING

Some economists have sought to explain the Phillips curve in a context in which markets clear, where wages are fully flexible but adjust slowly because expectations are temporarily wrong. In the 1960s, Milton Friedman and Edmund Phelps developed models in which, when nominal wages go up because prices have risen, workers mistakenly believe their real wage has risen and are willing to work more.[3] Thus, in the short run, until workers realize that the higher nominal wage is merely a result of a higher price level, an increase in the nominal wage is associated with a higher level of output and less unemployment. In these models, the slow adjustment of wages arises from workers' slow reactions to or imperfect information about changes in prices.

This explanation was put in an explicit rational expectations context by Robert Lucas. In the Lucas model (developed in Chapter 9), workers do not know the current price level at the time they have to decide whether to work at the going nominal wage.[4] When they see the wage they are paid rising, they realize it may have risen either because the overall price level has increased *or* because the wage for their type of labor has risen. If the cause of the wage increase is a higher price level, then their real wage has not changed, and they should not increase the amount of work they offer. But if the wage for their type of labor has risen, then the real wage is up, and they should work more. Since the workers cannot know at the time they have to decide whether to work more or not, they compromise, working a bit more, but not as much more as they would if they were *sure* the real wage had risen. In this way, Lucas develops a short-run tradeoff between higher wages and higher employment, which depends on the workers being imperfectly informed.

COORDINATION PROBLEMS

The coordination approach to the Phillips curve focuses more on the process by which firms adjust their prices when demand changes than on wages.[5] Suppose that there is an increase in the money stock. Ultimately, prices will go up in the same proportion as the money supply, and output will be unchanged. But if any one firm raises its price in proportion to the increase in the money stock, and no other firm does, then the single firm that has raised its prices will lose business to the others. Of course, if all firms raised their price in the same proportion, they would move immediately to the new equilibrium. But because the firms in an economy cannot get together to coordinate their price increases, each will raise prices slowly as the effects of the change in the money stock are felt through an increased demand for goods at the existing prices.

Coordination problems also can help explain why wages are sticky downward, that is, why they do not fall immediately when aggregate demand declines. Any firm cutting its wages while other firms do not will find its workers both annoyed and leaving the firm. If firms coordinated, they could all reduce wages together, but since they generally cannot coordinate, wages go down slowly as individual firms cut the

---

[3]Milton Friedman, "The Role of Monetary Policy," *American Economic Review*, March 1968, and Edmund S. Phelps, "Phillips Curves, Expectations of Inflation, and Optimal Unemployment Over Time," *Economica*, August 1967. See also Edmund Phelps, "A Review of *Unemployment*," *Journal of Economic Literature*, September 1992.

[4]Robert E. Lucas, "Some International Evidence on Output-Inflation Tradeoffs," *American Economic Review*, June 1973.

[5]See the papers under the heading "Coordination Failures" in N. Gregory Mankiw and David Romer (eds.), *New Keynesian Economics*, vol. 2 (Cambridge, Mass.: MIT Press, 1991).

nominal wages of their employees, with probably those firms whose profits have been hardest hit moving first.[6]

EFFICIENCY WAGES AND COSTS OF PRICE CHANGE

Efficiency wage theory focuses on the wage as a means of motivating labor. The amount of effort workers make on the job is related to how well the job pays relative to alternatives. Firms may want to pay employees wages above the market-clearing wage, to ensure they work hard so as not to lose their good jobs. This theory by itself does not explain why the average *nominal* wage is slow to change, but it does help explain the existence of unemployment.

However, taken in combination with the fact that there are costs of changing prices, efficiency wage theory can generate some stickiness in nominal wages even if the costs of resetting prices are quite small.[7] By combining that stickiness with problems of coordinating, this theory can help account for wage stickiness.

Contracts and Long-Term Relationships

In developing the explanation of wage stickiness, we build on the foregoing theories and on one central element—the fact that the labor market involves long-term relations between firms and workers. Most members of the labor force expect to continue in their current job for some time. Working conditions, including the wage, are renegotiated periodically, but not frequently. That is because frequent resetting of wages is costly. Typically, firms and workers reconsider wages and adjust them once a year.[8]

Wages are usually set in nominal terms in economies with low rates of inflation.[9] Thus the agreement is that the firm will pay the worker so many dollars per hour or

---

[6]A very similar explanation for downward wage rigidity was presented by Keynes in the *General Theory*. Some recent work suggests that wage cutting has become reasonably common in the United States in recent years. See, for instance, Alan S. Blinder and Don H. Choi, "A Shred of Evidence on Theories of Wage Stickiness," *Quarterly Journal of Economics*, November 1990.

[7]See George A. Akerlof and Janet L. Yellen, "A Near-Rational Model of the Business Cycle, with Wage and Price Inertia," *Quarterly Journal of Economics*, Supplement, 1985, and, edited by the same authors, *Efficiency Wage Models of the Labor Market* (New York: Cambridge University Press, 1986). See, too, the papers on "Costly Price Adjustment" in N. Gregory Mankiw and David Romer (eds.), *New Keynesian Economics*, vol. 1 (Cambridge, Mass.: MIT Press, 1991), and the discussion in Richard Layard, Stephen Nickell, and Richard Jackman, *Unemployment: Macroeconomic Performance and the Labor Market* (New York: Oxford University Press, 1991).

[8]The frequency with which wages (and prices) are reset depends on the stability of the level of output and prices in the economy. In extreme conditions, such as hyperinflations, wages might be reset daily or weekly. The need to reset prices and wages frequently is one of the important costs of high and unstable rates of inflation.

[9]In economies with high inflation, wages are likely to be *indexed* to the price level, that is, they adjust automatically when the price level changes. Even in the United States, some long-term labor contracts contain indexing clauses under which the wage is increased to compensate for past price increases. The indexing clauses typically adjust wages once a quarter (or once a year) to compensate for price increases in the past quarter (or year).

per month for the next quarter or year. Some formal union labor contracts last 2 or 3 years and may fix nominal wages for the period of the contract. Frequently labor contracts include separate wage rates for overtime hours, which implies that the wage rate paid by firms is higher the more hours are worked. That is one reason the *WN* curve in Figure 8-5 is positively sloped.

At any moment, firms and workers will have agreed, explicitly or implicitly, on the wage schedule that is to be paid to currently employed workers. There will be some base wage that corresponds to a given number of hours of work per week and depends on the type of job, with perhaps a higher wage for overtime. The firm then sets the level of employment each period.

Now consider how wages adjust when the demand for labor shifts and firms increase the hours of work. In the short run, wages rise along the *WN* curve. With demand up, workers will press for an increase in the base wage at the next labor negotiation. However, it will take some time before all wages are renegotiated. Further, not all wages are negotiated simultaneously. Rather, wage-setting dates are *staggered*, that is, they overlap.[10] Assume that wages for half the labor force are set in January and the other half in July. Suppose the money stock went up in September. In the first instance, prices will be slow to adjust because no wage is adjusted until 3 months after the change in the money stock. Second, when the time comes to renegotiate half the contracts, in January, both the firms and the workers negotiating know that other wages will not change for the next 6 months.

Workers do not adjust their base wage all the way to the level that will take the economy to the long-run equilibrium because if they did, their wages would be very high relative to other wages for the next 6 months. Firms will prefer to employ workers whose wages have not yet risen; there is thus a danger of unemployment to the January wage-setting workers if the renegotiated wages go too high. Wages are therefore adjusted only partway toward equilibrium.

Then in July, when the time comes to reset the other half of the wages, those too are not driven all the way to the equilibrium level because the January wages will then be relatively lower. So the July wages will go above the January wages, but still only partway to the full-employment equilibrium base wage.

This process keeps on going, with the supply curve rising from period to period as wages leapfrog each other, with first one wage and then another being renegotiated. The position of the aggregate supply curve in any period will depend on where it was last period because each unit renegotiating wages has to consider the level of its wage relative to the wages that are not being reset. And the level of the wages that are not being reset is reflected in last period's wage rate. That is why there is a W_{-1} term on the right-hand side of the Phillips curve equation (4).

During the adjustment process, firms will also be resetting prices as wages (and thus firms' costs) change. The process of wage and price adjustment continues until the economy is back at the full-employment equilibrium with the same real balances. The real-world adjustment process is more complicated than the January–July example because wages are not reset quite as regularly as that and, also, because both wage

---

[10]The adjustment process we present here is based on John Taylor, "Aggregate Dynamics and Staggered Contracts," *Journal of Political Economy*, February 1980.

and price adjustment matter.[11] But the January–July example gives the essence of the adjustment process.

This account of slow wage and price adjustment raises at least two serious questions. First, why do firms and workers not adjust wages more frequently when clearly understandable disturbances affect the economy? If they did, then perhaps they could adjust wages so as to maintain full employment. Recent research emphasizes that even comparatively small costs of resetting wages and prices can keep adjustment processes from operating quickly.[12] Further, the problems of coordinating wage and price adjustments so that wages and prices move back rapidly to equilibrium are formidable in a large economy in which there are many different forces affecting supply and demand in individual markets.

Second, when there is high unemployment why do firms and unemployed workers not get together on wage cuts that create jobs for the unemployed? The main reason, discussed in the efficiency wage theory approach, is that such practices are bad for the morale and therefore the productivity of those in the labor force who are on the job.[13]

To summarize, the combination of wages that are preset for a period of time and wage adjustments that are staggered generates the gradual wage and output adjustment we observe in the real world. This accounts for the dynamics. The upward-sloping aggregate supply curve, to which we now turn, is accounted for by overtime wages for some workers and by the fact that wages in those contracts that are renegotiated within the period (such as a quarter) do respond to market conditions.

Insider-Outsider Models

Finally, we draw attention to an approach that emphasizes the implications for the link between wage behavior and unemployment resulting from this simple fact: the unemployed do not sit at the bargaining table.[14] Firms effectively negotiate with the workers who have jobs, not with the people who are unemployed. This has an immediate implication. It is costly for firms to turn over their labor force—firing costs, hiring costs, training costs—and as a result *insiders* have an advantage over outsiders.

More important, threatening insiders with unemployment unless they accept wage cuts is not very effective for two reasons. First, people who are threatened may have to give in, but they will respond poorly in terms of morale, effort, and productivity. Second, if the firm actually fired high-wage workers and brought in the unemployed at low wages, the unemployed would now become insiders and present exactly the

---

[11]For an interesting study of the frequency of price adjustments (for newspapers) see Stephen G. Cecchetti, "Staggered Contracts and the Frequency of Price Adjustment," *Quarterly Journal of Economics*, Supplement, 1985.

[12]See the references in footnote 7.

[13]See Robert M. Solow, *The Labor Market as a Social Institution* (Cambridge: Basil Blackwell, 1990), for a discussion of the relation between pay and productivity.

[14]See Assar Lindbeck and Dennis Snower, *The Insider-Outsider Theory of Employment and Unemployment* (Cambridge, Mass.: MIT Press, 1988) and Assar Lindbeck, "Macroeconomic Theory and the Labor Market," *European Economic Review,* vol. 36, 1992.

same resistance to wage cuts as the previous generation of insiders. Thus the firm would face the prospect of many costly rounds of labor turnover before getting a docile labor force. Far better to reach a deal with the insiders, to pay them good wages even if there are unemployed workers who would be eager to work for less.

The insider-outsider model predicts that wages will not respond substantially to unemployment and thus offers another reason why we do not quickly return to full employment once the economy experiences recession.

8-3 THE AGGREGATE SUPPLY CURVE

Now we are ready to derive the aggregate supply curve. It will take four steps. First, we relate output to employment. Second, we relate the prices firms charge to their costs. Third, we use the Phillips curve relationship between wages and employment. Then we put the three components together to derive an upward-sloping aggregate supply curve.

The Production Function

The production function links the level of employment of labor to the level of output. The simplest production function is one in which output is proportional to the input of labor:

$$Y = aN \tag{5}$$

Here Y is the level of output produced and N is the amount of labor input or employment (measured in hours of work, for example). The coefficient a is called the input coefficient, or *labor productivity*. Labor productivity is the ratio of output to labor input, Y/N, that is, the amount of output produced per unit of labor employed. For instance, if a is equal to 3, then one unit of labor (1 hour of work) will produce three units of output.[15]

Costs and Prices

The second step in developing the theory of supply is to link firms' prices to their costs. Labor costs are the main component of total costs. The guiding principle here is that a firm will supply output at a price that at least covers its costs. Of course, firms would like to charge more than cost, but competition from existing firms and firms

---

[15]We assume for simplicity that labor productivity is constant, even though in practice it changes over the business cycle and over time. Productivity tends to grow over long periods, as workers become better trained, educated, and equipped with more capital. It also changes systematically during the business cycle. Productivity tends to fall before the start of a recession and rises during the recession and at the beginning of the recovery.

that might enter the industry to capture some of the profits prevent prices from getting far out of line with costs.

We assume that firms base price on the labor cost of production. Since each unit of labor produces a units of output, the labor cost of production per unit is W/a. For instance, if the wage is \$15 per hour and a is 3, then the labor cost is \$5 per unit. The ratio W/a is called the *unit labor cost*. Firms set price as a *markup, z,* on labor costs:

$$P = \frac{(1 + z)W}{a} \tag{6}$$

The markup over labor costs covers the cost of other factors of production that firms use, such as capital and raw materials, and includes an allowance for the firms' normal profits. If competition in the industry is less than perfect, then the markup will also include an element of monopoly profit.[16]

Employment and Wages and the Aggregate Supply Curve

The three components of the aggregate supply curve are the production function (5), the price-cost relation (6), and the Phillips curve (4). The price level is proportional to the wage [from equation (6)]. But today's wage is linked through the Phillips curve (4) to the level of employment and to past wages. Using the wage equation, we replace the wage in equation (6) to obtain a link between the level of employment and the price level:

$$P = \left(\frac{1 + z}{a}\right) W_{-1}\left[1 + \epsilon\left(\frac{N - N^*}{N^*}\right)\right] \tag{7}$$

which, since $P_{-1} = [(1 + z)/a]W_{-1}$, reduces to

$$P = P_{-1}\left[1 + \epsilon\left(\frac{N - N^*}{N^*}\right)\right] \tag{7a}$$

Further, the level of output is proportional to employment [from the production function, equation (5)]. Thus we can replace N and N^* in equation (7a) by Y/a and Y^*/a. Making these changes, we obtain

$$P = P_{-1}\left[1 + \epsilon\left(\frac{Y - Y^*}{Y^*}\right)\right]$$

---

[16]In microeconomics the competitive industry price is determined by the market, rather than set by firms. That is quite consistent with equation (6), for if the industry were competitive, z would cover only the costs of other factors of production and normal profits, and the price would thus be equal to the competitive price. Equation (6) is slightly more general, because it allows also for price setting by firms in industries that are less than fully competitive.

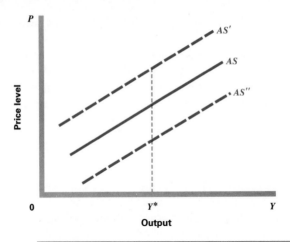

FIGURE 8-6

THE AGGREGATE SUPPLY CURVE. The aggregate supply curve, *AS*, is derived from the *WN* curve, with the added assumptions that output is proportional to employment and that prices are set as a markup on labor costs. The *AS* curve, too, shifts over time, depending on the level of the output. For instance, if output this period is above the full-employment level, *Y**, the *AS* curve will shift upward to *AS'* next period.

Finally, defining $\lambda \equiv \epsilon/Y^*$, we obtain the *aggregate supply curve*

$$P = P_{-1}[1 + \lambda(Y - Y^*)] \tag{8}$$

Figure 8-6 shows the aggregate supply curve implied by equation (8). The supply curve is upward-sloping. Like the *WN* curve on which it is based, the *AS* curve shifts over time. If output this period is above the full-employment level, *Y**, then next period the *AS* curve will shift up to *AS'*. If output this period is below the full-employment level, the *AS* curve next period will shift down to *AS"*. Thus the properties of the *AS* curve are those of the *WN* curve. This results from two assumptions: (1) the markup is fixed at *z*, and (2) output is proportional to employment.

The *AS* curve is the aggregate supply curve under conditions in which wages are less than fully flexible. Prices increase with the level of output because increased output implies increased employment, reduced unemployment, and therefore increased labor costs. The fact that prices in this model rise with output is entirely a reflection of the adjustments in the labor market, in which higher employment increases wages.

Properties of the Aggregate Supply Curve

We have now provided a derivation of the aggregate supply schedule, *AS*, and can, with the help of equation (8), explore its properties.

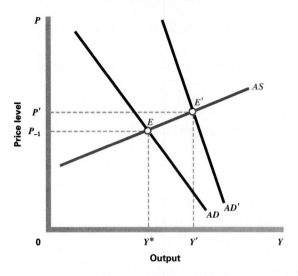

FIGURE 8-7

THE SHORT-RUN EFFECT OF AN INCREASE IN THE MONEY STOCK. The initial equilibrium at *E* is disturbed by an increase in the money stock that shifts the aggregate demand curve from *AD* to *AD'*. Short-run equilibrium is at *E'*, at which both the price level and output have increased. Prices are higher because the output expansion has caused an increase in wages, which is passed on into prices. The *AS* schedule is drawn quite flat, reflecting the assumption that wages are quite sticky.

1. The aggregate supply schedule is flatter the smaller the impact of output and employment changes on current wages. If wages respond very little to changes in unemployment, then the *AS* schedule shown in Figure 8-6 will be very flat. The coefficient λ in equation (8) captures this employment–wage-change linkage.
2. The position of the aggregate supply schedule depends on the past level of prices. The schedule passes through the full-employment level of output, Y^*, at $P = P_{-1}$. For higher output levels there is overemployment, and hence prices today are higher than those last period. Conversely, when unemployment is high, prices today will be below those last period.
3. The aggregate supply schedule shifts over time. If output is maintained above the full-employment level, Y^*, then over time wages continue to rise and the wage increases are passed on into increased prices.

   In Figures 8-7 and 8-8 we use the aggregate supply curve to examine the effects of a monetary expansion. This will give us a full understanding of both the short-run and long-run implications of the wage-price aggregate supply model.

8-4 THE EFFECTS OF A MONETARY EXPANSION

In Figure 8-7 we show the economy in full-employment equilibrium at point E. The aggregate supply schedule, AS, is drawn for a given past price level, P_{-1}. It passes through the full-employment output level, Y^*, at the price level P_{-1} because when output is at the full-employment level, there is no tendency for wages to change, and hence prices are also constant from period to period. The aggregate supply schedule is drawn relatively flat, suggesting a small effect of output and employment changes on wages.

Short-Run Effects

Suppose now that the nominal money stock is increased. At each price level real balances are higher, interest rates are lower, and hence the demand for output rises. The AD schedule shifts upward, proportionately to AD'. At the initial price level, $P = P_{-1}$, there is now an excess demand for goods. Firms find that their inventories are running down and accordingly hire more labor and raise output until the economy reaches E', the short-run equilibrium point. Note that at E' both output and prices have risen. A monetary expansion has led to a short-run increase in output. The rise in prices is due to the increase in labor costs as production and employment rise.

Compare now the short-run result with the Keynesian and classical models of Chapter 7 and the neoclassical model of this chapter. Our new equilibrium at E' has a feature of each: output is higher, and prices have risen. Whether we are more nearly in the classical or Keynesian situation depends entirely on the slope of the aggregate supply schedule, that is, on the coefficient λ, which translates employment changes into wage changes.

Medium-Term Adjustment

The short-run equilibrium at point E' is not the end of the story. At E' output is above normal. Therefore, as equation (7) indicates, prices *will keep on rising*. Consider now in Figure 8-8 what happens in the second period. Once we are in the second period, looking back, the price in the preceding period was P' at point E'. Therefore, the second-period supply curve passes through the full-employment output level at a price equal to P'. We show this by shifting the aggregate supply schedule up to AS', reflecting the increase in wages that has taken place since last period in response to the high level of employment.

With the new aggregate supply schedule, AS', and with the aggregate demand schedule unchanged at the higher level AD', the new equilibrium is at E''. Comparing E' and E'', we note that output now has fallen compared with the first period and prices have risen further. The increase in wages has been passed on by firms as an upward shift of the AS schedule, and the resulting price increase reduces real balances, raises interest rates, and lowers equilibrium income and spending. Thus, starting in the second period, we enter a phase of the adjustment process in which the initial expansion begins to be reversed—although output in period 2 is still above the full-employment level, Y^*. We continue this process by looking at the long-term adjustment.

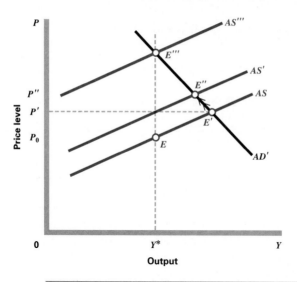

FIGURE 8-8

THE LONGER-TERM EFFECTS OF AN INCREASE IN THE MONEY STOCK. The increase in money stock led to a short-run equilibrium at E'. But because output is above the full-employment level, wages are rising and the *AS* curve is shifting upward. In the next period the *AS* curve shifts to AS', leading to equilibrium in that period at E'', with a higher price level than in the previous period, but lower output. The adjustment from E to E' reflects cost pressures that arise in an overemployed economy. Prices continue to rise and output to fall until the economy reaches equilibrium at E''', with aggregate supply curve AS''', at which point prices have risen in the same proportion as the money stock and output is back at Y^*.

Long-Term Adjustment

As long as output is above normal, employment is above normal, and therefore wages are rising. Because wages are rising, firms experience cost increases, and these are passed on, at each output level, as an upward shift of the aggregate supply schedule. As long as the short- and medium-term equilibrium positions of the economy (points E', E'', etc.) lie to the right of Y^*, the *AS* schedule is shifting upward and to the left. As a result, output will be declining toward the full-employment level and prices will keep rising. This adjustment is shown in Figure 8-8.

The upward-shifting *AS* schedule gives us a series of equilibrium positions on the *AD* schedule, starting with E' and moving up toward E'''. During the entire adjustment process, output is above the full-employment level, and prices are rising. The *AS* curve keeps shifting up, until the aggregate supply curve, AS''', intersects the aggregate demand curve at E''', at which point the economy has returned to full employment.

At E''', prices have risen in the same proportion as the nominal money stock, and so the real money stock, M/P, is again at the initial level. When real balances and therefore interest rates are again at the initial level, so are aggregate demand, output, and employment.

The Neutrality of Money

In the long run, once wages and prices have had time to adjust fully, the model has the same predictions as the classical case of Chapter 7: an increase in the money stock has no real effects. In the long run, according to our dynamic model of aggregate supply, *money is neutral*—it has no real effects, and it only affects prices.

But there is a crucial difference: *In this more realistic model of aggregate supply, money is neutral in the long run but not in the short run.* In the classical case a monetary expansion leads immediately to an equiproportionate rise in prices with no real expansion. Here, *both* output and prices rise in the short and medium term, and only in the long run do we reach the classical case. By assumption, though, the real wage remains constant in the adjustment process. In the short run the predictions of our model resemble the Keynesian case, and the more slowly wages adjust to changes in employment, the greater the resemblance.

Because the adjustments of wages and prices are, in fact, slow, the short- and medium-term adjustments are an essential aspect of macroeconomics. This is a point on which different groups of macroeconomists agree. We have developed the aggregate demand-supply model from the modern Keynesian approach and concluded that money is neutral in the long run but not the short run. Modern quantity theorists make the same point: monetary policy does have important effects on output in the short run, even if money is neutral in the long run.

8-5 SUPPLY SHOCKS

From the 1930s to the late 1960s, it was generally assumed that movements in output and prices in the economy were caused by shifts in the aggregate demand curve—by changes in monetary and fiscal policy (including wars as fiscal expansions) and investment demand. But the macroeconomic story of the 1970s was largely a story of *supply shocks.*

A supply shock is a disturbance to the economy whose first impact is to shift the aggregate supply curve. In the 1970s, the aggregate supply curve was shifted by two major oil price shocks, which increased the cost of production, and therefore increased the price at which firms were willing to supply output. In other words, the oil price shocks shifted the aggregate supply curve, in a way we shall shortly show.

Figure 8-9 shows the real or relative price of oil since 1971.[17] The first OPEC shock, which produced a quadrupling of the real price of oil between 1971 and 1974, helped push the economy into the 1973–1975 recession, up to then the worst recession of the post–World War II period. The second OPEC price increase, in 1979–1980,

---

[17]The relative price of oil is defined here as the world crude oil price deflated by the U.S. GNP deflator. It is expressed as an index, with the first quarter of 1981—the highest level attained over the period—as 100.

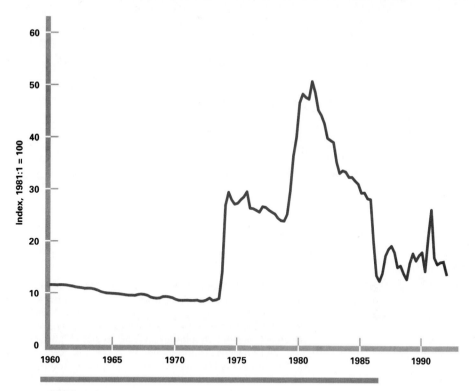

FIGURE 8-9
THE REAL PRICE OF OIL, 1971–1992. (in 1987 dollars).
(SOURCE: DRI/McGraw-Hill.)

doubled the price of oil and sharply accelerated the inflation rate. The high inflation led in 1980–1982 to a tough monetary policy to fight the inflation, with the result that the economy went into even deeper recession than in 1973–1975. After 1982 the relative price of oil fell throughout the 1980s, with a particularly sharp decline in 1985–1986. There was a brief oil price shock in the second half of 1990, as a result of the Iraqi invasion of Kuwait. That temporary oil price shock played a part in worsening the recession of 1990–1991, though the recession began in July, before Kuwait was invaded.

The two oil-price-shock–related recessions of the 1970s leave no doubt that supply shocks matter. We analyze their effect by incorporating prices of raw materials into the aggregate supply curve.

Incorporating Materials Prices in the Analysis

In equation (6) labor costs (and the markup) were the only determinants of output prices. Materials such as energy or copper or cotton were not explicitly included. But

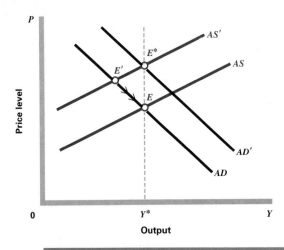

FIGURE 8-10

AN ADVERSE SUPPLY SHOCK. An increase in the real price of oil shifts the aggregate supply schedule upward and to the left because the cost of production is now higher at each level of output. Because wages do not adjust enough in the short run, the economy moves into an unemployment equilibrium at *E'*. Prices are higher and output is lower because of the reduction in real balances. Over time, wages decline because of unemployment and the economy returns to the initial equilibrium at *E*. Accommodating monetary or fiscal policies could shift the *AD* schedule to *AD'*, reducing the unemployment effects of the supply shock but increasing its inflationary impact.

these goods are used as inputs, and their prices, too, have an impact on the prices of final goods.

We incorporate materials prices in our analysis by modifying the price equation to include not only labor costs and the markup, but also *materials prices*, which we denote by P_m:

$$P = \frac{W(1 + z)}{a} + \Theta P_m \tag{9}$$

In equation (9) the term Θ denotes the materials requirement per unit of output (including a markup), and hence ΘP_m is the component of unit costs that comes from materials inputs.

The wage rate, we recall, increases with the level of output. Hence from equation (9) we still get an upward-sloping supply curve. Further, any increase in the price of materials will increase the price level at a given W. Thus an increase in P_m shifts the *AS* curve upward, as in Figure 8-10.

Alternatively, we can write the price equation in terms of the *relative* or *real* price of materials, which we denote by the lowercase p_m. The relative price is given by

$$p_m = \frac{P_m}{P} \tag{10}$$

Substituting from equation (10) into (9) gives us a modified equation linking wages and prices:

$$P = \frac{1 + z}{1 - \Theta p_m} \frac{W}{a} \qquad 1 > \Theta p_m \tag{11}$$

Equation (11) shows that for given wages, profit margins, and labor productivity, an increase in the real price of materials will increase prices simply because it raises costs. The impact of a change in real materials prices, therefore, is to shift the aggregate supply schedule upward at each level of output, as in Figure 8-10.

An Adverse Supply Shock

An *adverse supply shock* shifts the aggregate supply curve up. Figure 8-10 shows the effects of such a shock—an increase in the price of oil—reflecting an increase in p_m in equation (11). The *AS* curve shifts upward to *AS'*, and the equilibrium of the economy moves from *E* to *E'*. The immediate effect of the supply shock is thus to raise the price level and reduce the level of output. An adverse supply shock is doubly unfortunate: it causes *higher* prices and *lower* output.

There are two points to note about the impact of the supply shock. First, the shock shifts the *AS* curve upward because each unit of output now costs firms more to produce. Second, we are assuming that the supply shock does not affect the level of potential output, which remains at Y^*.[18]

What happens after the shock has hit? In Figure 8-10, the economy moves from *E'* back to *E*. The unemployment at *E'* forces wages and thus the price level down. The adjustment is slow because wages are slow to adjust. The adjustment takes place along the *AD* curve, with wages falling until *E* is reached.

At *E* the economy is back at full employment, with the price level the same as it was before the shock. But the nominal wage rate is lower than it was before the shock, because the unemployment in the meantime has forced the wage down. Thus the *real* wage, too, is lower than it was before the shock: the adverse supply shock reduces the real wage.[19]

---

[18] The increase in the price of oil in the 1970s both shifted up the *AS* curve and reduced the level of potential output because firms reduced their use of oil and could not use capital as efficiently as before. But we are assuming in Fig. 8-12 that the supply shock does not affect Y^*.

[19] In the problem set, we give you relevant data from the 1973–1975 period and ask you to apply the analysis of Fig. 8-10 to the case of the first OPEC oil shock.

Accommodation of Supply Shocks

Both fiscal and monetary policy barely responded when the first oil price shock hit the economy at the end of 1973. Because supply shocks were then a new phenomenon, neither economists nor policy makers knew what, if anything, could be done about them. But when the unemployment rate went above 8 percent at the end of 1974, both monetary and fiscal policy turned stimulatory in 1975–1976. These policies helped the economy recover from the recession more rapidly than it otherwise would have.

But why not always respond to an adverse supply shock with stimulatory policy? To answer that question, we look again at Figure 8-10. If the government had, at the time of the oil price increase, increased aggregate demand enough, the economy could have moved to E^* rather than E'. Prices would have risen by the full extent of the upward shift in the aggregate supply curve. Money wages would have remained unchanged, and the economy would have stayed at full employment. Of course, the real wage would have been lower, but in the end it is lower anyway.

The monetary and fiscal policies that shift the *AD* curve to *AD'* in Figure 8-10 are known as *accommodating* policies.[20] There has been a disturbance that requires a fall in the real wage. Policy is adjusted to make possible, or accommodate, that fall in the real wage *at the existing nominal wage*.

So the question now is why accommodating policies were not undertaken in 1973–1975. The answer is that there is a tradeoff between the inflationary impact of a supply shock and its recessionary effects. The more accommodation there is, the greater the inflationary impact of the shock and the smaller the unemployment impact. The policy mix actually chosen resulted in an intermediate position—some inflation (quite a lot) and some unemployment.

The Effects of a Favorable Oil Shock

The short-run analysis shows an adverse supply shock increasing the price level and decreasing GNP, and also decreasing the real wage. A favorable oil price shock should reduce the price level, increase GNP, and raise the real wage. What effect did the favorable oil shock of 1986, in fact, have? Although it is difficult to disentangle the timing of the impact of the lower oil prices in 1986, the oil price decline helped increase and maintain rapid low-inflation growth in the industrialized economies in 1987 and 1988. Table 8-1 shows the growth rate of real GNP and inflation for the seven largest economies (taken together) between 1986 and 1989. The combination of increased growth and low inflation is at least in part a result of the decline of oil prices in 1986.

Inflation and Unemployment, 1961–1992

In Figure 8-1 we showed how data on inflation and unemployment after 1969 were not consistent with the simple Phillips curve relationship shown in Figures 8-4 and

---

[20] In Chapter 5 we defined an accommodating monetary policy as one that increases the money supply when there is a fiscal expansion, so as to keep interest rates from rising. The term is also used more generally, as in this paragraph.

TABLE 8-1

GROWTH AND INFLATION OF INDUSTRIALIZED COUNTRIES*
(percent per annum)

	1986	1987	1988	1989
Real GNP growth	2.7	3.4	4.1	3.3
Inflation (GNP deflator)	3.1	3.2	3.6	4.5

*Data are for the seven largest OECD economies: the United States, Japan, Germany, France, Italy, the United Kingdom, and Canada.

SOURCE: OECD.

8-2, and we said that evidently something other than unemployment affects the rates of change of wages and prices. We have now introduced one additional element—supply shocks, which shift the aggregate supply curve. In several periods after 1969, inflation and unemployment increased together. That happened especially between 1973 and 1975, and 1979 and 1981. Supply shocks help account for those changes in inflation and unemployment.

The final element that has to be added to the theory of aggregate supply is *expectations of inflation*. That task will be addressed in Chapters 9 and 16.

8-6 SUMMARY

This chapter has covered a lot of hard ground. The major point is that in the short run, the aggregate supply curve is positively sloped. Over time, however, wages, costs, and prices will keep rising if output is above normal and keep falling if output is below normal, and the long-run aggregate supply curve is accordingly vertical.

We summarize the contents of the chapter as follows:

1. The frictions that exist in real-world labor markets as workers enter the labor market and look for jobs, or shift between jobs, mean that there is always some frictional unemployment. The amount of frictional unemployment that exists at full employment is the *natural rate* of unemployment.
2. The labor market does not adjust quickly to disturbances. Rather the adjustment process takes time. The Phillips curve shows that nominal wages change slowly in accordance with the level of employment. Wages tend to rise when employment is high and fall when employment is low.
3. The theory of aggregate supply is not yet settled. Several explanations have been offered for the basic fact that the labor market does not adjust quickly to shifts in aggregate demand: the imperfect information market clearing approach, of which the rational expectations equilibrium approach is a special case; coordination problems; efficiency wages and costs of price changes; and contracts and long-term relationships between firms and workers. All tend to point in the same

direction, a positively sloped short-run supply curve and a vertical long-run supply curve.

4. In deriving the supply curve, we emphasize the long-run relationships between firms and workers and the fact that wages are generally held fixed for some period, such as a quarter or, more frequently, a year. We also take into account the fact that wage changes are not coordinated among firms.

5. The short-run aggregate supply curve is derived in four steps: output is assumed proportional to employment; prices are set as a markup over costs; the wage is the main element of cost and adjusts according to the Phillips curve; and the Phillips curve relationship between the wage and unemployment is therefore transformed into a relationship between the price level and output.

6. The short-run aggregate supply curve shifts over time: if output is above (below) the full employment level this period, the aggregate supply curve shifts up (down) next period.

7. A shift in the aggregate demand curve increases the price level and output. The increase in output and employment increases wages somewhat in the current period. The full impact of changes in aggregate demand on prices occurs only over the course of time. High levels of employment generate increases in wages that feed into higher prices. As wages adjust, the aggregate supply curve shifts until the economy returns to equilibrium.

8. The aggregate supply curve is derived from the underlying assumptions that wages (and prices) are not adjusted continuously and that they are not all adjusted together. The positive slope of the aggregate supply curve is a result of some wages being adjusted in response to market conditions and of previously agreed overtime rates coming into effect as employment changes. The slow movement of the supply curve over time is a result of the slow and uncoordinated process by which wages and prices are adjusted.

9. Materials prices, along with wages, are a determinant of costs and prices. Changes in materials prices are passed on as changes in prices and, therefore, as changes in real wages. Materials price changes have been an important source of aggregate supply shocks.

10. Supply shocks pose a problem for macroeconomic policy. They can be accommodated through an expansionary aggregate demand policy, with the effect of increased prices but stable output. Alternatively, they can be offset, so that prices remain stable because of deflationary aggregate demand policy, but then output falls.

KEY TERMS

Frictionless neoclassical model
Frictional unemployment
Natural rate of unemployment
Phillips curve
Unit labor cost
Markup

Sticky wages
Coordination problem
Contracting approach
Labor productivity
Supply shock
Accommodation of supply shocks

PROBLEMS

1. Using Figures 8-7 and 8-8, analyze the effects of a reduction in the money stock on the price level and on output when the aggregate supply curve is positively sloped and wages adjust slowly over time.

2. In problem 1, what happens to the level of real balances as a result of the reduction in the nominal money stock?

3. Suppose that the productivity of labor rises—coefficient a in equation (1) increases. What are the short- and long-run impacts on prices, output, and the real wage?

4. Discuss the short-run and long-run adjustments to an increase in government spending, using diagrams similar to Figures 8-7 and 8-8.

5. Suppose the economy is in a recession. How can monetary and fiscal policies speed the recovery? What would happen in the absence of these policies?

6. The government increases income taxes. What are the effects of output, prices, and interest rates (a) in the short run and (b) in the long run?

7. Discuss why wages move only sluggishly.

8. Use the aggregate supply and demand framework to show the effect of a decline in the real price of materials. Show the effects (a) in the short run and (b) in the long run.

9. Suppose a policy could be found to shift the AS curve down.
    (a) What are the effects?
    (b) Why do you think there is great interest in such policies? [In Chapter 17 we discuss the use of *income policies* that are intended to shift the AS schedule down.]

10. Suppose that an increase in materials prices is accompanied by a fall in the level of potential output. There is no change in monetary or fiscal policy, and so the AD curve does not shift.
    (a) What is the long-run effect of the disturbance on prices and output? Compare the effect with the case in the text in which potential output does not fall.
    (b) Assume that the upward shift of the AS schedule leads initially to a decline in output below the new potential level. Then show the adjustment process by which output and prices reach the new long-run equilibrium.

11. The accompanying table presents data from the period 1973–1975, the first oil price shock. Use a diagram similar to Figure 8-10 to explain whether these data are consistent with the aggregate demand-supply model.

	1974	1975
Real fuel price, 1973 = 100	122.6	138.8
GNP deflator, 1973 = 100	108.8	118.9
Real GNP growth, % per year	−0.6	−1.2
Real wage change % per year	−2.8	0.8

COMPUTER EXERCISES

1. Constuct a table with three columns, (a) through (c), to record the effects of the following three simulations on output (Y), prices (P), and wages (W):
    (a) Foreign producers of raw materials (such as petroleum) increase P_m by 0.5 to 1.5.

(b) In response to the increase in P_m find a fiscal policy ($\Delta\overline{A}$) that would stabilize Y (shorten the recession). Fill in the value of $\Delta\overline{A}$ in the column heading.

(c) In response to the increase in P_m there is no change in $\overline{A}$, but the Fed reduces the money supply by 20 to 80 in order to fight inflation.

Construct your table of responses with twelve rows, four for each of the three key variables, in order to track each variable from the (1) BASE value, to the (2) INITIAL value, to the (3) INTERMEDIATE value, and ending with the (4) FINAL value.

2. Which response to the increase in raw materials prices would you favor, 1(b) or 1(c)? Defend your choice. (What would happen if you tried to do both?)

3. Construct a parallel table to the one you created in exercise 1, with four columns to record the effects of the following four simulations on Y, P, and W (remembering to reset the BASE solution before each successive exercise):

(a) As a result of demographic change the labor force (LF) increases by 10 percent to 63.8.

(b) As a result of technical change labor productivity (a) increases by 10 percent to 11.

(c) Government spending increases by 50 ($\Delta\overline{A} = 50$).

(d) Government spending increases by 50 ($\Delta\overline{A} = 50$), but the sensitivity of wages to unemployment (e) increases to 3.0.

Once again construct your table of responses with twelve rows, four for each of the three key variables, in order to track each variable from the (1) BASE value, to the (2) INITIAL value, to the (3) INTERMEDIATE value, and ending with the (4) FINAL value.

4. Contrast the effects of 3(a) and 3(b).

5. What happens to the effectiveness of government policy (the amount by which output changes when either fiscal or monetary policy changes) when the sensitivity of wages to unemployment increases [comparing 3(d) with 3(c)]? Why?

9

THE RATIONAL EXPECTATIONS EQUILIBRIUM APPROACH

*R*ational expectations represented a revolution in macroeconomics when it was introduced 20 years ago and when it reached full flower 10 years later. At the time it seemed it would change forever the teaching of macroeconomics and especially its practice by policy makers. Some of that dramatic promise has failed to materialize, in part because empirical support for the challenging ideas discussed here has not been as full and convincing as its proponents had hoped. But even so, the impact has been massive. Macroeconomics should not be taught or practiced without an idea of the rational expectations equilibrium school. In a nutshell, the approach argues that markets clear and that there is nothing systematic that monetary policy can do to affect output or unemployment.

We start with the frictionless neoclassical model of the labor market, to illustrate how the labor market would work in an idealized model. Then we develop a powerful theoretical model advanced by Robert Lucas of the University of Chicago. This model is the most important example of the rational expectations equilibrium approach to macroeconomics.

The name identifies two key features of this approach. First, it places weight on the role of expectations and specifically *rational* expectations. Economic agents do not know the future with certainty and therefore have to base their plans and decisions, including price setting, on their forecasts or expectations of the future. The approach insists categorically that these expectations be made in a rational fashion, which means that agents use all available information as well as possible to come out with the best possible forecasts. Second, the model insists on *equilibrium*; the approach leaves no room for markets not to clear. Anyone who knows that he or she is unemployed makes a deal to get a job. In other words, markets work and such phenomena as insider-outsider effects or costs of price changes seen in the preceding chapter simply do not come into play.

Why study so extreme a model? The reason is that it sets a rigorous benchmark for what would happen in an economy if there were no frictions and if information

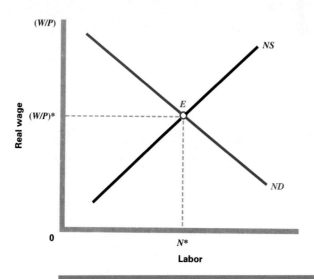

FIGURE 9-1

LABOR MARKET EQUILIBRIUM AND FULL EMPLOYMENT. The labor supply curve, *NS*, shows the quantity of labor supplied increasing with the real wage. Along *ND* a reduction in the real wage causes an increase in the quantity of labor demanded. The labor market is in equilibrium at point *E*, with real wage $(W/P)^*$ and employment N^*. Corresponding to the labor supply N^* there is a full-employment output level Y^*.

were used efficiently. It offers a challenge to competing approaches in showing where, specifically, they diverge from this very sharply drawn theory, particularly in explaining unemployment.

The chapter starts with the microeconomic foundations for the classical aggregate supply curve. From there we move to the Lucas model, followed by a very similar Keynesian model with rational expectations. We conclude with a discussion of *real business cycle* models, rational expectations equilibrium models in which economic fluctuations are caused entirely by real shocks—such as crop failures or changes in oil prices—that hit the economy, changing prices and output in markets that are always in equilibrium.

9-1 THE FRICTIONLESS NEOCLASSICAL MODEL OF THE LABOR MARKET

In this section we derive the classical, vertical, aggregate supply curve used in Chapter 7, starting from microeconomic foundations. Figure 9-1 presents a microeconomic analysis of the labor market. Both the demand for and supply of labor depend on the real wage. The real wage, W/P, is the ratio of the wage rate (W) to the price level (P), or the amount of goods that can be bought with an hour of work. The downward-sloping demand curve for labor, ND, shows that firms want to hire more labor when the real wage is lower: the quantity of labor demanded is greater the lower is the hourly real wage. Also shown is an upward-sloping supply curve of labor, NS, indicating that more labor is supplied the higher the real wage.

The full derivation of the demand curve for labor in Figure 9-1 is presented in the appendix to this chapter. Firms are assumed to be competitive and are therefore willing to pay a real wage equal to the value of the marginal product of labor. Firms' capital stock is fixed in the short run, and the marginal product of labor is therefore assumed to decrease as more labor is employed. As more labor is added, each new worker has less machinery with which to produce than the previous workers, and therefore the amount that each new worker adds to output (the marginal product of labor) is lower than the amount added by previous workers. Since firms are willing to employ labor up to the point where the marginal product of labor is equal to the real wage, they are willing to hire more labor only if the real wage is lower: the demand curve for labor slopes downward.

The supply curve of labor is shown as upward-sloping both because existing workers may be willing to work more when the real wage rises, and because as the wage rises, more workers come into the labor force seeking work. But the aggregate supply curve could be vertical (or completely inelastic) if the amount of labor supplied is insensitive to the real wage.[1]

The labor supply and demand curves intersect at point E, with a corresponding level of labor input or employment, N^*, and an equilibrium real wage, $(W/P)^*$. N^* is the *full-employment level of employment*. In this idealized, frictionless neoclassical model, everyone is working precisely as much as he or she wants to at the real wage, $(W/P)^*$, at point E. And firms are hiring precisely the amount of labor they want at the real wage, $(W/P)^*$, at point E. There is always full employment in the frictionless neoclassical world.

Corresponding to the full-employment level of employment, N^*, is the full-employment level of output, Y^*. That is the level of output that is produced using the existing amounts of other factors (the capital stock, land, and raw materials) and the full-employment amount of labor, N^*.[2]

In the frictionless neoclassical model, the equilibrium level of output is independent of the price level. That is, the aggregate supply curve is vertical as already shown for this classical case in Chapter 7. We can see this point most clearly by considering

---

[1]If you have studied microeconomics, you have probably seen the "backward-bending" labor supply curve, which is negatively sloped at high wages. That occurs because when the wage rises, individuals can both work less and earn more income. They may therefore choose to respond to higher wages by working less. Although the labor supply curve may well slope backward in the long run (we work fewer hours than our grandparents did and have much higher wages than they had), the supply curve of labor *for the economy* in the short run of a few years is positively sloped. That is because as the wage rises, people who were not working decide it is worthwhile to take a job rather than work at home, and they enter the labor force. Further, people already on the job may, in the short run, want to work longer hours when the real wage rises.

[2]In our description here, technology and the stock of capital are given. But these can change over time, and as a result, the full-employment level of output will change too. An increase in the capital stock, or an improvement in technology, raises full-employment output.

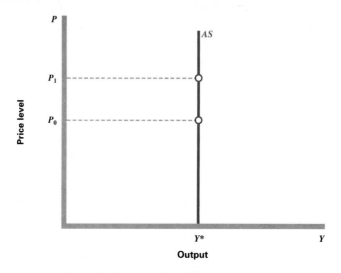

FIGURE 9-2

THE PRICE LEVEL AND FULL EMPLOYMENT: THE AGGREGATE SUPPLY
CURVE. The frictionless neoclassical model implies the vertical
aggregate supply curve of the classical case in Chapter 7. The full-
employment level of output Y^*, corresponding to full employment
N^* in Figure 9-1, is supplied no matter what the price level. If the
price level increases, say, from P_0 to P_1, the nominal wage increases
in the same proportion and the labor market continues in
equilibrium.

what happens in the labor market when the price level changes. Full employment
prevails for an initial price level at N^* with a money wage W_0. If the price level were
to change, say, to increase from P_0 to P_1 in Figure 9-2, the wage rate would increase
in the same proportion—recall that wages are fully flexible—so that the real wage
would remain unchanged, and output would also be unchanged. Hence the aggregate
supply curve is vertical, as shown in Figure 9-2.

*The full neoclassical theory of aggregate supply thus asserts that unemployment
is always at the natural rate, output always at the full-employment level, and any
unemployment is purely frictional.* Changes in the price level, for example, as a result
of an increase in the money stock, leave output and employment unchanged. Money
wages will rise, but since the real wage is unchanged, neither the quantity of labor
supplied nor that demanded will change. The analysis of the classical case in Chapter
7 applies in full: neither monetary nor fiscal policy changes will have *any* effect on
output. The Lucas model, which we now study, offers a qualified departure from
that conclusion.

9-2 THE MARKET-CLEARING APPROACH: THE LUCAS SUPPLY CURVE

Robert Lucas is the intellectual founder of the *rational expectations equilibrium* approach to macroeconomics, which seeks to explain all macroeconomic phenomena

starting from microeconomic foundations and assuming that markets clear and expectations are rational. The aggregate supply curve we derive in this section is the leading example of this approach.[3]

The model is the neoclassical labor market which we just saw, with one changed assumption: some people do not know the aggregate price level but do know the absolute (dollar) wage or price at which they can buy and sell. For instance, at a given moment, a worker knows that the going wage rate is $12 per hour but does not know all prices in the economy and hence the aggregate price level, and thus does not know the real wage (the nominal wage divided by the price level, equal to the amount of goods the wage will buy).

Assume as in the neoclassical model that labor supply depends on the *real* wage. Since it is the real wage, not the nominal wage, that determines whether and how many hours she wants to work, the worker has somehow to estimate the aggregate price level. In Figure 9-1 we showed the upward-sloping labor supply curve, NS, and downward-sloping labor demand curve, ND. If both firms and workers have full information, the real wage will adjust to the level $(W/P)^*$, at which there is full employment of labor at the level N^*; corresponding to labor employment of N^*, output is at its full-employment level, Y^*.

W/P^* is the *full-employment real wage*. Next we assume that workers and firms do not have the same information about the actual aggregate price level at the time that they decide how much work is to be done. Suppose that beforehand both firms and workers expected the price level to be P^e. Figure 9-3 shows the *nominal* wage, W, on the vertical axis, and labor supply and demand curves. Labor supply curve NS^* corresponds to the supply curve when workers think the actual price level is P^e. Labor demand curve ND^* shows the labor demand curve when firms also believe the actual price level is P^e. If each is correct, the level of employment will be N^* at wage rate W^*, corresponding to the equilibrium real wage $(W/P)^*$ $(= W^*/P^e)$ in Figure 9-3.

Now suppose that at any given time the firms know the *actual* price level, P, whereas workers are not informed about the actual price level and believe it is P^e. Suppose in particular that the actual price level, P, exceeds the expected price level, P^e. Here comes the crucial point: at any given nominal wage, firms now demand more labor than they would have if the price level were P^e. Why? Because at the actual price level, P, and any given nominal wage, say W_0, the *real* wage (W_0/P) is lower than it would be at the same nominal wage and P^e [i.e., with $P > P^e$, $(W_0/P) < W_0/P^e)$].

In Figure 9-3 ND' shows the labor demand curve of firms when they know the price level is P (which is greater than P^e). As a result of the shift in the labor demand curve to ND', the nominal wage rises from W^* to W'. At the same time, the level of employment rises from N^* to N'. *Thus as a result of the imperfect information of the workers, a rise in the price level leads to an increase in the level of employment, and therefore of output.* We could similarly show that if the actual price level is below the

[3]The model we present here is presented in Lucas's famous article, "Some International Evidence on Output-Inflation Tradeoffs," *American Economic Review*, June 1973. A full range of articles in this tradition is presented in Robert E. Lucas and Thomas Sargent (eds.), *Rational Expectations* (Minneapolis: University of Minnesota Press, 1981), 2 vols. For other expositions, see Steven Sheffrin, *Rational Expectations* (New York: Cambridge University Press, 1983), Kevin Hoover, *The Classical Macroeconomics* (Oxford: Basil Blackwell, 1988), and Olivier Blanchard and Stanley Fischer, *Lectures on Macroeconomics* (Cambridge, Mass.: MIT Press, 1989).

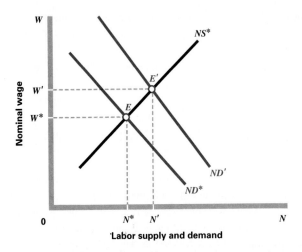

FIGURE 9-3

THE EFFECT OF AN UNANTICIPATED INCREASE IN THE PRICE LEVEL. The
labor supply and demand curves are now shown as functions of the
nominal wage, which is on the vertical axis. Their position thus
depends on the price level expected by firms (the labor demand
curve) and workers (labor supply), respectively. With the price level
equal to and expected by both firms and workers to be P^e, the
equilibrium nominal wage is W^* and employment is N^*. When the
price level increases to P, but workers do not know that, the labor
demand curve shifts to ND' but the supply curve stays put. The
nominal wage and output both rise, to W' and N', respectively.
Workers willingly supply more labor in the mistaken belief that their
real wage has risen. Firms willingly employ more workers in the
correct belief that the real wage has fallen.

predicted level, the demand-for-labor curve would shift to the left, the nominal wage
and employment would fall, and accordingly output would fall.

We want to explore in a bit more detail the mechanism that causes an increase
in the price level to raise output in Figure 9-3. The key assumption is the difference
in information between firms and workers. When the price level rises, workers do not
know that. All they can see is that the nominal wage they are being offered has risen.
Therefore they think the real wage is higher, and they are willing to work more. Thus
at point E' in Figure 9-3, there is a difference of views between firms and workers on
what the real wage is. Firms know that at E' the real wage is lower than $(W/P)^*$ in
Figure 9-1; workers by contrast believe the real wage is higher than $(W/P)^*$. Without
that difference in views, the increase in the price level would not have increased output.

Shouldn't workers refuse to work any more than N^* when there is an increase
in the demand for their services? After all, they know the firms are better informed
than they are and should suspect they will end up with a lower real wage than
$(W/P)^*$. This would be true if the demand in a given market were affected only by

TABLE 9-1
THE LUCAS SUPPLY CURVE

	underpredicted	correctly predicted	overpredicted
P/P^e	> 1	$= 1$	< 1
$(W/P)/(W/P)^*$	< 1	$= 1$	> 1
Y/Y^*	> 1	$= 1$	< 1

increases in aggregate demand or the aggregate price level. However, so long as there are also relative shifts in demand, so that a worker in a given market *may* be facing a relative increase in the demand for her or his services, workers will respond to increases in the wages they are offered—on the basis that the increase in demand may be a result of a relative shift in demand.[4]

We summarize by writing the aggregate supply curve that emerges from this model with imperfect information:

The Lucas supply curve:
$$Y = \psi \frac{P}{P^e} \qquad (1)$$

where output increases with P/P^e through the mechanism described in Figure 9-3. The Lucas supply curve shows that the amount of output firms are willing to supply increases as the ratio of the actual to the expected price level increases.[5]

Table 9-1 shows how the actual real wage, employment, and output are related to P/P^e. To give an example, if price predictions are too high, so that the actual price level is below the expected price level (third column), then the actual real wage turns out to be too high for full employment and the level of output will be below the full-employment level. The Lucas supply curve is shown in Figure 9-4. For instance, at point B, P is greater than P^e, the actual real wage will be lower than $(W/P)^*$, and output will be above Y^*.

Adding the Demand Side

The next step is to close the model by talking about how the expected price level is determined. In Box 7-1 we developed an equation for the equilibrium price level along the AD demand schedule:

---

[4]This is worked out in detail in the article by Lucas cited in footnote 3.

[5]The particular justification for the Lucas supply function offered in Fig. 9-4 was developed by Milton Friedman in "The Role of Monetary Policy," *American Economic Review*, March 1968. Lucas's contribution was to develop the microeconomic foundations for the incomplete information approach and show that they resulted in a supply equation of the form of equation (1). For the Lucas supply curve to take the form of equation (1), it is not necessary that firms know the aggregate price level while workers do not. Rather, the assumption is that firms have a more accurate estimate of the price level than workers.

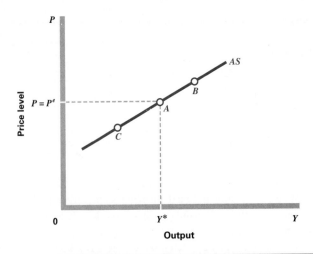

FIGURE 9-4
THE LUCAS SUPPLY CURVE. The *AS* curve represents equation (1) and is drawn for a given expected price level, P^e. If the actual price level is equal to the expected price level, that is, $P = P^e$, the amount of output supplied is Y^*. If prices are higher, and hence real wages are lower, firms supply more output than Y^*, and conversely if prices are lower.

Aggregate demand:
$$P = \frac{\beta \overline{M}}{Y - \gamma \overline{A}}$$
(2)

We turn now to the *rational expectations* aspect of this approach. How are firms and workers to form expectations of the price level? The rational expectations approach assumes people use all relevant information in forming expectations of economic variables. In particular, we assume that workers and firms will think through the economic mechanisms underlying the determination of the expected price level. How should they figure that out?

Households and firms expect that full employment will prevail. To determine that level of output, they need to figure out the expected price level. At the expected price level

- There are no expectational errors, $P = P^e$, and output is expected to be at the full-employment level, Y^*.

- The price level must be such as to equate aggregate demand and supply, that is, $AS = AD$.

The combination of these restrictions assures that, in forming expectations, people expect there to be market clearing, which is implied by the conditions $AS = AD$, and that there are no conscious forecasting errors. The combination of these restrictions characterizes the rational expectations equilibrium approach.

Households will therefore use equation (2) to forecast prices, setting $Y = Y*$. They set output for forecasting purposes at the full-employment level because, being rational, they do not expect to make forecasting errors, and only forecasting errors can lead to divergences between actual and expected real wages or actual and full-employment output. Here is a central implication of the rational expectations approach: people may not always get forecasts right, but they do not anticipate making *systematic* errors.

In using equation (2) to calculate the expected price level, it is not enough to assume that the economy will be at full employment. People also need to predict the money stock (and the level of autonomous demand, which we shall assume they know). Whatever way people predict the money stock, let M^e be the expected money stock. Then our prediction of the price level, P^e, under rational expectations, is

$$P^e = \frac{\beta M^e}{Y* - \gamma \bar{A}} \tag{3}$$

Note how price prediction now revolves around predicting the money stock.

We are now ready to see the implications of the Lucas supply curve approach, namely, the distinction between anticipated and unanticipated changes in the money supply. In Figure 9-5 we show aggregate supply and demand curves. The aggregate demand curves are familiar from earlier figures. The aggregate supply curve is based on equation (1), the Lucas supply curve. The position of the aggregate supply curve depends on the expected price level.

Consider Figure 9-5a. The AS curve is the aggregate supply curve for a given initial expected price level P_0^e. Now suppose the money supply is increased and the increase was expected. We are thus dealing with an *anticipated* increase in the money stock. The aggregate demand curve certainly shifts up in proportion to the increase in the money stock. But at output level $Y*$, so does the aggregate supply curve: as equation (1) shows, at $Y*$, P^e increases in the same proportion as the expected increase in money stock.

Accordingly the new equilibrium of the economy is at E', with a price level, P, equal to P_1^e, corresponding to the higher money stock, and unchanged output. Underlying this result are adjustments in the labor market: both firms and workers knew that the money stock and aggregate demand were going to increase in the proportion P_1^e/P_0^e, and accordingly the nominal wage went up in that same proportion.[6] Thus with anticipated increases in money there are no *real* effects (just as in the classical case before!); money, nominal wages, prices—actual and expected—all increase in the same proportion.

Consider next the case of *un*anticipated money. Now, because there is no change in the price level expected by workers, we have the situation illustrated in Figure 9-5b. The increase in the money stock causes the aggregate demand curve to move to

---

[6]You may want to use a figure like Fig. 9-3 to make sure that you understand why the nominal wage rises in the same proportion as the price level is expected to rise when both firms and workers have the same expectations.

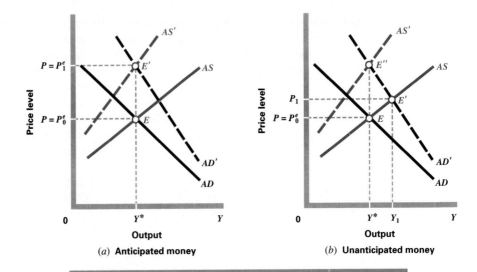

(a) **Anticipated money**
(b) **Unanticipated money**

FIGURE 9-5
EXPECTED AND UNEXPECTED INCREASES IN MONEY. (a) An anticipated increase in money is fully reflected in expected prices and hence in the supply curve. With an anticipated increase in money *both* the *AS* and *AD* schedules shift upward in the same proportion at output level Y^*. Hence, at the new equilibrium, at E', output remains at the level Y^*. Thus anticipated money increases have no *real* effects. (b) An unanticipated increase in money is not reflected in expected prices. Therefore initially only the *AD* schedule shifts. The short-run equilibrium is at E' with output higher. But because prices exceed expected prices, expectations will now be revised upward, the *AS* schedule will shift, and the economy will move eventually to E''. Unexpected money increases therefore have real effects, but the effects will be transitory.

AD', as in Figure 9-5a. But because the workers did not expect the price level to rise, the aggregate supply curve, *AS*, does not shift. As a result we move to a new equilibrium at point E'. Here actual prices have increased above expected prices, that is, $P > P_0^e$, and as a result output has increased. Thus unanticipated (by the workers) monetary expansion leads to an increase in output.

But note immediately that under rational expectations this state of affairs, point E', cannot last for long. Prices are above expectations, and households and firms will revise their forecasts. For example, if households and firms expect the increase in the money stock to be maintained, they revise their price expectations upward, to P_1^e. Then the *AS* schedule shifts upward to AS'. Thus changes in money matter only while they are unexpected, and an increase in money cannot be unexpected forever: money has only a short-lived influence on activity and is soon *fully* reflected in prices.

Equivalently, this is another theory that predicts that changes in the money stock will have real effects only in the (very) short run, but will be fully neutral in the long run. In fact, they will be fully neutral the very moment economic agents find out about the change in money and use the new information to recalculate the equilibrium wages and prices corresponding to full employment. The central assumptions leading to this result are that expectations are formed rationally and that markets clear.

Policy Irrelevance

At first sight, the Lucas model seems to be almost the same as the classical model; both models predict that neither monetary nor fiscal policy can affect the equilibrium level of income in the long run. The Lucas model is more interesting, though, than the classical model because it offers at least *transitory* deviations from full employment. But the key point about these transitory deviations from full employment is that they are the result of expectations errors and they last only as long as the errors last, and that cannot be very long.[7]

Moreover, there is no room for monetary policy systematically to affect output in this world of rational expectations and market clearing. If agents make forecasting mistakes, the government need simply announce the new statistics and the market will immediately go back to full employment. There is no need for accommodating monetary or fiscal policy to hasten the return to full employment. In fact, in some versions of this approach, policy responses are problematic because they make it more complicated for economic agents to determine exactly what is happening in their economy and how best to adjust to it. This is a radically different perspective from a Keynesian world where an accommodating policy can offer relief from unemployment.

The Rational Expectations Equilibrium Approach: An Evaluation

There is no question that the rational expectations approach is not only intellectually challenging, but also original and impressive. The key question about any economic theory, though, is whether it helps us understand the economy. The aggregate demand–supply model we outlined here, with its implication that only unanticipated changes in monetary policy affect output, met originally with some empirical success. Early studies seemed to show that only unanticipated changes in the money stock increase output.[8] However, these results did not stand up to further testing.[9]

Nonetheless, several features of the approach developed by Lucas have become pervasively influential. First, the basic methodological viewpoint that, wherever possible, macroeconomic models should be developed from microeconomic foundations

---

[7]We have to make allowance here for more elaborate models in the tradition of rational expectations and market clearing. The output and employment response to a change in money can be persistent because the initial expectations effects trigger investment decisions, which change equilibrium employment and output over time.

[8]See, for instance, Robert Barro, "Unanticipated Money, Output, and the Price Level in the United States," *Journal of Political Economy*, August 1978.

[9]Two influential, if difficult, articles are John Boschen and Herschel Grossman, "Tests of Equilibrium Macroeconomics with Contemporaneous Monetary Data," *Journal of Monetary Economics*, November 1982, and Frederic Mishkin, "Does Anticipated Monetary Policy Matter? An Econometric Investigation," *Journal of Political Economy*, February 1982.

has become dominant. Second, the notions that expectations are important and that individuals should be assumed to form expectations rationally unless there is good reason for another assumption are also broadly accepted. The rational expectations equilibrium view survives in the real business cycle approach that we discuss in Section 9-4. It also plays a key role in the discussion of the question whether government, by creating unanticipated inflation, can fool workers and firms to produce more than full-employment output. The answer is simple: you cannot fool most people most of the time. Inflation policy cannot raise the level of output produced for any length of time.

9-3 A NEW KEYNESIAN ALTERNATIVE

A rigorous theoretical alternative to the equilibrium model is the *contracting approach* that is identified with the new Keynesian macroeconomics. The contracting approach also starts from the labor market and the frictionless neoclassical model of Section 8-1, but it assumes that the wage is fixed by contract at the beginning of a period (say a year) while prices of goods may change within the period.

The assumption is that both firms and workers set the wage at the level that they expect will produce equilibrium in the labor market. Thus in terms of Figure 9-1, they set a nominal wage, W_n, which they hope will correspond to a real wage, $(W/P)^*$, that is, the equilibrium real wage. Let P^e be the expected price level. Then the workers and firms will agree to set the wage at that level which is expected to make the real wage equal to $(W/P)^*$. This means that

$$(W_n/P^e) = (W/P)^*$$

Assuming for convenience that $(W/P)^*$ is equal to some constant v^*, then the nominal wage is set such that

$$W_n = v^*P^e \tag{4}$$

Once the wage has been set, firms will produce for the market, taking the cost of labor as given. Because of the assumed diminishing marginal productivity of labor, firms will want to supply more output the lower the real wage they face—or, since the nominal wage is fixed by contract, the higher the price level. Accordingly, there is in the short run a positively sloped aggregate supply curve:

$$Y = f(P/W_n) \tag{5}$$
$$= f(P/v^*P^e)$$

Note that, remarkably, this very different approach reaches exactly the same aggregate supply curve as the Lucas supply curve. Combined with the rational expectations assumption, this approach, too, implies that unanticipated changes in the money stock have real effects on output while anticipated changes do not. This simple form of the contracting approach is therefore also rejected by the evidence cited in footnote 9.

The contracting approach does, however, provide for an increased possibility of slow adjustment of prices when it is recognized that contracts are not all signed for only one period, and that they are not all renegotiated at the same time. Under those conditions, there can be room for the supply curve to shift slowly over time, as old contracts are renegotiated, and there is room for anticipated monetary policy changes to affect output for several years so long as there are some contracts in the economy with a longer life than that.

9-4 REAL BUSINESS CYCLES

The weakness of the empirical evidence for the view that only unanticipated money affects real output, implied by the Lucas model of Section 9-2, led to two reactions. Some economists believed that better explanations would have to be found for the role of money in the business cycle. Others questioned the evidence linking money with the business cycle at all.

In particular, economists working in the rational expectations equilibrium approach developed *equilibrium real business cycle* theory.[10] Real business cycle theory asserts that fluctuations in output and employment are the result of a variety of real shocks hitting the economy, with markets adjusting rapidly and remaining always in equilibrium.

There is a considerable amount of evidence that changes in the money stock are correlated with changes in output, even though the evidence is not consistent with the proposition that only unanticipated changes in money affect output. Real business cycle theorists explain this correlation as a result of changes in money *accommodating to* changes in output, rather than causing output changes.[11] The argument is that when output increases, the banking system expands money to finance the higher level of spending. Thus changes in the quantity of money do not cause the business cycle, even though they are correlated with it.

With monetary causes of the business cycle assumed out of the way, real business cycle theory is left with two tasks. The first is to explain the *shocks*, or *disturbances*, that hit the economy, causing fluctuations in the first place. The second is to explain the *propagation mechanisms*. A propagation mechanism is a mechanism through which a disturbance is spread through the economy. In particular, the aim is to explain why shocks to the economy seem to have long-lived effects. We start with propagation mechanisms.

[10]For a recent review of the real business cycle approach, see Chan Huh and Bharat Trehan, "Real Business Cycles: A Selective Survey," Federal Reserve Bank of San Francisco, *Economic Review*, Spring 1991. For a forceful negative view of real business cycle theory, see Lawrence Summers, "Some Skeptical Observations on Real Business Cycle Theory," Federal Reserve Bank of Minneapolis, *Quarterly Review*, Fall 1986. See also Charles Plosser, "Understanding Real Business Cycles," and N. Gregory Mankiw, "Real Business Cycles: A New Keynesian Perspective," both in *Journal of Economic Perspectives*, Summer 1989, and Gary D. Bensen and Randall Wright, "The Labor Market in Real Business Cycle Theory," Federal Reserve Bank of Minneapolis, *Quarterly Review*, Spring 1992.

[11]This view is developed in a technically advanced paper by Robert King and Charles Plosser, "Money, Credit and Prices in a Real Business Cycle Model," *American Economic Review*, June 1984.

Propagation Mechanisms

Among the mechanisms that real business cycle theory relies on to explain why a shock to the economy affects output for several years are movements in inventories and changes in investment caused by shifts in profitability. These are part of anyone's theory of the business cycle, and they will be discussed in more detail in Chapter 12.

The mechanism that is most associated with equilibrium business cycles, though, is *the intertemporal substitution of leisure*. Any theory of the business cycle has to explain why people work more at some times than at others: during booms employment is high and jobs are easy to find; during recessions people work less.

A simple equilibrium explanation would be that people work more in booms because wages are higher. That way they would voluntarily be supplying more labor in response to a higher wage. (Remember that the equilibrium approach requires people to be on their supply-and-demand curves at all times.) However, the facts are not strongly in favor of that argument because the real wage changes very little over the business cycle. People are thus not obviously working more in response to higher wages.

In the Keynesian approach developed in Chapter 8, changes in employment are caused primarily by shifts in aggregate demand, while the real wage stays constant as a result of markup pricing. People are unemployed in recessions because they cannot get work despite their willingness to work at the going wage. But the equilibrium approach assumes markets are in equilibrium. It therefore explains large movements in output with small movements in wages as follows: there is a high elasticity of labor supply in response to *temporary* changes in the wage. Or, as the argument is put, people are very willing to substitute leisure intertemporally.

The argument is that people care very little about when in any given period of a year or two they work. Suppose that within a 2-year period they plan to work 4,000 hours at the going wage (50 weeks each year for 40 hours a week). If wages are equal in the 2 years, they would work 2,000 hours each year. But if wages were just 2 percent higher in one year than the other, they might prefer to work, say, 2,200 hours in one year, forgoing vacations and working overtime, and 1,800 hours in the other. That way they work the same total amount and earn more total income.

Note that the intertemporal substitution of leisure does not mean that labor supply is sensitive to *permanent* changes in wages. If the wage rises, and will stay higher, then there is nothing to be gained by working more this period than next. So it is quite possible for the response of labor supply to a permanent change in wages to be very small, even though the response to a temporary wage change is large.[12]

This intertemporal substitution of leisure is clearly capable of generating large movements in the amount of work done in response to small shifts in wages—and thus could account for large output effects in the cycle accompanied by small changes in wages. However, there has not been strong empirical support for this view either.

Disturbances

The inventory, investment, and intertemporal substitution of leisure mechanisms that propagate business cycles are set in motion by events or *disturbances* that change the

---

[12]In problem 10, we ask you to show what this statement means for the slope of the labor supply curve in Fig. 9-1.

equilibrium levels of output and employment in individual markets and the economy as a whole.

The most important disturbances isolated by equilibrium business cycle theorists are shocks to *productivity*, or supply shocks, and shocks to *government spending*. A productivity shock changes the level of output produced by given amounts of inputs. Changes in the weather and new methods of production are examples. Suppose there is a temporary favorable productivity shock this period. Then individuals will want to work harder to take advantage of the higher productivity. In working more this period they raise output. They will also invest more, thus spreading the productivity shock into future periods by raising the stock of capital. If the effect of the intertemporal substitution of leisure is strong, even a small productivity shock could have a relatively large effect on output.

Increased government spending is another type of shock. To provide the extra goods the government needs, individuals will work harder if the real wage rises and save more and consume less if the real (after-inflation) interest rate rises. Thus we should expect an increase in government spending to raise the real wage and the interest rate.[13]

Research on real business cycles continues in the 1990s, though it probably peaked in the second half of the 1980s. The influence of the rational expectations equilibrium approach is sure to survive though, especially in its goal of building macroeconomics on sound microeconomic foundations. There is no doubt, too, that some of the mechanisms, such as inventory accumulation and investment dynamics, that underlie the theory's explanation of the dynamics of the business cycle will form part of future business cycle models, as they have of past and current business cycle models. But there is increasing recognition even among early proponents of real cycle theory that business cycle models should include an important role for monetary factors.

9-5 SUMMARY

1. With wages and prices freely flexible, the equilibrium level of employment is determined in the labor market. The labor market is continuously in equilibrium at the full-employment level of employment. Aggregate supply would therefore be the amount of output produced by that amount of labor. Given that the labor market is always in equilibrium, the aggregate supply curve is vertical at the full-employment level of output.

2. An increase in prices leaves the equilibrium in the labor market unchanged: firms are willing to increase the wages they pay at the full-employment level of employment in proportion to the price increase. Workers require an increase in wages proportional to prices in order to supply an unchanged level of effort. Hence equilibrium wages rise in proportion to prices, and employment and hence output are unchanged.

3. The rational expectations equilibrium approach builds on *imperfect* information. With imperfect information there is room to make errors, but there is no excuse to make systematic or persistent errors.

---

[13]Note that an increase in government spending raises the interest rate in the *IS-LM* model too, though it is usually assumed in that model that government spending crowds out investment more than consumption.

4. The market-clearing feature of the rational expectations equilibrium approach is borrowed from the classical model: wages and prices are fully flexible. As a result, the labor market and the product market always clear.

5. The basic model of the rational expectations equilibrium approach has wages set on the basis of *expected* prices, using all available information to make price forecasts. If prices actually are higher than expected, firms find it profitable to hire more workers and produce more output. But this situation cannot last because workers will use the new information to revise upward their price forecasts and hence their wage demands. As a result, unanticipated money has real effects, while anticipated money does not.

6. The rational expectations equilibrium approach has not fared well in empirical testing. Specifically, anticipated money does have effects on employment in direct contradiction of the basic hypothesis.

7. Even though the rational expectations approach has been unsuccessful in empirical terms, it has become an important part of macroeconomics. There are three main reasons. First, it is a very elegant construction. Second, the idea of rational expectations is attractive. Why would economic agents not make the best forecasts they can possibly make; why would they not use information efficiently? Third, the approach is built on clear and simple microeconomic foundations.

8. The rational expectations approach has clarified where macroeconomics must search for explanations of persistent unemployment and the real effects of monetary policy. The most fruitful direction to look is toward the labor market for institutional arrangements that have economic motives (such as raising productivity) but have as a counterpart limits on wage cutting.

9. The new Keynesian approach builds the transitory effects of a money supply change on the idea that contracts *predetermine* wages. As a result, when money increases in an unanticipated fashion but wage contracts are locked in, there can be a real expansion at least for a while.

10. The equilibrium real business cycle theory denies any causal role for money in the business cycle. Rather the cycle is seen as resulting from real shocks or disturbances that hit the economy and are then propagated to other markets and through time. The main distinctive propagation mechanism is the intertemporal substitution of leisure. The main real shocks are to productivity and government spending.

11. The appendix shows how to derive a demand curve for labor from a production function. Firms' optimal employment strategy is to hire labor to the point where the marginal product of labor is equal to the real wage.

KEY TERMS

Classical labor market
Market-clearing approach
Production function
Marginal product of labor
Lucas model
Rational expectations

Unanticipated money
Real business cycle approach
Economic disturbances
Propagation mechanism
Intertemporal substitution of leisure

PROBLEMS

1. In the frictionless neoclassical model, assume that the capital stock increases and labor becomes more productive, with the labor demand curve shifting upward and to the right.
   (a) What is the effect of this change on the full-employment levels of employment and output?
   (b) What is the effect on the full-employment real wage?
   (c) How would your answers to (a) and (b) be affected if the labor supply curve were vertical?

2. What is the effect of an increase in the productivity of labor on the equilibrium price level in the frictionless neoclassical model? (Recall from Chapter 7 the type of aggregate supply curve implied in this case.) Compare your answers to questions 1 and 2.

3. (a) Explain why the short-run aggregate supply curve slopes up in both the rational expectations equilibrium approach and the contracting approach.
   (b) Explain why anticipated changes in the money stock would have no effect on output in these models.

4. Consider a fiscal expansion in the Lucas model.
   (a) What is the short-run effect on output and on prices? Why does output rise?
   (b) What is the long-run effect?

5. Assume two situations of unanticipated money. In one case the government permanently increases the money stock. In the other case it raises it for one period and then (again unexpectedly) reduces it permanently. What happens in each case to output in period 1, period 2, and the long run?

6. (a) Suppose the money stock in the current period increases by 10 percent, and that the increase was fully anticipated. What happens to output and the price level?
   (b) Suppose, on the contrary, that the public expected a 10 percent increase, but the actual rise was 20 percent. What happens to output and prices? Specifically, do they rise by 10 percent, 20 percent, somewhere between 10 and 20 percent, or what? Explain your answer.

7. (a) Where do you see the central difference between the dynamic model of aggregate demand and supply in Chapter 8 and the Lucas model?
   (b) State which model is more plausible and why you think so.

8. Supply shocks affect output in both the aggregate supply model of Chapter 8 and real business cycle models. However, the mechanisms are different. To show this, use the frictionless neoclassical model outlined in the appendix, and assume that a productivity disturbance shifts the production function and the demand curve for labor. Show graphically how this disturbance affects the level of output.

9. Now go back to the analysis of a supply shock in Chapter 8, and explain how the analysis there differs from your answer to problem 8.

*10. (a) Explain the aim of the real business cycle approach to macroeconomics.
   (b) Show in the standard labor market diagram, Figure 9-1, how, according to the view that consumers are willing to substitute leisure intertemporally, the labor supply curve differs for temporary and permanent changes in wages.

---

*The asterisk denotes a more difficult problem.

APPENDIX: THE NEOCLASSICAL MODEL OF THE LABOR MARKET AND AGGREGATE SUPPLY

The frictionless classical model is an idealized case in which wages and prices are *fully* flexible, there are no costs either to workers in finding jobs or to firms in increasing or reducing their labor force, and firms behave competitively and expect to sell all they produce at prevailing prices. The neoclassical model both serves as a benchmark for the discussion of more realistic cases and also allows us to introduce such useful concepts as the production function and the demand for labor. Throughout, we assume that labor is the only *variable* factor of production and that the capital stock is given.

The Production Function

A *production function* provides a relation between the quantity of factor inputs, such as the amount of labor used, and the maximum quantity of output that can be produced using those inputs. The relation reflects only technical efficiency. In equation (A1) we write the production function

$$Y = F(N, \ldots) \tag{A1}$$

where Y denotes real output, N is labor input, and the dots denote other cooperating factors (capital, for example) that are in short-run fixed supply. The production function is shown in Figure 9-A1. The production function exhibits *diminishing returns* to labor, which means that the increase in output resulting from the employment of one more unit of labor declines as the amount of labor used increases.

Diminishing returns are shown in the production function by its shape, which is neither a straight line through the origin (constant returns) nor an upward-curving line (increasing returns). Diminishing returns are explained by the fact that as employment increases and other inputs remain constant, each laborer on the job has fewer machines with which to work. An increase in the labor force will always raise output, but progressively less so as employment expands. The marginal contribution of increased employment is indicated by the slope of the production function, $\Delta Y/\Delta N$. The slope flattens out as employment increases, thus showing that increasing employment makes a diminishing, but still positive, contribution to output.

Labor Demand

From the production function we proceed to the demand for labor. We ask how much labor a firm would want to hire. The rule of thumb is to hire additional labor and expand production as long as doing so increases profits, bringing in more in revenue than the additional cost in wages.

The contribution to output of additional labor is called the *marginal product of labor*. It is equal, in Figure 9-A1, to the slope of the production function. The marginal product, as we have seen, is both positive—additional labor is productive—and diminishing, which means that additional employment becomes progressively less productive. *A firm will employ additional labor as long as the marginal product of labor* (MPN) *exceeds the cost of additional labor*. The cost of additional labor is given by the real wage, that is, the nominal wage divided by the price level. The real wage measures the amount of real output the firm has to pay each worker. Since hiring one more worker results in an output increase of *MPN* and a cost to the firm of the real wage, firms will hire additional labor if the *MPN* exceeds the real wage. This point is formalized in Figure 9-A2, which looks at the labor market.

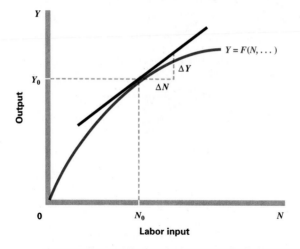

FIGURE 9-A1

THE PRODUCTION FUNCTION AND THE MARGINAL PRODUCT OF LABOR.
The production function links the amount of output produced to the
level of labor input, given other factors of production, such as
capital. The schedule shows diminishing returns. Successive
increases in labor yield less and less extra output. The marginal
product of labor is shown by the slope of the production function,
$\Delta Y/\Delta N$, that is, the increase in output per unit increase in
employment. The flattening of the slope shows that the marginal
product of labor is declining.

The downward-sloping schedule in Figure 9-A2 is the demand for labor schedule, which
is the *MPN* schedule; firms hire labor up to the point at which the *MPN* is equal to the real
wage. The *MPN* schedule shows the contribution to output of additional employment. It follows
from our reasoning that the *MPN* is positive but that additional employment reduces it, so that
the *MPN* schedule is negatively sloped.

Now consider a firm that currently employs a labor force N_1, and assume that the real
wage is $(W/P)_0$, where W is the money wage and P is the price of output. At employment level
N_1, in Figure 9-A2, the firm is clearly employing too much labor, since the real wage exceeds
the *MPN* at that level of employment. What would happen if the firm were to reduce employment
by one unit? The reduction in employment would decrease output by the amount of the *MPN*,
and therefore reduce revenue to the firm. On the other side of the calculation, we have the
reduction in the wage bill. For a unit reduction in employment, the wage bill would fall by the
real wage $(W/P)_0$. The net benefit of a reduction in the employment level is thus equal to the
vertical excess of the real wage over the *MPN* in Figure 9-A2. It is apparent that at a level of
employment N_1, the excess is quite sizable, and it pays the firm to reduce the employment level.
Indeed, it pays to reduce employment until the firm gets to point N_0. Only at that point does
the cost of additional labor—the real wage—exactly balance the benefit in the form of increased output.

The same argument applies to employment level N_2. Here employment is insufficient
because the contribution to output of additional employment, MPN_2, exceeds the cost of additional
employment, and it therefore pays to expand the level of employment. It is readily seen that

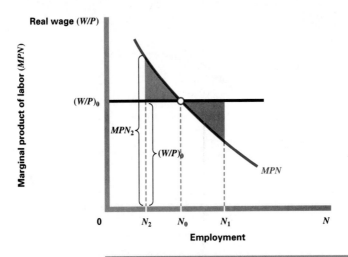

FIGURE 9-A2

THE OPTIMAL EMPLOYMENT CHOICE FOR A GIVEN REAL WAGE. The marginal product of labor, *MPN*, is a declining function of the level of employment because of diminishing returns. Given a real wage $(W/P)_0$, the optimal employment choice is N_0. At N_1, the marginal product of labor is less than the real wage, so that the firm would save by reducing employment. Conversely, at N_2 the marginal product exceeds the real wage, so that the firm would gain by hiring additional workers.

with real wage $(W/P)_0$, the firm's profits are maximized when employment is N_0. In general, given *any* real wage, the firm's demand for labor is shown by the *MPN* curve.

The firm's optimal employment position is formalized in equation (A2). At the optimal employment level the marginal product of labor (which is a declining function of employment), *MPN*, is equal to the real wage:

$$MPN = \frac{W}{P} \tag{A2}$$

Equilibrium in the Labor Market

We have now developed the relation between output and employment (the production function) and the implied demand for labor. It remains to consider labor supply and the determination of the real wage as part of labor market equilibrium.

We assume that labor supply increases with the real wage (W/P). In Figure 9-A3 the labor supply curve, *NS*, intersects the labor demand curve, *MPN*, at *E*. The equilibrium real wage is $(W/P)_0$, and the equilibrium level of employment is N^*.

How would the labor market get to that equilibrium? Suppose that the real wage fell whenever there was an excess supply of labor and that it rose whenever there was an excess demand. In terms of Figure 9-A3, the real wage would decline whenever it was above $(W/P)_0$.

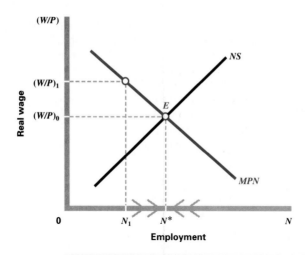

FIGURE 9-A3

EQUILIBRIUM IN THE LABOR MARKET. The labor supply curve is *NS*. The demand for labor is the marginal product schedule, *MPN*. Labor market equilibrium obtains at real wage $(W/P)_0$. At that real wage the demand for labor equals the quantity of labor supplied. At a lower real wage there is an excess demand for labor; at a higher real wage there is an excess supply, or unemployment.

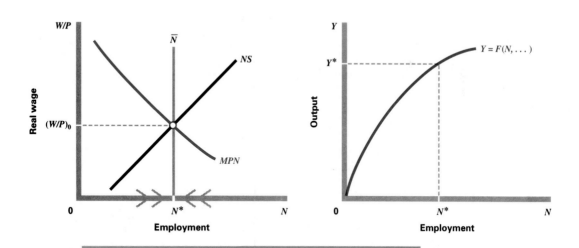

FIGURE 9-A4

FULL-EMPLOYMENT OUTPUT. The production function shows the full-employment level of output, Y^*, which corresponds to the equilibrium full-employment level of employment, N^*.

259

At $(W/P)_1$, for example, labor demand is only N_1 and thus falls short of the labor supply. This would put downward pressure on the real wage, causing the real wage to fall and making it profitable to expand employment. Exactly the reverse argument holds for real wages lower than $(W/P)_0$, where there is an excess demand for labor.

Figure 9-A3 shows that adjustment of the real wage would bring the labor market into full-employment equilibrium at real wage $(W/P)_0$ and employment level N^*. Figure 9-A4 shows the level of *full-employment output, Y**, which is the level of output associated with N^*, where labor is fully employed.

LONG-TERM GROWTH AND PRODUCTIVITY

O ver the past 100 years, U.S. real GNP has grown at an average annual rate of 3.2 percent.[1] Over the same period, *per capita* real GNP grew at the slower rate of 1.8 percent, doubling every 39 years.[2] With such a growth rate, a 20-year-old college student could anticipate per capita GNP doubling before she reaches retirement—and thus the material standard of living will roughly double during her working life.

Despite this record of sustained long-term growth, there is a heightening perception in the United States today that growth has been slowing, that future generations might be worse off than their parents, and that the United States has been falling behind its competitors, especially Japan and Germany.[3] The political debate in the United States focuses on economic growth as the single most important policy issue of the 1990s.

Table 10-1 presents comparative per capita GNP in dollars and growth rates.[4] These estimates are calculated by dividing GNP per capita, measured in the local currency, by the exchange rate. Two numbers jump out of the first row. First, by this measure, per capita income in the United States in 1990 was *already* 15 percent below

---

[1] Because GNP was until recently the main indicator of the economy's output, growth rate data over long periods generally refer to GNP rather than GDP. The growth rates of GNP and GDP for the United States are essentially the same.

[2] The so-called rule of 70 says that to calculate the (approximate) length of time it takes for a variable to double, divide 70 by the percentage growth rate of the variable.

[3] See, for instance, Lester Thurow, *Head to Head* (New York: Morrow, 1992).

[4] For historical international comparisons see Angus Maddison, *Phases of Capitalist Development* (London: Oxford University Press, 1982), *The World in the Twentieth Century* (Paris: OECD, 1989), and the data from that publication presented on the endpaper of this book, and *Dynamic Forces in Capitalist Development: A Long-Run Comparative View* (New York: Oxford University Press, 1992). See, too, A. Bergson, "Comparative Productivity," *American Economic Review,* June 1987.

TABLE 10-1

COMPARATIVE PER CAPITA INCOME LEVELS

	U.S.	Japan	Korea	Brazil	Mexico	India
Per capita GNP (1990), 1990 $	21,790	25,430	5,400	2,680	2,490	350
Growth rate (1965–1990), % per year	1.7	4.1	7.1	3.3	2.8	1.9
Per capita GDP, ICP method (1990 $)	21,360	16,950	7,190	4,780	5,980	1,150
Relative to U.S., ICP method	100	78	33	22	27	5

SOURCE: World Bank, *World Development Report*, 1992, Tables 1 and 30.

that of Japan. Second, India's per capita GNP of $350 is unbelievably low; no one in the United States could survive on $350 per year.

The purchasing powers of different currencies in their home countries are not equal and also fluctuate a great deal with exchange rates. To correct for this factor, the third row presents data from the *International Comparisons Project* (ICP), which tries to calculate incomes in different countries using *the same prices* for each country.[5] Just as real GDP data are calculated using the same prices to compare output in different years, the ICP data use the same prices to compare output and income in different places.

According to the ICP, real per capita income in the United States in 1990 was about 20 percent above that of Japan, and *twenty times* per capita real GDP in India. The ICP comparison shows Indian income at $100 per month, an income that reflects enormous poverty. That is indeed the situation in India.

Table 10-1 also shows that while the *level* of per capita income in the United States is very high, our *growth* in per capita income is relatively low. Korea's growth is remarkable by historical standards. If Korean real income continues to grow at 7.1 percent and U.S. income at 1.7 percent, Korea will catch up to the United States (using the ICP measures) in 20 years. That may sound impossible, but it is close to what Japan achieved: between 1950 and 1990, Japan's ICP income rose relative to that of the United States from 18 percent to 78 percent.

Evidently, over the long term—and even over periods as short as 25 years—differences in growth rates of a few percentage points produce enormous changes in living standards and in the relative economic standing of different countries. Growth really matters.

This chapter is therefore focused on two key questions. First, what determines the growth rate of output over long periods? And second, will the lower-income countries eventually catch up to the higher-income countries, and perhaps even overtake them?

There are two complementary approaches to these questions. One is *growth theory*, which models the interactions among factor supplies, productivity growth,

---

[5] For the most recent version of the ICP data, see Robert Summers and Alan Heston, "The Penn World Table (Mark 5): An Expanded Set of International Comparisons, 1950–1988," *Quarterly Journal of Economics,* May 1991. These data have been used extensively in empirical work on international growth in the last few years.

saving, and investment in the process of growth. The other is *growth accounting*, which attempts to quantify the contribution of different determinants of output growth. The two approaches draw on a common analytical framework, which we now outline.

10-1 SOURCES OF GROWTH IN REAL INCOME

In this section we use the production function to study the sources of growth. Output grows through increases in the inputs of factors of production—labor and capital— and through improvements in technology. To understand growth and differences in income levels among countries, we need to understand what determines the growth of factors of production and of technical knowledge.

The Production Function

In the appendix to Chapter 9 we introduced the concept of a production function. The *production function* links the amount of output produced in an economy to the inputs of factors of production and to the state of technical knowledge. Equation (1) represents the production function in symbols:

$$Y = AF(K, N) \tag{1}$$

where K and N denote the inputs of capital and labor and A denotes the state of technology. The production function $AF(K, N)$ in equation (1) states that the output produced depends on factor inputs K and N and on the state of technology. Increases in factor inputs and improved technology lead to an increase in output supply.

The next step is to make these links more precise by looking at an expression for the growth rate of output. In the *growth accounting equation* (2), which is derived in the appendix, we show the determinants of output growth.[6]

$$\Delta Y/Y = [(1 - \theta) \times \Delta N/N] + (\theta \times \Delta K/K) + \Delta A/A \tag{2}$$

$$\begin{array}{c} \text{Output} \\ \text{growth} \end{array} = \left(\begin{array}{c} \text{labor} \\ \text{share} \end{array} \times \begin{array}{c} \text{labor} \\ \text{growth} \end{array} \right) + \left(\begin{array}{c} \text{capital} \\ \text{share} \end{array} \times \begin{array}{c} \text{capital} \\ \text{growth} \end{array} \right) + \begin{array}{c} \text{technical} \\ \text{progress} \end{array}$$

where $(1 - \theta)$ and θ are weights equal to the income shares of labor and of capital in production.

Equation (2) summarizes the contributions of growth of inputs and of improved productivity to growth of output:

- Labor and capital each contribute an amount equal to their individual growth rates *multiplied by the share of that input in income*.

---

[6]Equation (2) applies when there are *constant returns to scale* in production; that is, increases in both inputs, in the same proportion, increase output in that proportion.

■ The rate of improvement of technology, called *technical progress,* or the *growth of total factor productivity*, is the third term in equation (2).

The growth rate of total factor productivity is the amount by which output would increase as a result of improvements in methods of production, with all inputs unchanged. In other words, there is growth in total factor productivity when we get more output from the same factors of production.[7]

EXAMPLE: Suppose the income share of capital is 0.25; and that of labor is 0.75. These values correspond approximately to the actual values for the U.S. economy. Furthermore, let labor force growth be 1.2 percent and growth of the capital stock be 3 percent, and suppose total factor productivity grows at the rate of 1.5 percent per annum. What is the growth rate of output? Applying equation (2) we obtain a growth rate of $\Delta Y/Y = 3.15$ percent $[= (0.75 \times 1.2 \text{ percent}) + (0.25 \times 3 \text{ percent}) + 1.5 \text{ percent}]$.

The growth rates of capital and labor in equation (2) are weighted by the respective income shares. The reason for these weights is that the importance to production of, say, a one-percentage-point change in labor differs from the same percentage-point change in capital. But if each of capital and labor grows by 1 percent, so does output.

The weighting of factor growth by factor shares is critical when we ask how much extra growth we get from faster growth in factor inputs, say by supply-side policies. Suppose, with everything else the same, capital growth had been twice as high—6 percent instead of 3 percent. Using equation (2), output growth would increase to 3.9 percent, rising by less than a percentage point even though capital growth rose by three percentage points.

ADDING HUMAN CAPITAL

Each of K and L in the production function (2) is an aggregate of many different types of capital and labor, respectively, that are used in production. For instance, K includes trucks, computers, and factory buildings, added together by their value.

Sometimes, to emphasize the potential contribution of education and training to economic growth, the production function is written with *human capital* as a separate input. Human capital is the value of the income-earning potential embodied in individuals. It includes native ability and talent as well as education and acquired skills.

With human capital as a separate input, the production function is written

$$Y = AF(K, H, N) \tag{3}$$

where H represents human capital. An equation corresponding to equation (2) can be written, showing that, with constant returns to scale, the growth rate of output is equal

---

[7]There is a distinction between *labor productivity* and total factor productivity. Labor productivity is just the ratio of output to labor input, Y/N. Labor productivity grows as a result of technical progress, but it also grows because of the accumulation of capital per worker.

to the growth rates of the inputs, each weighted by its share in income, plus the growth rate of productivity.

INCREASING RETURNS TO SCALE

The result cited in the preceding paragraphs—namely, if each input grows by 1 percent, so does output—holds only when there are constant returns to scale. If there are increasing returns to scale, then a 1 percent increase in each input results in a greater than 1 percent increase in output. Whether there are increasing or constant returns to scale is an empirical matter, with much of the evidence suggesting that returns to scale are roughly constant. We now turn to the evidence.

10-2 EMPIRICAL ESTIMATES OF THE SOURCES OF GROWTH

Equation (2) prepares us for an analysis of empirical studies that deal with sources of growth. An early and famous study by Nobel laureate Robert Solow of MIT dealt with the period 1909–1949 in the United States.[8] Solow's surprising conclusion was that over 80 percent of the growth in output per labor hour over that period was due to technical progress.

Specifically, Solow used an equation for the United States similar to equation (2) that identifies capital and labor growth along with technical progress as the sources of the output growth. Of the average annual growth of total GNP of 2.9 percent per year over that period, he concluded that 0.32 percent was attributable to capital accumulation, 1.09 percent per annum was due to increases in the input of labor, and the remaining 1.49 percent was due to technical progress. Per capita output grew at 1.81 percent, with 1.49 percent of that increase resulting from technical progress.

Because technical progress is calculated as output growth minus the part accounted for by increased factor inputs, the term functions as a catchall for omitted factors and poor measurement of the capital and labor inputs. Further work therefore turned quite naturally to explore this residual, that is, growth not explained by capital accumulation or increased labor input.

One of the most comprehensive of the subsequent studies is that by Edward Denison, summarized in Table 10-2.[9] Using data for the period 1929–1982, Denison attributed 1.9 percent of the 2.9 percent annual rate of increase in real output to increased factor inputs. Output per labor hour grew at the rate of 1.58 percent, of which 1.02 percent was due to technical progress. Denison's findings thus support Solow's estimate that most of the growth in output per labor hour is due to technical progress.

---

[8] "Technical Change and the Aggregate Production Function," *Review of Economics and Statistics*, August 1957.

[9] *Accounting for United States Economic Growth, 1929–1969* (Washington, D.C.: The Brookings Institution, 1974). See also Denison's *Trends in American Economic Growth, 1929–1982* (Washington, D.C.: The Brookings Institution, 1985), and *Estimates of Productivity Change by Industry* (Washington, D.C.: The Brookings Institution, 1989).

TABLE 10-2

SOURCES OF GROWTH OF TOTAL NATIONAL INCOME, 1929–1982

source of growth	growth rate, % per year

Total factor input
  Labor: 1.34
  Capital: 0.56
	1.90

Output per unit of input
  Knowledge: 0.66
  Resource allocation: 0.23
  Economies of scale: 0.26
  Other: −0.03
	1.02

National income	2.92

SOURCE: Edward Denison, *Trends in American Economic Growth, 1929–1982* (Washington, D.C.: The Brookings Institution, 1985), Table 8-1.

Consider now Denison's breakdown of the sources of U.S. growth over the period 1929–1982, in Table 10-2. Here increases in the labor force get a very large credit for their contributions to growth. Why? The answer is provided by equation (2), which shows that labor's growth rate has a relatively large weight mainly because labor's share of income is relatively large.

Next we look at the sources of increased factor productivity or increased output per unit of factor input. The striking fact is that advances in knowledge account for almost two-thirds of the contribution of technical progress toward growth. Two other sources of increased factor productivity are worth recording. One is the increase in productivity that stems from improved resource allocation—for example, people leaving low-paying jobs and moving to better jobs, thus contributing to increased output or income growth. An important element is relocation from farms to cities.

The remaining significant part of technical progress is *economies of scale*. This is a bit troublesome because we explicitly assumed constant returns to scale in deriving equation (2), but we find now that more than 10 percent of the average annual growth in income is attributed to the expanding scale of operation in the economy. As the scale of operation of the economy expands, fewer inputs are required per unit of output, presumably because we can use techniques that are economically inefficient at a small-scale level but yield savings at a larger scale of production.

The significance of Denison's work, and the work in this area of others, including Nobel laureate Simon Kuznets (1901–1985) and J. W. Kendrick, is to highlight technical progress. The early finding by Solow that growth in the capital stock makes a minor, though not negligible, contribution to growth stands up well to the test of later research.[10]

---

[10]The major exception is in work by Dale Jorgenson and his associates. The results of a massive study are presented in Dale Jorgenson, Frank Gollop, and Barbara Fraumeni, *Productivity and U.S. Economic Growth*

TABLE 10-3
GROWTH PERFORMANCE IN MAJOR ECONOMIES (percent per year)*

	U.S.	Japan	Germany	France	U.K.
1960–1973	4.0	9.6	4.4	5.7	3.1
1973–1986	2.4	3.7	1.8	2.3	1.4
1986–1990	2.6	5.1	3.4	3.3	3.1
1990–1992†	0.8	3.2	2.2	1.7	−0.9

*Data are for GDP through 1990; for GNP, 1990–1992.

†Data include projections by OECD.

SOURCE: OECD, *Historical Statistics*, 1960–1986, and *Economic Outlook*, June 1992.

Capital investment is necessary—particularly because some technological improvements require the use of new types of machines—but other sources of growth can make an important contribution. Furthermore, since for many purposes we are interested in output per head, we have to recognize that we are left with only technical progress and growth in capital to achieve increased output per head. Here we have to ask, What are the components of technical progress? *Advances in knowledge and efficiency stand out as the major sources and point to the roles of research, education, and training as important sources of growth.*

The Decline of Growth

Output growth in the United States declined in the 1970s. So did growth in most other industrialized countries, as can be seen in Table 10-3. In each of the major countries in Table 10-3, there was a significant decline in GNP growth after 1973, and then an increase in the second half of the 1980s. But only for the United Kingdom does the growth rate for the last four years of the 1980s match that for 1960–1973. In the first part of the 1990s, growth again slowed in all the major economies.

Table 10-4 spotlights the cause of the worsened growth performance: in the 1970s average growth rates of productivity declined throughout the industrialized world. There was an improvement in the United States, Japan, and the United Kingdom between 1980 and 1990, but for none of the five largest economies has the growth

---

(Cambridge, Mass.: Harvard University Press, 1987). Working with data for the period 1948–1979, for which the overall growth rate was 3.4 percent, Jorgenson et al. estimate that capital inputs contributed 1.6 percentage points of that growth, labor inputs 1.05 percentage points, and productivity growth only 0.8 percentage points. One-quarter of the increased capital input is attributed to quality improvements, and thus fully 1.2 percentage points of growth are attributed to an increased input of capital—significantly more than Denison's estimate.

TABLE 10-4

PRODUCTIVITY TRENDS IN MAJOR ECONOMIES (business sector, total factor productivity*; percent per year)

	U.S.	Japan	Germany	France	U.K.
1960–1973	1.6	5.8	2.6	4.0	2.3
1973–1979	−0.4	1.4	1.8	1.7	0.6
1979–1990	0.2	2.0	0.8	1.8	1.6

*The rate of increase of total factor productivity corresponds to $\Delta A/A$, the rate of technical progress, in equation (2).

SOURCE: OECD, *Economic Outlook*, June 1992.

rate of productivity returned to anywhere close to the growth rate of 1960–1973. There is as yet no fully satisfactory explanation.[11] Among the possible causes are[12]

- A worsened age-skill mix of the labor force (the baby-boom generation and more part-timers coming into the labor force)

- An increase in government regulation

- The costs of investment in pollution abatement and crime prevention

- The very sharp increases in the price of oil during this period

- A slowdown in the rate of innovation[13]

The rise in the price of oil would have had an effect by making much existing capital (gas-guzzlers, for example) obsolete and requiring new investment to be used to replace existing capital rather than expanding productive capacity.

Increased government regulation includes antipollution requirements as well as rules that make it very expensive to fire workers and therefore increase the costs of reallocating labor in response to changing prices and opportunities. An emphasis on reducing government regulation was one aspect of the supply-side approach to economic policy pursued during the early 1980s in the United States.

Government regulations (and labor unions) have been especially blamed for the

[11] See "Symposium on the Slowdown in Productivity Growth," *Journal of Economic Literature*, Fall 1988, as well as A. Maddison, "Growth and Slowdown in Advanced Capitalist Economies: Techniques of Quantitative Assessment," *Journal of Economic Literature*, June 1987.

[12] For detailed accounting of the decline in growth see Denison's works, cited above, and J. W. Kendrick, "The Implications of Growth Accounting Models," in Charles Hulten and Isabel Sawhill (eds.), *The Legacy of Reaganomics* (Washington, D.C.: Urban Institute Press, 1984). See, too, William Cullison, "The U.S. Productivity Slowdown: What the Experts Say," Federal Reserve Bank of Richmond *Economic Review*, July/August 1989.

[13] A. Steven Englander, Robert Evenson, and Masaharu Hanazaki, "R&D, Innovation and the Total Factor Productivity Slowdown," *OECD Economic Studies*, no. 11 (Autumn 1988), present evidence that the large slowdown in innovation in the 1970s contributed significantly to the slowdown in economic growth.

European growth slowdown, also called "Eurosclerosis," in the 1980s. But in interpreting the role of regulation, we should also recall that some of the benefits of increased regulation, such as reduced pollution, do not show up in GNP even though they make people better off.

The period of the productivity slowdown after 1973 was also a period in which the use of computers spread rapidly and an electronic revolution took place. It remains to be seen how the information technology revolution and other high-tech investments might translate into major productivity growth.[14]

Productivity growth in manufacturing was extremely strong in the 1980s—3 percent per year—but economywide growth fell to a record-low, less than 1 percent rate. Increasingly, the period from the end of World War II to 1973 is being seen as a golden age of rapid growth, perhaps a period of catch-up from the effects of the great depression and World War II. As the time since 1973 passes, it looks as if we have to get used to the idea that productivity growth is not what it used to be, and that the prospects for future growth and future standards of living are correspondingly diminished.

10-3 GROWTH THEORY: THE NEOCLASSICAL MODEL

The goal of growth theory is to explain the determinants of growth rates within a country and the reasons for differences in growth rates and per capita incomes across countries.

There have been two periods of intense work on growth theory, the first in the late 1950s and 1960s, and the second 30 years later, in the late 1980s and 1990s. Research in the first period created *neoclassical growth theory*. The best-known contribution in that period was by Robert Solow.[15] More recent research is known as *endogenous growth theory*. The early contributions here were by Robert Lucas of the University of Chicago and Paul Romer of Berkeley.[16]

We outline neoclassical growth theory in this section, and endogenous growth theory in the next.

We develop neoclassical growth theory using equations (1) and (2):

$$Y = AF(K, N) \tag{1}$$

$$\Delta Y/Y = [(1 - \theta) \times \Delta N/N] + (\theta \times \Delta K/K) + \Delta A/A \tag{2}$$

---

[14] See Charles Steindel, "Manufacturing Productivity and High-Tech Investment," Federal Reserve Bank of New York *Quarterly Review,* Summer 1992.

[15] "A Contribution to the Theory of Economic Growth," *Quarterly Journal of Economics,* February 1956, and *Growth Theory: An Exposition* (New York: Oxford University Press, 1988). The collection of papers in Joseph Stiglitz and Hirofumi Uzawa (eds.), *Readings in the Theory of Economic Growth* (Cambridge, Mass.: MIT Press, 1969), contains many of the most important papers of that period.

[16] Robert E. Lucas, Jr., "On the Mechanics of Economic Development," *Journal of Monetary Economics,* July 1988; and Paul Romer, "Increasing Returns and Long-Run Growth," *Journal of Political Economy,* October 1986. The volume edited by Alwyn Young, *Readings in Endogenous Growth* (Cambridge, Mass.: MIT Press, 1993), contains many of the key papers.

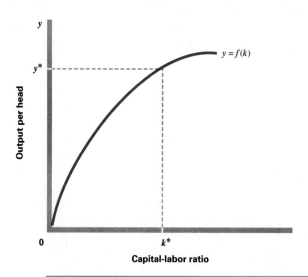

FIGURE 10-1

OUTPUT PER HEAD AND THE CAPITAL-LABOR RATIO. The production function shows output per head as a function of the amount of capital per head, or the capital-labor ratio. The higher the capital-labor ratio, the higher is output per head. But due to diminishing returns, the increment to output that results from raising the capital-labor ratio grows progressively smaller as the capital-labor ratio rises.

For convenience, we shall assume a given and constant rate of labor force growth, $\Delta N/N = n$, and also that there is no technical progress, that is, $\Delta A/A = 0$.[17]

It is useful also to express the production function in *per worker* or *per capita* terms,[18] as

$$y = f(k) \qquad (3)$$

where y is output per worker and k is capital per worker. Figure 10-1 shows the per worker production function (3). It has the familiar diminishing returns of capital:[19] as the amount of capital per worker rises, output per worker increases, but at a diminishing rate.

Given the assumptions of no technical progress and a fixed population growth rate, the only variable element left in equation (2) is the growth rate of capital. Capital growth is determined by saving, which, in turn, depends on income. Income, or output,

---

[17] Since $\Delta A/A = 0$, A is constant and can be set equal to one, so that we do not have to show it explicitly when we write out the production function.

[18] For further simplicity we also assume that the entire population works, so that the labor force and the population are the same.

[19] With constant returns to scale, there are diminishing returns to either factor separately.

in turn, depends on capital. We are thus set with an interdependent system in which capital growth depends, via saving and income, on the capital stock. How does this system work?

Steady State

We start by discussing the steady state of the economy. Here we ask whether in an economy with population growth and saving, and therefore growth in the capital stock, we reach a point at which output per head and capital per head become constant. The idea of a steady state is this: if capital per head is unchanging, given technology, so is output per head. But for capital *per head* to remain unchanging even though population is growing, capital must grow at just the same rate as population.

Substituting in equation (2) that

$$\Delta Y/Y = \Delta N/N = \Delta K/K = n \tag{4}$$

and with $\Delta A/A = 0$, we can confirm that equation (2) is satisfied. Thus there can be a steady state in which aggregate output, the capital stock, and the labor force all grow at the rate n, and output per head is constant.

We show the steady state graphically in Figure 10-1. In steady state, the economy settles down to a fixed capital-labor ratio, k^*. The production function shows the corresponding amount of output per head y^*.

Saving and Growth

Now we examine the link between saving and growth in capital. In a closed economy without a government sector, investment, or the gross increase in capital, is equal to saving. To obtain the increase in the capital stock, however, we have to deduct depreciation. Therefore the net addition to the capital stock is equal to saving less depreciation.

$$\Delta K = \text{saving} - \text{depreciation} \tag{5}$$

Two assumptions take us from equation (5) to a complete description of the steady state. We assume first that saving is a constant fraction, s, of income, Y. Second, we assume that depreciation is at a constant rate of d percent of the capital stock. Concretely, we might assume that people save $s = 15$ percent of their income and that depreciation is at a rate of 10 percent per year, so that every year 10 percent of the capital stock needs to be replaced to offset wear and tear.

Substituting these assumptions in equation (5) yields

$$\Delta K = sY - dK \tag{6}$$

and, using equation (4), that $\Delta K/K = n$, we arrive at the following result, which describes the steady state:

$$sY = (n + d)K \tag{6a}$$

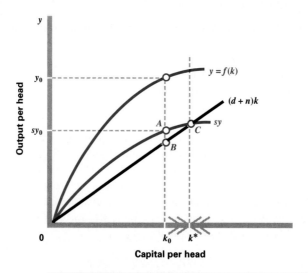

FIGURE 10-2
SAVING, INVESTMENT, AND CAPITAL ACCUMULATION. The saving
function shows the part of income that is saved, sy, at each capital-
labor ratio. The straight line $(d + n)k$ shows the amount of
investment required just to maintain the capital-labor ratio constant.
At low capital-labor ratios, saving exceeds the investment
requirement, and hence output per head grows. Conversely, at high
capital-labor ratios, saving is less than the investment requirement,
and capital per head is falling. The steady-state capital-labor ratio is
k^*, at which saving is just sufficient to maintain the capital-labor
ratio constant.

Equation (6a) states that in the steady state, saving (sY) is just sufficient to
provide for enough investment to offset depreciation (dK) *and* to equip new members
of the labor force with capital (nK). If saving were larger than this amount, capital per
head would grow, leading to rising income per head. Conversely, if not enough were
saved, capital per head would fall and with it income per head.

The Growth Process

In Figure 10-2 we study the adjustment process that leads the economy from some
initial capital-labor ratio over time to the steady state. The critical element in this
transition process is the rate of saving and investment compared with the rate of
depreciation and population growth.

With individuals saving a constant fraction of their income, the curve sy, which
is just a constant proportion of output, shows the level of saving at each capital-labor
ratio. The straight line $(d + n)k$ shows the amount of investment that is needed at
each capital-labor ratio to keep the capital-labor ratio constant.

The key to understanding the neoclassical growth model is that when saving, *sy*, exceeds the amount needed to keep the capital-output ratio, *k*, constant, then *k* is increasing.[20] Accordingly, when *sy* exceeds $(n + d)k$, *k* must be increasing, and the economy is moving to the right in Figure 10-2. For instance, if the economy starts at capital-output ratio k_0, then with saving at *A* exceeding the investment needed to hold *k* constant at *B*, the horizontal arrow shows *k* increasing.

The adjustment process comes to a halt at point *C*. Here we have reached a capital-labor ratio k^*, for which saving and investment associated with that capital-labor ratio exactly match the investment requirement. Given the exact matching of actual and required investment, the capital-labor ratio neither rises nor falls. We have reached the steady state.

At that steady state, both *k* and *y* are constant. With per capita income constant, aggregate income is growing at the same rate as population, that is, at rate *n*. *It follows that the steady-state growth rate is not affected by the saving rate.* This is one of the key results of neoclassical growth theory.

An Increase in the Saving Rate

In Figure 10-3 we show how an increase in the saving rate affects growth. In the short run, an increase in the saving rate raises the growth rate of output. It does not affect the *long-run growth rate* of output, but *it raises the long-run level of capital and output per head.*

In Figure 10-3, the economy is initially in steady-state equilibrium at point *C*, at which saving precisely matches the investment requirement. Now people want to save a larger fraction of income. This causes an upward shift of the saving schedule, to the dashed schedule.

At point *C*, at which we initially had a steady-state equilibrium, saving has now risen relative to the investment requirement, and as a consequence, more is saved than is required to maintain capital per head constant. Enough is saved to allow the capital stock per head to increase. The capital stock per head, *k*, will keep rising until we reach point C'. At C', the higher amount of saving is just enough to maintain the higher stock of capital. At point C', both capital per head and output per head have risen.

However, at point C', the economy has returned to its steady-state growth rate of *n*. Thus with this constant-returns-to-scale production function, an increase in the saving rate will in the long run raise only the level of output and capital per head, and not the growth rate of output per head.

Why should the long-run growth rate be independent of the saving rate? Shouldn't it be true that an economy in which 10 percent of income is set aside for additions to

---

[20] The percentage growth rate of the capital-labor ratio is equal to the difference between the growth rate of capital and the growth rate of labor, or $\Delta k/k = \Delta K/K - n$. Now using equation (6) to replace ΔK, we have

$$\frac{\Delta k}{k} = \frac{sY}{K} - d - n = \frac{s(Y/N)}{K/N} - (d + n) = \frac{sy}{k} - (d + n)$$

Multiplying both sides by *k*, we see that *k* will be rising so long as *sy* exceeds $(d + n)k$.

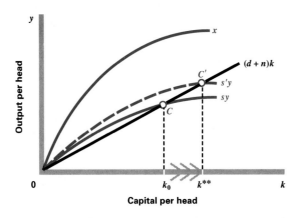

FIGURE 10-3
AN INCREASE IN THE SAVING RATE. An increase in the saving rate implies that at each capital-labor ratio a larger fraction of output is saved. The saving schedule shifts upward to $s'y$. At the initial steady state, saving now exceeds the investment requirement, and hence the capital-labor ratio rises until point C' is reached. An increase in the saving rate raises steady-state per capita income. The growth rate rises only in the transition from C to C'.

the capital stock is one in which capital and therefore output grow faster than in an economy in which only 5 percent of income is saved?

In the transition process, in fact, the higher saving rate increases the growth rate of output and the growth rate of output per head. This follows simply from the fact that the capital-labor ratio raises from k^* at the initial steady state to k^{**} in the new steady state. The only way to achieve an increase in the capital-labor ratio is for the capital stock to grow faster than the labor force (and depreciation).

Figure 10-4 summarizes the effects of an increase in the saving rate. Figure 10-4a shows the level of per capita output. Starting from an initial long-run equilibrium at time t_0, the increase in the saving rate causes saving and investment to increase, the stock of capital per head grows, and so does output per head. The process will continue at a diminishing rate. In Figure 10-4b we focus on the growth rate of output in the initial steady state. The increase in the saving rate immediately raises the growth rate of output because it implies faster growth in capital and therefore in output. As capital accumulates, the growth rate decreases, falling back toward the level of population growth.

POPULATION GROWTH

An increase in the population growth rate affects the $(n + d)k$ line in the diagram, rotating it up and to the left. In the problem set we ask you to show the following results:

■ An increase in the rate of population growth *reduces* the steady-state *level* of capital per head, k, and ouput per head, y.

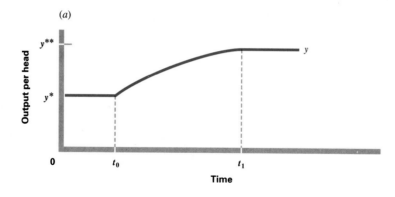

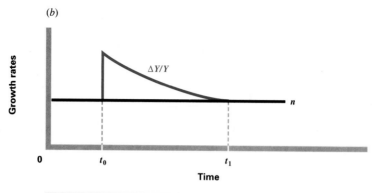

FIGURE 10-4

(a) THE TIME PATH OF PER CAPITA INCOME. A rise in the saving rate leads to a rising capital-labor ratio and therefore to increasing output per head until a new steady state is reached.

(b) THE TIME PATH OF THE GROWTH RATE OF OUTPUT. An increase in the saving rate raises investment above the investment requirement and thus leads to capital accumulation. Output growth transitorily rises and then falls back to the growth rate of population.

■ An increase in the rate of population growth *increases* the steady-state rate of growth of *aggregate* output.

The decline in output per head as a consequence of increased population growth points up the problem faced by many developing countries, discussed in Section 10-5.

Summary

There are four key results of neoclassical growth theory. The first two are:

■ From equation (4), and Figure 10-2, the growth rate of output in steady state is exogenous; in this case it is equal to n. *It is therefore independent of the saving rate, s.*

■ From Figure 10-3 and 10-4, although an increase in the saving rate does not affect the steady-state growth rate, by increasing the capital-output ratio, it does increase the steady-state *level* of income.

When we allow for productivity growth, we can show that if there is a steady state:

■ The steady-state growth rate of output remains exogenous. The steady-state rate of growth of per capita income is determined by the rate of technical progress. The steady-state growth rate of aggregate output is the sum of the rate of technical progress and the rate of population growth.

The final result of neoclassical theory concerns *convergence*:

■ If two countries have the *same* rate of population growth, the same saving rate, and have access to the same production function, they will eventually reach the same level of income. In this framework, poor countries are poor because they have less capital, but if they save at the same saving rate as rich countries, and have access to the same technology, they will eventually catch up.

Further, if countries have different saving rates, then according to this simple neoclassical theory, they will reach different *levels* of income in the steady state, but if their rates of technical progress and population growth are the same, their steady-state growth rates will be the same.

$10\text{-}4$ ENDOGENOUS GROWTH THEORY

In neoclassical growth theory, the steady-state growth rate is exogenous, and countries with the same technology and population growth rates eventually converge to the same steady-state growth rate—though the steady-state *level* of income could be different.

It is clear from Table 10-1, though, that differences in growth rates persist among countries for long periods, such as the 25 years shown there. Further, there are countries like India, seen in Table 10-1, that show no signs of converging to the income levels of the richer countries, even though they start with a much lower capital-labor ratio, k, and have if anything a higher saving rate than the United States.

Endogenous growth theory attempts to make the growth rate endogenous, that is, determined within the theory. The proponents of endogenous growth theory are driven by the view that government policy and economic behavior more generally must be able to affect the growth rate in the long run, and thus seek theories that will permit that to happen.

There are two basic ways of endogenizing the steady-state growth rate. First, the rate of technical progress, $\Delta A/A$, can be made endogenous.[21] It should, for instance, be affected by the share of the economy's resources devoted to research and development.

---

[21] For a comprehensive, but difficult, review of endogenous growth theory, see Xavier Sala-i-Martin, "Lecture Notes on Economic Growth (II): Five Prototype Models of Endogenous Growth," NBER Working Paper 3564, December 1990. See, too, Paul Romer, "Capital Accumulation in the Theory of Long Run Growth," in Robert Barro (ed.), *Modern Business Cycle Theory* (Cambridge, Mass.: Harvard University Press, 1989).

Second, if there are constant returns to factors of production that can be accumulated,[22] then the steady-state growth rate will be affected by the rate at which those factors are accumulated. This can be shown using the simplest possible production function, in which there is only capital, and assuming constant returns to scale.

Assume specifically that

$$Y = aK \tag{7}$$

that is, that output is proportional to the capital stock. Now suppose that the saving rate is constant at rate *s*. For simplicity, assume there is no population growth and no depreciation of capital. Then all saving goes to increase the capital stock. Accordingly:

$$\Delta K = sY = saK$$

or

$$\Delta K/K = sa \tag{8}$$

Then the growth rate of capital is affected by the saving rate. Further, since output is proportional to capital, it is also true that the growth rate of output is

$$\Delta Y/Y = sa \tag{8a}$$

In this example, the growth rate of output will be higher, the higher the saving rate. The general result is that *the steady-state growth rate is affected by the rate at which factors of production are accumulated if there are constant returns to the factors that can be accumulated.*

Empirical Evidence

The renewal of interest in growth theory has led to an explosion of empirical work on growth.[23] Most of this work uses the ICP data base, mentioned in footnote 5, which attempts to put data from different countries on a comparable basis. We review the most important results, and in Box 10-1 we summarize their policy lessons for growth in the United States.

CONDITIONAL CONVERGENCE

Endogenous growth theory implies that there should be persistent differences in growth rates among countries with different saving and investment rates. Neoclassical theory predicts that these differences affect the growth rate of output only for a (possibly lengthy) transitional period.

---

[22] This may require overall increasing returns, implying that output would go up more than proportionately if *all* factors of production increase in the same proportion.

[23] Much of this work is reviewed in Ross Levine and David Renelt, "A Sensitivity Analysis of Cross-Country Growth Regressions," *American Economic Review,* September 1992.

box 10-1

PROGROWTH POLICIES

What do growth theory and empirical work on growth tell us a country can do to increase growth? Some of the ingredients are those of the supply-side approach:

1. Increase investment by reducing budget deficits to crowd in private investment and by providing tax incentives
2. Reduce unnecessary regulation
3. Encourage investment in human capital, that is, spend more resources and effort on education and training
4. Increase infrastructure investment
5. Provide tax incentives for research and development spending

The obvious question is why, if it is all so simple, it hasn't already happened. In part, it is because these measures require current sacrifices for future gains. Cutting budget deficits is painful: it requires higher taxes or lower spending, and the U.S. political system has been incapable of doing that for a decade. Further, cutting the deficit means slower growth initially. Increased infrastructure investment sounds like a good idea, but given the budget deficit in the United States, it would need to be financed through higher taxes or else come at the expense of other priorities.*

---

*See Henry Aaron and Charles Schultze (eds.), *Setting Domestic Priorities: What Can Government Do?* (Washington, D.C.: The Brookings Institution, 1992), and Joseph A. Pechman and Michael S. McPerson (eds.), *Fulfilling America's Promise* (Washington, D.C.: The Brookings Institution, 1992).

Perhaps surprisingly, the tentative conclusion is that the evidence tends to favor the neoclassical view of the world. The industrialized countries appear to be converging toward the income level of the richest country, which, using the ICP measure of income, is still the United States.[24]

More generally, in a series of papers, Robert Barro[25] has shown that while countries that invest more tend to grow faster, the impact of higher investment on growth seems to be transitory—the higher investors will end in a steady state with higher per capita income but not a higher growth rate. This is as predicted by neoclassical theory. Barro refers to this result as *conditional convergence*, that is, countries are converging to steady states which are conditional on the share of investment in GDP. The levels are also contingent on other variables, such as the share of government spending in GNP and the rate of investment in human capital.

---

[24] See William J. Baumol, Anne B. Blackman, and Edward N. Wolff, *Productivity and American Leadership: The Long View* (Cambridge, Mass.: MIT Press, 1989), Chap. 5.

[25] For example, "Economic Growth in a Cross Section of Countries," *Quarterly Journal of Economics,* May 1991.

Moreover, in some areas we are already doing a lot, and maybe we need to do things differently rather than doing more. For instance, the United States spends heavily on education, so perhaps it is educational reform rather than more spending that is needed. The tax system already provides incentives to research and development spending; incentives must be financed by less spending on something else or higher taxes, and perhaps we are already doing enough.

Questions of political economy are central in discussing growth policies. First, the size of the budget deficit is obviously determined by political as much as economic factors. Second, many argue that the United States should, like Japan and Korea, take a far more active role in helping particular industries, through an industrial policy.[†] Critics argue that any such policy attempts in the United States would immediately be captured by special interests and would lead only to greater inefficiency. Third, in an influential book, Mancur Olsen[‡] of the University of Maryland argues that special interests tend to gain power in stable societies, and that they gradually encrust the economy with a host of restrictions that slow its progress. In Olsen's view, societies that have gone through major shakeups, such as the loss of a war (applying obviously to Japan and Germany) or a revolution, have the opportunity for a few years to redesign the economy along more rational lines.

Of course, it takes more than a revolution to restore growth. The new government has also to establish a reasonably stable economic framework, to pursue progrowth policies, and to allow private initiative to develop freely. For the United States, Olsen's work raises the crucial question of whether countries can reform effectively without a major shakeup or shock, such as a great depression. ∎

[†]Council on Competitiveness, *Gaining New Ground: Technology Priorities for America's Future* (Washington, D.C., 1991).

[‡]*The Rise and Decline of Nations* (New Haven, Conn.: Yale University Press, 1982).

Barro's evidence suggests that conditional convergence is taking place at a rate of 2 percent per year. For instance, if India's income level is now 5 percent that of the United States, in 35 years it would be approximately 10 percent of the U.S. level—provided that the other variables that affect the level of income, such as the saving rate, are the same between the two countries. This convergence is very slow; people now alive in India cannot look forward to catching up with the United States merely by relying on the "natural" neoclassical force of convergence.

INVESTMENT IN PHYSICAL CAPITAL, EQUIPMENT INVESTMENT, AND INFRASTRUCTURE

Countries that invest a greater share of GDP tend to grow faster, even if only for a transitional period. The investment–growth relationship bears closer examination, in two respects. First, Bradford De Long and Lawrence Summers[26] have shown that

---

[26]Bradford De Long and Lawrence Summers, "Equipment Investment and Economic Growth," *Brookings Papers on Economic Activity*, No. 2, 1992.

investment in machinery in particular appears to be associated with higher growth. Their work leads them to the conclusion that the rate of return on investment in machinery is about 20 percent per annum, an extraordinarily high rate.

Based on their results, De Long and Summers argue that machinery investment should be subsidized, through an investment tax credit, as discussed in Chapter 5. This suggestion raises the question of whether the 20 percent returns accrue to the people doing the investment, in which case it is not clear why any subsidy is needed, or whether these are returns to society which for some reason do not accrue to the investor. In that case a subsidy might be desirable.

The second aspect is the role of government infrastructure investment. As anyone who attends a public school or travels on the public highways can tell, government investment also contributes to economic productivity. There has been much recent work on the productivity of government capital, with the original contribution by David Aschauer arguing that the decline in government investment in the 1970s and 1980s bears a significant share of the blame for the decline in U.S. growth.[27]

Critics focus on the question of causality. They say that infrastructure investment is needed to complement private investment: roads and sewers are needed when industry expands. But building roads and sewers will not cause output growth without private investment. The critics are right to argue that some types of public investment, like sewers, will not contribute much to productivity unless private investment takes place. But in other cases, such as roads and schools, they are probably wrong.[28]

The public sector capital stock is large, more than 50 percent of the private sector nonresidential capital stock.[29] That is another reason to think that infrastructure investment contributes to growth.

HUMAN CAPITAL

The evidence supports the view that investment in human capital, education and training, tends to increase the growth rate, at least for a transitory period. This finding is consistent with a neoclassical production function like equation (3). Further, as shown in a paper by Gregory Mankiw, David Romer, and David Weil,[30] the explicit inclusion of human capital in a neoclassical model can account for some of the phenomena, such as long-lived differences in growth rates, that had been thought to require endogenous growth models.

---

[27] "Is Public Expenditure Productive?" *Journal of Monetary Economics,* March 1989. Aschauer's findings are basically supported by Alicia Munnell in "Why Has Productivity Growth Declined? Productivity and Public Investment," *New England Economic Review,* January/February 1990. A more skeptical view is taken in Laura S. Rubin, "Productivity and the Public Capital Stock: Another Look," Federal Reserve Board Working Paper, May 1991.

[28] For further discussion see Robert Eisner, "Infrastructure and Regional Economic Performance: Comment," Federal Reserve Bank of Boston *New England Economic Review,* September/October 1991, and *The American Prospect,* Fall 1992.

[29] See "Fixed Reproducible Tangible Wealth in the United States, 1988–1991," *Survey of Current Business,* August 1992.

[30] "A Contribution to the Empirics of Economic Growth," *Quarterly Journal of Economics,* May 1992.

PRODUCTIVITY GROWTH

The research associated with endogenous growth theory has not made any major inroads into the question of why productivity growth has slowed down and what can be done to revive it. Indirectly, though, the literature suggests that generally free-market policies tend to produce faster productivity growth: countries with smaller governments that maintain open markets, do not put up barriers to imports, and encourage foreign trade grow faster.[31]

A particularly striking piece of evidence comes from a detailed comparison by Alwyn Young[32] of two city-states, Singapore and Hong Kong. Both these cities experienced per capita growth rates of nearly 6 percent over the period since 1960. But in one of them, Hong Kong, the share of investment in GDP averaged about 20 percent over the period. In Singapore, the share of investment rose from 9 percent of GDP to around 40 percent in 1985. Corresponding to these great differences in investment shares, Young finds that productivity growth in Hong Kong averaged 3.5 percent per year over the last 20 years, while productivity growth in Singapore was essentially zero.

What accounts for this remarkable difference? Young draws attention to the fact that Hong Kong has an essentially laissez-faire, free market, government, whereas Singapore's government maintains tight control over the economy, with most of the economy's investments being indirectly directed by the government. He argues that the government of Singapore has tried to force the pace of development, relying on foreign investment to bring in new technologies, but moving on too rapidly to ever-more-sophisticated goods, before local entrepreneurs and workers have mastered the current technology.

Supply-Side Economics

In the 1980s, *supply-side economics* attracted much attention. Supply-side economists argue that growth could be significantly increased through policies designed to promote greater efficiency, reduced regulation, greater willingness to work, and investment.[33]

Supply-siders are associated with some extreme and implausible views, such as the view that cutting tax rates in the United States would reduce the deficit, as lower tax rates would encourage so much extra work that total taxes would rise and the deficit decline. Rather than discuss these views here (we do so in Chapter 18), we focus on the conventional aspects of supply-side economics.

We can interpret supply-side economics using the production function (1). The supply-siders' view is that increased incentives to work will increase the input of labor for a given population, that increased incentives to save and invest will make more

---

[31] See the work summarized in Levin and Renelt's paper referred to in footnote 23.

[32] "A Tale of Two Cities: Factor Accumulation and Technical Change in Hong Kong and Singapore," *NBER Macroeconomics Annual,* 1992.

[33] On supply-side economics see Hulten and Sawhill, *The Legacy of Reaganomics;* Martin Feldstein, "Supply Side Economics: Old Truths and New Claims," *American Economic Review,* May 1986; and for a view from the inside, Robert L. Bartley, *The Seven Fat Years, And How to Do It Again* (New York: The Free Press, 1992).

capital available, and that reduced regulation will increase A, the efficiency with which factors operate. All these changes would lead to increased output and, at least in the short run, more growth. The supply-siders were also (implicitly) endogenous growth theorists, in believing that these policies would permanently increase the growth rate.

On labor supply, the after-tax real wage should affect labor supply, but for people already working a higher real wage has an ambiguous effect on labor supply. The substitution effect of a higher wage encourages more work, while the income effect encourages more leisure. This ambiguity is absent for people who are not working, in which case there is only a substitution effect. Work by Jerry Hausman of MIT suggests that the aggregate effect of an increase in the after-tax real wage is to significantly increase labor supply, mainly by bringing more people into the labor force.[34]

On saving and investment, the supply-siders argued that the U.S. tax system discourages saving and that individuals would save more if the return to saving were higher.[35] However, the evidence does not provide much support for the view that increased after-tax rates of return to saving would significantly raise saving in the United States.[36]

The supply-siders' complaints about regulation did and do draw a responsive chord. Estimates by Denison, reported in Table 10-2, suggest that regulation has slowed measured growth. There is no doubt much unnecessary regulation, but some regulation improves the environment and its impacts are not correctly measured in GDP.

The conventional supply-siders, such as Martin Feldstein and Lawrence Summers of Harvard University, place a heavy emphasis on capital accumulation and on the need to reduce the budget deficit so as to crowd in investment. They support larger investment tax credits.

At first sight, equation (2) does not support the view that changes in investment would have a very big impact on the growth rate. Here is the arithmetic. Suppose, to be generous, that the share of capital is 0.33, and that investment is increased by 3 percent of GDP—a large increase. Since the ratio of capital to GDP is about 2, an increase of investment by 3 percent of GDP is an increase in the growth rate of capital by about 1.5 percent. This implies that an increase in investment by 3 percent of GDP would increase growth in the short run by about 0.5 percent. Although this seems small in the context of a Korean growth rate of 7.1 percent, it is in fact very large relative to the growth rate of per capita GDP in the United States of about 1.5 percent. Per capita growth in the United States would increase by one-third!

Indeed, that is very much the overall assessment of conventional supply-side economics. Most of the impacts would be quite small, but in the area of growth, even small increases in growth rates amount over time to big changes in the level of GDP.

---

[34] See Jerry Hausman, "Labor Supply and the Natural Unemployment Rate," in Laurence Meyer (ed.), *The Supply Side Effects of Economic Policy,* Federal Reserve Bank of St. Louis, 1981.

[35] In "Symposium on the Slowdown in Productivity Growth," *Journal of Economic Perspectives,* Fall 1988, the chairman of the Council of Economic Advisers in the Bush administration (1989–1993), Michael Boskin, presents evidence for the view that the current tax system discriminates strongly against saving.

[36] Gerald A. Carlino, "Interest Rate Effects and Intertemporal Consumption," *Journal of Monetary Economics,* March 1982, reviews and extends the (ambiguous) evidence. See, too, Larry Kotlikoff, "Taxation and Savings: A Neoclassical Perspective," *Journal of Economic Literature,* December 1984.

Of course, while in the 1980s supply-side economics ran high, the results in terms of savings—public and private—and investment were appalling.[37]

10-5 GROWTH AND DEVELOPMENT

Most of the world's people are poor and have no prospect of living at even the standard of the United States a century ago. The branch of economics that deals with the problems of the poor countries, also called the developing countries, is *development economics.*

Economic development takes place when the economic welfare of a country's people increases over a long period. We measure the state of development by a variety of economic indicators, including primarily per capita real GDP, but also indicators such as health, literacy, and longevity—indicating that the issue of development concerns far more than just the material standard of living.

The data in Table 10-1 also indicate the wide range of incomes among developing countries. Average income levels in many developing countries, particularly in Latin America, are at about the level in the United States a century ago. But in other developing countries, in Asia and in Africa, per capita incomes are far lower. Further, there are very big gaps in incomes within each country, with some people in those countries living very well indeed, and others at well below the very low average income level.

In discussing some of the problems of the developing countries, we draw on the analytic and empirical insights of modern growth theory.

Growth Performance

Table 10-5 shows a number of developing countries that differed vastly in their growth performance in the 1965–1990 period. Zaire, for example, had a declining level of per capita income—by 1990, income per head was 43 percent less than it had been in 1965! But there is also Korea, whose per capita income more than quintupled in the period.

What accounts for the differences in performance? The production function is a good starting point. Growth occurs as a result of the accumulation of factors of production and the improvement of resource utilization or increases in factor productivity.

Drawing on the production function, equation (3), we focus on the question

■ How much does a country invest?

■ How fast is population growing?

---

[37] See Ethan S. Harris and Charles Steindel, "The Decline in U.S. Saving and Its Implications for Economic Growth," Federal Reserve Bank of New York *Quarterly Review,* Winter 1991; Keith Carlson, "On Maintaining a Rising U.S. Standard of Living into the Mid-21st Century," Federal Reserve Bank of St. Louis *Economic Review,* March/April 1990; and M. A. Akhtar and Ethan S. Harris, "The Supply-Side Consequences of U.S. Fiscal Policy in the 1980s," Federal Reserve Bank of New York *Quarterly Review,* Spring 1992.

TABLE 10-5

GROWTH PERFORMANCE OF DEVELOPING COUNTRIES, 1965–1990 (percent)

	per capita income growth	population growth	investment/GDP
Argentina	−0.3	1.5	18.0
Brazil	3.3	2.3	21.8
China	5.8	1.7	32.8*
India	1.9	2.2	21.8
Korea	7.1	1.5	28.9
Mexico	2.8	2.4	22.4
Zaire	−2.2	3.1	14.2

*For the period 1970–1990.

SOURCE: World Bank, *World Development Report*, 1992, and *World Tables*, 1992.

- What is the quality of the human capital input?
- How effectively are the given productive resources utilized?

In the short run, as in Figure 10-3, changes in any of these variables will affect the growth rate. It therefore makes sense to ask with respect to each of these determinants of growth, What are policies that do or do not promote economic growth?

SAVING AND INVESTMENT

Physical capital has always been at the center of explanations for economic progress. In order to invest a country must either save or else have access to foreign saving through loans or aid. If domestic saving is the prerequisite for capital accumulation, then attention must focus on policies to promote high saving. For free market and reasonably stable economies, there is little evidence that higher interest rates increase saving, as the discussion of supply-side economics emphasizes.

Saving does depend on the availability of saving instruments—a banking system that offers convenient deposit services, for example. There is also abundant evidence that extreme financial instability, with large and negative real interest rates, interferes with saving. When the return on saving becomes negative one of three things happens: households sharply reduce their savings, or they shift their saving abroad (which is called capital flight), or they accumulate their saving in unproductive assets, such as gold. The financial environment for saving is thus an important factor in channeling saving from households, via financial intermediaries, to investing firms.[38]

In addition to the private sector, the government affects national saving through its budgetary policies. Beyond the domestic economy, countries can draw on foreign

---

[38] See Mark Gersovitz, "Saving and Development," in H. Chenery and T. N. Srinivasan (eds.), *Handbook of Development Economics* (Amsterdam: North Holland, 1988).

saving to finance investment. A developing country can tap foreign saving in three ways. One possibility is that foreign firms invest *directly* in a country. For example, in the late nineteenth century, European companies built railroads in Latin America; today, Japanese firms build plants in Indonesia and U.S. corporations invest in Mexico. The second way a country can tap foreign resources is by borrowing in the world capital market or from institutions such as the World Bank. Third, a country may be able to receive foreign aid from industrialized countries.

The importance of these three sources of external saving has varied over time and between countries. But there is little doubt that external saving has always been important in supplementing domestic saving. Of course, foreign saving is all the more important the lower the per capita income.

Many of the industrialized countries provide aid, in the form of grants and loans, to developing countries. The total volume of official development assistance in the 1989[39] was nearly $50 billion, about 0.33 percent of the income of the donor countries. The largest single donor is Japan, with the United States and France following closely behind. Aid received was more than 1.3 percent of the income of developing economies: in many sub-Saharan African countries aid amounted to more than 10 percent of their GNP, and according to the data, Mozambique received aid equal to 76 percent of GNP in 1989.

The amount of saving, domestic and foreign, private and public, determines how much investment will take place in a country. But the productivity of the resulting investment can vary widely. Governments often invest in unproductive ventures, or they might pursue policies that give incentives for unproductive private investments.

The large differences in the productivity of investment across countries focuses attention on development policies and strategies that affect the efficiency of resource utilization. We examine alternative development strategies shortly.

POPULATION GROWTH

We saw in the model of steady-state growth that the rate of population growth affects the steady-state *level* of per capita income. Given the saving rate, higher population growth means lower per capita income. Here is an immediate and stark implication of growth theory. Two countries with the same saving rate can have radically different levels of per capita income simply because one has, say, twice the growth rate of population of the other.[40]

Many developing countries are faced with the problem of very high rates of population growth. As we saw in developing the neoclassical model, if per capita income is to grow, there has to be enough investment in physical and human capital to equip each new worker with the tools that will make it possible to earn a higher level of income. But with a rapid rate of population growth, it takes a lot of resources to feed and educate the young. There are very poor countries in which population is

---

[39] Comprehensive data on aid are published each year by the OECD in the report of the Development Assistance Committee, *Development Co-Operation.*

[40] On population as a factor in economic development, see Allen Kelley, "Economic Consequences of Population Change in the Third World," *Journal of Economic Literature,* December 1988.

box 10-2

REFORM AND GROWTH IN EASTERN EUROPE

In the early 1990s, the formerly communist countries of Eastern Europe and the former Soviet Union are facing an economic growth and reform challenge of unprecedented nature and scale. Each of these economies had been run through a highly centralized planning system. In most countries, virtually all property and all industry were owned by the state. Unemployment had been virtually unknown. Several of these countries, including Poland and the former Soviet Union, ended the communist period with massive budget deficits and large external debts.

As the countries themselves, international agencies such as the World Bank and the International Monetary Fund, and academic economic advisers to the new governments wrestled with the question of how to reform, a basic reform strategy was developed:*

1. Restore macroeconomic stability by bringing the budget close to balance and pursuing tight monetary and credit policies.
2. Liberalize prices by removing price controls and allowing markets to begin operating.
3. Privatize government-owned firms by selling them, or even by giving them away to the citizens.
4. Liberalize foreign trade, allowing domestic firms and consumers access to world markets.
5. Establish a social safety network, so that people who become unemployed do not become destitute.
6. Develop as rapidly as possible the legal framework that a market economy needs to operate, for instance, contract and bankruptcy laws.

This agenda is overwhelming and will take decades to put in place. It includes such things as the necessity to develop banks and to train business managers and accountants. Since the changes are interdependent, ideally they should all take place at once. However, no government can operate that fast—least of all a new government made up of people who have spent their working lives in a very different type of economy. That is why the reform process is bound to look chaotic and will take time.

The initial stages of reform are very difficult. Table 1 shows estimates of the decline in output in the period 1990–1992. These data are very rough, but they

---

*See the "Symposium on Economic Transition in the Soviet Union and Eastern Europe," *Journal of Economic Perspectives*, Fall 1991.

---

growing above a rate of 3 percent per year. It thus takes income growth of 3 percent just to keep per capita income constant.

Some governments are beginning to recognize the need to reduce population growth—in the less repressive countries, by trying to persuade people to use contraceptives; in other countries, by policies of force that include sterilization. In China, for example, population growth has been reduced in the past 20 years from 2.7 to only 1.5 percent. But it often turns out to be difficult to reduce the rate of population growth

TABLE 1
GDP DECLINES IN
FORMERLY SOCIALIST
ECONOMIES, 1990–1992
(percent)

Russia	25
East Germany	37
Poland	19
Czechoslovakia	23
Albania	52

SOURCE: World Bank. Data include forecasted declines for 1992.

show massive declines in all countries. For comparison, note that real output in the United States declined by 30 percent in the great depression, between 1929 and early 1933. In Albania, the economy essentially stopped working.

East Germany is a special case. Since its unification with West Germany, it has been receiving massive subsidies from the western part of the country. The unification made the adjustment more difficult in some respects, for the wages of eastern Germans have risen very fast, and they are therefore less employable than they otherwise would be. The German government is spending massively on retraining, on subsidizing investment in the eastern part of Germany, and on welfare payments to eastern Germans. The estimate is that half of the income of eastern Germans comes from the German government. Still, there is no doubt that the living standards of eastern Germans have risen and will continue to rise far more rapidly than those of the citizens of other countries that had been behind the iron curtain.

How long will it take for the situation to turn around? That varies from country to country. There are some signs that the bottom was reached in Poland in 1992. In Russia and the rest of the former Soviet Union there are more years of decline to come. Even after these economies reach bottom, it will take some time—possibly a decade—to get back to the level they were at when the revolutions began. In the much longer run, the standard of living in these countries will be higher than it would have been in the old system. ∎

in very poor countries, where a large family may be acting as a social security system for the family, with the large number of children ensuring that the parents are taken care of in their old age.

HUMAN CAPITAL

Recent empirical work in neoclassical and endogenous growth theory emphasizes the role of human capital in growth. Human capital is produced through formal education and informal training as well as on-the-job experience. The problem for the developing countries is that it is extremely difficult to accumulate factors of production, physical or human capital, at the low levels of income characteristic of developing economies. The little that is left after providing for subsistence does not buy much education or much physical capital. The choice for children between working at a very young age or going to school is a critical one for families at very low income levels.

Also critical is the choice for a government of how to use the very limited resources it has at its command. And even if the financial resources were available, it still takes years to build up the group of teachers who can spread education and training. Thus growth is bound to take time as factors of production are accumulated very gradually; education is the slowest but quite possibly also the most powerful growth factor.

Countries that have been growing fastest, especially in East Asia, have educated populations, with high rates of literacy. This contrasts, for example, with educational attainment in most of the African countries.

GROWTH, NATURAL RESOURCES, AND THE ENVIRONMENT

There were fears in the 1970s that the world was rapidly running out of natural resources—not only oil, but also such commodities as copper, coal, and land (under the pressure of growing populations). These shortages, it was feared, would impose *limits to growth*.

Economists argued that price increases would cause people to conserve resources, that new technologies would develop, and thus that there was not too much to worry about. The use of energy per unit of GDP has indeed declined sharply since 1973, and so has the price of oil. Most other commodity prices have also dropped. Thus the concern that a shortage of natural resources would force a rapid end to growth has sharply decreased since the 1970s.

Since then, however, the fear that growing populations put pressure on resources and cause environmental degradation has increased, as tropical forests begin to disappear. Some calculations suggest that growth rates in developing countries have been significantly overstated because they have not taken into account the damage done to the environment.

There is also some evidence that the global climate may be warming. Economic mechanisms can be used to modify the trend to global warming, for instance, by imposing taxes on the use of carbon fuels and making the proceeds available for the development of alternative technologies. Governments in industrialized countries appear unwilling to impose such taxes to limit the use of carbon fuels that may cause global warming, in part because there is so much uncertainty about whether global warming is taking place and at what rate.[41]

Environmental issues often pit developing countries against the industrialized countries. The world is anxious for Brazil to protect its rain forests with their unique biological resources. Many Brazilians ask why they should forgo the potential benefits

---

[41] The World Bank's *World Development Review*, 1992, presents a comprehensive examination of the relationship between economic growth and the environment.

of developing the Amazon basin when other countries destroyed their forests centuries ago. Similarly, the industrialized countries want the developing countries to curb their polluting activities, for instance, China's use of coal. Presumably these issues will be settled through environmentally targeted aid from the industrialized to the developing countries.

There is no question that additional resources will have to be devoted to environmental protection, and that this will slow measured growth. In the meantime, we have to rely on human ingenuity to continue to produce the improvements in technology that have made modern standards of living possible, and that have overcome the limits of natural resources, the need to preserve the environment, and diminishing returns to capital and labor.

Convergence

To conclude, we return to the question of convergence. Will the developing economies ever catch up to the industrialized economies? The answer is, some. Growth at the rate of the newly industrializing economies (NIEs) will enable them to catch up fast, as Korea appears to be doing and as Japan has done. Economic leadership changes: according to Angus Maddison of the University of Groningen in the Netherlands, the Netherlands had the highest per capita income in 1700, the United Kingdom in 1800, and the United States in 1900.[42] If present trends continue, Japan will have the highest per capita income in the year 2000, even when measured by ICP standards.

But while the NIEs are growing fast, some countries in Africa are falling back, with per capita incomes declining. Similarly, at the turn of this century Argentina was one of the world's richest countries; now its annual income is only about $2,500 per capita. In short, there is nothing inevitable about the poorer countries catching up, or for that matter about the current leaders staying ahead. That is why growth is a major concern of U.S. economic policy.

10-6 SUMMARY

1. A production function links factor inputs and technology to the level of output. Growth of output—changes in technology aside—is a weighted average of input growth with the weights equal to income shares. The production function directs attention to factor inputs and technological change as sources of output growth.
2. In U.S. history since 1889, output per head has grown at an average rate of 1.8 percent. Over the 1929–1982 period, growth in factor inputs accounted for two-thirds and technical progress for one-third of the average growth rate of 2.9 percent of output. Growth in the stock of knowledge, along with growth in labor input, was the most important source of growth.
3. The growth rate of output in the major economies decreased sharply in the 1970s, recovered somewhat in the 1980s, and slowed again in the early 1990s. The

---

[42] See Maddison, *Phases of Capitalist Development.* See, too, the data on the first back endpaper of this book.

slowdown reflects a decline in productivity growth, which has been ascribed to several factors, most of which began reversing themselves in the late 1980s and in the early 1990s. Even so, predictions are for slower growth rates in the 1990s than earlier in the post–World War II period.

4. In neoclassical growth theory, the concept of steady-state equilibrium points (in the absence of technical change) to the conditions required for output per head to be constant. With a growing population, saving must be just sufficient to provide new members of the population with the economywide amount of capital per head.

5. The steady-state level of income is determined by the saving rate and by population growth. In the absence of technical change, the steady-state growth rate of total output is equal to the rate of population growth.

6. An increase in the saving rate transitorily raises the growth rate of output. In the new steady state, the growth rate remains unchanged, but the level of output per head is increased.

7. With technical change, per capita output in the steady state grows at the rate of technical progress. Total output grows at the sum of the rates of technical progress and population growth. Thus, in neoclassical growth theory, the steady-state rate of growth is exogenous.

8. Endogenous growth theory attempts to determine the steady-state growth rate within the theory. It does this either by making the rate of technical progress endogenous or by assuming that there are constant returns to scale to factors of production that can be accumulated.

9. The empirical work associated with endogenous growth theory tends to support neoclassical growth theory in finding conditional convergence. It emphasizes the rate of investment, especially in machinery investment, infrastructure, and human capital, as determinants of the growth rate of output in the short run and the steady-state level of income in the long run.

10. Supply-side economics proposes to raise the level and growth rate of full-employment output by creating improved incentives for work, saving, and investment and by reducing regulation. Empirical research suggests that incentives would be successful on the labor supply side and that reduced government deficits would stimulate investment.

11. Economic development takes place as a result of the accumulation of factors of production, including human capital, operating in a stable economic and political framework.

KEY TERMS

Production function

Growth accounting

Sources of growth

Technical progress

Steady state

Human capital

Development economies

Neoclassical growth theory

Endogenous growth theory

Infrastructure investment

Growth of total factor productivity

Newly industrializing economies (NIEs)

Convergence

PROBLEMS

1. Which of the following government activities have effects on the long-term growth rate: (a) monetary policy, (b) labor market policies, (c) educational and research policies, (d) fiscal policy, (e) population control programs. Explain how they can do so.

2. Suppose the share of capital in income is 0.4 and the share of labor is 0.6. Capital grows by 6 percent, and labor supply declines by 2 percent.
   (a) What happens to output? (Assume there is no technical change.)
   (b) How long does it take for output to double?

3. Since 1973, the growth rate of productivity has sharply declined in most industrialized countries. List several of the factors that are responsible for this decline and discuss why the decline in productivity growth is an important issue.

4. An earthquake destroys one-quarter of the capital stock. Discuss in the context of the growth model the adjustment process of the economy, and show, using Figure 10-2, what happens to growth in the short run and the long run.

5. (a) Show graphically (using a diagram like Figure 10-2) how an increase in the population growth rate affects the growth rate of output per capita and aggregate output in the short run and the long run.
   (b) Use a diagram like Figure 10-4 to show the time paths of per capita income and the per capita capital stock following the change.

6. Evaluate this statement: "The saving rate cannot affect the growth of output in the economy. That is determined by the growth of labor input and by technical progress." (*Hint:* You may want to use an endogenous growth model.)

7. Suppose we assume a production function of the form

$$Y = AF(K, N, Z)$$

where Z is a measure of the natural resources going into production. Assume this production function obeys constant returns to scale and diminishing returns to each factor [like equation (1)].
   (a) What will happen to output per head if capital and labor grow together but resources are fixed?
   (b) What if Z is fixed but there is technical progress?
   (c) In the 1970s there were fears that we were running out of natural resources and therefore that there were limits to growth. Discuss this view using your answers to (a) and (b).

8. Equation (1) includes human capital as a separate factor of production. (In this case N should be thought of as untrained labor.) Derive a growth accounting equation like equation (2) for the production function (3).

9. (a) Using the data in the two top rows of Table 10-1, calculate how long it would take for per capita income in India to reach that of the United States.
   (b) How long would it take India to catch up to Korea?
   (c) Explain why you believe or don't believe these answers.

*10. Use the neoclassical model of long-run growth to incorporate the government. Assume that an income tax at the rate t is levied and that, accordingly, saving per head is equal to $s(1 - t)y$. The government spends the tax revenue on public consumption.

---

*An asterisk denotes a more difficult problem.

(a) Use Figure 10-2 to explore the impact of an increase in the tax rate on the steady-state output level and capital per head.

(b) Draw a chart of the time path of capital per head, output per head, and the growth rate of output.

(c) Discuss the statement: "To raise the growth rate of output, the public sector has to run a budget surplus to free resources for investment."

11. Use Figure 10-2 to explore the impact of a *once-and-for-all* improvement in technology.

(a) How does technical progress affect the level of output per head at a given capital-labor ratio?

(b) Show the new steady-state equilibrium. Has saving changed? Is income per head higher? Has the capital stock increased?

(c) Show the time path of the adjustment to the new steady state. Does technical progress transitorily raise the ratio of investment to capital?

12. The chapter started with two questions. First, what determines the growth rate of output over long periods? And second, will the lower-income countries eventually catch up to the higher-income countries, and perhaps even overtake them? What are the answers?

🖫 COMPUTER EXERCISES

For this set of exercises, raise population growth (*n*) to 6 percent per year.

1. Study the effect on the steady-state equilibrium of this 6 percent increase in the population growth rate. What happens to output per capita (*y*), the per capita capital stock (*k*), and the per capita level of savings (*s* × *y*)?

2. Look at the graphs for the growth rate and the adjustment paths over time. Why are they shaped as they are? Explain what happens during adjustment to the new steady state.

3. By how much would the savings rate (*s*) have to increase to offset the decline in output per capita? How will such an increase affect *k* and the savings *level* (*s* × *y*)?

4. Compare the new adjustment path to your answer to exercise 2.

APPENDIX: PROPERTIES OF THE PRODUCTION FUNCTION

In this appendix we briefly show how the fundamental growth equation (2) is obtained. The material is presented for completeness; it is not essential to an understanding of the text.

We start with a production function that exhibits constant returns: increasing *all* inputs in the same proportion raises output in that same proportion. Thus if we double all inputs, output will double. With that property, the change in output due to technical progress and to changes in inputs can be written as

$$\Delta Y = F(K, N) \, \Delta A + MPK \, \Delta K + MPN \, \Delta N \tag{A1}$$

where *MPK* and *MPN* are the marginal products of capital and labor, respectively. We remember that the marginal product of a factor tells us the contribution to output made by employing one extra unit of the factor. Dividing both sides of the equation by $Y = AF(K, N)$ yields the expression

$$\frac{\Delta Y}{Y} = \frac{\Delta A}{A} + \frac{MPK}{Y} \Delta K + \frac{MPN}{Y} \Delta N \tag{A2}$$

Equation (A2) is further simplified by multiplying and dividing the second term on the right-hand side by K and the third term by N.

$$\frac{\Delta Y}{Y} = \frac{\Delta A}{A} + \left(K\frac{MPK}{Y}\right)\frac{\Delta K}{K} + \left(N\frac{MPN}{Y}\right)\frac{\Delta N}{N} \tag{A3}$$

We now argue that the terms in parentheses are the income shares of capital and labor. In a competitive market, factors are paid their marginal product. Thus the term $N(MPN/Y) = wN/Y$, where w is the real wage: the right-hand side is recognized as the ratio of labor income to total income or the share of labor in income. Similarly, the term $K(MPK/Y)$ is the share of capital in income. With constant returns and competition, factor payments exhaust the total product. Therefore the shares of capital and labor sum to unity. Denoting the share of capital in income by θ and the labor share by $1 - \theta$, we arrive at equation (2) in the text.

We note a further property of the constant-returns production function. When returns to scale are constant, we can write the production function as follows:

$$Y = AF(K, N) = NA\, F\left(\frac{K}{N}, 1\right) \tag{A4}$$

or using the notation $y = Y/N$ and $k = K/N$

$$y = Af(k) \tag{A5}$$

This is the form used in the growth theory section of the text, where output per head is a function of the capital-labor ratio and A has been set equal to one.

part three

BEHAVIORAL FOUNDATIONS

CONSUMPTION AND SAVING

There are two big reasons to go more deeply into consumption than we did in Chapter 3. First, consumption purchases account for more than 60 percent of aggregate demand; to understand the forces that affect aggregate demand, we have to understand what drives consumption. Second, income that is not consumed is saved, and the low U.S. rate of saving is often cited as a prime reason other countries are overtaking the United States as the richest industrial country in the world. As Table 11-1 shows, the U.S. national saving rate is extremely low by international standards. To understand saving, we have to understand consumption.[1] There is a third reason to study consumption: the economics of consumption is fascinating, something we are all interested in because we all have to make the decisions that the theories describe.

TABLE 11-1
INTERNATIONAL COMPARISONS OF SAVING RATES, 1980s (percent)

	U.S.	Japan	Germany	U.K.	Canada
Gross national saving*	16.3	31.6	22.5	16.6	20.7
Net national saving†	3.7	20.8	11.6	5.4	9.4

*As percentage of GNP.

†Net saving (= gross saving − depreciation) as percentage of NNP.

SOURCE: OECD, *Annual National Accounts.*

---

[1] Table 11-1 draws attention to the difference between the gross and net rates of saving, where net saving is gross saving minus depreciation. In addition, we see in Sec. 11-4 that there is a difference between household saving rates and *national* saving rates because both the government and the business sectors save (or maybe dissave) and thus contribute to national saving.

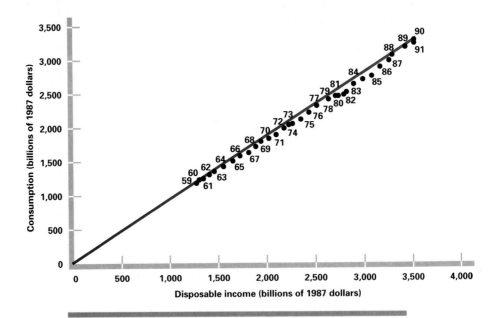

FIGURE 11-1

THE CONSUMPTION-INCOME RELATION, 1959–1992. There is a close relationship in practice between consumption spending and disposable income. Consumption spending rises on average by about 92 cents for every extra dollar of disposable income. The solid line is the fitted regression line that summarizes the relationship shown by the points for the individual years.

Our starting point is the consumption function we have been using in previous chapters. So far we have assumed that consumption (C) is determined by disposable income (YD):

$$C = \overline{C} + cYD \qquad 1 > c > 0 \tag{1}$$

We have already seen in Box 3-1 that the facts broadly support the relationship described by equation (1), but with the constant, $\overline{C}$, equal to zero. Figure 11-1 reproduces the Box 3-1 figure, which shows a very close link between consumption and disposable income, represented by the solid line, whose equation is[2]

$$C = 0.92YD \qquad \text{(annual data, 1948–1991)} \tag{2}$$

---

[2] The line drawn in Fig. 11-1 is represented by equation (2). That line is calculated by minimizing the sum of the squares of the vertical distances of the points in Fig. 11-1 from the line, and it provides a good description of the general relationship between the two variables. Those familiar with the method should note that we have corrected for serial correlation in calculating equation (2). For further details on the fitting of such lines, called least-squares regression lines, see Robert S. Pindyck and Daniel L. Rubinfeld, *Econometric Models and Economic Forecasts*, 3rd ed. (New York: McGraw-Hill, 1989).

Equation (2) implies that the average propensity to consume, C/YD, is constant and equal to 0.921.

As a first approximation, equation (2) provides a reasonable summary of consumption behavior. However, it is quite inaccurate in some years. For instance, in 1989 predicted consumption was below $3,191, which is $32 billion less than actual consumption.[3] This is an error of 0.7 percent of GDP. Errors of that size strongly suggest that the simplest consumption function can be improved upon.

We will now develop the two basic modern theories of consumption. They are the *life-cycle* theory, associated primarily with Franco Modigliani of MIT, the 1985 Nobel prizewinner in economic science,[4] and the *permanent-income* theory, associated primarily with Milton Friedman of the University of Chicago, the 1976 winner of the same prize. The theories are quite similar. Like much of good macroeconomics, they pay careful attention to microeconomic foundations. The life-cycle theory in particular starts from an individual's lifetime consumption planning, and goes on to develop from that a macroeconomic theory of consumption and saving. Then in Section 11-4 we turn to national saving rates and the international differences seen in Table 11-1.

11-1 THE LIFE-CYCLE THEORY OF CONSUMPTION AND SAVING

The consumption function (1) assumes that individuals' consumption behavior in a given period is related to their income in that period. The *life-cycle hypothesis* views individuals, instead, as planning their consumption and saving behavior over long periods with the intention of allocating their consumption in the best possible way over their entire lifetimes. The life-cycle hypothesis views savings as resulting mainly from individuals' desires to provide for consumption in old age. As we shall see, the theory points to a number of unexpected factors affecting the saving rate of the economy; for instance, the theory identifies the age structure of the population as an important determinant of consumption and saving behavior.

To anticipate, we state here that we will derive a consumption function of the form

$$C = aWR + cYL \tag{3}$$

where WR is real wealth, a is the marginal propensity to consume out of wealth, YL is *labor income*, and c is the marginal propensity to consume out of labor income—income earned by current work, rather than other incomes such as rents and profits. We will show what determines the marginal propensities a and c, and why wealth should affect consumption. Figure 11-2 helps you follow the argument.

---

[3] See the data appendix at the end of this chapter.

[4] Modigliani developed the life-cycle theory together with Richard Brumberg, who died tragically young, and Albert Ando of the University of Pennsylvania. Modigliani's Nobel Prize lecture, "Life Cycle, Individual Thrift, and the Wealth of Nations," appears in the June 1986 *American Economic Review.*

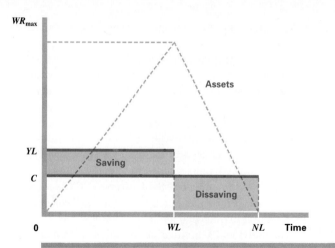

FIGURE 11-2

LIFETIME INCOME, CONSUMPTION, SAVINGS, AND WEALTH IN THE LIFE-
CYCLE MODEL. During the working life, lasting *WL* years, the
individual saves, building up assets. At the end of the working life,
the individual begins to live off these assets, dissaving for the next
(*NL* − *WL*) years, till the end of life. Consumption is constant at
level *C* throughout the lifetime. All assets have been used up at the
end of life.

Consider a person who expects to live for *NL* years, work and earn income of
YL each year for *WL* years, and then to live in retirement for (*NL* − *WL*) years.[5] The
individual's year 1 is the first year of work. We shall, in what follows, ignore any
uncertainty about either life expectancy or the length of working life. We assume, too,
that no interest is earned on savings and that prices are constant, so that current saving
translates dollar for dollar into future consumption possibilities.

With these assumptions, we can approach the saving or consumption decision
with two questions. First, what are the individual's lifetime consumption possibilities?
Given *WL* years of working life, *lifetime income* (from labor) is (*YL* × *WL*): income
per working year times the number of working years. Consumption over someone's
lifetime cannot exceed this lifetime income unless that person is born with wealth,
which we initially assume is not the case. Accordingly, we have determined that over
the lifetime, the individual can spend a maximum of (*YL* × *WL*).

The second question is how will the individual choose to distribute his or her
consumption over a lifetime? We assume he or she prefers to have a flat or even flow
of consumption—the preferred profile is to consume exactly equal amounts in each

---

[5] You may find it useful to follow the argument using the numerical example on p. 301. In that case, *NL* is
60, *WL* is 45, and *YL* is $30,000.

period.[6] Clearly, this assumption implies that consumption is geared not to *current income* (which is zero during retirement), but rather to *lifetime income*.

With lifetime consumption equal to lifetime income, the planned level of consumption, *C*, which is the same in every period, times the number of years of life, *NL*, equals lifetime income:

$$C \times NL = YL \times WL \tag{4}$$

Dividing through by *NL*, we have planned consumption per year, *C*, which is proportional to labor income:

$$C = \frac{WL}{NL} \times YL \tag{5}$$

The factor of proportionality in equation (5) is *WL/NL*, the fraction of the lifetime spent working. Accordingly, equation (5) states that in each year of working life a fraction of labor income is consumed, where that fraction is equal to the proportion of working life in total life.

NUMERICAL EXAMPLE: Suppose a person starts working at age 20, plans to work until 65, and will die at 80. The working life, *WL*, is thus 45 years (= 65 − 20) and the number of years of life, *NL*, is 60 years (= 80 − 20). Annual labor income, *YL*, is $30,000. Then

$$\text{Lifetime income} = YL \times WL$$
$$= \$30,000 \times 45 = \$1,350,000$$

This person will receive a total of $1,350,000 over her working lifetime. The consumer wants to spread the $1,350,000 evenly over the lifetime, and so

$$C = \frac{\$1,350,000}{60} = \$22,500 = \frac{WL}{NL} \times YL$$

$$= \frac{45}{60} \times 30,000 = 0.75 \times 30,000$$

---

[6] Why? The basic reason is the notion of diminishing marginal utility of consumption. Consider two alternative consumption plans. One involves an equal amount of consumption in each of two periods; the other involves consuming all in one period and none in the other. The principle of diminishing marginal utility of consumption implies that in the latter case, we would be better off by transferring some consumption from the period of plenty toward that of starvation. The loss in utility in the period of plenty is *more* than compensated for by the gain in utility in the period of scarcity. And there is a gain to be made by transferring consumption so long as there is any difference in consumption between the two periods. The principle of diminishing marginal utility of consumption conforms well with the observation that most people choose stable life styles—not, in general, saving furiously in one period to have a huge spending spree in the next but, rather, consuming at about the same level every period.

In this example, 0.75 of labor income is consumed each year the person works. Why? Because 0.75 is the fraction of his or her lifetime the person works. One-quarter of each year's income is saved for consumption during the one-quarter of the lifetime that she will be retired.

Saving and Dissaving

The counterpart of equation (5) is the saving function. Remembering that saving is equal to income less consumption, we have

$$S = YL - C = \frac{NL - WL}{NL} \times YL \tag{6}$$

As the numerical example and equation (6) show, the saving rate during working life is equal to the proportion of life spent in retirement.

Figure 11-2 shows the lifetime pattern of consumption, saving, and dissaving.[7] Over the whole lifetime, there is an even flow of consumption at the rate of C, amounting in total to $C \times NL$. That consumption spending is financed during working life out of current income. During retirement the consumption is financed by drawing down the savings that have been accumulated during working life. Therefore the shaded areas $(YL - C) \times WL$ and $C \times (NL - WL)$ are equal, or, equivalently, saving during working years finances dissaving during retirement.

Figure 11-2 demonstrates the key idea of the life-cycle theory of consumption: *consumption plans are made so as to achieve a smooth or even level of consumption by saving during periods of high income and dissaving during periods of low income.* This is an important departure from the treatment of consumption as being based on current income. It is an important difference because, in addition to current income, the whole future profile of income enters into the calculation of lifetime consumption. Before developing that aspect further, however, we return to Figure 11-2 to consider the role of assets.

ASSETS

As a result of her saving during her working life, the individual builds up assets. Figure 11-2 shows how the individual's wealth or assets increase over working life and reach a maximum at retirement age. From that time on, assets decline as they are sold or cashed in to pay for current consumption.

What is the maximum level that assets reach? Remember that assets are built up to finance consumption during retirement. Total consumption during retirement is equal to $C \times (NL - WL)$. All that consumption is financed out of the assets accumulated by the date of retirement, which is when assets are at their peak. Denote the maximum level of assets by WR_{max}. Then

$$WR_{max} = C \times (NL - WL)$$

---

[7] Figure 11-2 was developed by Franco Modigliani in "The Life Cycle Hypothesis of Saving, the Demand for Wealth and the Supply of Capital," *Social Research*, vol. 33, no. 2, 1966.

In the numerical example above, where C was \$22,500 and $(NL - WL)$ was equal to 15, the individual would have \$22,500 $\times$ 15 = \$337,500 saved at the date of retirement. Equivalently, the person has worked for 45 years, saving \$7,500 each year, thus accumulating \$337,500 at age 65.

SUMMARY

This simple case, in which income is constant during the working life, there is no uncertainty, the individual has no initial wealth, and so on, gives the spirit of the life-cycle theory of consumption and saving. People save and dissave so as to consume their lifetime incomes in the pattern they want. Typically, the theory argues, they will save while working, and then use the savings to finance spending in their retirement years. More generally, *the life-cycle theory of saving predicts that people save a lot when their income is high relative to lifetime average income and dissave when their income is low relative to the lifetime average.*

Introducing Wealth

The next step is to extend this model by allowing for initial assets, or wealth.[8] We draw on the previous insight that the consumer will try to achieve an even lifetime consumption profile. A person who is at some point T in life, with a stock of wealth, WR, and with labor income accruing for another $(WL - T)$ years at the rate of YL, and with a life expectancy of $(NL - T)$ years to go, has lifetime consumption possibilities

$$C \times (NL - T) = WR + (WL - T) \times YL \tag{7}$$

Now wealth, WR, as well as lifetime labor income, is a source of finance for lifetime consumption. From equation (7), consumption in each period is equal to

$$C = aWR + cYL \qquad a \equiv \frac{1}{NL - T} \qquad c \equiv \frac{WL - T}{NL - T} \qquad WL > T \tag{8}$$

where the coefficients a and c are, respectively, the marginal propensities to consume out of wealth[9] and out of labor income.

In the numerical example above, we considered a person starting to work at age 20 who will retire at 65 and die at 80. Thus $WL = (65 - 20) = 45$; and $NL = (80 - 20) = 60$. We also assumed $YL = 30,000$. Now suppose the person is 40 years old. Accordingly, $T = 20$, meaning that the person is in the twentieth year of

---

[8] The individual may receive wealth through gifts or bequests. In the fully developed life-cycle model, the individual, in calculating lifetime consumption, has also to take account of any bequests he or she may want to leave. We discuss the role of bequests in Box 11-1.

[9] Note that wealth changes over time, as a result of saving, changes in asset (e.g., stock) prices, and gifts and bequests. The coefficient a, which changes over the individual's lifetime, is the propensity to consume out of current wealth.

working life. We can calculate the propensity to consume out of wealth, a, and the propensity to consume out of income, c, from equation (8). For this person, at age 40 (i.e., for $T = 20$):

$$a = \frac{1}{NL - T} = \frac{1}{60 - 20} = 0.025$$

$$c = \frac{WL - T}{NL - T} = \frac{45 - 20}{60 - 20} = 0.625$$

Suppose now that the individual's wealth is $200,000. Then from the consumption function, equation (8), we find:

$$C = (0.025 \times 200,000) + (0.625 \times 30,000) = 23,500$$

The consumption level here is higher than in the previous example. That is because this individual has more wealth at age 40 than he or she would have if all this wealth came from saving out of labor income. (That amount would be $150,000, since the individual in the previous example saved $7,500 per year, and at $T = 20$, has been working 20 years.) We must be dealing here with someone who started out working life with inherited wealth.

Thus, in our model of individual lifetime consumption, we have derived a consumption function like equation (3), in which both wealth and labor income affect the individual's consumption decisions. It is important to recognize from equation (8) that the marginal propensities are related to the individual's position in the life cycle. The closer a person is to the end of lifetime, the higher the marginal propensity to consume out of wealth. Thus, someone with 2 more years of life will consume half his or her remaining wealth in each of the remaining 2 years. The marginal propensity to consume out of labor income is related both to the remaining number of years during which income will be earned, $WL - T$, and to the number of years over which these earnings are spread, $NL - T$.

It is quite clear from equation (8) that an increase in either wealth or labor income will raise consumption expenditures. It is apparent, too, that lengthening working life relative to retirement will raise consumption because it increases lifetime income and reduces the length of the period of dissaving.

To summarize, we note that in this particular form of the life-cycle model:

1. Consumption is constant over the consumer's lifetime.
2. Consumption spending is financed by lifetime income plus initial wealth.
3. During each year a fraction, $1/(NL - T)$, of wealth will be consumed, where $(NL - T)$ is the individual's life expectancy.
4. Current consumption spending depends on current wealth and lifetime income.

Extensions

The model as outlined makes very strong simplifying assumptions. It can be extended to remove most of the strong assumptions without affecting the underlying result of equation (8), namely, that consumption is related to both labor income and wealth.

The first extension is very important. In practice, (1) labor income changes over time, and (2) one never knows exactly what lifetime labor income will be. *It follows that lifetime consumption plans have to be made on the basis of predictions of future labor income.*

This immediately raises the question of how to predict future income. We leave this issue to the next section on permanent income, which is an estimate of lifetime income. However, *expected* lifetime labor income would be related to *current* disposable labor income, leading to a form of the consumption function like equation (3), perhaps with other variables also included. Second, it is necessary to take account of the possibility that savings earn interest, so that a dollar not consumed today provides more than a dollar's consumption tomorrow. In addition, the analysis has to be extended to allow for the fact that individuals are uncertain of the length of their lifetimes and, also, that they sometimes want to leave bequests to their heirs. In the latter case, they would not plan to consume all their resources over their own lifetimes. We discuss the role of bequests in Box 11-1. Similarly, the model has to be extended to take account of the composition of the family over time, so that some consumption is provided for children before they begin to work. These extensions are important and have interesting implications for the behavior of consumption, but—to repeat—they do not change the basic result contained in equation (8).

Aggregate Consumption and Saving

The theory outlined so far is strictly a microeconomic theory about an individual's lifetime consumption and saving patterns. How does it relate to aggregate consumption, which is, after all, the focus of macroeconomic interest in consumption? Imagine an economy in which population and the GNP were constant through time. Each individual in that economy would go through the life cycle of saving and dissaving outlined in Figure 11-2. The economy as a whole, though, would not be saving. At any one time, the saving of working people would be exactly matched by the dissaving of retired people.

However, if the population were growing, there would be more young people saving than when the population is constant, thus more saving in total than dissaving, and there would be net saving in the economy. Thus, aggregate consumption and saving depend in part on the age distribution of the population. With more people of saving age, net saving increases. Some economists argue that these demographic factors help account for the fact that household saving rates in Japan are much higher than those in the United States: the proportion of retired people is lower in Japan than in the United States. Because the percentage of the elderly in the Japanese population is rising rapidly, some economists expect the Japanese saving rate will start falling before the end of the century.[10]

Aggregate saving also depends on such characteristics of the economy as the average age of retirement[11] and the presence or absence of a social security program.

---

[10] See, for instance, Alan J. Auerbach, Laurence J. Kotlikoff, Robert P. Hagemann, and Giuseppe Nicoletti, "The Economic Dynamics of an Ageing Population: The Case of Four OECD Countries," *OECD Economic Studies,* Spring 1989, whose calculations suggest that Japanese saving rates would be below those in the United States by the year 2030.

[11] The older the retirement age, the less an individual needs to save for retirement.

box 11-1

THE LIFE-CYCLE HYPOTHESIS, CONSUMPTION BY THE ELDERLY, AND BEQUESTS

Although the life-cycle hypothesis remains the leading microeconomic theory of consumption behavior, recent empirical evidence raises questions about the particular form of the theory developed in this chapter. In the form of the theory developed by Modigliani, the assumption is that people save mainly for retirement and draw down their savings during that period. Laurence Kotlikoff and Lawrence Summers* have made calculations suggesting, on the contrary, that most saving is done to provide bequests rather than consumption when old. Of course, the savings are there for the old to use in retirement, but, they argue, the amount of wealth in the economy is far too large for people to have been saving only for their retirement. Rather, they conclude, people are saving mainly to pass wealth on to their descendants.

A detailed examination of the consumption propensities of the elderly by Sheldon Danziger, Jacques van der Gaag, Eugene Smolensky, and Michael Taussig[†] contains the remarkable conclusion that the elderly save a higher proportion of their incomes than the young. This fact is inconsistent with the simple form of the life-cycle hypothesis set out in the chapter.

How might this evidence be reconciled with existing theories? First, the facts are not yet definitive. Franco Modigliani has taken strong issue with the detailed calculations that underlie the Kotlikoff-Summers claim.[‡] In Japan, where similar results have been found,[§] the elderly typically move in and pool their wealth with their children. They are thus probably drawing down wealth during their retirement, but their wealth cannot be distinguished from that of the children, who are saving.

The behavior of the old has to be explained by taking into account their increasing fears of being left alone without financial help from family, and with possibly large medical expenses, as they get older. The need for wealth may increase with age if complete insurance against medical expenses is not available—as it is not. Whether people save for their own lifetimes, or also save to pass wealth on to their children—including transfers that take place during the parents' lifetime, such as paying for college education—does not affect the fact that wealth belongs in the consumption function, as in equation (3). ∎

---

*"The Role of Intergenerational Transfers in Aggregate Capital Accummulation," *Journal of Political Economy*, August 1981.

†"The Life Cycle Hypothesis and the Consumption Behavior of the Elderly," *Journal of Post-Keynesian Economics*, Winter 1982–1983.

‡"The Role of Intergenerational Transfers and Life Cycle Saving in the Accumulation of Wealth," *Journal of Economic Perspectives*, vol. 2, Spring 1988. See also the discussion of this article by Laurence Kotlikoff that follows.

§See Albert Ando and Arthur Kennickell, "How Much (or Little) Life Cycle Saving Is There in Micro Data?" in Rudiger Dornbusch, Stanley Fischer, and John Bossons (eds.), *Macroeconomics and Finance: Essays in Honor of Franco Modigliani* (Cambridge, Mass.: MIT Press, 1986).

If there is a social security system, which provides retirement income for individuals, then individuals need to save less for their retirement. What happens to aggregate saving then depends on whether the government saves in order to fund future social security payments to retirees. If the government does not increase its saving, planning rather to use taxes to finance payments to retirees, aggregate saving decreases when social security replaces private saving.[12]

The life-cycle hypothesis also provides a channel for the stock market to affect consumption behavior. The value of stocks held by the public is part of wealth and is included in *WR* in equation (8). When the value of stocks is high—when the stock market is booming—*WR* is high and tends to increase consumption, and the reverse occurs when the stock market is depressed (see Box 11-2).

We continue now to the permanent-income theory of consumption, bearing in mind that we have not yet discussed the determinants of expected lifetime labor income in any detail, and recalling that the two theories should be thought of as complementary rather than competing.

11-2 PERMANENT-INCOME THEORY OF CONSUMPTION

Like the life-cycle hypothesis, the permanent-income theory of consumption argues that consumption is related not to current income, but to a longer-term estimate of income, which Milton Friedman, who introduced the theory,[13] calls *permanent income*.

Friedman provides a suggestive example. Consider a person who is paid or receives income only once a week, on Fridays. We do not expect that person to consume only on Friday, with zero consumption on the other days of the week. People prefer a smooth consumption flow rather than plenty today and scarcity tomorrow or yesterday. On that argument, consumption on any one day of the week would be geared to average daily income—that is, income per week divided by the number of days per week.

It is clear that in this extreme example, income for a period longer than a day is relevant to the consumption decision. Similarly, Friedman argues, there is nothing special about a period of the length of one quarter or one year that requires the individual to plan consumption within the period solely on the basis of income within the period; rather, consumption is planned in relation to income over a longer period.

The idea of consumption spending that is geared to long-term or average or permanent income is appealing and essentially the same as the life-cycle theory. In its simplest form the theory argues that consumption is proportional to permanent income:

$$C = cYP \tag{9}$$

where *YP* is permanent (disposable) income.

Now we have to ask how to make the concept of permanent income operational, that is, how to define and estimate it.

---

[12] We return to this issue in Sec. 11-4, when we discuss government saving.

[13] Milton Friedman, *A Theory of the Consumption Function* (Princeton, N.J.: Princeton University Press, 1957).

box 11-2 ## CONSUMPTION AND THE 1987 STOCK MARKET CRASH

On October 19, 1987, when the New York stock market crashed (other stock markets all around the world suffered similar huge falls that day or the next), with stocks losing over 20 percent of their value in a single day, economists used a consumption function like (8) to estimate the likely effect of the crash on the level of consumption. Stocks lost over $500 billion in value on October 19, 1987. The figure 1 shows an index of household real net worth. In the fourth quarter of 1987 this index fell by 4 percent.

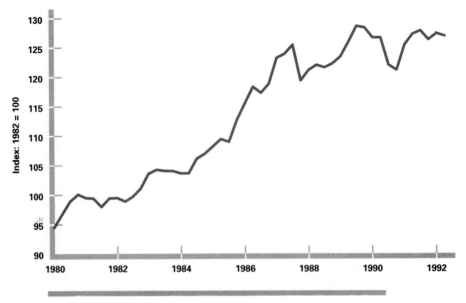

FIGURE 1
HOUSEHOLD REAL NET WORTH, 1983–1992. (Source: DRI/McGraw-Hill.)

Estimating Permanent Income

We define permanent income as follows:[14] *permanent income* is the steady rate of consumption a person *could* maintain for the rest of his or her life, given the present level of wealth and income earned now and in the future. To think about the measurement

---

[14] There is no standard definition of permanent income in Friedman's exposition of his theory. The definition given here is similar to average lifetime income. But it is not quite the same, because it effectively converts wealth into income in defining permanent income. Those with no labor income and only wealth are defined as having permanent income equal to the amount they could consume each year by using up wealth at a steady rate over the remainder of their lives.

TABLE 1
U.S. HOUSEHOLD SAVING RATE, 1987:1–1988:3 (percent of disposable income)

1987:1	1987:2	1987:3	1987:4	1988:1	1988:2	1988:3
5.7	3.1	3.5	5	4.7	4.3	4.3

SOURCE: DRI/McGraw-Hill.

The coefficient of real wealth, a, in equation (8) is typically estimated to be about 0.045. Accordingly, the stock market crash would have reduced consumption by about $25 billion, or just over 0.5 percent of GNP at the time. This is a sizable fall, whose effects on GNP could, however, be overcome through an expansionary monetary policy.

Table 1 shows the behavior of the household saving rate in the quarters around the stock market crash, which took place near the beginning of the fourth quarter of 1987. The crash was followed by an increase in the saving rate of about 1.5 percentage points. This would imply a decrease in consumption of about $50 billion at an annual rate (disposable personal income was $3.3 trillion in 1987:4). Thus the stock market crash was followed by a bigger decline in consumption than can be accounted for by the wealth term in the consumption function.

There are at least two possible reasons for this. First, the stock market crash made people much more uncertain about the future of the economy, and increased uncertainty usually leads to more saving. And second, the estimates of the impact of changes in wealth on consumption are in any case not exact. ∎

of permanent income, imagine someone trying to figure out what his or her permanent income is. The person has a current level of income and has formed some idea of the level of consumption he or she can maintain for the rest of life. Now income goes up. The person has to decide whether that increase is permanent or is merely a *transitory*, or temporary, change. In any particular case, the individual may know whether the increase is permanent or transitory. An associate professor who is promoted to professor will think that the change is permanent; a worker who has exceptionally high overtime in a given year will likely regard that year's increased income as transitory. But in general, a person is not likely to be so sure whether a change is permanent or transitory. The difference matters, because transitory income is assumed not to have any substantial effect on consumption.

The question of how to infer what part of an increase in income is permanent is typically resolved in a pragmatic way by assuming that permanent income is related to the behavior of current and past incomes. To give a simple example, we might estimate permanent income as being equal to last year's income plus some fraction of the change in income from last year to this year:

$$YP = Y_{-1} + \theta(Y - Y_{-1}) \qquad 0 < \theta < 1$$
$$= \theta Y + (1 - \theta)Y_{-1} \qquad\qquad (10)$$

where θ is a fraction and Y_{-1} is last year's income. The second line in equation (10) shows permanent income as a *weighted average* of current and past income. The second formulation is, of course, equivalent to that in the first line.

To understand equation (10), assume we had a value of $\theta = 0.6$, that this year's income was $Y = \$25,000$, and that last year's income was $Y_{-1} = \$24,000$. The value of permanent income would be $YP = \$24,600$ $(= 0.6 \times \$25,000 + 0.4 \times \$24,000)$. Thus, permanent income is an average of the two income levels. Whether it is closer to this year's or last year's income depends on the weight, θ, given to current income. Clearly, in the extreme, with $\theta = 1$, permanent income is equal to current income.

Some special features of equation (10) deserve comment. First, if $Y = Y_{-1}$, that is, if this year's income is equal to last year's, then permanent income is equal to the income earned this year and last year. This guarantees that an individual who had always earned the same income would expect to earn that income in the future. Second, if income rises this year compared with last year, then permanent income rises by *less* than current income. The reason is that the individual does not know whether the rise in income this year is permanent. Not knowing, the individual guesses that some but not all of the increase will be maintained.

Rational Expectations and Permanent Income

An estimate of permanent income that uses only current and last year's income is likely to be an oversimplification. Friedman forms the estimate by looking at incomes in many earlier periods, as well as current income, but with weights that are larger for the more recent, as compared with the more distant, incomes.[15]

The rational expectations approach, discussed in Chapter 9 and in the following section, emphasizes that there is no simple theory that would tell us how expectations are or should be formed without looking at how income changes in practice. If, in practice, changes in income are typically permanent or long-run changes, then consumers who see a given change in their income will believe that it is mostly permanent. Such consumers would have a high θ, as in equation (10). Consumers whose income is usually highly variable will, however, not pay much attention to current changes in income in forming an estimate of permanent income. Such consumers will have low values of θ. At the same time, any sensible theory of expectations, including rational

---

[15] Friedman also adjusts his estimates of permanent income by taking into account the growth of income over time.

expectations, would emphasize that a formula like (10), based on the behavior of income in the past, cannot include all the factors that influence a person's beliefs about future income. The discovery of a vast amount of oil in a country, for instance, would raise the permanent incomes of the inhabitants of the country as soon as it was announced, even though a (mechanical) formula like equation (10), based on past levels of income, would not reflect such a change.

Permanent Income and the Dynamics of Consumption

Using equation (10), we can now rewrite the consumption function:

$$C = cYP = c\theta Y + c(1 - \theta)Y_{-1} \tag{11}$$

The marginal propensity to consume out of *current* income is then just $c\theta$, which is clearly less than the long-run average propensity to consume, c. Hence, the permanent-income hypothesis implies that there is a difference between the short-run marginal propensity to consume and the long-run marginal (equal to the average) propensity to consume.[16]

The reason for the lower short-run marginal propensity to consume has already been discussed: when current income rises, the individual is not sure that the increase in income will be maintained. However, if the increase turns out to be permanent, that is, if (in this example) next period's income is the same as this period's, then the person will (next year) fully adjust consumption spending to the higher level of income.[17]

The argument is illustrated in Figure 11-3. Here we show the long-run consumption function as a straight line through the origin with slope c, which is the constant average and marginal propensity to consume out of permanent income. The lower flat consumption function is a short-run consumption function drawn for a given history of income which is reflected in the intercept $c(1 - \theta)Y_0$. Assume that we start out in long-run equilibrium with actual and permanent income equal to Y_0 and consumption therefore equal to cY_0, as shown at the intersection, point E, of the long-run and short-run consumption functions. Assume next that income increases to the level Y'. In the short run, which means during the current period, we revise our estimate of permanent income upward by θ times the increase in income and consume a fraction, c, of that increase in permanent income. Accordingly, consumption moves up along the short-run consumption function to point E'.

Note that in the short run the ratio of consumption to income declines as we move from point E to E'. Going one period ahead and assuming that the increase in

---

[16] There is another reason consumption may adjust relatively slowly even to changes in permanent income: the consumer may take time to purchase consumer durables. For instance, someone whose permanent income has doubled will at some point end up in a more luxurious house, but will take some time to buy such a house and the furnishings that go with it.

[17] Note, though, that the adjustment here is completed in 2 years only because we assumed, in equation (10), that permanent income is an average of 2 years' income. Depending on how expectations of permanent income are formed, the adjustment could be much slower.

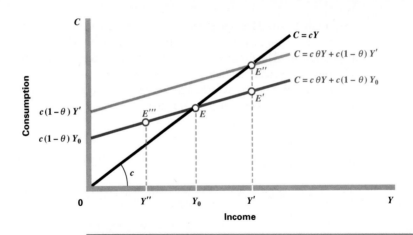

FIGURE 11-3
THE EFFECTS ON CONSUMPTION OF A SUSTAINED INCREASE IN INCOME.
The short-run consumption functions, shown in color, have a
marginal propensity to consume of $c\theta$. The position of the short-run
consumption function depends on the level of income in the
previous period. The long-run consumption function is shown by
the black line and has average and marginal propensity to consume
equal to c. When the level of income rises from Y_0 to Y',
consumption rises only to E' in the short run. But with income
remaining at Y', the short-run consumption function shifts up and
consumption rises to point E'', as consumers realize their permanent
income has changed.

income persists, so that income remains at Y', the short-run consumption function
shifts. It shifts upward because, as of the given higher level of income, the estimate
of permanent income is now revised upward to Y'. Accordingly, consumers want to
spend a fraction, c, of their new estimate of permanent income, Y'. The new consumption
point is E'', at which the ratio of consumption to income is back to the long-run level.

Like the life-cycle hypothesis, the permanent-income hypothesis has some unexpected and interesting implications. For instance, we noted above that an individual
whose income is very unstable would have a low value of θ, whereas one whose
income is more stable would have a higher value of θ. In looking at equation (11),
this means that the short-run marginal propensity to consume of someone whose income
is highly variable will be relatively low because the short-run marginal propensity to
consume is $c\theta$. Friedman showed that this implication is borne out by the facts. Farmers,
for instance, have highly variable incomes and a low marginal propensity to consume
out of current income.

The Life-Cycle and Permanent-Income Hypotheses

To conclude this section, it is worth briefly considering again the relationship between
the life-cycle and permanent-income hypotheses. The two hypotheses share the same

view that consumption is related to some measure of long-term income. The life-cycle hypothesis pays more attention to the motives for saving than the permanent-income hypothesis does, and it provides convincing reasons to include wealth as well as income in the consumption function. The permanent-income hypothesis, by contrast, pays more careful attention to the way in which individuals form expectations about their future incomes than the original life-cycle hypothesis does.

Modern theories of the consumption function combine the expectations emphasis of the permanent-income approach with the emphasis on wealth and demographic variables suggested by the life-cycle approach. A simplified version of a modern consumption function would be

$$C = aWR + b\theta YD + b(1 - \theta)YD_{-1} \tag{12}$$

where YD in equation (12) would be disposable labor income. Equation (12) combines the main features that are emphasized by modern consumption theory. It also shows the role of wealth, which is an important influence on consumption spending.

We end this section by repeating a warning. An equation like (12) performs quite well on average in predicting consumption. But it is important to remember the underlying theory when using it. If we have knowledge about some particular change in income—for example, that it is transitory—then we should use that knowledge in predicting consumption. For instance, a temporary 1-year tax increase that reduced current disposable income would reduce current consumption by less than a tax increase of the same size that was known to be permanent, even though equation (12) does not show that.

11-3 EXCESS SENSITIVITY, LIQUIDITY CONSTRAINTS, AND UNCERTAINTY

Much of the empirical work on consumption has tested implications of the life-cycle–permanent-income hypothesis that suggest consumption should not respond much to changes in current income, unless those changes are permanent. If consumption does respond "excessively" (in a sense to be defined shortly), the implication is that the simple Keynesian consumption function (2) is still relevant to aggregate consumption.

Modern research in this area, originating with work by Robert Hall of Stanford University and Marjorie Flavin of the University of Virginia, focuses on the combined implications of rational expectations and the life-cycle–permanent-income theory of consumption.[18] As noted in Section 11-2, if expectations are rational, consumers' estimates of their permanent incomes should be consistent with the way income actually changes in the real world. For example, historically a \$1 increase in current income might typically have represented a 25-cent increase in permanent income, with the

---

[18] Robert E. Hall, "Stochastic Implications of the Life Cycle–Permanent Income Hypothesis: Theory and Evidence," *Journal of Political Economy,* vol. 86, December 1978; and Marjorie Flavin, "The Adjustment of Consumption to Changing Expectations about Future Income," *Journal of Political Economy,* vol. 89, October 1981.

remaining 75 cents being transitory. Let θ be the fraction of a dollar increase in current income that represents the permanent increase. Then the consumption function in equation (9) together with this extra information about the current–permanent-income relation will yield a propensity to consume out of current income equal to $c\theta$. Thus if $c = 0.9$ and $\theta = 0.25$, the marginal propensity to consume out of current income should be 0.225, as implied by equation (11).

The researcher estimates how income behaves and can then tell how much on average of a given income change is permanent. The next step is to see whether consumption reacts appropriately to changes in income as implied by the combined rational expectations–permanent-income theory. The striking finding, for instance in Flavin's 1981 paper referred to earlier, is that consumption *systematically* responds too much to current income, or is excessively sensitive. When income rises, consumption goes up by more than $c\theta$, and when income falls, consumption goes down by more than $c\theta$. Similar results have been found for other countries.[19]

On the assumption, still, that the permanent-income hypothesis serves as a correct framework of consumption behavior, there are two possible explanations for this overreaction.[20] The first is that households are not forecasting in the best possible way and using all available information about how income behaves. This shortcoming would be a failure of the rational expectations hypothesis; for simplicity, we can refer to this as the *myopia hypothesis*, where myopia means shortsightedness. The alternative hypothesis is that while households in fact understand how income changes are divided between those that are permanent and those that are transitory, they fail to adjust to these changes properly because of liquidity constraints.

Excess Sensitivity, Liquidity Constraints, and Myopia

A liquidity constraint exists when a consumer cannot borrow to sustain current consumption in the expectation of higher future income. Students in particular should appreciate the possibility that liquidity constraints exist. Most students can look forward to a much higher income in the future than they receive as students. The life-cycle theory says they should be consuming on the basis of their lifetime incomes, which means they should be spending much more than they earn. To do that, they would have to borrow. They can borrow to some extent, through student loan plans. But it is entirely possible that they cannot borrow enough to support consumption at its permanent level.

Such students are liquidity-constrained. When they leave college and take jobs, their incomes will rise, and their consumption will rise, too. According to the life-cycle theory, consumption should not rise much when income rises, so long as the

---

[19] See John Campbell and N. Gregory Mankiw, "The Response of Consumption to Income," *European Economic Review,* 1991.

[20] There is not yet unanimity on the finding of excess sensitivity. Angus Deaton of Princeton University has argued that consumption may be too *insensitive* to changes in income or, as he puts it, excessively smooth. See, for instance, his "Life-Cycle Models of Consumption: Is the Evidence Consistent with the Theory?" in Truman Bewley (ed.), *Advances in Econometrics, Fifth World Congress,* vol. 2 (New York: Cambridge University Press, 1987). The issue turns on the nature of the behavior of income, with Deaton arguing that changes in income tend to be more permanent than other researchers have believed.

increase was expected. In fact, because of the liquidity constraint, consumption will rise a lot when income rises. Thus consumption will be more closely related to *current* income than is implied by the theory. Similarly, individuals who cannot borrow when their incomes decline temporarily would be liquidity-constrained.

How serious are these liquidity constraints in fact? There is substantial evidence that liquidity constraints help account for the excess sensitivity of consumption to income, and there is separate evidence that low-income households are indeed liquidity-constrained.[21] Indeed, estimates are that about half of U.S. consumption is accounted for by people who act as life-cycle–permanent-income consumers, and the other half by people who essentially consume all their current income.[22]

The alternative explanation for the sensitivity of consumption to current income, that consumers are myopic, is hard to distinguish in practice from the liquidity constraints hypothesis. For instance, David Wilcox of the Federal Reserve Board of Governors has shown that the announcement that social security benefits will be increased (which always happens at least 6 weeks before the change) does not lead to a change in consumption *until the benefit increases are actually paid.*[23] Once the increased benefits are paid, recipients certainly do adjust spending—primarily on durables. The delay could be either because recipients do not have the assets to enable them to adjust spending before they receive higher payments (liquidity constraints), or because they fail to pay attention to the announcements (myopia), or perhaps because they do not believe the announcements.

Uncertainty and Buffer Stock Saving

The life-cycle hypothesis is that people save largely to finance retirement. The evidence on bequests in Box 11-1 suggests that some saving is done to provide for bequests. There is also a growing amount of evidence to support the view that some saving is *precautionary*, undertaken to guard against rainy days. Equivalently, saving is used as a *buffer stock*, to maintain consumption when times are bad and to add to when times are good.

One piece of evidence is that old people rarely dissave. They tend to live off the income (e.g., interest and dividends) from their wealth, rather than reduce wealth. An explanation is that the older they are, the more they fear having to pay large bills for medical care, and therefore the more reluctant they are to spend. When consumers are asked in surveys why they are saving, their responses also point to saving being undertaken to meet emergency needs.

---

[21] For instance, Marjorie Flavin, "Excess Sensitivity of Consumption to Current Income: Liquidity Constraints or Myopia?" *Canadian Journal of Economics,* February 1985; Stephen P. Zeldes, "Consumption and Liquidity Constraints: An Empirical Investigation," *Journal of Political Economy,* April 1989; and Tullio Jappelli, "Who Is Credit Constrained in the U.S. Economy?" *Quarterly Journal of Economics,* February 1990.

[22] See Campbell and Mankiw, "Consumption, Income and Interest Rates: Reinterpreting the Time Series Evidence," *NBER Macroeconomic Annual,* 1989.

[23] David W. Wilcox, "Social Security Benefits, Consumption Expenditure, and the Life Cycle Hypothesis," *Journal of Political Economy,* April 1989.

This evidence is consistent with a version of the life-cycle model in which uncertainty about future income and future needs is explicitly included.[24] But it does lead to a different emphasis on the factors influencing saving, with more attention being paid to uncertainty than the simplest version of the life-cycle hypothesis implies.[25]

Summary

There is by now substantial evidence that aggregate consumption cannot be fully explained by the life-cycle–permanent-income hypothesis. Rather, some consumption is accounted for by life-cycle–permanent-income consumers, and some by simple Keynesian consumers of the type represented by equations (1) and (2). There is little doubt that this is in part due to the existence of liquidity constraints. There is also evidence to support the existence of buffer stock saving.

11-4 FURTHER ASPECTS OF CONSUMPTION BEHAVIOR

In this section we briefly review three topics in consumption, starting with international comparisons of saving behavior.

International Differences in Saving Rates

The U.S. saving rate is lower than that in other major countries, as Table 11-1 shows. This difference is especially striking when we look at *net* saving rates, net saving ($=$ total saving minus depreciation) as a share of net national product (NNP). The net saving rate is a measure of the rate at which a country is adding to its wealth, and the very low rate of national saving in the United States causes concern to Americans because other countries are increasing their wealth at so much higher a rate.

It is useful to look at the different sectors of the economy that save, starting with the government and private sectors:

$$\text{Gross national saving} = \text{government saving} + \text{private saving} \tag{13}$$

The government saves when it spends less than it receives, that is, when it runs a budget surplus. Table 11-2 shows government and private saving rates for major industrial countries. Clearly, the large government budget deficit helps account for the low saving rate in the United States. For example, the difference in private saving rates between Germany and the United States was only 2 percent of GNP, while the

---

[24] For example, Stephen Zeldes, "Optimal Consumption with Stochastic Income: Departures from Certainty Equivalence," *Quarterly Journal of Economics,* May 1989.

[25] See, for example, Christopher D. Carroll, "Buffer Stock Saving and the Permanent Income Hypothesis," Board of Governors of the Federal Reserve System Working Paper, February 1991.

TABLE 11-2
GOVERNMENT AND PRIVATE GROSS SAVING RATES, 1980s (percent)

	U.S.	Japan	Germany	U.K.	Canada
Gross national saving*	16.3	31.6	22.5	16.6	20.7
Government saving	−2.1	4.9	2.0	0.1	−1.6
Private saving	18.5	26.8	20.5	16.4	22.2

*All data are gross saving relative to GNP. Components may not sum to totals, due to rounding error.

SOURCE: OECD, *Annual National Accounts.*

TABLE 11-3
COMPOSITION OF U.S. SAVING, 1981–1990

Gross national saving rate*	15.1
Government saving	−2.5
Business saving	13.0
Household saving	4.6

*All ratios are sectoral saving as a percentage of GDP.

SOURCE: *Economic Report of the President,* 1992.

German government saved 4 percent of GNP more than the U.S. government. *It seems that one way to raise the U.S. saving rate is to reduce government budget deficits.*[26]

Next we look in Table 11-3 at the difference between business and personal saving in the United States:

$$\text{Private saving} = \text{business saving} + \text{personal saving} \qquad (14)$$

Business saving consists of retained earnings, that amount of profits not paid out to the owners of the business. A business saves when it does not pay income out to its owners, rather keeping those funds to plow back into the business.

The fact, seen in Table 11-3, that business saving is three times as large as personal saving in the United States has not received the attention it should.[27] That is

---

[26] Two points: (1) The government sector in Table 11-2 consists of federal, state, and local governments. (2) We examine later, under the heading of Ricardian equivalence, an argument that an increase in government spending would be completely offset by a reduction in private saving.

[27] International comparisons of the breakdown of saving between the business and personal sectors are difficult because data are not standardized. National data on saving may differ substantially—so much so that some economists contend, for example, that the U.S. and Japanese saving rates are the same when measured on a comparable basis. This view is not generally accepted.

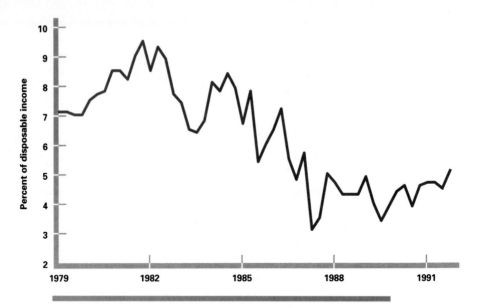

FIGURE 11-4

THE PERSONAL SAVING RATE, 1979–1992. The diagram shows personal saving as a percentage of disposable income. Despite tax cuts starting in 1981, the personal saving rate did not increase as the Barro-Ricardo hypothesis suggests it should have. (SOURCE: DRI/McGraw-Hill.)

partly because for a long time it seemed that households "pierced the corporate veil"— they treated business saving as if it was being done on their behalf and adjusted their own saving correspondingly.[28] The more recent evidence, though, is that households reduce their saving by about 50 cents for every extra dollar of saving done by business.[29] This means that reductions in business saving would reduce total private saving and, equivalently, that policies that increase business saving would increase total private saving. Given the relative neglect of the determinants of corporate saving, we expect significant amounts of research on this question in the 1990s.

Private saving trended downward in the United States in the 1980s (Figure 11-4). There has been no convincing single explanation for this trend. Among the reasons is the fact that the stock market did very well in the 1980s, so that wealth increased during the decade, increasing consumption and reducing saving.[30]

---

[28] This is known as *Denison's law,* after Edward Denison of the Brookings Institution. See Paul David and Jon Scadding, "Private Savings: Ultrarationality, Aggregation, and 'Denison's Law,' " *Journal of Political Economy,* March/April 1974.

[29] James Poterba, "Tax Policy and Corporate Savings," *Brookings Papers on Economic Activity,* 2, 1987.

[30] It has also been argued that the increase in house prices in the 1980s made consumers feel wealthier and therefore increased their spending. However, the impact of an increase in the price of houses on consumption

So why does the United States save less than other countries? First, the U.S. government runs large deficits, while other governments even run surpluses. Second, demographic factors referred to in Section 11-3 account for some of the remaining difference. A third reason, which we have not yet referred to, is that it is easier to borrow in the United States than in most other countries. In many countries, people have to save in order to make major purchases—a house or a car—whereas in the United States they can borrow for that purpose.

These factors do not fully account for international differences in saving rates. Some economists will in the end argue that there may simply be differences in national attitudes toward saving, but most still hope to find economic explanations for those underlying attitudes.

Consumption, Saving, and Interest Rates

Anyone who saves receives a return in the form of interest or of dividends and capital gains (an increase in the price) on stocks. It seems, then, that the natural way to raise saving is to raise the return available to savers. Think of someone saving and receiving an interest rate of 5 percent each year for each dollar saved. Surely an increase in the rate to, say, 10 percent would make that person save more. This thinking has at times influenced tax policy in the United States. For instance, the interest received on savings in individual retirement accounts is exempt from the payment of taxes. This means the return received by the saver is raised compared with what it would be if the return were taxed.

But should we really expect an increase in the interest rate to increase savings? It is true that when the interest rate rises, saving is made more attractive. But it is also less necessary. Consider someone who has decided to save an amount which will ensure that $10,000 per year will be available for retirement. Suppose the interest rate is now 5 percent, and the person is saving $1,000 per year. Now let the interest rate rise to 10 percent. With such a high interest rate, the individual needs to save less to provide the given $10,000 per year during retirement. It may be possible to provide the same retirement income by saving only about $650 a year. Thus an increase in the interest rate might reduce saving.

What do the facts show? Does saving rise when the interest rate increases because every dollar of saving generates a higher return? Or does saving fall because there is less need to save to provide a given level of future income? The answers from the data are ambiguous. Many researchers have examined this question, but few have found strong positive effects of interest rate increases on saving. Typically, research suggests the effects are small and certainly hard to find.[31]

---

is quite complicated, since people who intend to continue living in their current house or buy a new one are not made any better off by a general increase in the price of houses.

[31] The best-known study finding positive interest rate effects is that by Michael Boskin, chairman of the Council of Economic Advisers from 1989 to 1993. See his "Taxation, Saving, and the Rate of Interest," *Journal of Political Economy*, part 2, April 1978. For more typical negative results, see Campbell and Mankiw, referred to earlier.

Tax Cuts, the Barro-Ricardo Hypothesis, and Saving

It is often argued that the surest way to increase national saving is to increase government saving by raising taxes. The Barro-Ricardo hypothesis claims, by contrast, that changes in taxes would be precisely offset by an opposite change in private saving. The debate centers around an argument originally noted and rejected by David Ricardo in the nineteenth century, which was revived and supported in 1974 by Robert Barro of Harvard University.[32] Suppose the budget is balanced initially, and the government cuts taxes. There will be a budget deficit, financed by borrowing. The debt that is issued today must be retired next year or in some future year, along with the interest that it carries. To repay the debt the government will have to raise taxes in the future. Thus a tax cut today means a tax increase in the future. Hence changes in taxes should have no effect on consumption because *permanent* income is really unaffected by this intertemporal jiggling of taxes. But if permanent income is unaffected by the tax cut, then consumption should be unaffected. When taxes are cut today, households save the tax cut so that they can pay the higher taxes tomorrow.

We review this theory in more detail in Chapter 19, which deals with the government budget, but a look at saving behavior in the early 1980s, when the Reagan administration cut taxes substantially, will provide useful clues. On the Barro-Ricardo theory, the tax cuts should have been saved, and the household saving rate should have risen. Figure 11-4 shows that the personal saving rate was lower in 1985 than it was in 1980. How can we interpret the behavior of the saving rate? Liquidity constraints already noted are one element in the explanation. Another is that households may not in fact behave exactly in the way prescribed by the Barro-Ricardo hypothesis. They see themselves as recipients of present tax cuts, but (perhaps rationally) they see others, future generations (in whose well-being they are not especially interested),[33] as responsible for paying off the debt. A third possibility is that the Barro-Ricardo view is correct and that national saving did not fall despite the decline in government and household saving, because corporations increased their saving. In fact, though, the national saving rate did fall over this period.

The evidence thus suggests that tax changes *do* have an effect on consumption and saving, quite likely as a result of liquidity constraints.[34] This means that national saving in the United States would increase if the government were to reduce the budget deficit.

---

[32] "Are Government Bonds Net Wealth?" *Journal of Political Economy,* November/December 1974. Theory and evidence on this topic are extensively analyzed in Douglas Bernheim, "Richardian Equivalence: An Evaluation of Theory and Evidence," *NBER Macroeconomics Annual,* 1987, and Lawrence Kotlikoff, *What Determines Saving?* (Cambridge, Mass.: MIT Press, 1989).

[33] If parents are concerned enough about their children, they will regard future taxes to be paid by their children as equivalent to taxes on themselves, and the Ricardian view then is more likely to be true. Thus the discussion in Box 11-1 of the importance of bequests also has implications for the effectiveness of fiscal policy in affecting aggregate demand.

[34] Evidence on the effects of tax cuts on consumption has been examined by James Poterba, "Are Consumers Forward Looking? Evidence from Fiscal Experiments," *American Economic Review, Papers and Proceedings,* vol. 78, May 1988. Poterba concludes that tax cuts do increase consumption.

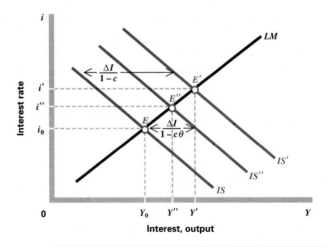

FIGURE 11-5

THE DYNAMICS OF ADJUSTMENT TO A SHIFT IN INVESTMENT DEMAND.
Autonomous investment demand rises by amount ΔI, but it is not
known whether the shift is permanent or transitory. It is in fact
permanent, so that the *IS* curve will eventually be at *IS'*, shifted to
the right by an amount $\Delta I/(1 - c)$, where $1/(1 - c)$ is the long-run
multiplier. But in the first period, the *IS* curve shifts only to *IS''*, by
amount $\Delta I/(1 - c\theta)$, which is determined by the short-run
consumption function and multiplier. Over time, the economy
moves gradually from E'' to E', as individuals come to recognize that
the shift in investment demand is permanent.

11-5 CONSUMPTION AND THE *IS-LM* FRAMEWORK

In this section we discuss briefly how the more sophisticated theories of consumption
we have developed in this chapter affect the *IS-LM* analysis of Chapters 4 and 5.
We focus on one important implication, that the response of consumption to various
changes—for instance, in autonomous spending—may take time, as individuals gradually adjust their estimates of permanent income.[35]

In Section 11-3 and Figure 11-3, we examined the dynamic response of consumption spending to a shift in disposable income. Now we want to embody that dynamic
adjustment in a full *IS-LM* model. The slow adjustment of consumption to a given
change in disposable income will mean that income itself adjusts slowly to any given
shift in autonomous spending that is not at first recognized as permanent, as we now
show. Figure 11-5 illustrates the effects of a permanent shift in autonomous demand,

---

[35] The inclusion of wealth in the consumption function is another implication of the theories developed in
this chapter. In the problem set, we ask you to show graphically in an *IS-LM* diagram how a change in
wealth shifts the *IS* curve and the equilibrium interest rate and output.

the nature of which (permanent or transitory) is not initially known to consumers. Suppose that the economy starts in equilibrium at point E. Now there is a shift in autonomous investment demand. In the long run, such a shift will move the IS curve to IS'. The extent of the shift is determined by the *long-run* multiplier $1/(1 - c)$, where c is the long-run propensity to consume. When expectations of income have fully adjusted, the economy will be at position E', with output level Y' and interest rate i'. But in the short run the marginal propensity to consume is not c, but only $c\theta$. This means that the short-run multiplier is only $1/(1 - c\theta)$. In the short run, the IS curve shifts only to IS''.

Thus the immediate effect of the shift in investment demand is to raise income to Y'' and the interest rate to i''. Next period, the IS curve shifts again. It does not shift all the way to IS' though. Consumers have adjusted their estimate of permanent income upward, but they have not yet adjusted it all the way to Y', because income last period was only Y'' and not Y'. (To keep the diagram simple, we do not show the IS curve for the second or later periods.) Income and the interest rate will rise above Y'' and i'' but still fall short of Y' and i'.

This process continues, with the consumption function gradually shifting up over time, as people come to realize that their permanent incomes have risen. A single shock to autonomous demand therefore produces a slow, or *distributed lag*, effect on output. Figure 11-6 shows how income adjusts gradually to its new equilibrium level. The time pattern of changes in income caused by the increase in investment demand is called the *dynamic multiplier* of income with respect to autonomous investment.

Policy Implications

Suppose we have a permanent decline in investment expenditure. As we have seen, the decline in spending would lead to a fall in output and employment, occurring over a period of time. Suppose the government wants to offset the reduction in aggregate demand by using tax cuts to keep income at the full-employment level. Since consumption adjusts only gradually to the changes in income resulting from both the initial fall in investment and tax cuts, the policy maker who wants to stabilize output *over time* will have to know about the adjustment pattern of consumption so as not to overreact. The problems may be further complicated by the fact that frequently the policy maker, too, reacts only with a lag to changed circumstances.

In the short run, consumption does not respond fully to changes in income. Therefore, it takes a relatively large tax cut to obtain a given change in consumption with which to offset the decline in investment. Over time, though, consumption adjusts to the change in disposable income, and the tax cut that was initially just sufficient to offset reduced investment now turns out to be too generous. The compensating policy must therefore be one of a tax cut that is *front-loaded* and gradually phased down to the long-run level.

Recall that we assumed consumers had no special knowledge about the nature of the changes in income they experienced as a result of the initial change in investment and of subsequent tax adjustments. Remarkably enough, if consumers knew that the investment shift was permanent, and if they could be persuaded that the change in government policy was permanent, a one-time reduction in taxes, calculated using the

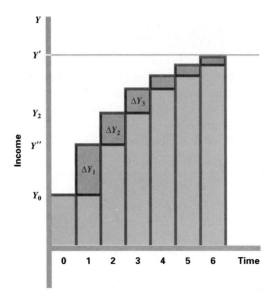

FIGURE 11-6

THE INCOME ADJUSTMENT PROCESS. The figure shows the *dynamic multiplier* of investment spending on income. This is how a given change in autonomous investment spending affects the level of output over time. Income rises in the first period from Y_0 to Y''. Then in subsequent periods it continues to rise toward its long-run equilibrium level, Y'.

long-run multiplier implied by the consumption function, would precisely stabilize income. In that case, the response to the fall in investment would recognize the permanent nature of the change, implying that the long-run multiplier is relevant; and the response to the tax change would also recognize the permanent nature of the change. Consumption would adjust immediately, rather than gradually.

The conclusion of this section is that policy making, and understanding the behavior of the economy, cannot be successful unless careful attention is paid to the formation of expectations—bearing in mind that expectations depend in part on how the policy makers are perceived to be acting. This is the message of rational expectations, which we introduced in Chapter 9.

11-6 SUMMARY

1. The simple Keynesian consumption function

$$C = 0.921YD \tag{2}$$

accounts well for observed consumption behavior. The equation implies that about 92 cents of each extra dollar of disposable income is spent on consumption and that the ratio of consumption to income, C/YD, is constant.

2. Because the ratio C/YD fluctuates, it is necessary to examine consumption behavior more deeply. Modern theories of consumption assume that individuals want to maintain relatively smooth consumption profiles over their lifetimes. Their consumption behavior is geared to their long-term consumption opportunities— permanent income or lifetime income plus wealth. With such a view, current income is only one of the determinants of consumption spending. Wealth and expected income play a role, too.

3. A consumption function that represents this idea is

$$C = aWR + b\theta YD + b(1 - \theta)YD_{-1} \tag{12}$$

which allows for the role of real wealth, WR, current disposable income, YD, and lagged disposable income, YD_{-1}.

4. The life-cycle hypothesis suggests that the propensities of an individual to consume out of disposable income and out of wealth depend on the person's age. It implies that saving is high (low) when income is high (low) relative to lifetime average income. It also suggests that aggregate saving depends on the growth rate of the economy and on such variables as the age distribution of the population.

5. The permanent-income hypothesis emphasizes the formation of expectations of future income. It implies that the propensity to consume out of permanent income is higher than the propensity to consume out of transitory income.

6. Both theories do well, in combination, in explaining aggregate consumption behavior. But there are still some consumption puzzles, including the excess sensitivity of consumption to current income and the fact that the elderly do not appear to draw down their savings as they age. In addition, differences in national saving rates have not been well explained.

7. The excess sensitivity of consumption to current income is partly caused by liquidity constraints that prevent individuals from borrowing enough to maintain smooth consumption patterns. It could also be accounted for by myopia about future income prospects.

8. The U.S. saving rate is very low by international standards. Most private saving in the United States is done by the business sector.

9. The rate of consumption, and thus of saving, could in principle be affected by the interest rate. But the evidence for the most part shows little effect of interest rates on saving.

10. The Barro-Ricardo hypothesis implies that cuts in tax rates that produce deficits will not affect consumption. The evidence seems to show that tax cuts do, however, affect consumption.

11. Lagged adjustment of consumption to income results in a gradual adjustment of the level of income in the economy to changes in autonomous spending and other economic changes. This adjustment process is described by dynamic multipliers that show by how much income changes in each period following a change in autonomous spending (or other exogenous variables).

KEY TERMS

Net national saving

Life-cycle hypothesis

Dissaving

Permanent income

Rational expectations

Excess sensitivity

Liquidity constraints

Myopia

Buffer-stock saving

Government saving

Private saving

Business saving

Barro-Ricardo hypothesis

Dynamic multiplier

PROBLEMS

1. What is the significance of the ratio of consumption to GNP in terms of the level of economic activity? Would you expect it to be higher or lower than normal during a recession (or depression)?

The Life-Cycle Hypothesis

2. The text implies that the ratio of consumption to accumulated savings declines over time until retirement.

(a) Why? What assumption about consumption behavior leads to this result?

(b) What happens to this ratio after retirement?

3. (a) Suppose you earn just as much as your neighbor but are in much better health and expect to live longer than she does. Would you consume more or less than she does? Why? Derive your answer from equation (4).

(b) According to the life-cycle hypothesis, what would be the effect of the Social Security system on your average propensity to consume out of (disposable) income?

(c) How would equation (7).be modified for an individual who expects to receive $X per year of retirement benefits? Verify your result in problem 3b.

4. Give an intuitive interpretation of the marginal propensity to consume out of wealth and income at time T in the individual's lifetime in equation (8).

5. In equation (4), consumption in each year of working life is given by

$$C = \frac{WL}{NL} \times YL \qquad (4)$$

In equation (8), consumption is given as

$$C = aWR + cYL \qquad a \equiv \frac{1}{NL - T} \qquad c \equiv \frac{WL - T}{NL - T} \qquad (8)$$

Show that equations (4) and (8) are consistent for an individual who started life with zero wealth and has been saving for T years. [*Hint:* First calculate the individual's wealth after T years of saving at rate $YL - C$. Then calculate the level of consumption implied by equation (8) when wealth is at the level you have computed.]

Permanent-Income Hypothesis

6. In terms of the permanent-income hypothesis, would you consume more of your Christmas bonus if (a) you knew there was a bonus every year; (b) this was the only year such bonuses were given?

7. Suppose that permanent income is calculated as the average of income over the past 5 years; that is,

$$YP = \frac{1}{5}(Y + Y_{-1} + Y_{-2} + Y_{-3} + Y_{-4}) \tag{P1}$$

Suppose, further, that consumption is given by $C = 0.9YP$.
   (a) If you have earned $20,000 per year for the past 10 years, what is your permanent income?
   (b) Suppose next year (period $t + 1$) you earn $30,000. What is your new YP?
   (c) What is your consumption this year and next year?
   (d) What is your short-run marginal propensity to consume (MPC)? Long-run MPC?
   (e) Assuming you continue to earn $30,000 starting in period $t + 1$, graph the value of your permanent income in each period, using equation (P1).

8. Explain why successful gamblers (and thieves) might be expected to live very well even in years when they don't do well at all.

9. The graph (below) shows the lifetime earnings profile of a person who lives for four periods and earns incomes of $30, $60, and $90 in the first three periods of the life cycle. There are no earnings during retirement. Assume that the interest rate is 0.

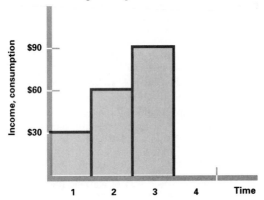

   (a) Determine the level of consumption, compatible with the budget constraint, for someone who wants an even consumption profile throughout the life cycle. Indicate in which periods the person saves and dissaves and in what amounts.
   (b) Assume now that, contrary to 9a, there is no possibility of borrowing. The credit markets are closed to the individual. Under this assumption, what is the flow of consumption the individual will pick over the life cycle? In providing an answer, continue to assume that, if possible, an even flow of consumption is preferred. (*Note:* You are assuming here that there are liquidity constraints.)
   (c) Assume next that the person described in 9b receives an increase in wealth, or nonlabor income. The increase in wealth is equal to $13. How will that wealth be allocated over the life cycle with and without access to the credit market? How would your answer differ if the increase in wealth were $23?
   (d) Relate your answer to the problem of excess sensitivity of consumption to current income.

10. Consider the consumption function in equation (12). Assume autonomous investment spending is constant, as is government spending. The economy is close to full employment and the government wishes to maintain aggregate demand precisely constant. In these circumstances, assume there is an increase in real wealth of $10 billion. What change in income taxes will maintain the equilibrium level of income constant in the present period? What change is required to maintain income constant in the long run?

11. Equation (12) shows consumption as a function of wealth and current and lagged disposable income. To reconcile that consumption function with the formation of permanent-income expectations, use equation (10) and the consumption function

$$C = 0.045WR + 0.55YD + 0.17YD_{-1}$$

to determine the magnitude of θ and $(1 - \theta)$ that is implied by equation (12).

12. (a) Explain why the interest rate might affect saving.
    (b) Why does this relation matter?

13. The consumption function (12) includes wealth. Show in an *IS-LM* diagram how an increase in wealth affects the level of output and the interest rate.

14. Here is a challenge to your ability to develop diagrams. You are asked to show short-run and long-run income determination in the 45° diagram of Chapter 3. Assume that investment demand is totally autonomous and does not respond to the interest rate. Thus, you do not need to use the full *IS-LM* model.
    (a) Draw the short-run and long-run consumption functions and the aggregate demand schedule, with $I = \bar{I}$.
    (b) Show the initial full equilibrium.
    (c) Show the short-run and long-run effects of increased investment on equilibrium income.

⊟ COMPUTER EXERCISES

Life-Cycle Model

1. Construct a table with five columns, (a) through (e), to record the effects of the following five simulations on annual consumption (C), marginal propensity to consume (MPC), and maximum wealth (W_{max}):
    (a) BASE solution (write the values in from the base solution before any simulation is carried out).
    (b) Increase annual labor income from $20,000 to $22,000.
    (c) Increase initial bequest from $0 to $90,000.
    (d) Increase retirement age from 65 to 69.5.
    (e) Decrease life expectancy from 80 to 74.5.

    Remember to reset to the BASE solution before each successive simulation.

2. (a) Why do simulations (b)–(e) give the same level of annual consumption?
    (b) Why does *MPC* increase the same amount in (d) and (e)?
    (c) Why does maximum wealth differ across the simulations?

Permanent-Income Model

3. For *all* of the following five simulations *increase income from $25,000 to $35,000.* Construct a table with five columns, (a) through (e), to record the effects of the following five simulations on short-run and long-run consumption:

(a) BASE parameter values (long-run $MPC = 0.9$ and $\theta = 0.2$).

(b) Lower long-run MPC to 0.8.

(c) Increase θ to 0.31 (leaving $c = 0.8$).

(d) Increase θ to 0.54 (leaving $c = 0.8$).

(e) Increase θ to 0.99 (returning MPC to original level, $c = 0.9$).

The three rows of the table will record (1) the starting level of consumption, (2) the short-run consumption level, and (3) the long-run consumption level.

Remember to reset to the BASE solution before each successive simulation.

4. Relate the values for short-run consumption in simulations (b)–(e) to the values of starting, short-run, and long-run consumption under the base parameter settings. When are they approximately equal? Can you say why?

DATA APPENDIX

This following table shows U.S. data in 1987 dollars for disposable income (YD), total consumption (C), consumption of durable goods (CD), household net worth (WR), the average personal saving rate (S/YD), and the average propensity to consume (C/YD).

DATA FOR CONSUMPTION STUDIES (1987 dollars in billions)

	YD	C	CD	WR	S/YD	C/YD
1959	1,284.85	1,178.92	114.41	6,490.05	6.35	91.76
1960	1,313.00	1,210.75	115.40	6,566.27	5.71	92.21
1961	1,356.40	1,238.36	109.39	6,950.14	6.63	91.30
1962	1,414.83	1,293.25	120.22	6,929.06	6.48	91.41
1963	1,461.10	1,341.87	130.30	7,271.17	5.89	91.84
1964	1,562.20	1,417.18	140.66	7,629.26	6.93	90.72
1965	1,653.45	1,496.98	156.15	7,924.09	7.05	90.54
1966	1,734.33	1,573.82	166.02	8,053.07	6.85	90.74
1967	1,811.40	1,622.37	167.17	8,618.60	8.06	89.56
1968	1,886.78	1,707.50	184.51	9,124.99	7.10	90.51
1969	1,947.45	1,771.22	190.78	9,287.41	6.53	90.94
1970	2,025.30	1,813.47	183.72	9,035.04	7.97	89.53
1971	2,099.90	1,873.72	201.39	9,570.36	8.33	89.23
1972	2,186.18	1,978.44	225.23	10,132.05	7.04	90.49
1973	2,334.13	2,066.74	246.64	10,283.64	8.99	88.52
1974	2,316.98	2,053.81	227.21	9,729.60	8.92	88.65
1975	2,355.40	2,097.50	226.78	10,106.62	8.71	89.05

	YD	C	CD	WR	S/YD	C/YD
1976	2,440.90	2,207.25	256.38	10,701.19	7.36	90.43
1977	2,512.63	2,296.57	279.97	10,983.78	6.32	91.39
1978	2,638.33	2,391.82	292.89	11,525.29	6.87	90.65
1979	2,710.05	2,448.35	288.99	12,176.86	7.04	90.34
1980	2,733.60	2,447.07	262.75	12,676.96	7.88	89.51
1981	2,795.83	2,476.90	264.59	12,872.18	8.82	88.58
1982	2,820.35	2,503.66	262.54	12,965.22	8.60	88.77
1983	2,893.55	2,619.44	297.69	13,507.45	6.76	90.53
1984	3,080.08	2,746.07	338.49	13,652.35	8.04	89.16
1985	3,162.10	2,865.81	370.11	14,266.96	6.43	90.64
1986	3,261.93	2,969.12	401.98	15,255.28	5.99	91.03
1987	3,289.60	3,052.22	403.72	15,973.36	4.32	92.79
1988	3,404.25	3,162.38	428.75	15,819.75	4.39	92.89
1989	3,464.90	3,223.28	440.68	16,439.10	4.02	93.03
1990	3,516.50	3,260.37	439.25	16,119.62	4.34	92.72
1991	3,509.05	3,240.76	414.68	16,647.92	4.74	92.35
1992	3,584.13	3,312.45	438.86	16,798.38	4.80	92.40

SOURCE: DRI/McGraw-Hill.

INVESTMENT SPENDING

*I*nvestment spending is a central topic in macroeconomics for two reasons. First, fluctuations in investment account for much of the movement of GDP in the business cycle. Second, investment spending determines the rate at which the economy adds to its stock of physical capital, and thus helps determine the economy's long-run growth and productivity performance. Faster-growing countries, including Japan and Germany, generally invest a higher share of their GDP than slower-growing countries. Anyone worried about the slow long-term growth of the U.S. economy would like to find policies to encourage investment in the economy.

Before getting down to business, we have to clarify terminology. In common terms, investment often refers to *buying* financial or physical assets. For example, we say someone "invests" in stocks, or bonds, or a house when he or she buys the asset. The usage in macroeconomics is more restricted: investment is the flow of spending that adds to the physical stock of capital.

In Table 12-1 we show the rate of investment, the stock of capital, and GDP for 1991. Capital is a *stock*, the given dollar value of all the buildings, machines, and inventories, at a point in time, in this case the end of 1991. Both GDP and investment refer to spending *flows*. Investment is the amount spent by businesses to *add* to the stock of capital over a given period, 1991 in Table 12-1. The capital stock has been created by past investment and is always being reduced by depreciation, so that some investment spending is needed just to keep the capital stock from declining.[1]

A second distinction concerns the components of investment spending. We disaggregate investment spending into three categories. The first is *business fixed investment*, business spending on machinery, equipment, and structures such as factories. As Table 12-2 shows, this category accounts for most of investment, about 10.4 percent of GDP on average over the past three decades. The second category is *residential investment*,

---

[1]The distinction between gross and net investment was drawn in Chap. 2.

TABLE 12-1

CAPITAL, GDP, AND INVESTMENT:
1991 (billions of current dollars)

capital*	GDP	investment†
13,559	5,673	727

*Stock of reproducible assets (excluding government assets), from Federal Reserve Board, *Balance Sheets for the U.S. Economy 1960–91.*

† *Gross private domestic investment.*

TABLE 12-2

INVESTMENT AS A SHARE OF GDP: AVERAGES 1960–1991 (1987 dollars, percent)

	period average	average at peak	average at trough
Investment	16.0	16.5	13.9
Fixed investment	15.5	15.7	14.6
Business structures	4.1	4.4	4.3
Equipment	6.3	6.5	6.0
Business fixed investment	10.4	10.9	10.2
Residential investment	4.9	4.8	4.3
Inventory investment	0.6	0.8	−0.7

SOURCE: DRI/McGraw-Hill.

consisting largely of investment in housing. And the third is *inventory investment*, consisting of additions to the stock of inventories.

Table 12-2 sets out the averages for each kind of investment over the past three decades. The table also shows the averages of the rates during business cycle peak and trough years. The point of the comparison is to show the large peak-to-trough swings in investment rates, especially for inventory investment.[2] This chapter focuses on the determinants of investment spending and seeks to explain both why investment is so volatile and what policies can be used to increase investment. We first discuss fixed investment and, at the end of the chapter, turn to inventory investment.

12-1   FIXED INVESTMENT: THE NEOCLASSICAL APPROACH

Figure 12-1 shows fixed investment as a share of GDP. In recessions or shortly before, the share of investment in GDP falls sharply, and then investment begins to recover

---

[2]Inventory investment is negative when firms are reducing inventories, selling off their stocks without replacing them.

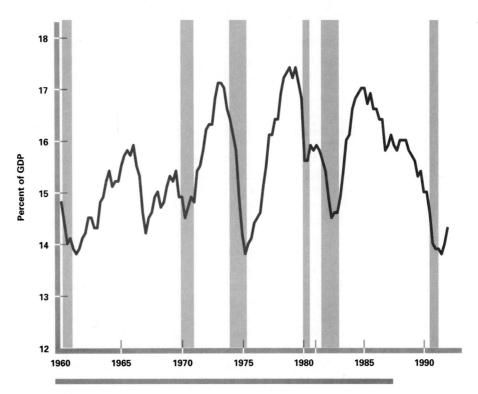

FIGURE 12-1

FIXED INVESTMENT SPENDING AS A PERCENTAGE OF GDP, 1960–1992.
Shaded bars mark periods of recession. (Source: DRI/McGraw-Hill.)

as the recovery gets under way. The cyclical relationships extend much further back in history. For instance, in the great depression, gross investment fell to less than 4 percent of GDP in both 1932 and 1933. Understanding investment, then, will go a long way toward helping us understand the business cycle.

In this section, we provide a foundation for the essential component of the simple investment function of Chapter 4—that investment demand is reduced by increases in the interest rate—and, also, go beyond that investment function by discussing the roles of output, financial constraints, and taxes in determining investment. We also examine how investment spending can be affected by policy. Our focus here is on business decisions to add to the stock of equipment or structures. We leave for the next section the discussion of housing, or residential, investment.

Our analysis proceeds in two stages. First, we ask how much capital firms would like to use, given the costs and returns of using capital and the level of output they expect to produce. That is, we ask what determines the *desired capital stock*. The desired capital stock is the capital stock that firms would like to have in the long run, abstracting from the delays they face in adjusting their use of capital. However, because it takes time to order new machines, build factories, and install the machines, firms cannot instantly adjust the stock of capital used in production. Second, therefore, we discuss the rate at which firms adjust from their existing capital stock toward the desired level over time. Investment spending thus depends on two considerations: where we want to go and how fast we want to get there.

The Desired Capital Stock: Overview

Firms use capital, along with labor, to produce goods and services for sale. Their goal is, of course, to maximize profits. In deciding how much capital to use in production, firms have to balance the contribution that more capital makes to their revenues against the cost of using more capital. The *marginal product of capital* is the increase in output produced by using one more unit of capital in production. The *rental (user) cost of capital* is the cost of using one more unit of capital in production.

To derive the rental cost of capital, we think of the firm as financing the purchase of the capital (whether the firm produces the capital itself or buys it from some other firm) by borrowing, at an interest rate i. Since the firm must pay the interest cost, i, each period, for each dollar of capital that it uses, the basic measure of the rental cost of capital is the interest rate.[3] Later we shall go into more detail about the rental cost of capital, but for the meantime we shall think of the interest rate as the chief determinant of the rental cost.

The value of the marginal product of capital is the increase in the *value* of output obtained by using one more unit of capital. For a competitive firm, the value of the marginal product of capital is equal to the price of output times the marginal product of capital. So long as the value of the marginal product of capital is above the rental cost, it pays the firm to add to its capital stock. Thus the firm will keep investing until the value of the output produced by adding one more unit of capital is equal to the cost of using that capital—the rental cost of capital. In equilibrium, we must have

$$\text{Value of marginal product of capital} = \text{rental cost of capital} \qquad (1)$$

To give content to this basic relationship, we have to specify what determines the productivity of capital and what determines the user (rental) cost of capital.

The Marginal Productivity of Capital

To understand the marginal productivity of capital, it is important to note that firms can substitute capital for labor in the production of output. A given level of output can be produced using different combinations of capital and labor. If labor is relatively cheap, the firm will want to use relatively more labor; and if capital is relatively cheap, the firm will want to use relatively more capital.

---

[3]Even if the firm finances the investment out of profits it has made in the past—retained earnings—it should still think of the interest rate as the basic cost of using the new capital, since it could have lent those funds and earned interest on them, or paid them out as dividends to shareholders.

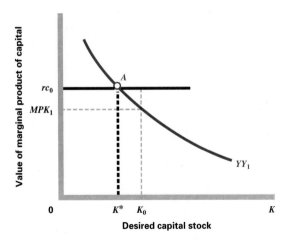

FIGURE 12-2

THE MARGINAL PRODUCT OF CAPITAL IN RELATION TO THE CAPITAL
STOCK. The marginal product of capital decreases as relatively more
capital is used in producing any given level of output. Thus the
schedule YY_1 is downward-sloping. With a rental cost of capital rc_0,
the equilibrium capital stock is K^*. The higher the level of output,
for any given capital input, the higher the marginal product of
capital. Thus an increase in output shifts the marginal product
schedule out and to the right.

The general relationship among the desired capital stock (K^*), the rental cost of
capital (rc), and the level of output is given by

$$K^* = g(rc, Y) \qquad (2)$$

Equation (2) indicates that the desired capital stock depends on the rental cost of capital
and the level of output. The lower the rental cost of capital, the larger the desired
capital stock. And the greater the level of output, the larger the desired capital stock.
We now explain in more detail the factors underlying equation (2).

As the firm combines progressively more capital with relatively less labor in the
production of a *given* amount of output, the marginal product of capital declines. This
relation is shown in the downward-sloping schedule in Figure 12-2. This schedule
shows how the marginal product of capital falls as more capital is used in producing
a given level of output. The schedule YY_1 is drawn for a level of output Y_1. Suppose
the rental cost of capital is rc_0 indicated by the horizontal line. Then the desired capital
stock will be K^*. If a higher capital stock were selected, say K_0, the marginal product
of capital would be less than the rental cost and the firm would do better to cut back
on capital. Conversely, for a lower capital stock some expansion is justified because
the benefit from using an extra unit of capital—the marginal product of capital—still
exceeds the rental cost.

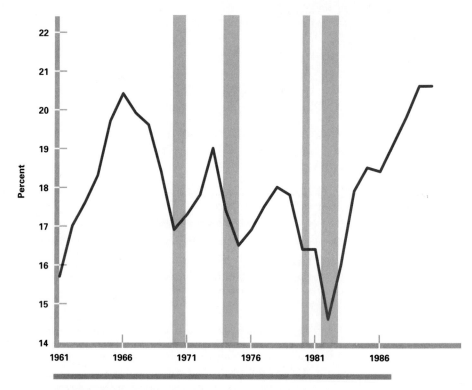

FIGURE 12-3
THE GROSS PROFITABILITY OF CAPITAL IN THE UNITED STATES, 1960–1990.
Shaded bars mark periods of recession. (SOURCE: *European Economy*, December 1991.)

Figure 12-2 can also be used to think about the effects of an increase in output. If output were higher, say Y_2, then the marginal product schedule would shift out and to the right. At an unchanged rental cost of capital the desired capital stock would therefore increase.

ESTIMATING THE RETURN TO CAPITAL

The value of the marginal product of capital is the increase in the value of output that is obtained by increasing the capital stock by one unit. Since we do not have data on the economywide return to capital, we need to use roundabout methods to estimate it. One proxy for the return to capital is the ratio of gross operating profits of firms to the capital stock. This is shown in Figure 12-3. It ranges between 15 and 20 percent.[4] The data are only a proxy because the gross income of capital is not measured exactly, and because no adjustments are made for taxes and for depreciation of capital. (See Box 12-1.)

[4]See "The Profitability of Fixed Capital and Its Relation to Investment," *European Economy*, December 1991. The article also reports estimates for various European economies.

box 12-1

INVESTMENT: GROSS, NET, AND MORE INCLUSIVE CONCEPTS

In this box, we discuss both the differences between gross and net investment, and some more inclusive concepts of investment. The distinction between gross and net investment is essential even though the difference, depreciation, is hard to measure. Depreciation is more than just the physical wear and tear that results from use and age. Economic depreciation may be much more rapid than physical depreciation. A piece of capital may become economically obsolete, for instance, because input prices change—as gas-guzzlers became obsolete when oil prices increased. Technological obsolescence may also cause rapid economic depreciation. This is particularly true for computers, where quality improvements have been dramatic.

The rate of depreciation depends on the type of capital. For example, the useful life of structures is decades whereas that of office equipment is only a few years. This has an important implication: if investment shifts toward capital goods with a short life (computers), then they make up a larger share of the capital stock, and, as a result, the overall rate of depreciation will rise. This is what happened in the United States in the 1980s, as can be seen in Table 1. Net investment declined by more than gross investment because depreciation increased.

TABLE 1
GROSS AND NET INVESTMENT (percent of GDP)

	1960–80	1980–90
Gross investment	18.1	17.6
Net investment	6.6	5.5

SOURCE: OECD, *Historical Statistics*, 1992.

Although it is traditional, the focus on private sector additions to the capital stock in this chapter takes a too restricted view of investment, in two respects. First, it ignores *government investment*.

Second, individuals invest not only in physical capital, but also in *human capital*, through schooling and training. In his comprehensive work, *Total Incomes System of Accounts*,[†] Robert Eisner of Northwestern University estimates that the stock of human capital in the United States is almost as large as the stock of physical capital. There is much evidence that this investment, like that in physical capital, yields a positive real return; indeed the return on human capital typically exceeds that on physical capital.

In thinking about investment as spending that increases future productivity, we should look beyond just private sector gross investment. ∎

---

†Chicago: University of Chicago Press, 1989.

In estimates that include these adjustments, Lawrence Summers calculated the return in the United States for the period 1960–1979 at 9.1 percent, followed by only 6.9 percent in 1980–1987.[5] These data mean that $1 of investment today generates a return of 7 to 9 cents per year on average.[6] Of course, the return to capital is lower in recessions and higher during booms. If a $1 increase in the capital stock generates a return of about 8 to 9 cents in the form of increased output in future years, many would argue that the tradeoff is well worth having, and that the United States should therefore seek ways to encourage investment.

Expected Output

Equation (2) shows that the desired capital stock depends on the level of output. But that must be the level of output for some future period, during which the capital will be in production. For some investments the future time at which the output will be produced is a matter of months or only weeks. For other investments—such as power stations—the future time at which the output will be produced is years away.

This suggests that the notion of permanent income (in this case, permanent output) introduced in Chapter 11 is relevant to investment as well as consumption. The firm's demand for business fixed capital, which depends on the normal or permanent level of output, thus depends on expectations of future output levels, rather than the current level of output. However, current output is likely to affect expectations of permanent output.[7]

The Desired Capital Stock: Summary

It is worthwhile stepping back for a moment to summarize the main results so far:

1. The firm's demand for capital—the desired capital stock, K^*—depends on the rental cost of capital, rc, and the expected level of output.

---

[5]See Lawrence Summers, "What Is the Social Return to Capital Investment?" Mimeo, Harvard University, 1989.

[6]An alternative estimate of the marginal product of capital can be obtained using the fact that the share of output received by capital is about 0.20. The share of capital in output, in turn, is equal to the marginal product of capital times the capital stock, divided by the level of output:

$$\text{Share of capital} = MPK \times \frac{K}{Y}$$

With the capital-output ratio (K/Y) in manufacturing at about 2 and the share of capital at 20 percent, we obtain

$$MPK = \frac{0.20}{2.0} = 10\%$$

This estimate of 10 percent is in the same ballpark as Summers's estimate.

[7]The role of permanent income in investment has been emphasized by Robert Eisner. Much of his work is summarized in his *Factors in Business Investment* (Cambridge, Mass.: Ballinger, 1978).

2. Firms balance the marginal costs and benefits of using capital. The lower the rental cost of capital, the higher the optimal level of capital relative to output. This relation reflects the lower marginal productivity of capital when it is used relatively intensively.
3. The higher the expected level of output, the larger the desired capital stock. The firm plans its capital stock in relation to expected future or permanent output. Current output affects capital demand to the extent that it affects expectations about future output.

The Rental Cost of Capital Again

As a first approximation, we identified the rental cost of capital, rc, with the interest rate, on the argument that firms would have to borrow to finance their use of capital. Now we go into more detail on the cost per period of using capital.

To use capital for a single period, say a year, the firm can be thought of as buying the capital with borrowed funds and paying the interest on the borrowing. But the capital is likely to depreciate over the course of the year, as a result of wear and tear, and that depreciation is also part of the cost of using that capital.

Why is depreciation considered as a cost? We can think of the firm having to spend money on repairs to keep the capital working as well as it did when it was new. We assume that, per dollar of capital, d dollars per period are required to keep the capital working at full efficiency. This is the depreciation cost of using the capital.

Leaving aside taxes, the rental or user cost of using capital now consists of interest plus depreciation costs:

$$rc = \text{interest rate} + d \qquad (3)$$

The Real Rate of Interest

We have next to take a careful look at the interest rate term in equation (3). The distinction between the *real* and *nominal* interest rates, described in Box 5-1, is essential here. As described there, the real interest rate is the nominal (stated) rate of interest minus the rate of inflation.

It is the *expected real* rate of interest that should enter the calculation of the rental cost of capital. Why? The firm is borrowing in order to produce goods for sale in the future. On average, the prices of the goods the firms sell will be rising along with the general price level. Thus the nominal value of the marginal product of capital will be rising with the price level, but the nominal amount of interest the firm has to pay does not rise with the price level. Equivalently, the real value of the firm's debt will be falling over time, as a result of inflation, and the firm should take that reduction in the real value of its outstanding debts into account in deciding how much capital to employ.

Accordingly, we can be more precise in the way we write equation (3) for the rental cost of capital. We write the rental cost of capital, taking account of expected inflation at the rate π^e, as

$$rc \equiv r + d \equiv i - \pi^e + d \qquad (4)$$

where r is the real interest rate, i is the nominal interest rate, and

$$r \equiv i - \pi^e \qquad\qquad (5)$$

Equation (5) states that the real rate of interest is the nominal interest rate minus the expected rate of inflation.[8]

The firm's cost of capital is determined by the *real* rate, and not the nominal rate of interest. Indeed, the nominal rate may not be a good guide to the rental cost of capital. If the expected rate of inflation is zero and the nominal interest rate is 5 percent, then the real interest rate is 5 percent. By contrast, if the nominal interest rate is 10 percent and the expected inflation rate is 10 percent, the real interest rate is zero. Other things equal, the desired capital stock in this example would be higher with the nominal interest rate of 10 percent than with the nominal rate of 5 percent.

Investment spending tends to be higher when the rental cost of capital is lower. But because of the distinction between real and nominal interest rates, that is *not* the same as saying that investment tends to be higher when the nominal rate of interest is lower.

Taxes and the Rental Cost of Capital

In addition to interest and depreciation, the rental cost of capital is affected by taxes. The two main tax variables are the corporate income tax and the investment tax credit. The corporate income tax is an essentially proportional tax on profits, whereby the firm pays a proportion, say t, of its profits in taxes. Since the mid-1980s the corporate tax rate has been 34 percent, down from 46 percent in the early 1980s.

The investment tax credit was in place for most of the period 1962–1986 but was discontinued in 1986. It allowed firms to deduct from their taxes a certain fraction, say τ, of their investment expenditures in each year. Thus a firm spending $1 million for investment purposes in a given year could deduct 10 percent of the $1 million, or $100,000, from the taxes it would otherwise have to pay the federal government. The investment tax credit reduces the price of a capital good to the firm by the ratio τ, since the Treasury returns to the firm a proportion, τ, of the cost of each capital good. The investment tax credit therefore reduces the rental cost of capital.

To a first approximation, the corporate income tax has no effect on the desired stock of capital. In the presence of the corporate income tax, the firm will want to equate the *after-tax* value of the marginal product of capital with the *after-tax* rental cost of capital in order to ensure that the marginal contribution of the capital to profits is equal to the marginal cost of using it. The key to understanding the impact of the corporate income tax is the fact that interest payments are deducted from the firm's income before its taxes are calculated.

Now consider the following example. Suppose there were no corporate income

---

[8]Accordingly, the real interest rate in equation (6) is the *expected* real rate. At the end of the period, when the rate of inflation is known, we can also state what the *actual*, or realized, real rate of interest for the period was—namely, the nominal interest rate, i, minus the actual rate of inflation.

tax, no inflation, no depreciation, and an interest rate of 10 percent. The desired capital stock would be that level of the capital stock, say, K_0^*, such that the marginal product of capital was 10 percent. Next suppose that the corporate income tax rises to 34 percent and the interest rate remains constant. At the capital stock K_0^*, the after-tax marginal product of capital is now 6.6 percent (since 34 percent of the profits are paid in taxes). But if the interest rate stays at 10 percent and the firm gets to deduct 34 percent of its interest payments from taxes, the after-tax cost of capital will be 6.6 percent too. In this example, the desired capital stock is unaffected by the rate of corporate taxation.

However, this sharp message is no longer true when investment is financed in part by equity, as it often is. When dividends are paid out to equity holders, they are not deducted from the firm's income for tax purposes. This means the cost of capital tends to rise with the corporate tax rate. We now look further at the role of equity in financing investment.

The Stock Market and the Cost of Capital

Rather than borrowing, a firm can also raise the financing it needs to pay for its investment by selling shares, or equity. The people buying the shares expect to earn a return from dividends and/or, if the firm is successful, from the increase in the market value of their shares, that is, *capital gains*.

When its share price is high, a company can raise a lot of money by selling relatively few shares. When stock prices are low, the firm has to sell more shares to raise a given amount of money. The owners of the firm, the existing shareholders, will be more willing for the firm to sell shares to raise new money if they have to sell few shares to do so, that is, if the price is high. Thus we expect corporations to be more willing to sell equity to finance investment when the stock market is high than when it is low.

In estimating the rental cost of capital, economists sometimes assume that the investment project will be financed by a mixture of borrowing and equity. The cost of equity capital is frequently measured by the ratio of the firm's dividends to the price of its stock.[9] Then, obviously, the higher the price of the stock, the lower the cost of equity capital, and the lower the overall cost of capital.[10] That is why a booming stock market is good for investment.[11]

---

[9] An alternative measure is the ratio of the firm's *earnings* (some of which are not paid out to shareholders) to the price of its stock. However, neither measure is really correct, for the cost of equity capital is the amount the investment is expected to yield *in the future* to the people who buy it now.

[10] An alternative approach to the firm's investment decision, Tobin's *q* theory of investment, focuses on the stock market as the primary source of funds. The basic approach is outlined in James Tobin, "A General Equilibrium Approach to Monetary Theory," *Journal of Money, Credit and Banking*, February 1969. For an empirical implementation, see Lawrence H. Summers, "Taxation and Corporate Investment: A *q*-Theory Approach," *Brookings Papers on Economic Activity*, 1, 1981. In Sec. 12-3 we outline the *q* theory in discussing housing investment.

[11] In a controversial study Randall Mork, Andrei Shleifer, and Robert Vishny, "The Stock Market and Investment: Is the Market a Sideshow?" *Brookings Papers on Economic Activity*, 2, 1990, ask just how important the stock market in fact is in guiding investment decisions.

The Effects of Fiscal and Monetary Policy on the Desired Capital Stock

Equation (2) states that the desired capital stock increases when the expected level of output rises and when the rental cost of capital falls. The rental cost of capital in turn falls when the real interest rate and the rate of depreciation fall, and when the investment tax credit rises. An increase in the corporate tax rate is likely, through the equity route, to reduce the desired capital stock.

The major significance of these results is that they imply that monetary and fiscal policy can affect the desired capital stock. Fiscal policy exerts an effect through both the corporate tax rate, t, and the investment tax credit, τ.

Fiscal policy also affects capital demand by its overall effects on the position of the *IS* curve and thus the interest rate. A high-tax–low-government-spending policy keeps the real interest rate low and encourages the demand for capital. (At this point you may want to refer to Figure 5-6.) A low-tax–high-government-spending policy that produces large deficits raises the real interest rate and discourages the demand for capital.

Monetary policy affects capital demand by affecting the market interest rate. A lowering of the nominal interest rate by the Federal Reserve (given the expected inflation rate) induces firms to desire more capital. This expansion in capital demand, in turn, will affect investment spending.

From Desired Capital Stock to Investment

Equation (2) specifies the desired capital stock. The actual capital stock will often differ from the capital stock firms would like to have. At what speed do firms invest to move toward the desired capital stock?

Since it takes time to plan and complete an investment project, and because investing quickly is likely to be more expensive than gradual adjustments of the capital stock, firms do not try to adjust their capital stocks to the long-run desired level instantaneously. Very rapid adjustment of the capital stock would require expensive crash programs that would interfere with regular production. Thus, firms generally plan to adjust their capital stocks gradually over a period of time rather than immediately.

Capital Stock Adjustment

There are a number of hypotheses about the speed at which firms plan to adjust their capital stock over time; we single out the *gradual adjustment hypothesis*, or *flexible accelerator model*.[12] The basic notion behind the gradual adjustment hypothesis is that *the larger the gap between the existing capital stock and the desired capital stock, the more rapid a firm's rate of investment.*

---

[12]The term *flexible accelerator* is used because the model is a generalized form of the older *accelerator* model of investment, in which investment is proportional to the *change* in the level of GDP. We discuss the accelerator model in Sec. 12-2.

The hypothesis is that the firm plans to close a fraction, λ, of the gap between the desired and actual capital stocks each period. Denote the capital stock at the end of the last period by K_{-1}. The gap between the desired capital stock and actual capital stock is $(K^* - K_{-1})$. The firm plans to add to last period's capital stock (K_{-1}) a fraction (λ) of the gap $(K^* - K_{-1})$ so that the actual capital stock at the end of the current period (K) will be

$$K = K_{-1} + \lambda(K^* - K_{-1}) \tag{6}$$

Equation (6) states that the firm plans to have the capital stock at the end of the period, K, be such that a fraction, λ, of the gap (between K^* and K_{-1}) is closed. To increase the capital stock from K_{-1} to the level of K indicated by equation (6), the firm has to achieve an amount of net investment, $I \equiv K - K_{-1}$, indicated by equation (6). We can therefore write net investment as

$$I = \lambda(K^* - K_{-1}) \tag{7}$$

which is the gradual adjustment formulation of net investment.[13]

In Figure 12-4 we show how the capital stock adjusts from an initial level of K_1 to the desired level K^*. The assumed speed of adjustment is $\lambda = 0.5$. Starting from K_1, one-half the gap between target capital and current actual capital is made up in every period. First-period net investment is therefore $0.5(K^* - K_1)$. In the second period, investment will be one-half the previous period's rate, since the gap has been reduced by half. Investment continues until the actual capital stock reaches the level of target capital. The larger λ is, the faster the gap is reduced.

In equation (7), we have reached our goal of deriving an investment function that shows current investment spending determined by the desired stock of capital, K^*, and the actual stock of capital, K_{-1}. Any factor that increases the desired capital stock increases the rate of investment. Therefore, an increase in expected output, a reduction in the real interest rate, or an increase in the investment tax credit will each increase the rate of investment.

In addition, the theory of investment in equation (7) contains aspects of *dynamic behavior*—that is, behavior that depends on values of economic variables in periods other than the current period. There are two sources of dynamic behavior in equation (7). The first arises from expectations. The K^* term depends on the firm's estimate of future or permanent output. If the firm estimates permanent output as a weighted average of past output levels, there will be lags in the adjustment of the level of permanent output to the actual level of output. The second source of dynamic behavior arises from adjustment lags. Firms plan to close only a proportion of the gap between the actual and desired capital stocks each period. The adjustment lags produce a lagged response of investment to changes in the variables that affect the desired capital stock.

---

[13]Gross investment, as opposed to the net investment described in equation (7), includes, in addition, depreciation. Thus, gross investment is $I + dK_{-1}$, where d is again the rate of depreciation.

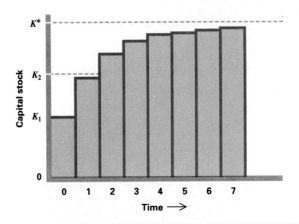

FIGURE 12-4
THE GRADUAL ADJUSTMENT OF THE CAPITAL STOCK. The desired capital stock is K^*, and the current capital stock is K_1. The firm plans to close half the gap between the actual and the desired capital stock each period ($\lambda = 0.5$). Thus, in period 1 the firm moves to K_2, with (net) investment equal to $K_2 - K_1$, which in turn is equal to one-half of $K^* - K_1$. In each subsequent period the firm closes half the gap between the capital stock at the beginning of the period and the desired capital stock, K^*.

The Timing of Investment and the Investment Tax Credit

The flexible accelerator model provides a useful summary of the dynamics of investment. But it does not sufficiently emphasize the *timing* of investment. Because investment often requires several years to complete, there is flexibility in the dates on which it is undertaken. For example, suppose a firm wanted to have some machinery in place within 3 years. Suppose that it knew the investment tax credit would be raised substantially a year from now. The firm might be smart to delay the investment for a year and then to invest at a faster rate during the next 2 years, receiving the higher investment tax credit as the reward for waiting the extra year. Similarly, if a firm anticipated that the cost of borrowing next year would be much lower than this year, it might wait a year to undertake its investment project.

This timing flexibility leads to an interesting contrast between the effects of the investment tax credit and the income tax. We saw in Chapter 11 that a *permanent* change in the income tax has a much larger effect on consumption than a *transitory* change. However, the rate of investment *during the period* that a *temporary* investment tax credit is in effect would be higher than the rate of investment that would occur over the same period during which a *permanent* credit of the same magnitude was in effect. Why? If firms know the investment tax credit is temporary, they try to squeeze their investments into the current period to take advantage of the higher credit. If there is a permanent change in the investment tax credit, then the desired capital stock will rise and there will on that account be more investment, but there will not be a bunching of investment.

It is for this reason that temporary changes in the investment tax credit have been suggested as a highly effective countercyclical policy measure. However, this is not a simple policy tool, as expectations about the timing and duration of the credit might conceivably worsen the instability of investment.

Empirical Results

How well does the neoclassical model, summarized in equation (7), do in explaining the behavior of investment?[14] To use equation (7), it is necessary to substitute some specific equation for K^*, the desired capital stock. Frequently, the Cobb-Douglas form (see Appendix 12-2) is chosen and yields a (net) investment function of the form

$$I = \lambda\left(\frac{\gamma Y}{rc} - K_{-1}\right) \tag{8}$$

Accordingly, investment depends positively on *current* output (since expected output is not being taken into account), and negatively on the rental cost of capital.

Early empirical evidence showed that an investment function including the variables in equation (8) provided a reasonable explanation of business fixed investment.[15] However, equation (8) could be improved upon by allowing investment to respond slowly to changes in output. In fact, the adjustment of investment to output takes the bell-shaped form in Figure 12-5, rather than the shape seen in Figure 12-4. The major impact of a change in output on actual investment occurs with a 2-period (year) lag.

As already discussed, the behavior shown in Figure 12-5 has two potential sources. First, the lag pattern may reflect the way in which expectations about future output are formed. In that view, only a sustained increase in output will persuade firms that the capital stock should be increased in the long run. The second explanation relies on the delays in the investment process. In that interpretation Figure 12-5 reflects the long time it takes for a change in the desired capital stock to be translated into the planning and execution of investment spending. No doubt, both explanations are relevant, and both imply lags in the response of business fixed investment to changes in the economy.

How important are tax variables? While it is reasonable to conclude that tax changes affect investment, empirical work—even that examining the impact of the major U.S. tax reforms in 1980–1981 and 1986—has not succeeded in pinning down the size of those effects.[16]

---

[14]For a recent survey, see Robert Ford and Pierre Poret, "Business Investment: Recent Performance and Some Implications for Policy," *OECD Economic Studies*, no. 16, Spring 1991.

[15]See Dale W. Jorgenson, "Econometric Studies of Investment Behavior: A Survey," *Journal of Econometric Literature*, December 1971.

[16]See Barry Bosworth and Gary Burtless, "Effects of the Tax Reform on Labor Supply, Investment and Saving," *Economic Perspectives*, Winter 1992, and Robert Corker, Owen Evans, and Lloyd Kenward, "Tax Policy and Business Investment in the United States. Evidence from the 1980s," *IMF Staff Papers*, March 1989.

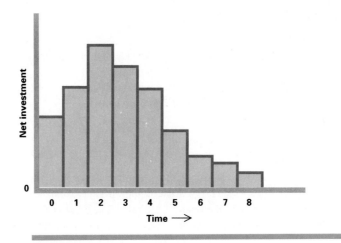

FIGURE 12-5

EFFECTS OF AN INCREASE IN OUTPUT IN PERIOD ZERO ON NET
INVESTMENT IN SUBSEQUENT PERIODS.

Summary

The main conclusions of the neoclassical theory of business fixed investment are that

1. Net investment spending is governed by the discrepancy between actual and desired capital.
2. Desired capital depends on the rental cost of capital and the expected level of output. Capital demand rises with expected output and the investment tax credit, and declines with an increase in *real* interest rates. This last point both justifies and modifies (by distinguishing real from nominal interest rates) the standard investment demand function, in which investment is negatively related to the nominal interest rate.
3. Monetary and fiscal policies affect investment via the desired capital stock, although with long lags.
4. The empirical evidence is broadly consistent with the neoclassical theory but leaves room for improvement.

12-2 BUSINESS FIXED INVESTMENT: ALTERNATIVE APPROACHES

In this section we discuss the way a firm approaches its investment decisions and also describe some departures from the neoclassical model.

The Business Investment Decision: The View from the Trenches

Business people making investment decisions typically use *discounted cash flow analysis*. The principles of discounting are described in Appendix 12-1. Consider a business

TABLE 12-3
DISCOUNTED CASH FLOW ANALYSIS AND PRESENT VALUE (dollars)

	year 1	year 2	year 3	present discounted value
Cash or revenue	-100	$+50$	$+80$	
Present value of $1	1	$1/1.12$ $= 0.893$	$(1/1.12^2)$ $= 0.797$	
Present value of costs or revenue	-100	50×0.893 $= 44.65$	80×0.797 $= 63.76$	$(-100 + 44.65$ $+ 63.76) = 8.41$

person deciding whether to build and equip a new factory. The first step is to figure out how much it will cost to get the factory into working order and how much revenue the factory will bring in each year after it starts operation.

For simplicity consider a very short-lived project, one that costs $100 to set up in the first year and then generates $50 in revenue (after paying for labor and raw materials) in the second year and a further $80 in the third year. By the end of the third year the factory has disintegrated.

Should the project be undertaken? Discounted cash flow analysis says that the revenues received in later years should be *discounted* to the present in order to calculate their present value. As Appendix 12-1 shows, if the interest rate is 10 percent, $110 a year from now is worth the same as $100 now. Why? Because if $100 were lent out today at 10 percent, a year from now the lender would end up with $110. To calculate the value of the project, the firm calculates its present discounted value at the interest rate at which it can borrow. If the present value is positive, then the project is undertaken.

Suppose that the relevant interest rate is 12 percent. The calculation of the present discounted value of the investment project is shown in Table 12-3. The $50 received in year 2 is worth only $44.65 today: $1 a year from now is worth $1/1.12 = $0.893 today, and so $50 a year from now is worth $44.65. The present value of the $80 received in year 3 is calculated similarly. The table shows that the present value of the net revenue received from the project is positive ($8.41); thus the firm should undertake the project.

Note that if the interest rate had been much higher—say, 18 percent—the decision would have been *not* to undertake the investment. We thus see that *the higher the interest rate, the less likely the firm will be to undertake any given investment project.*

At any time, each firm has an array of possible investment projects and estimates of the costs and the revenues from those projects. Depending on the level of the interest rate, the firm will want to undertake some of the projects and not undertake others. Adding the investment demands of all the firms in the economy, we obtain the total demand for investment in the economy at each interest rate.

This approach to the investment decision, which can be applied to investment projects of any duration and complexity, seems far from the description of Section 12-1 in terms of a desired capital stock and rate of adjustment. Actually, the two approaches are quite consistent. First, we should think of the desired capital stock as being the stock of capital that will be in place when the firms have their factories and new equipment on line. Second, the adjustment speed tells us how rapidly firms on average succeed in installing that capital.

Because the two approaches are consistent, the analysis of investment decisions could be made using either approach. For instance, using discounted cash flow analysis, the effects of expectations of future output can be analyzed by asking what determines the firms' projections of their future revenues (corresponding to the $50 in year 2 and $80 in year 3 in the example above); expected demand for their products must be relevant. Similarly, taxes are embodied by analyzing how taxes affect the amount of after-tax revenue the firm has left in each future year; for example, the investment tax credit reduces the net amount the firm has to lay out to build the project.

Finally, the firm makes decisions about the speed of adjustment by considering the cash flows associated with building the project at different speeds. If the project can be built more rapidly, the firm will decide on the speed with which it wants the project brought on line by considering the present discounted costs and revenues associated with speeding it up.

The Accelerator Model and Cost of Capital Effects

The flexible accelerator model developed in Section 12-1 is actually a generalization of an earlier model of investment; the simple *accelerator model.* The accelerator model asserts that investment spending is proportional to the *change* in output and is not affected by the cost of capital.

The simple accelerator model was based on the view that firms install new capital when they need to produce more. Therefore, firms would invest if output was expected to change, but they would not otherwise undertake *net* investment. The simple accelerator model did a reasonable job of explaining the data but was regarded as inadequate since it failed to take the costs of investing into account.

Much research has been devoted to the question of whether the cost of capital significantly affects investment.[17] If the accelerator model is extended by relating investment to current and past changes in income, it seems in some studies to do a better job of explaining investment than the neoclassical model. This finding would imply that the cost of capital is not a major determinant of the rate of investment.

There are also findings that the rental cost of capital does affect investment.[18] The conflicting findings mean that the evidence is not strong enough to decide the precise relative roles of the cost of capital and expectations of future output. No doubt both are major determinants of investment spending. But there are reasons and evidence to question whether the cost of capital is the only financial variable that affects investment.

---

[17]Usually, researchers in the neoclassical tradition use an equation like equation (9), in which the cost of capital, rc, enters only in the form (Y/rc), which means its effects are not estimated separately.

[18]For a comprehensive review of the evidence, see Robert S. Chirinko, "Business Fixed Investment and Tax Policy: A Perspective on Existing Models and Empirical Evidence," *National Tax Journal,* 1992, and Ford and Poret, "Business Investment."

TABLE 12-4
SOURCES OF FUNDS, U.S. MANUFACTURING FIRMS, 1970–1984

firm size	SOURCE OF FUNDS,* % OF TOTAL				% of long-term debt from banks	average retention ratio, %
	short-term bank debt	long-term bank debt	other long-term debt	retained earnings		
All firms	0.6	8.4	19.9	71.1	29.6	60
Asset class						
Under $10 million	5.1	12.8	6.2	75.9	67.3	79
Over $1 billion	−0.6	4.8	27.9	67.9	14.7	52

*Equity financing is excluded but is very small. Minus sign indicates firm has net assets (rather than liabilities) in this category.

SOURCE: Steven M. Fazzari, R. Glenn Hubbard, and Bruce C. Petersen, "Financing Constraints and Corporate Investment," *Brookings Paper on Economic Activity*, 1988.

Credit Rationing and Internal Sources of Finance

Table 12-4 shows the sources of manufacturing firms' funding in the United States during the period 1970–1984. The predominance of retained earnings as a source of financing stands out. Firms of all sizes use outside funding from banks, the bond markets, and equity only to a limited extent.[19] Instead they rely on retained earnings, profits that they do not pay out to stockholders, to finance investment. As the last column of the table shows, retained earnings exceed 50 percent of earnings for all firms and are relatively most important for the smallest firms.

What do these facts mean for the investment decision? They suggest that there is a close link between the earnings of firms and their investment decisions. If firms cannot readily obtain funding from outside sources when they need it, then the amount of assets they have on hand will affect their ability to invest. This would mean that the state of a firm's balance sheet and not just the cost of capital is a financial determinant of investment decisions.[20]

Box 12-2 describes the important phenomenon of *credit rationing*, which occurs when individuals cannot borrow even though they are willing to do so at the existing interest rates. There are good reasons for credit rationing, all stemming from the risk that the borrower will not repay the lender, for instance, because the borrower goes bankrupt. These arguments suggest that credit rationing is more likely for small firms without an established reputation than for large firms with a track record. The fact that the retention ratio in Table 12-4 declines with firm size is consistent with this implication. These data, as well as the experience of those who want to borrow, are consistent with the assumption that firms are rationed in their access to funding.

---

[19]Equity funding is excluded from the table, but independent evidence, noted in the article by Fazzari, Hubbard, and Petersen (cited in Table 12-4), shows that it provides very little financing for firms, especially small ones.

[20]See Mark Gertler and R. Glenn Hubbard, "Financial Factors in Business Investment," Federal Reserve Bank of Kansas, *Financial Market Volatility* (Kansas City, 1989).

box 12-2 **CREDIT RATIONING**

In the *IS-LM* model, interest rates are the only channel of transmission between financial markets and aggregate demand. Credit rationing is an important additional channel of transmission of monetary policy.* Credit rationing takes place when lenders limit the amount individuals can borrow, even though the borrowers are willing to pay the going interest rate on their loans.

Credit rationing can occur for two different reasons. First, a lender often cannot tell whether a particular customer (or the project the customer is financing) is good or bad. A bad customer will default on the loan and not repay it. Given the risk of default, the obvious answer seems to be to raise the interest rate.

However, raising interest rates works the wrong way: honest or conservative customers are deterred from borrowing because they realize their investments are not profitable at higher interest rates. But customers who are reckless or dishonest will borrow because they do not expect to pay if the project turns out badly. However carefully they try to evaluate their customers, the lenders cannot altogether escape this problem. The answer is to limit the amount lent to any one customer. Most customers get broadly the same interest rate (with some adjustments), but the amount of credit they are allowed is rationed, according to both the kind of security the customer can offer and the prospects for the economy.

When times are good, banks lend cheerfully because they believe that the average customer will not default. When the economy turns down, credit rationing intensifies—and this may happen even though interest rates decline.

Credit rationing provides another channel for monetary policy. If lenders perceive that the Fed is shifting to restraint and higher interest rates to cool down the economy, lenders fearing a slowdown will tighten credit. Conversely, if they believe policy is expansionary and times will be good, they ease credit, via both lower interest rates and expanded credit rations.

A second type of credit rationing can occur when the central bank imposes credit limits on commercial banks and other lenders. Banks are then not allowed to expand their loans during a given period by more than, say, 5 percent, or even less. Such a credit limit can put an abrupt end to a boom. A striking example occurred in the United States in early 1980. Concerned with the risk of double-digit inflation, the Fed clamped on credit controls. In no time the economy fell into a recession, with output falling at an annual rate of 9 percent.

Credit controls thus are an emergency brake for the central bank. They work, but they do so in a very blunt way. For that reason their use is very infrequent and remains reserved for occasions when dramatic, fast effects are desired. ■

---

*For a comprehensive survey on credit rationing see Dwight Jaffee and Joseph Stiglitz, "Credit Rationing," in Ben Friedman and Frank Hahn (eds.), *Handbook of Monetary Economics* (Amsterdam: North-Holland, 1990).

tion. These data, as well as the experience of those who want to borrow, are consistent with the assumption that firms are rationed in their access to funding.

Under such conditions, firms' investment decisions will be affected not only by the interest rate, but also by the amount of funds they have saved out of past earnings and by their current profits. The cost of capital must still affect the investment decision, because firms that retain earnings have to consider the alternative of holding financial assets and earning interest rather than investing in plant and equipment. There is indeed evidence that the rate of investment is affected by the volume of retained earnings and by profits, as well as the cost of capital.

In the early 1990s, in the aftermath of severe banking problems due to losses in real estate, credit rationing was held responsible for the slow rate of investment despite low short-term interest rates. Banks were lending very little, especially to small and medium sized firms. The problem was especially severe in depressed regions, because small business can only borrow locally, from banks, but banks in a depressed region are especially unwilling to lend.[21]

Why Does Investment Fluctuate?

The facts with which we started this chapter show that investment fluctuates much more than consumption spending. The accelerator model, which links investment to *changes* in output, provides one explanation for these fluctuations. There are two other basic explanations: the uncertain basis for expectations and the flexibility of the timing of investment.

UNCERTAIN EXPECTATIONS

Keynes, in the *General Theory*, emphasized the uncertain basis on which investment decisions are made. In his words, "We have to admit that our basis of knowledge for estimating the yield ten years hence of a railway, a copper mine, a textile factory, the goodwill of a patent medicine . . . amounts to little and sometimes to nothing."[22] Thus, he argued, investment decisions are very much affected by how optimistic or pessimistic the investors feel.

The term "animal spirits" is sometimes used to describe the optimism or pessimism of investors; the term indicates that there may be no good basis for the expectations on which investors base their decisions. If there is no good basis for expectations, then they could change easily—and the volume of investment could well change along with expectations.

---

[21] See the discussion in Richard Syron, "Are We Experiencing a Credit Crunch?" Federal Reserve Bank of Boston, *New England Economic Review*, July/August 1991, especially Fig. 9, which shows responses of small business in New England and nationwide to a credit-rationing survey.

[22] J. M. Keynes, *The General Theory of Employment, Interest and Money* (London: Macmillan, 1936), pp. 149–150.

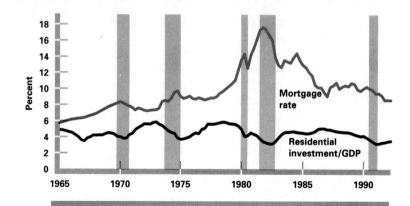

FIGURE 12-6
HOUSING INVESTMENT AND THE MORTGAGE INTEREST RATE, 1965–1992.
The mortgage rate is for new houses. Housing investment is
measured as a percentage of GDP. Shaded bars mark periods of
recession. (SOURCE: DRI/McGraw-Hill.)

THE TIMING OF INVESTMENT DECISIONS

The second additional reason for fluctuations in investment is that, as already discussed,
investment decisions can be delayed. Suppose a firm is considering an investment
project, but the economy is currently in a recession and, indeed, at present the firm
cannot even usefully employ all the capital it already has. Such a firm might choose
to wait until the prospects for the economy look better—when the recovery gets under
way—before starting the investment project. In fact, one can go a step ahead and argue
that a project will be executed not just when it becomes profitable but rather when it
does not pay to wait for any further improvement in profitability.[23]

Either or both of those factors could help account for the substantial fluctuations
that are seen in business investment spending. Indeed, they may also explain the success
of the accelerator theory of investment, for if firms wait for a recovery to get under
way before investing, their investment will be closely related to the change in GDP.

12-3 RESIDENTIAL INVESTMENT

We study residential investment separately from business fixed investment to introduce
a slightly different model of investment.

Figure 12-6 shows residential investment spending as a percentage of GDP for
the 1965–1992 period, together with the nominal mortgage interest rate. Residential

---

[23]This statement is based on a sophisticated argument in terms of financial option theory. See Robert Pindyck,
"Irreversibility, Uncertainty, and Investment," *Journal of Economic Literature*, September 1991.

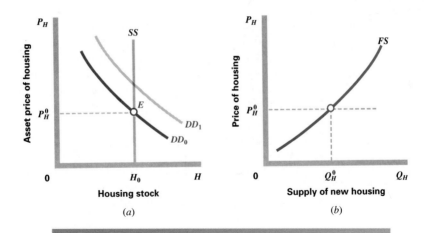

FIGURE 12-7

THE HOUSING MARKET: DETERMINATION OF THE ASSET PRICE OF HOUSING AND THE RATE OF HOUSING INVESTMENT. The supply of and demand for the stock of housing determine the asset price of housing (P_H^0) in panel (*a*). The rate of housing investment (Q_H^0) is determined by the flow supply of housing at price P_H^0 in panel (*b*).

investment declines in all recessions. Thus in 1969–1970, 1973–1975, 1980, 1981–1982, and 1990–1991 there are dips in residential investment. The same is true for the 1966–1967 minirecession.

Theory

Residential investment consists of the building of single-family and multifamily dwellings, which we call *housing* for short. Housing is distinguished as an asset by its long life. Consequently, investment in housing in any one year tends to be a very small proportion—about 3 percent—of the existing stock of housing. The theory of residential investment starts by considering the demand for the existing *stock* of housing. Housing is viewed as one among the many assets that a wealthholder can own.[24]

In Figure 12-7 we show the demand for the stock of housing in the downward-sloping DD_0 curve. The lower the price of housing (P_H), the greater the quantity demanded. The position of the demand curve itself depends on a number of economic variables. First, the more wealthy individuals are, the more housing they desire to own.

---

[24]The theory of housing investment of this section is outlined in James R. Kearl, "Inflation, Mortgages, and Housing," *Journal of Political Economy*, October 1979. See, too, James Poterba, "House Price Dynamics: The Role of Tax Policy and Demography," *Brookings Papers on Economic Activity*, 2, 1991, Robert Topel and Sherwin Rosen, "Housing Investment in the United States," *Journal of Political Economy*, November/December 1988, and James Poterba, "Taxation and Housing: Old Questions, New Answers," NBER Working Paper 3963, 1992.

Thus an increase in wealth would shift the demand curve from DD_0 to DD_1. Second, the demand for housing as an asset depends on the real return on other assets. If returns on other forms of holding wealth—such as bonds—are low, then housing looks like a relatively attractive form in which to hold wealth. A reduction in the return on other assets, such as bonds or common stock, shifts the demand curve from DD_0 to DD_1.

Third, the demand for the housing stock depends on the net real return obtained by owning housing. The gross return—before taking costs into account—consists either of rent, if the housing is rented out, or of the implicit return that the homeowner receives by living in the home plus capital gains arising from increases in the value of the housing. In turn, the costs of owning the housing consist of interest costs, typically the mortgage interest rate, plus any real estate taxes, and depreciation. These costs are deducted from the gross return and, after tax adjustments, constitute the net return. An increase in the net return on housing, caused, for example, by a reduction in the mortgage interest rate, makes housing a more attractive form in which to hold wealth and shifts the demand curve for housing from DD_0 to DD_1.

The price of housing is determined by the interaction of this demand with the stock supply of housing. At any time the stock supply is fixed—there is a given stock of housing that cannot be changed quickly. The supply curve of the stock of housing is therefore the SS curve of Figure 12-7a. The equilibrium *asset price of housing*, P_H^0, is determined by the intersection of the supply and demand curves. The asset price of housing is the price of a typical house or apartment. At any one time, the market for the stock of housing determines the asset price of housing.

THE RATE OF INVESTMENT

We now consider the determinants of the rate of investment in housing, and for that purpose turn to Figure 12-7b. The FS curve represents the supply of new housing as a function of the price of housing. This curve is the same as the regular supply curve of any industry. The supply curve shows the amount of a good that suppliers want to sell at each price. In this case, the good being supplied is new housing. The position of the FS curve is affected by the costs of factors of production used in the construction industry and by technological factors affecting the cost of building.

The FS curve is sometimes called the flow supply curve, since it represents the *flow* of new housing into the market in a given time period. In contrast, the *stock* supply curve, SS, represents the total amount of housing in the market at a moment of time.

Given the price of housing established in the asset market, P_H^0, building contractors supply the amount of new housing, Q_H^0, for sale at that price. The higher the asset price, the greater the supply of new housing. Thus, the supply of new housing is nothing other than gross investment in housing—total additions to the housing stock. Figure 12-7 thus represents our basic theory of housing investment.

Any factor affecting the demand for the existing stock of housing will affect the asset price of housing, P_H, and thus the rate of investment in housing. Similarly, any factor shifting the flow supply curve, FS, will affect the rate of investment.

Suppose the interest rate—the rate that potential homeowners can obtain by investing elsewhere—rises. Then the asset demand for housing falls and the price of housing falls; that, in turn, induces a decline in the rate of production of new housing, or a decline in housing investment. Or suppose that the mortgage interest rate rises: once again there is a fall in the asset price of housing and a reduction in the rate of construction.

Because the existing stock of housing is so large relative to the rate of investment in housing, we can ignore the effects of the current supply of new housing on the price of housing in the short run. However, over time, as the new construction increases the housing stock it shifts the *SS* curve of panel (*a*) to the right. The long-run equilibrium in the housing industry would be reached, in a nongrowing economy, when the housing stock became constant. Constancy of the housing stock requires gross investment to be equal to depreciation or net investment to be equal to zero. The asset price of housing would have to be at the level at which the rate of construction was just equal to the rate of depreciation of the existing stock of housing in long-run equilibrium. If population or income and wealth were growing at a constant rate, the long-run equilibrium would be one in which the rate of construction was just sufficient to cover depreciation and the steadily growing stock demand. In an economy subjected to continual, nonsteady changes, the long-run equilibrium is not necessarily ever reached.

Minor qualifications to the basic theoretical structure arise chiefly because new housing cannot be constructed immediately in response to changes in P_H. Thus, the supply of new housing responds, not to the actual price of housing today, but to the price expected to prevail when the construction is completed. However, the lags are quite short; it takes less than a year to build a typical house. Another qualification stems from that same construction delay. Since builders have to incur expenses before they sell their output, they need financing over the construction period. They frequently obtain mortgages to provide the needed funds. Hence, the position of the flow supply curve is affected by the mortgage interest rate as well as the amount of lending undertaken by mortgage lenders.

THE q THEORY OF INVESTMENT

Step aside for a moment to note that the model of the housing market that emphasizes the asset market and the rate of addition to the stock can similarly be used to analyze business fixed investment—this is the q theory, which focuses on the stock market (see footnote 10).

The q theory can be cast in terms very similar to those of the housing model. At any one moment, there is a given stock of shares (equity) in the economy. Stock market investors place a value on those shares, with the price of shares in the stock market corresponding to P_H in Figure 12-7.

The price of a share in a company is the price of a claim on the capital in the company. The managers of the company can then be thought of as responding to the price of the stock by producing more new capital—that is, investing—when the price of shares is high and producing less new capital—or not investing at all—when the price of shares is low.

What is q? It is an estimate of the value the stock market places on a firm's assets relative to the cost of producing those assets. When the ratio is high, firms will want to produce more assets, so that investment will be rapid. Similarly, P_H can be

TABLE 12-5
MONTHLY PAYMENTS ON MORTGAGES

Interest rate, %	5	10	15
Monthly payment, $	292	454	640

NOTE: The assumed mortgage is a loan for $50,000, paid back over 25 years, with equal monthly payments throughout the 25 years.

thought of as the price of an existing house relative to the cost of building a new one. When that ratio is high, there will be lots of building.[25]

Monetary Policy and Housing Investment

Monetary policy has powerful effects on housing investment. Part of the reason is that most houses are purchased with mortgages. Since the 1930s, a mortgage has typically been a debt instrument of very long maturity, 20 to 30 years, with fixed monthly repayments until maturity.[26]

Monetary policy has powerful effects on housing investment because the demand for housing is sensitive to the interest rate. There is sensitivity to both the *real* and *nominal* interest rates. The reason for this sensitivity can be seen in Table 12-5, which shows the monthly payment that has to be made by someone borrowing $50,000 through a conventional mortgage at different interest rates. All these interest rates have existed at some time during the last 25 years: 5 percent at the beginning of the sixties, 10 percent at the end of the seventies and end of the eighties, and 15 percent in 1981 and 1982.

The monthly repayment by the borrower approximately doubles when the interest rate doubles. Thus an essential component of the cost of owning a home rises almost proportionately with the interest rate. It is therefore not surprising that the demand for housing is very sensitive to the interest rate.

The preceding statements have to be qualified. First, there are substantial tax advantages to financing a home through a mortgage, because the interest payments can be deducted from income before calculating taxes. Second, we should be concerned with the *real* and not the nominal interest cost of owning a house—and certainly much of the rise of the mortgage interest rate between 1960 and 1981 was a result of increases in the expected rate of inflation.

But because of the form of the mortgage, the *nominal* interest rate also affects

[25]See Chirinko, "Business Fixed Investment and Tax Policy," for a review of the evidence on this model.

[26]So-called ARMS (adjustable rate mortgages) were introduced in the 1970s. The interest rate on such mortgages is adjusted in accordance with some reference rate, such as the 1-year Treasury bill rate. Both fixed rate mortgages and ARMs are now used to finance housing.

FIGURE 12-8

THE INVENTORY TO FINAL SALES RATIO, 1960–1992. Shaded bars mark periods of recession. (SOURCE: DRI/McGraw-Hill.)

the homeowner. The conventional mortgage makes the borrower pay a fixed amount each month over the lifetime of the mortgage. Even if the interest rate rises only because the expected rate of inflation has risen—and thus the real rate is constant—the payments that have to be made *today* by a borrower go up. But the inflation has not yet happened. Thus the real payments made today by a borrower rise when the *nominal* interest rate rises, even if the real rate does not rise. Given the higher real monthly payments when the nominal interest rate rises, we should expect the nominal interest rate also to affect housing demand. And the data shown in Figure 12-6 are consistent with the view that the nominal interest rate affects housing demand.

12-4 INVENTORY INVESTMENT

Inventories consist of raw materials, goods in the process of production, and completed goods held by firms in anticipation of the products' sale. The ratio of inventories to annual final sales in the United States shown in Figure 12-8 has been in the range of

18.5 to 30 percent over the past 25 years. The trend has been declining, so that at present firms hold inventories that average just under 3 months of their final sales.

Firms hold inventories for several reasons:

- Sellers hold inventories to meet future demand for goods, because goods cannot be instantly manufactured or obtained to meet demand.

- Inventories are held because it is less costly for a firm to order goods less frequently in large quantities than to order small quantities frequently—just as the average householder finds it useful to keep several days' supplies in the house so as not to have to visit the supermarket daily.

- Producers may hold inventories as a way of smoothing their production. Since it is costly to keep changing the level of output on a production line, producers may produce at a relatively steady rate even when demand fluctuates, building up inventories when demand is low and drawing them down when demand is high.[27]

- Some inventories are held as an unavoidable part of the production process; there is an inventory of meat and sawdust inside the sausage machine during the manufacture of sausage, for example.

Firms have a desired ratio of inventories to final sales that depends on economic variables. The smaller the cost of ordering new goods and the greater the speed with which such goods arrive, the smaller the inventory-sales ratio. The inventory-sales ratio may also depend on the level of sales, with the ratio falling with sales because there is relatively less uncertainty about sales as their level increases.

Finally, there is the *interest rate*. Since firms carry inventories over time, the firms must tie up resources in order to buy and hold the inventories. There is an interest cost involved in such inventory holding, and the desired inventory-sales ratio should be expected to fall with increases in the interest rate.

Figure 12-8 shows the inventory-sales ratio falling over the last 20 years. This reduction is generally attributed to improved methods of inventory and production management.

Anticipated versus Unanticipated Inventory Investment

Inventory investment takes place when firms increase their inventories. The central aspect of inventory investment lies in the distinction between anticipated (desired) and unanticipated (undesired) investment. Inventory investment could be high in two circumstances. First, if sales are unexpectedly low, firms would find unsold inventories

---

[27]This so-called *production-smoothing* reason for holding inventories has been the focus of much recent research. Although most evidence has been against the production-smoothing model (see, for instance, Jeffrey A. Miron and Stephen P. Zeldes, "Seasonality, Cost Shocks, and the Production Smoothing Model of Inventories," *Econometrica*, July 1988), there is some evidence suggesting that the data, rather than the theory, may be at fault. See, too, Spencer Krane and Steven Braun, "Production Smoothing Evidence from Physical-Production Data," *Journal of Political Economy*, June 1991.

accumulating on their shelves; that constitutes unanticipated inventory investment. Second, inventory investment could be high because firms plan to build up inventories; that is anticipated or desired investment.

The two circumstances obviously have very different implications for the behavior of aggregate demand. Unanticipated inventory investment is a result of unexpectedly low aggregate demand. By contrast, planned inventory investment adds to aggregate demand. Thus rapid accumulation of inventories could be associated with either rapidly declining aggregate demand or rapidly increasing aggregate demand.

Inventories in the Business Cycle

Inventory investment fluctuates proportionately more in the business cycle than any other component of aggregate demand. In every post–World War II recession in the United States there has been a decline in inventory investment between peak and trough. As a recession develops, demand slows down and firms add involuntarily to the stock of inventories. Thus the inventory-sales ratio rises. Then production is cut, and firms meet demand by selling goods from inventories. This pattern is apparent in Figure 12-8, where the peaks clearly mark recession years. At the end of every recession firms have been reducing their inventories, meaning that inventory investment has been negative in the final quarter of every recession.

The role of inventories in the business cycle is a result of a combination of unanticipated and anticipated inventory change. Figure 12-9 illustrates the combination using data from the recession at the start of the 1980s. In the quarter before the 1981–1982 recession began, GDP increased rapidly, recovering from the previous recession. From the beginning of 1981 firms began to accumulate inventories, as output exceeded their sales. Firms were probably anticipating high sales in the future and decided to build up their stocks of goods for future sale. Thus there was *intended* inventory accumulation.

Final sales turned down in the middle of 1981, but GDP stayed above sales until the end of the year. Then firms realized their inventories were too high and cut production to get them back in line. In the first quarter of 1982, firms had cut output way back and finally were successfully and *intentionally* reducing their inventories; hence, sales exceed output. This stage, in which output falls sharply as firms intentionally cut back production to get inventories back in line, has been typical in post–World War II recessions, and continued until the end of this recession. Finally inventories were built up *intentionally* as the recovery got under way in 1983 (not shown in the figure).

Note that the behavior of inventories reflects the adjustment mechanism for output that we discussed in Chapter 3 and described there as the *inventory cycle*. To understand the inventory cycle, consider the case of a hypothetical automobile dealer who sells, say, thirty cars per month, and holds an average of 1 month's sales—namely, thirty cars—in inventory. As long as sales stay steady at thirty cars per month, the dealer will be ordering thirty cars per month from the factory. Now suppose sales drop to twenty-five cars per month, and it takes the dealer 2 months to respond to the change. During those 2 months inventories will have climbed to forty cars. In the future the dealer will want an inventory of only twenty-five cars on hand. Thus when responding to the fall in demand, the dealer cuts the order from the factory from thirty cars to ten

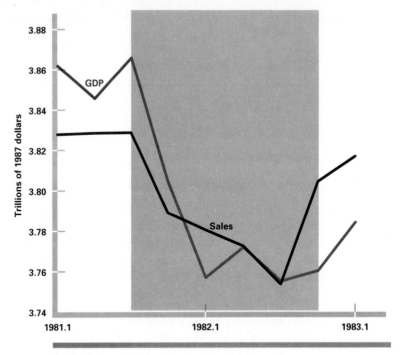

FIGURE 12-9

SALES AND OUTPUT IN RECESSION AND RECOVERY, 1981–1983. Shaded
bar marks period of recession. (Source: DRI/McGraw-Hill.)

in the third month, to get the inventory back to 1 month's sales. After the desired
inventory-sales ratio has been restored, the order will be twenty-five cars per month.
We see in this extreme case how the drop in demand of five cars, instead of leading
to a simple drop in car output of five cars per month, causes a drop in output of twenty
cars in 1 month, followed by the longer-run drop in output of five cars per month.

JUST-IN-TIME INVENTORY MANAGEMENT

If inventories could be kept more closely in line with sales, or aggregate demand,
fluctuations in inventory investment and in GDP would be reduced. As business methods
are improving all the time, the hope is often expressed that new methods of management
will enable firms to keep tighter control over their inventories and thus that the prospects
for steadier growth can be improved. "Just-in-time" inventory management techniques
imported from Japan emphasize the synchronization of suppliers and users of materials,
allowing firms to operate with small inventories, so that production is "lean" in inventories. These improved methods help account for the downward trend in inventories in

Figure 12-8.[28] Indeed, in the 1990–1991 recession, the inventory-final sales ratio increased very little, much less than in previous recessions. These facts suggest that the role of inventory spending in the business cycle may have changed.

12-5 SUMMARY

1. Investment is spending that adds to the capital stock. Investment usually constitutes less than 17 percent of aggregate demand in the United States, but fluctuations in investment account for a large share of business cycle movements in GDP. We analyze investment in three categories: business fixed investment, residential investment, and inventory investment.

2. The neoclassical theory of business fixed investment sees the rate of investment being determined by the speed with which firms adjust their capital stocks toward the desired level. The desired capital stock is bigger the larger is the *expected* output the firm plans to produce and the smaller the rental or user cost of capital.

3. The real interest rate is the nominal (stated) interest rate minus the inflation rate.

4. The rental cost of capital is higher the higher the real interest rate, the lower the price of the firm's stock, and the higher the rate of depreciation of capital. Taxes also affect the rental cost of capital, in particular through the investment tax credit. The investment tax credit is, in effect, a government subsidy for investment.

5. In practice, firms decide how much to invest using discounted cash flow analysis. This analysis gives answers that are consistent with those of the neoclassical approach.

6. Because credit is rationed, firms' investment decisions are affected also by the state of their balance sheets, and thus by the amount of earnings they have retained.

7. Empirical results show that business fixed investment responds with long lags to changes in output. The accelerator model, which does not take into account changes in the rental cost of capital, does almost as good a job of explaining investment as the more sophisticated neoclassical model.

8. The theory of housing investment starts from the demand for the *stock* of housing. Demand is affected by wealth, the interest rates available on alternative investments, and the mortgage rate. The price of housing is determined by the interaction of the stock demand and the given stock supply of housing available at any given time. The rate of housing investment is determined by the rate at which builders supply housing at the going price.

9. Housing investment is affected by monetary policy because housing demand is sensitive to the mortgage interest rate (real and nominal). Credit availability also plays a role.

10. Monetary and fiscal policy both affect investment, particularly business fixed investment and housing investment. The effects take place through changes in real (and nominal in the case of housing) interest rates and through tax incentives for investment.

---

[28]See Dan M. Bechter and Stephen Stanley, "Evidence of Improved Inventory Control," *Federal Reserve Bank of Richmond Economic Review*, January–February 1992 and Jane Sneddon Little, "Changes in Inventory Management: Implications for the U.S. Recovery," *New England Economic Review*, November/December 1992.

11. Inventory investment fluctuates proportionately more than any other class of investment. Firms have a desired inventory-sales ratio. That may get out of line if sales are unexpectedly high or low, and then firms change their production levels to adjust inventories. For instance, when aggregate demand falls at the beginning of a recession, inventories build up. Then when firms cut back production, output falls even more than did aggregate demand. This is the inventory cycle.

KEY TERMS

Business fixed investment
Residential investment
Inventory investment
Desired capital stock
Flexible accelerator model
Marginal product of capital
Rental (user) cost of capital

Real interest rates
Gradual adjustment hypothesis
Discounted cash flow analysis
Credit rationing
q theory
Inventory cycle

PROBLEMS

1. We have seen in Chapters 11 and 12 that *permanent* income and output, rather than current income and output, determine consumption and investment.
   (a) How does this affect the *IS-LM* model built in Chapter 4? (Refer to Figure 11-5.)
   (b) What are the policy implications of the use of "permanent" measures?

2. In Chapter 4 it was assumed that investment rises during periods of low interest rates. That, however, was not the case during the 1930s, when investment and interest rates were both very low. Explain how this can occur. What would have been appropriate fiscal policy in such a case?

3. According to the description of business fixed investment in this chapter, how would you expect a firm's investment decisions to be affected by a sudden increase in the demand for its product? What factors would determine the speed of its reaction?

4. Describe how a car rental agency would calculate the price at which it rents cars, and relate your description to equation (4).

5. It is often suggested that investment spending is dominated by animal spirits—the optimism or pessimism of investors. Is this argument at all consistent with the analysis of Sections 12-1 and 12-2?

6. Here are the cash flows for an investment project:

year 1	year 2	year 3
−200	100	120

Should the firm undertake this project?
(a) If the interest rate is 5 percent?
(b) If the interest rate is 10 percent?

7. What is the relationship between the neoclassical theory of investment and the way firms make their investment decisions in practice?

8. (a) Give at least two reasons why higher profits may increase the rate of investment.
   (b) Explain why lenders may ration the quantity of credit rather than merely charge higher interest rates to more risky borrowers.

9. Suppose that an explicitly temporary tax credit is enacted. The tax credit is at the rate of 10 percent and lasts only 1 year.
   (a) What is the effect of this tax measure on investment in the long run (say, after 4 or 5 years)?
   (b) What is the effect in the current year and the following year?
   (c) How would your answers in 9a and 9b differ if the tax credit were permanent?

10. Using Figure 12-7, trace carefully the step-by-step effects on the housing market of an increase in interest rates. Explain each shift and its long-run and short-run effects.

11. (a) Explain why the housing market usually prospers when (real) mortgage rates are low.
    (b) In some states, usury laws prohibit (nominal) mortgage rates in excess of a legal maximum. Explain how this could lead to an exception to the conclusion in (a).

12. (a) Explain how final sales and output can differ.
    (b) Point out in Figure 12-9 periods of planned and unplanned inventory investment and drawing down.
    (c) During a period of slow but steady growth, how would you expect final sales and output to be related? Explain. Draw a hypothetical figure like Figure 12-9 for such a period.

13. At the end of 1988 and the beginning of 1989, the inventory-sales ratio, although very low, was beginning to rise. Business cycle forecasters argued that this was a worrisome sign (among other signs, including a rising dollar and higher interest rates) and that there could be a recession later in 1989. Explain why this would be a recessionary signal, and check the data to see whether there was a recession or slowdown after 1989.

14. In the 1990–1991 recession, the inventory-sales ratio did not rise appreciably. How do you explain this fact?

*15. For this question use the Cobb-Douglas production function and the corresponding desired capital stock given by equation (8). Assume that

$$\gamma = 0.3 \qquad Y = \$5.0 \text{ trillion} \qquad rc = 0.12$$

   (a) Calculate the desired capital stock, K^*.
   (b) Now suppose that Y is expected to rise to $6 trillion. What is the corresponding desired capital stock?
   (c) Suppose that the capital stock was at its desired level before the change in income was expected. Suppose further that $\lambda = 0.4$ in the gradual adjustment model of investment. What will the rate of investment be in the first year after expected income changes? In the second year?
   (d) Does your answer in (c) refer to gross or net investment?

⊟ COMPUTER EXERCISES

1. Increase government spending by 90 and compare the flexible accelerator cycles to the simple accelerator cycles. What happens as λ increases from 0.40 to 0.50 to 0.60? Why?

---

*An asterisk denotes a more difficult problem.

2. How does a decline in government spending of 90 change your analysis in exercise 1?

3. Suppose the saving rate rises, reducing MPC to 0.60. By how much will long-run GDP decline? Now find a value of MPC that will cause an equivalent rise in long-run GDP. Why are the cycles in these two simulations so different from each other and different from the cycles in exercises 1 and 2?

4. How does increasing the rental cost of capital to 7 percent affect GDP and the capital stock? Why does the accelerator give you cycles?

APPENDIX 12-1: INTEREST RATES, PRESENT VALUES, AND DISCOUNTING

In this appendix we deal with the relationships among bond coupons, interest rates and yields, and the prices of bonds. In doing so, we shall introduce the very useful concept of present discounted value (*PDV*).

Section 1

We start with the case of a perpetual bond, or perpetuity. Such bonds have been issued in a number of countries, including the United Kingdom, where they are called Consols. The Consol is a promise by the British government to pay a fixed amount to the holder of the bond every year and forever. Let us denote the promised payment per Consol by Q_c, the *coupon*.[29]

The *yield* on a bond is the return per dollar that the holder of the bond receives. The yield on a savings account paying 5 percent interest per year is obviously just 5 percent. Someone paying $25 for a Consol that has a coupon of $2.50 obtains a yield of 10 percent [($2.50/25) $\times$ 100 percent].

The yield on a Consol and its price are related in a simple way. Let us denote the price of the Consol by P_c and the coupon (as before) by Q_c. Then, as the above example suggests, the yield, i, is just

$$i = \frac{Q_c}{P_c} \qquad \text{(A1)}$$

which says that the yield on a perpetuity is the coupon divided by the price.

Alternatively, we can switch equation (A1) around to

$$P_c = \frac{Q_c}{i} \qquad \text{(A2)}$$

which says that the price is the coupon divided by the yield. So, given the coupon and the yield, we can derive the price, or given the coupon and the price, we can derive the yield.

None of this is a theory of the determination of the yield or the price of a perpetuity. It merely points out the relationship between price and yield. The theory of interest rate determination is

---

[29]The *coupon rate* is the coupon divided by the face value of the bond, which is literally the value printed on the face of the bond. Bonds do not necessarily sell for their face value, though customarily the face value is close to the value at which the bonds are sold when they first come on the market.

presented in Chapter 4; the interest rate corresponds to the yield on bonds, and we tend to talk interchangeably of interest rates and yields.

We shall return to the Consol at the end of this appendix.

Section 2

Now we move to a short-term bond. Let us consider a bond that was sold by a borrower for $100 and on which the borrower promises to pay $108 after 1 year. This is a 1-year bond. The yield on the bond to the person who bought it for $100 is 8 percent. For every $1 lent, the lender obtains both the $1 principal and 8 cents extra at the end of the year.

Next we ask a slightly different question. How much would a promise to pay $1 at the end of the year be worth? If $108 at the end of the year is worth $100 today, then $1 at the end of the year must be worth $100/108, or 92.6 cents, today. That is the value today of $1 in 1 year's time. In other words, it is the *present discounted value* of $1 in 1 year's time. It is the present value because it is what would be paid today for the promise of money in 1 year's time, and it is discounted because the value today is less than the promised payment in a year's time.

Denoting the 1-year yield or interest rate by i, we can write the present discounted value of a promised payment of Q_1 1 year from now as

$$PDV = \frac{Q_1}{1 + i} \qquad \text{(A3)}$$

Let us return to our 1-year bond and suppose that the day after the original borrower obtained the money, the yield on 1-year bonds rises. How much would anyone *now* be willing to pay for the promise to receive $108 after 1 year? The answer must be given by the general formula (A3). That means that the price of the 1-year bond will fall when the interest rate or yield on such bonds rises. Once again, we see that the price of the bond and the yield are invariably related, given the promised payments to be made on the bond.

As before, we can reverse the formula for the price in order to find the yield on the bond, given its price and the promised payment Q_1. Note that the price, P, is equal to the present discounted value, so we can write

$$1 + i = \frac{Q_1}{P} \qquad \text{(A4)}$$

Section 3

Next we consider a 2-year bond. Such a bond would typically promise to make a payment of interest, which we shall denote Q_1, at the end of the first year, and then a payment of interest and principal (usually the amount borrowed), Q_2, at the end of the second year. Given the yield, i, on the bond, how do we compute its *PDV*, which will be equal to its price?

We start by asking first what the bond will be worth 1 year from now. At that stage, it will be a 1-year bond, promising to pay the amount Q_2 in 1 year's time, and yielding i. Its value 1 year from now will accordingly be given by equation (A3), except that Q_1 in equation (A3) is replaced by Q_2. Let us denote the value of the bond 1 year from now by PDV_1, and note that

$$PDV_1 = \frac{Q_2}{1 + i} \qquad \text{(A5)}$$

To complete computing the *PDV* of the 2-year bond, we can now treat it as a 1-year bond that promises to pay Q_1 in interest 1 year from now and, also, to pay PDV_1 1 year from now, since it can be sold at that stage for that amount. Hence, the *PDV* of the bond, equal to its price, is

$$PDV = \frac{Q_1}{1 + i} + \frac{PDV_1}{1 + i} \qquad (A6)$$

or

$$PDV = \frac{Q_1}{1 + i} + \frac{Q_2}{(1 + i)^2} \qquad (A6a)$$

As previously, given the promised payments Q_1 and Q_2, the price of the bond will fall if the yield rises, and vice versa.

It is now less simple to reverse the equation for the price of the bond to find the yield than it was before; that is because, from equation (A6), we obtain a quadratic equation for the yield, which has two solutions.

Section 4

We have now outlined the argument whereby the present discounted value of *any* promised stream of payments for any number of years can be computed. Suppose that a bond, or any other asset, promises to pay amounts $Q_1, Q_2, Q_3, \ldots, Q_n$ in future years 1, 2, 3, $\ldots$, *n*. By pursuing the type of argument given in Section 3, it is possible to show that the *PDV* of such a payments stream will be

$$PDV = \frac{Q_1}{1 + i} + \frac{Q_2}{(1 + i)^2} + \frac{Q_3}{(1 + i)^3} + \cdots + \frac{Q_n}{(1 + i)^n} \qquad (A7)$$

As usual, the price of a bond with a specified payments stream will be inversely related to its yield.

Section 5

The formula (A7) is the general formula for calculating the present discounted value of any stream of payments. Indeed, the payments may also be negative. Thus in calculating the *PDV* of an investment project, we expect the first few payments, for example, Q_1 and Q_2, to be negative. Those are the periods in which the firm is spending to build the factory or buy machinery. Then in later years the Q_i become positive as the factory starts generating revenues.

Firms undertaking discounted cash flow analysis are calculating present values using a formula such as (A7).

Section 6

Finally, we return to the Consol. The Consol promises to pay the amount Q_c forever. Applying the formula, we can compute the present value of the Consol by

$$PDV = Q_c \left[\frac{1}{(1 + i)} + \frac{1}{(1 + i)^2} + \frac{1}{(1 + i)^3} + \cdots + \frac{1}{(1 + i)^n} + \cdots \right] \qquad (A8)$$

The brackets on the right-hand side contain an infinite series, the sum of which can be calculated as $1/i$. Thus,

$$PDV = \frac{Q_c}{i} \tag{A9}$$

This section casts a slightly different light on the commonsense discussion in Section 1 of this appendix. Equations (A8) and (A9) show that the Consol's price is equal to the *PDV* of the future coupon payments.

APPENDIX 12-2: THE DESIRED CAPITAL STOCK: A COBB-DOUGLAS EXAMPLE

The Cobb-Douglas production function is written in the form

$$Y = N^{1-\gamma}K^{\gamma} \qquad 1 > \gamma > 0 \tag{A-10}$$

where N is the amount of labor used. This production function is particularly popular because it is easy to handle and also because it appears to fit the facts of U.S. economic experience reasonably well. The coefficient γ of equation (8) is the same as the γ of the production function.

The Cobb-Douglas production function implies a very specific and simple form of equation (2) for the desired capital stock:

$$K^* = \frac{\gamma Y}{rc} \tag{A-11}$$

In this case, the desired capital stock varies in proportion to output and inversely with the rental cost of capital.

We also draw attention here to a subtle point: in general, the desired capital stock is determined not only by the rental rate on capital, but also by the real wage rate. Firms will want to use more capital to produce a given level of output, the lower is the rental cost of capital *relative to* the real wage. Implicitly, in writing equation (2) in the text, we assume that the real wage paid to labor is given and does not change as the rental cost of capital changes. In general, the rental cost of capital relative to the real wage determines the desired capital stock, given Y.

THE DEMAND FOR MONEY

*M*oney is the means of payment or medium of exchange. More informally, money is whatever is generally accepted in exchange. In the past, seashells or cocoa or gold coins served as money in different places. In the United States, $M1$, consisting of currency plus checkable deposits, comes closest to defining the means of payment. At the end of 1991, $M1$ was $898 billion, about $3,500 per person. There is a lively discussion today whether a broader group of monetary assets discussed below, $M2$ or even $M3$, might better meet the definition of money in a modern payments system.

What is money? Discussions of the meaning of money are fluid for a simple reason: in the past, money was the means of payment generally accepted in exchange, but it also had the characteristic that it did not pay interest. Thus the sum of currency and demand deposits (which did not earn interest) was the accepted definition of money for a long time. This aggregate is now known as $M1$. In the course of the 1980s, however, a widening range of interest-bearing assets also became checkable. That has forced an ongoing review on where to draw the line between assets that form part of our definition of money and those that are just financial assets and not money proper. The issue is important not only conceptually but also for the evaluation of what aggregate the Fed should try to control.

The demand for money has been studied very intensively at both the theoretical and empirical levels. There is by now almost total agreement that the demand for real balances should, as a theoretical matter, increase as the level of real income rises and decrease as the nominal interest rate rises—as we assumed in Chapter 4. Much empirical work bears out these two properties of the demand-for-money function.

However, the money demand function has been a problem for almost two decades. Until 1973, empirical work showed a very *stable* simple demand-for-money function, with real balances demanded increasing with the level of income and decreasing with interest rates. But then, from about 1974 on, the demand-for-money function seemed to shift several times. Explaining these shifts in money demand, or money demand instability, has been a major, though so far not very successful, area for research. Many of the problems are undoubtedly due to a series of changes in the financial system that we discuss in this chapter.

13-1 COMPONENTS OF THE MONEY STOCK

There is a vast array of financial assets in any economy, from currency to complicated claims on other financial assets. Which part of these assets is called money? In the United States, there are four main monetary aggregates: currency, *M*1, *M*2, and *M*3. Box 13-1 describes the components of the different measures of money.

*M*1 comprises those claims that can be used *directly*, *instantly*, and *without restrictions* to make payments. These claims are *liquid*. An asset is liquid if it can immediately, conveniently, and cheaply be used for making payments. *M*1 corresponds most closely to the traditional definition of money as the means of payment. *M*2 includes, in addition, claims that are not instantly liquid—withdrawal of time deposits, for example, may require notice to the depository institution; money market mutual funds may set a minimum on the size of checks drawn on an account. But with these qualifications, the claims also fall into a broader category of money. Finally, in *M*3 we include items that most people never see, namely, large negotiable deposits and repurchase agreements. These are held primarily by corporations, but also by wealthy individuals.

As we move from the top to the bottom of the list in Box 13-1, the liquidity of the assets decreases, while their interest yield increases. Currency earns zero interest, NOW accounts[1] earn less than money market deposit accounts, and so on. This is a typical economic tradeoff—in order to get more liquidity, asset holders have to give up yield.

We now run briefly down the list of assets in Box 13-1. Currency consists of notes and coin in circulation, mainly notes. Checkable deposits (demand deposits and other checkable deposits) are, as the name suggests, deposits against which checks can be written. They are held in commercial banks and thrift institutions. The financial institutions referred to as thrifts are savings and loan associations, mutual savings banks, and credit unions. Information on the distribution of the ownership of demand deposits is available,[2] but there are no systematic records of the ownership of currency. About a third of demand deposits are held by consumers, with businesses holding most of the rest.

A 1984 survey of cash holdings of U.S. households, undertaken for the Federal Reserve System, showed that the average amount of currency held per person surveyed then was about $100.[3] At that time, total currency outstanding divided by population was $675. Thus the vast majority of the currency outstanding is not held by U.S.

---

[1] A NOW (negotiable order of withdrawal) account is an interest-bearing checking account.

[2] The data, available each quarter, are published in the *Federal Reserve Bulletin*.

[3] "The Use of Cash and Transaction Accounts by American Families," *Federal Reserve Bulletin*, February 1986, and "Changes in Family Finances from 1983 to 1989: Evidence from the Survey of Consumer Finances," *Federal Reserve Bulletin*, January 1992.

households—or at least they do not admit to holding it. Some currency is held by legitimate businesses, but large amounts must be held to finance illegal activities, particularly drug-related ones, or are held outside the United States. In many foreign countries $100 bills are regularly used to conduct large, and frequently illegal, transactions.

M2 and Other Monetary Aggregates

All the assets described in Box 13-1 are to some extent substitutes for one another, and there is therefore no clear point at which to draw the line in defining money. *M2* adds to *M*1 assets that are close to being usable as a medium of exchange. The largest part of *M2* consists of savings and small (less than $100,000) time deposits at banks and thrift institutions. These can be used almost without difficulty for making payments. In the case of a savings deposit, the bank has to be notified to transfer funds from the savings deposit to a checking account; for time deposits, it is in principle necessary to wait until the time deposit matures, or else to pay an interest penalty.

The second largest category of assets in *M2* consists of money market mutual funds and deposit accounts. A money market mutual fund (MMMF) is one that invests its assets in short-term interest-bearing securities, such as certificates of deposit (CDs)[4] and Treasury bills. MMMFs pay interest and permit the owner of the account to write checks (typically the checks have to be for more than $500) against the account. Money market deposit accounts (MMDAs) are MMMFs held in commercial banks. A limited number of checks can be written against MMDAs each month. Obviously MMDAs and MMMFs are close to being checkable deposits—only the limits on the size and number of checks that can be written against these accounts keep them out of *M*1.

Until 1987, *M*1 was the most closely watched money stock, both because it comes closest to the theoretical definition of money as a medium of exchange and because its demand function was reasonably stable. But after the demand for *M*1 became difficult to predict, many economists, including those at the Federal Reserve Board, began to pay more attention to the behavior of *M2* than that of *M*1. Until 1987 the Fed set target growth rates for *M*1, *M2*, and *M3*.[5] Then it stopped specifying an *M*1 target and emphasized *M2*. Since the early 1990s, the behavior of *M2* has also become unpredictable, but *M3* is not better.[6]

Unpredictability of the demand for the monetary aggregates complicates the task of monetary policy, as we shall see in Chapter 14.

---

[4]CDs are liabilities of the banks that can be bought and sold in the open market like other securities. Typically they come in large denominations ($100,000 or more).

[5]See Board of Governors of the Federal Reserve *Annual Report*, which reports each year on the behavior of various monetary aggregates, velocity, and the Fed's targeting.

[6]Two further aggregates are regularly reported by the Federal Reserve: liquid assets (*L* in Box 13-1) and debt. The former includes in addition to *M3* all short-term debt instruments of the government and the private sector. The aggregate "debt" is the most comprehensive measure, including the entire debt of the nonfinancial sector. Neither the liquid assets nor the debt aggregates are regarded as monetary aggregates.

box 13-1 **COMPONENTS OF THE MONETARY AGGREGATES**

We briefly describe here the components of the monetary aggregates.

1. *Currency*: Coins and notes in circulation.
2. *Demand deposits*: Non-interest-bearing checking accounts at commercial banks, excluding deposits of other banks, the government, and foreign governments.
3. *Traveler's checks*: Those checks issued by nonbanks (such as American Express). Traveler's checks issued by banks are included in demand deposits.
4. *Other checkable deposits*: Interest-earning checking accounts, including NOW and ATS (automatic transfers from savings) accounts. With ATSs a deposit holder keeps assets in a savings account and the bank transfers them automatically to the checking account when a payment has to be made.

$$M1 = (1) + (2) + (3) + (4)$$

5. *Overnight repurchase agreement* (RP or REPO): Transaction in which a bank borrows from a nonbank customer by selling a security (for example, a Treasury bill) to the customer today and promising to buy it back at a fixed price tomorrow. That way the bank gets to use the amount borrowed for a day.
6. *Overnight Eurodollars*: Deposits that pay interest and mature the next day, held in Caribbean branches of U.S. banks.
7. *Money market mutual fund (MMMF) shares*: Interest-earning checkable deposits in mutual funds that invest in short-term assets. Some MMMF shares are held by institutions; these are excluded from $M2$ but included in $M3$.
8. *Money market deposit accounts (MMDAs)*: MMMFs run by banks, with the advantage that they are insured up to $100,000. Introduced at the end of 1982 to allow the banks to compete with MMMFs.
9. *Savings deposits*: Deposits at banks and other thrift institutions that are

Financial Innovation

Changes in the definitions of the monetary aggregates followed financial innovations, frequently a result of attempts to get around government regulations. For instance, thrifts, which pay interest on deposits and had been forbidden to offer checkable accounts, invented NOW accounts as a way of getting around the prohibition. A NOW, a negotiable order of withdrawal, looks and smells like a check, but was not, legally speaking, a check. Banks were trying to compete by finding ways of paying interest on demand deposits, again something they were forbidden from doing. As ways were found around the prohibitions, deposits formerly called savings deposits in fact became demand deposits, and eventually the definitions changed. Similarly, money market mutual funds were invented only in 1973. Until 1982, banks were not allowed to issue money market deposit accounts, but as soon as they were permitted to do so, there was a rapid inflow of such deposits to banks: MMDA deposits rose from zero in November 1982 to $320 billion in March 1983.

not transferrable by check, often recorded in a separate passbook kept by the depositor.

10. *Small time deposits*: Interest-bearing deposits with a specific maturity date. Before that date they can be used only if a penalty is paid. "Small" means less than $100,000.

$$M2 = M1 + (5) + (6) + (7) + (8) + (9) + (10)$$

11. *Large-denomination time deposits*: Interest-earning deposits of more than $100,000 denomination. The total excludes amounts held by MMMFs or MMDAs (and some other institutions) to make sure the same asset is not counted twice in the monetary aggregates.
12. *Term repurchase agreements*: RPs sold by thrift institutions, typically for longer than overnight.

$$M3 = M2 + (11) + (12) + \text{MMMFs held by institutions}$$

13. *Other Eurodollar deposits*: Longer-term (than overnight) Eurodollars.
14. *Savings bonds*: U.S. government bonds, typically sold to the small saver.
15. *Banker's acceptances*: Obligations of banks to pay a specific amount at a specific time. These arise largely in international trade.
16. *Commercial paper*: Short-term liabilities of corporations.
17. *Short-term Treasury securities*: Securities issued by the U.S. Treasury that have less than 12 months to maturity.

$$L = M3 + (13) + (14) + (15) + (16) + (17) \qquad ∎$$

SOURCE: See *Federal Reserve Bulletin,* which reports the data and definition in each monthly issue. For further discussion see Daniel J. Larkins, "The Monetary Aggregates: An Introduction to Definitional Issues," *Survey of Current Business,* January 1983; *Handbook of Securities of the United States Government and Federal Agencies,* First Boston Corporation; Data Resources, Inc.

There is no unique set of assets that will always and everywhere constitute the money supply, nor are present definitions beyond question. For instance, should credit cards be regarded as a means of payment? If so—and the argument is certainly persuasive—we should probably count the amounts that people are allowed to charge by using their credit cards as part of the money stock. And there are even arguments for using a less broad definition than *M*1—for example, should $1,000 bills, which are not easily used to buy groceries, be included? What is certain is that over the course of time, the particular assets that serve as a medium of exchange, or means of payment, will change further, and so will the definitions of the monetary aggregates.

13-2 THE FUNCTIONS OF MONEY

Money is so widely used that we rarely recognize how remarkable a device it is. It is impossible to imagine a modern economy operating without the use of money or something very much like it. In a mythical barter economy in which there is no money, every transaction has to involve an exchange of goods (and/or services) on both sides of the transaction. The examples of the difficulties of barter are endless. The economist wanting a haircut would have to find a barber wanting to listen to a lecture on economics; the actor wanting a suit would have to find a tailor wanting to watch movies; and so on. Without a medium of exchange, modern economies could not operate.

Money, as a medium of exchange, makes it unnecessary for there to be a "double coincidence of wants" in exchanges. By the double coincidence, we have in mind the preceding examples. The wants of two individuals would have to be identically matched for the exchange to take place. For instance, the man selling movie tickets would have to find a buyer whose goods he wanted to buy (the suit), while, at the same time, the woman selling suits would have to find a buyer whose goods she wanted to buy (the movie tickets).

There are four traditional functions of money, of which the medium of exchange is the first.[7] The other three are store of value, unit of account, and standard of deferred payment. These stand on a different footing from the medium-of-exchange function. A *store of value* is an asset that maintains value over time. Thus, an individual holding a store of value can use that asset to make purchases at a future date. If an asset were not a store of value, then it would not be used as a medium of exchange. Imagine trying to use ice cream as money in the absence of refrigerators. There would hardly ever be a good reason for anyone to give up goods for money (ice cream) if the money were sure to melt within the next few minutes. And if the sellers were unwilling to accept the ice cream in exchange for their goods, then the ice cream would not be a medium of exchange. But there are many stores of value other than money—such as bonds, stocks, and houses.

The *unit of account* is the unit in which prices are quoted and books kept. Prices are quoted in dollars and cents, and dollars and cents are the units in which the money stock is measured. Usually, the money unit is also the unit of account, but that is not essential. In many high-inflation countries, dollars become the unit of account even though the local money continues to serve as the medium of exchange.

Finally, as a *standard of deferred payment*, money units are used in long-term transactions, such as loans. The amount that has to be paid back in 5 or 10 years is specified in dollars and cents. Dollars and cents are acting as the standard of deferred payment. Once again, though, it is not essential that the standard of deferred payment be the money unit. For example, the final payment of a loan may be related to the behavior of the price level, rather than being fixed in dollars and cents. This is known as an indexed loan. The last two of the four functions of money are, accordingly, functions that money *usually* performs, but not functions that it *necessarily* performs. And the store-of-value function is one that many assets perform.

There is one final point we want to emphasize once more. *Money is whatever is generally accepted in exchange.* In the past an astounding variety of monies have been used: simple commodities such as seashells, then metals, pieces of paper representing claims on gold or silver, pieces of paper that are claims only on other pieces of

---

[7]For the classic statement of the functions of money, see W. S. Jevons, *Money and the Mechanism of Exchange* (London: C. Kegan Paul & Co., 1875).

paper, and then paper and electronic entries in banks' accounts.[8] However magnificently engraved a piece of paper may be, it is not money if it is not accepted in payment. And however unusual the material of which it is made, anything that is generally accepted in payment is money. There is thus an inherent circularity in the acceptance of money. Money is accepted in payment only because it is believed that it will later also be accepted in payment by others.

13-3 THE DEMAND FOR MONEY: THEORY

In this section we review the three major motives underlying the demand for money and concentrate on the effects of changes in income and the interest rate on money demand. Before we take up the discussion we must make an essential point about money demand: *the demand for money is a demand for real balances.* In other words, people hold money for its purchasing power, for the amount of goods they can buy with it. They are not concerned with their *nominal* money holdings, that is, the number of dollar bills they hold. Two implications follow:

1. *Real* money demand is unchanged when the price level increases, and *all* real variables, such as the interest rate, real income, and real wealth, remain unchanged.
2. Equivalently, *nominal* money demand increases in proportion to the increase in the price level, given the real variables just specified.

There is a special name for the behavior described here. An individual is free from *money illusion* if a change in the level of prices, holding all real variables constant, leaves the person's real behavior, including real money demand, unchanged. By contrast, an individual whose real behavior is affected by a change in the price level, all real variables remaining unchanged, is said to suffer from money illusion.

The theories we are about to review correspond to Keynes's famous three motives for holding money:[9]

- The transactions motive, which is the demand for money arising from the use of money in making regular payments;

- The precautionary motive, which is the demand for money to meet unforeseen contingencies; and

- The speculative motive, which arises from uncertainties about the money value of other assets that an individual can hold.

In discussing the transactions and precautionary motives, we are mainly discussing $M1$, whereas the speculative motive refers more to $M2$ or $M3$, as we shall see.

---

[8] See Paul Einzig, *Primitive Money* (New York: Pergamon, 1966).

[9] J. M. Keynes, *The General Theory of Employment, Interest and Money* (New York: Macmillan, 1936), chap. 13.

Although we examine the demand for money by looking at the three motives for holding it, we cannot separate a particular person's money holdings, say, $500, into three neat piles of, say, $200, $200, and $100, each being held from a different motive. Money being held to satisfy one motive is always available for another use. The person holding unusually large balances for speculative reasons also has those balances available to meet an unexpected emergency, so that they serve, too, as precautionary balances. All three motives influence an individual's holdings of money.

These theories of money demand are built around a tradeoff between the benefits of holding more money versus the interest costs of doing so. Money (*M*1, currency and some checkable deposits) generally earns no interest or less interest than other assets. The higher the interest loss from holding a dollar of money, the less money we expect the individual to hold. In practice, we can measure the cost of holding money as the difference between the interest rate paid on money (perhaps zero) and the interest rate paid on the most nearly comparable other asset, such as a savings deposit or, for corporations, a certificate of deposit or commercial paper. The interest rate on money is referred to as the *own* rate of interest, and the *opportunity cost* of holding money is equal to the difference between the yield on other assets and the own rate.

Transactions Demand

The transactions demand for money arises from the use of money in making regular payments for goods and services. In the course of each month, an individual makes a variety of payments for rent or a mortgage, groceries, the newspaper, and other purchases. In this section we examine how much money an individual would hold to finance these purchases.

The tradeoff here is between the amount of interest an individual forgoes by holding money and the costs and inconveniences of holding a small amount of money. To make the problem concrete, consider someone who is paid, say, $1,800 (after taxes) each month. Assume the person spends the $1,800 evenly over the course of the month, at the rate of $60 per day. Now at one extreme, the individual could simply leave the $1,800 in cash (whether in currency or as demand deposits) and spend it at the rate of $60 per day. Alternatively, on the first day of the month the individual could take the $60 to spend that day and put the remaining $1,740 in a daily-interest savings account. Then every morning the person could go to the bank to withdraw that day's $60 from the savings account. By the end of the month the depositor would have earned interest on the money retained each day in the savings account. That would be the *benefit* of keeping the money holdings down as low as $60 at the beginning of each day. The *cost* of keeping money holdings down is simply the cost and inconvenience of the trips to the bank to withdraw the daily $60.

In more detail, we assume that the nominal monthly income of the individual is Y_N.[10] If held in a savings account, the deposit earns interest at a rate of i per month. It earns zero interest as cash.[11] The cost to the individual of making a transfer between

---

[10] As a reminder, nominal income, Y_N, is defined as real income, Y, times the price level, P: $Y_N = P \times Y$.

[11] In general, we should think of i as the opportunity cost of holding cash, which may be the difference between the interest rate on a savings account and the interest rate on a checking account.

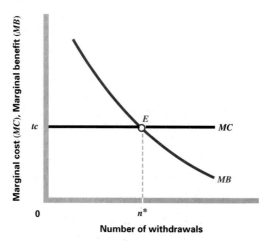

FIGURE 13-1

OPTIMAL CASH MANAGEMENT DETERMINING THE OPTIMAL NUMBER OF WITHDRAWALS. The marginal cost of making another transaction, *tc*, is constant, as shown by the *MC* curve. The marginal benefit (*MB*) of making another transaction is the amount of interest saved by holding smaller money balances. The marginal benefit decreases as the number of withdrawals from the savings account increases. Point *E* is the point at which the cost of managing money holdings is minimized. Corresponding to point *E* is *n**, the optimal number of withdrawals to make from the savings account into money.

cash and the savings account (which we henceforth call bonds for convenience) is $tc. That cost may be the individual's time, or it may be a cost explicitly paid to someone else to make the transfer. For convenience we refer to it as a broker's fee.

In the appendix, we derive in detail the implications of this *inventory-theoretic approach* to the demand for money, whose basic assumptions we have just set out.[12] The inventory-theoretic approach applies equally well, with small changes in terminology and assumptions, to firms and households. The derivation in the appendix involves a comparison of the marginal benefit of making one more trip to the bank (which enables the individual to hold a lower stock of money on average during the month), with the marginal cost of making one more trip (the transaction cost).

Figure 13-1 illustrates this. The cost of making another transaction is always

---

[12] The theory was originally developed to determine the inventories of goods a firm should have on hand. In that context, the amount Y_N would be the monthly sales of the good, *tc* the cost of ordering the good, and *i* the interest rate for carrying the inventory. The inventory-theoretic approach to the demand for money is associated with the names of William Baumol and James Tobin: William Baumol, "The Transactions Demand for Cash: An Inventory Theoretic Approach," *Quarterly Journal of Economics*, November 1952; and James Tobin, "The Interest Elasticity of Transactions Demand for Cash," *Review of Economics and Statistics*, August 1956.

equal to *tc*, as shown by the horizontal marginal cost curve, *MC*. The financial benefit from making another transaction is represented by the *MB* (marginal benefit) curve, which represents the interest *saved* by making another withdrawal and thus holding a smaller average cash balance. The reduction of the interest cost that is obtained by making more transactions falls off rapidly as the number of withdrawals increases. This means that the marginal benefit of making more withdrawals decreases as the number of withdrawals increases. The *MB* curve in Figure 13-1 is, accordingly, down-ward-sloping.[13] In Figure 13-1, the optimal number of transactions is given by *n**, the number at which the marginal benefit in terms of interest saved is equal to the marginal cost of making a transaction. Given the number of transactions and the individual's income, the appendix shows that the optimal holding of money is given by the famous *square-root formula* for money demand, developed by William Baumol and James Tobin:[14]

$$M^* = \sqrt{\frac{tc \times Y_N}{2i}} \qquad (1)$$

Equation (1) shows that the transactions demand for money increases with the brokerage fee, or the cost of transacting, and with the level of income. The demand for money decreases with the interest rate.

MONEY DEMAND ELASTICITIES

Equation (1) shows that the ratio of money to income, M/Y_N, declines with the level of income. A person with a higher level of income holds proportionately less money. This point is sometimes put in different words by saying that there are *economies of scale* in cash management. Another way of saying the same thing is that the income elasticity of the demand for money is less than 1 [it is equal to ½ in equation (1)]. The income elasticity measures the percentage change in the demand for money due to a 1 percent change in income.[15] Similarly, equation (1) implies that the elasticity of the demand for money with respect to the brokerage fee is ½, and the elasticity with respect to the interest rate is $-$½.

---

[13] We have, for convenience, drawn the curves as continuous, even though it is possible to make only an integral number of transactions, and not, for example, 1.6 or 7.24 transactions.

[14] See footnote 12.

[15] The income elasticity of demand is

$$\frac{\frac{\Delta(M/P)}{M/P}}{\frac{\Delta Y}{Y}}$$

Similarly, the interest elasticity is

$$\frac{\frac{\Delta(M/P)}{M/P}}{\frac{\Delta i}{i}}$$

What accounts for the fact that people can somehow manage with less cash per dollar of spending as income increases? The reason is that cash management is more effective at high levels of income because the average cost per dollar of transaction is lower with large-size transactions. It costs as much to transfer $10 as $10 million, so the average cost per dollar transferred is lower for large transfers. However, in the case of households, we should recognize that the "brokerage cost" (*tc*, the cost of making withdrawals from a savings account) is in part the cost of time and the nuisance of having to go to the bank. Since the cost of time to individuals is likely to be higher the higher their income, *tc* may rise with Y_N. In that case, an increase in income would result in an increase in the demand for money by more than the income elasticity of $\frac{1}{2}$ indicates, because *tc* goes up together with Y.[16]

THE DEMAND FOR REAL BALANCES

We noted earlier that the demand for money is a demand for real balances. The inventory-theoretic approach should, and does, imply that the demand for real balances does not change when all prices double (or increase in any other proportion). When all prices double, both Y_N and *tc* in equation (1) double; that is, both nominal income and the nominal brokerage fee double. Accordingly, the demand for nominal balances doubles, so that the demand for real balances is unchanged. The square-root formula does not imply any money illusion in the demand for money.

Thus we should be careful when saying that the income elasticity of demand for money implied by equation (1) is $\frac{1}{2}$. The elasticity of the demand for *real* balances with respect to *real* income is $\frac{1}{2}$. But if income rises only because all prices (including *tc*) rise, then the demand for *nominal* balances rises proportionately.

QUALIFICATIONS

The Baumol-Tobin formula (1) implies that the elasticities of money demand with respect to real income and the interest rate are exactly $\frac{1}{2}$ and $-\frac{1}{2}$, respectively. Once we take account of the fact that individuals can make only an integer number of transactions—1, 2, 3, and so on—and that it is not possible to make 1.25 or 3.57 transactions, we find that many individuals would make only one or two transactions per month between money and bonds. As a result, it can be shown, the income elasticity of money demand implied by the inventory-theoretic approach is *between* $\frac{1}{2}$ and 1, and the interest elasticity *between* $-\frac{1}{2}$ and 0.[17]

In addition, once the integer constraints are taken into account, it can be shown that the transactions demand for money depends on the frequency with which individuals are paid (the payment period). The reason is that in practice some people receive their monthly income in their checking account and do not make transactions between money

---

[16] See Kevin Dowd, "The Value of Time and the Transactions Demand for Money," *Journal of Money, Credit and Banking*, February 1990.

[17] See Robert J. Barro, "Integer Constraints and Aggregation in an Inventory Model of Money Demand," *Journal of Finance*, 1976.

and bonds in the way described by the Baumol-Tobin model. For such people, average money holdings are half of monthly income. If income were paid weekly, their average money holdings would be one-half of weekly income, or only one-quarter as much as when income is paid monthly. Accordingly, the longer the payments period, the larger are average money holdings.

SUMMARY

The inventory-theoretic approach to the demand for money gives a precise formula for the transactions demand for money: the income elasticity of the demand for money is ½, and the interest elasticity is − ½. When integer constraints are taken into account, the limits on the income elasticity of demand are between ½ and 1, and the limits on the interest elasticity are between − ½ and 0. We have outlined the approach in terms of an individual's demand for money, but a similar approach is relevant for firms.

Some of the assumptions made in deriving the square-root formula are very restrictive. People do not spend their money evenly over the course of the month, and they do not know exactly what their payments will be. Their checks are not paid into savings accounts, and so on. It turns out, though, that the major results we have derived are not greatly affected by the use of more realistic assumptions. There is thus good reason to expect the demand for money to increase with the level of income and to decrease as the interest rate on other assets (or, generally, the cost of holding money) increases.

The Precautionary Motive

In discussing the transactions demand for money, we focused on transactions costs and ignored uncertainty. In this section, we concentrate on the demand for money that arises because people are uncertain about the payments they might want, or have, to make.[18] Suppose, realistically, that an individual does not know precisely what payments he or she will be receiving in the next few weeks and what payments will have to be made. The person might decide to have a hot fudge sundae, or need to take a cab in the rain, or have to pay for a prescription. If he or she does not have money with which to pay, he or she will incur a loss. For concreteness, we shall denote the loss incurred as a result of being short of cash by q. The loss clearly varies from situation to situation, but as usual we simplify.

The more money an individual holds, the less likely he or she is to incur the costs of illiquidity (that is, not having money immediately available). But the more money the person holds, the more interest he or she is giving up. We are back to a tradeoff situation similar to that examined in relation to the transactions demand. Somewhere between holding so little money that it will almost certainly be necessary to forgo some purchase (or to borrow in a hurry) and holding so much money that there is little chance of not being able to make any payment that might be necessary, there must be an optimal amount of precautionary balances to hold.

---

[18] See Edward H. Whalen, "A Rationalization of the Precautionary Demand for Cash," *Quarterly Journal of Economics*, May 1966.

Once more, we write down the total costs of holding an amount of money, M.[19] This time we are dealing with expected costs, since it is not certain what the need for money will be. We denote the probability that the individual is illiquid during the month by $p(M, \sigma)$. The function $p(M, \sigma)$ indicates that the probability of the person's being illiquid at some time during the month depends on the level of money balances, M, being held and the degree of uncertainty, σ, about the net payments that will be made during the month. The probability of illiquidity is lower the higher is M, and higher the higher the degree of uncertainty, σ. The *expected cost* of illiquidity is $p(M, \sigma)q$—the probability of illiquidity times the cost of being illiquid. The interest cost associated with holding a cash balance of M is just iM. Thus, we have

$$\text{Expected costs} = iM + p(M, \sigma)q \tag{2}$$

To determine the optimal amount of money to hold, we compare the marginal cost of increasing money holding by \$1 with the expected marginal benefit of doing so. The marginal cost is again the interest forgone, or i. That is shown by the MC curve in Figure 13-2. The marginal benefit of increasing money holding arises from the lower expected costs of illiquidity. Increasing precautionary balances from zero has a large marginal benefit, since that takes care of small, unexpected disbursements that are quite likely to occur. As we increase cash balances further, we continue to reduce the probability of illiquidity, but at a decreasing rate. We start to hold cash to insure against quite unlikely events. Thus, the marginal benefit of additional cash is a decreasing function of the level of cash holdings, as shown by the MB curve in Figure 13-2.

The optimal level of precautionary demand is reached where the two curves intersect. That level of money is shown as M^* in Figure 13-2. It is apparent from Figure 13-2 that precautionary balances will be larger when the interest rate is lower. A reduction in the interest rate shifts the MC curve down and increases M^*. The lower cost of holding money makes it profitable to insure more heavily against the costs of illiquidity. An increase in uncertainty leads to increased money holdings because it shifts up the MB curve. With more uncertainty about the flow of spending, there is more scope for unforeseen payments and thus a greater danger of illiquidity. It therefore pays to insure more heavily by holding larger cash balances. Finally, the lower the costs of illiquidity, q, the lower the money demand. A reduction in q moves the MB curve down.

The model of precautionary demand is a broad theory that applies to any commodity inventory that is held as insurance against contingencies. For instance, cars carry spare tires. You can work out circumstances under which you would want to have more than one spare tire in a car, and even circumstances in which zero would be the optimal number. The idea of the precautionary demand for money or for goods is quite general. So, too, are the determinants of the precautionary demand: the alternative cost in terms of interest forgone, the cost of illiquidity, and the degree of uncertainty that determines the probability of illiquidity.

---

[19]This paragraph contains technical material that is optional and can easily be skipped.

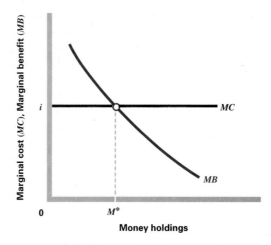

FIGURE 13-2

THE PRECAUTIONARY DEMAND FOR MONEY. The *MC* schedule shows the marginal cost of holding an extra dollar of money; holding an extra dollar means losing interest, and so the *MC* curve is horizontal at a level equal to the interest rate (or, more generally, the opportunity cost of holding money). The marginal benefit (*MB*) of holding an extra dollar is that the consumer is less likely to be short of money when it is needed. The marginal benefit declines with the amount of money held. The optimal amount of money to hold is shown by *M**, at which marginal cost is equal to marginal benefit.

The Speculative Demand for Money

The transactions demand and the precautionary demand for money emphasize the medium-of-exchange function of money, for each refers to the need to have money on hand to make payments. Each theory is most relevant to the *M*1 definition of money, though the precautionary demand could certainly explain part of the holding of savings accounts and other relatively liquid assets that are part of *M*2. Now we move over to the store-of-value function of money and concentrate on the role of money in the investment portfolio of an individual.

An individual who has wealth has to hold that wealth in specific assets. Those assets make up a *portfolio*. One would think an investor would want to hold the asset that provides the highest returns. However, given that the return on most assets is uncertain, it is unwise to hold the entire portfolio in a single *risky asset*. You may have the hottest tip that a certain stock will surely double within the next 2 years, but you would be wise to recognize that hot tips are far from infallible and that you could lose a lot of money in that stock as well as make money. A prudent, risk-averse investor does not put all his or her eggs in one basket. *Uncertainty about the returns on risky assets leads to a diversified portfolio strategy.*

As part of that diversified portfolio, the typical investor will want to hold some amount of a safe asset as insurance against capital losses on assets whose prices change in an uncertain manner. Money is a safe asset in that its nominal value is known with certainty.[20] In a famous article, James Tobin argued that money would be held as the safe asset in the portfolios of investors.[21] The title of the article, "Liquidity Preference as Behavior toward Risk," explains the essential notion. In this framework, the demand for money—the safest asset—depends on the expected yields as well as on the riskiness of the yields on other assets. The riskiness of the returns on other assets is measured by the variability of the returns. Using reasonable assumptions, Tobin shows that an increase in the expected return on other assets—an increase in the opportunity cost of holding money (that is, the return forgone by holding money)—lowers money demand. By contrast, an increase in the riskiness of the returns on other assets increases money demand.

An investor's aversion to risk certainly generates a demand for a safe asset. However, that asset is not likely to be $M1$. From the viewpoint of the yield and risks of holding money, it is clear that time or savings deposits or MMDAs have the same risks as currency or checkable deposits, while paying a higher yield. The risks in both cases are the risks arising from uncertainty about inflation. Given that the risks are the same, and with the yields on time and savings deposits higher than on currency and demand deposits, portfolio diversification explains the demand for assets such as time and savings deposits, which are part of $M2$, better than the demand for $M1$.

The implications of the speculative demand for money are similar to those of the transactions and precautionary demands. An increase in the interest rate on non-money assets, such as long-term bond yields or equity yields, will reduce the demand for $M2$. An increase in the rate paid on time deposits will increase the demand for time deposits, perhaps even at the cost of the demand for $M1$, as people take advantage of the higher yields they can earn on their investment portfolios to increase the size of those portfolios.

One final point on speculative demand. Many individuals will indeed hold part of that wealth in savings accounts in order to diversify their portfolios. But bigger investors are sometimes able to purchase other securities which pay higher interest and also have fixed (that is, risk-free) nominal values. Large CDs (in excess of $100,000) are an example of such assets, as are Treasury bills. For such individuals or groups, the demand for a safe asset is not a demand for money.

13-4   EMPIRICAL EVIDENCE

This section examines the empirical evidence—the studies made using actual data—on the demand for money. We know from Chapter 5 that the *interest elasticity* of the demand for money plays an important role in determining the effectiveness of monetary and fiscal policies. We showed in Section 13-3 that there are good theoretical reasons for believing the demand for real balances should depend on the interest rate. Empirical

---

[20] Of course, when the rate of inflation is uncertain, the real value of money is also uncertain, and money is no longer a safe asset. Even so, the uncertainties about the values of equity are so much larger than the uncertainties about the rate of inflation in the United States that money can be treated as a relatively safe asset.

[21] James Tobin, "Liquidity Preference as Behavior toward Risk," *Review of Economic Studies*, February 1958.

studies have indeed established that the demand for money is negatively related to the interest rate.

The theory of money demand also predicts that the demand for money should depend on the level of income. The response of the demand for money to the level of income, as measured by the *income elasticity* of money demand, is also important from a policy viewpoint. As we shall see, the income elasticity of money demand provides a guide to the Fed as to how fast to increase the money supply in order to support a given rate of growth of GNP without changing the interest rate.

Lagged Adjustment

The empirical work on the demand for money has introduced one complication that we did not study in the theoretical section—that the demand for money adjusts to changes in income and interest rates *with a lag*. When the level of income or the interest rate changes, there is first only a small change in the demand for money. Then, over the course of time, the change in the demand for money increases, slowly building up to its full long-run change.

There are two basic reasons for these lags. First, there are costs of adjusting money holdings; second, money holders' expectations are slow to adjust. The costs of adjustment include the costs of figuring out the new best way to manage money and the cost of opening a new type of account if that is needed. On the expectations side, if people believe that a given change in the interest rate is temporary, they may be unwilling to make a major change in their money holdings. As time passes and it becomes clearer that the change is not transitory, they are willing to make a larger adjustment.

Empirical Results for *M*1 Demand

Until the mid-1970s the standard *M*1 demand-for-money function was the one estimated by Stephen Goldfeld of Princeton University in a comprehensive 1973 study.[22] Goldfeld studied the demand for *M*1 using quarterly postwar data and, of course, the 1973 definition of *M*1.

Table 13-1 summarizes Goldfeld's results. In the short run (one quarter), the elasticity of demand with respect to real income is 0.19. This means that a 1 percent increase in real income raises money demand by 0.19 percent, which is considerably less than proportionately. The table shows that an increase in interest rates reduces money demand. The short-run interest elasticities are quite small. An increase in the rate on time deposits from 4 percent to 5 percent, that is, a 25 percent increase ($\frac{5}{4} = 1.25$), reduces the demand for money by only 1.12 percent ($= 0.045 \times 25$ percent).

[22]This work, along with a vast amount of more recent material, is summarized in Stephen Goldfeld and Daniel Sichel, "The Demand for Money," in B. M. Friedman and F. H. Hahn (eds.), *Handbook of Monetary Economics*, vol. 1 (Amsterdam: North-Holland, 1990), chap. 8. See also the comprehensive review of theory and empirical work in David Laidler, *The Demand for Money*, 3rd ed. (New York: Harper and Row, 1985).

TABLE 13-1

ELASTICITIES OF REAL *M*1 MONEY

	Y	i_{TD}	i_{CP}
Short run	0.19	−0.045	−0.019
Long run	0.68	−0.160	−0.067

SOURCE: Stephen M. Goldfeld, "The Demand for Money Revisited," *Brookings Papers on Economic Activity,* Vol. 3, 1973.

An increase in the rate on commercial paper (an alternative asset for firms to hold) from 4 to 5 percent would reduce money demand by only 0.47 percent.

The long-run elasticities exceed the short-run elasticities by a factor of more than 3, as Table 13-1 shows. The long-run real income elasticity is 0.68, meaning that in the long run the increase in real money demand occurring as a result of a given increase in real income is only 68 percent as large as the proportional increase in income. Real money demand thus rises less than proportionately to the rise in real income. The long-run interest elasticities sum to a little over 0.2, meaning that an increase in *both* i_{TD} and i_{CP} from 4 percent to 5 percent would reduce the demand for money by less than 6 percent.

This early work by Goldfeld established four essential properties of money demand that continue to hold:

■ The demand for real money balances responds negatively to the rate of interest. An increase in interest rates reduces the demand for money.

■ The demand for money increases with the level of real income.

■ The short-run responsiveness of money demand to changes in interest rates and income is considerably less than the long-run response. The long-run elasticities are estimated to be over 3 times the size of the short-run elasticities.

■ The demand for nominal money balances is proportional to the price level. There is no money illusion; in other words, the demand for money is a demand for *real* balances.

Rethinking the Money Demand Function

Until 1973, the demand for real money balances was considered one of the best understood and most highly stable equations in the U.S. macroeconomy—and in those of other countries too. Since then, *M*1 demand has been shifting, and it has not yet settled down to the extent that there is agreement on the empirically correct form of the money demand function.[23] However, there is general agreement on the fact that money demand is affected primarily by income and interest rates.

The continuing difficulty of accounting for shifts in money demand has prompted a widening search for an explanation.[24] Although none of these suggestions has produced a stable money demand function, most contribute to better understanding of money demand. We briefly describe the leading candidates, many of which are designed to deal with the effect that financial innovations have had on the demand for money.

DEFINITIONS OF THE MONEY SUPPLY

As is clear from Box 13-1, current money stock definitions, even for $M1$, include several different types of assets. $M1$, for instance, includes both noninterest- and interest-bearing assets. For a time it seemed that the demand function for $M1A$, the current $M1$ minus interest-bearing deposits, was quite stable, and therefore that the real problem with $M1$ demand was the inclusion of interest-bearing deposits. However, the $M1A$ demand function has not been stable recently.

An alternative approach is to seek a wider money demand concept for which the demand is stable. $M2$, the obvious candidate here, includes several types of assets on which checks can be written. We review the most promising demand function for $M2$ shortly.

The most ambitious attempts to redefine the money stock have been undertaken by William Barnett and Paul Spindt.[25] Their approach recognizes that assets have differing degrees of "moneyness." Currency and demand deposits are all money, whereas MMDA accounts are part money and part store of value. They therefore form monetary aggregates that weight the different components of money according to their degree of moneyness.

The procedures used by Barnett and Spindt differ somewhat, and we briefly outline the Barnett approach. It is to assume that non-interest-bearing assets are all money, and that some very illiquid asset, generally corporate bonds, is not at all money. Suppose the interest rate on corporate bonds is 8 percent. Then an asset that earns 5 percent will be regarded as $\frac{3}{8}$ money and $\frac{5}{8}$ nonmoney and will receive a weight of $\frac{3}{8}$ in being added to the monetary aggregate. Equivalently, assets are weighted by the *opportunity cost* of holding them.

This approach is appealing because it deals directly with the differing degrees of liquidity of different assets that are partly used as medium of exchange. While there

---

[23] However, Robert Rasche, "M1-Velocity and Money-Demand Functions: Do Stable Relationships Exist?" in Karl Brunner and Allan H. Meltzer (eds.), *Carnegie-Rochester Conference Series on Public Policy*, vol. 27, Autumn 1987, suggests that it is possible to find money demand functions that fit the data quite well, provided that shifts in 1975 and 1982 are taken into account.

[24] The paper by Goldfeld and Sichel referred to in footnote 22 provides an excellent guide to the literature.

[25] See, for instance, William Barnett, Edward Offenbacher, and Paul Spindt, "The New Divisia Monetary Aggregates," *Journal of Political Economy*, December 1984; in "Are Weighted Monetary Aggregates Better than Simple-Sum M1?" Federal Reserve Bank of St. Louis *Review*, June/July 1985, Dallas Batten and Daniel Thornton provide a very clear summary of the issues. See, too, W. Barnett, "The Divisia Monetary Aggregates" Working Paper No. 161, Department of Economics, Washington University, St. Louis, 1991.

have been shifts in the demand for these aggregates too, empirical work is proceeding along these lines.

Another way of proceeding is to move in the opposite direction and try to estimate separate demand functions for each of the different assets listed in Box 13-1. The demand function for any particular monetary aggregate, then—econometric complications aside—is the sum of the demand functions for its components.

SCALE VARIABLE, OPPORTUNITY COSTS, AND THE PAYMENTS TECHNOLOGY

Several other aspects of the Goldfeld specification have been reexamined. One questions the role of GNP or GDP as the basic measure of the transactions that have to be undertaken with money. In particular, since GNP does not include exchanges of current assets, it is possible that the volume of financial transactions, for instance, in the stock market, should also affect money demand. It has also been argued that since money is part of wealth, the demand for money should be influenced by consumers' wealth.

Second, there have been attempts to specify the opportunity cost of holding money more precisely. For instance, several researchers have argued that the expected inflation rate should affect money demand (see Box 13-2). Others have attempted to include the rate of return on equity as one of the opportunity costs of holding money.

Finally, the transactions demand model points to tc, the cost of making transactions, as an important determinant of money demand. In the period since 1973, the entire technology of portfolio management has changed. Not only have new assets been invented; the speed with which checks are cleared has been increased, and computer technology has developed at a fantastic pace. It has been difficult to measure the implied changes in tc, but there is little doubt these changes must have affected the demand for money.

M2 Money Demand

The demand for $M2$ has shown more stability than the demand for $M1$.[26] We would expect real money demand to depend positively on the own rate of interest on $M2$ (a weighted average of the interest rates paid on various kinds of deposits) and negatively on the alternative cost of holding $M2$. The alternative cost can be measured by the rate on money market instruments such as Treasury bills. We also expect real $M2$ money demand to depend positively on the level of income.

These hypotheses are, indeed, confirmed by the empirical evidence. An estimate with quarterly data for the period 1961–1988 yields the elasticities shown in Table 13-2. The table confirms that the elasticity with respect to the own rate is positive and the elasticity with respect to the commercial paper rate is negative. The short-run

---

[26]See the discussion in David Small and Richard Porter, "Understanding the Behavior of M2 and V2," *Federal Reserve Bulletin*, April 1989; see also Robert Hetzel and Yash Mehra, "The Behavior of Money Demand in the 1980s," *Journal of Money, Credit and Banking*, November 1989; see also Peter Ireland, "Financial Evolution and the Long-Run Behavior of Velocity: New Evidence from U.S. Regional Data," Federal Reserve Bank of Richmond *Economic Review*, December 1991; and Seungmook Choi and Kim Sosin, "Structural Change in the Demand for Money," *Journal of Money, Credit and Banking*, May 1992.

box 13-2 ⁻ **MONEY DEMAND AND HIGH INFLATION**

The demand for real balances depends on the alternative cost of holding money. That cost is normally measured by the yield on alternative assets, say Treasury bills, commercial paper, or money market funds. But there is another margin of substitution. Rather than holding their wealth in financial assets, households or firms can also hold real assets: stocks of food or houses or machinery. This margin of substitution is particularly important in countries in which inflation is very high and capital markets do not function well. In that case it is quite possible that the return on holding goods can even be higher than that on financial assets.

Consider a household deciding whether to hold $100 in currency or a demand deposit or to hold its wealth in the form of groceries on the shelf. The advantage of holding groceries is that, unlike money, they maintain their real value. Rather than having the purchasing power of money balances eroded by inflation, the household gets rid of money, buying goods and thus avoiding a loss.

This "flight out of money" occurs systematically when inflation rates become high. In a famous study of hyperinflations (defined in the study as inflation rates of more than 50 percent *per month*), Phillip Cagan of Columbia University found large changes in real balances taking place as inflation increased.* In the most famous hyperinflation, that in Germany in 1922–1923, the quantity of real balances at the height of the hyperinflation had fallen to one-twentieth of its preinflation level. The increased cost of holding money leads to a reduction in real money demand and with it to changes in the public's payments habits as everybody tries to pass on money like a hot potato. We shall see more on this in Chapter 18, in which we study money and inflation.

In well-developed capital markets, interest rates will reflect expectations of inflation, and hence it will not make much difference whether we measure the alternative cost of holding money by interest rates or inflation rates. But when capital markets are not free because interest rates are regulated or have ceilings, it is often appropriate to use inflation, not interest, rates as the measure of the alternative cost. Franco Modigliani has offered the following rule of thumb: the right measure of the opportunity cost of holding money is the higher of the two, interest rates or inflation. ∎

---

*Phillip Cagan, "The Monetary Dynamics of Hyperinflation," in Milton Friedman (ed.), *Studies in the Quantity Theory of Money* (Chicago: University of Chicago Press, 1956).

---

elasticities are smaller than the long-run elasticities, and the own-rate elasticity is less than the elasticity with respect to the commercial paper rate. The latter property implies that an equiproportionate increase in the own rate and the commercial paper rate will reduce the demand for $M2$. Thus even though a large share of $M2$ is interest-bearing, an (equiproportionate) increase in the level of all interest rates reduces $M2$.

The long-run income elasticity of $M2$ is clearly positive and is approximately equal to unity. This implies that, other things equal, the ratio of real balances to real GNP will remain constant over time. We return to this property later—and also to the question of the stability of the demand function for $M2$ shown in Table 13-2.

TABLE 13-2

ELASTICITIES OF *M*2 MONEY DEMAND, 1961–1988

	own rate	commercial paper rate	income
Short run	0.023	−0.039	0.136
Long run	0.176	−0.293	1.030

SOURCE: From equations estimated by the authors and based on results in D. Small and R. Porter, "Understanding the Behavior of *M*2 and *V*2," *Federal Reserve Bulletin,* April 1989.

13-5 THE INCOME VELOCITY OF MONEY AND THE QUANTITY THEORY

The *income velocity of money* is the number of times the stock of money is turned over per year in financing the annual flow of income. It is equal to the ratio of GDP to the money stock. Thus in 1991 GDP was about $5,677 billion, the money stock (*M*1) averaged $862 billion, and velocity was therefore 6.59. The average dollar of (*M*1) money balances financed $6.59 of spending on final goods and services, or the public held an average of just over 15 cents of *M*1 per dollar of income.[27]

Income velocity (from now on we shall refer to velocity rather than income velocity) is defined as

$$V \equiv \frac{Y_N}{M} \tag{3}$$

that is, the ratio of nominal income to the nominal money stock. An alternative way of writing equation (3) recognizes that Y_N (nominal GDP) is equal to the price level, P, times real income, Y. Thus

$$M \times V = P \times Y \tag{4}$$

The Quantity Theory

Equation (4) is the famous *quantity equation*, linking the price level and the level of output to the money stock. The quantity equation became the (classical) *quantity theory of money* when it was argued that both *V*, the income velocity of money, and *Y*, the

---

[27] Why do we say income velocity and not plain velocity? There is another concept, transactions velocity, which is the ratio of *total transactions* to money balances. Total transactions far exceed GDP for two reasons. First, many transactions involving the sale and purchase of assets do not contribute to GDP. Second, a particular item in final output typically generates total spending on it that exceeds the contribution of that item to GDP. For instance, $1 worth of wheat generates transactions as it leaves the farm, as it is sold by the miller, and so forth. Transactions velocity is thus higher than income velocity.

level of output, were fixed. Real output was taken to be fixed because the economy was at full employment, and velocity was assumed not to change much. Neither of these assumptions holds in fact, but it is, nonetheless, interesting to see where they lead. *If both V and Y are fixed, then it follows that the price level is proportional to the money stock.* Thus the classical quantity theory was a theory of the price level and of inflation.

The classical quantity theory is the proposition that the price level is proportional to the money stock:

$$P = \frac{V \times M}{Y} \tag{4a}$$

The classical quantity theory applies in the *classical case* supply function examined in Chapter 7. Recall that in that case, with a vertical aggregate supply function, changes in the quantity of money result in changes in the price level, with the level of output remaining at its full-employment level. When the aggregate supply function is not vertical, increases in the quantity of money increase both the price level and output, and the price level is therefore not proportional to the quantity of money. Of course, if velocity is constant, *nominal GDP* (the price level times output) is proportional to the money stock.

Velocity and Policy

Velocity is a useful concept in economic policy making. We see how to use it by rewriting (3) as

$$Y_N \equiv V \times M \tag{3a}$$

Given the nominal money stock and velocity, we know the level of nominal GDP. Thus if we can predict the level of velocity, we can predict the level of nominal income, given the money stock.

Further, *if* velocity were constant, changing the money supply would result in proportionate changes in nominal income. Any policies, including fiscal policies, that did not affect the money stock would not affect the level of income. You will probably now recognize that we previously discussed a case of constant velocity. In Chapter 5, we discussed the effectiveness of fiscal policy when the demand for money is not a function of the interest rate and the *LM* curve is therefore vertical. That vertical *LM* curve is the same as the assumption of constant velocity.

Velocity and the Demand for Money

The concept of velocity is important largely because it is a convenient way of talking about money demand. Let the demand for real balances be written $L(i, Y)$, consistent with Chapter 4. Recall that Y is real income. When the supply of money is equal to the demand for money, we have

$$\frac{M}{P} = L(i, Y) \tag{5}$$

or $M = P \times L(i, Y)$. Now we can substitute for M, the nominal money supply, in equation (3) to obtain

$$V = \frac{Y_N}{P \times L(i, Y)} = \frac{Y}{L(i, Y)} \tag{3b}$$

where we have recognized that $Y_N/P = Y$ is the level of real income. Income velocity is the ratio of the level of real income to the demand for real balances.

From equation (3b) we note that velocity is a function of real income and the interest rate. An increase in the interest rate reduces the demand for real balances and therefore increases velocity: when the cost of holding money increases, money holders make their money do more work and thus turn it over more often. The way in which changes in real income affect velocity depends on the income elasticity of the demand for money. If the income elasticity of the demand for real balances were 1, then the demand for real balances would change in the same proportion as income. In that case, changes in real income would not affect velocity. In Table 13-2, we saw that the long-run income elasticity of $M2$ demand is approximately 1. That means that changes in income do not cause changes in $M2$ velocity over the long run. In Table 13-1, we saw that the long-run income elasticity of $M1$ demand is less than 1. That means that $M1$ velocity *increases* with increases in real income. For example, suppose that real income rose by 10 percent and the demand for real balances increased only by 6.8 percent ($= 0.68 \times 10$ percent), as Goldfeld's results suggest. Then the numerator of equation (3b) would increase by more than the denominator, and velocity would rise.

The empirical work reviewed in Section 13-4 makes it clear that the demand for money, and thus also velocity, does react systematically to changes in interest rates. The empirical evidence therefore decisively refutes the view that velocity is unaffected by changes in interest rates and that fiscal policy is, accordingly, incapable of affecting the level of nominal income. In terms of equation (3b), and using the analysis of Chapter 4, expansionary fiscal policy can be thought of as working by increasing interest rates, thereby increasing velocity, and thus making it possible for a given stock of money to support a higher level of nominal GDP.

Velocity in Practice

The empirical evidence we reviewed in Section 13-4 is useful in interpreting the behavior of velocity. Figure 13-3 shows a very striking change in the behavior of $M1$ velocity. From 1960 to approximately 1980, velocity steadily increased at an average rate of roughly 3 percent per year: in the mid-1950s velocity was about 3, whereas by 1981 it was above 7. Then the velocity of $M1$ stopped rising, and velocity has fluctuated between 6 and 7 since the early 1980s.

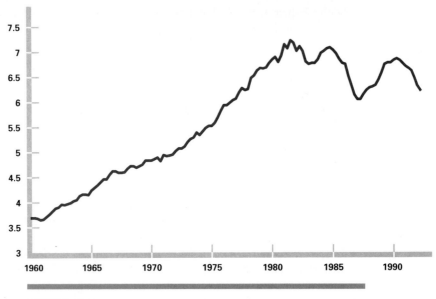

FIGURE 13-3
THE INCOME VELOCITY OF *M*1, 1960–1992. (SOURCE: DRI/McGraw-Hill.)

*M*2 VELOCITY (*V*2)

At the end of the previous section, we showed that it is possible to find a stable demand function for *M*2, for the years 1961–1988. Correspondingly, the velocity of *M*2 has also been reasonably stable, as Figure 13-4 shows. Over the period since 1960, *V*2 has fluctuated only between 1.54 and 1.8. Further, as the figure shows, for most of that period, variations in the opportunity cost of holding money explain a good part of these fluctuations.

As Table 13-3 confirms, there has been no trend in *M*2 velocity over a period of more than 30 years. The interesting fact that the *V*2 averages for the periods up to 1988 are essentially the same can be explained by the combination of three factors. First, as we already saw in Table 13-2, the income elasticity of demand for *M*2 is about unity, which implies that income growth does not affect velocity. Second, interest rates on money market instruments have risen from the 1960s to the 1980s, but so has the own rate of interest on *M*2. As a result the opportunity cost of holding *M*2 changed very little. Third, even though the opportunity cost has risen from 2 to 3 percent, the elasticity of demand with respect to the opportunity cost is exceedingly small. As a result there is an increase in velocity, but it is almost negligible.

If *M*2 velocity were constant or highly predictable, then the Federal Reserve could use equation (3*a*) to set monetary policy: by choosing the path of *M*2, it could produce its desired path of nominal GDP. We return to this point in Chapter 14 when we discuss monetary policy.

We conclude with a word of caution. Often (some say always) when a stable relationship is discovered and starts to be used, it breaks down. This pattern is referred

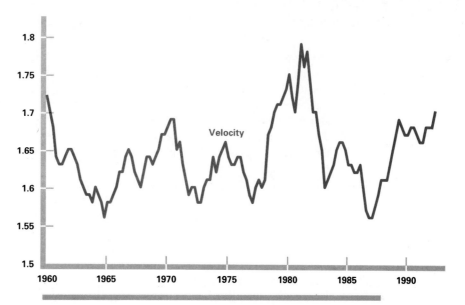

FIGURE 13-4

THE INCOME VELOCITY OF *M*2 AND THE OPPORTUNITY COST, 1960–1992.
(SOURCE: DRI/McGraw-Hill and Federal Reserve System.)

TABLE 13-3

THE VELOCITY OF *M*2 (period averages)

	1960–1969	1970–1979	1980–1988	1989–1991
Velocity	1.63	1.65	1.65	1.65
Own rate	2.32	4.06	6.61	5.53
Commercial paper rate	4.54	7.16	9.75	7.53
Opportunity cost	2.22	3.10	3.14	2.00

SOURCE: DRI/McGraw-Hill, Federal Reserve Board.

to as *Goodhart's law*, after Charles Goodhart of the London School of Economics. Certainly the disappearance of a stable *M*1 money demand equation was an instance of Goodhart's law.

Interestingly, the behavior of *M*2 velocity since 1988 is beginning to provide another example of Goodhart's law. Since 1988, *V*2 has stayed constant even though the opportunity cost of holding *M*2 has fallen. The money demand function has not performed well, just at the time the Fed began to place more weight on the *M*2 money supply.

13-6 SUMMARY

1. The demand for money is a demand for real balances. It is the purchasing power, not the number, of their dollar bills that matters to holders of money.
2. The money supply, $M1$, is made up of currency and checkable deposits. A broader measure, $M2$, includes as well savings and time deposits at depository institutions along with some other interest-bearing assets.
3. The chief characteristic of money is that it serves as a means of payment. The three classic reasons to hold money are for transactions purposes ($M1$) and for precautionary ($M1$ and $M2$) and speculative reasons ($M2$ and $M3$).
4. Decisions to hold money are based on a tradeoff between the liquidity of money and the opportunity cost of holding it when other assets have a higher yield.
5. The inventory-theoretic approach shows that an individual will hold a stock of real balances that varies inversely with the interest rate but increases with the level of real income and the cost of transactions. According to the inventory approach, the income elasticity of money demand is less than unity, implying that there are economies of scale.
6. Uncertainty about payments and receipts in combination with transactions costs give rise to a precautionary demand for money. Precautionary money holdings are higher the greater the variability of net disbursements, the higher the cost of illiquidity, and the lower the interest rate.
7. Portfolio diversification involves the tradeoff between risk and return. Some assets that are in $M2$ form part of an optimal portfolio because they are less risky than other assets—their nominal value is constant. Because they earn interest, assets such as saving or time deposits, or MMMF shares, dominate currency and demand deposits for portfolio diversification purposes. Thus the speculative demand is a demand for $M2$ or even $M3$ and not $M1$.
8. The empirical evidence provides support for a negative interest elasticity of money demand and a positive income elasticity. Because of lags, short-run elasticities are much smaller than long-run elasticities.
9. The demand function for $M1$ started showing instability in the mid-1970s, leading to many attempts to improve the specification. These have contributed to greater understanding of $M1$ demand but have not yet led to a stable demand function. The demand function for $M2$ appears to be more stable, showing a unit income elasticity, a positive elasticity with respect to the own rate, and a negative elasticity with respect to the commercial paper rate. Even this demand function has not been very successful since 1989.
10. The income velocity of money is defined as the ratio of income to money or the rate of turnover of money. Since the 1950s, $M1$ velocity has doubled to a level in excess of 6. The behavior of velocity is closely tied to the demand for money, so that an increase in the opportunity cost of holding money leads to an increase in velocity.
11. The velocity of $M2$ has been roughly constant over long periods of time. The constancy is a reflection of small changes in the opportunity cost of holding money and of a unit income elasticity of demand for $M2$.
12. Inflation implies that money loses purchasing power, and inflation thus creates a cost of holding money. The higher the rate of inflation, the lower the amount

of real balances that will be held. Hyperinflations provide striking support for this prediction. Under conditions of very high expected inflation, money demand falls dramatically relative to income. Velocity rises as people use less money in relation to income.

KEY TERMS

Real balances

Money illusion

*M*1

*M*2

Liquidity

Medium of exchange

Store of value

Unit of account

Standard of deferred payments

Transactions demand

Inventory-theoretic approach

Square-root formula

Precautionary demand

Speculative demand

Income velocity of money

Quantity equation

Quantity theory of money

Goodhart's law

Hyperinflation

PROBLEMS

1. To what extent would it be possible to design a society in which there was no money? What would the problems be? Could currency at least be eliminated? How? (Lest all this seems too otherworldly, you should know that some people are beginning to talk of a "cashless society" in the next century.)

2. Evaluate the effects of the following changes on the demand for *M*1 and *M*2. Which of the functions of money do they relate to?
   (a) "Instant cash" machines that allow 24-hour withdrawals from savings accounts at banks
   (b) The employment of more tellers at your bank
   (c) An increase in inflationary expectations
   (d) Widespread acceptance of credit cards
   (e) Fear of an imminent collapse of the government
   (f) A rise in the interest rate on time deposits

3. (a) Do you think credit card credit limits should be counted in the money stock?
   (b) Should MMDAs be part of *M*1?

4. Discuss the various factors that go into an individual's decision regarding how many traveler's checks to take on a vacation.

5. In the text, we said that the transactions demand-for-money model can also be applied to firms. Suppose a firm sells steadily during the month and has to pay its workers at the end of the month. Explain then how it would determine its money holdings.

6. In the 1970s, corporations received permission to hold savings accounts. It has been argued that this caused a decline in the demand for money.
   (a) For which demand-for-money concept is this true? For which is it false?
   (b) Explain why this change would have been more important for small firms than for large ones.

7. Explain why the $M1$ demand function shifted during the seventies and eighties.

8. (a) Is V high or low relative to trend during recessions? Why?
   (b) How can the Fed influence velocity?

9. (a) Explain the concept of the opportunity cost of holding money.
   (b) At the end of the chapter, we include data that allow you to calculate the opportunity cost of holding $M2$. Calculate this opportunity cost for the years 1988–1991, and explain what impact those changes should have had on the demand for $M2$.
   (c) What impact should they have had on velocity? How does this compare with what actually happened to velocity?

10. This chapter emphasizes that the demand for money is a demand for real balances. Thus the demand for nominal balances rises with the price level. At the same time, inflation causes the real demand to fall. Explain how these two assertions can both be correct.

11. "Muggers favor deflation." Comment.

The next two questions are related to the material in the appendix.

*12. (a) Determine the optimal strategy for cash management for a person who earns $1,600 per month, can earn 0.5 percent interest per month in a savings account, and has a transaction cost of $1. [*Hint:* Integer constraints matter here.]
   (b) What is the individual's average cash balance?
   (c) Suppose income rises to $1,800. By what percentage does the individual's demand for money change?

*13. The assumption was made in the appendix that, in the transactions demand-for-cash model, it is optimal to space transactions evenly throughout the month. Prove this as follows in the case where $n = 2$. Since one transaction must be made immediately, the only question is when to make the second one. For simplicity, call the beginning of the month $t = 0$ and the end of the month $t = 1$. Then consider a transaction strategy that performs the second transaction at the time t. If income is Y_N, then this will require moving tY_N into cash now and $(1 - t)Y_N$ at time t. Calculate the total cost incurred under this strategy, and try various values of t to see which is optimal. (If you are familiar with calculus, prove that $t = \frac{1}{2}$ minimizes total cost.)

🖫 COMPUTER EXERCISES

Please see exercises at the end of Chapter 14.

APPENDIX: THE BAUMOL-TOBIN TRANSACTIONS DEMAND MODEL

The assumptions of the Baumol-Tobin transactions demand model are set out in the text and summarized here. An individual receives a payment, Y_N, at the beginning of each month and spends it at an even pace during the month. He or she can earn interest at the rate i per month by holding money in a savings account (equivalently, bonds). There is a cost of tc per transaction

---

*An asterisk denotes a more difficult problem.

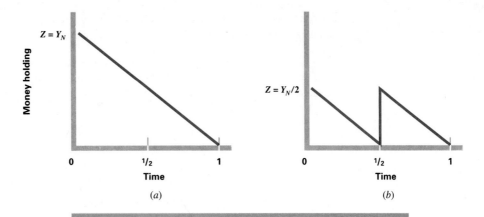

FIGURE 13A-1
THE AMOUNT OF CASH HELD DURING THE MONTH RELATED TO THE
NUMBER OF WITHDRAWALS. Panel (*a*) shows the pattern of money
holding during the month when the individual makes just one
transaction from the savings account to cash during the month. At
the beginning of the month the individual transfers the entire
amount to be spent, Y_N, into cash, and then spends it evenly over
the month. Panel (*b*) shows the pattern of money holding when
there are two transactions, one at the beginning of the month and
one in the middle of the month. In panel (*a*) average cash holdings
for the month are $Y_N/2$; in panel (*b*) they are $Y_N/4$.

for moving between bonds and money. We denote by n the number of transactions per month
between bonds and money, and we assume for convenience that monthly income is paid into
the savings account or paid in the form of bonds.

The individual minimizes the cost of money management during the month. Those costs
consist of the transactions cost, $(n \times tc)$, plus the interest forgone by holding money instead
of bonds during the month. The interest cost is $(i \times M)$, where M is the average holdings of
money during the month.

M, the average holdings of money, depends on n, the number of transactions. Suppose
that each time the individual makes a transaction, she transfers amount Z from bonds into
money.[28] If the individual makes n equal-sized withdrawals during the month, the size of each
transfer is Y_N/n, since a total of Y_N has to be transferred. Thus

$$nZ = Y_N \tag{A1}$$

Now, how is the *average* cash balance related to n? Figure 13A-1 helps answer the
question. In Figure 13A-1*a*, the average cash balance held during the month is $Y_N/2 = Z/2$,

---

[28] With simple interest being paid on the savings account, the individual's transactions between bonds and
cash should be evenly spaced over the month. We leave the proof of that for the case in which there are
two transactions to problem 13.

since the cash balance starts at Y_N and runs down in a straight line to zero.[29] In the case of Figure 13-A1b, the average cash balance for the first half of the month is $Y_N/4 = Z/2$, and the average cash balance for the second half of the month is also $Z/2$. Thus, the average cash balance for the entire month is $Y_N/4 = Z/2$. In general, the average cash balance is $Z/2$, as you might want to confirm by drawing diagrams similar to Figure 13A-1 for $n = 3$ or other values of n. By using equation (A1), it follows that the average cash balance is $Y_N/2n$.

The total cost of cash management is accordingly

$$\text{Total cost} = (n \times tc) + \frac{iY_N}{2n} \tag{A2}$$

The optimum number of transactions is found by minimizing total cost with respect to n.[30] That implies

$$n^* = \sqrt{\frac{iY_N}{2tc}} \tag{A3}$$

where n^* is the optimal number of transactions. As we should expect, the individual makes more transactions the higher the interest rate (since it is then more costly to hold money rather than bonds), the higher is income (this is explained in the text), and the lower the transaction cost.

The Baumol-Tobin result, equation (1) in the text, is obtained using equation (A3) and the fact that $M = iY_N/2n$.

In addition to deriving the square-root formula, we want also to show why for many people it is optimal to make only one transaction between bonds and money or, equivalently, why the integer constraints may matter. Consider the example in the text of an individual who receives $1,800 per month. Suppose that the interest rate on deposits is as high as 0.5 percent per month. The individual cannot avoid making one initial transaction, since income is paid into the savings account to start with. Does it pay to make a second transaction? For $n = 2$, the average cash balance is $1,800/2n = $450, so that interest earned would be $(0.005 \times $450) = 2.25.

If the transaction cost exceeds $2.25, the individual will not bother to make more than one transaction. And $2.25 is not an outrageous cost in terms of the time and nuisance of making a transfer between bonds (or a savings account) and money.

For anyone making only one transaction, the average cash balance is half his or her income. That means the interest elasticity of money demand for that person is zero—up to the point that the interest rate becomes high enough to make a second transaction worthwhile. And the *real* income elasticity is one, up to the point that income rises high enough to make a second transaction worthwhile. Since for some people the income elasticity is one, and for others the Baumol-Tobin formula is closer to applying, we expect the income elasticity to be between one-half and one; similarly, since for some the interest elasticity is zero, while for others it is closer to minus one-half, we expect the interest elasticity to be between minus one-half and zero.

---

[29] The average cash balance is the average of the amount of cash the individual holds at each moment during the month. For instance, if the balance held is $400 for 3 days and zero for the rest of the month, the average cash balance would be $40, or one-tenth (3 days divided by 30 days) of the month times $400.

[30] If you can handle calculus, derive equation (A3) by minimizing the total cost with respect to n in equation (A2).

DATA APPENDIX

In the following table, PGDP is the GDP deflator, set at 1.00 in 1987; OWN is the own rate of return on $M2$; and COMM is the commercial paper rate.

year	M1	M2	PGDP	V1	V2	OWN	COMM
1960	140.350	304.325	0.260	3.644	1.651	1.393	3.733
1961	143.067	324.867	0.263	3.675	1.595	1.550	2.811
1962	146.500	350.142	0.269	3.881	1.588	2.100	3.124
1963	151.033	379.658	0.272	3.935	1.542	2.238	3.430
1964	156.825	409.367	0.277	4.054	1.535	2.342	3.849
1965	163.508	442.500	0.284	4.208	1.541	2.505	4.281
1966	171.000	471.408	0.294	4.486	1.611	2.670	5.481
1967	177.775	503.692	0.303	4.462	1.562	2.720	5.032
1968	190.092	545.342	0.318	4.540	1.582	2.793	5.842
1969	201.425	579.125	0.334	4.715	1.635	2.853	7.931
1970	209.200	603.183	0.352	4.729	1.623	3.130	7.714
1971	223.233	676.367	0.371	4.815	1.553	3.163	5.045
1972	239.108	760.925	0.389	4.889	1.514	3.248	4.663
1973	256.383	836.292	0.413	5.171	1.579	4.023	8.203
1974	269.283	887.292	0.449	5.333	1.612	4.485	10.015
1975	281.475	970.175	0.492	5.528	1.563	3.858	6.250
1976	297.283	1095.792	0.523	5.810	1.538	3.938	5.236
1977	320.083	1234.575	0.559	5.993	1.544	4.138	5.547
1978	346.392	1339.883	0.603	6.266	1.618	4.658	7.942
1979	372.825	1450.600	0.656	6.510	1.668	5.930	10.970
1980	395.975	1567.142	0.717	6.593	1.666	7.080	12.658
1981	425.150	1715.000	0.789	6.999	1.706	8.978	15.325
1982	453.183	1874.983	0.838	6.686	1.625	7.965	11.893
1983	503.342	2109.892	0.871	6.548	1.565	6.575	8.878
1984	538.825	2282.492	0.910	6.890	1.608	7.413	10.097
1985	587.283	2485.567	0.944	6.580	1.582	6.165	7.954
1986	666.717	2689.033	0.969	6.021	1.531	5.160	6.495
1987	744.167	2867.100	1.000	6.023	1.561	4.865	6.813
1988	775.775	3015.242	1.038	6.234	1.601	5.300	7.656
1989	783.350	3132.175	1.086	6.641	1.637	6.165	8.989
1990	812.000	3298.308	1.132	6.701	1.655	5.830	8.061
1991	860.367	3402.617	1.178	6.378	1.655	4.595	5.865
1992	1016.800	3502.600	1.208	5.847	1.698	2.840	3.573

SOURCE: DRI/McGraw-Hill, Federal Reserve Board.

THE FED, MONEY, AND CREDIT

*I*n the recession of 1990–1991 and in 1992, the Fed cut interest rates twenty-three times to try to revive growth. Some critics said the Fed acted too late and too little, and that the slow rates of growth of $M2$ and $M3$ (see Table 14-1) proved it. Other critics emphasized the slow growth of *credit* as a sign that monetary policy was not expansionary enough. Credit consists of loans, short- and long-term, to firms, households, and the government. The Fed said it had acted prudently and decisively, and that the rapid declines in interest rates proved it.

Judged by the outcome—recession and slow growth—the critics were right. But it is always easy to be right after the event, and the data in Table 14-1 raise difficult questions. Should the Fed have been guided more by monetary targets or by interest rates? Why did bank credit grow so slowly? Should the Fed have cut interest rates more rapidly? Could the Fed have made $M2$ grow faster if it had wanted to? And what precisely does the Fed do to cut interest rates?

We start this chapter with a brief discussion of the mechanics of money supply determination. Then we go on to discuss monetary policy: both how the Fed conducts monetary policy—precisely what the Fed does to cut interest rates—and controversies about how it should do so. In particular, we ask whether the Fed should aim to affect the money supply, or the interest rate, or the quantity of credit—or some or all of them.

14-1 MONEY STOCK DETERMINATION: THE COMPONENTS

The money supply consists mostly of deposits at banks,[1] which the Fed does not control directly. In this section we begin to develop the details of the process by which the money supply is determined, and particularly the role of the Fed.

---

[1]We shall refer to all deposit-taking institutions, including savings and loan associations, mutual savings banks, and credit unions, as banks.

TABLE 14-1

MONETARY POLICY 1988–1992 (percent per annum)

	1988	1989	1990	1991	1992
Growth rate of M1	4.9	0.9	4.0	8.7	14.2
Growth rate of M2	5.5	5.1	3.5	3.0	2.3
Growth rate of M3	6.6	3.5	1.3	1.4	0.4
Growth rate of debt	9.3	8.0	6.8	4.2	4.3
Growth rate of bank loans	9.1	7.7	4.4	−0.1	−0.3
Treasury bill rate	6.7	8.1	7.5	5.4	3.8
10-year bond rate	8.9	8.5	8.6	7.9	7.3
Real GDP growth	3.9	2.5	1.0	−0.7	2.1
Inflation (GDP deflator)	3.9	4.4	4.1	3.7	2.5

NOTE: Money growth rates for 1989–1992 are for December relative to previous December; interest rates are averages for the period shown.

SOURCE: DRI/McGraw-Hill.

We ignore the distinction between various kinds of deposits (and thus the distinction between different M's) and consider the money supply process as if there were only a uniform class of deposits, D. Using that simplification, the money supply consists of currency (CU) plus deposits:

$$M \equiv CU + D \tag{1}$$

The behavior of both the public and the banks affects the money supply. The public's demand for currency affects the currency component, CU, and its demand for deposits affects the deposit component, D. The banks have a role because deposits, D, are a debt the banks owe their customers. And of course the Fed has a part (the most important) in determining the money supply. The interactions among the actions of the public, the banks, and the Fed determine the money supply.

We summarize the behavior of the public, the banks, and the Fed in the money supply process by three variables: the *currency-deposit ratio,* the *reserve ratio,* and the *stock of high-powered money.*

The Currency-Deposit Ratio

The payment habits of the public determine how much currency is held relative to deposits. In December 1991, the currency-deposit ratio was 0.084.[2] The currency-deposit ratio is affected by the cost and convenience of obtaining cash; for instance,

---

[2]We use here the $M2$ definition of the money stock; the currency stock in December 1991 averaged $267.3 billion and $M2$ averaged $3,439.3 billion.

if there is a cash machine nearby, individuals will on average carry less cash with them because the costs of running out are lower. The currency-deposit ratio has a strong seasonal pattern, being highest around Christmas.

For the remainder of the chapter we shall for convenience treat the currency-deposit ratio as independent of interest rates and constant.[3]

The Reserve-Deposit Ratio

Bank reserves consist of notes and coin held by banks and deposits the banks hold at the Fed. Banks hold reserves to meet (1) the demands of their customers for cash and (2) payments their customers make by checks that are deposited in other banks.

Banks have to keep reserves in the form of notes and coin because their customers have a right to currency on demand. They keep accounts at the Fed mainly to make payments among themselves.[4] Thus, when I pay you with a check drawn on my bank account, which you deposit in your bank, my bank makes the payment by transferring money from its account at the Fed to your bank's account at the Fed.[5] Banks can also use their deposits at the Fed to obtain cash; the Fed sends the cash over in an armored truck on request.

THE BANKS' BALANCE SHEET AND DETERMINANTS OF THE RESERVE-DEPOSIT RATIO

A balance sheet is a complete listing of the amounts owned by a person or institution (the *assets*) and the amounts it owes (the *liabilities*). A balance sheet is presented as in Table 14-2, with the assets listed on the left and the liabilities on the right. Reserves are an asset of the banks, and deposits—amounts they owe their depositors—are liabilities.

We denote by *re* the ratio of bank reserves to deposits, or the reserve-deposit ratio. The reserve ratio is less than 1, since banks hold assets other than reserves, such as loans they make to the public and securities. In December 1991, banks held $57.9 billion in reserves, deposits were $3,172 billion, and *re* was accordingly 1.83 percent.

The reserve-deposit ratio is determined by two sets of considerations. First, the Fed sets *minimum reserve requirements.*[6] Reserves have to be held against "transactions deposits," deposits against which more than three checks can be written per month. No reserves are required against MMDAs. Reserve requirements are lower for small banks than large. The reserve requirements are imposed partly to make sure that the

---

[3]In fact the currency-deposit ratio rose fairly steadily from 1960 to the early 1980s, declined quite rapidly from 1984 on, and then turned up in the early 1990s. With interest paid on demand deposits, it is possible that the currency-deposit ratio is negatively related to the interest rate.

[4]At the end of 1991, banks' reserves held at the Fed accounted for 52 percent of total reserves; notes and coin held by the banks accounted for the remaining 48 percent.

[5]Many banks, particularly small ones, hold their reserves in the form of deposits at other banks. These *interbank deposits* serve the same function as reserves but are not included in the U.S. measure of reserves. They are excluded from the definitions of the money stock.

[6]The *Federal Reserve Bulletin* includes a table listing reserve requirements.

TABLE 14-2

BANK BALANCE SHEET

assets	liabilities
Reserves	Deposits
Bank credit	
Loans	
Investments	
Less	
Borrowing from Fed	
Borrowing in the Fed funds market (net)	

banks have cash available when depositors demand it, and partly because they help the Fed control the money supply, as we shall see later.[7]

Second, banks may want to hold *excess reserves* beyond the level of required reserves. In deciding how much excess reserves to hold, a bank's economic problem is similar to the problem of an individual in deciding on a precautionary demand for money. That is, the bank has to compare the cost of holding more reserves with the benefit of doing so.

We see from Table 14-2 that the alternative to reserves is loans or other investments. The cost of holding more reserves is that the bank could instead hold interest-bearing assets. We denote the return on other assets by the market interest rate, i, and expect excess reserves to fall when i rises.

The benefit of holding more reserves is that the bank is able to meet demands for cash (or deposits at the Fed, to pay other banks) immediately. This benefit is greater the more uncertain its net flow of deposits: the greater the uncertainty (which we denote σ), the more likely a bank is to have to come up with cash quickly. Thus excess reserves rise with σ.

A bank that runs short of reserves can borrow to make good the deficiency. It may borrow either from the Fed or from other banks that have spare reserves. The cost of borrowing from the Fed is the *discount rate*. The discount rate is the interest rate charged by the Fed to banks that borrow from it to meet temporary needs for reserves. The discount rate is the explicit cost of Fed borrowing, but there is also an implicit cost, since the Fed frowns on banks that try to borrow from it too often.

The cost of borrowing from other banks is the *federal funds rate*. Federal funds are reserves that some banks have in excess and others borrow. The federal funds rate varies together with other market rates, and can be affected by the Fed.

---

[7]Reserve requirements usually constitute a tax on banks or their depositors. This is because reserves usually pay no interest to the banks, and the banks therefore can pay less interest to their depositors. In effect, a bank holding non-interest-paying reserves is making an interest-free loan to the government. Thus governments can help finance their budget deficits by imposing high reserve requirements. Frequently reserve requirements are very high in countries where governments have large deficits and high inflation. In the United States, reserve requirements have been gradually reduced over time to improve banks' ability to compete with nonbank institutions such as money market mutual funds.

We summarize this discussion by writing the bank's reserve-deposit ratio, *re,* as a function of the market interest rate, *i,* the discount rate, i_D, the required reserve ratio, r_R, and σ:[8]

$$re = r\,(i,\, i_D,\, r_R,\, \sigma) \tag{2}$$

An increase in the market rate, *i,* reduces excess reserves, while increases in the other variables in equation (2) increase *re.* We do not explicitly include the federal funds rate since it and the market interest rate, *i,* move very similarly.

The important point about equation (2) is that the reserve ratio is a function of market interest rates. This implies that the supply of money itself may also be a function of market interest rates, as we shall see.

DEPOSIT INSURANCE AND BANK RUNS

Excess reserves in the postwar period have been small compared with levels reached in the 1930s. Many banks failed in the 1930s. That is, they were unable to meet the demands of their depositors for cash. If you have a deposit in a failed bank, you cannot "get your money out."

A bank that holds few reserves is in danger of not being able to meet its depositors' demands for currency. Anyone who believes his or her bank may run out of cash will rush to the bank to try to withdraw money before the other depositors. A *run* on a bank occurs when depositors rush to try to withdraw cash because they believe others will also try to do so. There may be good reasons for the running investors to worry about the bank's safety, or it is even possible that a run on a bank may occur precisely because its depositors believe that a run on the bank is likely to occur.[9]

In a general atmosphere of instability, as in the 1930s, banks need to hold large reserves to prevent runs by persuading depositors that the bank is in no possible danger. That is one reason the banks that survived in the 1930s held large excess reserves.[10]

The massive bank failures of the 1930s, as a consequence of runs on banks, gave rise to an important institutional reform, the creation of the *Federal Deposit Insurance Corporation* (FDIC). That institution insures bank depositors and as a result bank runs have been rare since the 1930s.[11] As shown in Appendix 14-2, bank failures virtually

---

[8]The precise behavior of excess reserves depends on how the Fed is conducting monetary policy. One possible method is for the Fed to allow banks to borrow as much as they want to meet the required reserve ratio, r_R. If banks hold exactly to that ratio, there are never any excess reserves, so excess reserves are unaffected by the discount rate. In that case, an increase in the discount rate would not affect excess reserves (which would remain at zero) or the reserve ratio (which would remain equal to r_R). More generally, we should expect the relationship stated in equation (2), in which the reserve ratio declines when the discount rate increases.

[9]The notion of self-justifying runs on banks has both intuitive appeal and historical support. It has been formalized in an ingenious but very difficult article by Douglas Diamond and Philip Dybvig, "Bank Runs, Deposit Insurance and Liquidity," *Journal of Political Economy,* June 1983.

[10]Another reason is that *i* was so low in the 1930s that holding excess reserves was cheap.

[11]In the 1980s there were runs on thrift institutions in Ohio and Rhode Island whose deposits were not covered by federal insurance.

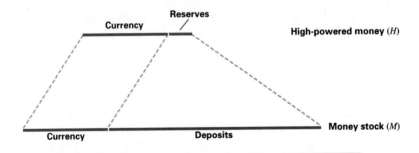

FIGURE 14-1

THE MONEY MULTIPLIER. The money multiplier is the ratio of the money stock (the base of the diagram) to high-powered money. The multiplier is larger than 1. It is larger the smaller the ratio of currency to deposits and the smaller the ratio of reserves to deposits.

disappeared between 1940 and 1979 but have since become a more serious problem. The scale today is still less than in the early 1930s, and—because of the FDIC—the economic consequences are much less serious now.

There are two main reasons why excess reserves are now so small. First, deposit insurance reduces the threat of runs. Second, the development of financial markets and communications has reduced the cost to banks of managing their balance sheets in such a way as to keep excess reserves small.

High-Powered Money

High-powered money (or the monetary base) consists of currency (notes and coin) and banks' deposits at the Fed. Part of the currency is held by the public. The remaining currency (around 10 percent) is held by banks as part of their reserves. The Fed's control over the monetary base is the main route through which it determines the money supply.

14-2 THE MONEY MULTIPLIER

In this section we develop a simple approach to money stock determination, using as the key variables the currency-deposit ratio, the reserve-deposit ratio, and high-powered money. The approach is organized around the supply of and demand for high-powered money. The Fed can control the *supply* of high-powered money. The total *demand* for high-powered money comes from the public, who want to use it as currency, and the banks, which need it as reserves.

Before going into details, we want to think briefly about the relationship between the money stock and the stock of high-powered money (Figure 14-1). At the top of the figure we show the stock of high-powered money. At the bottom we show the stock of money. They are related by the *money multiplier*. The money multiplier is the ratio of the stock of money to the stock of high-powered money.

The money multiplier is larger than 1. It is clear from the diagram that the multiplier is larger the larger are deposits as a fraction of the money stock. This is true because currency uses up one dollar of high-powered money per dollar of money. Deposits, by contrast, use up only amount *re* of high-powered money (in reserves) per dollar of money stock. For instance, if the reserve ratio, *re*, is 10 percent, every dollar of the money stock in the form of deposits uses up only 10 cents of high-powered money. Equivalently, each dollar of high-powered money held as bank reserves can support ten dollars of deposits.

The precise relationship among the money stock, *M*, the stock of high-powered money, *H*, the reserve-deposit ratio, *re*, and the currency-deposit ratio, *cu*, is derived in Appendix 14-1.[12] Here we present the resulting expression for the money supply expressed in terms of its principal determinants, *re*, *cu*, and *H*:[13]

$$M = \frac{1 + cu}{re + cu} H \equiv mm \times H \tag{3}$$

where *mm* is the money multiplier given by

$$mm \equiv \frac{1 + cu}{re + cu} \tag{4}$$

It is thus clear that

■ *The money multiplier is larger the smaller the reserve ratio, re.*

■ In addition, *the money multiplier is larger the smaller the currency deposit ratio, cu.* That is because the smaller is *cu*, the smaller the proportion of the high-powered money stock that is being used as currency (which translates high-powered money only one for one into money) and the larger the proportion that is available to be reserves (which translates much more than one for one into money).

The Multiplier in Practice

Since the Fed controls *H,* it would be able to control the money stock, *M, exactly* if the multiplier were constant or fully predictable. Actual data for the money multiplier for *M*2 are shown in Figure 14-2. It is clear that the money multiplier is neither constant

---

[12]See the appendix for the key equations.

[13]Using the actual values for December 1991, we have, as ratios to *M*2 deposits, *cu* = 0.0843 and *re* = 0.0183; and *H* = 325.2. Thus we obtain *M*2 = [(1.0843)/(0.0843 + 0.0183)] × 325.2 = 3,437. Rounding error accounts for the difference between $3,437 billion and the true figure of $3,439 billion.

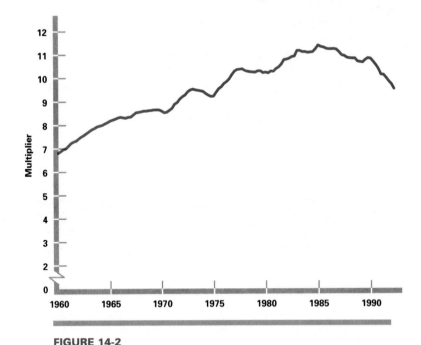

FIGURE 14-2
THE *M*2 MONEY MULTIPLIER, 1960–1992. (SOURCE: DRI/McGraw-Hill.)

nor exactly predictable.[14] This means that the Fed cannot exactly determine the money stock in any period by setting the base at a specific level.

We next examine more closely the process by which the Fed determines *H*. We then turn to the question of how the Fed conducts monetary policy in practice and to an examination of the role of credit in the economy.

14-3 CONTROLLING THE STOCK OF HIGH-POWERED MONEY

Table 14-3 shows a highly simplified form of the Fed's balance sheet, designed to illustrate the sources of the monetary base—the way the Fed creates high-powered money—and the uses of, or demand for, the base.[15]

The reason to focus on the Federal Reserve balance sheet is to see how operations by the Fed affect the stock of high-powered money outstanding. High-powered money

---

[14] A sophisticated method of predicting the money multiplier is presented in James M. Johannes and Robert H. Rasche, *Controlling the Growth of the Monetary Aggregates* (Norwell, Mass.: Kluwer, 1987).

[15] We have simplified the balance sheet by lumping together a number of assets and liabilities in the entry "Net other assets." More detail on the Fed's balance sheet and the monetary base can be obtained by examining the tables in the *Federal Reserve Bulletin*.

TABLE 14-3

SIMPLIFIED FORM OF THE FED BALANCE SHEET, SHOWING SOURCES AND USES OF HIGH-POWERED MONEY, APRIL 1992 (billions of dollars)

assets (sources)			liabilities (uses)		
Gold and foreign exchange		$ 21.1	Currency		$304.8
Federal reserve credit		305.2	Held by the public	$273.7	
Loans and discounts	$ 0.9		Vault cash	31.1	
Government securities	273.3		Bank deposits at the Fed		22.9
Net other credit	31.0				
Plus					
Net other assets		1.4			
Monetary base (sources)		$327.7	Monetary base (uses)		$327.7

SOURCE: *Federal Reserve Bulletin*, July 1992.

is created when the Fed acquires assets and pays for them by creating liabilities. **The two main classes of liabilities, or *uses* of the base, are currency and bank deposits at the Fed.**

An Open Market Purchase

The method by which the Fed most often changes the stock of high-powered money is an open market operation. We examine the mechanics of an open market *purchase*, an operation in which the Fed buys, say, $1 million of government bonds from a private individual. An open market purchase *increases* the monetary base.

The accounting for the Fed's purchase is shown in Table 14-4. The Fed's ownership of government securities rises by $1 million, which is shown in the "Government securities" entry on the assets side of the balance sheet. How does the Fed pay for the bond? It writes a check on itself. In return for the bond, the seller receives a check instructing the Fed to pay (the seller) $1 million. The seller takes the check to his or her bank, which credits the depositor with the $1 million and then deposits the check

TABLE 14-4

EFFECTS OF AN OPEN MARKET PURCHASE ON THE FED BALANCE SHEET (millions of dollars)

assets		liabilities	
Government securities	+1	Currency	0
All other assets	0	Bank deposits at Fed	+1
Monetary base (sources)	+1	Monetary base (uses)	+1

at the Fed. That bank has an account at the Fed; the account is credited with $1 million, and the "Bank deposits at Fed" entry on the "Liabilities" side of the balance sheet rises by $1 million. The commercial bank has just increased its reserves by $1 million, which are held in the first instance as a deposit at the Fed.

The only unexpected part of the story is that the Fed can pay for the securities it bought by giving the seller a check on itself. The eventual owner of the check then has a deposit at the Fed. That deposit can be used to make payments to other banks, or it can be exchanged for currency. Just as the ordinary deposit holder at a bank can obtain currency in exchange for deposits, the bank deposit holder at the Fed can acquire currency in exchange for its deposits. When the Fed pays for the bond by writing a check on itself, it creates high-powered money with a stroke of the pen. The Fed can create high-powered money at will merely by buying assets, such as government bonds, and paying for them with its liabilities.

The Fed Balance Sheet

We return now to the balance sheet and start by examining the assets. The purchase of assets generates high-powered money. The gold and foreign exchange that the Fed owns were acquired in the past, when the Fed paid for them too by writing checks on itself. There is, accordingly, almost no difference between the way in which a purchase of gold affects the balance sheet and the way in which an open market purchase of bonds affects the balance sheet.[16]

The Fed sometimes buys or sells foreign currencies in an attempt to affect exchange rates. These purchases and sales of foreign exchange—*foreign exchange market intervention*—affect the base. Note from the balance sheet that if the central bank buys gold or foreign exchange, there is a corresponding increase in high-powered money, as the Fed pays with its own liabilities for the gold or foreign exchange that is purchases. Thus foreign exchange market operations affect the base.[17]

LOANS AND DISCOUNTS

The Fed's role as a lender is reflected by the "Loans and discounts" item in Table 14-3. The Fed provides high-powered money to banks that need it by lending to them at the discount rate (see Section 14-1). Banks' willingness to borrow from the Fed is affected by the discount rate, which accordingly influences the volume of borrowing. Since borrowed reserves are also part of high-powered money, the Fed's discount rate has some effect on the monetary base.

---

[16]The Fed's 1992 holdings of gold were about $11 billion, valued at $42 an ounce. The market value of the gold is much higher, since the market price of gold is far above $42 per ounce. In problem 5, you are asked to show how the balance sheet would be affected if the Fed decided to value its gold at the free market price. For that purpose you will have to adjust the item "Net other assets" appropriately.

[17]Details of this impact may be complicated by the fact, which we do not pursue, that the Fed and the Treasury usually collaborate in foreign exchange intervention.

Financing Federal Deficits

The U.S. Treasury maintains an account at the Fed and makes payments to the public by writing checks on its Fed account. An understanding of the relationship between the Fed and the Treasury helps clarify the financing of government budget deficits.

Budget deficits can be financed by the Treasury's borrowing from the public. In that case, the Treasury sells bonds to the public. The public pays for the bonds with checks, which the Treasury deposits in an account it holds in a commercial bank, thereby making sure it does not affect the stock of high-powered money. When the Treasury uses the proceeds of the bond sales to make a payment, it moves the money into its Fed account just before making the payment. As a result, the monetary base is not affected by the Treasury's deficit financing, except for the short time between which the Treasury moves the money into its Fed account and then pays it out.

Alternatively, the Treasury can finance its deficit by borrowing from the Fed. It is simplest to think of the Treasury's selling a bond to the Fed instead of to the public. When the bond is sold, the Fed's holdings of government securities increase, and simultaneously the asset "Net other assets" falls because Treasury deposits, a liability of the Fed, have risen. But then when the Treasury uses the borrowed money to make a payment, the stock of high-powered money rises. Accordingly, when a budget deficit is financed by the Treasury borrowing from the Fed, the stock of high-powered money is increased.

We often talk of central bank financing of government deficits as financing through the printing of money. Typically, the deficit is not literally financed by the central bank through the printing of money, but it is true that central bank financing increases the stock of high-powered money, which comes to much the same thing.

In some countries the central bank automatically finances the Treasury and may be subordinated to the Treasury. In the United States, by contrast, the Federal Reserve answers to the Congress and is not legally obliged to finance government deficits by buying bonds.[18] Thus it still retains its ability to control the stock of high-powered money even when the Treasury is running a budget deficit. This is an essential characteristic of an independent central bank.

Summary

1. The main point of this section is that the Fed controls the stock of high-powered money primarily through open market operations.
2. The Fed can also influence the stock of high-powered money by changing the discount rate and thereby affecting the volume of member bank borrowing.
3. Treasury financing of its budget deficits through borrowing from the public leaves the stock of high-powered money unaffected, whereas Treasury financing by borrowing from the Fed increases the monetary base.

---

[18]See Sayre Ellen Dykes, "The Establishment and Evolution of the Federal Reserve Board: 1913–1923," *Federal Reserve Bulletin*, April 1989, and the special seventy-fifth anniversary issue of the Federal Reserve Bank of New York's *Quarterly Review*, Spring 1989.

box 14-1

THE FED AS LENDER OF LAST RESORT

An important function assigned to central banks since the nineteenth century is to act as lender of last resort. When financial panic threatens the collapse of the financial system, swift action by the Fed can restore confidence and avoid a systemwide run on financial intermediaries, a freezing of credit lines, or, worse, a calling in of loans. The Fed does assume this role whenever major financial institutions go under or when, as when the stock market fell 20 percent on one day in the October 1987 collapse, there is a serious risk of instability.

The need for a lender of last resort emerges from the following consideration. The credit system is by its very nature *illiquid*, though not *insolvent*—various debtors can, given time, repay their loans, but they cannot do so on demand. But many liabilities, for example, bank deposits or large CDs of banks and corporations, have very short maturities. If all creditors ask for their assets, many of the debtors would not be able to pay and would have to default.

Now imagine that a major financial institution, say First Bank of Nowhere (First for short), has payment difficulties. Other financial institutions may well have lent to First and will want to recover their money before anyone else. A bank run starts. Yet other financial institutions are aware that *some* institutions have lent to First, cannot recover their loans, and are therefore vulnerable themselves, as are their creditors in turn. There arises a general uncertainty as to who lent to whom and who is in trouble because someone (or many) in the many layers of credit and intermediation cannot meet redemption demands. As a result *all* credit freezes; nobody wants to lend to anyone because everyone is afraid to be pulled into the default. But if nobody wants to lend, short-term credit lines cannot be rolled over, and many institutions become illiquid. The process deteriorates in a 1930s-style financial collapse as assets are liquidated to recover liquidity.

The Fed enters in such a situation by *isolating* the center of the storm, guaranteeing the assets of the individual financial institution (beyond the guarantees of the FDIC). The guarantee assures everybody that third parties will not suffer losses and hence not become a risk. Thus the lender-of-last-resort function prevents spillover effects to the credit market of individual payment difficulties. But the function also comes into its own when there is a marketwide problem. Walter Bagehot (1826–1877) in his famous 1873 book, *Lombard Street*, gave the classic prescription: "*During crisis discount freely!*"

14-4 THE MONEY MULTIPLIER AND THE ADJUSTMENT PROCESS

We now develop the economics of the money multiplier by showing how adjustments by banks and the public following an increase in the monetary base produce a multiple expansion of the money stock. We sketch the argument here and refer to Appendix 14-1 for the basic equations.

A Fed open market purchase increases the monetary base. To start with, the increase in the base shows up as an increase in bank reserves. This is because the Fed pays for the securities by writing a check on itself, which the seller of the securities deposits in his or her bank account. The bank in turn presents the check for collection

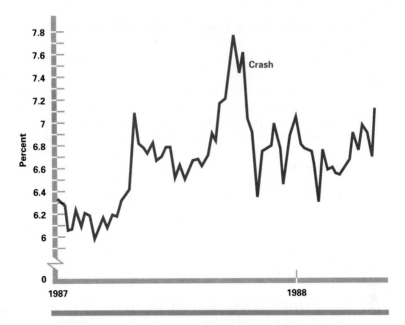

FIGURE 1

THE CRASH AND THE FEDERAL FUNDS RATE, 1987–1988. Friday
quotations of the federal funds rate, percent per year. (Source: DRI/
McGraw-Hill.)

Milton Friedman and Anna Schwartz, in their *A Monetary History of the United
States*, blamed the Fed for not responding to the systemwide problems induced
by the stock market crash of 1929, thus violating Bagehot's prescription. But during
the stock market crash of 1987, the lesson had been learned. Fed chairman Alan
Greenspan did not hesitate. He announced that the Fed stood behind the banking
system. The Fed immediately reduced interest rates, as shown in Figure 1, providing
the much-needed liquidity that would help stem the risk of a credit collapse. ∎

to the Fed; the bank then will be credited with an increase in its reserve position at
the Fed.

At this stage the public has increased its deposits but not its currency holdings.
That means the currency-deposit ratio, *cu*, is out of line—it is too low. The public will
therefore convert deposits into currency, thus reducing bank reserves and deposits.

More important in the story is the fact that the bank in which the original check
was deposited now has a reserve ratio, *re*, that is too high. Its reserves and deposits
have gone up by the same amount. Therefore, its ratio of reserves to deposits has risen.
To reduce the ratio of reserves to deposits, it increases its lending.

When the bank makes a loan, the person receiving the loan gets a bank deposit.

At this stage, when the bank makes a loan, *the money supply has risen by more than the amount of the open market operation.* The person who sold the security to the Fed has increased his or her holdings of money—some in currency and some in deposits—by the value of the bonds sold. The person receiving the loan has a new bank deposit—and thus the process has already generated a multiple expansion of the money stock.

In the subsequent adjustment, part of the increase in high-powered money finds its way into the public's holdings of currency, and part serves as the basis for an expansion of lending by the banking system. When banks lend, they do so by crediting the deposits of their loan customers with the loan. Banks therefore create money whenever they make loans.

The expansion of loans, and hence money, continues until the reserve-deposit ratio has fallen to the desired level and the public again has achieved its desired currency-deposit ratio. The money multiplier summarizes the total expansion of money created by a dollar increase in the monetary base.

14-5 THE MONEY SUPPLY FUNCTION AND THE INSTRUMENTS OF MONETARY CONTROL

We summarize the discussion so far by returning to equation (3) and writing a *money supply function* that takes account of the behavior of the public, the banking system, and the Fed:

$$M = \frac{1 + cu}{re + cu} H$$

$$= mm(i, i_D, r_R, cu, \sigma) H \tag{5}$$

In equation (5) we write the money multiplier, *mm*, as a function of market interest rates, the discount rate, required reserves, the currency-deposit ratio, and the variability of deposit flows. Given H, the supply of money increases with the money multiplier, *mm*. The multiplier, in turn, increases with the level of market interest rates and decreases with the discount rate, the required reserve ratio, and the currency-deposit ratio. Note that the Fed affects the money supply through three routes: H, controlled primarily through open market operations; the discount rate, i_D; and the required reserve ratio, r_R. Of these three *instruments of monetary control*, open market operations are the most frequently used.

Why can the Fed not control the money stock exactly? The reasons emerge by looking at the money multiplier formula in equation (5). We have assumed *cu* is constant—but, in fact, *cu* varies, and the Fed does not know in advance exactly what the value of *cu* will be. Similarly, the reserve ratio, *re*, varies, both because deposits move among banks with different reserve ratios and because banks change the amount of excess reserves they want to hold.

In brief, the Fed cannot control the money stock exactly because the money multiplier is neither constant nor fully predictable.

14-6 EQUILIBRIUM IN THE MONEY MARKET

We now combine the money supply function in equation (5) with the money demand function to study money market equilibrium. For that purpose we will assume that the price level is given at the level P_0, and that the level of real income is constant at $Y = Y_0$. With both the price level and level of income fixed, money demand depends only on the interest rate, and the money market equilibrium will determine the equilibrium interest rate and quantity of money for given P_0 and Y_0.

The equilibrium condition in the money market is that the real money supply, M/P, equals the demand for real balances, or

$$\frac{M}{P} = L(i, Y) \tag{6}$$

Substituting expression (5) for M in the money market equilibrium condition (6), and noting that $P = P_0$ and $Y = Y_0$ by assumption, we obtain

$$mm(i, i_D, r_R, cu, \sigma)\frac{H}{P_0} = L(i, Y_0) \tag{7}$$

We now have the money market equilibrium condition in terms of interest rates and the other variables affecting the supply of, and demand for, money.

In Figure 14-3 we show the real money demand function (LL) as a downward-sloping schedule, drawn for a given level of real income. The real money supply function (MS), given i_D, r_R, cu, σ, and P_0, is upward-sloping and is drawn for a given stock of high-powered money, H. The positive slope of MS reflects the fact that at higher interest rates banks prefer to hold fewer reserves, so that the money multiplier is higher.[19] The equilibrium money supply and interest rate are jointly determined at point E.

Figure 14-3 also shows the effects of an open market purchase on interest rates and the money stock, given the price level and the level of income. An increase of ΔH in the monetary base shifts the MS curve to the right to MS', increasing the money stock and reducing the interest rate. Because the interest rate falls, the money multiplier declines as a result of the increase in H. But despite the decline in the interest rate, the money stock unquestionably increases.

In Figure 14-3, we are implicitly looking at the effects of a change in the stock of high-powered money on the LM curve. Figure 14-4 shows the IS and LM curves. The LM curve represents the combinations of income levels and the interest rate at which the money market is in equilibrium. What happens to the LM curve when the stock of high-powered money is increased? In Figure 14-3 we saw that for any given level of income, Y_0, an increase in H reduces the equilibrium interest rate. That means that the LM curve in Figure 14-4 shifts down to LM' when H increases. The equilibrium

---

[19]At sufficiently high interest rates, the money supply schedule becomes vertical. This is because excess reserves become zero at very high interest rates and the banks cannot squeeze out any more loans on the basis of the reserves they have.

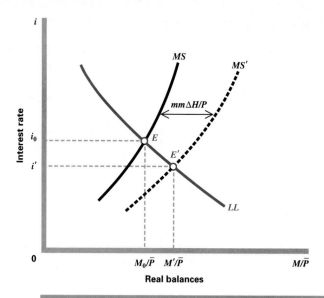

FIGURE 14-3

EQUILIBRIUM IN THE MONEY MARKET AND THE EFFECTS OF AN INCREASE IN H. The downward-sloping curve is the demand for money. The quantity of money demanded is greater the lower the interest rate. The upward-sloping curve is the money supply function. This slopes up because, given the quantity of high-powered money, banks reduce their demand for excess reserves when the interest rate rises. Thus the reserve ratio is lower and the money multiplier higher at higher interest rates. The equilibrium interest rate and stock of money are determined at the intersection point, E. An increase in the monetary base shifts the money schedule to MS' and the new equilibrium to E', with a larger money supply and lower interest rate.

shifts from E to E', with output rising and the interest rate falling. Thus our analysis confirms that the Fed, by increasing the stock of high-powered money, can reduce the interest rate and increase the level of income.[20]

Changes in the Discount Rate

We can also analyze the effects of an increase in the discount rate on the position of the LM curve and thus on the interest rate and output. With a higher discount rate,

---

[20]The way in which the central bank conducts monetary policy varies from country to country. For a description of other countries, see Dallas S. Batten et al., "The Conduct of Monetary Policy in the Major Industrial Countries," IMF Occasional Paper 70, July 1990, and Bruce Kasman, "A Comparison of Monetary Policy Operating Procedures in Six Industrial Countries," Federal Reserve Bank of New York *Quarterly Review*, Summer 1992.

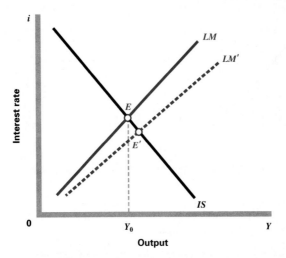

FIGURE 14-4

THE EFFECTS OF AN INCREASE IN HIGH-POWERED MONEY IN THE *IS-LM* MODEL. For any given level of output, an increase in the stock of high-powered money reduces the interest rate at which the money market is in equilibrium. That means the *LM* curve shifts down when *H* is increased; as the economy moves from *E* to *E'*, the interest rate falls and output rises.

banks will hold higher reserves because it is more expensive to borrow to cover any reserve shortage that may occur. An increase in the discount rate therefore reduces the money multiplier.

In problem 7 we ask you to show how an increase in the discount rate affects the *MS* curve in Figure 14-3, and then how it affects the *LM* curve. You will be able to show that an increase in the discount rate causes *i* to rise and output to fall. Accordingly, an increase in the discount rate is a contractionary monetary policy.

14-7 CONTROL OF THE MONEY STOCK AND CONTROL OF THE INTEREST RATE

We make a simple but important point in this section: *The Fed cannot simultaneously set both the interest rate and the stock of money at any given target levels that it may choose.*

Figure 14-5 illustrates this point. Suppose that the Fed, for some reason, wants to set the interest rate at a level i^* and the money stock at a level M^*, and that the demand-for-money function is as shown by *LL*. The Fed can move the money supply function around, as in Figure 14-3, but it cannot move the money demand function around. It can set only the combinations of the interest rate and the money supply that

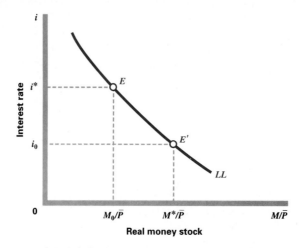

FIGURE 14-5

CONTROLLING THE MONEY STOCK AND INTEREST RATES. The Fed
cannot simultaneously set both the interest rate and the money
stock at levels it wants. Suppose it wanted the interest rate to be $i*$
and the money stock to be M. These two levels are inconsistent with
the demand for money, LL. If the Fed insists on interest rate level $i*$,
it will have to accept a money stock equal to M_0. If instead the Fed
wants to set the money stock at $M*$, it will end up with an interest
rate equal to i_0.

lie along LL. At interest rate $i*$, it can have money supply $M_0/\bar{P}$. At target money
supply $M*/\bar{P}$, it can have interest rate i_0. But it cannot have both $M*/\bar{P}$ and $i*$.

The point is sometimes put more dramatically, as follows. When the Fed decides
to set the interest rate at some given level and keep it fixed—a policy known at *pegging*
the interest rate—it loses control over the money supply. If the money demand curve
were to shift, the Fed would have to supply whatever amount of money is demanded
at the pegging interest rate.

As an operational matter, the Fed in its day-to-day operations can more accurately
control interest rates than the money stock. The Fed buys and sells government securities
through its *open market desk* in the New York Fed every day. If it wants to raise the
price of government securities (lower the interest rate), it can buy the securities at that
price. If it wants to reduce prices of government securities (raise the interest rate), it
can sell a sufficient amount of securities from its large portfolio. Thus, on a day-to-
day basis, the Fed can determine the market interest rate quite accurately.[21]

However, the Fed cannot determine the money supply precisely on a day-to-day
basis. For one thing, there is a lag before reasonably good money supply data for a

---

[21]For a description of techniques of monetary control, see Daniel Thornton, "The Borrowed-Reserves
Operating Procedure: Theory and Evidence," Federal Reserve Bank of St. Louis *Review*, January/Febru-
ary 1988.

given date become available. That would not affect the Fed's ability to control the money stock if the money multiplier were constant, for then the Fed would be able to deduce, from the behavior of the monetary base, what the money stock was. But as we have seen, the multiplier cannot be accurately predicted.

These are *technical* reasons why the Fed cannot hit the target stock of money exactly even if it wants to. But over a slightly longer period, the Fed can determine the money supply fairly accurately. As data on the behavior of the money stock and the money multiplier become available, the Fed can make midcourse corrections to its setting of the base. For example, if the Fed were aiming for monetary growth of 5 percent over a given period, it might start the base growing at 5 percent. If it found halfway into the period that the multiplier had been falling, and the money stock therefore growing by less than 5 percent, the Fed would step up the growth rate of the base to compensate.

The main reasons the Fed does not hit its money growth targets are not technical, but rather have to do with its having both interest rate *and* money stock targets, and as we have seen in this section, it cannot hit them both at the same time.

14-8 MONEY STOCK AND INTEREST RATE TARGETS

Over the period since the 1950s, the emphasis the Fed has placed on controlling the interest rate versus controlling the money supply has changed. Initially the emphasis was almost entirely on interest rates—indeed, it was not until 1959 that the Fed even began to publish money stock data. Until 1982 the emphasis on monetary targets increased more or less steadily. Since then the emphasis has shifted back increasingly toward interest rates, and to a more eclectic approach to monetary policy.[22]

In this section we discuss the issues involved in the choice between interest rate and money stock targets.

Making Monetary Policy

Monetary policy is made by the Fed's Open Market Committee (FOMC), which meets eight times a year and also holds frequent consultations between meetings. At these meetings the Fed issues a *monetary policy directive* to the open market desk in New York, describing the type of monetary policy it wants.[23]

In recent years, the directive has instructed the open market desk to conduct open market operations to produce money stock growth within given target ranges. The target ranges for *M*2 since 1976 are given in Table 14-5. Between 1976 and 1986 the Fed also specified a target range for *M*1, but it dropped that target as the behavior

---

[22]See Ann-Marie Meulendyke, "A Review of Federal Reserve Policy Targets and Operating Guides in Recent Decades," Federal Reserve Bank of New York *Quarterly Review*, Autumn 1988.

[23]A summary of the FOMC's discussions and the directive are published in the *Federal Reserve Bulletin*. You may find it useful to read one of these reports, to see if you can understand the Fed's arguments. See, too, the Fed's monetary policy report to Congress published each spring and fall.

TABLE 14-5
TARGET AND ACTUAL GROWTH RATES OF *M2**

period	target range	actual	period	target range	actual
1976	7.5–10.5	10.9	1985	6–9	8.7
1977	7–10	9.8	1986	6–9	9.2
1978	6.5–9	8.7	1987	5.5–8.5	4.3
1979	5–8	8.2	1988	4–8	5.2
1980	6–9	8.9	1989	3–7	4.8
1981	6–9	9.3	1990	3–7	3.8
1982	6–9	9.1	1991	2.5–6.5	3.1
1983	7–10	12.2	1992	2.5–6.5	
1984	6–9	8.0			

*Money definitions are those in effect at the time targets were set. Rates are for a 1-year period ending in the fourth quarter of the specified year.

Source: Various issues of the *Federal Reserve Bulletin*.

of *M*1 became harder to predict. There are also target ranges for *M*3 and, since 1982, for total nonfinancial debt in the economy. This latter total is the amount of lending to spending units in the economy.

Comparison of the actual money growth rate with the target range in Table 14-5 shows a persistent tendency for *M*2 growth to be at the top end of or above the target range, through 1986. Since then *M*2 growth has been below the midpoint of the range, and sometimes below the range.

Interest Rate or Money Targets?

Although the formal language of monetary policy directives now refers almost entirely to money growth ranges, the Fed has in the period 1990–1993 focused on interest rates, repeatedly cutting the discount rate and publicly talking about its hope that long-term interest rates will decline. In this section we ask whether the Fed makes the economy more stable by aiming for a particular money stock or for a particular interest rate.[24]

We assume that the Fed's aim is for the economy to reach a particular level of output. The analysis, known as the Poole analysis, uses the *IS-LM* model and applies to a short period such as 3 to 9 months.[25] In Figure 14-6, the *LM* curve labeled *LM(M)* is the *LM* curve that exists when the Fed fixes the money stock. The *LM* curve labeled

---

[24]In problem 13 we ask you to analyze a closely related problem, whether in seeking to hit a particular money target, the Fed should set an interest rate or *H*.

[25]The analysis we present here is based on a classic article by William Poole, "Optimal Choice of Monetary Policy Instruments in a Simple Stochastic Macro Model," *Quarterly Journal of Economics*, May 1970.

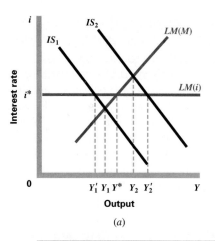
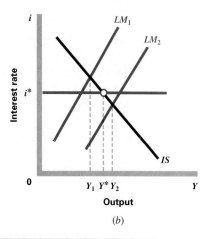

FIGURE 14-6

MONEY AND INTEREST RATE TARGETS. In panel (*a*), the *IS* curve shifts. If the Fed targets the money stock, the *LM* curve is shown by *LM*(*M*). *LM*(*i*) is the *LM* curve when the interest rate is held constant. The aim of policy is to hit output level *Y**. If the *LM* curve is *LM*(*M*), the output levels will be either Y_1 or Y_2, depending on where the *IS* curve turns out to be. In the case of an interest rate target, the corresponding levels of output are Y_1' and Y_2', both further from the desired level of output, *Y**. Thus, monetary targeting leads to more stable output behavior. In panel (*b*) it is the *LM* curve that is shifting, because of shifts in the demand for money. With *LM* shifting and the *IS* curve stable, output will be at the target level *Y** if the interest rate is held constant at *i** but will be at either Y_1 or Y_2 if the money stock is held constant. Therefore, the Fed should target the interest rate if the demand-for-money function is unstable.

LM(*i*) describes money market equilibrium when the Fed fixes the interest rate. It is horizontal at the chosen level of the interest rate, *i**.

The problem for policy is that the *IS* and *LM* curves shift unpredictably. When they shift, output ends up at a level different from the target level. In Figure 14-6*a* we show two alternative positions for the *IS* curve: IS_1 and IS_2. We assume that the Fed does not know in advance which *IS* curve will obtain: the position depends, for instance, on investment demand, which is difficult to predict. The Fed's aim is to have income come out as close as possible to the target level, *Y**.

In Figure 14-6*a* we see that the level of output stays closer to *Y** if the *LM* curve is *LM*(*M*). In that case the level of output will be Y_1 if the *IS* curve is IS_1 and Y_2 if the *IS* curve is IS_2. If policy had kept the interest rate constant, we would in each case have a level of income that is further from *Y**: Y_1' instead of Y_1, and Y_2' instead of Y_2.

Thus we have our first conclusion: *If output deviates from its equilibrium level mainly because the IS curve shifts about, then output is stabilized by keeping the money stock constant. The Fed should, in this case, have monetary targets.*

We can see from Figure 14-6a why it is more stabilizing to keep M rather than i constant. When the *IS* curve shifts to the right and the *LM(M)* curve applies, the interest rate rises, thereby reducing investment demand and moderating the effect of the shift. But if the *LM(i)* curve applies, there is no resistance from monetary policy to the effects of the *IS* shift. Monetary policy is thus automatically stabilizing in Figure 14-6a when the *IS* curve shifts and the money stock is held constant.

In Figure 14-6b we assume that the *IS* curve is stable. Now the uncertainty about the effects of monetary policy results from shifts in the *LM* curve. Assuming that the Fed can fix the money stock, the *LM* curve shifts because the demand function shifts. The Fed does not know when it sets the money stock what the interest rate will be. The *LM* curve could end up being either LM_1 or LM_2. Alternatively, the Fed could simply fix the interest rate at level i^*. That would ensure that the level of output is Y^*.

If the Fed were to fix the money stock, output could be either Y_1 or Y_2. If it fixes the interest rate, output will be Y^*. Thus we have our second conclusion: *If output deviates from its equilibrium level mainly because the demand-for-money function shifts about, then the Fed should operate monetary policy by fixing the interest rate.* That way it automatically neutralizes the effects of the shifts in money demand. In this case the Fed should have interest rate targets.

The Poole analysis helps explain why the Fed stopped specifying M_1 targets from 1987 on while continuing to target M_2 (and M_3 and total nonfinancial debt). The increasing instability of the demand for M_1 limited its usefulness as a monetary target. Similarly, the unpredictability of the growth of all the monetary aggregates in the last few years has led to the increasing weight on interest rates.

THE SHORT RUN AND THE LONG RUN

It is important to note that the Poole argument discusses Fed targeting over short periods. The Fed is *not* to be thought of as announcing or desiring that the interest rate will be, say, 8 percent forever. Rather, the Fed should readjust its targets in light of the changing behavior of the economy. The target interest rate might be 5 percent at the bottom of a recession and 15 percent when the economy is overheating. Similarly, the money growth targets could also be adjusted in response to the state of the economy.

Monetarist proponents of money stock targeting might agree with the technical details of the Poole analysis but still argue that it is a mistake to target interest rates rather than money. They argue that increases in the money stock lead eventually to inflation and that the only way to avoid inflation in the long run is by keeping money growth moderate. The problem with focusing on interest rates, they suggest, is that while the Fed keeps its eye on interest rates, the growth rate of money and the inflation rate often tend to increase.[26] This argument appears to fit the facts of the 1960s and 1970s well.

However, that experience has led the Fed to watch inflationary trends very closely and to tighten policy when inflation threatens. That experience, and the monetarist

---

[26]Another argument for money targeting arises from the distinction between real and nominal interest rates. The nominal interest rate can rise because inflation is expected. If the Fed fights this increase in the nominal rate by increasing the money stock, it is only feeding the inflation. We examine this argument in more detail in Chap. 18.

analysis, has also led the Fed to set monetary targets for itself and to appraise carefully the reasons when it misses the targets. At the same time, the Fed pays attention to interest rates and is ready to revise them should the economy appear to be heading for either inflation or recession.

Monetarism and the Fed

Since the 1960s the Fed has been criticized by monetarists, who argue that it should conduct monetary policy by targeting the money stock (typically either M_1 or M_2). The monetarist criticism seemed to be having an impact as the Fed adopted monetary targets in the 1970s and then in 1979 announced that it was giving them greater weight. Even so monetarist critics such as Milton Friedman describe the Fed's use of monetary targets as "rhetorical camouflage," a perfectly reasonable comment.

Their criticisms of the Fed's monetary policy take place at several levels. First, as noted above, monetarists argue that the Fed's propensity to try to stabilize interest rates tends to make it follow inflationary policies. That criticism no longer seems justified. Certainly the inflation rate in the long expansion from 1982 to 1989 stayed low even as the economy in 1989 reached the lowest unemployment rate in 15 years.

In reply to the analysis that shows the interest rate as a good guide for monetary policy when money demand is unstable, critics of the Fed argue that velocity changes are infrequent. The instability of the demand for M_1 in the 1980s makes this claim less plausible, though that instability results in part from deregulation of interest rates. Further, they contend, money demand would be more stable if the Fed followed steady policies.

At a second level, monetarist critics argue that the Fed's operating procedures—the procedures by which it attempts to control the money stock—are technically defective. At an even more basic level, the critics argue that the Fed should simply attempt to keep the growth rate of money constant, quarter by quarter and year by year, rather than change its targets frequently. The argument—discussed further in Chapter 15—is that policy that reacts to the way the economy is behaving may end up causing more instability rather than less.

Our own views in this area are that rigid commitment to monetary targets is unwise in light of shifts in the money demand function and that the Fed should target interest rates as well as the stock of money. We note also that on a year-to-year basis (excepting the period of deregulation in 1981–1983) the Fed has maintained quite stable growth of $M2$—not much less stable than that of other leading countries, such as Japan and Germany. The record since 1976 does not show that the Fed has let money growth get out of hand even if it has also been informally targeting interest rates.

14-9 MONEY, CREDIT, AND INTEREST RATES

The Fed targets not only $M2$ and $M3$ but also the increase in the total *debt* of the nonfinancial sectors, that is, the debt of the government, households, and firms other than financial firms. Their debt is equal to the credit (lending) that has been extended to them. Thus the Fed can also be described as having *credit targets*.

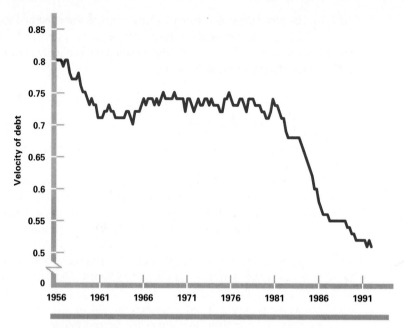

FIGURE 14-7
THE RATIO OF GDP TO PRIVATE DEBT, 1956–1992. (Source: DRI/McGraw-Hill.)

Why? In the first instance, this is a very old approach of the Fed, which had credit targets already in the 1950s. The Fed returned to them in 1982 in part because of econometric evidence by Benjamin Friedman of Harvard,[27] showing that there was a tighter link between the volume of debt and GNP than between money and nominal GNP. As shown in Figure 14-7, the velocity of debt was remarkably stable up to 1983, just after the time the Fed adopted it as a target of monetary policy. But then the ratio of GNP to debt (the velocity of debt) began to drop fast, as the volume of debt in the economy started growing rapidly.[28]

Why might the amount of credit be closely related to GDP? Spending can be financed by borrowing, so that debt growth and spending growth should move together. In particular, investment spending is likely to be financed by borrowing, that is, by credit, and investment spending is a key to the business cycle. Thus we should expect the amount of lending to be related to GDP, but it is of course an empirical question whether the velocity of credit is more stable than that of money; the recent evidence is that it is not more stable than the velocity of $M2$, though up to 1982 it was.

---

[27]"The Roles of Money and Credit in Macroeconomic Analysis," in James Tobin (ed.), *Microeconomics, Prices, and Quantities* (Washington, D.C.: The Brookings Institution, 1983).

[28]This is another example of the operation of Goodhart's law, which was introduced at the end of Chapter 13.

Proponents of the credit view, such as Ben Bernanke of Princeton and Mark Gertler of New York University, emphasize the importance of the extent of financial intermediation—the volume of lending and borrowing through financial institutions—in the economy. Financial intermediation occurs when financial institutions channel funds from savers to investors, as banks do when they lend funds deposited with them to borrowers who want to invest. Bernanke's research suggests that a large part of the decline in output in the great depression was the result of the breakdown of the financial system and the collapse in the quantity of credit, rather than the decline in the quantity of money.[29] The slow growth of credit in 1989–1991 has also been blamed for the recent recession (see Box 14-2).

Proponents of the central role of credit also argue that *credit rationing* (discussed in Box 14-2) makes interest rates an unreliable indicator of monetary policy. Credit is rationed when individuals cannot borrow as much as they want at the going interest rate. Credit is rationed because lenders fear that borrowers who are willing to borrow may nonetheless not be able to repay. But if credit is rationed at a given interest rate, then that interest rate does not fully describe the impact of monetary policy on investment and aggregate demand. Proponents of the credit view argue that the Fed should rather focus directly on the volume of credit to judge what impact monetary policy is having on aggregate demand.

What do these arguments imply for the importance of credit and for monetary policy? First, of course a well-functioning financial system is important for the efficient allocation of investment in the economy; a collapse of the financial system, and thus of credit, would severely reduce investment and GNP. Second, credit rationing does take place, and its extent varies with the lenders' views of economic prospects. Thus, the volume of credit contains relevant information about the impact of monetary policy on the economy. Third, in practice the velocity of credit has not recently been stable. Fourth, the Fed does not directly control the quantity of credit, since the overall volume of lending and borrowing in the economy is not under its direct control. These conflicting considerations suggest we need to clarify our thinking about the notion of "targets" of monetary policy, which we do in the next section. We should also recognize that over time the relative importance of different transmission channels changes and therefore the targets of monetary policy might have to change with them.[30]

14-10 WHICH TARGETS FOR THE FED?

We are now ready to set monetary policy in a broader perspective, by discussing the ultimate goals of monetary policy. There are three points to note before we get down

---

[29]Ben Bernanke, "Non-Monetary Effects of the Financial Crisis in the Propagation of the Great Depression," *American Economic Review*, June 1983. See, too, Mark Gertler and R. Glenn Hubbard, "Financial Factors in Business Fluctuations," in Federal Reserve Bank of Kansas, *Financial Market Volatility*, 1989; and Anil Kashyap, Jeremy Stein, and David Wilcox, "Monetary Policy and Credit Conditions: Evidence from the Composition of External Finance," NBER Working Paper 4015, 1992. A major review of the money versus credit issue is offered in Christina Romer and David Romer, "New Evidence on the Monetary Transmission Mechanism," *Brookings Papers on Economic Activity*, vol. 1, 1990.

[30]See Patricia Mosser, "Changes in Monetary Policy Effectiveness: Evidence from Large Econometric Models," Federal Reserve Bank of New York *Quarterly Review*, Spring 1992, and Cara Lown, "Banking and the Economy: What Are the Facts?" Federal Reserve Bank of Chicago *Economic Review*, September 1990.

box 14-2

MONEY GROWTH, INTEREST RATES, AND CREDIT IN THE 1990–1991 RECESSION

In the 1990–1991 recession, fiscal policy was completely immobilized by the size of the budget deficit. The burden of dealing with the recession therefore fell on monetary policy, which ran into severe difficulties as banks appeared unwilling to lend and the different monetary aggregates grew at very different rates.

The starting point for the 1990–1991 recession is the gradually rising inflation rate at the end of the 1980s. From a low of 1.9 percent in 1986, the CPI inflation rate reached 4.8 percent in 1989. With the unemployment rate in 1989 at 5.2 percent, perhaps even below the natural rate, the Fed's main concern was to fight inflation.

The main indicators of monetary policy showed a tightening in 1989 (see Table 14-1). The most visible sign was the rise in the Treasury bill rate from an average of 6.7 percent in 1988 to 8.1 percent in 1989; in addition the growth rate of each of the monetary aggregates and debt declined between 1988 and 1989—though M1 growth virtually collapsed while M2 fell very little. The Fed entered 1990 with inflation on its mind, and viewing the 2.5 percent GDP growth in 1989 as at about the sustainable rate.

The recession dates from July 1990, before the Iraqi invasion of Kuwait. We know now that GDP growth was negative in both the third and fourth quarters of 1990, though the third quarter decline showed up only in revised data in July 1992. But the Fed, then preoccupied with the question of how to deal with the 40 percent rise in the price of oil that followed the Iraqi invasion, held its interest rates constant through the end of the year. Then, as the recession continued, the Fed kept reducing the interest rate, very slowly through 1991, always concerned not to go too far in case it reignited inflation.

At the end of 1991, with the recession already over, the data again began to show signs of weakening production and output. There was much talk of a *double-dip recession*. This time the Fed moved decisively, cutting the discount rate from 4.5 to 3.5 percent. Treasury bill rates moved to their lowest level in 20 years, and then as growth continued sluggish, they fell to their lowest level in 30 years.

to the details:

1. A key distinction is between *ultimate targets* of policy and *intermediate* targets. Ultimate targets are variables such as the inflation rate and the unemployment rate (or real output) whose behavior matters. The interest rate and the rate of growth of money or credit are intermediate targets of policy—targets the Fed aims at so that it can hit the ultimate targets more accurately. The discount rate, open market operations, and reserve requirements are the *instruments* the Fed has with which to hit the targets.[31]

2. It matters how often the intermediate targets are reset. For instance, if the Fed

---

[31]See Benjamin Friedman, "Targets and Indicators of Monetary Policy," in B. Friedman and F. Hahn (eds.), *Handbook of Monetary Economics* (Amsterdam: North-Holland, 1991).

Interestingly, though, long-term interest rates were very slow to come down, as can be seen by looking at the 10-year bond rate in Table 14-1. The explanation is that markets believed that inflation would soon return.

It is striking that in the 1990–1992 period, the Fed conducted monetary policy almost entirely with reference to interest rates. The reason can be seen in Table 14-1: the growth rates of the different monetary aggregates diverged wildly. One explanation for the slow growth of M2 and M3 in this period is that as interest rates on these assets fell, people moved into stocks, which were still doing well, and into longer-term bonds, whose interest rates stayed high.

There was one other special feature of the recession: a view that credit was unusually difficult to get. Even before the recession began, business executives and policy makers were complaining about the difficulty of getting loans. The credit crunch—the reluctance of banks and thrifts to lend—seemed to worsen as the recession continued. The volume of bank loans declined in the recession, confirming the existence of the problem.*

Why was there a crunch? First, bank regulators, worried about bank failures, were tightening their standards, trying to make sure the banks did not make bad loans. Banks in response tended to move to safety, to hold government securities rather than make loans to business. Second, banks were extremely cautious in lending because they had made so many bad loans in the 1980s, especially in real estate. They wanted to rebuild their portfolios by making only very safe loans.

By the second half of 1992, the U.S. economy was recovering slowly and hesitatingly from the recession—but the recovery was much weaker than typical in the post–World War II period. The big question in the 1990s is whether this slow recovery is also the beginning of a decade of exceptionally slow growth. ∎

---

*See Paul Francis O'Brien and Frank Browne, "A 'Credit Crunch'? The Recent Slowdown in Bank Lending and Its Implications for Monetary Policy," OECD Working Paper No. 107, 1992, and Raymond Owens and Stacey Schreft, "Identifying Credit Crunches," Federal Reserve Bank of Richmond, Working Paper No. 92-1, 1992. See too Ben Bernanke and Cara Lown, "The Credit Crunch," *Brookings Papers on Economic Activity*, 2, 1991.

---

were to commit itself to 5.5 percent money growth over a period of several years, it would have to be sure that the velocity of money was not going to change unpredictably; otherwise, the actual level of GDP would be far different from the targeted level. If the money target were reset more often, as velocity changed, the Fed could come closer to hitting its ultimate targets.

3. The need for targeting arises from a lack of knowledge. If the Fed had the right ultimate goals and knew exactly how the economy worked, it could do whatever was needed to keep the economy as close to its ultimate targets as possible.

Intermediate targets then give the Fed something concrete and specific to aim for in the next year. That enables the Fed itself to focus on what it should be doing. It also helps the private sector know what to expect. If the Fed announces and will stick to its targets, firms and consumers have a better idea of what monetary policy will be. Of course, it would not help the private sector much to know about future monetary policy unless that policy increased the predictability of future outputs and prices.

Another benefit of specifying targets for monetary policy is that the Fed can then be monitored concretely and held *accountable* for its actions. It has a job to do. By announcing targets the Fed makes it possible for outsiders to discuss whether it is aiming in the right direction, and then later to judge whether it succeeded in its aims.

The ideal intermediate target is a variable that the Fed can control exactly and that at the same time has an exact relationship with the ultimate targets of policy. For instance, if the ultimate target could be expressed as some particular level of nominal GDP, and if the money multiplier and velocity were both constant, the Fed could hit its ultimate target by having the money base as its intermediate target.

In practice, life is not so simple. Rather, *in choosing intermediate targets, the Fed has to trade off between those targets it can control exactly and those targets that are most closely related to its ultimate targets.*[32]

Targeting the Monetary Base

Sometimes proposed, at one extreme, is *monetary base targeting*.[33] The Fed can essentially control the monetary base exactly. If that were the intermediate target, the Fed would have no trouble hitting the bull's eye. Further, it could certainly be held accountable for not hitting the target, since it could not plausibly blame factors beyond its control for any failures.

The problem with monetary base targeting is that the Fed might be hitting the bull's eye on the money base target while completely missing the ultimate targets of policy. Unpredictable changes in the money multiplier and in velocity break the tight link between the money base and nominal GNP.

Targeting Nominal GDP

Nominal GDP targeting is at the other end of the tradeoff. In this scheme the Fed would announce a target path for nominal GDP—for instance, that it wants nominal GNP to grow by 10 percent. But since the Fed does not directly control nominal GDP, it would have each period to calculate the money stock or money base that would enable it to come closest to hitting the GDP target. Relative to money stock targeting, nominal GDP targeting implies that the Fed automatically adjusts money targets for velocity shifts.

By targeting nominal GDP growth, the Fed builds in an automatic policy tradeoff between inflation and output. If inflation turns out high, the nominal income growth

---

[32]A major review by the Federal Reserve staff of the targeting issue is *Intermediate Targets and Indicators for Monetary Policy. A Critical Survey*, Federal Reserve Bank of New York, July 1990.

[33]See Bennett T. McCallum, "Could a Monetary Base Rule Have Prevented the Great Depression?" NBER Working Paper 3162, November 1989.

target implies that the Fed will be aiming for a lower level of output growth than it otherwise would have.[34]

With nominal GDP targeting, the Fed might well not be to blame if the target is missed—fiscal policy or supply shocks could be just as responsible as monetary policy. Thus those who believe the main problem in monetary policy is controlling the Fed typically argue for monetary base or money stock rules. Those who believe the Fed can be trusted to do the right thing tend to prefer nominal GDP targeting.

Beyond the issue of trusting the Fed lie questions of whether the economy would be more stable if over periods of a year or so nominal GDP growth were held constant or if money base growth or interest rates were held constant. There are no simple answers at this stage: the answer depends on what shocks are likely to hit the economy, as the Poole analysis above illustrates.

Which targets should the Fed have? The Fed should have and announce ultimate targets for monetary policy, such as the path of nominal GDP it would like to attain over the next few years. At the same time, it should announce money stock targets for the next year and explain why those targets are consistent with its ultimate targets of policy. It should be willing to adjust the intermediate targets as velocity and the shocks hitting the economy change.

This is not far from what the Fed actually does. Judged by the behavior of the ultimate targets, it was very successful between 1982 and 1989. But since 1989, the economy has done badly. Is that the Fed's fault? The implicit answer found in Box 14-2 is "Only partly." Would the Fed have done better with a monetary rule? Probably not, because none of the monetary aggregates gave reliable signals throughout the period.

What do we conclude? That targeting has an important role in monetary policy, that public discussion about monetary policy is important, and that—because the economy is always evolving unpredictably—the Federal Reserve Board cannot avoid using its judgment in deciding which targets to follow and which to change.

14-11 SUMMARY

1. The stock of money is determined by the Fed through its control of the monetary base (high-powered money); the public, through its preferred currency-deposit ratio; and the banks, through their preferred reserve holding behavior.
2. The money stock is larger than the stock of high-powered money because part of the money stock consists of bank deposits, against which the banks hold less than one dollar of reserves per dollar of deposits.
3. The money multiplier is the ratio of the money stock to high-powered money. It is larger the smaller the reserve-deposit ratio and the smaller the currency-deposit ratio.

---

[34]See Michael D. Bradley and Dennis W. Jansen, "Understanding Nominal GNP Targeting," *Federal Reserve Bank of St. Louis Review*, November/December 1989; see, too, Jeffrey A. Frankel and Menzie Chinn, "The Stabilizing Properties of a Nominal GNP Rule in an Open Economy," working paper, Department of Economics, University of California Berkeley, May 1991, for an extension of the analysis to the open economy.

4. The Fed creates high-powered money in open market purchases when it buys assets (for example, Treasury bills, gold, foreign exchange) by creating liabilities on its balance sheet. These purchases increase banks' reserves held at the Fed and lead, through the multiplier process, to an increase in the money stock which is larger than the increase in high-powered money.

5. The money multiplier builds up through an adjustment process in which banks make loans (or buy securities) because deposits have increased their reserves above desired levels.

6. The Fed has three basic policy instruments: open market operations, the discount rate, and required reserves for depository institutions.

7. Because the desired reserve-deposit ratio of banks decreases as the interest rate rises, the supply-of-money function is interest-elastic.

8. The Fed cannot independently control both the interest rate and the money stock at the same time. It can only choose combinations of the interest rate and money stock that are consistent with the demand-for-money function.

9. The Fed operates monetary policy by specifying target ranges for both the money stock and the interest rate. In order to hit its target level of output, the Fed should concentrate on its money targets if the *IS* curve is unstable. It should concentrate on interest rate targets if the money demand function is the major source of instability in the economy.

10. The Fed targets not only *M2* and *M3* and interest rates, but also total nonfinancial debt, or the volume of credit, in the economy. The velocity of debt was more stable than that of money through 1983, but it has changed sharply since then.

11. Because of credit rationing, the volume of credit is likely to convey additional information about future levels of spending, particularly investment spending, than is conveyed by interest rates. Credit targets therefore can make sense. However, the relation between credit and nominal GNP became very unstable in the 1980s.

12. The Fed faces a tradeoff between targets that it can hit exactly but that may be far from the ultimate targets of policy and targets that are closer to ultimate targets but are more difficult to hit. Critics of the Fed argue that in addition the Fed should choose targets that will make it easy to judge its success in achieving its goals. This suggests the Fed should select intermediate targets that it can hit quite accurately.

KEY TERMS

Currency-deposit ratio

Reserve-deposit ratio

High-powered money (monetary base)

Money multiplier

Discount rate

Excess reserves

FDIC

Credit

Multiple expansion of money stock

Money supply function

Money stock and interest rate targets

Intermediate targets

Ultimate targets

PROBLEMS

1. Use Figure 14-1 to discuss how (a) an increase in the currency-deposit ratio and (b) an increase in the reserve-deposit ratio affect the money stock, given the monetary base.

2. Show how an open market sale affects the Fed's balance sheet and also the balance sheet of the commercial bank of the purchaser of the bond sold by the Fed.

3. When the Fed buys or sells gold or foreign exchange, it automatically offsets, or *sterilizes*, the impact of these operations on the monetary base by compensating open market operations. What it does is to buy gold and at the same time sell bonds from its portfolio. Show the effects on the Fed balance sheet of a purchase of gold and a corresponding sterilization through an open market sale.

4. How much does bank credit increase when the Fed increases the monetary base by $1? Give the answer in terms of *cu* and *re*.

5. Explain how the Fed's balance sheet would be affected if it valued gold at the market price.

6. A proposal for "100 percent banking" involves a reserve-deposit ratio of unity. Such a scheme has been proposed for the United States in order to enhance the Fed's control over the money supply.
   (a) Indicate why such a scheme would help monetary control.
   (b) Indicate what bank balance sheets look like under this scheme.
   (c) Under 100 percent money, how would banking remain profitable?

7. Use Figures 14-3 and 14-4 to show the effect of an increase in the discount rate on (a) the equilibrium money supply, (b) interest rates, and (c) the equilibrium level of income.

8. The Federal Deposit Insurance Corporation insures commercial bank deposits against bank default. Discuss the implications of that deposit scheme for the money multiplier, and thus for the money supply, given H.

9. Under what circumstances should the Fed conduct monetary policy by targeting mainly (a) interest rates or (b) the money stock?

10. (a) Why does the Fed not stick more closely to its target paths for money?
    (b) What are the dangers of targeting nominal interest rates?

11. Categorize the following as either an ultimate or intermediate target, or an instrument of monetary policy: nominal GDP, the discount rate, the monetary base, $M1$, the Treasury bill rate, the unemployment rate.

12. The Fed's target for monetary policy should be to produce constant growth of real GNP at a rate of 3.5 percent per year. Discuss.

*13. This lengthy problem asks you to analyze the following question. Suppose the Fed has already decided that it wants to target the money stock: Will the Fed come closer to the target by setting the interest rate at a given level, or will it do better by fixing H? You should think of this analysis as applying to a very short horizon of a few weeks—about the period between meetings of the Open Market Committee.

    The analysis should use a diagram like Figure 14-3, and then apply an analysis similar to that of Figure 14-6. The result of such an analysis involves the relative stability of money demand and the money multiplier. Show that:
    (a) If the demand-for-money function is stable, then fixing interest rates ensures that the Fed will come closer to hitting the target money stock.

---

*An asterisk denotes a more difficult problem.

(b) If the demand-for-money function is relatively unstable (compared to the money multiplier), then the Fed should target H if it wants to hit its target level of the money stock more closely.

💾 COMPUTER EXERCISES

1. Construct a table with four rows, (1) through (4), and five columns, (a) through (e), to record the effects of the following five simulations on (1) real balances (M/P), (2) the interest rate (i), (3) the money multiplier (mm), and (4) velocity (V):

   (a) BASE solution (write the values in from the base solution before any simulation is carried out).
   (b) Increase Y by 175 to 775.
   (c) Increase Y by 220 to 820.
   (d) Keeping Y at 820, lower the reserve requirement to 10 percent.
   (e) Increase the monetary base (high-powered money, H) by 30 to 130.

   Remember to reset to the BASE solution before each successive simulation.

2. Explain each change from (a) to (b).

3. Comparing (b) to (c), why do certain of the four variables change whereas others do not?

4. Why does lowering the reserve requirement in (d) change the variables that did not change from (b) to (c)?

5. Compare the effect of expanding H in (e) to increasing Y in (b). How are they similar and how do they differ?

APPENDIX 14-1: THE MONEY STOCK AND THE MONEY MULTIPLIER

We derive the equilibrium money stock and the multiplier by looking at the demand for and supply of money and high-powered money. Consider, first, equilibrium between the supply of money and the demand for money, which, in turn, equals deposits plus currency:

$$M = D + CU \equiv (1 + cu)D \qquad (A1)$$

where we have substituted for $CU = cu \times D$.

Equilibrium between the supply of high-powered money and the demand for high-powered money, which equals reserves (RE) plus currency, implies

$$H = RE + CU \equiv (re + cu)D \qquad (A2)$$

Again we have expressed the demand side in terms of the desired ratio of currency to deposits and of the banks' desired reserve-deposit ratio, re. When equations (A1) and (A2) both hold, we are in monetary equilibrium because people hold their money balances in the preferred ratio and banks hold just the right ratio of reserves to deposits.

Dividing equation (A2) by (A1) yields an expression for the money multiplier (*mm*):

$$\frac{M}{H} \equiv mm = \frac{1 + cu}{re + cu} \qquad (A3)$$

The money multiplier thus depends on the *cu* and *re* ratios.

We can also use equation (A3), multiplying both sides by *H*, to obtain the money supply in terms of the principal determinants *mm* and *H*:

$$M = mm \times H \qquad (A4)$$

In writing equation (A4) we remember that *mm* depends on the currency-deposit preferences of the public and the reserve-deposit preferences of banks. It thus takes into account preferences about the composition of balance sheets.

APPENDIX 14-2: THE DEPOSIT INSURANCE MESS: THE SAVINGS AND LOANS AND THE BANKS

The federal government insures deposits in federally chartered savings and loan associations (S&Ls), as well as banks. Until 1989, S&L deposits were insured by FSLIC (pronounced "fizz-lick"), the Federal Savings and Loan Insurance Corporation. Like the FDIC, FSLIC financed itself by charging premiums on the deposits it insured.

During the 1980s it became clear that FSLIC had spectacularly run out of funds. In 1989 the federal government abolished FSLIC and moved its insurance responsibilities to the FDIC. More important, the federal government had to cover the losses from S&L deposit insurance. The total paid by the federal government over the period 1988–1992 was an astounding $277 billion—and there is more to come.

What happened? From the great depression until 1980, the interest rates banks and thrifts could pay on their deposits were controlled. As market interest rates rose in the late 1970s, the S&Ls started losing deposits. The S&Ls thus supported the gradual deregulation of interest rates that began in 1980, and they began to compete for funds by offering higher interest rates.

Depositors, covered by deposit insurance, went where the rates were highest. They did not have to worry about what the S&Ls were doing with the funds. The owners and managers of S&Ls were thus free to lend those funds out on high-yielding and therefore risky investments—including high-yielding junk bonds. If the investments succeeded, the S&L owner became rich. If the investments failed, the federal government picked up the bill. This is an example of *moral hazard*, a situation in which a party to a contract can benefit by taking advantage in a way not covered by the original contract.

Many of the S&Ls' risky investments, especially in real estate, did fail. In addition, some S&L owners engaged in outright fraud. As a result, one-third of the S&Ls in the United States failed between 1987 and 1991. The federal insurers had to step in to protect the depositors. Typically, they arranged for some other institution, such as a more sound S&L or a business person, to take over the failed S&L. The takeovers were costly because the federal government had to provide funds to make sure the reorganized S&L would be profitable.

One expensive lesson from this episode is that interest rate deregulation in the presence of deposit insurance has to be handled very carefully. With deposit insurance, depositors did not worry about where they put their money, and reckless competition for deposits could thus take place. Of course, the dangers should have been foreseen by FSLIC, which should also have monitored S&L portfolios more closely.

TABLE A14-1

NUMBER AND DEPOSITS OF FDIC-INSURED BANKS CLOSED BECAUSE OF FINANCIAL
DIFFICULTIES (annual averages)

	number of closed banks	deposits at closed banks, $ millions	percent of total deposits at insured banks
1934–1939	52.5	49.0	0.1
1940–1949	10.0	23.5	0.02
1950–1959	3.1	10.5	0.005
1960–1969	4.4	28.5	0.008
1970–1979	7.6	513.0	0.06
1980–1983	27.5	4,848.0	0.32
1984–1987	130.2	6,937.3	0.34
1988–1991	174.5	29,311.7	1.19

SOURCE: FDIC *Annual Report,* 1991.

When the federal government pays the depositors in a failed S&L, it is transferring money from one set of taxpayers to another. Since this is just a transfer, its net economic cost could be small. However, analysis by the Congressional Budget Office (CBO) points to the main economic cost of the S&L failures: resources that could have been used to finance good investments were wasted on bad investments.[35] CBO calculations suggest this cost was as high as $400 billion over the period 1981–1992.

As the S&L debacle continued, the number of commercial bank failures in the United States increased (Table A14-1). Bank failures are much more frequent in the United States than in other countries, and the question is therefore whether banking insurance, the structure of the banking system, or both are responsible for U.S. banking problems.[36]

In the early 1990s the administration and the Congress have been wrestling with the issues of bank deposit insurance and bank reform. Problems in deposit insurance arise from moral hazard, from slow reactions by the regulators, and on the "too big to fail" doctrine, which we now explain.

Legally, deposits are insured up to only $100,000. In practice, when a big bank fails, the FDIC treats all depositors alike, large and small, even though the holders of large deposits are formally not insured beyond $100,000. The reason is that the FDIC fears that large depositors would run on the banks if they were to believe they are not covered by insurance. If the large banks in the United States were to fail, the financial system and the economy would be in deep trouble. Accordingly, some banks are "too big to fail," even though their depositors are not fully insured. Obviously, the FDIC loses when it covers depositors who are not paying for their insurance.

One special feature of the U.S. banking system is that branching is very limited across state lines, and frequently limited within a state. This means that U.S. banks cannot diversify

---

[35]See the Congressional Budget Office Study, "The Economic Effects of the Savings and Loan Crisis," January 1992. See also Edward J. Kane, *The S&L Insurance Mess: How Did It Happen?* (Washington, D.C.: Urban Institute Press, 1990).

[36]See R. Dan Brumbaugh, Jr., and Kenneth E. Scott, "A Political Logjam Still Blocks Banking Reform," *Challenge,* March–April 1992.

their portfolios as widely as banks in many foreign countries do. When Texas is in trouble, Texan banks fail. In other countries, where banks operate nationwide, losses in one region can be offset by gains in another.

Banking reforms introduced in the 1990s aim to make nationwide branching easier. There have also been a variety of proposals to deal with the deposit insurance and moral hazard problems. One idea is that insurance should be limited to "narrow" or "core" banks, banks that are allowed to hold only completely safe assets, such as Treasury bills. That way there is no chance of their failing. Critics of this proposal argue that institutions just like banks would develop, that the failure of several of these institutions would constitute a danger to the financial system, and therefore that in practice, the federal government would step in to protect their depositors just as it does now for the big banks' depositors.

These issues are certain to be discussed and legislated throughout the first half of the 1990s.

DATA APPENDIX

This appendix reports annual data, in current dollars, for currency, reserves, monetary base (high-powered money), all deposits included in *M*2, and the federal funds rate.

DATA FOR MONEY SUPPLY PROCESS

year	currency	reserves	base	deposits	fed funds
1960	28.767	11.254	40.021	282.233	3.216
1961	29.200	11.465	40.665	304.200	1.956
1962	30.200	11.515	41.715	329.767	2.682
1963	32.000	11.578	43.578	359.167	3.178
1964	33.767	11.966	45.732	388.367	3.497
1965	35.800	12.147	47.974	420.267	4.073
1966	37.833	12.209	50.042	440.033	5.112
1967	39.767	13.133	52.900	481.633	4.219
1968	42.700	13.648	56.348	519.533	5.658
1969	45.467	14.081	59.548	541.367	8.207
1970	48.333	14.503	62.836	574.333	7.181
1971	51.867	15.229	67.096	654.800	4.662
1972	55.700	16.426	72.126	741.433	4.431
1973	60.300	16.974	77.274	794.367	8.728
1974	66.467	17.451	83.917	838.333	10.503
1975	72.300	17.753	90.053	942.000	5.824
1976	79.067	18.268	97.335	1,070.433	5.046
1977	86.633	18.988	105.622	1,191.733	5.538
1978	95.200	19.911	115.111	1,285.133	7.931
1979	104.433	20.498	124.931	1,387.467	11.194
1980	114.533	21.771	136.304	1,510.733	13.356
1981	121.467	22.359	143.826	1,655.133	16.378
1982	131.667	23.281	154.948	1,806.367	12.258

(continued on next page)

DATA FOR MONEY SUPPLY PROCESS *(continued)*

year	currency	reserves	base	deposits	fed funds
1983	145.200	25.406	170.606	2,030.167	9.087
1984	155.467	26.570	182.037	2,194.167	10.225
1985	167.067	30.979	198.046	2,386.600	8.101
1986	179.533	37.567	217.100	2,609.367	6.805
1987	195.133	39.446	234.579	2,713.433	6.658
1988	211.100	40.526	251.626	2,849.467	7.568
1989	221.233	40.343	261.577	2,985.700	9.217
1990	245.467	41.246	286.713	3,090.267	8.099
1991	266.033	44.841	310.875	3,163.733	5.688
1992	290.300	53.897	344.197	3,212.300	3.530

STABILIZATION POLICY: PROSPECTS AND PROBLEMS

S tabilization policy seems to be easy in the basic macroeconomic models set out in Chapters 3–8: in recession, use expansionary monetary and fiscal policy; in booms and when inflation is too high, use contractionary policy.

If stabilization policy were that simple, recessions would be rare and brief, and inflation would always be low. Evidently stabilization policy is not so simple. In part that is because the goals of keeping both inflation and unemployment low sometimes conflict. We have already discussed the Phillips curve in Chapters 7 and 8, and we will return to the tradeoffs between inflation and unemployment in Chapters 16 and 17.

In this chapter we discuss other problems in using stabilization policies. The modern approach to stabilization policy developed out of the great depression, knowledge of which is still, 60 years later, essential to understanding both modern economics and the U.S. economy. We start by describing the events of the great depression and the New Economics that it spawned, with its emphasis on the potential for active policy, particularly fiscal policy, to help stabilize the economy.

Then we turn to technical problems in policy making, which imply that policy cannot be expected to keep the economy always close to full employment with low inflation. In a nutshell, we will argue that a policy maker who (1) observes a disturbance, (2) does not know whether it is permanent or not, and (3) takes time to develop a policy that (4) takes still more time to affect behavior and (5) has uncertain effects on aggregate demand, is very poorly equipped to do a perfect job of stabilizing the economy. When the economy is far from full employment, stabilization policy has a clear target and is bound to work. Near full employment, however, policies intended to stabilize the economy can easily go wrong.

15-1 THE GREAT DEPRESSION

The great depression shaped modern macroeconomics as well as many institutions in the economy, including the Fed. The essential facts about the depression are presented in Figure 15-1 and in Table 15-1.

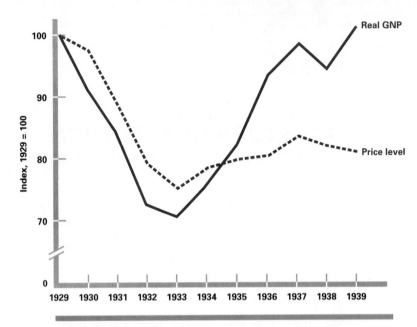

FIGURE 15-1
OUTPUT AND PRICES IN THE GREAT DEPRESSION, 1929–1939. (SOURCE:
U.S. Department of Commerce, *The National Income and Product
Accounts of the United States,* 1929–1974, and *Economic Report of
the President,* 1957.)

The best-known fact about the great depression is the stock market crash. Between September 1929 and June 1932, the market fell by 85 percent, which means that stocks worth $1,000 at the stock market peak were worth only $150 at the bottom of the market in 1932. The depression and the stock market crash are popularly thought of as almost the same thing. In fact, the economy started turning down in August 1929, before the stock market crash, and continued falling until 1933.

Between 1929 and 1933, GNP fell by nearly 30 percent and the unemployment rate rose from 3 to 25 percent. Until early 1931, the economy was suffering from a very severe depression, but not one that was out of the range of the experience of the previous century.[1] It was in the period from early 1931 until Franklin Roosevelt became president in March 1933 that the depression became "great." More than anything else, the great depression is remembered for the mass unemployment that it brought. For the 10 years 1931 to 1940, the unemployment rate averaged 18.8 percent, ranging

---

[1]The classic work by Milton Friedman and Anna J. Schwartz, *A Monetary History of the United States, 1867–1960* (Princeton, N.J.: Princeton University Press, 1963), gives a very detailed account of the great depression, comparing it with other recessions and emphasizing the role of the Fed.

TABLE 15-1

ECONOMIC STATISTICS OF THE GREAT DEPRESSION

year	GNP, 1972, $ billion (1)	I/GNP, % (2)	G, 1972, $ billion (3)	unemploy- ment rate, % (4)	CPI, 1929 = 100 (5)	commer- cial paper rate, % (6)	AAA rate, % (7)	Stock market index (8)	M1, 1929 = 100 (9)	full- employ- ment surplus/ Y*, % (10)
1929	314.7	17.8	40.9	3.2	100.0	5.9	4.7	83.1	100.0	−0.8
1930	285.2	13.5	44.6	8.7	97.4	3.6	4.6	67.2	96.2	−1.4
1931	263.3	9.0	46.2	15.9	88.7	2.6	4.6	43.6	89.4	−3.1
1932	226.8	3.5	44.0	23.6	79.7	2.7	5.0	22.1	78.0	−0.9
1933	222.1	3.8	42.8	24.9	75.4	1.7	4.5	28.6	73.5	1.6
1934	239.4	5.5	48.7	21.7	78.0	1.0	4.0	31.4	81.4	0.2
1935	260.8	9.2	49.8	20.1	80.1	0.8	3.6	33.9	96.6	−0.1
1936	296.1	10.9	58.5	16.9	80.9	0.8	3.2	49.4	110.6	−1.1
1937	309.8	12.8	56.3	14.3	83.3	0.9	3.3	49.2	114.8	1.8
1938	297.1	8.1	61.3	19.0	82.3	0.8	3.2	36.7	115.9	0.6
1939	319.7	10.5	63.8	17.2	81.0	0.6	3.0	38.5	127.3	−0.1

NOTE: Stock market index is Standard & Poor's composite index, which includes 500 stocks; September 1929 = 100. *Y** denotes full-employment output.

SOURCES: *Cols. 1, 2, 3:* U.S. Department of Commerce, *The National Income and Product Accounts of the United States,* 1929–1974. *Col. 4:* Revised Bureau of Labor Statistics data taken from Michael Darby, "Three-and-a-Half Million U.S. Employees Have Been Mislaid: Or, an Explanation of Unemployment, 1934–1941," *Journal of Political Economy,* February 1976. *Cols. 5, 6, 7: Economic Report of the President,* 1957. *Col. 8:* Standard & Poor's Statistical Service, *Security Price Index Record,* 1978. *Col. 9:* Milton Friedman and Anna J. Schwartz, *A Monetary History of the United States, 1867–1960* (Princeton, N.J.: Princeton University Press, 1963), table A1, col. 7. *Col. 10:* E. Cary Brown, "Fiscal Policy in the Thirties: A Reappraisal," *American Economic Review,* December 1956, table 1, cols. 3, 5, and 19.

between a low of 14.3 percent in 1937 and a high of 24.9 percent in 1933.[2] By contrast, the post–World War II high, reached in 1982, was under 11 percent.

Investment collapsed in the great depression; indeed, net investment was negative from 1931 to 1935. The consumer price index fell nearly 25 percent from 1929 to 1933; the stock market fell 80 percent between September 1929 and March 1933.

In the recovery, from 1933 to 1937, real GNP grew at a rapid annual rate of nearly 9 percent, but even that did not get the unemployment rate down to normal levels. Then, in 1937–1938 there was a major recession within the depression, pushing the unemployment rate back up to nearly 20 percent. In the second half of the decade, short-term interest rates, such as the commercial paper rate, were near zero.

---

[2]Michael Darby, "Three-and-a-Half Million U.S. Employees Have Been Mislaid: Or, an Explanation of Unemployment, 1934–1941," *Journal of Political Economy,* February 1976. Darby argues that unemployment is mismeasured after 1933 because those on government work relief programs were counted as unemployed. Adjusted for those individuals, the unemployment rate fell rapidly from 20.6 percent in 1933 to below 10 percent in 1936. See also Thomas Mayer, "Money and the Great Depression: A Critique of Professor Temin's Thesis," *Explorations in Economic History,* April 1978, and Karl Brunner (ed.), *The Great Depression Revisited* (Boston: Martinus Nijhoff, 1981).

The two most important questions raised by these events are, Why did this happen? and Could it have been prevented? Whenever the economy is in recession economists are asked—and they ask themselves—Could "it" happen again?

Economic Policy

What was economic policy during this period? The money stock already fell nearly 4 percent from 1929 to 1930, and then fell rapidly in 1931 and 1932 and continued falling through April 1933.

The fall in the money stock was in part the result of large-scale bank failures. Banks failed because they did not have the reserves with which to meet customers' cash withdrawals,[3] and in failing they destroyed deposits and hence reduced the money stock. But the failures went further in reducing the money stock, because they led to a loss of confidence on the part of depositors and hence to an even higher desired currency-deposit ratio. Furthermore, banks that had not yet failed adjusted to the possibility of a run by holding increased reserves relative to deposits. The rise in the currency-deposit ratio and the reserve-deposit ratio reduced the money multiplier and hence sharply contracted the money stock.

The Fed took very few steps to offset the fall in the money supply. For a few months in 1932 it did undertake a program of open market purchases, but otherwise it seemed to acquiesce in bank closings and certainly failed to understand that the central bank should act vigorously in a crisis to prevent the collapse of the financial system.[4]

Fiscal policy, too, was weak. The natural impulse of politicians then was to balance the budget in times of trouble, and much rhetoric was devoted to that proposition. The presidential candidates campaigned on balanced budget platforms in 1932. In fact, as Table 15-2 shows, the federal government ran large deficits, particularly for that time, averaging 2.6 percent of GNP from 1931 to 1933 and even more later. (These actual deficits are lower as a percentage of GNP than those in the early 1990s.) The belief in budget balancing was more than rhetoric, however, for state and local governments raised taxes to match their expenditures, as did the federal government, particularly in 1932 and 1933. President Roosevelt tried seriously to balance the budget—he was no Keynesian. The full-employment surplus shows fiscal policy (combined state, local, and federal) as most expansionary in 1931 and moving to a more contractionary level from 1932 to 1934. In fact, the full-employment surplus was positive in 1933 and 1934, despite the actual deficits. Of course, the concept of the full-employment surplus had not yet been invented in the 1930s.

Economic activity recovered in the period from 1933 to 1937, with fiscal policy becoming more expansionary and the money stock growing rapidly. The growth of the money stock was based on an inflow of gold from Europe. This provided high-

---

[3]We discussed bank runs in Chap. 14.

[4]Friedman and Schwartz speculate on the reasons for the Fed's inaction; the whodunit or who didn't do it on pp. 407–419 of their book (cited in footnote 1) is fascinating.

TABLE 15-2
GOVERNMENT SPENDING AND REVENUE (percent)

year	TOTAL GOVERNMENT		FEDERAL GOVERNMENT		total government: full-employment surplus/Y*
	expenditure/ GNP	actual surplus/ GNP	expenditure/ GNP	actual surplus/ GNP	
1929	10.0	1.0	2.5	1.2	−0.8
1930	12.3	−0.3	3.1	0.3	−1.4
1931	16.4	−3.8	5.5	−2.8	−3.1
1932	18.3	−3.1	5.5	−2.6	−0.9
1933	19.2	−2.5	7.2	−2.3	1.6
1934	19.8	−3.7	9.8	−4.4	0.2
1935	18.6	−2.8	9.0	−3.6	−0.1
1936	19.5	−3.8	10.5	−4.4	−1.1
1937	16.6	0.3	8.2	0.4	1.8
1938	19.8	−2.1	10.2	−2.5	0.6
1939	19.4	−2.4	9.8	−2.4	−0.1

NOTE: Total government includes federal, state, and local. Y* denotes potential output.

SOURCES: *Cols. 1, 2, 3, 4: Economic Report of the President*, 1972, tables B1 and B70. *Col. 5:* E. Cary Brown, "Fiscal Policy in the Thirties: A Reappraisal," *American Economic Review*, December 1956, table 1, cols. 3, 5, and 19.

powered money for the monetary system. It was in the 1930s that the Fed acquired most of its current holdings of gold.

Institutional Change

The period from 1933 to 1937 also saw substantial legislative and administrative action—the *New Deal*—from the Roosevelt administration. The Fed was reorganized, and the Federal Deposit Insurance Corporation (FDIC) was established.

The Social Security Administration was set up so that the elderly would not have to rely on their own savings to ensure themselves a minimally adequate standard of living in retirement. By the mid-1990s, social welfare payments will be the biggest single item in the federal budget.

A number of regulatory agencies were also created, most notably the Securities and Exchange Commission, which regulates the securities industry. Its purpose was to prevent speculative excesses that were thought to be largely responsible for the stock market crash. The Roosevelt administration also believed that the route to recovery lay in increasing wages and prices, so it encouraged trade unionization, as well as price-raising and price-fixing schemes by business, through the National Recovery Administration.

TABLE 15-3

WORLD PRODUCTION AND TRADE, 1929–1935

(1929 = 100)

	1929	1932	1933	1935
Production	100	69	78	95
Trade				
Volume	100	75	76	82
Prices	100	53	47	42

SOURCE: League of Nations, *World Economic Survey 1935/36.*

International Aspects

The great depression was virtually worldwide. To some extent, this was the result of the collapse of the international financial system.[5] It resulted, too, from the mutual adoption by many countries (including the United States) of high-tariff policies, which were intended to protect domestic producers by keeping out foreign goods.

The policies were called "beggar-thy-neighbor" strategies (see Chapter 6) since they attempted to "export" unemployment by improving one country's trade position and hence demand for its goods at the expense of its trading partners. And, of course, if each country keeps out foreign goods, the volume of world trade declines, providing a contractionary influence on the world economy. Table 15-3 documents the decline in *world* production and in world trade.

Almost every country suffered a deep recession in the 1930s, but some countries did better than the United States. Sweden began an expansionary policy in the early 1930s and reduced its unemployment relatively fast in the second half of the decade. Britain's economy suffered high unemployment in both the 1920s and the 1930s. In 1931, Britain went off gold and the devaluation set the stage for at least some improvement. Germany grew rapidly after Hitler came to power and expanded government spending. China escaped the recession until after 1931, essentially because it had a floating exchange rate. As always, there is much to be learned from the exceptions.[6]

In 1939, real GNP in the United States rose above its 1929 level for the first time in the decade. But it was not until 1942, after the United States formally entered World War II, that the unemployment rate finally fell below 5 percent.

---

[5]This aspect of the depression is emphasized by Charles Kindleberger, *The World in Depression, 1929–1939* (Berkeley: University of California Press, 1986), and Gottfried Haberler, *The World Economy, Money and the Great Depression* (Washington, D.C.: American Enterprise Institute, 1976).

[6]A particularly valuable source on the international experience is Barry Eichengreen, *Golden Fetters* (New York: Oxford University Press, 1992). The central thesis of this book is that adherence to the gold standard forced countries into deflation and only after gold was abandoned could recovery start. The devaluation of sterling in 1931 is also discussed in Alec Cairncross and Barry Eichengreen, *Sterling in Decline* (Oxford: Basil Blackwell, 1983).

15-2 THE GREAT DEPRESSION: THE ISSUES AND IDEAS

The depression was the greatest economic crisis the western world had experienced. In the 1930s, by contrast with 1990, it was the economy of the Soviet Union that was booming while western economies seemed to be collapsing. The questions of what caused the great depression, whether it could have been avoided, and whether it could happen again have therefore to be taken seriously.

The classical economics of the time had no well-developed theory that would explain persistent unemployment nor any policy prescriptions to solve the problem. Many economists then did, in fact, recommend government spending as a way of reducing unemployment, but they had no macroeconomic theory by which to justify their recommendations.

Keynes wrote his great work, *The General Theory of Employment, Interest and Money,* in the 1930s, after Britain had suffered during the 1920s from a decade of double-digit unemployment and while the United States was in the depths of its depression. He was fully aware of the seriousness of the issues. As Don Patinkin of the Hebrew University puts it:[7]

> ... the period was one of fear and darkness as the Western world struggled with the greatest depression that it had known. ... [T]here was a definite feeling that by attempting to achieve a scientific understanding of the phenomenon of mass unemployment, one was not only making an intellectual contribution, but was also dealing with a critical problem that endangered the very existence of Western civilization.

Keynesian theory explained what had happened, what could have been done to prevent the depression, and what could be done to prevent future depressions. The explanation soon became accepted by most macroeconomists, in the process described as the Keynesian revolution, even though the Keynesian revolution did not have much impact on economic policy making in the United States until the 1960s.

The Keynesian Explanation

The essence of the Keynesian explanation of the great depression is contained in the simple aggregate demand model. Growth in the 1920s, in this view, was based on the mass production of the automobile and radio and was fueled by a housing boom. The collapse of growth in the 1930s resulted from the drying up of investment opportunities and a downward shift in investment demand. The collapse of investment, shown in Table 15-1, fits in with this picture. Some researchers also believe there was a downward shift in the consumption function in 1930.[8] Poor fiscal policy, as reflected in the perverse behavior of the full-employment surplus from 1931 to 1933, shares the blame, particularly for making the depression worse.

---

[7] In "The Process of Writing *The General Theory*: A Critical Survey," in Don Patinkin and J. Clark Leith (eds.), *Keynes, Cambridge and the General Theory* (Toronto: University of Toronto Press, 1978), p. 3. For a biography of Keynes, see D. E. Moggridge, *John Maynard Keynes* (New York: Macmillan, 1990).

[8] Peter Temin, *Did Monetary Forces Cause the Great Depression?* (New York: Norton, 1976).

It was also widely believed that the experience of the depression showed that the private economy was inherently unstable in that it could self-depress with no difficulty if left alone. The experience of the 1930s was, implicitly or explicitly, the basis for the belief that an active stabilization policy was needed to maintain good economic performance.

The Keynesian model not only offered an explanation of what had happened, but also suggested policy measures that could have been taken to prevent the depression, and that could be used to prevent future depressions. Vigorous use of countercyclical fiscal policy was the preferred method for reducing cyclical fluctuations. If a recession ever showed signs of deteriorating into a depression, the cure would be to cut taxes and increase government spending. And those policies would, too, have prevented the depression from being as deep as it was.

What about monetary factors in the depression? The Fed argued in the 1930s that there was little it could have done to prevent the depression, because interest rates were already as low as they could possibly go. A variety of sayings of the type, "You can lead a horse to water but you can't make it drink," were used to explain that further reductions in interest rates would have had no effect if there was no demand for investment. Investment demand was thought to be very unresponsive to the rate of interest—implying a very steep *IS* curve. At the same time, the *LM* curve was believed to be quite flat, though not necessarily reaching the extreme of a liquidity trap. In this situation, monetary expansion would be relatively ineffective in stimulating demand and output.

There is nothing in the *IS-LM* model developed in Chapter 4 that suggests that fiscal policy is more useful than monetary policy for stabilization of the economy. Nonetheless, it is true that until the 1950s, Keynesians tended to give more emphasis to fiscal than to monetary policy.

The Monetarist Challenge

The Keynesian emphasis on fiscal policy, and its downplaying of the role of money, was challenged by Milton Friedman and his coworkers during the 1950s.[9] They emphasized the role of monetary policy in determining the behavior of both output and prices.

If monetary policy was to be given an important role, though, it was necessary to dispose of the view that monetary policy had been tried in the great depression and had failed. In other words, the view that "You can lead a horse to the water, etc.," had to be challenged.

The view that monetary policy in the thirties had been impotent was attacked in 1963 by Friedman and Schwartz in their *Monetary History*. They argued that the depression, far from showing that money does not matter, "is in fact a tragic testimonial to the importance of monetary factors."[10] They argued, with skill and style, that the failure of the Fed to prevent bank failures and the decline of the money stock from

---

[9] See, in particular, Milton Friedman (ed.), *Studies in the Quantity Theory of Money* (Chicago: University of Chicago Press, 1956).

[10] Friedman and Schwartz, *A Monetary History of the United States,* p. 300.

the end of 1930 to 1933 was largely responsible for the recession's being as serious as it was. This monetary view, in turn, came close to being accepted as the orthodox explanation of the depression.[11]

Synthesis

Both the Keynesian and the monetarist explanations of the great depression fit the facts, and both provide answers to the questions of why it happened and how to prevent it from happening again. Both inept fiscal and inept monetary policies made the great depression severe. If there had been prompt, strong, expansive monetary and fiscal policy, the economy would have suffered a recession but not the trauma it did.

On the question of whether it could happen again, there is agreement that it could not, except, of course, in the event of truly perverse policies. But these are less likely now than they were then. For one thing, we have history to help us avoid its repetition. Taxes would not again be raised in the middle of a depression, nor would attempts be made to balance the budget. The Fed would seek actively to keep the money supply from falling, and it would not allow bank failures to reduce the money stock. In addition, the government now has a much larger role in the economy than it did then, and automatic stabilizers, including the income tax and unemployment insurance, reduce the size of the multiplier and hence the impact of demand shocks on output.

One example of policy makers responding rapidly to the threat of financial crisis was seen immediately after the worldwide October 19, 1987, stock market crash. On that day and the next, stock markets around the world fell by 15–20 percent. Conscious of the history of the great depression, the Fed publicly and clearly stated that it would lend as needed to prevent financial collapse, and it immediately undertook open market operations, driving down the interest rate sharply as it undertook expansionary monetary policy. The Fed's actions, and those of other major central banks, helped to contain the panic and prevented it from affecting output.

If, as we argue, there is no inherent conflict between the Keynesian and monetarist explanations of the great depression, why has there been controversy over its causes? The reason is that the 1930s are seen as the period that set the stage for massive government intervention in the economy. Those opposed to an active role for government have to explain away the debacle of the economy in the 1930s. If the depression occurred because of, and not despite, the government (particularly the Fed), the case for an active government role in economic stabilization is weakened. Further, the 1930s are a period in which the economy behaved in such an extreme way that competing theories have to be subjected to the test of whether they can explain that period.

---

[11] Ben Bernanke, in "Nonmonetary Effects of the Financial Crisis in the Propagation of the Great Depression," *American Economic Review,* June 1983, takes issue with the monetary view, arguing instead that the destruction of the financial system made it difficult for borrowers to obtain funds needed for investment. However, there is no conflict between that argument and the view that more decisive monetary policy by the Fed in 1930 and 1931 would have mitigated the depression.

15-3 THE NEW ECONOMICS

Following the 1930s and the writing of Keynes and his followers, Keynesian economics was rapidly accepted by most macroeconomists, but it affected policy less rapidly. The budget was used as a countercyclical policy tool in Britain in the entire post–World War II period. In the United States, the Employment Act of 1946 required that the government follow policies to produce high employment. Nonetheless, it was not until the Kennedy administration in the early 1960s that a U.S. administration began to follow avowedly Keynesian policies.

The approach was described as the *New Economics*. The analytical approach of the New Economics consists basically of the tools we have outlined in Chapters 3 through 13 (with the exception of Chapter 9). The philosophy characterizing that approach to economics is a mix of activism and optimism. It is well characterized by an excerpt from the 1962 *Economic Report of the President*:[12]

> Insufficient demand means unemployment, idle capacity, and lost production. Excessive demand means inflation—general increases in prices and money incomes, bringing forth little or no gains in output and real income. The objective of stabilization policies is to minimize these deviations, i.e., to keep overall demand in step with the basic production potential of the economy.
>
> Stabilization does not mean a mere leveling off of peaks and troughs in production and employment. . . . It means minimizing deviations from a rising trend, not from an unchanging average. In a growing economy, demand must grow in order to maintain full employment of labor and full utilization of capacity at stable prices. The economy is not performing satisfactorily unless it is almost continuously setting new records of production, income, and employment. . . .

In the 1930s, policy fumbled, and badly, for some way to get the economy moving again. The Roosevelt administration did run budget deficits, but most unwillingly, and it had no concept of the full-employment surplus. In the 1960s, in marked contrast, policy makers came into a not very difficult economic situation with well-thought-out theories and policies to apply. Those policies were based on the Keynesian analysis that developed in the 1930s and on the experience of that decade. The Kennedy-Johnson administration made the concept of the full-employment budget a central tenet of fiscal policy. It called for a tax cut in 1963–1964 even though the budget was already in deficit, and it sold the policy to a skeptical Congress.

We briefly review the basic analytical concepts of the New Economics before concluding this section by discussing what was new in the New Economics.

Potential Output and the GNP Gap

To focus attention on the target of full employment and for use as an operating guide to policy, the *Council of Economic Advisers* (CEA), and particularly the late Arthur

---

[12]President Kennedy's Council of Economic Advisers was served by many distinguished economists, among them three who later won the Nobel Prize: James Tobin of Yale, Kenneth Arrow of Stanford, and Robert Solow of MIT. A fourth Nobel laureate, Paul Samuelson, served as an unofficial adviser.

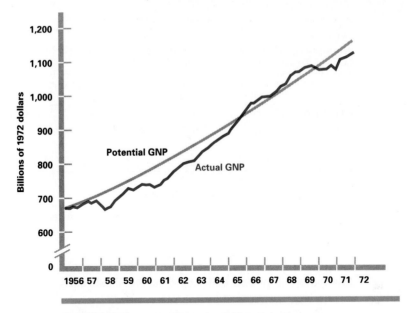

FIGURE 15-2

ACTUAL AND POTENTIAL GNP, 1956–1971. (SOURCE: *Survey of Current Business,* April 1982 and 1983, and DRI/McGraw-Hill.)

Okun, developed and stressed the concept of potential output. Potential output or full-employment output, introduced in Chapter 1, measures the level of real GNP the economy can produce with full employment. The full-employment rate of unemployment used in defining potential output in the 1960s was about 4 percent, below the rates of 5 to 6 percent used more recently. Figure 15-2 shows potential output for the 1956–1971 period.

Along with the concept and measurement of potential output went the notion of the GNP gap.[13] The gap is the difference between actual and potential real output. For the years 1961–1965, actual GNP was below its potential level, and the GNP gap was therefore positive. At the beginning of 1961, the GNP gap was more than 7 percent of GNP. A gap of that magnitude clearly called for expansionary monetary or fiscal policy to raise aggregate demand to a level closer to the economy's potential.

Although the notions of potential output and the GNP gap seem very simple, they dramatize the costs of unemployment in easily understood terms—and that is very important in the political context in which economic policy decisions are made.

The Full-Employment Budget Surplus

The full-employment budget concept is important and useful because it directs attention away from the automatic effect of the business cycle on the actual budget. In recessions

---

[13] Until 1992, the U.S. used GNP rather than GDP as its basic measure of output.

TABLE 15-4

BUDGET DEFICITS, 1985–1992 (percent of GNP, federal government)

	actual deficit	full-employment deficit	unemployment rate
1985–1989	4.0	3.4	6.2
1990	4.0	2.7	5.5
1991	4.8	2.9	6.8
1992*	6.3	3.1	7.2

*Estimate.

SOURCE: Congressional Budget Office and DRI/McGraw-Hill.

there are deficits in the actual budget, but that should not be an obstacle to antirecessionary stimuli.

The New Economists planned to use fiscal policy as the instrument with which to close the GNP gap. It was important for them to get across to Congress and the public the idea of the full-employment surplus because the federal budget was in actual deficit. Herbert Stein, chairman of the CEA under President Nixon, reviews the progress toward the major policy measure of the early 1960s, the 1964 tax cut, in his book *The Fiscal Revolution in America*.[14] He shows how both the Kennedy administration and the Congress had to get accustomed to the idea that a tax cut that increased the budget deficit during a recession was not necessarily a step toward fiscal irresponsibility.

The contrast between the scope for fiscal policy in the sluggish economies of the early 1960s and early 1990s is very clear. In the early 1960s, the full-employment budget was in surplus so that a tax cut was very plausible. In 1990–1992, even though the economy was sluggish, the full-employment budget had been in deficit for a decade, and the easy arguments of the 1960s could no longer be marshaled to support further fiscal stimulus (see Table 15-4).

Growth and Inflation

The New Economics emphasized economic growth in two ways. First, aggregate demand needed to grow in order to achieve full employment. In that respect, growth was a matter of achieving full employment and maintaining it. Second, there was an emphasis on achieving a high rate of growth of potential output itself. The focus was on investment spending to encourage growth in productive potential—a supply side emphasis. To that end the administration introduced an investment tax credit in 1962.

The New Economics emphasized the behavior of money wages in affecting the rate of inflation. Early in the Kennedy-Johnson years, in 1962, the CEA set up *guideposts*

---

[14]Herbert Stein, *The Fiscal Revolution in America* (Chicago: University of Chicago Press, 1969).

for the behavior of money wages.[15] The basic guidepost was that money wages should not grow faster than the average rate at which labor productivity was increasing in the economy. Labor productivity is the ratio of output to labor input.

When productivity is growing, less labor is being used to produce the same amount of goods. Thus if wages are growing as fast as productivity, the labor costs of producing a good are constant. Assuming, as the New Economics did, that prices are set as a markup on labor costs, prices would not rise if wages were rising no faster than productivity. This argument also implies that more rapid investment—which contributes to productivity increases—can help reduce inflation from the supply side.

What was new in the New Economics was not the analysis, which was by then standard macroeconomics, but rather the active and successful use of that analysis in the operation of U.S. macroeconomic policy.

The New Economics and the Economy

The most ambitious and successful policy action of the Kennedy-Johnson administration was the tax cut of 1964.[16] The tax cut kept the economy growing rapidly through the mid-1960s, thus reducing the unemployment rate. At the same time, as Figure 15-3 shows, the inflation rate stayed below 3 percent per year.

Through the middle of the 1960s, the economy was behaving as well as it ever has. Productivity growth was high, output was growing fast, unemployment was falling, and the inflation rate was low. It is little wonder that there was considerable optimism about the possibilities of the New Economics.

Things began to go wrong in the late 1960s. Much of the problem was political. Government spending for the Vietnam war was rising rapidly, but President Johnson feared that a tax increase would make the war more unpopular. In 1966 and 1967, it was left to monetary policy to fight the increasing expansionary pressure of fiscal policy. Only in 1968 was the Johnson administration willing to ask Congress for a tax increase to try to contain the expansionary pressure of military spending.

A transitory tax increase was enacted, but the contractionary effect was less than expected and the impact on inflation negligible.[17] Thus by 1969 the inflation rate exceeded 5 percent. To be sure, the unemployment rate was below 4 percent, and the economy was still in the longest economic expansion on record.

The record of the 1960s is one of full employment, expansion, and rising inflation. Keynesian economics, or the New Economics, received the popular credit for the expansion of the mid-1960s following the tax cut. Similarly, it received the blame for

---

[15] For an interesting, and sometimes amusing, discussion of the guideposts, see George P. Shultz (a University of Chicago economist and later Secretary of State) and Robert Z. Aliber (eds.), *Guidelines* (Chicago: University of Chicago Press, 1966).

[16] The classic analysis of the tax cut is presented in Arthur Okun's "Measuring the Impact of the 1964 Tax Reduction," in his book *Economics for Policymaking* (Cambridge, Mass.: MIT Press, 1983).

[17] For an explanation, which relies on the fact that a temporary tax increase has only a small effect on permanent income and therefore on consumption, see Robert Eisner, "What Went Wrong?" *Journal of Political Economy,* May/June 1971.

FIGURE 15-3
INFLATION AND UNEMPLOYMENT, 1961–1970. (Source: DRI/McGraw-Hill.)

the rising inflation. The rising inflation that accompanied the expansion in output opened up the question of whether active monetary and fiscal policy could be used successfully to control the economy, to which we now turn.

15-4 LAGS IN THE EFFECTS OF POLICY

Suppose that the economy is at full employment and has been affected by an aggregate demand disturbance that reduces the equilibrium level of income below full employment. Suppose further that there was no advance warning of this disturbance and that, consequently, no policy actions were taken in anticipation of its occurrence. Policy makers now have to decide *whether to respond at all* and *how* to respond to the disturbance.

The first concern is to distinguish whether a disturbance is *permanent,* or at least very persistent, or *transitory* and short-lived. Suppose the disturbance is only transitory, such as a one-period reduction in consumption spending. When the disturbance is transitory, so that consumption rapidly reverts to its initial level, the best policy may be to do nothing at all. Provided suppliers or producers do not mistakenly interpret the decrease in demand as permanent but, rather, perceive it as transitory, they will absorb it by production and inventory changes rather than by capacity adjustments. The disturbance will affect income in this period but will have very little permanent effect. Since today's policy actions take time to have an effect, today's actions would

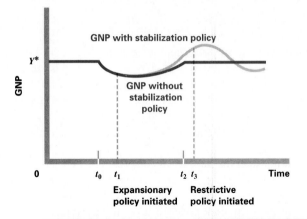

FIGURE 15-4
LAGS AND DESTABILIZING POLICY. A disturbance at time t_0 reduces
output below the full-employment level. It takes until t_1 before policy
responds, and there is a further lag until the policy starts working.
By the time the full effects of the policy are evident, output would
already have returned to the full-employment level even without
action. But because a policy action has been taken, output now rises
above the full-employment level and then fluctuates around Y^*. The
lags in policy thus have made policy a source of fluctuations in
output that would not otherwise have happened.

be hitting an economy that would otherwise have been close to full employment, and
would tend to move the economy *away* from the full-employment level. Thus, if a
disturbance is temporary and it has no long-lived effects and policy operates with a
lag, then the best policy is to do nothing.

Figure 15-4 illustrates the main idea. Assume that an aggregate demand disturbance reduces output below potential, starting at time t_0. Without active policy intervention output declines for a while but then recovers and reaches the full-employment
level again at time t_2. Consider next the path of GDP under an active stabilization
policy, but one that works with the disadvantage of lags. Thus, expansionary policy
might be initiated at time t_1 and start taking effect some time after. Output now tends
to recover faster as a consequence of the expansion but, because of poor dosage and/
or timing, actually overshoots the full-employment level. By time t_3, restrictive policy
is initiated, and some time after, output starts turning down toward full employment
and may well continue cycling for a while.

If this were an accurate description of the potency or scope of stabilization policy,
then one has to ask whether it is worth trying to stabilize output or whether the effect
of stabilization policy is, in fact, to make things worse. Stabilization policy may actually
destabilize the economy.

One of the main difficulties of policy making is in establishing whether or not
a disturbance is temporary. It was clear enough in the case of World War II that a
high level of defense expenditures would be required for some years. However, in the

case of the Arab oil embargo of 1973–1974, it was not at all clear how long the embargo would last or whether the high prices for oil that were established in late 1973 would persist. At the time, there were many who argued that the oil cartel would not survive and that oil prices would soon fall—that is, that the disturbance was temporary. "Soon" turned out to be 12 years.

Let us suppose, however, that it is known that the disturbance will have effects that will last for several quarters and that the level of income will, without intervention, be below the full-employment level for some time. What lags do policy makers encounter?

We now consider the steps required before action can be taken after a disturbance has occurred, and then the process by which that policy action affects the economy. There are delays, or lags, at every stage. These can be divided into two stages: an *inside lag,* which is the time period it takes to undertake a policy action—such as a tax cut or an increase in the money supply—and an *outside lag,* which describes the timing of the effects of the policy action on the economy. The inside lag, in turn, is divided into recognition, decision, and action lags.

The Recognition Lag

The *recognition lag* is the period that elapses between the time a disturbance occurs and the time the policy makers recognize that action is required. This lag could, in principle, be *negative* if the disturbance could be predicted and appropriate policy actions considered *before* it even occurs. For example, we know that seasonal factors affect behavior. Thus it is known that at Christmas the demand for currency is high. Rather than allow this to exert a restrictive effect on the money supply, the Fed will accommodate this seasonal demand by an expansion in high-powered money.

In other cases the recognition lag has been positive, so that time has elapsed between the disturbance and the recognition that active policy was required. Solow and Kareken long ago studied the history of policy making and concluded that on average the recognition lag had been about 5 months.[18] The lag was found to be somewhat shorter when the required policy was expansionary and somewhat longer when restrictive policy was required. The speed with which tax cuts follow sharp increases in unemployment was clearly evident in both 1975 and 1980.

The Decision and Action Lags

The *decision lag*—the delay between the recognition of the need for action and the policy decision—differs between monetary and fiscal policy. The Federal Reserve System's Open Market Committee meets frequently to discuss and decide on policy. Thus, once the need for a policy action has been recognized, the decision lag for monetary policy is short. Further, the *action lag*—the lag between the policy decision

---

[18] See John Kareken and Robert Solow, "Lags in Monetary Policy," in *Stabilization Policies,* prepared for the Commission on Money and Credit (Englewood Cliffs, N.J.: Prentice-Hall, 1963).

and its implementation—for monetary policy is also short. The major monetary policy actions, we have seen, are open market operations and changes in the discount rate. These policy actions can be undertaken almost as soon as a decision has been made. Thus, under the existing arrangements of the Federal Reserve System, the decision lag for monetary policy is short and the action lag practically zero.

However, fiscal policy actions are less rapid. Once the need for a fiscal policy action has been recognized, the administration has to prepare legislation for that action. Next, the legislation has to be considered and approved by both houses of Congress before the policy change can be made. That may be a lengthy process. Even after the legislation has been approved, the policy change has still to be put into effect. If the fiscal policy takes the form of a change in tax rates, it may be some time before the change in tax rates begins to be reflected in paychecks—that is, there may be an action lag. On occasion, though, as in early 1975 when taxes were reduced, the fiscal decision lag may be short; in 1975 it was about 2 months.

Built-in Stabilizers

The existence of the inside lag in policy making focuses attention on the built-in or automatic stabilizers that we discussed in Chapter 3. One of the major benefits of automatic stabilizers is that their inside lag is zero. The most important automatic stabilizer is the income tax. It stabilizes the economy by reducing the multiplier effects of any disturbance to aggregate demand. The multiplier for the effects of changes in autonomous spending on GNP is inversely related to the income tax rate. Similarly, unemployment compensation is another automatic stabilizer. When workers become unemployed and reduce their consumption, that reduction in consumption demand tends to have multiplier effects on output. Those multiplier effects are reduced when a worker receives unemployment compensation because disposable income is reduced by less than the loss in earnings.

Figure 15-5 shows the practical importance of automatic stabilizers (and active fiscal policy) in the U.S. economy. The figure shows personal disposable income as a percentage of GDP. Personal disposable income is the income that actually accrues to households after all taxes and inclusive of all transfers. The figure brings out the fact that during periods of recession personal disposable income rises relative to GDP. In those periods, transfer payments rise and the growth in income tax collection slows. To be precise, the chart reflects both automatic stabilizers and discretionary changes in taxes and transfers. Thus, the increase in the ratio in 1975 reflects not only automatic transfers but also the tax rebate of early 1975.

Although built-in stabilizers have desirable effects, they cannot be carried too far without also affecting the overall performance of the economy. The multiplier could be reduced to 1 by increasing the tax rate to 100 percent, and that would appear to be a stabilizing influence on the economy. But with 100 percent marginal tax rates, the desire to work, and consequently the level of output, would be reduced to zero. Thus there are limits on the extent to which automatic stabilizers are desirable.[19]

---

[19] For a discussion of the history of automatic stabilizers, see Stein, *The Fiscal Revolution in America*.

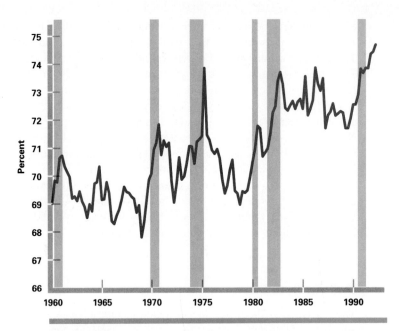

FIGURE 15-5

AUTOMATIC STABILIZERS: THE RATIO OF PERSONAL DISPOSABLE INCOME TO GDP, 1960–1992. Shaded bars mark periods of recession. (SOURCE: DRI/McGraw-Hill.)

The Outside Lag

The inside lag of policy is a *discrete* lag—so many months—from recognition to decision and implementation. The outside lag is generally a *distributed* lag: once the policy action has been taken, its effects on the economy are spread over time. There may be a small immediate effect of a policy action, but other effects occur later.

The idea that policy operates on aggregate demand and income with a distributed lag is illustrated by the dynamic multiplier in Figure 15-6. There we show the effects over time of a once-and-for-all increase in bank reserves in period zero. The impact is initially very small, and it continues to increase over a long period of time. The lags of monetary policy are represented by the fact that any significant impact of money on spending and output takes several quarters and builds up only gradually.

What are the policy implications of the distributed lag encountered in the outside lag? If it were necessary to increase the level of employment rapidly to offset a demand disturbance, a large open market purchase would be necessary. But in later quarters, the large initial open market purchase would build up large effects on GNP, and those effects would probably overcorrect the unemployment, leading to inflationary pressures. It would then be necessary to reverse the open market purchase and conduct open market sales to avoid the inflationary consequences of the initial open market purchase.

Why are there such long outside lags? Consider the example of monetary policy. Because aggregate demand depends heavily on lagged values of income, interest rates,

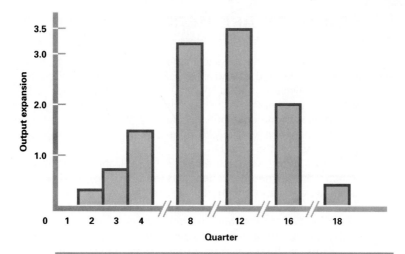

FIGURE 15-6

MONETARY POLICY MULTIPLIER FROM THE DRI MODEL. The figure shows the dynamic multiplier for a one-time increase of 3 percent in the nominal stock of M_1. For each quarter the figure shows the increase in the level of real output relative to the path the economy would otherwise have taken. Thus for the eighth quarter, for example, the 3 percent increase in money implies a rise of real GDP of 3.2 percent. By the eighteenth quarter, output is nearly back to its normal path. (SOURCE: DRI/McGraw-Hill.)

and other economic variables, an open market purchase initially has effects mainly on interest rates and not on income. The interest rates, in turn, affect investment with a lag and also affect consumption by affecting the value of wealth. When aggregate demand is ultimately affected, the increase in spending itself produces a series of induced adjustments in output and spending. When policy acts slowly, with the impacts of policy building up over time as in Figure 15-6, considerable skill is required of policy makers if their own attempts to correct an initially undesirable situation are not to lead to problems that themselves need correcting.

Monetary versus Fiscal Policy Lags

Fiscal policy—and certainly changes in government spending, which act directly on aggregate demand—affect income more rapidly than monetary policy. However, while fiscal policy has a shorter outside lag, it has a considerably longer inside lag. The long inside lag makes fiscal policy less useful for stabilization and means that fiscal policy tends to be used relatively infrequently to try to stabilize the economy.

Our analysis of lags clearly indicates one difficulty in undertaking stabilizing short-term policy actions: it takes time to set the policies in action, and then the policies

box 15-1 HOW GOOD ARE MACROECONOMIC FORECASTS?

In business and finance and in government, knowing what will happen in the economy next quarter and next year is critical as an ingredient for planning, for portfolio selection, and for policy making. The demand for forecasts is met by a broad group of professional forecasters. The methods used range from informal, almost back-of-the-envelope calculations to the use of sophisticated macroeconometric models where literally hundreds of equations representing the economy are the basis of the outlook.

How good are the forecasts? Table 1 shows the forecasts and the actual results from two sources. The first is the Congressional Budget Office (CBO), which uses macroeconometric models as the background for revenue and outlay projections. The other source is the Blue Chip forecast, a consensus of private forecasters. The projections in the table are obviously off—the forecasters did not predict the declines in output in either 1990 or 1991.

How can forecasters go wrong? They may not predict disturbances (the Gulf War, for example); they may misread the current state of the economy and hence base their forecasts on a wrong picture of the present situation; and they may misjudge the timing or vigor of the government's monetary and fiscal responses to booms or recessions. The fact is that forecasting has not reached perfection, particularly at major turning points in the economy, as illustrated in the table.*

---

*Stephen McNees, "How Large Are Economic Forecast Errors?" *New England Economic Review,* July/August 1992, provides a detailed examination of the historical record of forecasters and identifies what they are good at and what they seemingly do not do well.

---

themselves take time to affect the economy. But that is not the only difficulty. Further difficulties arise because policy makers cannot be certain about the size and the timing of the effects of policy actions.

15-5 EXPECTATIONS AND REACTIONS

Uncertainty about the effects of policies on the economy arise because, unlike in our supposition in early chapters of this book, policy makers do not know the precise values of multipliers. The government is always uncertain how the economy will react to policy changes. In practice, governments work with econometric models of the economy in estimating the effects of policy changes. An econometric model is a statistical description of the economy, or some part of it.

Government uncertainty about the effects of policy arises partly because it does not know the true model of the economy and partly because it does not know what expectations firms and consumers have. In this section we concentrate on the role of expectations.

TABLE 1

HOW ACCURATE ARE MACROECONOMIC FORECASTS (GNP growth, 4th quarter over 4th quarter)

forecast date	1989	1990	1991	1992	1993
February 1989					
CBO	2.9	2.2			
Blue Chip	2.3	1.9			
January 1990					
CBO		1.8	2.5		
Blue Chip		1.8	2.4		
March 1991					
CBO			1.3	3.4	
Blue Chip			0.9	2.8	
March 1992					
CBO				2.8	3.3
Blue Chip				2.9	3.1
Actual	1.8	−0.3	−0.3		

Source: Congressional Budget Office and DRI/McGraw-Hill.

There is no shortage of jokes about economists and their forecasts. For example, economists have predicted nine of the last seven recessions; if you must forecast, forecast often; if you have to forecast, predict either a quantity or a date, but never a quantity for a given date.

Reaction Uncertainties

Suppose that in early 1993, because of weakness in the economy, the government decides to cut taxes. But because the deficit is so large, the tax cut is meant to be strictly transitory—a brief shot in the arm to get the economy moving and nothing more.

In figuring out how big a tax cut is needed, the government has to guess how the public will react to a temporary tax cut. One possible answer is that the tax cut raises permanent income by very little and hence leads to only a very small increase in spending. This suggests that to be useful, a transitory tax cut would have to be large. Alternatively, perhaps consumers will believe that the tax cut will last much longer than the government says—after all, the public knows that raising taxes is difficult. In this case the marginal propensity to spend out of a tax cut announced as transitory would be larger. A smaller tax cut would be enough to raise spending a lot. If the government is wrong in its guess about consumers' reactions, it could destabilize rather than stabilize the economy.

Changes in Policy Regime

A special problem emerges when the government changes the way it has traditionally responded to disturbances. For example, a government that has typically cut taxes in recessions and now no longer does so (perhaps because the deficit is large) may find that the cut had been expected, and that there is an extra drop in demand when consumers realize taxes will not be cut this time.

It is particularly important to consider the effects of a given policy action itself on expectations, since it is possible that a new type of policy will affect the way in which expectations are formed.[20] Suppose that the Federal Reserve System announced that from now on its policy would be aimed *solely* at maintaining price stability, and that in response to any price level increase it would reduce the money supply (and vice versa). If people believed the announcement, they would not base expectations of money growth and inflation on the past behavior of the inflation rate.

However, people are not likely to believe such an announcement fully immediately. The policy makers are likely to lack full credibility. Policy makers have credibility when their announcements are believed by economic agents. Typically, policy makers have to earn credibility, by behaving consistently over long periods, so that people learn to believe what they say.

That learning is likely to be costly. Consider what happens if the Fed announces it will keep inflation low and is not believed. Then the expected inflation rate is above the actual inflation rate, and—as the Phillips curve shows—a recession follows. Only over time, as the new policies are understood, is credibility earned.

Credibility issues are always a problem when governments promise to keep exchange rates fixed. For example, in the 1980s, governments in the European Monetary System of quasi-fixed exchange rates announced that they would no longer respond to increases in wages and prices with devaluations. Initially, the policy makers lacked credibility, and inflation stayed high. But eventually, by holding fast, and with the aid of recessions, policy makers gained credibility and inflation came down. Then in 1992, under the macroeconomic impact of German unification, major devaluations were forced on reluctant governments, and their credibility was seriously dented.

Econometric Policy Evaluation Critique

The public's reactions to changes in income, interest rates, or exchange rates depend on what they expect to be happening in the economy and what the policy responses of the government will be. This poses an acute dilemma for policy research. We would like to know what the public will do in response to this or that new policy. But we cannot find the answer from historical relationships between variables and policies unless we know what expectations people held about policy.

This difficulty has been identified by Robert Lucas of the University of Chicago in a challenge to stabilization policy. He argues in his wider *econometric policy evaluation critique* that existing macroeconometric models cannot be used to study the effects of policy changes *because the way private agents (firms and consumers)*

---

[20]The interactions of policy and expectations have been the focus of the rational expectations approach to macroeconomics, introduced in Chap. 9. For a very early statement, see Thomas J. Sargent and Neil Wallace, "Rational Expectations and the Theory of Economic Policy," *Journal of Monetary Economics,* April 1976.

respond to changes in income and prices depends on the types of policy being followed.[21]

Lucas claims that problems of this sort are pervasive in macroeconometric models. He does not argue that it will never be possible to use econometric models to study policy—only that existing models cannot be used for that purpose.

Accordingly, the Lucas critique is not one that rules out the use of econometric models. It suggests rather that very careful modeling of the responses of consumers and firms to changes in income and prices, and particularly to changes in policy, is necessary for serious policy analysis.

15-6   UNCERTAINTY AND ECONOMIC POLICY

Uncertainty about the expectations of firms and consumers is one reason that policy makers can go wrong in using active stabilization policy. Another reason is that it is difficult to forecast disturbances such as changes in the price of oil, that might disturb the economy before policy takes effect.

A third reason is that economists and therefore policy makers do not know enough about the true structure of the economy. We distinguish between uncertainty about the correct model of the economy and uncertainty about the precise values of the parameters or coefficients within a given model of the economy, even though the distinction is not watertight.

First, there is considerable disagreement and therefore uncertainty about the correct model of the economy, as evidenced by the large number of macroeconometric models. Reasonable economists can and do differ about what theory and empirical evidence suggest are the correct behavioral functions of the economy. Generally, each economist will have reasons for favoring one particular form and will use that form. But, being reasonable, the economist will recognize that the particular formulation being used may not be the correct one and will thus regard its predictions as subject to a margin of error. In turn, policy makers will know that there are different predictions about the effects of a given policy and will want to consider the range of predictions that are being made in deciding on policy.

Second, even within a given model there is uncertainty about the values of parameters and multipliers. The statistical evidence does allow us to say something about the likely range of parameters or multipliers, so that we can at least get some idea of the type of errors that could result from a particular policy action.[22]

Uncertainty about the size of the effects that will result from any particular policy action—whether because of uncertainty about expectations or about the structure of the economy—is known as *multiplier uncertainty*. For instance, our best estimate of the multiplier of an increase in government spending might be 1.2. If GNP has to be

---

[21] See "Econometric Policy Evaluation: A Critique," in R. E. Lucas, Jr., *Studies in Business Cycle Theory* (Cambridge, Mass.: MIT Press, 1981).

[22] We are discussing here confidence intervals about estimates of parameters; see Robert Pindyck and Daniel Rubinfeld, *Econometric Models and Economic Forecasts* (New York: McGraw-Hill, 1991), for further discussion.

increased by $60 billion, we would increase government spending by $50 billion. But the statistical evidence might be better interpreted as saying only that we can be quite confident that the multiplier is between 0.9 and 1.5. In that case, when we increase government spending by $50 billion, we expect GNP to rise by some amount between $45 billion and $75 billion.

How should a policy maker react in the face of these uncertainties? The more precisely policy makers are informed about the relevant parameters, the more activist the policy can afford to be. Conversely, if there is a considerable range of error in the estimate of the relevant parameters—in our example, the multiplier—then policy should be more modest. With poor information, very active policy runs a large danger of introducing unnecessary fluctuations in the economy.

15-7 ACTIVIST POLICY

We started this chapter by asking why there are any fluctuations in the American economy when the policy measures needed to iron out those fluctuations seem to be so simple. The list of difficulties in the way of successful policy making that we have outlined may have raised a different question: Why should one believe that policy can do anything to reduce fluctuations in the economy?[23]

Indeed, considerations of the sort spelled out in the previous four sections have led Milton Friedman and others to argue that there should be no use of active countercyclical monetary policy and that monetary policy should be confined to making the money supply grow at a constant rate. The precise value of the constant rate of growth of money, Friedman suggests, is less important than the fact that monetary growth should be constant and that policy should *not* respond to disturbances. At various times, he has suggested growth rates for money of 2 or 4 or 5 percent. As Friedman has expressed it, "By setting itself a steady course and keeping to it, the monetary authority could make a major contribution to promoting economic stability. By making that course one of steady but moderate growth in the quantity of money, it would make a major contribution to avoidance of either inflation or deflation of prices."[24] Friedman thus advocates a simple monetary rule in which the Fed does not respond to the condition of the economy. Policies that respond to the current or predicted state of the economy are called *activist policies.* Interestingly, Friedman does make an exception to this rule in the face of extreme disturbances.

In discussing the desirability of activist monetary and fiscal policy, we want to distinguish between policy actions taken in response to major disturbances to the economy and *fine tuning,* in which policy variables are continually adjusted in response to small disturbances in the economy. We see no case for arguing that monetary and fiscal policy should not be used actively in the face of major disturbances to the economy. Most of the considerations of the previous sections of this chapter indicate

---

[23] An excellent discussion of the issues is Steven Sheffrin, *The Making of Economic Policy* (Oxford: Basil Blackwell, 1989).

[24] Milton Friedman, "The Role of Monetary Policy," *American Economic Review,* March 1968. See also his book, *A Program for Monetary Stability* (New York: Fordham University Press, 1959).

some uncertainty about the effects of policy, but sometimes there can be no doubt about which direction to move policy.

For instance, an administration coming to power in 1933 should not have worried about the uncertainties associated with expansionary policy that we have outlined. The economy does not move from 25 percent unemployment to full employment in a short time (precisely because of those same lags that make policy difficult). Thus, expansionary measures, such as a rapid growth of the money supply, or increased government expenditures, or tax reductions, or all three, would have been appropriate policy since there was no chance they would have an impact only after the economy was at full employment. Similarly, contractionary policies for private demand are called for in wartime. In the fall of 1982, with unemployment rising above 10 percent and the inflation rate falling, expansionary monetary policy was clearly appropriate and was implemented. In the event of large disturbances in the future, activist monetary and/or fiscal policy should once again be used.

Fine tuning presents more complicated issues. In the case of fiscal policy, the long inside lags make discretionary fine tuning virtually impossible, though automatic stabilizers are in fact fine tuning all the time. But with monetary policy decisions being made frequently, fine tuning of monetary policy is indeed possible. The question then is whether a small increase in the unemployment rate should lead to a small increase in the growth rate of money, or whether policy should not respond until the increase in unemployment becomes large, say more than 1.0 percent.

The problem is that the disturbance that caused the increase in unemployment may be either transitory or permanent. If it is transitory, nothing should be done. If it is permanent, policy should react to a small disturbance in a small way. Given uncertainty over the nature of the disturbance, the technically correct response is a small one, between the zero that is appropriate for a transitory shock and the full response that would be appropriate for a permanent disturbance. Accordingly fine tuning is appropriate provided that policy responses are always kept small in response to small disturbances.

However, the case for fine tuning is a controversial one. The major argument against it is that policy makers do not in practice behave as suggested—making only small adjustments in response to small disturbances. If allowed to do anything, they may do too much. Instead of merely trying to offset disturbances, policy makers shift toward fine tuning to keep the economy always exactly at full employment with the risk of overdoing a good thing. The "full-employment bias" in policies risks creating inflation.

The major lesson is not that activist policy is bound to be destabilizing, but that overly ambitious policy is risky. The lesson is to proceed with extreme caution, always bearing in mind the possibility that policy itself may be destabilizing.

Rules versus Discretion

If there is a risk that policy makers react to disturbances in unpredictable ways, and in a dosage that is excessively influenced by the perception of the day, and if all this is possibly one of the reasons for macroeconomic instability, why not put policy on automatic pilot? This is the issue of *rules versus discretion*. Should the monetary authority and also the fiscal authority conduct policy in accordance with preannounced rules that describe precisely how their policy variables will be determined in all future situations, or should they be allowed to use their discretion in determining the values of the policy variables at different times?

One example of a rule is the constant growth rate rule, say at 4 percent, for monetary policy. The rule is that no matter what happens, the money supply will be kept growing at 4 percent. Another example would be a rule stating that the money supply growth rate will be increased by 2 percent per year for every 1 percent unemployment in excess of, say, 5.5 percent. Algebraically, such a rule would be expressed as

$$\frac{\Delta M}{M} = 4.0 + 2(u - 5.5) \tag{1}$$

where the growth rate of money, $\Delta M/M$, is an annual percentage rate and u is the percentage unemployment rate.

The activist monetary rule of equation (1) implies that at 5.5 percent unemployment, monetary growth is 4 percent. If unemployment rises above 5.5 percent, monetary growth is *automatically* increased. Thus, with 7.5 percent unemployment, monetary growth would be 8 percent, using equation (1). Conversely, if unemployment dropped below 5.5 percent, monetary growth would be lowered below 4 percent. The rule therefore gears the amount of monetary stimulus to an indicator of the business cycle. By linking monetary growth to the unemployment rate, an activist, anticyclical monetary policy is achieved, but this is done without any discretion.

The issue of rules versus discretion has been clouded by the fact that most proponents of rules have been nonactivists, whose preferred monetary rule is a constant growth rate rule. Consequently, the argument has tended to center on whether activist policy is desirable or not. The fundamental point to recognize is that we can design *activist rules*. We can design rules that have countercyclical features without at the same time leaving any discretion about their actions to policy makers. The point is made by equation (1), which is an activist rule because it expands money supply when unemployment is high and reduces it when unemployment is low. The equation leaves no room for policy discretion and in this respect is a rule (see Box 15-2).

Given that both the economy and our knowledge of it are changing over time, there is no economic case for stating permanent policy rules that would tie the hands of the monetary and fiscal authorities permanently. Two practical issues then arise in the rules-versus-discretion debate. The first is where the authority to change the rule is located. At one extreme the growth rate of money could be prescribed by the Constitution. At the other it is left to the Fed or the "Fisc" (the equivalent fiscal policy-making body). In each case policy can be changed, but changing the Constitution takes longer than it takes the Fed to change its policy. In the tradeoff between certainty about future policy and flexibility of policy, activists place a premium on flexibility, and those in favor of rules that are difficult to change place a premium on the fact that the Fed has often made mistakes in the past. Because the financial system responds very quickly to shocks and is so interconnected, we believe it essential that the Fed have considerable discretion and thus flexibility to respond to disturbances. But that is far from a universal judgment.

box 15-2

DYNAMIC INCONSISTENCY AND RULES VERSUS DISCRETION

In the last 15 years economists have developed an intriguing argument in favor of rules rather than discretion. The argument is that policy makers who have discretion will be tempted to act inconsistently, even though it would be better for the economy in the long run if they were consistent.*

How can that be? Here is a noneconomic example. By threatening to punish their children, parents can generally make the children behave better. So long as the children behave well, all is well. But when a child misbehaves, the parent has a problem, since punishing the child is unpleasant for both parent and child. One solution is not to punish but to threaten to punish next time. But if there was no punishment this time, there is unlikely to be punishment next time either, and the threat loses its beneficial effect. The dynamically consistent parent will use punishment each time the child misbehaves, thereby producing better behavior in the long run despite its short-run cost.

What does this have to do with economics? Suppose the inflation rate has risen because of a supply shock. The Fed is considering whether or not to accommodate it by expanding the money supply. If the Fed accommodates, prices will rise more now, but there will be less unemployment. So that seems like a good thing to do. This is the equivalent of not punishing the misbehaving child. But—warn those in favor of rules who worry about dynamic consistency—if the Fed accommodates every inflationary pressure because it fears unemployment, people will soon come to expect it to do that, and they will build an allowance for expected inflation into the wages they set. The Fed will lose whatever reputation it had as an inflation fighter, and the economy will develop an inflationary bias, with the inflation rate creeping up over time.

Much better, says the dynamic consistency approach, that the Fed should have a rule that prevents it from making responses that are right from the short-run viewpoint but wrong for the long-run perspective. Those who nonetheless favor discretion for the Fed emphasize the importance of preserving flexibility for monetary policy. To the dynamic inconsistency argument, they counter that as long as the Fed is aware that having a good reputation helps it keep the inflation rate low, it will take any loss of reputation into account when it decides how to respond to particular shocks, and thus will not be dynamically inconsistent. ∎

---

*The basic reference is Finn Kydland and Edward Prescott, "Rules Rather than Discretion; The Inconsistency of Optimal Plans," *Journal of Political Economy,* June 1977. This is very difficult reading. See also V. V. Chari, "Time Consistency and Optimal Policy Design," Federal Reserve Bank of Minneapolis *Quarterly Review,* Fall 1988.

The second issue is whether the policy makers should announce in advance the policies they will be following for the foreseeable future. Such announcements are in principle desirable because they aid private individuals to forecast future policy. In fact, the chairperson of the Fed is required to announce to Congress the Fed's monetary targets (see Chapter 14). In practice, however, these announcements have not been a great help because the Fed does not stick to its targets. If the Fed is able to keep output close to potential and inflation low by departing from announced policy, then it helps private individuals forecast the variables in which they are really interested—their future incomes and, in the case of firms, the demand for their goods—rather than those, like the money supply, that they need know only as an intermediate step in forecasting.

15-8 SUMMARY

1. Despite the apparent simplicity of policies needed to maintain continuous full employment, the historical record of recessions and unemployment implies that successful stabilization policy is difficult to carry out.

2. The great depression shaped both modern macroeconomics and many of the economy's institutions. The extremely high unemployment and the length of the depression led to the view that the private economy was unstable and that government intervention was needed to maintain high employment levels.

3. Keynesian economics succeeded because it seemed to explain the causes of the great depression—a collapse of investment demand—and because it pointed to expansionary fiscal policy as a means of preventing future depressions.

4. Keynesian views did not much affect economic policy making in the United States until the New Economics of the Kennedy-Johnson administration. The greatest success of the New Economics was the tax cut of 1964. The New Economics is perceived by the public as having been responsible for increasing inflation during the 1960s. As confidence in the New Economics declined, its emphasis on active stabilization policy was reexamined.

5. The potential need for stabilizing policy actions arises from economic disturbances. Some of these disturbances, such as changes in money demand, consumption spending, or investment demand, arise from within the private sector. Others, such as wars, may arise for noneconomic reasons.

6. The three key difficulties of stabilization policy are that *(a)* policy works with lags; *(b)* the outcome of policy depends very much on private sector expectations, which are difficult to predict and which may react to policy; and *(c)* there is uncertainty about both the structure of the economy and shocks that hit the economy.

7. There are clearly occasions on which active monetary and fiscal policy actions should be taken to stabilize the economy. These are situations in which the economy has been affected by major disturbances.

8. Fine tuning—continuous attempts to stabilize the economy in the face of small disturbances—is more controversial. If fine tuning is undertaken, it calls for small policy responses in an attempt to moderate the economy's fluctuations, rather than to remove them entirely. A very active policy in response to small disturbances is likely to destabilize the economy.

9. In the rules-versus-discretion debate, it is important to recognize that activist rules are possible. The two important issues in the debate are how difficult it should be to change policy, and whether policy should be announced as far ahead as possible. There is a tradeoff between the certainty about future policy that comes from rules and the flexibility of the policy makers in responding to shocks.

KEY TERMS

New Deal
New Economics
Economic disturbances
Decision lag
Automatic stabilizers
Inside lag
Recognition lag
Rules versus discretion
Dynamic inconsistency

Action lag
Outside lag
Multiplier uncertainty
Econometric models
Activist policy
Policy rule
Fine tuning
Credibility

PROBLEMS

1. It is sometimes said that the great depression would have been a severe recession if it had stopped in 1931, but it would not have been the calamity it was.
   (a) From Table 15-1 calculate the rate at which GNP was falling from 1929 to 1931.
   (b) How does that rate compare with the rate at which real GNP fell during the 1990–1991 recession?
   (c) Do you agree with the first sentence in this question? Explain.

2. Using Table 15-2, explain why concentration on the actual budget deficit might have given a misleading impression of fiscal policy at some stages between 1929 and 1933.

3. In Table 15-1 examine the behavior of the short-term (commercial paper) interest rate and the growth rate of money. Explain why a Keynesian could have thought monetary policy was expansionary during the great depression, while a monetarist would argue that monetary policy was, on the contrary, contractionary.

4. Suppose that GDP is $40 billion below its potential level. It is expected that next-period GDP will be $20 billion below potential, and that two periods from now it will be back at its potential level. You are told that the multiplier for government spending is 2 and that the effects of the increased government spending are immediate. What policy actions can be taken to put GDP back on target each period?

5. The basic facts about the path of GDP are as above. But there is now a one-period outside lag for government spending. Decisions to spend today are translated into actual spending only tomorrow. The multiplier for government spending is still 2 in the period that the spending takes place.
   (a) What is the best that can be done to keep GDP as close to target as possible each period?
   (b) Compare the path of GDP in this question with the path in problem 4 after policy actions have been taken.

6. Life has become yet more complicated. Government spending works with a distributed lag. Now when $1 billion is spent today, GDP increases by $1 billion this period and $1.5 billion next period.
   (a) What happens to the path of GDP if government spending rises enough this period to put GDP back to its potential level this period?
   (b) Suppose fiscal policy actions are taken to put GDP at its potential level this period. What fiscal policy will be needed to put GDP on target next period?
   (c) Explain why the government has to be so active in keeping GDP on target in this case.

7. Suppose that you knew that the multiplier for government spending was between 1 and 2.5, but that its effects ended in the period in which spending was increased. How would you run fiscal policy if GDP would, without policy, behave as in problem 4?

8. Explain why monetary policy works with a distributed lag, as in Figure 15-6.

9. Check the *Federal Reserve Bulletin* where the forecasts of the Federal Reserve Board are presented twice a year following the February and July monetary policy reports to Congress.
(a) How well did the Fed anticipate the economic performance of 1993 or 1994?
(b) Explain why econometric forecasts are not totally accurate.

10. Evaluate the argument that monetary policy should be determined by a rule rather than discretion. How about fiscal policy?

11. Evaluate the arguments for a constant growth rate rule for money.

COMPUTER EXERCISES

The computer module allows you to study how the economy responds over time to changes in fiscal and monetary policy, $\overline{G}$ and $\overline{M}$. You can contrast the impact of a one-time change in $\overline{G}$ or $\overline{M}$ with an extended policy regime change in these variables. Note that the simulation starts with GDP below potential and, although the economy is growing, GDP stays below potential in the absence of a policy stimulus.

1. Start with a one-time increase in $\overline{G}$ of 4, i.e., $\overline{G}$ is up by 4 in each period starting with the second year. Compare this policy with increasing the *growth* of $\overline{G}$ from 2 per year to 4 per year. Note what happens to inflation and to interest rates, as well as to the gap between actual and potential GDP.

2. How much of a *one-time* increase in $\overline{G}$ do you need to eliminate the gap between GDP and potential GDP without going above potential in any year? How long does it take to eliminate the gap? How long does the gap stay close to zero?

3. Find a combination of a one-time increase in $\overline{G}$ and an increase in the annual growth in $\overline{G}$ that will eliminate the gap and keep GDP near its potential. Compare your results with exercise 2, contrasting the effects of each policy on inflation and investment. Do you see a tradeoff?

4. Now explore the dynamics of monetary policy. Start with a one-time increase in $\overline{M}$ of 15, i.e., $\overline{M}$ is up by 15 in each period starting with the second year. Compare this policy with increasing the *growth* of $\overline{M}$ from 5 per year to 15 per year. Compare what happens to inflation and to interest rates with respect to your results from exercise 1.

5. Redo exercises 2 and 3 using monetary rather than fiscal policy. Compare your results to the fiscal policy simulations of exercises 2 and 3.

Note: If you are interested in exploring economic policy material after reading this chapter, refer to the Policy Game contained in the *PC-Macroeconomics* program and the question material located at the end of the book. The Policy Game is a more realistic and complex representation of the economy than the simpler material found in earlier chapters.

part four

INFLATION, UNEMPLOYMENT, BUDGET DEFICITS, AND INTERNATIONAL ADJUSTMENT

16

THE DYNAMICS OF INFLATION AND UNEMPLOYMENT

*I*nflation cannot be eliminated without raising unemployment at least for some time, and moderate unemployment cannot be cut sharply without the risk of raising inflation. This is the fundamental tradeoff and problem of stabilization policy.

We have two main objectives in this chapter: first, to understand where the basic tradeoff comes from; and second, to adapt the model of aggregate supply and demand to make it easy to analyze *ongoing* inflation, as opposed to one-time changes in the price *level*. We will show that the analysis of ongoing inflation and unemployment can be readily handled by dynamizing the aggregate supply and demand model of earlier chapters.

The analysis developed in this chapter is used in all policy discussions of inflation and unemployment. For instance, it helps explain why, in the United States, the Fed has not set out to kill inflation once and for all. It also helps us see why Canada's decision to aim for zero inflation involves a costly period of transition. Inflation is a problem, but so is stopping it! Putting the economy on a (monetary) diet eventually has positive and sound effects, but the transition can be painful.

Figure 16-1 shows the actual U.S. inflation rate since 1960 as well as the average rate from one business cycle peak to the next. From the late 1950s through the end of the 1970s the inflation rate in the United States increased in every successive business cycle. During a recession, inflation would fall below its previous trend. But in the following recovery it would rise again and, before long, exceed its past level.

In late 1979 the Fed made a dramatic decision: monetary policy was to be changed decisively to stop inflation from rising and to force it back down from 10 percent to the 2 percent level of the 1950s. The decision was dramatic because there was little disagreement among economists of widely different macroeconomic persuasions that the move toward tight money would cause a recession along with a reduction in the inflation rate. The disinflation process created the worst post–World War II recession, in 1981–1982, but did cut inflation. From the business cycle peak in July 1981 to the

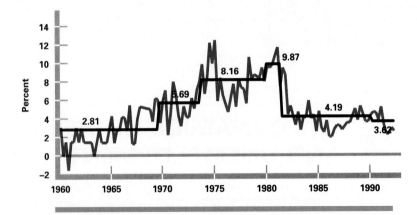

FIGURE 16-1
CYCLICAL AVERAGE INFLATION RATES, 1960–1992. Inflation rate is the GDP deflator; averages are peak to peak; last cycle is from 1990:2 to 1992:4. (SOURCE: DRI/McGraw-Hill.)

next peak in July 1990 inflation averaged 4 percent, down from nearly 10 percent in the previous cycle.

Through 1989 the U.S. economy succeeded in maintaining a low average rate of inflation—not as low as that of the 1950s, but well below that of the 1970s—while continuing strong growth. But in 1989 the inflation rate showed signs of rising to the 5 percent range, and the Fed was once again faced with the tough question of how far to go in fighting inflation, knowing that the tighter its monetary policy, the greater the risk that it would bring on a recession. Even as the recession developed in 1990 and 1991, the Fed was slow to cut interest rates, for fear that it would trigger a renewal of inflation.

The key question of this chapter is: Why is it apparently inevitable that inflation stabilization should cause unemployment and recession? The distinction between the short- and long-run aggregate supply curves is essential here. In the short run, inflation cannot be reduced without creating a recession; in the long run, though, there is no tradeoff between inflation and unemployment.

16-1 INFLATION, EXPECTATIONS, AND THE AGGREGATE SUPPLY CURVE

In this chapter we develop the aggregate supply curve in two directions. First, we modify it to include *expected inflation;* firms and workers take account of expected increases in the price level when they are fixing wages and prices. Second, we transform the aggregate supply curve into a relationship between output and the *inflation rate* rather than the price level. That way we can use the aggregate supply curve to model ongoing inflation, that is, continuing changes in the price level. We reproduce here the aggregate supply curve of Chapter 8:

$$P = P_{-1}[1 + \lambda(Y - Y^*)] \tag{1}$$

where P is the price level, Y the level of output, and Y^* the full-employment level of output. Define now the rate of inflation by the symbol π:

$$\pi = \frac{P - P_{-1}}{P_{-1}}$$

Using this definition and rearranging equation (1) we have already accomplished our first task:

$$\pi = \lambda(Y - Y^*) \tag{2}$$

The aggregate supply curve of Chapter 8 thus states that inflation is high when output exceeds the full-employment level. The reasoning, as a reminder, is this:

- The Phillips curve shows that wages increase more rapidly the lower the level of unemployment.
- The level of output is higher when the unemployment rate is lower.
- Firms' prices are set as a *markup* on labor costs, so that prices are rising when wages are rising.
- Thus, a tight labor market produces wage and price inflation.

The next step is to introduce expectations of inflation as an extra element on the supply side.

Wage Setting and Expected Inflation

The second factor in setting wage increases is the ongoing rate of inflation. In proposing a crucial amendment to the original Phillips curve, Milton Friedman and Edmund Phelps[1] each pointed out that the wage-Phillips curve ignores the effects of expected inflation on wage setting. Workers are interested in *real* wages (the amount of goods they can buy with their wages), not *nominal* wages (the dollar value of wages). It is clear that workers, who are concerned with the real wage they receive, will want the nominal wage to fully reflect the inflation they expect during the period between the time the wage is fixed and the time the wage is actually paid. In other words, quite

---

[1]Milton Friedman, "The Role of Monetary Policy," *American Economic Review*, March 1968; and Edmund Phelps, "Phillips Curves, Expectations of Inflation, and Optimal Unemployment Over Time," *Economica*, 1967. See also Chaps. 8 and 9.

independent of the effects of the level of employment on wage bargaining, workers will want compensation for expected inflation.

But what about the other side? Why do firms agree to raise wages more rapidly when they expect higher prices? The reason is that they can afford to pay higher nominal wages if they will be able to sell their goods at higher prices. And if all prices are rising, each firm can expect to be able to sell its output for a higher price because the prices of competing goods are increasing. Indeed, when wages and prices are rising at the same rate, both firms and workers are in essentially the same position as they would be if there were no inflation and the nominal wage were constant.

The Friedman-Phelps theory suggests that the inflation adjustment compensates for *expected* inflation. An alternative possibility is that wage increases compensate workers for *past* inflation. Wage contracts may provide explicitly for cost of living adjustments (COLAs) based on a formula, or it might be done instead as a rule of thumb.

As we will show below, it is critical to the adjustment process of the economy whether wage changes adjust for past inflation or for expected inflation. We shall also see that while it is simple to spell out the difference between past and expected inflation conceptually, empirically it is much harder.

Either way, inflation adjustment will be part of the wage increase. We denote by π^e the growth rate of wages that represents this inflation adjustment and, to be concrete, we call it expected inflation. We add the term π^e to the right-hand side of the aggregate supply curve in equation (2), to represent the inflation component of wage settlements:

$$\pi = \pi^e + \lambda(Y - Y^*) \tag{3}$$

In equation (3), actual inflation is determined by both expected inflation and unemployment (or the level of output). Expected inflation is passed on into wages, which are in turn passed through the fixed markup, into prices and inflation. Thus, according to equation (3), prices may be rising even when unemployment is high, provided expected inflation is sufficiently high.

Equation (3) is known as the *expectations-augmented* or dynamic aggregate supply curve; it is the original Phillips curve augmented to take account of expected inflation.

16-2   SHORT- AND LONG-RUN AGGREGATE SUPPLY CURVES

Expectations-augmented short-run aggregate supply curves are shown in Figure 16-2. There is an aggregate supply curve corresponding to each expected rate of inflation. For example, on *SAS* the expected inflation rate is 5 percent, as can be seen from the fact that when $Y = Y^*$, at point A on *SAS*, the inflation rate on the vertical axis is 5 percent. [Note from equation (3) that when $Y = Y^*$, $\pi = \pi^e$.] The short-run aggregate supply curve shows the relationship between the inflation rate and the level of output when the expected rate of inflation is held constant. The curves are called short run because it is assumed that the expected rate of inflation is constant (or at least does not change much) in the short run of a few months or as much as a year.

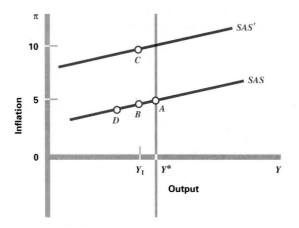

FIGURE 16-2

THE SHORT-RUN AGGREGATE SUPPLY CURVE. The expected inflation rate is constant on a short-run aggregate supply curve: it is 5 percent on *SAS*, 10 percent on *SAS'*. Each short-run aggregate supply curve is shown quite flat, reflecting the fact that, in the short run, it takes a large change in output to generate a given change in inflation.

Given the expected inflation rate, the short-run aggregate supply curve shows the inflation rate rising with the level of output: the higher the level of output, the higher the rate of inflation. This is a reflection of the effect of higher output levels on the rate of increase of wages and, through higher wages, on the rate of increase of prices.

The higher the expected inflation rate, the higher the aggregate supply curve. Thus on *SAS'*, the expected inflation rate is 10 percent. And for any expected inflation rate, there is a corresponding short-run aggregate supply curve, parallel to *SAS* and *SAS'*, with the vertical distance between any two short-run supply curves equal to the difference in expected inflation rates between them.

On each short-run aggregate supply curve there is a tradeoff between inflation and output. To reduce the inflation rate it is necessary to reduce the level of output, producing a recession, forcing the rate of wage increase down through unemployment, and thus achieving a lower inflation rate.

We show the short-run aggregate supply curves in Figure 16-2 as quite flat, reflecting the evidence that in the short run—up to a year or even two—it takes a large recession to bring about a substantial reduction in the inflation rate. That was the choice made, for example, in the United States in 1981–1983 when the inflation rate was reduced.

Changes in the Expected Inflation Rate

Each aggregate supply curve is drawn for a given expected rate of inflation. As the expected rate of inflation changes, the economy moves from one short-run aggregate supply curve to another. This means that the combination of the level of output and inflation rate that occurs depends on the expected inflation rate. For instance, the level of output of Y_1 in Figure 16-2 would be consistent with a low inflation rate at point B on SAS and a higher inflation rate at point C on SAS'.

Changes in the expected rate of inflation help explain why the simple Phillips curve relationship seen in Figure 8-3 for 1961–1969 seemed to break down later. Through the end of the 1960s, there was relatively little awareness of inflation, and the economy was basically moving along an SAS curve. When at the end of the 1960s people in the United States began to expect inflation to continue, the short-run aggregate supply curve began to shift, generating higher inflation at each given output level. The Friedman-Phelps analysis thus can explain why the simple Phillips curve of the sixties seemed to break down in the seventies—and recall that their analysis was made before the Phillips curve began to shift.

The conclusion of this section is the most important practical lesson macroeconomists and economic policy makers learned in the last 20 years. *The short-run aggregate supply curve shifts with the expected rate of inflation. The inflation rate corresponding to any given level of output therefore changes over time as the expected inflation rate changes. The higher the expected inflation rate, the higher the inflation rate corresponding to a given level of output.* That is one important reason why it is possible for the inflation rate and the unemployment rate to increase together, or for the inflation rate to rise while the level of output falls.[2]

The Vertical Long-Run Aggregate Supply Curve

On each short-run aggregate supply curve, the expected inflation rate is constant and, except at points such as A, at which $Y = Y^*$, will turn out to be different from the actual inflation rate. For instance, at point D on SAS in Figure 16-2 the expected inflation rate is 5 percent, but the actual inflation rate is only 4 percent.

If the inflation rate remains constant for any long period, firms and workers will expect that rate to continue, and the expected inflation rate will become equal to the actual rate. The assumption that $\pi = \pi^e$ distinguishes the *long-run* from the short-run aggregate supply curve. The long-run aggregate supply curve describes the relationship between inflation and output when actual and expected inflation are equal.

With the actual and expected inflation rates equal (that is, $\pi = \pi^e$), the aggregate supply curve (3) shows that $Y = Y^*$. Accordingly, the long-run aggregate supply curve, LAS, in Figure 16-3 is a vertical line joining points on short-run aggregate supply curves at which the actual and expected inflation rates are equal.

The meaning of the vertical long-run aggregate supply curve is that *in the long run the level of output is independent of the inflation rate.* Note the important contrast between the short and the long run: in the short run, with a given expected rate of inflation, higher inflation rates are accompanied by higher output; in the long run, with the expected rate of inflation equal to the actual rate, the level of output is independent of the inflation rate.

---

[2]The other important reason is that a supply shock may hit the economy.

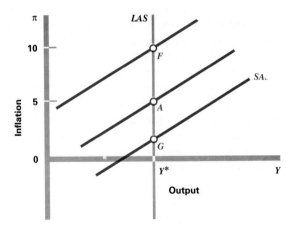

FIGURE 16-3
SHORT- AND LONG-RUN AGGREGATE SUPPLY CURVES. The long-run
aggregate supply curve (*LAS*) joins points on short-run aggregate
supply curves (*SAS*) at which expected inflation is equal to actual
inflation. The long-run curve is thus the vertical line *LAS*, at level of
output *Y**.

Assumptions About Expectations

In concluding this section we return to the issue of expected inflation. Many of the
controversies in macroeconomics are connected with the inclusion of expected inflation
in the aggregate supply function. The key questions are, Is it *expected* inflation rather
than compensation for *past* inflation that shifts the short-run aggregate supply curve?
and What determines expected inflation?

Why does it matter whether wage adjustments for inflation respond to yesterday's
actual inflation or tomorrow's expected inflation? The difference is very important
because the explanation has different implications for how long it takes for the inflation
rate to change. If wages for next year reflect last year's inflation and prices are based
on wages, as they are, then inflation today will reflect yesterday's inflation and inflation
rates will change only gradually. If it is only expected inflation that matters for wage
setting, then perhaps a radical change in policy that changes expectations can also
change the inflation rate quickly.

There are two main formulations about expected inflation. One hypothesis that
was used in the 1950s and 1960s, and that still commands some support, is that
expectations are *adaptive*. Expectations are adaptive if they are based on the past
behavior of inflation. Thus under adaptive expectations the rate of inflation expected
for next year might be the rate of inflation last year. Under this simplest adaptive
expectations assumption, we would have

$$\pi^e = \pi_{-1} \qquad\qquad (4)$$

Of course, the adaptive expectations assumption could be more complicated, for instance, if the expected inflation rate is the average of the last 3 years' inflation.

The leading alternative is the rational expectations approach, associated primarily with the names of Robert Lucas and Thomas Sargent, which we have discussed already in Chapter 9. *The rational expectations hypothesis implies that people do not make systematic mistakes in forming their expectations.* Systematic mistakes—for instance, always underpredicting inflation—are easily spotted. According to the rational expectations hypothesis, people correct such mistakes and change the way they form expectations. On average, rational expectations are correct because people understand the environment in which they operate. Of course people make mistakes from time to time, but they do not make *systematic* mistakes.

The rational expectations view cannot be captured in a simple mechanical form such as $\pi^e = \pi_{-1}$. Rather, it argues that there can be no formula for expected inflation that is independent of the actual behavior of inflation. It assumes that people base their expectations of inflation (or any other economic variable) on all the information economically available about the future behavior of that variable.[3]

Note that if expectations are adaptive, it becomes virtually impossible to tell whether the π^e term in the aggregate supply curve represents expected inflation or compensation for past inflation. If $\pi^e = \pi_{-1}$, there is no difference between past inflation and expected inflation.

For much of this chapter we work with the simple adaptive expectations assumption of equation (4), that the expected inflation rate is equal to the lagged inflation rate. The aggregate supply curve is thus

$$\pi = \pi_{-1} + \lambda(Y - Y^*) \tag{5}$$

We use this aggregate supply curve, together with an aggregate demand curve to be introduced in the next section, to study the dynamic adjustment of the economy to changes in policy. By way of contrast, we also use the rational expectations assumption and show just how radical are its implications.

16-3 DYNAMIC AGGREGATE DEMAND

The aggregate demand curve in Chapter 8 represents combinations of the *price level* and level of output at which the goods and assets markets are simultaneously in equilibrium. In this chapter, where we are studying continuing inflation, we work with an aggregate demand curve that shows the relationship between the level of output and the *inflation rate*. The dynamic aggregate demand curve shows the relationship between the rate of inflation and the change in aggregate demand.

---

[3]For a recent test of the rational expectations hypothesis for the case of inflation, see Michael Keane and David Runkle, "Testing the Rationality of Price Forecasts: New Evidence from Panel Data," *American Economic Review*, September 1990. Using new methods, the authors report *strong* evidence that price forecasts are rational; this finding is different from much of the previous literature.

The dynamic aggregate demand curve derived in the appendix,[4] is

$$Y = Y_{-1} + \phi(m - \pi) + \sigma f \tag{6}$$

where m is the growth rate of the nominal money stock. Thus $(m - \pi)$ is the rate of change of real balances: when m exceeds π, the money stock is increasing faster than prices, and so real balances (M/P) are increasing. The other term, σf, denotes the impact on demand of a fiscal expansion.

The curve is most simply understood as saying that the *change* in aggregate demand $(Y - Y_{-1})$ is determined by the growth rate of real balances and by fiscal expansion. The higher the level of real balances, the lower the interest rate and the higher the level of aggregate demand; therefore, as real balances grow more rapidly, the interest rate falls more rapidly and aggregate demand increases more rapidly. By the same line of argument an *increase* in government spending or a *cut* in taxes means an expansionary fiscal policy and hence an increase in demand over the previous period's level.

In the appendix to this chapter we show that the aggregate demand curve (6) is a simplified version of the aggregate demand curve obtained by using the full *IS-LM* model. The simplification is that we omit the expected rate of inflation that affects aggregate demand.[5] To start, we concentrate on presenting the aggregate demand schedule diagrammatically. For simplicity, we therefore suppress the term relating to fiscal policy changes. We return to fiscal policy changes later in the chapter.

In Figure 16-4 we plot the dynamic aggregate demand schedule, or *DAD*. The shape of that schedule is most clearly seen by rewriting equation (6) to put inflation on the left-hand side:

$$\pi = m - \frac{1}{\phi}(Y - Y_{-1}) \tag{6a}$$

The schedule is drawn for a given growth rate of money and is downward-sloping. Given the growth rate of money, a lower rate of inflation implies that real balances are higher and thus that the interest rate is lower and aggregate demand is higher. The negative slope results from this connection between lower inflation, implying higher growth in real balances, and higher spending.

The position of the aggregate demand curve depends on the level of output last period. The higher the level of output last period, the higher the inflation rate corresponding to any given level of current output on the aggregate demand curve.

A change in the growth rate of money will shift the aggregate demand curve. A change in the growth rate of money shifts the *DAD* curve vertically by precisely the same amount as changes in the growth rate of money. Thus the dynamic aggregate

---

[4]The parameters ϕ and σ are the money and fiscal multipliers familiar from the *IS-LM* model of Chap. 5.

[5]The expected rate of inflation enters because investment is affected by the *real* interest rate, whereas the demand for money is affected by the *nominal* interest rate. Thus when we say above that increases in real balances reduce interest rates, we should, to be more precise, say that while they reduce the nominal interest rate, whether they also reduce the real interest rate depends on how the expected inflation rate is changing.

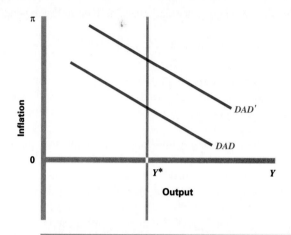

FIGURE 16-4
THE DYNAMIC AGGREGATE DEMAND SCHEDULE. The dynamic aggregate demand curve (*DAD*) is downward-sloping and drawn for a given rate of growth of money and lagged output level. The growth rate of money is higher on *DAD'* than on *DAD*.

demand curve, *DAD'* in Figure 16-4, lies above *DAD* by the same distance as the growth rate of money has increased between *DAD* and *DAD'*.

16-4 INFLATION AND OUTPUT

The inflation rate and level of output are determined by aggregate demand and supply. Figure 16-5 shows the intersection of the upward-sloping aggregate supply curve and the downward-sloping aggregate demand curve at point E. The inflation rate this period is π_0, and the level of output is Y_0.

The current rate of inflation and the level of output clearly depend on the positions of the aggregate supply and demand curves. Thus changes in any of the variables that shift the aggregate supply and demand curves will affect the current levels of inflation and output.

The Inflation Rate and Output in the Short Run

Any upward shift in the aggregate demand curve causes an increase in both the rate of inflation and the level of output, as can be seen in the shift from E to E_1 when the *DAD* curve shifts upward to *DAD'*. Such a shift would be caused by an increase in the growth rate of money. [It could also be caused by an increase in government spending or a reduction in taxes, though for the moment we do not explicitly include

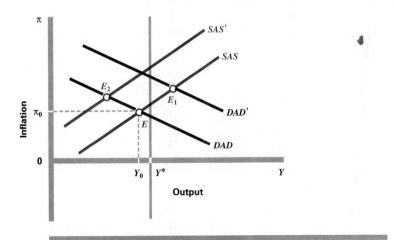

FIGURE 16-5
INFLATION AND OUTPUT IN THE SHORT RUN. Inflation and output are
determined by the intersection of the aggregate supply and demand
curves at point E. An upward shift of the aggregate demand curve
raises both output and inflation. An upward shift of the aggregate
supply curve increases the inflation rate while reducing the level of
output.

those variables in the aggregate demand curve $(6a)$.] In addition, the position of the
aggregate demand curve depends on the level of output last period. The higher the
level of output last period (Y_{-1}), the higher the aggregate demand curve.

An increase in the growth rate of money shifts the aggregate demand curve up
by exactly the same amount in Figure 16-5 as the rise in the growth rate of money.
Therefore output rises and inflation increases. But the increase in inflation is less than
the increase in the growth rate of money. In the short run a 1 percent increase in money
growth produces a less than 1 percent increase in inflation because some of the effects
of the increase in money stock show up in higher output.

Shifts in the aggregate supply curve also affect the rate of inflation and the level
of output. An upward shift of the aggregate supply curve, such as the shift from SAS
to SAS', moves the equilibrium from E to E_2, raising the inflation rate and reducing
the level of output. An increase in the expected rate of inflation would cause an upward
shift such as that from SAS to SAS'. The reason is that the higher expected rate of
inflation produces more rapid rises in wages, which cause more rapid inflation.

Summarizing, we see that in the short run:

- An increase in the growth rate of money causes higher inflation and higher output,
  but inflation rises less than the growth rate of money.

- An increase in the expected rate of inflation causes higher inflation and lower
  output.

We also note, and leave to you to show, that the factors we have omitted here from the aggregate supply and demand curves change the inflation rate and output in the short run:

- A supply shock that shifts the aggregate supply curve upward causes higher inflation and lower output.

- An increase in expected inflation shifts the aggregate demand curve upward and to the right. To understand this point note from the appendix that the analysis in the text has omitted changes in inflationary expectations as another determinant of dynamic aggregate demand.[6]

The Inflation Rate and Output in the Long Run

We move next to the hypothetical longest run, in which the growth rate of money is constant, in which expectations have adjusted to actual inflation, and in which output and inflation are constant. Such a situation is called a *steady state*, obviously because nothing is changing. Returning to the aggregate demand equation,

$$\pi = m - \frac{1}{\phi}(Y - Y_{-1}) \tag{6a}$$

we recognize that with output constant ($Y = Y_{-1}$), the inflation rate is equal to the growth rate of money. Thus *in the steady state, the inflation rate is determined solely by the growth rate of money.*

On the aggregate supply side,

$$\pi = \pi^e + \lambda(Y - Y^*) \tag{3}$$

We set $\pi = \pi^e$ and recognize that output is at its potential level Y^*. Thus *in the steady state, output is at its full-employment level.*

What is the real world importance of these steady-state relationships? The first thing to notice is that the economy never reaches a steady state. There are always disturbances affecting aggregate supply and demand: changes in expectations, or in the labor force, or in the prices of other factors of production, or in methods of production on the aggregate supply side; changes in fiscal policy, or in consumer tastes, or in monetary policy, on the aggregate demand side. In practice the economy moves toward ever-changing steady states; as it starts out on the route toward a steady state, some shock or disturbance will come along to bump it off that route onto another path.

Steady-state relationships are useful, though, in indicating the long-run tendency

---

[6] When we include inflation in the aggregate demand curve, an increase in expected inflation causes both the aggregate supply and demand curves to shift up, certainly increasing the inflation rate, but producing an uncertain effect on output. The net effect on output depends on which curve shifts up more. Typically, the aggregate supply curve would shift up more, implying higher inflation and lower output—which corresponds to the conclusion reached above when we omitted expected inflation from the aggregate demand curve.

of the economy. Over long periods, we can expect the economy on average to behave as if the steady-state relationships hold. On average, we expect output to be at its potential level.[7] And on average, we expect the inflation rate to be determined by the growth rate of money.

16-5 THE ADJUSTMENT PROCESS

In this section we ask how the economy moves toward the long-run equilibrium when a shock or disturbance affects aggregate supply or demand. We repeat here for convenience the two building blocks:

Dynamic aggregate supply: $\qquad\qquad\qquad \pi = \pi_{-1} + \lambda(Y - Y^*)$ $\qquad$ (3)

Dynamic aggregate demand: $\qquad\qquad\qquad \pi = m - \dfrac{1}{\phi}(Y - Y_{-1}) + \dfrac{\sigma}{\phi}f$ $\qquad$ (7)

We repeat also that we have made the adaptive expectations assumption that expected inflation is equal to last period's inflation rate. Note that we have brought fiscal policy expansion back as a source of aggregate demand expansion.

In Figure 16-6, the economy is initially at point E, with output at its potential level, Y^*, and with inflation equal to the growth rate of money, m_0, implying an initial inflation rate $\pi_0 = m_0$. This is a position of long-run equilibrium because real balances are not changing and expectations are in line with the actual rate of inflation. Thus there is no force to move the economy away from its equilibrium position.

A Fiscal Expansion

We saw in Chapter 8 that a sustained fiscal expansion leads to a cumulative increase in prices and a decline in the real money stock that raises interest rates until crowding out returns the economy to the initial equilibrium. We now establish the same result in the dynamic framework.

Equations (3) and (7) provide the framework for analyzing the dynamics of inflation for shocks in the growth rate of money—temporary or sustained—or for *changes* in fiscal policy. Since the term f in equation (7) denotes *changes* in fiscal policy, it is zero except in a period where fiscal policy shifts to be more or less expansionary as measured by changes in the full-employment budget. Given the growth rate of money, a fiscal expansion ($f > 0$) will increase the rate of inflation or shift the aggregate demand schedule upward and to the right.

Suppose now that we have a given growth rate of money, m_0, and that the economy is in an initial steady state such that $Y = Y^*$ and $\pi = \pi^e = m$. Now a

---

[7]Indeed, some economists define the natural rate of unemployment as the long-run average rate of unemployment. In that case by definition the unemployment rate is on average over long periods equal to the natural rate, to which the level of potential output corresponds.

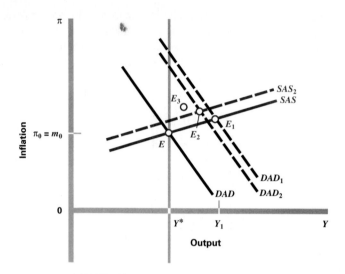

FIGURE 16-6

ADJUSTMENT TO A SUSTAINED FISCAL EXPANSION. Starting from the steady state at *E*, a fiscal expansion shifts aggregate demand to DAD_1 so that in the short run the economy moves to E_1. In the subsequent adjustment the aggregate demand schedule shifts back while the aggregate supply schedule shifts up and to the left as inflationary expectations increase. The economy thus suffers stagflation along a path shown by points E_2 and E_3.

permanent fiscal expansion takes place, meaning that in the current period f in equation (7) is positive, and for every period afterward f is zero because government spending now remains constant at the higher level. In Figure 16-6 we show the fiscal expansion as the rightward shift of the aggregate demand schedule from DAD to DAD_1. In the short run the economy moves to point E_1. Output unambiguously expands and inflation rises.

The subsequent adjustment process can be understood from equation (7). Note that in the second period $f = 0$ again. Hence the aggregate demand schedule will shift downward to DAD_2 because there is no new and extra fiscal stimulus. Since Y_1 exceeds Y^*, DAD_2 lies above DAD. On the supply side, using equation (3) the aggregate supply curve shifts upward to SAS_2. The equilibrium in period 2 already involves a return of output toward full employment. Inflation may be higher or lower than in period 1, depending on the relative shifts of the two schedules. Next period the curves shift again.

With an unchanged growth rate of money, in the long run, we return to the initial rate of inflation, $\pi = m_0$. The typical path of the adjustment to a sustained fiscal expansion would involve a transition period where inflation will have been higher than the growth rate of money and, as a result, real balances decline, interest rates rise, and real spending declines. The fact that the economy returns to full-employment output, with government spending higher, means that private demand has been crowded out.

In practice, the dynamics of adjustment are also affected by the impact of the fiscal expansion on the exchange rate—a factor which is not included in this model. As the domestic interest rate rises along with the fiscal expansion, the currency appreciates (as seen in Chapter 6), thus tending to reduce the prices of imported commodities. This appreciation tends to shift the aggregate supply curve down, thereby reducing the inflationary impact of the expansion. It is widely believed that the appreciation of the dollar in the period up to 1985 played an important role in the U.S. disinflation at the start of the 1980s.

Fiscal expansion cannot *permanently* raise output above normal. Nonetheless, after a fiscal expansion, output will be above normal for a time, and that may be enough of a motive for a government to implement a fiscal expansion, at the right time.

An Increase in Monetary Growth

Suppose next that the growth rate of money increases from an initial rate m_0 to a new, higher level, m_1, at which it now stays forever. We start again from a position of long-run equilibrium and investigate the adjustment process. To anticipate the results, we show that, after an initial expansion, output in the long run is back to full employment and inflation increases by exactly the increase in money growth. Figure 16-7 shows the analysis.

As a result of the increase in money growth, the aggregate demand curve shifts up from DAD_0 to DAD_1, by the amount of the increase in money growth. In the short run both inflation and output increase, to π_1 and Y_1, respectively. But those changes in turn set off further changes. On the aggregate supply side, the increase in inflation causes expected inflation to increase, with the SAS curve shifting up to SAS_2. The new aggregate supply curve intersects the Y^* line at precisely the same rate of inflation that occurred in period 1, that is, at π_1. The aggregate demand curve also shifts upward, because the level of output was higher last period. On the new aggregate demand curve, the rate of inflation is equal to m_1 at level of output Y_1 [from equation (7)].

The period 2 equilibrium is at point E_2. Because both the aggregate supply and aggregate demand curves have shifted upward, the inflation rate in period 2, π_2, is certainly higher than π_1. However, it is not clear whether the level of output in period 2, Y_2, is higher or lower than Y_1. That depends on whether the aggregate demand or the aggregate supply curve shifted more from period 1 to period 2.[8]

In Figure 16-7 we show output higher in period 2 than in period 1. The process now continues, with the aggregate supply and demand curves moving yet further upward. We show the third-period equilibrium, E_3, with a higher inflation rate and lower level of output than in the previous period.

16-6 EXPECTATIONS AND SLUGGISH ADJUSTMENT

We now draw out some aspects of the adjustment process in Figure 16-7 which highlight important features of inflationary experience in many countries.

---

[8]If $\lambda\phi < 1$, then output rises in period 2 relative to period 1. If ϕ is small, the aggregate demand curve moves up a great deal, thereby tending to cause output in period 2 to be higher than Y_1.

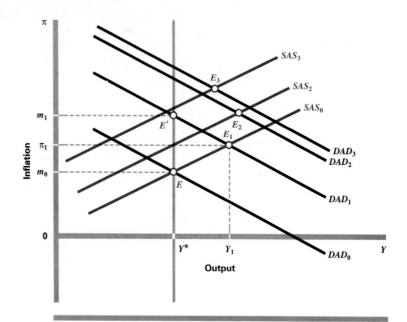

FIGURE 16-7

ADJUSTMENT TO A CHANGE IN THE GROWTH RATE OF MONEY. The increased growth rate of money shifts the aggregate demand curve up, from DAD_0 to DAD_1, raising the inflation rate and output. These changes in turn cause both the supply and demand curves to shift upward in the next period, raising the inflation rate. The process continues until the economy reaches the new steady state.

Stagflation

Two special features of the adjustment process can be seen in Figure 16-7. First, there are times when output decreases while the inflation rate increases. For instance, between E_2 and E_3 in Figure 16-7, the inflation rate increases while output decreases. This inverse relationship between the rate of inflation and output is a result of the shifts of the aggregate supply curve caused by changes in expected inflation.

The inverse relationship between the rate of inflation and output is important, for it often occurs in practice and is widely believed not to be consistent with accepted macroeconomics. This is *stagflation*. Stagflation occurs when inflation rises while output is either falling or at least not rising.

If one ignores the role of expected inflation in the Phillips curve, it is easy to conclude that periods in which output and inflation move in opposite directions—equivalently, periods in which both inflation and unemployment increase at the same time—are impossible. Indeed, it is not only changes in expectations, but any supply shock, such as an increase in oil prices, that shifts the aggregate supply curve that can produce stagflation. Nonetheless, during periods of stagflation, such as 1973–1974,

1980, and 1991, there are articles in the newspapers that the laws of economics are not working as they should because inflation is high or rising even though output is falling.

Overshooting

The most striking feature of Figure 16-7 is that the economy does not move directly to a new, higher inflation rate following the increase in money growth. Rather, given the adaptive expectations assumption we are making, the level of output can even at some stage fall below Y^*. Similarly, the inflation rate is sometimes above its long-run level, m_1, that is, it *overshoots* its new steady-state level. In fact, the economy may even fluctuate around the new long-run equilibrium at E'.[9]

There is one more major lesson from this section. It is that the details of the adjustment process depend on the formation of expectations. Since the shifts in the supply curve are determined by shifting expectations, that point is easy to see in a general way. We make the point more specifically now by replacing the adaptive expectations assumption by rational expectations.

Perfect Foresight Expectations

When there is no uncertainty, the rational expectations assumption is equivalent to the assumption of perfect foresight, namely, that firms and individuals correctly predict what will happen when policy changes. In that case we write $\pi^e = \pi$. Under rational expectations, and without uncertainty, we assume that people understand how the economy works and have enough information to figure out what the inflation rate will be.

Substituting the perfect foresight assumption into the aggregate supply curve (3), we obtain $Y = Y^*$. This is a radical result, for it means that, under perfect foresight, the economy is always at potential output. It is as if under rational expectations the long-run results take place in the short run.

How can that be? The underlying assumption of the Phillips curve mechanism that includes expected inflation is that firms and workers are trying to set wages at a level such that there will be full employment. In the Friedman-Phelps version of the Phillips curve, the only reason they might not achieve that is errors in expectations. If by assumption we remove errors in expectations, the economy will then always be at full employment.

Expected and Unexpected Changes in Monetary Policy

The timing of policy actions and the formation of expectations become very important under rational expectations. The Friedman-Phelps Phillips curve assumes that wages are set before the period begins. That would mean that wages cannot react to changes

---

[9] We show this formally in Sec. 16-7.

in the growth rate of money that are made after wages are set. So the rational expectations assumption would leave open the possibility that an *unexpected* change in monetary policy could affect output.[10]

The logic of rational expectations implies that people base their expectations of inflation on the policies they believe the government is following. Suppose the growth rate of money has been m_0 for a long time. Then we will have under rational expectations $\pi^e = m_0$, as long as m_0 is the expected growth rate of money.

Then if the Fed unexpectedly changes the growth rate of money to m_1, the initial impact will be exactly as in Figure 16-7, with the economy moving to point E_1, because the terms of wage contracts have not yet been changed. But one period later the adjustment under rational expectations will be very different from that in Figure 16-7. Namely, if everyone believes the Fed has indeed changed the growth rate of money, then the aggregate supply curve will move up by just that amount necessary for the economy to go back immediately to full employment, at Y^*. One period later the economy will be in the steady state, with output equal to Y^* and inflation equal to m_1. Thus, as noted in Chapter 9, the rational expectations assumption implies that monetary policy will not have real effects unless changes in monetary policy are unexpected.

Inflationary Inertia

The issue of how π^e gets into the aggregate supply function is clearly crucial. If instead of expected inflation, the π^e term reflects compensation for past inflation, or if it takes a period of years for changed inflation rates to be reflected in labor contracts, then the adjustment pattern seen in Figure 16-7 is more representative of what will happen than is the rapid adjustment that takes place under rational expectations.

This adjustment pattern displays *inflationary inertia*. Inflationary inertia occurs when the inflation rate reacts slowly to changes in policy. It is especially important to note that inflationary inertia may be present even if expectations are rational; for instance, if wages adjust for *past* inflation, then they—and therefore inflation—will adjust slowly to a change in the growth rate of money, even if people have correct expectations.

The key question for policy makers seeking to reduce the inflation rate is whether the economy displays inflationary inertia. It does if the π^e term in the aggregate supply curve reflects compensation for past inflation, or slow adjustment of wage setting because of long-term contracts. It does not if there were rational expectations *and* very quick readjustment of wages and prices.

Summary

1. If inflationary expectations are based on past inflation, an increase in the growth rate of money increases both the inflation rate and the level of output in the short

---

[10] We discussed unexpected monetary policy changes in Chap. 9.

run. Both the inflation rate and the level of output continue to fluctuate thereafter, tending eventually to move to the long-run equilibrium of the economy.

2. In the process of adjustment to a change in the growth rate of money, there are stages at which inflation and output move in opposite directions. This is because the aggregate supply curve is shifting. Stagflation occurs when output is falling while inflation stays high or rises.

3. Under rational expectations, a fully expected change in the growth rate of money does not affect the level of output at all, affecting only inflation. Even if the change in money growth was not expected, output is affected only until expectations adjust to the new growth rate of money.

4. The question of how expectations translate into wages is thus crucial to the dynamics. If it takes time for changed expectations to affect wages, then even with rational expectations, the process of adjustment to a change in the growth rate of money will be lengthy, and the economy is said to display inflationary inertia.

16-7 DYNAMIC ADJUSTMENT DONE MORE FORMALLY

In Figure 16-7 we looked at only the first few periods after a change in money growth. We now examine the adjustment to policy changes in more detail. The starting point is again the dynamic aggregate demand equation (6), in which aggregate demand and output rise whenever real balances are increasing. Conversely, when real balances are falling, so, too, are aggregate demand and output. We write this relation in equation (8), using the notation $\Delta Y = Y - Y_{-1}$:[11]

$$\Delta Y = \phi(m - \pi) \tag{8}$$

Assume now a given growth rate of money, m_0. In Figure 16-8a we show the schedule $\pi = m_0$ along which output is neither rising nor falling. Now we consider how output is changing at different points in Figure 16-8a. For points above the $\pi = m_0$ schedule, inflation exceeds the given growth rate of money. Hence real balances are falling and so, according to equation (8), is output. This is indicated by the arrow showing falling output. Conversely, below the schedule, inflation is lower than money growth, and hence real balances are increasing, and demand and output are growing.

The second relationship is the aggregate supply curve in equation (5). We focus on the case of adaptive expectations with $\pi^e = \pi_{-1}$. Using the notation $\Delta\pi = \pi - \pi_{-1}$, we can rewrite equation (5) as

$$\Delta\pi = \lambda(Y - Y^*) \tag{9}$$

In Figure 16-8b we show the arrows that indicate the direction in which inflation is moving. When output is below the full-employment level, inflation is falling, and when output is above the full-employment level, inflation is rising.

---

*Asterisk indicates a more difficult problem.

[11] We again omit the fiscal term.

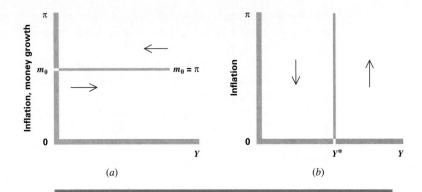

FIGURE 16-8

THE DYNAMICS OF INFLATION AND OUTPUT. Panel (*a*) shows the response of output to real balances. When inflation exceeds the growth rate of money, real balances are falling and hence demand and output are declining. Conversely, when inflation falls short of money growth, output is rising. Panel (*b*) shows that at output levels above *Y** inflation rises and at output levels below *Y** inflation declines.

Table 16-1 and Figure 16-9 combine the information in the two parts of Figure 16-8. The table shows the direction in which output and inflation are moving in each of the four regions of Figure 16-9. We use the arrows to show the combined movement or the path of inflation and output at each point.

Suppose the economy is at point *A* in region I. Because output is above the full-employment level, inflation is rising. But inflation is below money growth. Therefore, real balances are increasing, and hence demand and output are rising. Thus at point *A* output is rising, as is inflation, so that the economy moves in a northeasterly direction. We can establish the direction of movement at points *B*, *C*, and *D* in a similar fashion.

TABLE 16-1

THE DETERMINANTS OF
OUTPUT AND INFLATION

	$m > \pi$	$m < \pi$
$Y > Y^*$	I	II
	Y is ↑	Y is ↓
	π is ↑	π is ↑
$Y < Y^*$	III	IV
	Y is ↑	Y is ↓
	π is ↓	π is ↓

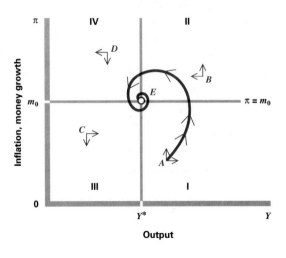

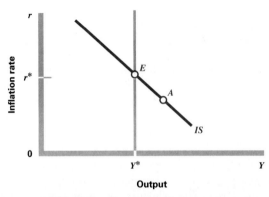

FIGURE 16-9

THE ADJUSTMENT PROCESS. The upper panel combines the
information in Figure 16-8 to show how output and inflation evolve
over time. The long-run equilibrium is at point *E*, at which inflation
equals money growth and output is at the full-employment level.
The lower panel shows the real rate of interest corresponding to
each level of output along the *IS* curve. For example, if the economy
is at point *A* in the upper panel, point *A* on the *IS* curve gives the
corresponding real interest rate. The long-run equilibrium real
interest rate is *r**.

Note that point *E* is the only point in the diagram at which *both* output and inflation are
constant. This is the long-run equilibrium to which the economy ultimately converges.

   In Figure 16-9 we complete the model by bringing in the *IS* schedule. On the
vertical axis in the lower diagram we show the *real*, or *inflation-adjusted*, interest rate,
defined as the nominal interest rate minus the expected inflation rate. Real aggregate
demand, as we saw in previous chapters, depends on the real interest rate—the amount

borrowers expect to pay for borrowing, after taking inflation into account. A higher real interest rate lowers aggregate demand and hence reduces equilibrium output, as shown by the *IS* schedule. The lower part of Figure 16-9 helps us track the real interest rate in the adjustment process. For each level of output in the upper part we can find the corresponding equilibrium real interest rate on the *IS* schedule. Thus we can follow output, inflation, and the real interest rate at the same time.

We show a typical adjustment path starting at point *A*. The corresponding point is also labeled *A* in the lower part of Figure 16-9. At *A* inflation is rising because of overemployment. But because inflation is low relative to money growth, real balances are rising and hence demand and output are growing. The economy thus moves in a northeasterly direction. The driving force is the increasing level of real balances, which reduces interest rates and pushes up demand and output. Over time, as the economy cycles back to point *E*, the real interest rate first declines and then, as the economy enters region II, starts rising. The interest rate overshoots the long-run equilibrium level, r^*, several times before it ultimately settles there.

An Increase in Money Growth

In Figure 16-10 we use this framework to examine once more the effects of a sustained increase in money growth. Of course, we will get the results we already saw in Figure 16-7. We start in long-run equilibrium at point *E*, where money growth is initially m_0. The inflation rate is equal to the growth rate of money, and output is at its full-employment level. Now the growth rate of money is permanently raised to m'. The new $\pi = m'$ schedule lies above the previous one (which is not drawn to avoid cluttering the diagram). The arrows on the path show the direction in which inflation and output are moving. The path starting at *E* shows the evolution of the economy.

At point *E* the growth rate of money, m', now exceeds the initial inflation rate $\pi = m_0$. As a result, the real money stock is increasing. Interest rates are pushed down, and thus aggregate demand and output will be rising. At the very beginning of the adjustment process the economy therefore moves horizontally to the right with output rising. But the moment output starts exceeding the full-employment level, inflation increases. Now the path starts pointing in a northeasterly direction with rising output because inflation, although rising, remains low relative to money growth.

Over time the economy moves to point *B*. Here real balances are constant because now inflation has risen to the level of money growth. But output is above the full-employment level. Therefore inflation is still increasing, and the economy is thus pushed into region II. We do not describe the whole path, but it is apparent that the economy will cycle its way gradually to point E'.

Rational Expectations

The exact details of the adjustment path in Figure 16-10 depend on the assumptions about expectations. But the general pattern—that increased monetary growth first raises output and ultimately is fully reflected in higher inflation—is valid for (almost) any assumption about expectations.

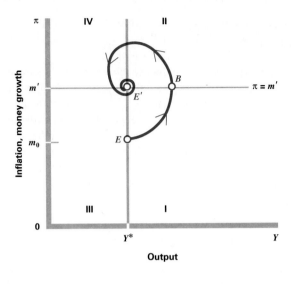

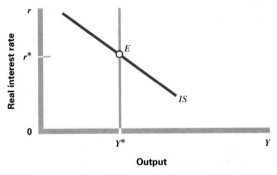

FIGURE 16-10

THE ADJUSTMENT TO AN INCREASE IN MONEY GROWTH. A sustained increase in money growth from m_0 to m' leads the economy along a path from E to E'. Output first expands, and inflation gradually builds up. In the long run, inflation rises to equal the growth rate of money. The economy returns to full employment at the real interest rate, r^*.

Only in a world of complete flexibility of wages and prices combined with rational expectations would the adjustment occur instantly without any dynamics whatsoever. In that case, if a change in the growth rate of money is expected, π^e in equation (3) will be equal to m' at the time the growth rate of money changes, and output will remain at its full-employment level throughout. Remarkably, in this case the inflation rate would generally start to rise before the growth rate of money increases, because people's expectations of inflation in the future reduce the quantity of real balances demanded, and the price level therefore starts moving up.

Once we move away from that extreme case—which requires both rational expectations and full flexibility of prices and wages—the pattern of adjustment is that shown in Figure 16-10. Alternative assumptions about expectations and the adjustment of wages and prices will primarily influence the speed of adjustment and the movement of nominal interest rates, but will generally imply a slow adjustment pattern.

How exactly adjustment to changes in money growth takes place in the real world depends in good part on people's experience with inflation. In economies in which inflation is the number-one issue—because of hyperinflation—it takes very little time for adjustment to occur. But in the U.S. economy, in which inflation has never become a way of life, a slowly adjusting response, as on the path of Figure 16-10, is a lot more likely.

$16\text{-}8$ INTEREST RATES AND INFLATION: THE FISHER EQUATION

We have noted at various points in this book the relationship among nominal interest rates, real rates, and the expected rate of inflation. The (expected) real rate of interest is the nominal rate less the expected rate of inflation:[12]

$$r^e \equiv i - \pi^e \tag{10}$$

Equation (10) is the Fisher equation, named after Irving Fisher (1867–1947), the most famous American economist of the first third of this century, who analyzed the inflation–interest rate linkage.

The Fisher equation draws attention to an important finding about money growth, inflation, and interest rates. We saw in Figures 16-9 and 16-10 that in the long run the economy returns to the full-employment level of output, that the real interest rate returns to its full-employment level (r^*), and that actual and expected inflation converge. Using these two facts ($r^e = r^*$, $\pi^e = \pi$) we write the long-run relationship as

$$i \equiv r^* + \pi \tag{11}$$

With r^* given, equation (11) implies a central result: *in the long run when all adjustments have occurred, an increase in inflation is reflected fully in nominal interest rates.* Nominal interest rates rise one for one with the increase in inflation. The reason we have such a strong inflation–nominal interest rate link is that in the long run the real interest rate is unaffected by monetary disturbances, which do affect the inflation rate.

---

[12] See Irving Fisher, *The Rate of Interest* (New York: Macmillan, 1907). Fisher taught at Yale and was an effective and sophisticated developer of the quantity theory of money. He had other interests, too; he was the inventor of the card index file still used for keeping addresses, and he was a health food enthusiast who wrote several books on the subject. Fisher was an early, if long forgotten in that regard, discoverer of the Phillips curve. See the reprinted version of his 1926 article, "A Statistical Relation between Unemployment and Price Changes," under the heading "Lost and Found," *Journal of Political Economy*, March/April 1973, pp. 496–502.

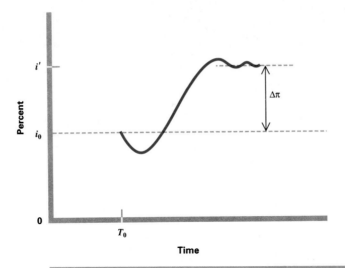

FIGURE 16-11

THE FISHER EFFECT. A sustained increase in money growth leads first to a reduction in nominal interest rates. Then, as output and inflation both increase, the interest rate gradually rises. In the long run it increases by the same amount as money growth and inflation.

Of course, we can see in Figure 16-10 that the constancy of the real interest rate holds only in long-run equilibrium.[13] During the adjustment process the real interest rate does change, and hence changes in the nominal interest rate reflect both changes in real rates and changes in inflationary expectations.

Alternative Expectations Assumptions

The way in which expectations of inflation are formed will influence the adjustment path of interest rates, real and nominal, to a change in money growth, though not the long-run implication of the Fisher equation. Depending on expectations, the nominal rate may start out rising, or it may first decline and then later rise.

Figure 16-11 shows a possible pattern which has received attention in empirical work. In response to increased growth in nominal money, at time T_0 the real money stock grows and initially pushes down the nominal interest rate. Then, as output rises and with it inflation, the nominal interest rate is pushed up until ultimately, after some cycling, it has increased by the full increase in money growth and inflation.

The initial declining phase of the nominal interest rate path is called the *liquidity effect* to denote the impact of increased real balances (liquidity) on the interest rate.

---

[13] In practice, there may be small changes in the long-run equilibrium of real interest rate when inflation changes, but those are of secondary importance.

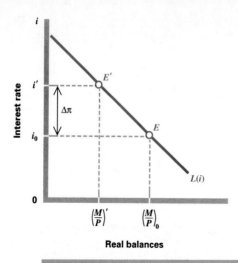

FIGURE 16-12

THE DEMAND FOR REAL BALANCES. An increase in inflation and accordingly in the nominal interest rate will reduce the equilibrium stock of real balances. As the interest rate increases in long-run equilibrium from i_0 to i', real balances decline from E to E'.

The phase of increasing nominal interest rates just after the bottom is reached is called the *income effect*. In this phase increasing nominal income pushes up interest rates by increasing the quantity of real balances demanded. The long-run effect is called the *Fisher effect*, or *expectations effect*, to represent the impact of an increase in inflationary expectations, at a constant real interest rate, on the nominal interest rate. These names are suggestive of the three phases of adjustment as the economy is initially surprised by increased money growth and gradually adjusts to it.[14]

Real Balances and Inflation

In Figure 16-12 we present the demand for real balances as a function of the nominal interest rate. We now study the effect of a sustained change in the growth rate of money on the long-run equilibrium level of real balances.

For that purpose we simply combine two of our results. We saw that in the long run a sustained change in monetary growth changes the rate of inflation and the nominal interest rate in the same direction and by the same amount. A three-percentage-point

---

[14]For an extensive discussion see Milton Friedman and Anna Schwartz, *Monetary Trends in the United States and the United Kingdom* (Cambridge, Mass.: National Bureau of Economic Research, 1982), chap. 10. For a recent discussion of the liquidity effect see Lawrence Christiano, "Modelling the Liquidity Effect of a Money Shock," Federal Reserve Bank of Minneapolis *Quarterly Review*, Winter 1991, and Eric Leeper and David Gordon, "In Search of the Liquidity Effect," International Finance Discussion Papers No. 403, Board of Governors of the Federal Reserve, 1991.

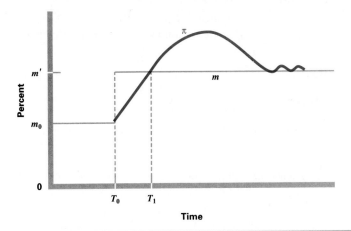

FIGURE 16-13

MONEY GROWTH AND INFLATION. An increase in money growth from m_0 to m' only gradually translates into increased inflation. In the adjustment process prices rise cumulatively more than money, as shown by the overshooting of inflation. This implies that real balances will be reduced in the long run.

increase in money growth raises the nominal interest rate by three percentage points in the long run. We therefore conclude from Figure 16-12 that *a sustained increase in money growth and in inflation ultimately leads to a reduction in the real money stock.*

Here is a very important result that might seem a bit puzzling: increased *nominal* money growth reduces the long-run *real* money stock. Conversely, reduced nominal money growth raises the long-run real money stock. The reason is that higher inflation raises the nominal interest rate and hence raises the opportunity cost of holding money. Hence money holders will reduce the amount of real balances they choose to hold. This reduction in real balances is an important part of the adjustment process to an increase in money growth. It means that, *on average, in the period of adjustment to an increase in money growth, prices must rise faster than money.*

Figure 16-13, which shows the time paths of inflation and money growth, helps explain the adjustment of real balances. At time T_0 money growth rises from m_0 to m'. At the very beginning nothing happens to inflation. Inflation builds up gradually until, with overshooting and cycling, it settles down at the higher level m'. In the phase up to time T_1 money growth exceeds inflation and real balances are rising. Then in the following phase real balances are falling as the inflation rate exceeds money growth.

The diagram is drawn to show that in the phase in which real balances are declining (when π is larger than m'), real balances fall more than they rise in the initial phase.[15] This is consistent with the decline in real balances that happens when the

_____

[15] This can be seen because the total excess of π above m' in the phase after T_1 exceeds the total amount by which π falls short of m' in the phase before T_1.

inflation rate rises, and it means that on average inflation exceeds m' when the money supply rises. Similarly, inflation on average falls short of the growth rate of money when money growth is cut in an effort to reduce inflation.

16-9   SUMMARY

1. The aggregate supply and demand curves introduced in this chapter show the relationship between output and the inflation rate rather than output and the price level.
2. The aggregate supply curve includes expected inflation. Wages increase more rapidly when inflation is expected, thus shifting the aggregate supply curve upward. The process through which a change in the expected inflation rate works its way into the aggregate supply curve may be quite slow. For this reason, the inflation process is often said to display inflationary inertia.
3. The short-run aggregate supply curve with constant expected inflation is nearly flat—because in the short run changes in output do not cause large changes in prices. The long-run aggregate supply curve, with the actual and expected inflation rates equal, is vertical: there is no long-run tradeoff between inflation and output.
4. Under adaptive expectations, expected inflation is based on the recent behavior of the inflation rate. A useful special case is the assumption that the expected inflation rate is equal to last period's inflation rate.
5. Under rational expectations, people are assumed to form expectations using all the information that is available about the determinants of the inflation rate (or other relevant variables).
6. The dynamic aggregate demand curve is a negatively sloped relationship between the inflation rate and the level of output. Its position is determined by the growth rate of money and by last period's level of output. The basic relationship follows from the link between aggregate demand and real balances: the more rapidly are real balances growing, the more rapidly is aggregate demand increasing. The dynamic aggregate demand curve is also shifted by changes in the aggregate demand curve and by fiscal policy changes.
7. The inflation rate and level of output are determined by the intersection of the aggregate supply and demand curves. In the short run, changes in the growth rate of money affect both output and inflation. In the long run, a change in the growth rate of money affects only the inflation rate.
8. During the process of adjustment to a change in the growth rate of money, assuming adaptive expectations, there are periods of stagflation during which inflation is increasing while output falls. Typically, there is also overshooting of the new inflation rate in the sense that on average during the adjustment process the increase in the inflation rate exceeds the increase in the growth rate of money.
9. The adjustment pattern is much more rapid under rational expectations. If the change in the growth rate of money is anticipated, then only the inflation rate changes when the money growth rate changes. If the change in monetary policy is unexpected, it does affect both the level of output and the inflation rate in the short run, but output returns to its potential level as soon as the new policy is understood.

10. The Fisher equation implies that, in long-run equilibrium, the nominal interest rate fully reflects changes in inflation.

KEY TERMS

Expectations-augmented aggregate
  supply curve
Short-run aggregate supply curve
Long-run aggregate supply curve
Adaptive expectations
Rational expectations
Dynamic aggregate demand curve

Overshooting
Inflationary inertia
Stagflation
Fisher equation
Liquidity effect
Expectations effect

PROBLEMS

1. Explain why the expected rate of inflation affects the position of the expectations-augmented aggregate supply curve.

2. (a) Define the long-run aggregate supply curve.
   (b) Explain why the expectations-augmented long-run supply curve is vertical.
   (c) Does the economy ever reach the long run?

3. (a) In Figures 16-7 and 16-10 we show how the economy responds to an increase in money growth. Starting at a steady state with 10 percent inflation, show how inflation would shift back to 4 percent if the growth rate of money were reduced immediately to 4 percent.
   (b) Comment on whether inflation displays inertia during this adjustment process.

4. Consider the adjustment to a *transitory* fiscal expansion. For one period only government spending increases. In the next period it falls back to the initial level. Use equations (3) and (7) to trace the adjustment path of inflation and of output. (*Note:* This is different from the analysis of Figure 16-6. Here we have $f > 0$ in period 1 and $f < 0$ in period 2.)

5. Using the assumptions $\pi^e = \pi_{-1}$, $\lambda = 0.4$, and $\phi = 0.5$, and starting from a steady state with money growth equal to the inflation rate equal to 4 percent, calculate the inflation rate and output in the first three periods following an increase in the growth rate of money to 8 percent.

6. Suppose that in problem 5, expectations are rational instead of adaptive.
   (a) Suppose the change in money growth is announced before it happens, and everyone believes it will take place. What happens to inflation and output?
   (b) Suppose that money growth is unexpectedly increased from 4 percent to 8 percent in period 1, but that people believe from period 2 on that money growth will be 8 percent. Calculate the inflation rate in period 1 and in subsequent periods.

7. The *sacrifice ratio* is the ratio of the total loss of output during a disinflation (i.e., the cumulative amount, as a percentage of GDP, that output falls below its potential level) to the reduction in inflation that is achieved by that disinflation.
   (a) Calculate the sacrifice ratio using the assumption that $\pi^e = \pi_{-1}$. (*Hint:* Given the expectations assumption, this problem can be solved by assuming that the entire reduction in inflation is achieved in one period.)
   (b) Confirm that the sacrifice ratio is greater the flatter the aggregate supply curve.

8. Consider an economy that experiences an adverse supply shock. We can model this by introducing into equation (3) a one-time shock, which we denote by x:

$$\pi = \pi_{-1} + \lambda(Y - Y^*) + x$$

The term x is positive during the supply shock. Show the adjustment process to such a disturbance.

9. The economy finds itself in a recession as a result of an adverse supply shock. Show that either a fiscal expansion or increased monetary growth can speed the return of the economy to full employment.

10. Suppose that a new policy mix of fiscal expansion and a permanent reduction in money growth goes into effect.
    (a) What are the long-run effects on output and inflation?
    (b) How does the fiscal expansion affect the adjustment relative to that which you discussed in answering problem 3?

*11. We stated in the text that under rational expectations and with full price and wage flexibility, the inflation rate rises immediately to its new steady-state level when the growth rate of money increases. We also stated that real balance holdings decline when the expected inflation rate rises. How can the level of real balances fall under rational expectations if the inflation rate is equal to the growth rate of money? (*Hint:* With prices fully flexible, they can change all at once when new information becomes available.)

🖫 COMPUTER EXERCISES

1. Increase YF by 15. Describe what happens to output, unemployment, inflation, interest rates, and investment over time. Find a level of U^* (at original YF) that gives the same result. Why is this?

2. Suppose inflationary expectations (π^e) increase to 10 percent. What happens to output and inflation in the short run and in the long run? Why do they differ?

3. What variable determines long-run inflation? Demonstrate how you would use it to cut long-run inflation by half. What happens over the adjustment path?

4. When fiscal growth is 1 percent per year, what happens to GDP, inflation, interest rates, and investment in the long run and in the short run? Can you explain why?

APPENDIX: DYNAMIC AGGREGATE DEMAND

In the text we use the simplified dynamic aggregate demand curve

$$Y = Y_{-1} + \phi(m - \pi) \tag{A1}$$

In this appendix we derive the dynamic aggregate demand curve carefully from the *IS-LM* model of aggregate demand and show where equation (A1) simplifies matters.

---

*Asterisk indicates a more difficult problem.

We start with the goods market equilibrium condition

$$Y = \alpha(\overline{A} - br) \tag{A2}$$

where $\overline{A}$ denotes autonomous spending, α is the multiplier, and r denotes the *real* rate of interest. Recall that investment demand is determined by the *real* and not the nominal interest rate.

Recognizing that the real interest rate is equal to the nominal interest rate, i, minus the expected rate of inflation, we rewrite equation (A2) as

$$Y = \alpha(\overline{A} - bi + b\pi^e) \tag{A3}$$

Goods market equilibrium thus depends on both the nominal interest rate *and* the expected inflation rate. Given the nominal interest rate, an increase in the expected rate of inflation increases aggregate demand—because the increase implies a lower real interest rate and larger investment demand.

Now we bring in the asset markets by rewriting the condition that the supply of real balances is equal to the demand. Putting the interest rate on the left-hand side, as we did in equation (11a) of Chapter 4, we obtain

$$i = \frac{1}{h}\left(kY - \frac{M}{P}\right) \tag{A4}$$

Substituting (A4) into (A3), we find that the level of output at which both the goods and assets markets are in equilibrium can be written as

$$Y = \alpha\left[\overline{A} - \frac{b}{h}\left(kY - \frac{M}{P}\right) + b\pi^e\right] \tag{A5}$$

or

$$Y = \gamma\left(\overline{A} + \frac{b}{h}\frac{M}{P} + b\pi^e\right)$$

where $\gamma = \alpha/[1 + (\alpha bk/h)]$.

The aggregate demand curve (A5) shows that the *level* of aggregate demand is determined by autonomous demand (including fiscal policy), real balances, and the expected inflation rate. An increase in any of these three factors will increase the level of aggregate demand.

The *change* in aggregate demand is determined by *changes* in autonomous demand, real balances, and the expected inflation rate. Assuming that the only change in autonomous demand comes from fiscal policy, we write

$$\Delta Y = \sigma f + \phi(m - \pi) + \eta(\Delta\pi^e) \tag{A6}$$

where Δ indicates the change in a variable, f is the *change* in fiscal policy, and $\eta = \gamma b$.

The term $(m - \pi)$ is the change in real balances, the difference between the growth rate of money and the rate of inflation: when money is growing faster than prices, real balances are increasing, and when money is growing more slowly than prices, real balances are decreasing: Rewriting equation (A6) by noting that $\Delta Y = Y - Y_{-1}$,

$$Y = Y_{-1} + \sigma f + \phi(m - \pi) + \eta(\Delta\pi^e) \tag{A7}$$

Equation (A7) is the complete aggregate demand relationship between the level of output and the inflation rate. Given last period's income, expectations, the change in fiscal policy, and the growth rate of money, higher inflation rates imply lower aggregate demand.

In the text we simplify by omitting the change in expected inflation, $\Delta\pi^e$.

THE TRADEOFFS BETWEEN INFLATION AND UNEMPLOYMENT

*T*he Gallup Organization regularly conducts opinion polls asking what is the most important problem facing the country. The answers could be anything from drugs, crime, or pollution, to nuclear war. In 1981, with the inflation rate in double digits, a majority named inflation as the most important problem facing the country. In 1983, with inflation down and unemployment up, a majority named unemployment as the country's most important problem. By 1989, after 7 years of expansion with low inflation, neither inflation nor unemployment was regarded as a major issue. In 1992, concern about unemployment was rising along with the unemployment rate.

Table 17-1 makes the point that when inflation, unemployment, or both are high, they are seen as *the* national issue. When they are low, they practically disappear from the list of concerns.

Inflation and unemployment should be avoided as far as possible; that is certainly the best first principle. But since there are tradeoffs between inflation and unemployment, it is also important to get a better understanding of the economic costs of inflation and unemployment. The information provides the input for policy makers' evaluation of the tradeoffs.

How do policy makers deal with the tradeoff in practice? One answer is given by the theory of the *political business cycle*, described at the end of the chapter. According to political business cycle theory, policy makers try to make the inflation and unemployment results come out just right at the time of elections. Of course, the inflation (or the recession to stop it) will come later, after the election.

17-1 THE ANATOMY OF UNEMPLOYMENT

Research on the U.S. labor market has revealed five key characteristics of unemployment:

TABLE 17-1
THE MOST IMPORTANT PROBLEM FACING THE COUNTRY?

	INFLATION		UNEMPLOYMENT	
	rate, %	problem #1, %*	rate, %	problem #1, %*
1981	10.4	73	7.5	8
1982	6.2	49	9.6	28
1983	3.2	18	9.5	53
1984	4.4	10	7.5	28
1985	3.6	7	7.2	24
1986	1.9	4	7.0	23
1987	3.7	5	6.2	13
1988	4.1	—‡	5.5	9
1989	4.8	3	5.3	6
1990	5.4	—‡	5.5	3
1991	4.2	—‡	6.8	23
1992†	3.2	—‡	7.3	25

*Percent of respondents.

†First half of year.

‡Less than 3 percent.

SOURCE: *Gallup Report*, various issues, and DRI/McGraw-Hill.

- There are large variations in unemployment rates across groups defined by age, sex, or experience.

- There is high turnover in the labor market. Flows in and out of employment and unemployment are high relative to the numbers of employed or unemployed.

- A significant part of this turnover is cyclical: layoffs and separations are high during recessions, and voluntary quits are high during booms.

- Most people who become unemployed in any given month remain unemployed for only a short time.

- Much of U.S. unemployment comprises people who will be unemployed for quite a long time.

These facts are critical to understanding what unemployment means and what can or should be done about it.[1]

The starting point for a discussion of unemployment is Table 17-2. The working-age (16 or older) population of the United States in 1991 was 191 million people, of

---

[1] For recent reviews see Kevin Murphy and Robert Topel, "The Evolution of Unemployment in the United States," *NBER Macroeconomics Annual*, 1987, and Chinhui Juhn, Kevin Murphy, and Robert Topel, "Why Has the Natural Rate of Unemployment Increased Over Time?" *Brookings Papers on Economic Activity*, vol. 2, 1991.

TABLE 17-2
U.S. LABOR FORCE AND
UNEMPLOYMENT IN 1991 (in millions
of persons 16 years and over)

Working-age population	191.3
Labor force	126.9
Employed	118.4
Unemployed	8.4
Not in the labor force	64.5

SOURCE: *Economic Indicators*, June 1992.

whom 64.7 percent were *in the labor force*. The size of the labor force is estimated from surveys. The labor force consists of people who respond that they are unemployed as well as those who say they are employed. An unemployed person in these surveys is defined as one who is out of work *and* who (1) has actively looked for work during the previous 4 weeks, or (2) is waiting to be recalled to a job after having been laid off, or (3) is waiting to report to a new job within 4 weeks. The condition of having looked for a job in the past 4 weeks tests that the person is *actively* interested in working.

The Unemployment Pool

Those who are of working age but not in the labor force might be retired, spouses working in the home, students, or people who would like to work but have given up looking. We will concentrate on that part of the labor force that is unemployed.

At any point in time there is a given number, or *pool*, of unemployed people, and there are flows in and out of the *unemployment pool* (Figure 17-1). A person may become unemployed and enter the unemployment pool for one of four reasons: (1) He or she may be a new entrant into the labor force—someone looking for work for the first time—or else be a reentrant—someone returning to the labor force after not having looked for work for more than 4 weeks. (2) A person may quit a job in order to look for other employment and register as unemployed while searching. (3) The person may be laid off. The definition of *layoff* is a suspension without pay lasting or expected to last more than 7 consecutive days, initiated by the employer "without prejudice to the worker."[2] (4) A worker may lose a job, either by being fired or because the firm closes down. This is referred to as an *involuntary quit*, or simply a job loss.

There are essentially three ways of moving out of the unemployment pool. (1) A person may be hired into a new job. (2) Someone laid off may be recalled to his

---

[2] The qualification means that the worker was not fired but, rather, will return to the old job if demand for the firm's product recovers. Until the 1990–1991 recession, over 75 percent of laid-off workers in manufacturing typically returned to jobs with their original employers. The proportion in 1990–1991 was much lower.

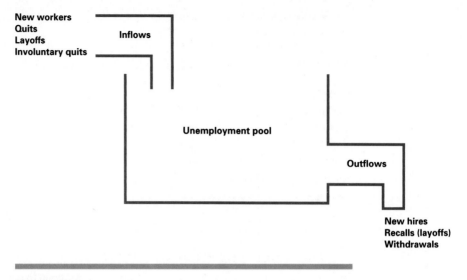

FIGURE 17-1
THE UNEMPLOYMENT POOL.

or her employer. (3) An unemployed person may stop looking for a job and thus, by definition, leave the labor force.

The concept of the unemployment pool gives a good way of thinking about changes in unemployment. Unemployment is rising when more people are entering the pool than leaving. Thus, other things equal, increases in quits and layoffs increase unemployment, as does an increase in the flow of new entrants into the labor market.

Table 17-3 gives a breakdown of the reasons people became unemployed in selected years.[3] Job loss is always the main reason for unemployment, but it is relatively more important in high-unemployment years.

TABLE 17-3
REASON FOR UNEMPLOYMENT (percent of unemployed persons)

	job losers	job leavers	reentrants	new entrants
1983	58.4	7.7	22.5	11.3
1988	46.1	14.7	27.0	12.2
1992*	57.7	10.5	22.7	9.0

*May 1992.

SOURCE: *Economic Indicators*, June 1992.

---

[3] The data source does not show layoffs separately.

TABLE 17-4
UNEMPLOYMENT RATES BY AGE AND RACE
(percent of group unemployed)

	1988	1992
Total	5.5	7.4
White	4.7	6.5
Black and other	10.4	12.7
Age 16–19	15.3	20.0
Men, 20 years and over	4.8	7.0

SOURCE: *Economic Indicators.*

Variation in Unemployment across Groups

At any point in time there is a given unemployment rate. For example, in May 1992, the unemployment rate was 7.4 percent. But this aggregate number conceals wide variations across sex and age groups.

The overall rate is a weighted average of the unemployment rates of the various groups:

$$u = w_1 u_1 + w_2 u_2 + \cdots + w_n u_n \tag{1}$$

The w_i weights are the fraction of the civilian labor force that falls within a specific group, say, black teenagers.

Equation (1) makes it clear that the overall unemployment rate either could be made up of unemployment rates that are similar for different groups in the labor force or could conceal dramatic differences in unemployment rates among groups categorized, say, by age, race, and sex.

Table 17-4 shows data for 1988, when unemployment was low, and 1992, when unemployment was higher. The pattern seen there is typical: unemployment rates are high for the young, and they are lower for white workers. The differences are very large. In 1992, the unemployment rate among blacks was double that among whites, and the unemployment rate among teenagers was more than three times the average.[4]

Cyclical and Structural Unemployment

Table 17-4 can also be used to make a distinction between *cyclical* and *structural* unemployment. The unemployment rates for 1988 correspond, roughly, to structural unemployment. *Structural unemployment* is the unemployment that exists when the economy is at full employment. Structural (or frictional) unemployment results from

---

[4]To check equation (1), you should use the data in Table 17-4 to verify that the aggregate unemployment rate in May 1992 corresponds to that in the table, given that the 16–19 age group made up 15.2 percent of the labor force.

TABLE 17-5

LABOR TURNOVER RATES IN MANUFACTURING IN 1981 (per 100
employees; average of monthly data)

ACCESSIONS			SEPARATIONS			
total	new hires	recalls	total	quits	layoffs	other
3.2	2.0	1.0	3.6	1.3	1.8	0.7

NOTE: Components do not add totals due to averaging and rounding. "Other"
includes involuntary separations.

SOURCE: *Employment and Earnings,* March 1982.

the structure of the labor market—from the nature of jobs in the economy and from
the social habits and labor market institutions, for example, unemployment benefits,
which affect the behavior of workers and firms. *Cyclical unemployment* is unemployment in excess of structural unemployment; it occurs when output is below its full-
employment level.

    With this preliminary discussion in mind, we now turn to a closer examination
of unemployment.

Labor Market Flows

Labor market *turnover*—flows into and out of unemployment and employment, and
between jobs—is large.[5] Table 17-5 shows the average of monthly flows in 1981 into
and out of employment. These data (which, unfortunately, are no longer collected)
show the movement, or turnover, in the labor market by splitting net employment
changes into the different components.

    Table 17-5 presents a remarkable picture of the movement in the labor force.
Accessions are names added to the payroll of a company in a given month. Thus, in
1981, manufacturing companies each month on average added 3.2 names to their
payrolls per 100 employees. *Separations* are names removed from payrolls during the
month. In 1981 manufacturing companies each month on average removed 3.6 names
from their payrolls per 100 employees.

    The data show that people are taking *and* leaving jobs even during times of high
unemployment. Even though the unemployment rate in 1981 was 7.5 percent, firms
were hiring new people and calling back workers who had earlier been laid off, despite
the high unemployment rate. Perhaps even more surprising, 1.3 percent of the workers
in manufacturing quit their jobs voluntarily.

---

[5]The important papers in this area include Robert E. Hall, "Why Is the Unemployment Rate So High at
Full Employment?" *Brookings Papers on Economic Activity,* vol. 3, 1970; Kim B. Clark and Lawrence H.
Summers, "Labor Market Dynamics and Unemployment: A Reconsideration," *Brookings Papers on Economic
Activity,* vol. 1, 1979; George Akerlof, Andrew Rose, and Janet Yellen, "Job Switching, Job Satisfaction
and the U.S. Labor Market," *Brookings Papers on Economic Activity,* vol. 2, 1988.

TABLE 17-6
UNEMPLOYMENT BY DURATION (percent of
unemployed by number of weeks)

	1989	1992*
Less than 5 weeks	48.6	36.4
5–14 weeks	30.3	27.8
15–26 weeks	11.2	14.8
27 weeks and over	9.9	21.1
Mean number of weeks	11.9	18.3
Median number of weeks	4.8	9.0

*May 1992.

SOURCE: *Economic Indicators*, June 1992.

Duration of Unemployment

A second way of looking at flows into and out of unemployment is to consider the *duration of spells of unemployment*. A spell of unemployment is a period in which an individual remains continuously unemployed. The duration of unemployment is the average length of time a person remains unemployed.

By looking at the duration of unemployment, we get an idea of whether unemployment is typically short-term—that is, people moving quickly into and between jobs—and whether long-term unemployment is a major problem. Table 17-6 shows data on the duration of unemployment for 1989 and 1992, years of low and high unemployment. In 1989, nearly half (48.6 percent) of the unemployed had been out of a job for less than 5 weeks; by 1992, people who became unemployed stayed unemployed much longer. As we should expect, the duration of unemployment is high when the unemployment rate is high.[6]

Table 17-6 tells us how long an unemployed person has been out of a job so far. But we are also interested in describing the duration of the typical spell of unemployment, and for that information we have to look at *completed* spells rather than spells in progress. These data are no longer reported, but an idea is conveyed by Table 17-7, which shows information for 1969 and 1975, years of full employment and high unemployment, respectively. Several striking characteristics of unemployment emerge:

- More than half the completed spells of unemployment finish within a month, whether labor markets are tight or slack. This means that a large part of unemployment experiences is of very short duration.

---

[6]Michael Baker, "Unemployment Duration: Compositional Effects and Cyclical Variability," *American Economic Review*, March 1992, shows that the duration of unemployment for all labor market groups tends to increase when unemployment goes up.

TABLE 17-7

COMPLETED SPELLS OF UNEMPLOYMENT

	1969	1975
Percent of spells ending within 1 month	79	55
Mean duration, months	1.42	2.22
Percent ending in withdrawal from the labor force	44	46

Source: Adapted from Kim B. Clark and Lawrence H. Summers, "Labor Market Dynamics and Unemployment: A Reconsideration," *Brookings Papers on Economic Activity*, vol. 1, 1979. Copyright by The Brookings Institution, Washington, D.C.

- The median duration of completed spells, although short, is affected by labor market conditions. For instance, in 1975, the median duration of a completed spell was more than 50 percent longer than in the boom year, 1969.

- Nearly half the spells of unemployment end with the person's leaving the labor force, independent of the state of the labor market. This means that the short median spell of unemployment must be interpreted with caution; it does not mean that people find new jobs in virtually no time.

The Unemployment Rate and the Time Unemployed

Table 17-8 provides information about the proportion of unemployment that consists of people who are unemployed for different lengths of time within the year. The total amount of time unemployed (over all spells of unemployment) is counted for those individuals who experience more than one spell in a given year.

These data establish that despite the substantial flows into and out of unemployment, much of aggregate unemployment is accounted for by people who remain unemployed for a substantial time. Thus, if one believes that unemployment is a more serious problem when it affects only a few people intensely, rather than many people a little, these data suggest that unemployment is a severe problem.[7]

The duration of unemployment differs across groups in the labor force, lengthening particularly with age.[8] Spells of unemployment are more likely to end in withdrawal from the labor force among young males than among older males; this difference does not exist between younger and older females.

---

[7] The role of nonemployment is emphasized by Juhn, Murphy, and Topel, in the article referred to in footnote 1.

[8] See Richard Layard, Stephen Nickell, and Richard Jackman, *Unemployment* (Oxford University Press, 1991), especially Chap. 5.

TABLE 17-8
PERCENTAGE OF UNEMPLOYMENT
ACCOUNTED FOR BY THE LONG-TERM
UNEMPLOYED

all groups	1974	1975
Unemployment rate	5.6	8.5
Weeks of unemployment		
1–4	4.2	2.6
5–14	22.4	15.6
15–26	31.7	27.0
27–39	21.1	22.3
40 or more	20.7	32.5
	100.0	100.0

SOURCE: Adapted from Kim B. Clark and Lawrence
H. Summers, "Labor Market Dynamics and Unemployment: A Reconsideration," *Brookings Papers
on Economic Activity*, vol. 1, 1979. Copyright by
The Brookings Institution, Washington, D.C.

The evidence tells an unambiguous story. Unemployment is much higher among the young than among the older. But the nature of the unemployment is different. The young tend to be unemployed more often and for shorter spells, whereas older workers are unemployed less often but for longer periods. It should also be noted that about half the teenagers unemployed are, in fact, at school and looking for part-time work.

17-2 FULL EMPLOYMENT

The notion of full employment, or the natural rate, or the structural rate of unemployment, plays a central role in macroeconomics and in macroeconomic policy. We start by discussing the theory of the natural rate and then turn to examine estimates of the rate.

Determinants of the Natural Rate

The determinants of the natural rate of unemployment, u^*, can be thought of in terms of the *duration* and *frequency* of unemployment. The duration of unemployment (the average length of time a person remains unemployed) depends on cyclical factors and in addition on the following structural characteristics of the labor market:

■ The organization of the labor market, including the presence or absence of employment agencies, youth employment services, and so on

■ The demographic makeup of the labor force

■ The ability and desire of the unemployed to keep looking for a better job, which depends in part on the availability of unemployment benefits

The last point deserves special notice. A person may quit a job to have more time to look for a new and better one. We refer to this kind of unemployment as *search* unemployment. If all jobs are the same, an unemployed person will take the first one offered. If some jobs are better than others, it is worthwhile searching and waiting for a good one. The higher are unemployment benefits, the more likely people are to keep searching for a better job, and the more likely they are to quit their current job to try to find a better one. Thus an increase in unemployment benefits will increase the natural rate of unemployment.

The behavior of workers who have been laid off is also important when considering the duration of unemployment. Typically, a worker who has been laid off returns to the original job and does not search much for another job. The reason is quite simple: a worker who has been with a firm for a long time has special expertise in the way that firm works and may have built up seniority rights, including a pension. Hence, such an individual is unlikely to find a better-paying job by searching. The best course of action may be to wait to be recalled, particularly if the individual is eligible for unemployment benefits while waiting.

Frequency of Unemployment

The *frequency of unemployment* is the average number of times, per period, that workers become unemployed. There are two basic determinants of the frequency of unemployment. The first is the variability of the demand for labor across different firms in the economy. Even when aggregate demand is constant, some firms are growing and some are contracting. The contracting firms lose labor, and the growing firms hire more labor. The greater this variability of the demand for labor across different firms, the higher the unemployment rate. The second determinant is the rate at which new workers enter the labor force: the more rapidly new workers enter the labor force—the faster the growth rate of the labor force—the higher the natural rate of unemployment.

The three factors affecting duration and the two factors affecting frequency of unemployment are the basic determinants of the natural rate of unemployment. These factors obviously change over time. The structure of the labor market and the labor force can change. The variability of the demand for labor by differing firms can shift. As Edmund Phelps has noted, the natural rate is *not* "an intertemporal constant, something like the speed of light, independent of everything under the sun."[9]

Estimates of the Natural Rate of Unemployment

Estimates of the natural rate keep changing, from about 4 percent in the 1960s, to 6 percent in the early 1980s, to 5.5 percent in the early 1990s. (See Figure 17-2.) The

---

[9] See E. S. Phelps, "Economic Policy and Unemployment in the Sixties," *Public Interest,* Winter 1974.

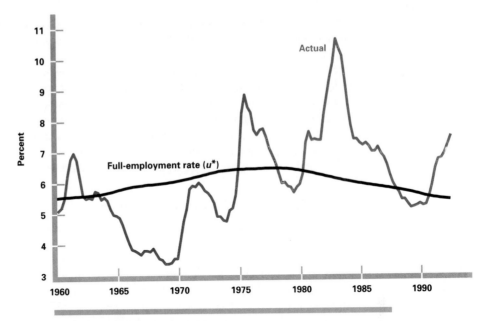

FIGURE 17-2
THE ACTUAL AND NATURAL RATES OF UNEMPLOYMENT, 1960–1992.
(SOURCE: DRI/McGraw-Hill.)

estimates are made pragmatically, using as a benchmark some period when the labor market was thought to be in equilibrium.

The basis for the estimate is an equation for the natural rate (which we denote u^*) that is very similar to equation (1):

$$u^* = w_1 u_1^* + w_2 u_2^* + \cdots + w_n u_n^* \tag{2}$$

Equation (2) says that the natural rate is the weighted average of the natural rates of unemployment of the subgroups in the labor force. The estimate usually starts from a period like the mid-1950s, when the overall unemployment rate was 4 percent. It is then adjusted for changes in the composition of the labor force (that is, the w weights) and for changes in the natural rates for the different groups (that is, the u^* for each group).

The first adjustment, for the changing composition of the labor force, takes into account such changes as the increasing weight of teenagers and women in the labor force and the declining share of adult males, for whom the natural rate of unemployment appears to be lower. These adjustments increase the natural rate, but very little.[10] The

---

[10] See, for example, the demographic adjustments in Brian Motley, "Has There Been a Change in the Natural Rate of Unemployment?" Federal Reserve Bank of San Francisco *Economic Review,* Winter 1990.

second set of adjustments tries in a variety of ways to take account of changes in the fundamental determinants of the natural rate, such as unemployment benefits.

Until the 1980s, there was an official full-employment–unemployment rate estimate. In the 1960s it was 4 percent. Adjustments for changes in the composition of the labor force raised the estimate to 4.9 percent in the early 1970s. Extrapolating to the 1980s and 1990s, the 4 percent rate of the 1960s corresponds to a range of 5 to 6 percent. Figure 17-2 shows the actual unemployment rate as well as the Data Resources, Inc. (DRI) estimate of a full-employment rate developed in this benchmark fashion. It is important to recognize that this full-employment rate, u^*, is nothing but a benchmark and it should properly be viewed as a band at least a percentage point wide.[11]

Hysteresis and the Rising Natural Rate of Unemployment

From 1973 to 1988 the unemployment rate stayed mostly above the natural rate estimated using the demographic adjustment method that underlies Figure 17-2. Even more strikingly, unemployment rates in Europe averaged 4.2 percent in the 1970s and nearly 10 percent in the 1980s. Some economists argue that the unemployment rate over long periods cannot move too far from the natural rate, and therefore that the natural rate in both the United States and Europe must have risen a lot in the 1980s.

One possible explanation is that extended periods of high unemployment raise the natural rate, a phenomenon known as *unemployment hysteresis*.[12] There are various ways in which this could happen. The unemployed might become accustomed to not working. They might find out about unemployment benefits, how to obtain them and how to spend the day doing odd jobs. Or the unemployed may become discouraged and apply less than full effort to locating a job.

The problem may be reinforced by the actions of potential employers. For instance, they may believe that the longer a person has been unemployed, the more likely it is that the person lacks either the energy or the qualifications to work. Long unemployment spells thus *signal* to firms the possibility (not the certainty!) that the worker is undesirable, and accordingly firms shy away from hiring such workers. Hence, the higher the unemployment rate (and therefore the longer the unemployment spells), the more unbreakable the vicious circle lengthening unemployment spells.

Reducing the Natural Rate of Unemployment

Discussion of methods for reducing the natural rate of unemployment tends to focus on the high unemployment rates of teenagers and on the very high proportion of total unemployment accounted for by the long-term unemployed.

---

[11] There is an important alternative estimate of the natural rate of unemployment, described as the NAIRU, or *nonaccelerating inflation rate of unemployment*. This terrible terminology arises from the use of a Phillips curve like $\pi = \pi_{-1} - \varepsilon(u - u^*)$, where π_{-1} may represent the expected inflation rate. It is then possible to get an estimate of u^*—the natural rate, or NAIRU—by looking for that unemployment rate at which inflation is neither accelerating nor decelerating (i.e., where $\pi = \pi_{-1}$). These estimates also tend to show an increasing NAIRU over time.

[12] See James Tobin, "Stabilization Policy Ten Years After," *Brookings Papers on Economic Activity,* vol. 1, 1980, and Olivier Blanchard and Lawrence Summers, "Hysteresis in the Unemployment Rate," *NBER Macroeconomics Annual,* 1986.

We start with teenage unemployment. Many of the unemployed teenagers are new entrants to the labor force, and teenagers are also more likely than adults to be reentrants into the labor force. Thus unemployment among teenagers could be reduced if the length of time teenagers take to find a first job was reduced. In order to reduce delays in the finding of jobs, it has been suggested that a youth employment service be set up to help those who leave school locate jobs. Apprenticeships would also be a powerful means of easing the transition from school to jobs.

Teenagers enter and leave the labor force often in part because the jobs are not particularly attractive. To improve jobs, the emphasis in some European countries, especially Germany, is to provide technical training for teenagers and thus make holding onto a job more rewarding. The European apprenticeship system, in which young people receive on-the-job training, is widely credited not only with providing serious jobs for the young, but also with making them productive workers for the long term.

THE MINIMUM WAGE

Teenagers' wages (on average) are closer to the minimum wage than are those of more experienced workers. Many teenagers earn the minimum wage, and some would earn less if that were permissible. Accordingly, reducing the minimum wage might be one way of reducing the teenage unemployment rate. There have, in fact, been a variety of programs, including a "summer special" that reduces the minimum wage by 25 percent during the summer months, designed to reduce the impact of the minimum wage on teenage unemployment.[13]

UNEMPLOYMENT BENEFITS

We come next to the implication of unemployment benefits for unemployment. A key concept is the *replacement ratio*. The replacement ratio is the ratio of after-tax income while unemployed to after-tax income while employed.

Unemployment benefits add in three separate ways to the *measured* rate of unemployment. First, unemployment benefits allow longer job search. The higher the replacement ratio, the less urgent it is for an unemployed person to take a job. Feldstein and Poterba have shown that high replacement ratios significantly affect the *reservation wage*, the wage at which a person receiving unemployment benefits is willing to take a new job.[14]

The effects of unemployment benefits on unemployment is a particularly lively issue in Europe. Many observers argue that high levels of European unemployment result from the very high replacement ratios there. Patrick Minford states: "The picture presented is a grim one from the point of view of incentives to participate in employment. The replacement ratios are such that, should a person 'work the system,' incentives to have a job are, on the whole, rather small for a family man."[15]

---

[13] However, Charles Brown, "Minimum Wage Laws: Are They Overrated?" *Journal of Economic Perspectives*, Summer 1988, finds little evidence that these measures have affected teenage unemployment.

[14] Martin Feldstein and James Poterba, "Unemployment Insurance and Reservation Wages," *Journal of Public Economics*, February–March 1984.

[15] Patrick Minford, *Unemployment: Cause and Cure* (Oxford: Blackwell, 1985), p. 39.

box 17-1 # UNEMPLOYMENT IN INTERNATIONAL PERSPECTIVE

At the end of the 1980s, there was full employment in the United States. But that was not the case in Europe, as can be seen in Table 1. European unemployment in the 1980s averaged more than twice its 1970s level, which in turn was almost twice the 1960s level, and was still very high at the end of the decade.

With the European unemployment rate averaging more than 9 percent for a decade, it became a prime public issue and topic of academic research. Many reasons have been advanced for the continuation of high unemployment, among them the hysteresis theory discussed in the text.

Other prominent explanations include the *inflexibility* of European labor markets and specifically the downward inflexibility of real wages and the high firing costs imposed by law. The argument is that firms were reluctant to hire workers because it would be so expensive to fire them if necessary later.*

The strength of European unions receives part of the blame. The *insider-outsider* theory of the labor market says that firms bargain with the insiders (the already employed) and have no reason to take account of the outsiders (the unem-

TABLE 1

UNEMPLOYMENT RATES IN INDUSTRIAL COUNTRIES

	1971–1980	1980–1985	1986–1991
United States	6.4	8.1	6.0
Europe	4.2	9.8	9.1
Japan	1.8	2.6	2.4

SOURCE: OECD, *Economic Outlook*, various issues.

*See Edmond Malinvaud, *Mass Unemployment* (Oxford: Basil Blackwell, 1988); Assar Lindbeck, *Unemployment and Macroeconomics* (Cambridge, Mass.: MIT Press, 1993); and Charles Bean, Richard Layard, and Stephen Nickell (eds.), *Unemployment* (Oxford: Basil Blackwell, 1987).

The second channel through which unemployment benefits raise the *measured* unemployment rate is through *reporting effects*. To collect unemployment benefits people have to be "in the labor force," looking for work even if they do not really want a job. They therefore get counted as unemployed. One estimate suggests that reporting effects raise the unemployment rate by about half a percentage point.

The third channel is *employment stability*. With unemployment insurance, the consequences of being in and out of jobs are less severe.[16] Accordingly, it is argued, workers and firms do not have much incentive to create highly stable employment,

[16]Randall Wright argues that European insurance compensates for short work, not only in case of total unemployment as is the case in the United States and Canada. He concludes that the European system results in less variability of employment, though higher variability in hours per worker. See his "The Labor

ployed). Of course, if unions were not so strong, the firms might be willing to hire the outsiders at lower wages, or new firms would be set up to take advantage of the cheap labor.[†] High European unemployment benefits also contribute to high unemployment, with some potential workers being better off unemployed than in a job.

European unemployment is a problem especially because of its incidence. The share of youth among the unemployed is very high, as is the share of the unemployed who experience long-term unemployment. The long-term unemployment has for many gone on so long that most have greatly reduced their lifetime earnings potential. For example, the share of the unemployed experiencing a spell of more than a year in the United States was 8.7 percent. This compared with 41 percent in Britain, 32 percent in France, and 69 percent in Belgium!

What can be done? One view is that aggregate demand should be increased. Another is that structural labor market policies, including training and reductions in unemployment benefits, would help cut unemployment. The idea of *work sharing*—everybody working fewer hours per day, so that more people have jobs, has also been proposed.[‡]

The European experience stands in sharp contrast to the minimal unemployment in Japan. Japanese workers typically receive part of their income in the form of a *bonus*, once or twice a year. This means in effect that firms can cut wages (i.e., the bonus) when times are bad, thus creating wage flexibility. Martin Weitzman has proposed a *profit-sharing* scheme for Europe and the United States, which would make the wage more flexible, but profit sharing has not caught on.[§]

In economics, where experiments are not usually possible, any extreme experience—like the great depression, or European unemployment—provides an opportunity to test and develop theories. That, along with the need to deal with a severe social problem, is why so much attention has been paid to the European unemployment of the 1980s. Unfortunately, that experience seems to be extending into the 1990s as well, and even worsening. ■

[†]See Assar Lindbeck and Dennis Snower, *The Insider-Outsider Theory* (Cambridge, Mass.: MIT Press, 1989).

[‡]Jacques Dreze, "Work Sharing: Some Theory and Recent European Experience," *Economic Policy*, October 1986.

[§]Martin Weitzman, "Macroeconomic Implications of Profit Sharing," *NBER Macroeconomics Annual*, 1986.

---

and firms are more willing to lay off workers temporarily than to attempt to keep them on the job.

There seems to be little doubt that unemployment compensation adds to the natural rate of unemployment.[17] This does not imply, though, that unemployment compensation should be abolished. Individuals need time to search for the right job if

---

Market Implications of Unemployment Insurance and Short-Time Compensation," Federal Reserve Bank of Minneapolis *Quarterly Review*, Summer 1991.

[17]Among the most convincing evidence is a finding that unemployment spells tend to end, with the worker going back to a job, at precisely the time that unemployment benefits run out (typically after 26 or 39 weeks of unemployment). See Lawrence Katz and Bruce Meyer, "Unemployment Insurance, Recall Expectations, and Unemployment Outcomes," NBER Working Paper 2594, 1988.

the economy is to allocate people efficiently among jobs. Thus even from the viewpoint of economic efficiency, zero is not the ideal level of unemployment benefits. Beyond that, society may be willing to give up some efficiency so that the unemployed can maintain a minimal standard of living. In designing unemployment benefits, there is a tradeoff between reducing the distress suffered by the unemployed and the likelihood that higher benefits raise the natural rate.[18]

It is sometimes argued that unemployment does not present a serious social problem because the unemployed choose to be unemployed and live off unemployment compensation. This argument is wrong in assuming that all unemployed people are covered by unemployment benefits. In fact, insured unemployment is less than two-thirds of total unemployment.

17-3 THE COSTS OF UNEMPLOYMENT

The unemployed as individuals suffer both from their income loss while unemployed and from the low level of self-esteem that long periods of unemployment cause. In addition, society on the whole loses from unemployment because total output is below its potential level.

This section provides some estimates of the costs of forgone output resulting from unemployment, and it clarifies some of the issues connected with the costs of unemployment and the potential benefits from reducing unemployment. We distinguish between cyclical unemployment, associated with short-run deviations of the unemployment rate from the natural rate, and "permanent," or structural, unemployment that exists at the natural rate.

The Costs of Cyclical Unemployment

A first measure of the cost of cyclical unemployment is the output lost because the economy is not at full employment. We can obtain an estimate of this loss by using Okun's law.

According to Okun's law, the economy loses about 2.5 percent of output for each 1 percent that the unemployment rate exceeds the natural rate. Using DRI's estimate that the natural rate in 1991 was 5.5 percent, and noting that the actual rate was 6.8 percent, we conclude that the recession caused a loss of 3.3 percent of GDP in 1991. That amounts to about $187 billion. With the unemployment rate averaging 7.3 percent in 1992, for which DRI estimates a natural rate of 5.4 percent, the output loss was 4.8 percent of GDP, about $280 billion.

These very large costs invite the question of why policy makers should tolerate such high unemployment.

---

[18] This tradeoff was the center of an argument between the Congress and the Reagan-Bush administrations during recent recessions: the Congress generally voted to extend the payment of unemployment benefits by 3 months, in order to help the unemployed, while the administration sometimes argued that this would raise unemployment.

DISTRIBUTIONAL IMPACT OF UNEMPLOYMENT

While the Okun's law estimate provides the basic measure of the overall costs of cyclical unemployment, the distributional impact of unemployment has also to be taken into account. Typically an increase in the overall unemployment rate of one percentage point is accompanied by a two percentage point increase in the unemployment rate among blacks (see Table 17-4). In general, unemployment hits poorer people harder than the rich, and this aspect should increase concern about the problem.

The Okun's law estimate encompasses *all* the lost income, including that of all individuals who lose their jobs. That total loss could in principle be distributed among different people in the economy in many different ways. For instance, one could imagine that the unemployed continue to receive benefit payments totaling close to their previous income while employed, with the benefit payments financed through taxes on working individuals. In that case, the unemployed would not suffer an income loss from being unemployed, but society would still lose from the reduction in total output available.

OTHER COSTS AND BENEFITS

Are there any other costs of unemployment or, for that matter, offsetting direct benefits? A possible offsetting benefit occurs because the unemployed are not working and have more leisure. However, the value that can be placed on that leisure is small. In the first place, much of it is unwanted leisure.

Second, because people pay taxes on their wages, society earns more from an hour's work than does the worker. Thus when a worker loses her job, society's loss is greater than the individual's. Therefore, the value of increased leisure provides only a partial offset to the Okun's law estimate of the cost of cyclical unemployment.

17-4 THE COSTS OF INFLATION

There is no direct loss of output from inflation, as there is from unemployment. The relevant distinction is between inflation that is *perfectly anticipated*, and taken into account in economic transactions, and imperfectly anticipated, or unexpected, inflation. We start with perfectly anticipated inflation.

Perfectly Anticipated Inflation

Suppose that an economy has been experiencing a given rate of inflation, say 5 percent, for a long time, and that everyone correctly anticipates that the rate of inflation will continue to be 5 percent. In such an economy, all contracts would build in the expected 5 percent inflation.

Borrowers and lenders would know and agree that the dollars in which a loan is repaid will be worth less than the dollars given up by the lender when making the loan. Nominal interest rates would be raised 5 percent to compensate for the inflation. Long-term labor contracts would increase wages at 5 percent per year to take account of the inflation, and then build in whatever changes in real wages are agreed to. Long-term leases would take account of the inflation. In brief, any contracts in which the passage of time is involved would take the 5 percent inflation into account. In that category we include the tax laws, which we are assuming would be indexed. The tax brackets themselves would be increased at the rate of 5 percent per year.[19]

In such an economy, inflation has no real costs—except for two qualifications. The first qualification arises because no interest is paid on currency (notes and coins), not least because it is very difficult to do so. This means that the costs of holding currency rise along with the inflation rate.

The cost to the individual of holding currency is the interest forgone by not holding an interest-bearing asset. When the inflation rate rises, the nominal interest rate rises, the interest lost by holding currency increases, and the cost of holding currency therefore increases. Accordingly, the demand for currency falls. Individuals have to make do with less currency, making more trips to the bank to cash smaller checks than they did before. The costs of these trips to the bank are often described as the "shoeleather" costs of inflation. They are related to the amount by which the demand for currency is reduced by an increase in the anticipated inflation rate, and they are estimated to be small.

The second qualification is the "menu costs" of inflation. These arise from the fact that with inflation—as opposed to price stability—people have to devote real resources to marking up prices and changing pay telephones and vending machines as well as cash registers. Those costs are there, but one cannot get too excited about them.

We should add that we are assuming here reasonable inflation rates, say in the single or low double digits, which are low enough not to disrupt the payments system. At such low to moderate inflation rates, the costs of fully anticipated inflation are small.

The notion that the costs of fully anticipated inflation are small does not square well with the strong aversion to inflation reflected in policy making and politics. The most important reason for that aversion is that the inflations in the United States have not been perfectly anticipated—and their costs therefore have been substantially different from those discussed in this section.

Imperfectly Anticipated Inflation

The idyllic scenario of full adjustment to inflation does not describe economies in the real world. Modern economies include a variety of institutional features representing different degrees of adjustment to inflation. Economies with long inflationary histories, such as those of Brazil and Israel, have made substantial adjustments to inflation through the use of indexing. Others, in which inflation has been episodic, such as the U.S. economy, have not.

WEALTH REDISTRIBUTION THROUGH INFLATION

One important effect of inflation is to change the real value of assets fixed in nominal terms. A tripling of the price level—as the United States experienced from 1966 to

---

[19]The taxation of interest would have to be on the *real* (after-inflation) return on assets for the tax system to be properly indexed.

TABLE 17-9

REAL ASSET RETURNS (percent per year)

	1960–1969	1970–1979	1980–1991
M2	−0.3*	−3.3	1.8
Treasury bills	1.4	−1.1	3.3
Bonds	1.9	−0.5	5.2

*1963–1969.

SOURCE: DRI/McGraw-Hill.

1990—cuts the purchasing power of all claims or assets fixed in money terms to one-third. Thus, someone who bought a 20-year government bond in 1970 and expected to receive a principal of, say, $100 in constant purchasing power at the 1990 maturity date actually winds up with a $100 principal that has a purchasing power of only $33 in 1970 dollars. The tripling of the price level has—if it was unanticipated—transferred wealth from the creditors, or holders of bonds, to the borrowers.

This redistribution effect operates with respect to all assets fixed in nominal terms, in particular, money, bonds, savings accounts, insurance contracts, and some pensions. It implies that *realized real interest rates* are lower than nominal interest rates on assets, and even possibly negative. Obviously, it is an extremely important effect since it can wipe out the purchasing power of a lifetime's saving that is supposed to finance retirement consumption. Table 17-9 shows real returns on various assets. We note that for money balances (*M2*), for example, there are negative real returns in the 1960s and 1970s, since few components paid interest and the rates were low relative to inflation.

Table 17-10 shows the asset and liability positions by sector in the U.S. economy. The *net* nominal creditor status of a sector is just equal to nominal assets less nominal liabilities. With this definition the household sector is a creditor in nominal terms, with the government and nonfinancial and financial business the offsetting major monetary debtors. Inflation therefore erodes the real value of households' net nominal creditor position. Nonfinancial corporations are net monetary debtors, reflecting their debt-financed capital structure. Financial corporations too are net monetary debtors.

In 1991 the total value of assets fixed in nominal terms held by households was $5.4 trillion. An increase of one percentage point in the price level would reduce the real value of these assets by $54 billion, or an amount equal to 1 percent of GDP.

That figure by itself seems to explain the public concern over inflation. There is a lot riding on each percentage-point change in the price level. But the figure is slightly misleading. While the household sector is a net creditor in nominal terms, some households—for instance, those with large mortgages—are net debtors, and some are net creditors. Even within the household sector, some gain from inflation and some lose. The borrowers gain from unanticipated inflation, and the creditors lose. This means that there is more than $54 billion riding on each percentage-point change in the price level.

TABLE 17-10

NET NOMINAL CREDITOR STATUS (billions of dollars; year-end 1991)

		ASSETS		liabilities (nominal)
	tangible	financia		
		nominal	real	
Households	9,102	5,371	9,819	4,190
Farm and unincorporated business	866	49		163
Nonfinancial corporate business	5,061	2,238		3,433
Financial business	508	10,189	1,844	11,553
Public sector (net)*				2,815

*Net public sector financial liabilities.

SOURCE: Federal Reserve Board, *Balance Sheets for the US Economy, 1960–91.*

Thus a change in the price level brings about a major *redistribution of wealth*, not only among sectors but also within sectors. In particular, with government as the major net nominal debtor, the main redistribution is between the government sector and the private sector.

We must go beyond Table 17-10 in two respects. First, that table really indicates the *vulnerability* of different sectors in inflation. It does not tell us to what extent inflation was anticipated when the contracts behind the figures in Table 17-10 were drawn. Inflation might have been correctly anticipated, so the wealth transfers occurring as a result of the inflation would not cause any surprises or upset.

Second, the gains and losses from the redistributions of wealth among sectors and individuals that takes place as a result of unanticipated inflation basically cancel out over the economy as a whole. When the government gains from inflation, the private sector may have to pay lower taxes later. When the corporate sector gains from inflation, owners of corporations benefit at the expense of others. If we really did not care about redistributing wealth among individuals, the costs of unanticipated inflation would be negligible. Included in the individuals of the previous sentence are those belonging to different generations, since the current owners of the national debt might be harmed by inflation—to the benefit of future taxpayers.

Who gains and who loses from unanticipated inflation? There is a presumption that the old are more vulnerable to inflation than the young in that they own more nominal assets. Offsetting this, however, is the fact that Social Security benefits are indexed, so that a substantial part of the wealth of those about to retire is protected from unanticipated inflation. There appears to be little evidence supporting the view that the poor suffer especially from unanticipated inflation.[20]

Inflation redistributes *wealth* between debtors and creditors. It could also redistribute *incomes*. A popular line of argument has always been that inflation benefits capital-

---

[20] See Rebecca Blank and Alan Blinder, "Macroeconomics, Income Distribution and Poverty," in Sheldon Danziger and Daniel Weinberg (eds.), *Fighting Poverty* (Cambridge, Mass.: Harvard University Press, 1986).

ists, or recipients of profit income, at the expense of wage earners. Unanticipated inflation, it is argued, means that prices rise faster than wages and therefore allow profits to expand. For the United States in the post–World War II period, there is no persuasive evidence to this effect. There is evidence that the real return on common stocks—that is, the real value of dividends and capital gains on equity—is reduced by unanticipated inflation. Thus, equity holders are hurt by unanticipated inflation.[21]

The last important distributional effect of inflation concerns the real value of tax liabilities. A failure to index the tax structure implies that inflation moves the public into higher tax brackets and thus raises the real value of its tax payments or reduces real disposable income. Inflation acts as though Congress had voted an increase in tax schedules. Tax brackets in the United States have been indexed since 1985.[22]

The fact that unanticipated inflation acts mainly to redistribute wealth has led to some questioning of the reasons for public concern over inflation. The gainers, it seems, do not shout as loudly as the losers. Since some of the gainers (future taxpayers) have yet to be born, this is hardly surprising. There is also a notion that the average wage earner is subject to an illusion when both the nominal wage and the price level increase. Wage earners are thought to attribute increases in nominal wages to their own merit rather than to inflation, while the general inflation of prices is seen as causing an unfair reduction in the real wage they would otherwise have received.

Inflation, the Efficiency of the Price System, and Growth

When people are uncertain about current and future price levels, they find it difficult to know exactly how to respond to changes in prices.[23] That means uncertain inflation reduces the efficiency of the price system, therefore reduces the efficiency with which the economy allocates goods and factors, and may affect the level of output.

A considerable body of evidence links higher inflation with lower growth, over the long term. For instance, Jarrett and Selody show that for Canada, over the period 1963–1979, output growth was 0.3 percent lower for each 1 percent increase in the inflation rate.[24] Similarly, international evidence shows that countries with high inflation grow slower.

It is not yet certain what mechanisms produce the inflation–slow growth link, in particular whether it relates to the reduced efficiency of the price system. Nor is it clear whether the relationship applies even at low rates of inflation, say below 5 percent. But there is no doubt that high inflation is bad for growth.

---

[21] See Charles R. Nelson, "Inflation and Rates of Return on Common Stocks," *Journal of Finance*, May 1976, for one of the earliest papers with this result—which has stood up to repeated testing. See also Franco Modigliani and Richard Cohn, "Inflation, Rational Valuation and the Market," *Financial Analysts Journal*, March–April 1979, for a controversial view of the reasons inflation affects the stock market.

[22] Inflation also affects the real rate of taxation of interest and other asset returns when taxes are not adjusted for inflation. The U.S. tax laws do not adjust the taxation of asset returns for inflation.

[23] Confusion over the meaning of nominal price changes is at the heart of the Lucas inflation model discussed in Chapter 9, for instance.

[24] This, and other evidence, is reviewed in Jack Selody, "The Goal of Price Stability," Bank of Canada Technical Report No. 54, May 1990.

17-5   INFLATION AND INDEXATION: INFLATION-PROOFING THE ECONOMY

In this section we look briefly at two kinds of contracts that are especially affected by inflation: long-term loan contracts and wage contracts. We then discuss the possibility of reducing the vulnerability of people in the economy to inflation by *indexation*, which ties the terms of contracts to the behavior of the price level.

Inflation and Interest Rates

There are many long-term nominal loan contracts, including 30-year government bonds and 25- or 30-year mortgages. For example, a firm may sell 20-year bonds in the capital markets at an interest rate of 8 percent per year. Whether the *real* (after-inflation) interest rate on the bonds turns out to be high or low depends on what the inflation rate will be over the next 20 years. The rate of inflation is thus of great importance to long-term lenders and borrowers, and this is especially true in housing.

INFLATION AND HOUSING

The typical household buys a home by borrowing from a bank or savings and loan institution. The interaction of inflation and taxes has a big impact on the real cost of borrowing. The mortgage—this is the term for the home loan—used to be a fixed nominal interest rate loan for a duration of 25 or 30 years. The interest payments are deductible in calculating federal income taxes, which reduces the effective interest cost of the loan. For instance, suppose the marginal tax rate is 30 percent; then the nominal interest cost is only 70 percent of the actual mortgage rate.

Now consider the economics of investing in a home, for example, for someone buying a home in 1963 and financing it with a 25-year fixed interest mortgage. The mortgage rate in 1963 was 5.9 percent, and the rate of inflation over the next 25 years averaged 5.4 percent. Thus the pretax actual real interest cost of borrowing was 0.5 percent. In addition, the home buyer could deduct the interest paid on the mortgage from his or her taxable income. At an interest rate of 5.9 percent and a tax rate of 30 percent, the tax reduction is worth 1.77 percent a year (30 percent of 5.9 percent), so the after-tax real cost of borrowing was *minus* 1.3 percent, not a bad deal! But of course inflation could have turned out to be lower than expected, and then the borrowers would have done worse than they expected.

Uncertainty about the outlook for inflation was one of the reasons a new financial instrument made its appearance: *the adjustable rate mortgage*, which is a particular example of a *floating rate* loan. These are long-term loans with an interest rate that is periodically (every year, for example) adjusted in line with prevailing short-term interest rates. To the extent that nominal interest rates roughly reflect inflation trends, adjustable rate mortgages reduce the effects of inflation on the long-term real costs of financing home purchases. Both adjustable rate and long-term fixed interest mortgages are now in use.

INDEXED DEBT

In countries where inflation rates are high and uncertain, long-term borrowing using nominal debt becomes impossible—lenders are simply too uncertain about the real value of the repayments they will receive. In such countries, governments typically issue indexed debt. A bond is indexed (to the price level) when either the interest or the principal or both are adjusted for inflation.

The holder of an indexed bond will typically receive interest equal to the stated real interest rate (for example, 3 percent) plus whatever the inflation rate turns out to be. Thus if inflation is 18 percent, the bondholder receives 21 percent; if inflation is 50 percent, the *ex post* nominal interest payment is 53 percent. That way the bondholder is compensated for inflation.

Many economists have argued that governments should issue indexed debt, so that citizens can hold at least one asset with a safe real return. However, it is generally only governments in high-inflation countries, such as Brazil, Argentina, and Israel, that issue these debts, and they do it because they could not otherwise borrow.

In low-inflation countries, only the U.K. government has issued indexed bonds, since 1979. The U.S. Treasury has studied the question repeatedly but has never quite made the decision; in 1992 it engaged in another study. Of course, since social security payments in many countries are effectively indexed, the citizens of those countries do hold an asset that protects them against inflation. However, it is not an asset they can buy and sell.

We will consider the arguments for and against indexation below.

Indexation of Wages

In Chapter 16 we discussed the role of automatic cost-of-living adjustment (COLA) provisions in wage contracts. COLA provisions link increases in money wages to increases in the price level. COLA clauses are designed to allow workers to recover, wholly or in part, purchasing power lost through price increases since the signing of the labor contract.

Indexation in some form is a common feature of labor markets in many countries. Indexation strikes a balance between the advantages of long-term wage contracts and the interests of workers and firms in not having *real* wages get too far out of line.

Because wage bargaining is time-consuming and difficult, wages are not negotiated once a week or once a month, but rather in the form of 1- or 3-year contracts. But since prices will change over the term of these contracts, some adjustment has to be made for inflation. Broadly, there are two possibilities. One is to index wages to the CPI or GDP deflator and, based on periodic, say quarterly, reviews, increase wages by the increase in prices over the period. The other is to schedule periodic, preannounced wage increases based on the expected rate of price increase. If inflation were known with certainty, the two methods would come to the same thing. But since inflation can differ from expectations, there will be discrepancies.

We should expect to find indexation rather than preannounced wage increases when uncertainty about inflation is high. Inflation is more uncertain when the inflation rate is high than when it is low, and therefore wage indexation is more prevalent in high-inflation than low-inflation countries.

TABLE 17-11

INFLATION AND COLA PROVISIONS (percent)

period	average inflation rate	workers with COLA coverage*
1963–1972	3.5	27
1973–1982	8.2	55
1983–1988	3.5	50
1989–1991	4.8	39

*Percentage of all workers covered in major collective bargaining agreements.

SOURCE: *Monthly Labor Review*, various issues, and DRI/McGraw-Hill.

In the U.S. economy more than 50 percent of workers who were covered in major collective bargaining agreements in the mid-1980s had contract provisions for automatic cost-of-living adjustments. Table 17-11 shows that these provisions were much more common after 1973, when inflation became higher and more variable, than before. They have again declined as inflation has stayed low.

Table 17-11 might give the impression that indexation is a very common feature of the U.S. labor market. But that is not the case once we note that major bargaining agreements cover only a small part of the labor force. In 1985, for example, about 10 million workers out of a total labor force pool of 110 million were covered by COLA provisions.

SUPPLY SHOCKS AND WAGE INDEXATION

Suppose real material prices increase, and firms pass these cost increases on into higher prices of final goods. Consumer prices will rise, and under a system of wage indexation, wages would rise. This leads to further price, material costs, and wage increases. Indexation here feeds an inflation spiral that would be avoided under a system of prefixed wage increases because then real wages could fall as a consequence of higher material prices.

The example makes it clear that in considering the effects of wage indexing, we must distinguish two possibilities: demand shocks and supply shocks. In the case of a demand shock, there is a "pure" inflation disturbance, and firms can afford to pay the same real wages and therefore would not mind 100 percent indexation. In the case of an adverse supply shock, however, real wages must fall, and full indexation prevents that happening.

Wage indexation thus greatly complicates the adjustment of an economy to supply shocks. In the 1970s and 1980s, the U.S. economy adjusted more easily to the oil shocks than did countries in Europe, where full indexation is more common. The limited extent of wage indexing in the United States helped bring this easier adjustment about.[25]

---

[25] See Michael Bruno and Jeffrey Sachs, *The Economics of Worldwide Stagflation* (Cambridge, Mass.: Harvard University Press, 1985).

Why Not Index?

Economists have often argued that governments should adopt indexation on a broad scale, indexing bonds, the tax system, and everything else they control. That way inflation would be much easier to live with, and most of the costs of unanticipated inflation would disappear. Governments, by contrast, have been very reluctant to index.

There are three good reasons. First, as we see in the case of wage indexation, indexing makes it harder for the economy to adjust to shocks whenever changes in relative prices are needed. Second, indexing is in practice complicated, adding another layer of calculation to most contracts. Third, governments are scared that by making inflation easier to live with, indexation will weaken the political will to fight inflation, lead to higher inflation, and possibly make the economy worse off since indexation can never deal perfectly with the consequences of inflation.[26]

This last argument is one of political economy, a subject to which we now turn.

17-6 THE POLITICAL ECONOMY OF INFLATION AND UNEMPLOYMENT

While the best of all worlds would tolerate neither inflation nor excess unemployment, that world is not available. In the short run, policy makers frequently have to decide how hard to fight an inflationary shock, knowing that the less they accommodate it, the more unemployment they will have. In the long run, policy makers have to decide whether to aim for a very low, or even zero, inflation rate, or rather to be willing to live with positive inflation.

Alternative Policy Paths

Figure 17-3 shows a long-run Phillips curve, *LPC*, which indicates that in the long run there is no tradeoff between inflation and unemployment. Suppose now that as a consequence of a disturbance, say an oil shock, the economy finds itself at point *A*, with high inflation and high unemployment. We show two possible adjustment paths. The solid path shows higher inflation rates in the transition and corresponds to a policy choice of rapid restoration of low unemployment levels and then a long period of decelerating inflation. An alternative is the dashed path along which there is an immediate reduction in inflation. Along this path inflation is falling, but the cost is that the reduction in unemployment is more gradual.

Figure 17-3 makes the point that policy makers do not choose between inflation and unemployment, but rather between *adjustment paths* that differ in the inflation-unemployment mix. The solid-line path corresponds to the gradualist disinflation policy in Chapter 16; the broken-line path is more like the cold turkey policy.

How do policy makers actually choose between paths such as those shown in Figure 17-3? There are two ways of thinking about this problem. One is to assume

---

[26]Indexation cannot be perfect because there are lags in measuring the price level and making payments.

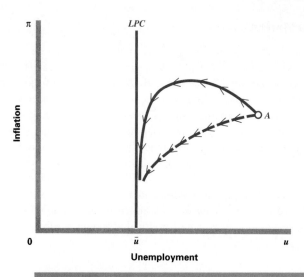

FIGURE 17-3

ALTERNATIVE PATHS OF INFLATION AND UNEMPLOYMENT. A disturbance moves the economy to point *A*, at which there is high inflation and high unemployment. There are alternative strategies for returning to full employment. The upper path emphasizes a rapid elimination of unemployment, the lower path a more rapid disinflation.

that policy makers are benevolent dictators who act in the interests of society. They form estimates of the social costs associated with alternative paths of inflation and unemployment and choose the path that minimizes the total cost of stabilization to society.

The second approach to policy choices recognizes the political nature of the decisions. In a democracy, policy makers respond to the electorate and choose policies that will maximize their chances of being kept in office. In economics and political science, this approach is called *political business cycle theory*.

Political Business Cycle Theory

Political business cycle theory studies the interactions between economic policy decisions and political considerations. The best-known prediction of the theory is that the business cycle mirrors the timetable of the election cycle.

We now review the building blocks of this theory.[27] We have already discussed the first, the tradeoffs from which a policy maker can choose. There are two more

[27] For a survey see Alberto Alesina, "Macroeconomics and Politics," *NBER Macroeconomics Annual*, 1988; and William Nordhaus, "Alternative Approaches to the Political Business Cycle," *Brookings Papers on Economic Activity*, vol. 2, 1989. For a critical view, see K. Alec Chrystal and David A. Peel, "What Can Economics Learn from Political Science, and Vice Versa?" *American Economic Review*, May 1986.

building blocks: how voters rate the issue, or inflation versus unemployment; and the optimal timing for influencing election results.

RATING THE ISSUES

Table 17-1 showed responses to Gallup opinion polls. We noted there that voters worry about inflation and unemployment when these are high. More careful study of the polls reveals a further important lesson: voters worry about both the *level* and the *rate of change* of the inflation and unemployment rates. *Rising* unemployment increases the public's concern over unemployment. Concern over inflation depends on the expectation of rising inflation as well as on the level of inflation. These facts influence the types of policies politicians will choose.

TIMING

The policy maker wants to be sure that at election time the economy is pointed in the right direction to yield a maximum of voter approval. The inflation rate and unemployment rate should be falling if possible—and should not be too high if that can be managed. The problem is how to use the period from inauguration to election to bring the economy into just the right position.

The answer of the political business cycle hypothesis is that politicians will use restrictive policies early in an administration, raising unemployment to reduce inflation. The need for restraint can often be blamed on a previous administration. But as the election approaches, expansion takes over to assure that falling unemployment brings voter approval even while the level of unemployment still checks inflation.

According to this hypothesis, there should be a systematic cycle in unemployment, rising in the first part of a presidential term and declining in the second.

The empirical evidence on the political business cycle remains mixed. The U.S. data do not show as clear a pattern over the 4-year presidential cycle in the United States as the theory would lead us to expect. Every now and then, though, as in 1969–1972, 1981–1984, and in 1988, the model seems to work to perfection.

In any event, there are factors that work against the political business cycle. One is that the president cannot use the business cycle fully because of midterm congressional elections. The second is that a president cannot indulge too openly in staging recessions and recoveries timed solely with a view to the election. There are risks to being caught in cynical manipulation of macroeconomic policies. Third, large macroshocks—oil shocks and wars—may on occasion overshadow the election cycle. Fourth, the executive does not control the full range of instruments. Specifically the Fed, in principle at least, is independent and therefore need not accommodate an attempt to move the economy in an election cycle. In fact, though, the Fed has not always spoiled the game. At least on one occasion, in 1972, the Fed very obviously provided expansion just at the right time. Fifth, if expectations are rational, then monetary policy expansions staged just for elections will have only small real effects and will mainly produce inflation.

Thus we should not be surprised that the electoral cycle is not completely regular. Nonetheless, the hypothesis should not be dismissed. No doubt, every administration would like to have the economy strongly expanding, with declining inflation, at election time. Some are skilled or lucky, and they are reelected. Others are less skilled, or unlucky, and they lose the election.

The U.S. election of 1992 is a case in point. There, the economy grew very slowly until the middle of 1992. Rapid growth began in the third quarter of 1992, and accelerated in the fourth quarter. But that was too late for President Bush.

The Independence of the Central Bank

In Box 15-2, we discussed the problem of dynamic inconsistency, in which policy makers who try to exploit the short-term Phillips curve tradeoff between inflation and unemployment end up with more inflation and no less unemployment than if they did not try to use the tradeoff. This happens because in the long run there is no Phillips curve tradeoff, and eventually the public catches on to the government's inflationary policies.

One solution to the problem of dynamic inconsistency is to require the central bank to follow a monetary rule, for instance, to increase the money supply at a low, constant rate. However, because the monetary rule may be wrong, and because there are good reasons for monetary policy to respond to some shocks, such as a supply shock, no country has adopted a rigid form of rule.

Another solution to the inflationary bias of discretionary policy is to set up a central bank that is independent of the electoral cycle, and that has a clear mandate to fight inflation. The Fed is in principle independent of the administration, though it does report to the Congress. Germany's central bank, the Bundesbank, is fiercely independent, and a determined inflation-fighter. There is strong empirical evidence showing that the more independent the central bank, the lower the inflation rate in a country.[28]

The question of the optimal degree of independence of the central bank is a complicated one. There *are* short-run tradeoffs, and there is always a question of just how fast a central bank should try to reduce inflation. Thus central banks end up exercising judgment, which ultimately depends on their evaluation of what the public's real interests are. But there is no way of knowing what those interests are without some democratic input. Whenever the Fed shows its independence, typically by refusing to expand as fast as the administration or the Congress wants—for example, in 1991 and 1992—there are calls to clip its wings. This is one way it gets the message.

THE ZERO INFLATION TARGET

The views that there is no long-run tradeoff between inflation and unemployment and that there are costs to inflation lead naturally to a conclusion that the optimal inflation rate is zero. Whereas the costs of a steady long-run inflation rate anywhere between zero and 5 percent are probably quite similar, zero has some big attractions: it is a round number, a clear goal, about which there can be no ambiguity. In short, proponents

---

[28] Vittorio Grilli, Donato Masciandaro, and Guido Tabellini, "Political and Monetary Institutions and Public Financial Policies in the Industrial Countries," *Economic Policy*, October 1991, show this result as well as results on the relation between institutions and fiscal policy.

say, it is a *credible* (believable) inflation target. Further, if a zero inflation rate were maintained for a long time, the price level 50 years from now would be the same as it is now, and that would facilitate making long-term nominal contracts.

Thinking like this has led several countries, most notably Canada and New Zealand, to give their central banks the goal of producing zero inflation.[29] This focus makes it clear that the central bank should not devote much effort to attempting to stabilize the business cycle. Supporters hope that a clear mandate and task will both ensure that the central bank keeps inflation low and create expectations of low inflation.[30]

The outcomes of these experiments still have to be seen. For our part, we believe central banks should have some responsibility to attempt to stabilize the business cycle as well as to keep inflation low. The strong emphasis that the central bank should keep the inflation rate low, say in the 0–4 percent range, is entirely appropriate.

17-7 SUMMARY

1. The anatomy of unemployment in the United States reveals frequent and short spells of unemployment. Nonetheless, a substantial fraction of U.S. unemployment is accounted for by those who are unemployed for a large portion of the time.

2. There are significant differences in unemployment rates across age groups and race. Unemployment among black teenagers is highest, and that of white adults is lowest. The young and minorities have significantly higher unemployment rates than middle-aged whites.

3. The concept of the natural, or structural, rate of unemployment singles out that part of unemployment which would exist even at full employment. This unemployment arises from the natural frictions of the labor market, as people move between jobs. The natural rate is hard to measure. The consensus is to estimate it at about 5.5 percent, up from the 4 percent of the mid-1950s.

4. Policies to reduce the natural rate of unemployment involve structural labor market policies. Disincentives to employment and training, such as minimum wages, and incentives to extended job search, such as high unemployment benefits, tend to raise the natural rate. It is also possible that unemployment displays hysteresis, with high unemployment today raising the natural rate.

5. The costs of unemployment are the psychological and financial distress of the unemployed as well as the loss of output. In addition, higher unemployment tends to hit the poorer members of society disproportionately.

6. The economy can adjust to perfectly anticipated inflation by moving to a system of indexed taxes and to nominal interest rates that reflect the expected rate of inflation. If inflation were perfectly anticipated and adjusted to, the only costs of inflation would be shoeleather and menu costs.

7. Imperfectly anticipated inflation has important redistributive effects among sectors. Unanticipated inflation benefits monetary debtors and hurts monetary credi-

[29] For a Canadian view supporting the goal, see the paper by Selody referred to in footnote 24.

[30] The argument is also being made that the Fed should have a zero inflation target. See, for instance, W. Lee Hoskins, "Defending Zero Inflation: All for Naught," Federal Reserve Bank of Minneapolis *Quarterly Review*, Spring 1991.

tors. The government gains real tax revenue, and the real value of government debt declines.

8. In the U.S. housing market, unanticipated increases in inflation combined with the tax deductibility of interest made housing a particularly good investment over the 1960–1980 period.

9. In the U.S. economy, indexation is neither very widespread nor complete. This absence of strong indexation probably eased the adjustment to supply shocks.

10. There is considerable evidence that higher rates of inflation accompany lower rates of growth, implying that inflation is bad for growth in the long run.

11. Stabilization policy involves choosing an optimal path of inflation and unemployment. The choice is between more or less rapid paths of recovery. The more rapid path reduces unemployment rapidly but does so without making large inroads on inflation. To reduce inflation quickly, unemployment must be high and/or recovery slow.

12. The political business cycle hypothesis emphasizes the direction of change of the economy. For incumbents to win an election, the unemployment rate should be falling and the inflation rate not worsening.

13. Countries with independent central banks have lower inflation on average. Several countries have recently given their central banks the target of attaining zero (say 0–2 percent) inflation.

KEY TERMS

Unemployment pool	Replacement ratio
Layoffs	Anticipated inflation
Structural unemployment	Unanticipated inflation
Quits	Redistribution of wealth
Cyclical unemployment	Indexation
Accessions	COLA
Separations	Political business cycle
Duration of spells of unemployment	Central bank independence
Natural rate of unemployment	Zero inflation target
Frequency of unemployment	

PROBLEMS

1. Discuss strategies whereby the government (federal, state, or local) could reduce unemployment in or among (a) depressed industries, (b) unskilled workers, (c) depressed geographical regions, (d) teenagers. Include comments on the *type* of unemployment you would expect in these various groups (that is, relative durations of unemployment spells).

2. Discuss how the following changes would affect the natural or structural rate of unemployment. Comment also on the side effects of these changes.
   (a) Elimination of unions
   (b) Increased participation of women in the labor market
   (c) Larger fluctuations in the *level* of aggregate demand
   (d) An increase in unemployment benefits

(e) Elimination of minimum wages

(f) Larger fluctuations in the *composition* of aggregate demand

3. Discuss the differences in unemployment between adults and teenagers. What does this imply about the types of jobs (on average) the different groups are getting?

4. The following information is to be used for calculations of the unemployment rate. There are two major groups: adults and teenagers. Teenagers account for 10 percent of the labor force, and adults for 90 percent. Adults are divided into men and women. Women account for 35 percent of the adult labor force. The following table shows the unemployment rates for the groups.

group	unemployment rate, %
Teenagers	19
Adults	
Men	6
Women	7

(a) How do the numbers in this table compare (roughly) with the numbers for the U.S. economy?

(b) Calculate the aggregate unemployment rate.

(c) Assume the unemployment rate for teenagers rises from 19 to 29 percent. What is the effect on the male unemployment rate? (Assume 60 percent of the teenagers are males.) What is the effect on the aggregate unemployment rate?

(d) Assume the share of women in the adult labor force increases to 40 percent. What is the effect on the adult unemployment rate? What is the effect on the aggregate unemployment rate?

(e) Relate your answers to methods of estimating the natural rate of unemployment.

5. Use the *Economic Report of the President* to find the unemployment data for the years 1975, 1979, and 1989. Use as labor force groups, males and females, 16 to 19 years of age and 20 and older (that is, four groups). Calculate what 1975 and 1989 unemployment would have been if each group in 1975 and 1989 had the unemployment rate of the group of 1979. What does the answer tell you?

6. In the *Economic Report of the President*, you will find data on the duration of unemployment. Compare the distribution of unemployment by duration in 1989 and 1992. What relationship do you find between duration and the overall unemployment rate?

7. A reduction in minimum wages during summer months reduces the cost of labor to firms, but it also reduces the income per hour that a teenager working for the minimum wage receives.

(a) Who benefits from the measure, firms that have access to cheaper labor, teenagers who otherwise would not have a job, or both?

(b) Who "pays" for the program, teenagers who would have a job anyway but who now receive less pay than they would have, and/or other workers who are displaced by the cheaper labor resulting from reduced minimum wages? Spell out what you think is the answer to these questions and decide whether you think the program is a good idea.

8. (a) What are the economic costs of inflation? Distinguish between anticipated and unanticipated inflation.

(b) Do you think anything is missing from the list of costs of inflation that economists present? If so, what?

9. Evaluate the following argument that attempts to dispose of the notion of the political business cycle. "The public is too sophisticated to think that it makes much difference which party is running the economy. Both the Democrats and Republicans want the economy to boom, and want to keep inflation low. Both have access to the best economists available. Why would anyone think economic performance would be different with one party than with the other?"

10. Explain what adjustments would be needed in the economy to make it as far as possible inflation-proof. Then evaluate the claim in the text that in practice indexation cannot be expected to work very well.

11. Some people say that inflation can be reduced in the long run without an increase in unemployment, and so we should reduce inflation to zero. Others say a steady rate of inflation at, say, 4 percent, is not so bad, and that should be our goal. Evaluate these two arguments and describe what, in your opinion, are good long-run goals for reducing inflation and unemployment. How would these be achieved?

12. We have discussed the case for the independence of the central bank. Can the same, or a similar, case be made for setting up an independent fiscal authority?

13. In a growing economy with moderate inflation, a president should expect to be reelected. What went wrong in 1992?

💾 COMPUTER EXERCISES

If you are interested in exploring economic policy material after reading this chapter, refer to the Policy Game contained in the *PC-Macroeconomics* program and the question material located at the end of the book. The Policy Game is a more realistic and complex representation of the economy than the simpler material found in earlier chapters.

18

MONEY, DEFICITS, AND INFLATION: EVIDENCE AND POLICY ISSUES

*I*n this chapter we concentrate on the effects of money growth on inflation and interest rates. We begin by examining the monetarist proposition that inflation is a monetary phenomenon, which means that inflation results entirely, or at least primarily, from excessive money growth.[1] We then study the linkages among interest rates, inflation, and money growth. Next we look at the links between budget deficits and money growth, asking whether or under what circumstances budget deficits cause money growth. Finally, we describe hyperinflations—extremely high inflations—and the role of money growth in them.

We will show that high inflation is indeed primarily a monetary phenomenon in the sense that inflation could not continue without continued money growth. But typically in conditions of high inflation there are also high budget deficits underlying the rapid money growth. This was the case, for instance, in the high inflation or hyperinflations in Israel, Bolivia, Argentina, and Brazil in the 1980s. Similarly, in conditions of high inflation nominal interest rates become very high as expected inflation becomes incorporated into nominal rates.

However, the role of money stands out less when inflation rates are lower, in the single-digit or low-double-digit range; then supply shocks may well play a relatively larger role. Similarly, more moderate budget deficits, such as those in the United States in the early 1980s, do not necessarily lead to higher money growth and inflation.

18-1 MONEY, INFLATION, AND INTEREST RATES: REVIEW

Our discussion of inflation dynamics in Chapter 16 yielded the following conclusions:

- A sustained increase in the growth rate of money will, in the long run when all adjustments have taken place, lead to an equal increase in the rate of inflation.

---

[1] See the discussion of monetarism in Chap. 7.

In the long run, the inflation rate is equal to the growth rate of money adjusted for trend growth in real income.

- A sustained increase in money growth will have no long-run effects on the level of output: there is no long-run tradeoff between inflation and output.[2]

This is consistent with the monetarist claim that inflation is caused by money growth, *in the long run*. But as one moves away from the long run, disturbances other than changes in the money stock—such as supply shocks—affect inflation and, conversely, changes in the money stock do have real effects.

Even if the disturbances are purely monetary, it will still generally take time before they are fully reflected in inflation and only in inflation. As we also saw in Chapter 16, expectations play a key role in determining the short-run dynamics of inflation. The short-run real effects of changes in money growth, and the role of expectations, are of course also recognized by monetarists.[3]

We also recall the relationship between money growth and interest rates, showing

- In the short run, increased money growth will reduce the real interest rate. But in the long run, after all adjustments have taken place, the real interest rate will return to its initial level.

- With the real interest rate unchanged, the nominal rate will rise by the increase in inflation. This is the Fisher effect.

18-2 EMPIRICAL EVIDENCE

What is the evidence on the links between money growth and inflation and among money growth, inflation, and interest rates?

The Money-Inflation Link

In examining the links between inflation and money growth, it is convenient to use the quantity theory of money. The quantity theory relates the level of nominal income (PY), the money stock (M), and the velocity of money (V):

$$MV = PY \tag{1}$$

Recall that the velocity of money is the number of times the money stock turns over each year in financing payments made to purchase the economy's output.

---

[2] We ask you in problem 1 at the end of the chapter to demonstrate the corresponding results for a sustained reduction in the growth rate of money.

[3] See, for instance, Milton Friedman, "Monetarism in Rhetoric and Practice," Bank of Japan, *Monetary and Economic Studies,* October 1983.

The quantity equation can also be written in terms of the percentage change over time of each of the four terms in equation (1):

$$m + v = \pi + y \tag{1a}$$

Putting the inflation rate on the left, we obtain the central result:

$$\pi = m - y + v \tag{1b}$$

where m is money growth, v is the percentage change in velocity, π is the inflation rate, and y is the growth rate of output.[4]

Equation (1b) can be used to account for the sources of inflation, that is, for the part that is due to velocity changes or to money growth or to output growth. The monetarist claim that inflation is predominantly a monetary phenomenon implies that velocity changes are small.

Now we turn to the data. Figure 18-1 shows annual $M2$ growth and the inflation rate of the GDP deflator for the United States. We see that the inflation rate and the growth rate of money have broadly moved together. But the relationship is *very* rough, especially in the first part of the 1970s. As equation (1b) shows, that means that either or both changes in output growth and velocity changes were affecting inflation.

In Table 18-1 we examine the link between money growth and inflation over longer periods, specifically decades, and also adjusting for growth in output. The growth adjustment is made as implied by equation (1b), that is, subtracting the growth rate of output from the growth of money.[5]

In Table 18-1, inflation is closely related to the growth rate of $M2$.[6] For example, in the 1960s money growth less real growth was 3.1 percent and actual inflation averaged 2.7 percent, not far off the mark. Likewise in the 1970s equation (1b) predicts 7 percent whereas actual inflation was 7.1 percent. And the same close forecast is evident once more in the 1980s, with a predicted inflation rate of 5.2 percent versus an actual rate of 5.0 percent.

The relationship between money growth and inflation is much looser for $M1$. This is a reflection of the instability of $M1$ money demand, especially in the 1980s. To obtain a stable relationship between money growth and inflation we need a stable real money demand.

---

[4]Examining equation (1b), we see that the long-run results of Chap. 16 correspond to a situation where the velocity of money is constant. That assumption is made implicitly in the dynamic aggregate demand curve, when we assume that the change in demand is determined by the change in real balances (holding fiscal policy constant).

[5]In making this adjustment for output growth, we are assuming that velocity is not systematically related to income. That means we are assuming a unit income elasticity of money demand. In general the inflation rate is equal to money growth less the product of the income elasticity and the growth rate of output.

[6]In Chap. 13 we saw that the demand for real money balances ($M2$) has an income elasticity of about unity. Thus the long-run relationship between $M2$ growth and inflation should be approximately 1:1 except for changes in velocity unrelated to income growth.

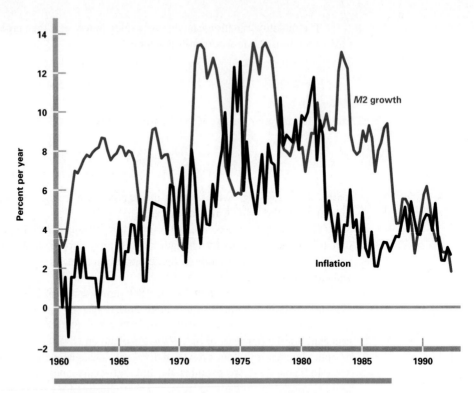

FIGURE 18-1

MONEY GROWTH AND INFLATION, 1960–1992. Inflation is depicted by the GDP deflator; money growth by *M*2. (SOURCE: DRI/McGraw-Hill.)

TABLE 18-1

MONEY, INFLATION, AND GROWTH (percent per year)

	*M*1	*M*2	inflation*	GNP growth
1960–1969	3.8	7.1	2.7	4.0
1970–1979	6.5	9.8	7.1	2.8
1980–1989	8.4	8.0	5.0	2.6
1960–1992	6.1	7.8	4.7	2.9

*Inflation rate of the deflator.

SOURCE: DRI/McGraw-Hill.

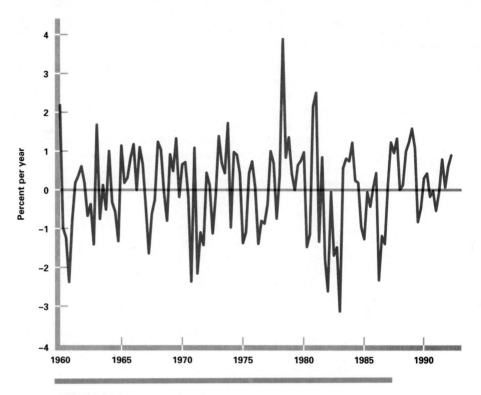

FIGURE 18-2
QUARTERLY CHANGE IN VELOCITY, 1960–1992. Percent change in the
velocity of *M*2. (Source: DRI/McGraw-Hill.)

FLUCTUATIONS OF VELOCITY

If the 10-year average *M*2 growth-inflation relation in Table 18-1 works well, why is
the year-to-year relationship in Figure 18-1 much poorer? One reason, of course, is
that we have adjusted for output growth in Table 18-1. But the more important reason
is fluctuations in velocity.

Figure 18-2 shows year-to-year percentage changes in *M*2 velocity—the *v* term
in equation (1*a*). Velocity frequently shifts by 3–4 percent per year, thus adding
considerable short-run variability to the money growth-inflation relationship. The velocity of *M*2 is affected in the short run by variations in output and interest rates. For
example, because the short-run income elasticity is much less than unity, a fall in real
income will reduce velocity. A rise in interest rates will raise velocity.

These shifts in interest rates or income that result in velocity changes could be
caused by changes in the money stock. They could also be caused by supply shocks,
such as the oil price increases of 1973–1974 and 1979–1980, which shifted the aggregate
supply curve upward, causing more rapid inflation and recessions. In addition, changes
in inflationary expectations can result in changes in output or interest rates that cause

MONETARISM AND MODERN MACROECONOMICS

In the early 1960s, monetarists began a serious challenge to the Keynesian macro-economics that had dominated the field since the great depression. Many leading economists in addition to Milton Friedman* have propounded the basic message of monetarism, that money is extremely important for macroeconomics, along with several other important positions.

Three decades later, many of the positions originally associated with mone-tarism are part of the agreed-upon core of macroeconomics, while others remain controversial. Most of the key propositions have been discussed in context earlier in this book. Here they are, along with the chapters in which they were discussed:

1. Money matters (this chapter).
2. A monetary rule: Monetarists argue that monetary policy would be better conducted by a rule—that is, that money grows at a constant rate—than by discretion (Chapters 14 and 15).
3. Monetary policy is better conducted by setting money targets rather than interest rate targets (Chapter 14).

---

*For a recent account of Friedman's views, see his *Money Mischief* (New York: Harcourt Brace Jovanovich, 1992). Among the most prominent monetarists are Anna J. Schwartz of the National Bureau of Economic Research, Friedman's co-author of (among other books and articles) the magisterial *A Monetary History of the United States 1867–1960* (Princeton, N.J.: Princeton University Press, 1963), and the late Karl Brunner of the University of Rochester, Allan Meltzer and Bennett McCallum of Carnegie-Mellon, Phillip Cagan of Columbia University, David Laidler and Michael Parkin of the University of Western Ontario, William Poole of Brown University, and many leading economists in other countries.

---

velocity changes. And velocity can change also because the demand for money shifts, for instance, because of changes in the financial system. There are thus many potential causes of the short-run instability of velocity that is evident in Figure 18-2.

Finally, a warning is in order: even the good long-run performance of the money ($M2$) growth-inflation relation may be the exception rather than the rule. There is no economic rule that says velocity in the long run must be constant; in fact, if the income elasticity of real money demand is not unity, velocity will change for that reason alone. With an income elasticity of, say, 0.5, velocity would be rising with real income.

The other critical factor affecting velocity is financial innovation. If innovation introduces substitutes for the particular monetary aggregate we study, we expect a fall in real money demand and hence a rise in velocity. Conversely, if the particular monetary aggregate being studied becomes more attractive to hold—for example, because it starts earning interest—we expect a fall in velocity. We regard a roughly constant velocity over long periods as therefore somewhat surprising and deserving further examination.

HISTORICAL AND FOREIGN TRENDS

In the United States, the $M2$ money-inflation link has not always been as tight as in the past 3 decades. In problem 10 we provide data for decadal averages in the period

4. Long and variable lags: Monetarists assert that monetary policy affects the economy with lags that are both long and variable. This is a position that was discussed and accepted in Chapters 14 and 15.

There are two other monetarist positions that should be noted:

5. The inherent stability of the private sector: Monetarists argue that the private sector is inherently stable, and that most disturbances to the economy are caused by mistaken government policy. They believe that less government is better than more, and that governments have an inherent tendency to grow. (Some of these issues are discussed in Chapter 19.)
6. Flexible exchange rates: In the 1950s Milton Friedman was the most outstanding proponent of the view that exchange rates should be flexible rather than fixed. Although this view is not necessarily monetarist—in the sense that it is independent of the argument that money matters—most monetarists (along with many other macroeconomists) accept it, regarding the exchange rate as just another price that the markets should be free to set, and that governments are likely to get wrong.

Where does the profession come out on the issues? As Franco Modigliani of MIT has said, "We are all monetarists now," in the sense that we all believe that *some* stock of money has major impacts on the economy, that sustained rapid money growth leads to inflation, and that inflation cannot be kept low unless money growth is low. While the other positions are generally more controversial, there is no question that monetarism has had major successes, including the adoption in many countries of money growth targets (Chapter 14). ■

1860 to 1989 and ask you to investigate the money-inflation link for that period. There are clearly some outliers, for example, the 1890s, when money growth (adjusted for real income growth) was high but prices were falling.

International data, shown in Table 18-2, give the same impression as the data for the United States: generally, higher growth rates of money (adjusted for output growth) are associated with higher inflation, but the relationship is not 1:1. For some countries, such as the United Kingdom, inflation is well below the "predicted" rate (the growth rate of money minus output growth), whereas for others, such as Italy, the converse is true. Once again, the relationship is not exact because of shifts in money demand, perhaps caused by financial deregulation, changes in interest rates that affect velocity, and income elasticities of money demand that are different from unity.[7]

SUMMARY: IS INFLATION A MONETARY PHENOMENON?

The answer to the question of whether inflation is a monetary phenomenon *in the long run* is yes. No major inflation can take place without rapid money growth, and rapid

---

[7]Definitions of monetary aggregates differ substantially among countries. The terms money plus quasi-money, or broad as opposed to narrow aggregates, in Table 18-2, describe the aggregate corresponding most closely to $M2$ in the United States.

TABLE 18-2
MONEY AND INFLATION IN INTERNATIONAL PERSPECTIVE, 1960–1990
(percent per year)

	money growth*	output growth	"predicted" inflation	actual inflation
Canada†	8.9	2.8	6.1	5.9
United States	8.9	3.2	5.7	4.8
Japan	13.8	6.3	7.5	5.4
Germany	8.6	3.1	5.5	3.5
France†	9.8	2.1	7.7	7.0
Italy	11.3	2.4	8.9	10.9
United Kingdom	14.5	2.4	12.1	7.7

*M1 plus quasi-money.

†For 1979–1990 only, previous data being unavailable for broad monetary aggregates.

SOURCE: OECD, *Historical Statistics*, 1992.

money growth will cause rapid inflation. Further, any policy that determinedly keeps the growth rate of money low will lead eventually to a low rate of inflation.

But at the same time the link between money growth and inflation is not precise. There are three reasons for that. First, nonmonetary shocks that change the level of output can change the inflation rate while the growth rate of money is unchanged. Second, changes in interest rates change the alternative cost of holding money and hence affect the desired ratio of income to money. And, very important, financial institutions change, the definition of money changes, and the demand for money may shift over time.

The first two reasons explain short-run instability of the money-inflation relationship. The third factor, financial innovation, has become very important in most industrialized countries since the 1980s. The payment of interest on a wide range of $M2$ components has raised the demand for $M2$ and hence reduced the inflation rate associated with a given money growth rate in the transition period.

Inflation and Interest Rates

With the real interest rate approximately constant in the long run, and with expectations of inflation adjusting to actual inflation, the Fisher equation asserts a positive link between nominal interest rates and inflation, as we saw in Chapter 16.

Figure 18-3 shows the nominal interest rate on 3-month Treasury bills and the rate of inflation over the period for which the bills are outstanding. The *realized* real interest rate is the difference between the nominal interest rate and the actual rate of inflation or, in symbols,

$$r \equiv i - \pi \tag{2}$$

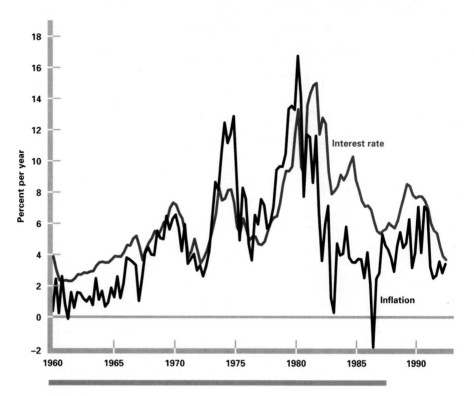

FIGURE 18-3

INFLATION AND NOMINAL INTEREST RATES, 1960–1992. The interest rate is the yield on 3-month Treasury bills. The inflation rate is the rate of inflation of the CPI over the following quarter. (SOURCE: DRI/ McGraw-Hill.)

In Chapter 16, we defined the *expected* real interest rate as the difference between the nominal interest rate and expected inflation. But we do not have reliable data on expected inflation and hence report only *realized* real rates rather than expected real rates of interest.[8] But in the short term, with inflation quite predictable, there are no big discrepancies between expected and actual real rates.

As can be seen in Figure 18-3, there were several episodes of negative real rates in the 1970s, particularly in 1974–1975 when inflation increased sharply and exceeded the interest rate by a significant margin. By contrast, in the period since 1980 the real rate of interest has been *persistently* positive, and in most years by a good margin. This is a quite new experience if we look back only a few years, but it certainly has precedents in U.S. experience in the past 100 years, during which real interest rates were significantly positive in several decades, as is shown in Table 18-3.

---

[8] In the United Kingdom, where indexed long-term bonds are available, there are measures of market long-term real interest rates.

TABLE 18-3

THE REAL INTEREST RATE, UNITED STATES
(average annual percent)

period	rate	period	rate
1860–1869	1.5	1930–1939	3.6
1870–1879	9.8	1940–1949	−4.6
1880–1889	7.2	1950–1959	0.4
1890–1899	4.2	1960–1969	2.1
1900–1909	2.3	1970–1979	−0.2
1910–1919	−3.6	1980–1989	4.1
1920–1929	−6.0		

SOURCE: Lawrence Summers, "The Non-Adjust-ment of Nominal Interest Rates: A Study of the Fisher Effect," in J. Tobin (ed.) *Macroeconomics, Prices and Quantities* (Washington, D.C.: The Brookings Institution, 1983), updated by the authors. Rate is for commercial paper.

Although there have been decades with positive and even high real interest rates, the average real rate over much longer periods has been low. Imagine an investor who put money into Treasury bills in the mid-1920s (which is when data on Treasury bill rates start) and reinvested (tax free) all the earnings every time the bills matured. The real return over the period 1925–1992 would have been barely positive, less than 0.5 percent per year. Table 18-4 shows the average real return on different assets over several time periods. The point of the table is that real returns—on Treasury bills, on long-term government bonds, and on stocks—are not constant, even over quite long periods.

Table 18-5 presents international evidence on the interest rate-inflation link. Two

TABLE 18-4

RETURNS ON DIFFERENT ASSETS

	1926–1991	1960–1991	1980–1991
Inflation	3.1	5.0	5.0
T bills	3.7	6.4	8.5
Long-term government bonds	4.8	6.8	12.6
Common stocks	10.4	10.4	16.7

SOURCE: *Stocks, Bonds, Bills, and Inflation 1992 Yearbook*, Ibbotson Associates, Chicago (annually updates work of Roger D. Ibbotson and Rex A. Sinquefield). Used with permission. All rights reserved.

TABLE 18-5
INTEREST RATES AND INFLATION, 1991*

country	interest rate, % per annum	inflation rate
Argentina	86.5[†]	92.3
Brazil	690[‡]	468.4
Canada	7.4	5.6
Finland	13.1	4.1
Germany	8.8	3.5
Italy	12.2	6.4
Mexico	19.3	22.7
United Kingdom	11.8	5.9
United States	5.7	4.3

*Interest rates are short-term market rates; the inflation rate is for the CPI, from December to December.

[†]Average of deposit and lending interest rates.

[‡]Rate on savings deposits.

SOURCE: *International Financial Statistics*, various issues.

features stand out. First, the countries with high inflation, such as Italy and Mexico, tend to have higher *nominal* interest rates. This is especially true when the inflation rate is very high, as for Argentina and Brazil. Second, real interest rates vary widely across countries.

The evidence is thus that inflation and nominal interest rates tend to move together, within a country over time and across countries. But the data do not support a very strict Fisher effect. Year-to-year changes in inflation are not reflected one for one in nominal interest rates. The real rate does move, and hence the Fisher equation is primarily a guide to nominal interest rates when inflationary disturbances are large relative to all other factors determining interest rates.

The evidence on the Fisher equation is thus very similar to that for the quantity theory. In both cases, the data support the basic prediction of the theory—that inflation tends to be higher when money growth is higher, and that the nominal interest rate tends to be higher when inflation is higher, respectively—but do not support a strict one-for-one interpretation of the theory.

18-3 ALTERNATIVE STRATEGIES TO REDUCE INFLATION

Suppose the inflation rate in the economy is 10 percent, and the government decides to try to get the economy down to inflation rates of around 2 to 3 percent. This is the decision that was made in the United States in 1979. By the mid-1980s the inflation rate was down to the 3 to 4 percent range, but in the meantime the economy went through two recessions, in 1980 and again in 1981–1982. The problem of how to

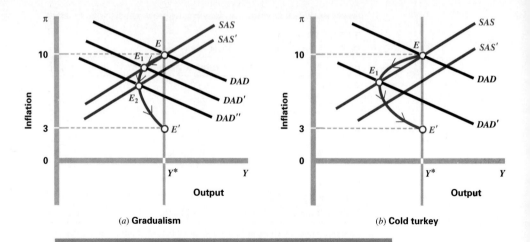

FIGURE 18-4

ALTERNATIVE DISINFLATION STRATEGIES. In panel (*a*) policy reduces the inflation rate gradually from 10 to 3 percent, seeking to keep output from falling much below the potential level. In panel (*b*), by contrast, the decision is made to try to end the inflation rapidly by starting with a large cut in the growth rate of money, which produces much lower inflation at the cost of a large recession.

disinflate is one that faces governments recurrently—and occasionally the problem is how to end a hyperinflation in which the *monthly* inflation rate is well into the double digits.

The key question for any government contemplating disinflation is how to disinflate as cheaply as possible—that is, with as small a recession as possible. In this section we consider alternative strategies for disinflation. The basic method of disinflation should be clear from Chapter 16: it is to reduce the growth rate of aggregate demand, shifting the *DAD* curve downward. That can be done by cutting back on money growth and, in the short run, by using fiscal policy. In this section we consider only monetary policy.

Gradualism versus Cold Turkey

Figure 18-4 shows the choices. A policy of *gradualism* attempts a slow and steady return to low inflation. The gradualist policy, shown in Figure 18-4*a*, begins with a small reduction in the money growth rate that shifts the aggregate demand curve down from *DAD* to *DAD'*, moving the economy a little way along the short-run aggregate supply curve, *SAS*, from *E* to E_1. In response to the lower inflation at E_1, the short-run aggregate supply curve shifts downward to *SAS'*. A further small cut in the money

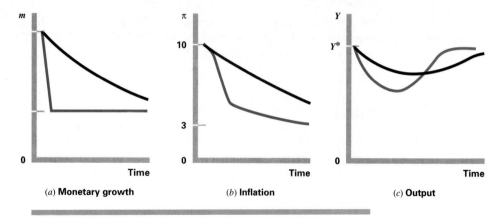

FIGURE 18-5

COLD TURKEY VERSUS GRADUALISM. This is an alternative way of comparing the two strategies. Cold turkey (colored curves) cuts the growth rate of money sharply, producing a massive but shorter recession. The gradualist strategy (black curves) produces much less unemployment but also a much less rapid reduction in the inflation rate.

growth rate moves the economy to E_2, the aggregate supply curve shifts down again, and the process continues.

Eventually output returns to its potential level, at point E', at a lower inflation rate. There is no massive recession during the adjustment process, although unemployment is above normal throughout.

Panel (*b*) of Figure 18-4 shows the *cold turkey* alternative. The cold turkey strategy tries to cut the inflation rate fast. The strategy starts with an immediate sharp cutback in money growth, shifting the aggregate demand curve from *DAD* to *DAD'* and moving the economy from E to E_1. The immediate recession is larger than under gradualism.

By creating a larger fall in the inflation rate than the gradualist policy, the cold turkey strategy causes the short-run supply curve to move down faster than it does in Figure 18-4*a*. The cold turkey strategy keeps up the pressure by holding the rate of money growth low. Eventually the rate of inflation falls enough that output and employment begin to grow again. The economy returns to point E' with full employment and a lower rate of inflation.

Figure 18-5 presents the gradualist and cold turkey strategies in an alternative form. In the gradualist strategy the growth rate of money is initially reduced only slightly, and the economy never strays far from the natural rate of unemployment. But the inflation rate comes down only slowly. The cold turkey strategy, by contrast, starts with a massive cut in the growth rate of money and a large recession. The recession is much worse than it ever is in the gradualist strategy, but the reduction in inflation is more rapid.

Which strategy should be chosen? Is moderate unemployment with higher inflation preferable to higher unemployment with lower inflation? U.S. policy makers in 1981–1982 chose a policy closer to cold turkey than to gradualism.

Credibility

The cold turkey strategy has one major point in its favor. It is much more clear in the case of cold turkey than gradualism that a decisive policy change has been made, with the firm aim of driving down the inflation rate. The cold turkey policy is more *credible* than a gradualist policy.[9] A credible policy is one that the public believes will be kept up and will succeed.

A belief that policy has changed will by itself drive down the expected rate of inflation and for that reason cause the short-run Phillips curve to shift down. Thus a credible policy earns a *credibility bonus* in the fight against inflation.

Throughout the period of disinflation in the United States, starting with the Fed's change in policy in October 1979, there was strong emphasis on the credibility of policy. Some proponents of rational expectations even believed that if policy could only be made credible, it would be possible to disinflate practically without causing any recession at all.[10]

The argument went like this. The expectations-augmented aggregate supply curve from Chapter 10 is

$$\pi = \pi^e + \lambda(Y - Y^*) \tag{3}$$

If the policy is credible, people instantly adjust their expectations of inflation when a new lower money growth rate is adjusted, and the short-run aggregate supply curve therefore moves down immediately. Accordingly, if policy is credible and if expectations are rational, the economy can move immediately to a new long-run equilibrium when there is a change in policy.

The experience of the United States in the early 1980s casts doubt on the relevance of this optimistic scenario. So does the experience of Britain in the same period, when the unmistakably tough-minded Thatcher government was pursuing a resolute anti-inflationary policy, but the unemployment rate still reached 13 percent.

There are two possible reasons the simple credibility-rational expectations argument does not work: first, credibility may be very difficult to obtain; second, as discussed in Chapter 8, the economy has, at any time, an overhang of past contracts embodying

---

[9] The credibility issue is treated in several interesting papers in "Anti-inflation Policies and the Problem of Credibility," *American Economic Review*, Papers and Proceedings, May 1982. In the European context, Thomas Egebo and Steven Englander investigate whether the European Exchange Rate System of quasi-fixed rates helped reduce the costs of disinflation. See their article "Institutional Commitments and Policy Credibility: A Critical Survey and Empirical Evidence from the ERM," *OECD Economic Studies*, Spring 1992.

[10] See John Fender, *Inflation* (Ann Arbor: University of Michigan Press, 1990), and Dean Croushore, "What Are the Costs of Disinflation?" Federal Reserve Bank of Philadelphia *Business Review*, May–June 1992.

past expectations, and the contract renegotiations take time. Thus, because of inflationary inertia, a rapid return to lower inflation in economies experiencing inflation rates in the 10 to 20 percent range is unlikely.

It is easiest to change the inflation rate when there are no long-term contracts that embody the ongoing inflation—for instance, by building in high rates of wage increase for the next several years—in the economy. There will be very few such contracts if inflation is high and uncertain, for instance, in a hyperinflation. Under such conditions negotiators will not want to sign an agreement in nominal terms because they will be gambling too much on the future behavior of the price level. Long-term nominal contracts disappear, and wages and prices are frequently reset. In these circumstances, a credible policy will have rapid effects. But such rapid success cannot be expected in an economy in which the structure of contracts has not yet been destroyed by extreme inflation.

It remains true, though, that whatever the structure of contracts, the more credible a policy that aims to disinflate the economy is, the more successful that policy will be.

Disinflation and the Sacrifice Ratio

Inflation reduction almost always costs a recession, but what exactly is the tradeoff? How much output is lost through different methods of disinflation, such as cold turkey and gradualism? Discussion of the costs of disinflation makes extensive use of the concept of the *sacrifice ratio.* The sacrifice ratio is the ratio of the cumulative percentage loss of GDP (as a result of a disinflation policy) to the reduction in inflation that is actually achieved.

Thus, suppose a policy reduces the inflation rate from 10 to 4 percent over a 3-year period, at the cost of levels of output that are 10 percent below potential in the first year, 8 percent below potential in the second year, and 6 percent below potential in the third year. The total loss of GDP is 24 percent $(10 + 8 + 6)$, the reduction in inflation is 6 percent $(10 - 4)$, and the sacrifice ratio is 4.

Before the disinflation of the 1980s, economists estimated sacrifice ratios that would apply if a disinflation program were undertaken. Estimates ranged between 5 and 10. In the 1980s experience, inflation was reduced from 9 percent in 1980 to 3 percent by 1986–1987. The cumulative loss in output (relative to the path of potential output) was 26 percent. Thus the sacrifice ratio was 4.3 $(= 26/6)$, a low number relative to previous estimates, but clearly in line with them. The estimate may understate the true cost of disinflation because events favorable for disinflation, such as declining oil prices and the strong dollar, influenced the path of actual inflation.

A study by the International Monetary Fund summarizes the factors that make for a less costly disinflation.[11] Disinflation is less costly "(1) if the policy is announced in advance; (2) the more gradually the deceleration is phased in; (3) the more credible is the policy of disinflation; (4) (given credibility) the greater is the relative importance

---

[11] See Bankim Chadha, Paul Masson, and Guy Meredith, "Models of Inflation and the Costs of Disinflation," *IMF Staff Papers*, June 1992.

box 18-2

THE RATIONAL EXPECTATIONS SCHOOL, MONETARISM, AND HYPERINFLATION

The rational expectations school in macroeconomics accepts many monetarist positions, including a preference for rules and the belief that government intervention usually makes the situation worse. Indeed, many of the leaders of the rational expectations school were students of Milton Friedman. Some, including Robert Lucas, studied under Friedman at the University of Chicago; others, such as Robert Barro and Thomas Sargent, studied his works while they were graduate students at other universities.

As in the case of monetarism, rational expectations views have already been discussed earlier in this book. These views include

1. The market-clearing rational expectations approach to the Phillips curve (Chapter 9)
2. Rational expectations as a theory of expectations (Chapter 9)
3. The emphasis on the credibility of policy makers (Chapter 15 and this chapter)
4. The preference for policy-making rules rather than discretion (Chapter 15)

Most of these views can be seen as developments of the monetarist approach. However, the monetarist and rational expectations schools differ on one key issue: whereas monetarists, like Keynesians, see the economy as reacting to disturbances and policy changes slowly and with long and variable lags and are willing to allow the possibility that markets may not clear, the rational expectations school generally insists that markets clear rapidly. Obviously, we do not share this latter view, nor does much of the profession. However, as we noted in Chapter 9, the rational

of expected future inflation in determining current inflation; and (5) the greater is the responsiveness of prices and wages to demand conditions."

Is There a Better Way?

The treatments for the inflation disease summarized in Figure 18-5 are painful and have led to a search for better ways. The most frequent alternative involves an attempt to control prices and wages directly.

INCOMES POLICY (OR WAGE AND PRICE CONTROLS)

Inflation stabilization takes time and involves unemployment because that is what is needed to get the rate of wage change down. *Incomes policies* are policies that attempt to reduce the rate of wage and price increases by direct action. Either wages and prices are controlled by law, or the government tries to persuade labor leaders and business expectations approach to expectations is widely shared. So is the emphasis on the *credibility* of policy makers.

While the rational expectations approach started influencing macroeconomic theory in the early 1970s, the single most influential article in the macroeconomic policy debate was Thomas Sargent's "The Ends of Four Big Inflations."* In this article, written while the United States was suffering from double-digit inflation, Sargent argued that the major European hyperinflations had, as a result of a *credible* reform of monetary and fiscal policy, ended rapidly and at very little cost in terms of forgone output. By implication, he suggested that the United States could do the same.

Critics of this view argued that it was one thing to end an inflation when all contracts and the economy had broken down, as in the hyperinflations, and another to end an inflation that was just barely in the double digits, with all contracts intact. In any event, the United States ended its inflation only following the deep recession of 1981–1982. Further research has shown that even the European hyperinflations did not end costlessly.[†]

All experience suggests that credibility is difficult to earn, and difficult to keep, and that the structure of contracts that exist in an economy has to be taken into account in analyzing the effects of policy changes. Thus while we do not doubt that credibility is an important aspect of policy making, we believe its role has generally been exaggerated, and we are suspicious of policy arguments in which credibility is the main reason for pursuing a policy that otherwise makes little economic sense. ∎

---

*In Robert E. Hall (ed.), *Inflation: Causes and Effects* (Chicago: University of Chicago Press, 1982).

†See Elmus Wicker, "Terminating Hyperinflation in the Dismembered Habsburg Monarchy," *American Economic Review*, June 1986; see also the articles on modern high inflations in Michael Bruno et al. (eds.), *Lessons of Economic Stabilization and Its Aftermath* (Cambridge, Mass.: MIT Press, 1991).

---

to raise wages and prices more slowly than they otherwise would. Incomes policies, if successful, shift the short-run aggregate supply curve down.

Wage and price controls are typically used in wartime in many countries and were also used in the United States in the period 1971–1974. The 1971 controls were imposed in an effort to break the back of an inflation that for 2 years had shown little sign of responding to restrictive monetary and fiscal policies.

A wage-price freeze certainly brings the inflation rate down. So why not get rid of inflation that way? The reason is that wages and prices have to change if resources are to be allocated efficiently in the economy. Anti-inflationary policy has to try to reduce the average rate of price increase without interfering with the role of prices in allocating resources.[12]

---

[12]During the 1970s there was considerable interest in using *tax incentive plans* (or TIPs) to help reduce inflation. Under such a plan, firms could reduce their taxes by reducing the increase in their prices, or they would have to pay higher taxes if their rate of price increase was higher. Aside from their technical complexity, TIPs also are problematic in that they may hinder the efficiency of the price system. The *Brookings Papers on Economic Activity*, 1978:2, contains several articles and discussions of TIPs.

Over a short period, misallocations of resources from frozen wages and prices will be small and not costly. But if wages and prices are kept fixed for a long time, shortages of labor and particular goods will develop. The problem then is to find a way out of controls that does not reignite inflation. The United States did not avoid that problem when, after many policy shifts, controls were lifted in 1973–1974—at the time when the oil price shock hit the economy.

One reason incomes policies have rarely been successful is that governments often fail to implement restrictive aggregate demand policies to accompany them.[13] Incomes policies aim to move the aggregate supply curve down, thereby reducing the inflation rate. So long as the aggregate demand curve moves down at the same time, the inflation rate will fall and can stay low. But if there is no accompanying change in the aggregate demand curve, the wage and price controls will only build up inflationary pressures that will eventually explode.

Wage and price controls can be used successfully when the right monetary and fiscal policy measures are taken. For instance, in 1985, Israel put into place a policy package to reduce the inflation rate from several hundred percent per year to the low double digits. In addition to sharply cutting the budget deficit and tightening credit, the package involved controls on wages and prices. These controls contributed to the success in making a rapid reduction in inflation possible without a big increase in unemployment.

At the same time, though, a similar-looking program in Argentina failed when fiscal policy was not kept sufficiently tight.

The potential for incomes policies to work arises from the role of expectations in the Phillips curve. However, all attempts to control inflation through direct means run into the difficulty that relative wages and prices in the economy do have to change if the price mechanism is to work. Thus these policies cannot be effective except during short transitional periods.

Is There Hope?

The disinflation that started in the United States at the beginning of the 1980s was still operating successfully in 1992. In the period 1982–1992 inflation averaged only 4.2 percent, far less than in the 1970s.

Around the world inflation was lower at the beginning of the 1990s than in the previous two decades, but many governments had become convinced that the costs of inflation were very high, and that inflation still had to be fought very hard. Germany, for instance, long committed to low inflation, was pursuing a very restrictive monetary policy to drive the inflation rate down from 4 percent. Given the fixed exchange rates in Europe, German tightening of money was producing a slowdown throughout Europe.

In Canada, too, the inflation problem was attacked by a stringent anti-inflationary policy, which involved important changes in the role of the central bank. Between

---

[13] For a careful account of wage and price controls, see Hugh Rockoff, *Drastic Measures: A History of Wage and Price Controls in the United States* (London: Cambridge University Press, 1984).

1983 and 1991, the annual Canadian inflation rate was in the range of 4 to 6 percent. Canadian researchers argued that inflation systematically slows economic growth. Based largely on this view, the Canadian government, with the Bank of Canada in the lead, concluded that Canada should aim for a target of *zero inflation*.[14] An agreement was reached between the Bank of Canada and the Ministry of Finance that the Bank would aim to reduce inflation gradually from 5.6 percent to 2 percent by the end of 1995. Inflation fighting meant, of course, recession, and the verdict remains open on whether Canada will achieve a lasting move to price stability.

In the United States, too, there was a move to make monetary policy responsible for achieving a stable price level, but inflation was too moderate and recession problems were too severe to generate much enthusiasm.[15]

18-4 DEFICITS, MONEY GROWTH, AND THE INFLATION TAX

We have seen that a sustained increase in money growth ultimately translates into increased inflation. But that still leaves the question of what determines the money growth rate. A frequent argument is that money growth is the result of government budget deficits. In this section we examine several possible relationships between the budget deficit and inflation.

The Government's Budget Constraint

The federal government, including the Fed as part of the government, can finance its budget deficit in two ways. It can either sell bonds or "print money." The Fed "prints money" when it increases the stock of high-powered money, typically through open market purchases that buy up part of the debt that the Treasury is selling.

The government budget constraint[16] is

$$\text{Budget deficit} = \text{sales of bonds} + \text{increase in money base} \tag{4}$$

There are two types of possible link between budget deficits and money growth. First, in the short run, an increase in the deficit caused by expansionary fiscal policy will tend to raise nominal and real interest rates. If the Fed is targeting interest rates in any way, it may increase the growth rate of money in an attempt to keep the interest rate from rising. Second, the government may deliberately be increasing the stock of money as a means of obtaining government revenue over the long term.

---

[14] See Richard Lipsey (ed.), *Zero Inflation* (Toronto: C. D. Howe Institute, 1990), and Jack Selody, "The Goal of Price Stability," Bank of Canada Technical Report No. 54.

[15] See the proposed legislation by Representative Richard Neal, *Congressional Record*, August 1, 1989.

[16] We show here the government's *flow*, or year-by-year budget constraint. In addition, the government faces a stock budget constraint that says the present value of all the government's future outlays (including debt repayment) has to be equal to the present value of all its future receipts. Technically, the stock budget constraint can be obtained by integrating the year-by-year flow constraints.

In the remainder of this section we examine first the short-run links between money and deficits that come from central bank policy and then the use of money printing as a means of financing government budgets. Finally, we link the short- and long-run aspects.

The Fed's Dilemma

The Fed is said to *monetize* deficits whenever it purchases a part of the debt sold by the Treasury to finance the deficit. In the United States the monetary authorities enjoy independence from the Treasury and therefore can choose whether to monetize or not.[17]

The Fed typically faces a dilemma in deciding whether to monetize a deficit. If it does not finance the deficit, the fiscal expansion, not being accompanied by accommodating monetary policy, raises interest rates and thus crowds out private expenditure. There is accordingly a temptation for the Fed to prevent crowding out by buying securities, thereby increasing the money supply and hence allowing an expansion in income without a rise in interest rates.

But such a policy of accommodation or monetization runs a risk. If the economy is near full employment, the monetization tends to feed inflation. Eventually higher aggregate demand will raise the real interest rate; crowding out will occur in any event. Thus the policy fails in its objective of preventing crowding out, and it has a cost in terms of higher inflation.

Much discussion of Fed policy centers on this question: Should the Fed control monetary aggregates or interest rates? In the context of an increase in budget deficits the answer must often be that the Fed should *not* accommodate; that is, it should let the interest rate increase and keep the growth rate of money constant. If the economy is close to full employment, an accommodating policy would simply feed inflation. An unwise fiscal expansion would be made even more potent by fueling it with a monetary expansion.

There are other circumstances, though, in which the risks of igniting inflation are much more remote. Certainly in a deep recession there is no reason to shy away from accommodating a fiscal expansion with higher money growth.

In any particular case, the Fed has to judge whether to pursue an accommodating monetary policy or whether, rather, to stay with an unchanged monetary target or even offset a fiscal expansion by a tightening of monetary policy. To make that decision, the Fed has to compare the relative costs of higher inflation with those of higher unemployment whenever expansionary policy threatens to cause inflation.

The U.S. Evidence

A number of studies have tried to determine how the Fed reacts to deficits in practice. The question here is whether there is a systematic link between monetary policy and

---

[17]In other countries the central bank may enjoy much less independence; for instance, it could be under the control of the Treasury, and then it might simply be ordered to finance part or all of the deficit by creating high-powered money.

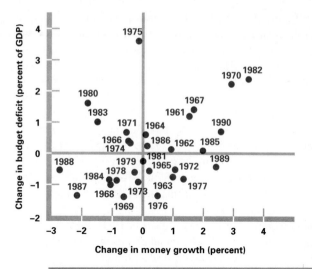

FIGURE 18-6

BUDGET DEFICITS AND MONEY ACCOMMODATION, 1960–1991. The change in the cyclically adjusted budget deficit is expressed as a fraction of GDP; money growth is for the high-powered money stock. (Source: DRI/McGraw-Hill.)

the budget. Specifically, does the Fed allow money growth to rise when the budget deficit increases?

Figure 18-6 is a scatter diagram showing the change in the growth rate of the monetary base and the change in the cyclically adjusted budget (expressed as a percentage of GDP).[18] There is no very clear pattern of accommodation. Nor does a diagram relating money growth to the *level* of the deficit show a closer relationship.

More sophisticated empirical work provides some evidence that the Fed does react in the direction of accommodation, monetizing deficits at least in part. But the evidence is not conclusive because it is difficult to know whether the Fed is reacting to the deficit itself or to other macroeconomic variables, specifically unemployment and the rate of inflation.[19]

The question of accommodation and the monetary-fiscal policy mix was certainly a major issue in the discussion leading up to the Gramm-Rudman-Hollings deficit

---

[18] The monetary base is the relevant aggregate because the deficit can be financed either by the sale of bonds or by the creation of high-powered money (or monetary base).

[19] See Alan Blinder, "On the Monetization of Deficits," in Laurence Meyer (eds.), *The Economic Consequences of Government Deficits* (Norwell, Mass.: Kluwer Nijhoff, 1983); Gerald Dwyer, "Federal Deficits, Interest Rates and Monetary Policy," *Journal of Money, Credit and Banking*, November 1985; and Douglas Joines, "Deficits and Money Growth in the United States: 1872–1983," *Journal of Monetary Economics*, November 1985.

control legislation of 1985. Fiscal and monetary policy combined in the early 1980s to take real interest rates to exceptionally high levels. As a result the dollar became very strong, hurting U.S. trade and hurting debtors both here and in the developing countries. The Fed was seen to be in a very unusual position: holding out on monetary accommodation, it raised the economic and political cost of an excessive fiscal expansion. It thus made the economy experience a "lopsided" recovery in which imports increased and exports fell.

The Federal Reserve explicitly held out the promise of easier money to continue the recovery if the Congress would cut the budget deficit. It increasingly and rightly insisted that at full employment the Federal Reserve could no longer help keep interest rates low; accommodation of continuing high demand growth would simply mean inflation, not high real growth. Starting in 1988 interest rates were pushed up gradually to cool an overheating economy.

Monetarist critics of the Fed argued in 1988–1989 that the Fed had allowed too high money growth for too long—an annual growth rate of 7 percent since 1983, far above the 2.5 percent trend growth. And in the face of a sharp deceleration of money growth in 1989 to only 3.6 percent they were quick to argue that the Fed was following its usual pattern of too much expansion and then a dramatic slamming on of brakes. Others saw the high growth of money in the 1980s as fully appropriate, given the initial recession and financial deregulation, and they also felt that the slowdown of money growth in 1986 was altogether appropriate, since the economy had reached full employment.

The tightening of monetary policy in 1989 helped bring about the recession of 1990–1991. Quite likely, the monetary tightening would not have been necessary if fiscal policy had tightened earlier, say in 1987–1988. But the inaction of fiscal policy meant that the task of stabilizing the economy had been left almost entirely to monetary policy through most of the 1980s.

The Inflation Tax

In discussing monetization of deficits in the United States we paid no attention to the fact that financing government spending through the creation of high-powered money is an alternative to explicit taxation. Governments can—and some do—obtain significant amounts of resources year after year by printing money, that is, by increasing high-powered money. This source of revenue is sometimes known as *seigniorage*, which is the government's ability to raise revenue through its right to create money.

When the government finances a deficit by creating money, it in effect keeps printing money, period after period, which it uses to pay for the goods and services it buys. This money is absorbed by the public. But why would the public choose to increase its holdings of nominal money balances period after period?

The only reason, real income growth aside, for the public's adding to its holdings of nominal money balances would be to offset the effects of inflation. Assuming there is no real income growth, in the long run the public will hold a constant level of *real* balances. But if prices are rising, the purchasing power of a given stock of *nominal balances* is falling. To maintain a constant real value of money balances, the public has to be adding to its stock of nominal balances at a rate that will exactly offset the effects of inflation.

When the public is adding to its stock of nominal balances in order to offset the effects of inflation on holdings of real balances, it is using part of its income to increase holdings of nominal money. For instance, suppose someone has an income of $20,000 (nominal) this year. Over the course of the year, inflation reduces the value of that person's real balances. He or she therefore has to add, say, $300, to a bank account just to maintain the real value of his or her money holdings constant. That $300 is not available for spending. The person seems to be saving $300 in the form of money holdings, but in fact in real terms is not increasing his or her wealth by adding the $300 to nominal balances. All that person is doing is preventing his or her wealth from falling as a result of inflation.

Inflation acts just like a tax because people are forced to spend less than their income and pay the difference to the government in exchange for extra money.[20] The government thus can spend more resources, and the public less, just as if the government had raised taxes to finance extra spending. When the government finances its deficit by issuing money, which the public adds to its holdings of nominal balances to maintain the real value of money balances constant, we say the government is financing itself through the inflation tax.[21]

How much revenue can the government collect through the inflation tax? The amount of revenue produced is the product of the tax rate (the inflation rate) and the object of taxation (the real monetary base). When real output is constant, inflation tax revenue is given by

$$\text{Inflation tax revenue} = \text{inflation rate} \times \text{real money base} \qquad (5)$$

Table 18-6 shows data on the inflation tax for Latin American countries in the 1983–1988 period. Clearly the amounts are very significant, as are the inflation rates at which these amounts of revenue are obtained by the government.

The amount of revenue the government can raise through the inflation tax is shown by the curve *AA* in Figure 18-7. When the inflation rate is zero, the government gets no revenue from inflation.[22] As the inflation rate rises, the amount of inflation tax received by the government increases. But, of course, as the inflation rate rises, people reduce their real holdings of the money base—because the base is becoming increasingly costly to hold. Individuals hold less currency, and banks hold as little excess reserves

---

[20] There is one complication in this analysis. As noted above, the amount that is received by the government is the increase in the stock of *high-powered* money, because the Fed is buying Treasury debt with high-powered money. But the public is increasing its holdings of both bank deposits and currency, and thus part of the increase in the public's holdings of money does not go to the government to finance the deficit. This complication in no way changes the essence of the analysis.

[21] Inflation is often referred to as the "cruelest tax." This does not refer to the inflation tax analyzed here but rather to the redistribution of wealth and income associated with unanticipated inflation, which was discussed in Chap. 17.

[22] When the economy is growing, the government obtains some revenue from seigniorage even if there is no inflation. That is because when the demand for real monetary base is growing, the government can create some base without producing inflation.

TABLE 18-6

INFLATION AND INFLATION TAX, 1983–1988 (percent)

| country | AVERAGE, 1983–1988 | | peak-year tax/GDP |
	tax/GDP*	inflation	
Argentina	3.7	359	5.2
Bolivia	3.5	1,797	7.2
Brazil	3.5	341	4.3
Chile	0.9	21	1.1
Colombia	1.9	22	2.0
Mexico	2.6	87	3.5
Peru	4.7	382	4.5

*Inflation tax.

SOURCE: M. Selowsky, "Preconditions Necessary for the Recovery of Latin America's Growth," The World Bank, June 1989 (mimeographed).

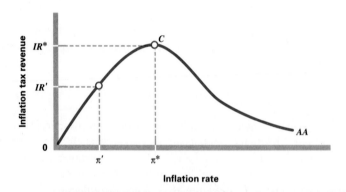

FIGURE 18-7

THE INFLATION TAX. At a zero inflation rate, the inflation tax revenue is zero. As the inflation rate rises, the government receives more revenue from inflation, up to point C, where the tax revenue reaches its maximum of IR^*. The corresponding inflation rate is π^*. Beyond point C the demand for real balances is falling so much as the inflation rate increases that total tax revenues decline.

as possible. Eventually the real monetary base falls so much that the total amount of inflation tax revenue received by the government falls. That starts to happen at point C and signifies that there is a maximum amount of revenue that government can raise through the inflation tax: the maximum is shown as amount IR^* in the figure. There is a corresponding inflation rate, denoted π^*: the steady-state inflation rate at which the inflation tax is at its maximum.

Suppose that in Figure 18-7, the economy is initially in a situation where there is no deficit and no printing of money. Inflation is zero and the economy is at point 0 in the figure. Now the government cuts taxes and finances the deficit by printing money. We assume that the deficit is equal to amount IR' in Figure 18-7, and thus it can be financed entirely through the inflation tax. Money growth is permanently increased, and inflation in the long run moves to the rate π', corresponding to the inflation tax revenue IR'.

It is clear from Figure 18-7 that the more revenue the government wishes to raise through the inflation tax, the higher the inflation rate must be—so long as the economy is on the rising part of the curve. The figure raises the question of what happens if the government tries to finance a deficit larger than IR^* by printing money. That cannot be done. We take up that issue in Section 18-5 on hyperinflation.

Inflation Tax Revenue

The amounts of inflation tax revenue obtained in the high-inflation developing countries in Table 18-6 are very large. In the more industrialized economies, in which the real money base is small relative to the size of the economy, the government obtains only small amounts of inflation tax revenue. For instance, in the United States the base is slightly above 5 percent of GDP. At a 10 percent inflation rate the government would, from equation (5), be collecting about 0.5 percent of GNP in inflation tax revenue. That is not a trivial amount, but it is not a major source of government revenue either.[23] It is hard to believe that the inflation rate in the United States is set with the revenue aspects of inflation as the main criterion. Rather the Fed and the administration choose policies to influence the inflation rate on the basis of an analysis of the costs and benefits of inflation.

In countries in which the banking system is less developed and in which people therefore hold large amounts of currency, the government obtains more revenue from inflation and is more likely to give high weight to the revenue aspects of inflation in setting policy. And, as we see in the next section, in conditions of high inflation in which the conventional tax system breaks down, the inflation tax revenue may be the government's last resort to keep paying its bills. But whenever the inflation tax is used on a large scale, inflation invariably becomes extreme.

18-5 HYPERINFLATION

Large budget deficits are inevitably part of the extreme inflations of 50 to 100 to 500 percent per year that took place in the mid-1980s in Latin America and Israel. They

---

[23] A measure of seigniorage different from the value of the printing of high-powered money is sometimes used in the United States. It is the value of the interest payments the Fed earns on its portfolio. Since the Fed's securities were obtained through open market purchases that increased the high-powered money stock, this is a measure of how much interest the Treasury saves (since the Fed pays its profits to the Treasury) as a result of *previous* Fed money printing. The printing of high-powered money is a measure of the current command over resources obtained as a result of money printing this period.

TABLE 18-7

RECENT HIGH-INFLATION EXPERIENCES (percent per year)

	1985	1986	1987	1988	1989	1990	1991	1992*
Argentina	672	90	131	343	3,080	2,314	172	92
Bolivia	11,750	276	15	16	15	17	21	16
Brazil	58	86	132	682	1,287	2,938	441	695
Israel	305	48	20	16	20	17	19	17
Mexico	58	86	132	114	20	27	23	16
Nicaragua	220	681	911	10,205	23,710	13,491	1,183	
Peru	163	78	86	825	3,399	7,482	410	88

*Latest 12-month data avaliable.

SOURCE: *International Financial Statistics* and United Nations.

are also part of the even more extreme cases of *hyperinflation.* Although there is no precise definition of the rate of inflation that deserves the star ranking of hyperinflation rather than high inflation, a working definition is that a country is in hyperinflation when its annual inflation rate reaches 1,000 percent per annum. When inflation becomes very high, inflation is reckoned in terms of *monthly* rates, not inflation per year. The power of compound interest is apparent when we look at the correspondence between monthly inflation rates and the same rate annualized. For example, a 20 percent inflation per month corresponds to an annualized rate of 791 percent. Table 18-7 shows recent extreme inflation experiences.[24]

It seems difficult to believe that countries can function for any length of time with extremely high inflation rates of several hundred percent or more. In fact, they do not function well, and sooner or later they will stabilize a high inflation simply because the economy turns chaotic. Thus, Israel successfully stabilized in 1985 as did Bolivia (see Box 18-3). But other countries, such as Brazil, were still in inflationary crises in 1992.

In a hyperinflationary economy, inflation is so pervasive and such a problem that it completely dominates daily economic life. People spend significant amounts of resources minimizing the inflationary damage. They have to shop often to try to get to the stores before the prices go up; their main concern in saving or investing is protecting themselves against inflation; they reduce holdings of real balances to a remarkable extent to avoid the inflation tax, but they have to compensate by going to the bank more often—daily or hourly instead of weekly, for example, to get currency.

---

[24]Hyperinflation is not a recent invention. Experience with extreme inflation can be found in history. See Edwin Seligman, *Currency Inflation and Public Debts: An Historical Sketch* (New York: The Equitable Trust Company, 1921). There was a wave in the 1920s, notably in Austria, Hungary, Germany, and Poland, and again in the 1940s. The most famous experience is that in Germany in the 1920s. For a recent discussion see Steven Webb, *Hyperinflation and Stabilization in Weimar Germany* (Oxford: Oxford University Press, 1989).

The classic hyperinflations have taken place in the aftermath of wars. The most famous of all—though not the most rapid—was the German hyperinflation of 1922–1923. The average inflation rate during the hyperinflation was 322 percent *per month*. The highest rate of inflation was in October 1923, just before the end of the hyperinflation, when prices rose by over 29,000 percent. In dollars that means that something that cost $1 at the beginning of the month would have cost $290 at the end of the month. The most rapid hyperinflation was that in Hungary at the end of World War II: the *average* rate of inflation from August 1945 to July 1946 was 19,800 percent per month, and the maximum monthly rate was 41.9 quadrillion percent.[25]

Keynes, in a masterful description of the hyperinflation process in Austria after World War II, tells of how people would order two beers at a time because they grew stale at a rate slower than that at which the price was rising.[26] This and similar stories appear in all hyperinflations. They include the woman who carried her (almost worthless) currency in a basket and found that when she set it down for a moment, the basket was stolen but the money left behind. And, it was said, it was cheaper to take a taxi than a bus because in the taxi you pay at the end of the ride and in the bus at the beginning.

Hyperinflationary economies are typically marked by widespread indexing, more to the foreign exchange rate than to the price level. That is because it becomes difficult to keep measuring prices on a current basis when they change so fast. So prices might be specified in terms of dollars, and the actual amount of the local currency (marks in the German case) that has to be paid in each transaction is calculated from the dollar price and the exchange rate. Wages are paid very often—at the end of the German hyperinflation, several times a day.

Deficits and Hyperinflation

The hyperinflationary economies all suffered from large budget deficits. In several cases the origin of the budget deficit was wartime spending, which generated large national debts and also destroyed the tax-gathering apparatus of the country.

But there is a two-way interaction between budget deficits and inflation. Large budget deficits can lead to rapid inflation by causing governments to print money to finance the deficit. In turn, high inflation increases the measured deficit. There are two main mechanisms through which inflation increases budget deficits.

THE TAX-COLLECTION SYSTEM

As the inflation rate rises, the real revenue raised from taxation falls. The reason is that there are lags in both the calculation and payment of taxes. Suppose, to take an

---

[25] At least, so we think. The price level rose 41.9×10^{15} percent in July 1946. Data are from Phillip Cagan, "The Monetary Dynamics of Hyperinflation," in Milton Friedman (ed.), *Studies in the Quantity Theory of Money* (Chicago: University of Chicago Press, 1956). This classic paper contains data on seven hyperinflations.

[26] John Maynard Keynes, *A Tract on Monetary Reform* (New York: Macmillan, 1923). This remains one of the most readable accounts of inflation. See also Thomas William Guttmann and Patricia Meehan, *The Great Inflation* (London: Gordon and Cremonsi, 1975); Adam Fergussan, *When Money Dies* (London: William Kimber, 1975); and Leland Yeager and associates, *Experiences with Stopping Inflation* (Washington, D.C.: American Enterprise Institute, 1981).

box 18-3

BOLIVIAN HYPERINFLATION AND STABILIZATION

In the 1920s, Europe experienced hyperinflation, and the experience is reviewed in an important paper by Thomas Sargent.* Latin America followed in the 1980s. In 1985 Bolivia experienced a full-fledged hyperinflation, as can be seen in Figure 1. At the peak, in mid-1985, inflation was, at an annual rate, 35,000 percent!

There were three main reasons for the hyperinflation. First, like other Latin American countries, Bolivia had overborrowed in the 1970s. When, in the early 1980s, interest rates increased in world markets, it could no longer service its debt by taking out new loans to pay the interest on the old loans. But without borrowing, the country did not have the budgetary resources to service the debt. The attempt to do so strained the budget and led to high rates of money creation. Second, commodity prices, especially of tin, fell sharply. For Bolivia this meant a large fall in real income and in revenues for the government. Third, substantial political instability led to capital flight: Bolivians attempted to move assets abroad and foreigners tried to get their assets out of Bolivia. The combination of factors set off an inflationary spiral that forced increasing depreciation of the currency and opened an ever wider gap between government outlays and revenues. Tax collection sharply dropped by more than half, as can be seen in Table 1.

By 1984–1985 the government was attempting to finance nearly 25 percent of GDP with money creation. But, of course, by this time the demand for real

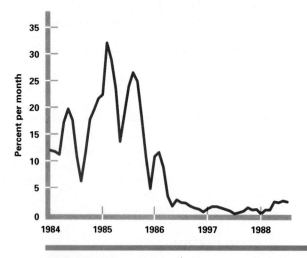

FIGURE 1
BOLIVIAN HYPERINFLATION, 1984–1992. (SOURCE: Banco Central de Bolivia.)

---

*See Thomas Sargent, "The Ends of Four Big Inflations," in R. Hall (ed.), *Inflation* (Chicago: University of Chicago Press, 1982).

TABLE 1

THE BOLIVIAN HYPERINFLATION

	1980–1983	1984	1985	1986
Budget deficit*	11.9	26.5	10.8	3.0
Tax collection*	6.7	2.3	3.1	6.6
Inflation[†]	123	1,282	11,750	276

*Percent of GDP.

†Percent per year.

SOURCE: World Bank and Banco Central de Bolivia.

balances had fallen to negligible levels because of the hyperinflation. It took ever-larger rates of inflation to finance the ever-growing deficit.

In August–September 1985 a new government came into power and, in a short time, imposed a drastic stabilization plan. By stopping external debt service and raising taxes the drain in the budget was brought under control; money creation was reduced from the extreme rates of the past years; and the exchange rate was stabilized. Within half a year the inflation rate had come down to less than 50 percent. Moreover, because the decrease in the budget deficit was maintained and reinforced, the gain in disinflation continued; by 1989, inflation rates had fallen to less than 10 percent per year.

The Bolivian stabilization is a good example of how a sharp cut in the fiscal deficit can stop a major inflation.[†] But there should be no illusion about the costs. As a result of austerity (and of poor export prices) Bolivian per capita income in 1992 was 30 percent less than it had been 10 years earlier, at its peak. Inflation had been brought under control, but confidence was not sufficient to bring back growth on a significant scale.

While Bolivia succeeded in controlling inflation, in several other Latin American countries inflation was exploding. An important question for these countries was whether *heterodox* programs, which add wage-price controls to the *orthodox* medicine of fiscal austerity, would help reduce the costs of stabilization. Stabilization attempts undertaken several times in 1985–1989 in Argentina and Brazil included very little orthodoxy, and failed. Argentina finally undertook a major program in early 1991; inflation was attacked vigorously and, for the time being, successfully. In Brazil stabilization was not in sight even by 1993.[‡] ∎

†See Juan A. Morales, "Inflation Stabilization in Bolivia," in M. Bruno et al. (eds.), *Inflation Stabilization* (Cambridge, Mass.: MIT Press, 1988), and J. Sachs, "The Bolivian Hyperinflation and Stabilization," *American Economic Review*, May 1987.

‡See E. Helpman and L. Leiderman, "Stabilization in High Inflation Countries: Analytical Foundations of Recent Experience," *Carnegie Rochester Conference Series on Public Policy*, no. 28 (1988); M. Kiguel and N. Liviatan, "Inflationary Rigidities and Orthodox Stabilization Policies: Lessons from Latin America," *The World Bank Economic Review*, no. 3 (1988); and Bruno et al. (eds.), *Lessons of Economic Stabilization and Its Aftermath* (Cambridge, Mass.: MIT Press, 1991).

extreme example, that people pay taxes on April 15 on the income they earned the previous year. Consider someone who earned $50,000 last year and has a tax bill of $10,000 due on April 15. If prices have in the meantime gone up by a factor of 10, as they might in hyperinflation, the real value of the taxes is only one-tenth of what it should be. The budget deficit can rapidly get out of hand. This impact of inflation on the real value of tax revenues is called the Tanzi-Olivera effect, so named after two economists who independently documented it.[27]

In principle the tax system can be indexed to adjust for the inflation. But that is in practice difficult, especially for business taxation, and in any event even indexing lags behind. For example, if the monthly rate of inflation is 20 percent (equivalent to an annual rate of nearly 800 percent), then even if the amount that has to be paid is fixed according to the most recent price index and it takes a month to collect taxes, inflation causes the government to lose 20 percent of the value of its taxes.

NOMINAL INTEREST RATES AND DEFICITS

The measured budget deficit includes the interest payments on the national debt. Since the nominal interest rate tends to rise when inflation increases, higher inflation generally increases the *nominal* interest payments that are made by the government, and the measured deficit therefore increases.

Of course, these high nominal rates are not necessarily high real rates of interest. If the inflation rate were reduced, the deficit would *automatically* fall as a result of the lower interest rates on the national debt. Accordingly, economists in high-inflation countries often calculate the *inflation-adjusted deficit*:

$$\text{Inflation-adjusted deficit} = \text{total deficit} - (\text{inflation rate} \times \text{national debt}) \quad (6)$$

The inflation adjustment removes that component of interest payments on the debt that is attributed directly to inflation and gives a more accurate picture of what the budget situation would be at a very low inflation rate than does the actual deficit.

The Inflation Tax and Accelerating Hyperinflation

Rates of money growth are also very high during hyperinflations, of the same order of magnitude as the inflation rate.[28] The high rates of money growth originate, of course, in monetary financing of the deficit.

But as the inflation progresses and the tax-collection system breaks down, the government reaches a point at which it tries to raise more revenue through money printing than the maximum amount, IR^*, that it can (see Figure 18-7). It can succeed in raising more than IR^* *temporarily* by printing money even faster than people

---

[27] Vito Tanzi of the IMF and Julio Olivera of the University of Buenos Aires.

[28] On average, though, the growth rate of money is below the inflation rate. That is because people are reducing their holdings of real balances during hyperinflation: if M/P is falling, then P on average has to be growing faster than M.

expected. That increased money growth causes the inflation rate to increase. And as the government continues to try to spend more than *IR**, it continues driving up the inflation rate. The amount of real money base that people hold becomes smaller and smaller as they try to flee the inflation tax, and the government prints even more rapidly to try to finance its expenditure. In the end the process will break down.

Stopping Hyperinflations

All hyperinflations come to an end. The dislocation of the economy becomes too great for the public to bear, and the government finds a way of reforming its budget process. Often a new money is introduced, and the tax system is reformed. Typically, too, the exchange rate of the new money is pegged to a foreign currency in order to provide an anchor for prices and expectations. Frequently, there are unsuccessful attempts at stabilization before the final success.

The presence of so many destabilizing factors in inflation, particularly the collapse of the tax system as the inflation proceeds, together with an economy that is extremely dislocated by inflation, raises the fascinating possibility that a coordinated attack on inflation may stop the inflation with relatively little unemployment cost. Monetary, fiscal, and exchange rate policies are combined with incomes policies in this *heterodox approach* to stabilization. This approach was used in Argentina and Israel in 1985 and in Brazil in 1986, when the governments froze wages and prices. That stopped the inflation at a single blow.

The Israeli stabilization succeeded, while the Argentinian and Brazilian did not. The difference, as noted previously, was fiscal policy. The Israelis corrected their fiscal deficit, whereas the two others did not. Wage and price controls alone cannot keep inflation in check if the underlying fundamentals of fiscal and monetary policy are not consistent with low inflation.

One more important feature of the stabilizations should be brought out. *Money growth rates following stabilization are very high.* Why? Because as people expect less inflation, nominal interest rates decline, and the demand for real balances rises. With the demand for real balances increasing, the government can create more money without creating inflation. Thus at the beginning of a successful stabilization there may be a bonus for the government: it can temporarily finance part of the deficit through the printing of money, without renewing inflation. But it certainly cannot do so for much more than a year without reigniting inflation.

18-6 SUMMARY

1. A monetary expansion typically expands output in the short run. In the long run sustained higher money growth is translated fully into inflation. Real interest rates and output return to the full-employment level. Only under rational expectations and with full wage and price flexibility does a monetary expansion translate instantly into an increased rate of inflation with no impact on output.

2. A sustained change in money growth ultimately raises the nominal interest rate

by the same amount. This positive association between inflation and nominal interest rates is called the Fisher effect.

3. A sustained monetary expansion ultimately raises nominal interest rates and hence reduces the demand for real balances. That means that prices must on average rise faster than money in the transition to the new long-run equilibrium.

4. In the U.S. economy, broad trends in money growth and in inflation do coincide. Money growth does affect inflation, but the effects occur with a lag that is not very precise. In the short term, inflation is affected by other than monetary shocks, for example, fiscal policy changes and supply shocks.

5. Nominal interest rates tend to reflect the rate of inflation in the U.S. economy. But the real interest rate is definitely not constant. In the early 1980s the real rate increased sharply compared with the levels of the 1970s and long-term average rates.

6. When fiscal policy turns expansionary, the Fed has to decide whether to monetize the deficit, printing money in order to prevent a rise in interest rates and crowding out; to keep the growth rate of money constant; or even to tighten monetary policy. If the government monetizes the deficit, it runs the risk of increasing the inflation rate. The evidence on deficit monetization in the United States remains ambiguous.

7. Inflation is a tax on real balances. To keep constant the purchasing power of money holdings in the face of rising prices, a person has to add to nominal balances. In this fashion resources are transferred from money holders to money issuers, specifically the government.

8. Hyperinflations have generally taken place in the aftermaths of wars. Large budget deficits are typical in hyperinflations. Governments can use the inflation tax to finance deficits to a limited extent, but if too large a deficit has to be financed, inflation explodes.

9. There is a two-way interaction between inflation and budget deficits. Higher deficits tend to cause higher inflation, since they are typically financed in part by money printing. As well, higher inflation causes higher deficits by reducing the real value of tax collection. Higher nominal interest rates raise the measured deficit by increasing the value of nominal interest payments in the budget. The inflation-corrected deficit adjusts for this latter effect.

10. Money growth rates are very high following a successful inflation stabilization, as people increase their holdings of real balances.

11. Incomes policies can help stop high inflation, but can never be a substitute for fiscal tightening.

KEY TERMS

Fisher effect
Monetization of deficits
Cold turkey
Gradualism
Sacrifice ratio

Hyperinflation
Inflation tax
Seigniorage
Inflation-adjusted deficit
Heterodox programs

PROBLEMS

1. (a) Show graphically the effects of a reduction in the growth rate of money on output and inflation.
   (b) Show also how the real interest rate adjusts over time. Be specific about the expectations assumption you are using.

2. In the above example show how the nominal interest rate adjusts to lower inflation.

3. (a) Study the growth rate of money and the inflation rate in the last 5 years in the tables on the inside covers of the book. How closely are they linked?
   (b) Calculate the real rate of interest on Treasury bills during the last 2 years and compare with the historical average.
   (c) What is the explanation for the high levels of real rates in the early 1980s relative to the historical average?

4. Suppose the ratio of money base to GDP is 10 percent. The government is considering raising the inflation rate from the current 0 rate to 10 percent per annum and believes it will obtain an increase in government revenue of 1 percent of GDP by doing so. Explain why that calculation overestimates the inflation tax the government will receive at a 10 percent inflation rate.

5. During 1981–1992 the U.S. government added massively to the national debt.
   (a) Explain why you might worry that this is inflationary.
   (b) Explain whether you actually worry that the high deficits of the 1980s will lead to high inflation later.

6. At the height of the German hyperinflation, the government was covering only 1 percent of its spending with taxes. Explain how the German government could possibly finance the remaining 99 percent of its spending. Refer to Figure 18-7.

7. (a) If the debt-GDP ratio is 30 percent, the nominal interest rate is 12 percent, the inflation rate is 7 percent, and the total budget deficit is 4 percent of GDP, calculate the inflation-adjusted deficit.
   (b) Suppose you were to discover in an inflationary economy that the inflation-corrected budget was in surplus. Explain why in that case the government might be able to sustain a low inflation rate if it could only find a way of getting the rate down to start with.
   (c) Then explain why governments in the mid-1980s used wage and price controls in trying to stop high inflations.

8. Explain how, following the end of hyperinflation, it was possible for the nominal money stock in Germany to increase by a factor of nearly 20 without restarting the inflation.

9. Why do budget deficits create such alarm? Distinguish the short from the long run in developing your answer.

10. The accompanying table shows growth rates of *M2*, inflation, and real growth for decadal averages since 1870. Discuss the extent to which money growth adjusted for output growth helps explain inflation.

	money growth	output growth	inflation
1870–1879	2.3%	5.5%	−3.0%
1880–1889	6.6	1.4	−1.1
1890–1899	5.0	3.7	−2.2
1900–1909	7.3	4.0	1.9
1910–1919	9.8	3.5	6.6
1920–1929	3.3	4.2	2.2
1930–1939	0.8	1.5	−1.9
1940–1949	11.5	3.4	5.6
1950–1959	3.8	3.3	2.5
1960–1969	7.1	4.0	2.7
1970–1979	9.8	2.8	7.1
1980–1989	8.0	2.6	5.4

NOTE: Money refers to *M*2 and inflation to the GNP deflator.

SOURCE: Until 1959, Milton Friedman and Anna Schwartz, *Monetary Trends in the United States and the United Kingdom* (Chicago: University of Chicago Press, 1982); thereafter, DRI/McGraw-Hill.

11. Calculate the real interest rates in Table 18-5. How might you explain the difference in real interest rates between countries? Remember that these are open economies where investors are concerned about returns in a common currency.

12. Hyperinflations occur in the aftermath of wars or major social upheavals. Explain the extreme inflation in Russia today in these terms.

COMPUTER EXERCISES

If you are interested in exploring economic policy material after reading this chapter, refer to the Policy Game contained in the *PC-Macroeconomics* program and the question material located at the end of the book. The Policy Game is a more realistic and complex representation of the economy than the simpler material found in earlier chapters.

BUDGET DEFICITS AND THE PUBLIC DEBT

S ince the early 1980s the United States has experienced the largest sustained budget deficits in its peacetime history. Right at the start of his administration, in February 1993 President Clinton announced an ambitious plan to reduce the budget deficit from 6 percent of GDP in 1992 to less than 3 percent of GDP by 1996. Many criticized the President for planning to raise taxes more than he planned to cut spending, but few criticized his intention to cut the deficit.

In this chapter we discuss the role of deficits and debt in the economy. We ask how budget deficits are financed, whether the public debt is a burden, and what are the implications of deficit financing for interest rates and growth.

Important aspects of this discussion revolve around a surprising question: Does it make any difference whether the government pays for its expenditures by raising taxes or by issuing debt? An influential group in the economics profession believes in the *Barro-Ricardo* view. This holds that, since borrowing today means higher future taxes to service the debt, there is no fundamental difference between tax (current taxes) and debt (future taxes) financing of deficits. We will discuss that view, which stands in sharp contrast to the argument made in earlier chapters that tax increases reduce aggregate demand.

We also consider another question: Under what conditions do budget deficits lead to an ever-growing ratio of debt to GDP, and what happens then? The issue is whether a given deficit policy is *sustainable* and, of course, how unsustainable policies end.

We start with an overview of federal public finances.

19-1 FEDERAL GOVERNMENT FINANCES: FACTS AND ISSUES

In this section we review the facts about the composition and trends of U.S. government spending and revenues, the deficit, and the public debt. The main question is, Why did the U.S. deficit reach such high levels in the mid-1980s and early 1990s?

TABLE 19-1

FEDERAL GOVERNMENT OUTLAYS (percent of GDP; fiscal year; unified budget)

	1960–1969	1970–1979	1980–1989	1990–1992
National defense	8.9	6.0	5.7	5.5
Entitlements and other mandatory spending	4.8*	9.2	11.1	11.3
Nondefense discretionary spending	4.8*	5.1	4.5	3.8
Net interest	1.3	1.7	2.9	3.5
Total outlays	19.0	20.5	23.1	23.3

*1962–1969.

SOURCE: Congressional Budget Office, *The Economic and Budget Outlook*, January 1993, and *Historical Tables, Budget of the United States Government*, fiscal year 1990. Columns do not seem to total because "offsetting receipts" are excluded.

Outlays

Table 19-1 shows the outlays of the federal government over the past 32 years. The table introduces some special terminology. There is a distinction between *mandatory* and *discretionary* outlays. The former are outlays that have to be made under *entitlement programs,* where the law specifies that a person meeting certain requirements is automatically entitled to receive payments. Examples of entitlement programs are Medicaid and Social Security. Discretionary spending, by contrast, is governed by the congressional appropriation process and includes, for example, defense expenditures and foreign aid.

Three points stand out in Table 19-1. First, defense expenditures have declined significantly as a fraction of GDP. Second, entitlement programs have doubled. Third, interest payments by the government have become an important part of government outlays. The share of federal interest payments in GDP has nearly tripled over the past 30 years.

For macroeconomic purposes there is an important distinction between the government's *purchases* of goods and services and *transfer payments.* The former are a component of aggregate demand—the G term in Chapter 3—whereas the latter affect aggregate demand indirectly, via changes in disposable income. By the late 1980s only a third of federal government outlays (less than 10 percent of GDP) represented spending on goods and services, while transfer payments accounted for two-thirds.

Receipts

Most of the federal government's revenues come from taxes. The sources of revenue and the total are shown in Table 19-2. The revenue sources are self-explanatory, except perhaps for social insurance taxes. These are taxes on wages paid by employers and by wage earners.

Total federal government revenue as a share of GDP has changed very little over the past 30 years. However, there has been a shift in the sources of revenue. Social

TABLE 19-2
SOURCES OF FEDERAL REVENUE (percent of GNP; period average)

	1960–1969	1970–1979	1980–1989	1990–1992
Individual income tax	8.0	8.3	8.8	8.3
Corporate income tax	3.9	2.8	1.8	1.7
Social insurance taxes and contributions	3.5	5.2	6.6	7.0
Other*	2.8	2.1	1.9	1.7
Total revenue	18.2	18.4	19.0	18.8

*This entry lumps together excise, or sales, taxes; estate and gift taxes; customs duties; and miscellaneous receipts.

SOURCE: Congressional Budget Office, *The Economic and Budget Outlook*, January 1993.

Security taxes and contributions have become a substantially higher source of revenue, corporate income taxes have declined by more than half, and personal income taxes have remained broadly unchanged.[1]

Deficits and Debt

In Table 19-3 we calculate the budget deficit, the excess of outlays over revenues. The growing deficits are accounted for by rising outlays rather than falling taxes. Moreover, the increase in net interest paid by the government is about half the increase in the deficit.

To complete the picture, we recall that deficits are financed by borrowing, which increases the government debt. Since the economy is growing, it is not a forgone conclusion that the debt must grow *relative* to GDP when there is a deficit. In the last decade, though, the U.S. debt has been rising relative to GDP, as is apparent from Table 19-3.

The Business Cycle and Deficits

The distinction between the actual and the *structural* deficit, introduced in Chapter 3, is widely used. The structural deficit, or the full-employment or high-employment or cyclically adjusted deficit, is the level at which the deficit would be if output were at its full-employment level. The *cyclical* deficit is the difference between the actual and the structural deficit.

If the budget were on average balanced over long periods, we would expect budget deficits in recessions and surpluses in boom years. That used to be the case,

---

[1]Note that the much-discussed cut in personal income tax *rates* in the 1980s has not in fact reduced the share of revenue from income taxes, because there was an offsetting closing of tax loopholes.

box 19-1 **SOCIAL SECURITY AND THE BUDGET**

In the United States the Social Security system collects contributions from workers and firms and disburses benefits to retirees. The system works on a "pay-as-you-go" basis, meaning that current revenues from contributions are used to pay current benefits. Such a system works well when inflows from contributions exceed outflows, and it has a crisis when payments to beneficiaries exceed current contributions. The net surplus or deficit of the Social Security system is part of the federal government budget in that general government resources must make up for any shortfall of the system and that any surplus of the system can be used to finance a deficit in the budget.

The financing of social security systems has become highly controversial in the United States and in other industrialized countries because demographic trends foretell serious difficulties 20 to 30 years from now. At the present time the Social Security system runs a surplus—contributions are high because the postwar baby boom is in the labor market. As a result the Social Security surplus helps reduce the size of the budget deficit, as shown in Table 1. But over time, starting in the late 1990s, the demographic balance will start to deteriorate.

TABLE 1

SOCIAL SECURITY AND THE BUDGET DEFICIT
(percent of GDP; fiscal year; unified budget)

	1992	1995	1997
On-budget deficit*	6.9	4.0	4.3
Off-budget deficit†	−0.9	−1.2	−1.4
Combined deficit	3.0	2.8	2.9

*Including deposit insurance.

†Social Security system.

SOURCE: Congressional Budget Office.

The number of retirees will rise relative to the contributing population and the Social Security surplus will turn into a deficit. In 1990 there were about five contributors for every retiree, and in the year 2020 there will be only four. In Japan the aging of the population is much more dramatic: from six workers per retiree in 1990 the drop is to only three in 2020. The emerging imbalance means that benefits have to be trimmed or retirement age has to be raised or taxes have to increase. Given that prospect many argue that early budget balancing is an important step to avoid a far sharper increase in taxes later.* ∎

*See Henry Aaron, Barry Bosworth, and Gary Burtless, *Can America Afford to Grow Old?* (Washington, D.C.: The Brookings Institution, 1989); Alan Auerbach et al., "The Economic Dynamics of an Ageing Population: The Case of Four OECD Countries," *OECD Economic Studies,* Spring 1989; and David Cutler, James Poterba, Louise Sheiner, and Lawrence Summers, "An Aging Society: Opportunity or Challenge?" *Brookings Papers on Economic Activity,* Vol. 1, 1990.

TABLE 19-3

COMPOSITION OF THE BUDGET DEFICIT (percent of GDP; fiscal year; unified budget)

	1960–1969	1970–1979	1980–1989	1990–1992
Outlays	19.0	20.5	23.1	23.3
Interest	1.3	1.7	2.9	3.5
Revenues	18.2	18.4	19.0	18.8
Deficit	0.8	1.9	4.1	4.6
Debt	39.4	27.4	35.9	47.6

SOURCE: See Table 19-2.

but there has been a gradual increase in the structural deficit over time, and now there are deficits even at business cycle peaks, such as 1990, as can be seen in Figure 19-1.

The *cyclical* component of deficits reflects the impact of recessions or booms on tax revenues and government outlays such as unemployment compensation.[2] When the economy goes into recession, the budget automatically worsens as government tax revenues fall and outlays increase. Conversely, in a boom the budget automatically improves.

Here is a convenient rule of thumb for assessing the quantitative impact of a recession on the budget:[3]

> *A percentage point rise in unemployment increases the budget deficit by about 1 percent of GDP.*

This rule of thumb helps explain why deficits were so large in recession years like 1975, 1980, 1982, and 1991. But in addition to the business cycle, other factors are at work. Revenue and expenditure policies are one factor and the other is debt service.

Discretionary Budget Changes

In recessions, the government has often reinforced the automatic effects of the cycle on the budget by *discretionary* fiscal policy expansion. Faced with a recession in 1975, the administration proposed and Congress enacted a tax cut to stimulate the economy. In 1982, the Reagan tax cuts (which were not enacted solely for short-run reasons) helped fuel a rapid recovery from the deep recession.

There are two ways to quantify the discretionary spending component of deficits. One is to look at the impact of the policy measure on the budget deficit. The other is

[2] Cyclical deficit data in this chapter are calculated as the difference between the actual and the structural deficit using the DRI/McGraw-Hill structural deficit series.

[3] See Congressional Budget Office, *The Economic and Budget Outlook,* January 1989.

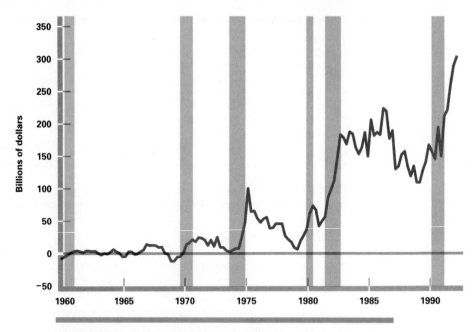

FIGURE 19-1
FEDERAL BUDGET DEFICITS, 1960–1961. Shaded areas represent
recessions. (SOURCE: DRI/McGraw-Hill.)

to ask how much stimulus the measure creates. Figure 19-2 shows a Federal Reserve
Board estimate of *fiscal impetus.* The fiscal impetus is a measure of fiscal policy effects
on GDP, calculated by weighting different spending programs and tax rate cuts with
the corresponding multipliers. For example, a spending program gets a higher multiplier
than a temporary tax rate cut (as we saw in Chapter 3).[4]

Note two points from Figure 19-2. First, discretionary expansions outweigh the
contractions in frequency and by size of action. A tendency to expand in recessions,
but not to contract during booms, means slipping into permanent deficits. Second, the
recession years 1975 and 1982 show up with a large expansionary impulse, as we
would expect. But in the 1990–1991 recession, under the stress of persistent U.S.
deficits, there was no discretionary fiscal expansion, and thus fiscal policy could not
help the economy move out of recession.

What Makes For Large Deficits?

There is an obvious answer to the question, What makes for the large deficits? Outlays
exceed income by a lot. But we can do better by identifying the factors that are
responsible for the *cumulative* growth of the deficit since the early 1980s.[5]

---

[4]See Darrel Cohen, "Models and Measures of Fiscal Policy," Board of Governors of the Federal Reserve
System, Working Paper Series, no. 70, March 1988.

[5]The best source on the deficit is the annual reports to Congress of the Congressional Budget Office published
in January and August.

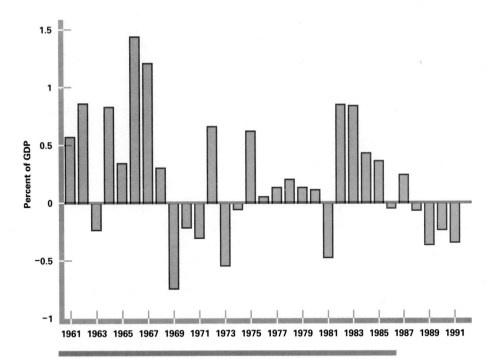

FIGURE 19-2
DISCRETIONARY FISCAL POLICY CHANGES, 1960–1991. (Source: Data
kindly provided by the Board of Governors of the Federal Reserve.)

The tightening of monetary policy in the early 1980s, in response to high and accelerating inflation, raised real interest rates, which stayed high for more than 10 years. Higher interest rates meant that more interest had to be paid on the outstanding debt. The impact of interest rates on the deficit is sizable. Here is another rule of thumb:[6]

A one percentage point increase in interest rates eventually increases interest payments on the debt by an amount equal to 1 percent times the ratio of the debt to GDP.

In the United States, the debt to GDP ratio is about 50 percent, so the long-run impact on the deficit of a one percentage point rise in the real interest rate would be about 0.5 percent of GDP. In the short run, the impact is smaller, because interest payments on outstanding debt are fixed, and actual interest changes only when those bonds mature and have to be rolled over. With the current structure of the debt, the estimate is that the interest cost rises by about 0.25 percent of GDP within a year.[7]

---

[6]See footnote 3.

[7]Technically, interest is not paid on Treasury bills but only on bonds. Treasury bills pay interest implicitly since they are sold at a discount. A Treasury bill is a promise by the Treasury to pay a given amount on a given date, say $100 on June 30. Before June 30, the Treasury bill sells at a discount, that is, at less than $100, with the discount implying a rate of interest.

The second factor in the ballooning of deficits is the political stalemate: higher taxes and spending cuts are both unpopular. Short of a crisis, few politicians are willing to take the blame for either, and the deficits therefore persist. In the meantime the debt grows and the growing debt brings with it rising interest payments that add to the deficit.

The combination of these two factors, a period of record interest rates and the political stalemate, accounts for much of the debt and deficit picture of the past decade. But the picture would not be complete without a look at the supply-side economics of taxes and the budget.

Supply-Side Economics, Tax Rates, and Deficits

In 1981–1983 tax rates were cut by 30 percent in a three-stage process known as the Kemp-Roth tax cuts. The tax structure was also simplified: by 1989 there were only two basic rates of income tax. One argument for these changes was efficiency. Proponents argued that high tax rates were a disincentive to work, to saving, and to investment, and that cutting taxes would reduce these disincentives.

Of course, tax rate cuts might also be expected to lead to larger deficits. How did the cuts of the 1980s pass when many warned that they would result in such large deficits?

The *supply-side economists* who supported the tax cuts argued that the tax cuts would produce *more,* not less, total tax revenue.[8] In the analysis of Chapters 3 and 5, a cut in taxes increases the deficit, even though the tax cuts cause an increase in output, which partly—but not wholly—offsets the effect of the tax cut on government revenue. The supply-siders, by contrast, concentrated on the *incentive effects* of tax cuts. Take the income tax as an example. Supply-siders argued that a cut in income tax rates would encourage people to work more because it would raise their after-tax wage.[9]

THE LAFFER CURVE

The supply-side story was made popular by a diagram proposed by Arthur Laffer, a former professor of economics and now an economics consultant in California. Figure 19-3 shows the *Laffer curve,* which relates tax revenues to the tax rate. The curve shows total tax revenue first increasing as the tax rate rises and then eventually decreasing.[10]

Suppose that we are discussing the income tax rate. When the tax rate is zero, government tax revenue is certainly zero. Hence we have point *A* on the curve. Further,

---

[8] See Paul Craig Roberts, *Supply Side Economics, Theory and Results: An Assessment of American Experience in the 1980s* (Washington, D.C.: Institute for Political Economy, 1989) and the provocative book by the editor of the *Wall Street Journal,* Robert Bartley, *The Seven Fat Years. And How to Do It Again* (New York: Free Press, 1992).

[9] If you have taken a course in microeconomics, you will recognize that the substitution effect of the increase in the after-tax wage causes the worker to work more, while the income effect reduces work. This theory alone cannot determine whether an income tax cut raises work effort.

[10] Note that Figure 18-7, relating the revenue from the inflation tax to the inflation rate, has the same Laffer curve shape as Figure 19-3.

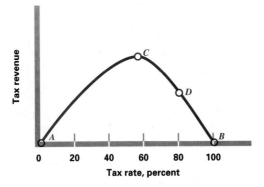

FIGURE 19-3
THE LAFFER CURVE.

suppose the tax rate were 100 percent. Then the government would be taking all the income that people earn. There would be no point in working for zero earnings, and so income in that case too would be zero. Then tax revenue would also be zero. Accordingly, point *B* is also a point on the Laffer curve.

Between *A* and *B*, though, the government certainly takes in some revenue from taxes. Thus we expect the curve to start to rise from point *A* as the tax rate is increased from zero to some very small rate, such as 3 percent. Eventually the curve has to come back down to *B*. Thus at some point it will turn around—perhaps at a tax rate of 60 percent, as shown in Figure 19-3. Here is the crucial point: beyond *C*, at tax rates above 60 percent, any increase in the tax rate *reduces* total revenue. Equivalently, at any tax rate above 60 percent, a *cut* in the tax rate will *increase* total tax revenue.

Looking at Figure 19-3, we have to ask where point *C* is in practice. Note that beyond point *C* a *cut* in the tax rate causes people to work so much more that the increased work effort outweighs the reduced taxes on the amount they used to work. But there is some question whether cuts in tax rates encourage people to work more. There are conflicting effects: the cut in the tax rate makes work more desirable relative to leisure; but with a higher after-tax wage, a worker needs to work less to support the same standard of living. Perhaps when the after-tax wage rises, the response is to work less, earn more income and have more leisure. Thus point *C* might be at a tax rate very close indeed to 100 percent, far from the tax rates in 1981.

Whatever the possibilities, the supply-side tax cuts of the early 1980s do not appear to have raised work effort or saving, and they unquestionably increased the deficit.

Controlling Deficits

The second—a political economy—argument made for tax cuts states that Congress will spend whatever revenue it receives and therefore the only way to get it to cut its spending is to cut revenue.[11] This argument too did not work out, since outlays rose during the 1980s despite the rising deficits.

Various attempts have been made over the past decade to find a solution that would *automatically* cut budget deficits by some formula that leaves no option for escape. These attempts started with the Gramm-Rudman budget deficit reduction plan of 1985, which was to reduce the deficit to zero by 1991. The most recent version is the *Budget Enforcement Act of 1990,* a budget pact agreed to between President Bush and the Congress, in which taxes were to be raised somewhat and a tight lid kept on spending.

The very large size of the deficits suggests that these attempts have been entirely unsuccessful. Surprisingly, that is not the case. The deficits would have been even larger otherwise! But success has been very limited, and in the meantime, the deficit persists. In 1992, the Congressional Budget Office projected deficits that would increase as a share of GDP after the mid-1990s unless policies change. It warned:[12]

> Such large budget deficits impair economic growth by reducing national saving and capital formation. Deficits also create a vicious cycle of more federal borrowing and higher debt service costs, which in turn make it still more difficult to reduce the deficit.

Against this background, we review two important questions: What are the mechanics of debts and deficits? and What damage, if any, do deficits cause?

19-2 THE MECHANICS OF DEFICIT FINANCING

The government pays for its spending by drawing on its bank accounts. Like an individual, the government must have funds in the accounts on which it draws. When tax receipts are insufficient to cover its expenditures—when there is a deficit—the government must borrow. As shown in Figure 19-4, it may borrow either by selling debt to the public or by borrowing from the central bank.

When the Treasury borrows from the central bank to finance its deficit, it engages in *money financing.* In the United States the Treasury rarely sells securities *directly* to the Fed. But in many developing countries, deficit financing often takes the form of direct borrowing from the central bank, and more often than not this means inflationary financing. When the Treasury finances its deficit by borrowing from the public, it engages in *debt financing.*

More formally, we use equation (1), the *government budget constraint,* to examine the financing of deficits. Let ΔB_f be the value of sales of bonds to the central bank and ΔB_p be the value of sales of government bonds to the private sector. Let H be the stock of high-powered money and BD the budget deficit measured in *real* terms. P is

---

[11]For evidence on this point, see Kevin Hoover and Stephen Sheffrin, "Causation, Spending, and Taxes: Sand in the Box or Tax Collector for the Welfare State?" *American Economic Review,* March 1992.

[12]See the analysis in the Congressional Budget Office, *The Economic and Budget Outlook,* issued in January of each year. The quote is from the 1992 issue.

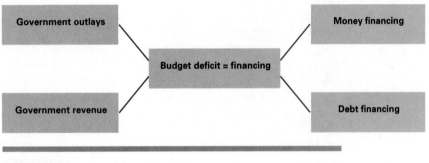

FIGURE 19-4
BUDGET DEFICITS AND THEIR FINANCING.

the price level. The last term in equation (1), ΔA, represents government asset sales. We thus have

$$P \times BD = \Delta B_f + \Delta B_p + \Delta A$$
$$= \Delta H + \Delta B_p + \Delta A \tag{1}$$

Equation (1) states that the nominal budget deficit is financed by borrowing either from the central bank (ΔB_f) or from the private sector (ΔB_p) or by selling assets (ΔA). The change in the central bank's holdings of Treasury debts causes a corresponding change in high-powered money (ΔH), so that it is in this sense that the central bank monetizes the debt.[13]

Financing by debt and money are the standard ways of financing deficits; asset sales are much less common but became important in the 1980s in Europe and in many developing countries. When a government sells public lands or a public sector enterprise (for example, privatizing the national airline), the receipts from the sale can be used to finance the deficit or to retire public debt. Of course, this form of financing has to be temporary, since ultimately the government will run out of assets to sell.

Deficits and the National Debt

The net stock of government debt outstanding is the *national,* or *public,* debt. The definition refers to the *net* debt stock since part of the Treasury's debt is held by other government agencies, including the Fed and the Social Security system. Since the interest on these debts is paid by one government agency to another, we concentrate on the net debt of the government, the net amount the government owes to the private sector of the economy and to foreigners.

---

[13]Note that the government budget constraint, equation (1), also shows that for a given value of the deficit, changes in the stock of high-powered money are matched by offsetting changes in the public's holdings of government debt. A positive ΔH matched by a negative ΔB_p is nothing other than an open market purchase.

If we disregard money financing[14] and assets sales, which have been very small in the United States, the national debt is the result of past federal budget deficits. The Treasury sells securities more or less continuously. It auctions Treasury bills to prospective buyers each week and issues longer-term debt less regularly. Issues of Treasury debt are not all made for the purpose of financing the budget deficit. Most debt issues are made to refinance parts of the national debt that are maturing. For example, 6 months after a 180-day Treasury bill is issued, the Treasury has to pay the face amount of the Treasury bill to the holder. Typically, the Treasury obtains the funds to make those payments by further borrowing. The process by which the Treasury (with the help and advice of the Fed) finances and refinances the national debt is known as *debt management*. Only a minor part of debt management is concerned with financing the current budget deficit, that is, with net debt issue as opposed to refinancing the large existing stock.

We have been focusing on deficits, but the same principles apply in the case of a budget surplus. When the government has an excess of tax revenues over outlays, there is a surplus. Rather than having to borrow, the government can *retire debt*. It can do this by not renewing maturing debt but, rather, paying off bonds or Treasury bills that are coming due. Thus the stock of public debt outstanding declines. There is little risk of the U.S. Treasury's reducing the stock of debt in the next few years. But this happened in the past, for example, after the Civil War, after World War I, and again after World War II.[15]

FED ACCOMMODATION

The Fed *accommodates* the budget deficit by buying more government bonds when the deficit increases. If the Fed accommodates deficits, then there is a clear argument that deficits cause money growth. But since the Fed determines on its own initiative how much high-powered money to create, it does not *have* to accommodate. If it chooses not to conduct open market purchases when the Treasury is borrowing, the stock of high-powered money is not affected by the Treasury's deficit.

Nonetheless, there have been occasions in the past when there was a more or less automatic Fed accommodation. This link was most direct when the Fed was committed to maintaining constant nominal interest rates on government bonds, in the period from 1941 to 1951. An increase in the government deficit tends to increase the nominal interest rate. If the Fed were committed to maintaining a constant nominal interest rate, an increase in the deficit would force the Fed to conduct an open market purchase to keep the nominal interest rate from rising. In this very special way, there would then be a direct link between Treasury borrowing and Fed open market purchases.

---

[14]In the United States, the Fed does not directly finance the deficit by extending loans to the Treasury. But if, over any period, the Fed on net buys government debt in open market operations, it is in effect helping finance the deficit by reducing the amount of debt the Treasury has to sell to the public.

[15]See E. Cary Brown, "Episodes in the Public Debt History of the United States," in R. Dornbusch and M. Draghi (eds.), *Public Debt Management: Theory and History* (Cambridge: Cambridge University Press, 1990).

The Fed's commitment to maintain constant nominal interest rates on government bonds ended formally in 1951 in the "Accord" between the Fed and the Treasury. Even after that, the Fed's longtime policy of having target nominal interest rates—which could change from time to time—also led to an association between deficits and Fed open market purchases. Given the Fed's target interest rates, Treasury borrowing, which would have led to interest rate increases, triggered Fed open market purchases to keep the interest rate from rising above its target level. Thus, for much of the 1950s and 1960s, there was a link between increased Treasury borrowing and Fed open market purchases.

If the Fed targets a monetary aggregate rather than interest rates, there is no longer any *automatic* link between budget deficits and the monetary base. In the 1979–1982 period, for example, the Fed emphasized monetary targets, and even when interest rates became extremely high, there was no automatic response of monetizing the deficits.

Summary

1. Federal government spending is financed through taxes and through borrowing; the latter is necessary when the budget is in deficit.
2. Borrowing may be from the private sector or indirectly from the Federal Reserve System.
3. Lending by the Fed to the Treasury changes the stock of high-powered money, whereas lending by the private sector to the Treasury does not affect the stock of high-powered money.
4. The net stock of government debt outstanding—the national debt—changes with Treasury borrowing. The national debt increases when the Treasury is on net borrowing and decreases when the Treasury is on net repaying debt.
5. Because the deficit can be financed in two ways, there is no *necessary* connection between the budget deficit and changes in the stock of high-powered money. Equation (1), the government budget constraint, says only that the *sum* of changes in the stock of debt and changes in high-powered money is approximately equal to the budget deficit.

19-3 THE DYNAMICS OF DEFICITS AND DEBTS

In this section we focus on the potential vicious cycle of debts and deficits. It is useful to distinguish between two components of the budget deficit: the *primary,* or *noninterest, deficit* and interest payments on the public debt.

$$\text{Total deficit} \equiv \text{primary deficit} + \text{interest payments} \tag{2}$$

TABLE 19-4

THE U.S. PRIMARY DEFICIT (percent of GDP; fiscal year)

	total deficit	primary deficit
1960–1969	0.8	−0.5
1970–1979	1.9	0.2
1980–1989	4.1	1.2
1990–1991	4.6	1.1

SOURCE: DRI/McGraw-Hill. See table 19-2.

The primary deficit (or surplus) represents all government outlays, except interest payments, less all government revenue. The primary deficit is also called the *noninterest* deficit.[16]

$$\text{Primary deficit} \equiv \text{noninterest outlays} - \text{total revenue} \qquad (3)$$

The distinction between interest and noninterest outlays highlights the role of the public debt in the budget. Interest has to be paid when there is debt outstanding. The overall budget will be in deficit unless the interest payments on the debt are more than matched by a primary surplus. Table 19-4 shows the total deficit and the two components over the period since 1960.

The key point in deficit financing is this: *If there is a primary deficit in the budget, then the total budget deficit will keep growing as the debt grows because of the deficit, and interest payments rise because the debt is growing.* The problem is exactly the same for an individual as for a country. Someone who is spending more than he or she earns, and borrowing to cover the difference, will need to borrow more and more each year just because the interest on past borrowings keeps rising. If the economy is not growing, any policy that leads debt to keep on growing cannot be viable, because ultimately the debt will be unmanageably large relative to the size of the economy.

Debt, Growth, and Instability

The national debt in the United States has risen almost every year for most of the past 50 years. Does that mean the government budget is bound to get out of hand, with

---

[16]We draw attention here to another budget concept, the *operational*, or *inflation-adjusted*, deficit, already discussed in Chap. 18. This is the budget deficit including *real* rather than nominal interest payments on the debt. The concept is especially useful in high-inflation countries, where high nominal interest payments reflect the erosion of the real value of the debt due to inflation. See Mario Blejer and Adrienne Cheasty, "The Measurement of Fiscal Deficits: Analytical and Methodological Issues," *Journal of Economic Literature,* December 1991.

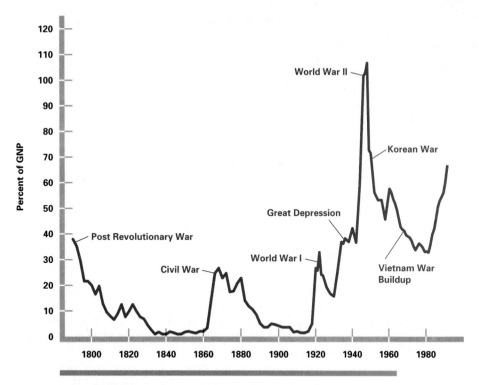

FIGURE 19-5

THE U.S. DEBT-INCOME RATIO IN HISTORICAL PERSPECTIVE. (SOURCE: Congressional Budget Office, from material cited in James R. Barth and Stephen O. Morrell, "A Primer on Budget Deficits," Federal Reserve Bank of Atlanta *Economic Review*, August 1982.)

interest payments rising so high that taxes have to keep rising, until eventually something terrible happens? The answer is no, because the economy has been growing.

Figure 19-5 shows the U.S. public debt as a fraction of GNP for a long stretch of time, starting in the early nineteenth century. The most striking fact is that the debt rises sharply as a result of large wartime deficits, and then declines in each postwar period. Over most of the period from World War II to 1974 the debt-income ratio was falling even though the debt itself was rising as the result of budget deficits.

How could this happen? It is helpful to look at the definition of the debt-income ratio:

$$\text{Debt ratio} = \frac{\text{debt}}{PY} \tag{4}$$

where *PY* represents nominal GDP.[17] The ratio of debt to GDP falls when nominal

---

[17]Since GNP and GDP are almost the same for the United States, it does not make a difference whether we discuss the debt to GNP or debt to GDP ratio.

TABLE 19-5

DETERMINANTS OF THE DEBT-INCOME RATIO

	$b(r - y) - z > 0$	$b(r - y) - z = 0$	$b(r - y) - z < 0$
Debt-income ratio is	Rising	Constant	Falling

GDP grows more rapidly than the debt. To see this point it is useful to look separately at the numerator and denominator of the debt-GDP ratio. The numerator, the debt, grows because of deficits. The denominator, nominal GDP, grows as a result of both inflation and real GDP growth.

Why is it useful to look at the ratio of debt to income rather than at the absolute value of the debt? The reason is that GDP is a measure of the size of the economy, and the debt-GDP ratio is thus a measure of the magnitude of the debt relative to the size of the economy. A national debt of $3 trillion would have been overwhelming in 1929 when U.S. GDP was about $100 billion—even if the interest rate had been only 1 percent, the government would have had to raise 30 percent of GDP in taxes to pay interest on the debt. But when GDP is near $6 trillion, a $3 trillion debt is not so overwhelming.

We can formalize this discussion by writing the equation for the debt-income ratio and considering explicitly how it changes over time.[18] We define the following symbols:

r = real, or inflation-adjusted, interest rate

z = noninterest or primary budget surplus measured as a fraction of GDP

y = growth rate of real GDP

b = debt-income ratio

In the appendix we show that the debt-income ratio is rising over time if

$$\Delta b = b(r - y) - z > 0 \tag{5}$$

The evolution of the debt-income ratio thus depends on the relationship among the real interest rate, the growth rate of output, and the noninterest budget surplus. The higher the interest rate and the lower the growth rate of output, the more likely the debt-income ratio is to be rising. A large noninterest surplus tends to make the debt-income ratio fall. Table 19-5 summarizes the conditions derived in the appendix that determine whether the debt-GDP ratio is rising or falling.

---

[18]For a recent evaluation of the sustainability of deficit strategies in industrial countries, see Olivier Blanchard, Jean-Claude Chouraqui, Robert Hageman, and Nicola Sartor, "The Sustainability of Fiscal Policy: New Answers to an Old Question," *OECD Economic Studies,* Autumn 1990.

The table brings out the reason why the debt-income ratio was falling during the 1950s and 1960s. The real interest rate was practically zero, output grew steadily, and the noninterest budget was in surplus or near balance. In these circumstances debt grows less rapidly than nominal income, and hence the debt-income ratio fell. In the 1980s, by contrast, real interest rates were very high, growth was sluggish, and the noninterest budget was in deficit. As a result the debt-income ratio was rising. In a period of slow growth and high real interest rates, deficits therefore translate into a rapidly rising debt-income ratio. That was, indeed, the case in the 1980s.

UNPLEASANT ARITHMETIC

What would happen if the deficit were so large that debt relative to income grew seemingly without bound? Such a process cannot go on forever. Ultimately, the public debt becomes so large, interest payments take up so much of the budget, and crowding out becomes so pervasive that *some* action has to be taken to balance the budget. This might involve inflation, special taxes, or highly unpopular major cuts in government spending. As an extreme measure, the government might even write down the value of the public debt, in essence paying back only a fraction of what it owes. This possibility has often been discussed in the aftermath of wars in which debts grew exceptionally large, and it has sometimes been implemented.[19]

Thomas Sargent and Neil Wallace of the University of Minnesota have pointed to an important implication of the government budget constraint, equation (1).[20] Specifically, *debt financing of a deficit may in the long run be more inflationary than money financing*. The argument is that persistent deficits ultimately lead to inflation because the government will build up a debt burden and interest payments that it cannot finance by taxes or more borrowing. The only way it can then meet its payments is to print money.

Interestingly, the longer the government keeps financing the deficit by borrowing, the higher the ultimate inflation. If the government starts money financing today, it needs to print money at a rate that finances the interest payments on the *existing* national debt. But if it waits 5 years to start money financing, it will have to create money at a rate that finances the interest payments on the national debt that will exist 5 years from now. Because interest on the debt will have accumulated in the meantime, the debt will be larger 5 years from now and, therefore, so will the inflation rate.

This example shows that because of the accumulation of interest, short-run debt financing that ends in money financing will generally ultimately be more inflationary than immediate money financing of a given deficit. The arithmetic is unpleasant for monetarists because it suggests that the future inflation rate may be more closely related to budget deficits than to the current growth rate of money.

The main question raised by this argument is whether the government will eventually be forced into money financing for *any* given current deficit, or whether it

---

[19]See Alberto Alesina, "The End of Large Public Debts," in Francesco Giavazzi and Luigi Spaventa (eds.), *High Public Debt* (Cambridge: Cambridge University Press, 1988) for a historical perspective.

[20]See T. Sargent and N. Wallace, "Some Unpleasant Monetarist Arithmetic," Federal Reserve Bank of Minnesota *Quarterly Review,* Fall 1981. As the title suggests, the treatment is technical.

can continue debt financing forever. As equation (5) suggests, that depends on the relationship between the growth rate of output and the real interest rate. If the real interest rate is above the growth rate of output, and given a zero (or positive) primary deficit, debt financing cannot continue forever because the debt becomes a larger and larger part of GDP and interest payments keep rising. At some point, then, the government will have to turn to money financing and higher inflation—or will have to cut spending and/or raise taxes.

If the real interest rate is below the growth rate of output, with a zero primary deficit, the government can continue debt financing without a resulting rise in the debt-GDP ratio. In that case debt financing is viable for the long term, and the hard choice posed by the Sargent-Wallace example can be avoided. Note also that if the government is willing to raise taxes at some future date to pay higher interest bills, there is no necessary link between current deficits and future money growth.

The Sargent-Wallace analysis does make clear why permanent deficits cause concern. If the national debt is growing relative to GDP, then ultimately the government will have to raise taxes or raise the inflation rate to meet its debt obligations. That is the long-run threat that leads people to worry about deficits. But the long run in this case may be decades away.

There is a further important point. The Sargent-Wallace concern is about *primary* deficits; if the *total* deficit is constant as a percentage of GDP, then ultimately the debt-GDP ratio will stabilize, provided the economy is growing at all. For instance, a statement that the deficit in the United States would be 5 percent of GDP forever would not mean that the debt would explode as a percentage of GDP. Rather, if the deficit were financed through debt, the debt-GDP ratio would eventually reach a steady state. The explanation is that when the deficit is measured to *include* interest payments, a statement that the deficit will be constant forever means that behind the scenes the primary deficit or surplus is being adjusted to ensure that interest payments are being made without the debt-GDP ratio exploding.

How does inflation help solve the deficit problem? First, the inflation tax (discussed in Chapter 18) can make some small contribution to financing the deficit. But more important, a large, *unanticipated* inflation will reduce the real value of the outstanding stock of government debt. The national debt in most countries is *nominal*, meaning that the government is obliged to pay only a certain number of dollars to the holders of the debt. A policy that raises the price level thus reduces the real value of the payments the government is obliged to make. The debt can therefore virtually be wiped out by a large enough unanticipated inflation—so long as the debt is a nominal debt.

It is important to have some perspective on the relevance of these extreme conditions to the world today. Table 19-6 presents deficit and debt data for the major industrialized countries. Italy in 1992 was in a highly precarious situation. By contrast, the United States was not close to a debt crisis. But it did face the prospect of a rise in the ratio of debt to income, back toward the levels of the 1950s. Herbert Stein, the distinguished expert on U.S. fiscal history, comments on such a situation in the following terms: "Something that cannot last forever ultimately comes to an end."

Debt problems are often clearly visible ahead of time. But on occasion debt problems emerge very suddenly, for instance, in the international debt crisis of the 1980s. Many developing countries had borrowed abroad during the 1970s and in 1980–

TABLE 19-6
DEBT AND DEFICITS IN INDUSTRIALIZED COUNTRIES (percent of GNP/GDP; general government)

	NET PUBLIC DEBT		PRIMARY BUDGET	
	1980	1992	1980	1992
United States	19.0	38.3	0.0	−1.6
Japan	17.3	5.4	−3.4	2.2
Europe	26.3	43.8	−1.4	−1.0
Germany	14.3	24.2	−1.6	−1.3
Italy	53.6	104.5	−3.9	−0.9
United Kingdom	47.5	32.2	−0.3	−2.9
Canada	13.0	50.9	−0.9	0.7

SOURCE: OECD, *Economic Outlook*, June 1992.

1981, when the real interest rate was still low. When the real interest rate rose sharply in 1982, their heavy indebtedness meant that they had to make large interest payments to foreigners, which for many of the countries was extremely difficult to do. The result was the developing countries' debt crisis of the 1980s.

19-4 ECONOMIC EFFECTS OF DEBT-FINANCED DEFICITS

In this section we discuss the consequences of deficits, concentrating on debt-financed deficits. We draw a distinction between transitory and persistent deficits. Two important questions are asked. First, what is the impact of a debt-financed deficit on aggregate demand, output, and interest rates? Second, do deficits today come at a cost or are they a "free lunch"?

A Debt-Financed Transitory Deficit

Figure 19-6 shows aggregate demand curves. We consider the effects of a tax cut. The tax cut is temporary, and the budget deficit is financed by selling debt to the private sector.

The initial effect of the cut in taxes is to shift the aggregate demand curve out from AD to AD_1. Because the private sector is buying bonds during the period of the deficit, it ends up holding a higher stock of government bonds. What effect does that higher stock of government debt held by the private sector have on aggregate demand?

Suppose that individuals holding government bonds regard those bonds as part of their wealth. Then, given the level of income, aggregate demand should rise when the stock of government bonds rises because individuals holding those bonds have higher wealth. The higher wealth increases consumption demand and the aggregate

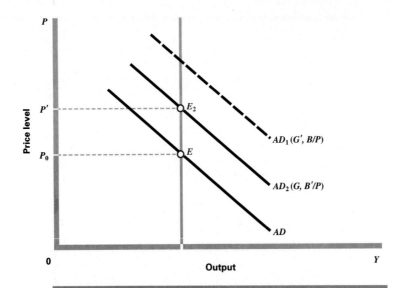

FIGURE 19-6

A TRANSITORY DEBT-FINANCED DEFICIT. A cut in taxes shifts the aggregate demand curve from AD to AD_1. In the short run, aggregate demand expands. Because the deficit is transitory, the tax cut is later reversed. The rise in public debt that financed the transitory deficit raises the wealth of the debt holders. Once the deficit has returned to normal, the effect of increased debt outstanding implies higher aggregate demand. AD_1 shifts back only to AD_2 rather than to AD. There is a permanent increase in the price level and, given nominal money, a rise in interest rates.

demand curve shifts out to the right.[21] Hence, we show the final aggregate demand curve—after government spending has returned to its original level—at AD_2, above the initial AD curve. The difference between the two aggregate demand schedules, AD and AD_2, arises from the higher stock of government bonds, B', compared with B on the initial aggregate demand curve. Since the effects of the higher wealth on consumption demand are likely to be small, we show the final aggregate demand curve, AD_2, below the aggregate demand curve AD_1.

There are two complications to this analysis. The first is that the existence of the higher stock of debt raises the amount of interest payments in the federal budget. If the budget was originally balanced at point E, it may not be balanced at E_2. Of course, since the price level at E_2 is higher than at E, bracket creep may have balanced the budget. (Bracket creep occurs when the *real* value of taxes paid rises with the price level because tax brackets are specified in nominal terms.) If it has not, then further

---

[21] Recall the discussion of the effect of wealth on consumption in Chap. 11.

financing of the deficit would have to be undertaken, and that would have subsequent effects on the equilibrium.

The Neoclassical Approach to Fiscal Policy

Fiscal policy as discussed in simple Keynesian models takes it for granted that a cut in personal taxes will lead to increased spending by households. Unless there is full employment, expansionary fiscal policy can therefore lead to an increase in output. Moreover, if households treat the debt with which the deficit is financed as net worth, there may be further demand expansion as a result of debt financing. This line of thinking has been sharply attacked and rejected by the neoclassical approach to fiscal policy.[22] The neoclassical approach to fiscal policy emphasizes the microeconomic linkages among government spending, debt, and tax policies and their effects on households and firms. It asserts that the scope for active fiscal policy is radically less than Keynesian approaches suggest.

THE BARRO-RICARDO PROBLEM

The neoclassical approach focuses on households' permanent income and ability to spend. If an individual's taxes are cut now, and that same person has to pay off the interest and principal on the debt floated to finance the tax cut, the person's permanent income has not changed. In this example, there is no reason, on permanent income grounds, to think that a tax cut will increase the person's spending.

At the aggregate level, suppose that everyone believed that the national debt would eventually be paid off. At some point in the future the federal government would have to run a surplus to pay off the debt. That means it would have to raise taxes in the future. Then an increase in the debt would increase individuals' wealth and at the same time suggest to them that their taxes would be higher in the future. The net effect on aggregate demand might then be zero.

The issue raised by this argument is sometimes posed as the question, Are government bonds wealth? The question goes back at least to the classical English economist David Ricardo. It has been given prominence in the work of the new classical economists, in particular Robert Barro.[23] Hence it is known as the *Barro-Ricardo equivalence proposition*, or *Ricardian equivalence*. The proposition is that debt financing by bond issue merely postpones taxation; therefore, in many instances it is strictly

---

[22]See Robert Barro, "The Neoclassical Approach to Fiscal Policy," in R. Barro (ed.), *Modern Business Cycle Theory* (Cambridge, Mass.: Harvard University Press, 1989).

[23]The original article is Robert Barro, "Are Government Bonds Net Wealth?" *Journal of Political Economy,* December 1974. A recent statement by the same author is "The Ricardian Approach to Budget Deficits," *Economic Perspectives,* Spring 1989. Recent theoretical challenges to the Barro-Ricardo view are Olivier Blanchard, "Debts, Deficits and Finite Horizons," *Journal of Political Economy,* April 1985, and Douglas Bernheim, "A Neoclassical Perspective on Budget Deficits," *Economic Perspectives,* Spring 1989. For a discussion in the context of the 1980s see Franco Modigliani, "Reagan's Economic Policies," *Oxford Economic Papers,* October 1988, and Benjamin Friedman, *The Day of Reckoning* (New York: Random House, 1988).

equivalent to current taxation. (Incidentally, after raising this as a theoretical possibility, Ricardo rejected its practical significance.)

The strict Barro-Ricardo proposition that government bonds are not net wealth turns on the argument that people realize their bonds will have to be paid off with future increases in taxes. If so, an increase in the budget deficit unaccompanied by cuts in government spending should lead to an increase in savings that precisely matches the deficit.

There are two main theoretical objections to the Barro-Ricardo proposition. First, given that people have finite lifetimes, the people who are receiving the tax cut today will not be paying off the debt tomorrow. This argument assumes that people now alive do not take into account the higher taxes their descendants will have to pay in the future. Second, it is argued that many people cannot borrow, and thus do not consume according to their permanent income. They would like to consume more today but because of *liquidity constraints*—their inability to borrow—are constrained to consuming less than they would want according to their permanent income. A tax cut for these people eases their liquidity constraint and allows them to consume more.

These theoretical disagreements mean that the Barro-Ricardo hypothesis has to be settled by examining the empirical evidence. The sharp decline of the U.S. private saving rate in the 1980s is one piece of evidence against the proposition. Less casual empirical research continues in an attempt to settle the issue of whether the debt is wealth.[24] We believe the evidence to date is on balance unfavorable to the Barro-Ricardo proposition but recognize that the issue has not yet been decisively settled.

Money and Debt Financing

There is one important difference between debt and money financing of a given short-run budget deficit. Compared with debt financing, money financing of the deficit tends to reduce the interest rate in the short run. That is because money financing increases the nominal money stock (shifting rightward the *LM* curve in the *IS-LM* model), whereas debt financing does not. In the short run, then, debt financing reduces the level of investment compared with money financing. That is an issue connected with the crowding out question.

We want also to compare the effects on the price level of money and debt financing of a temporary increase in government spending. The price level is higher with money financing than with debt financing. There are two reasons. First, money financing increases the money stock, and debt financing does not. The higher the money stock, the greater is aggregate demand at any given price level. Second, we attributed a price level rise in the case of debt financing to the wealth effect of a greater stock of debt on consumption. Although there is some argument about whether bonds are wealth, there is no question that money is wealth. So the wealth effect on consumption is larger in the case of money financing than of debt financing. That, too, means that

---

[24]See, for example, Leonardo Leiderman and Mario Blejer, "Modeling and Testing Ricardian Equivalence: A Survey," *IMF Staff Papers*, March 1988, and James Poterba and Lawrence Summers, "Finite Lifetimes and the Savings Effect of Budget Deficits," *Journal of Monetary Economics*, September 1987.

aggregate demand at any given price level will be higher with money than with debt financing.

We now summarize the effects of a temporary budget deficit. Deficit financing probably increases aggregate demand, but because of the possible effects of anticipated future tax liabilities on consumption, that is not certain. Debt financing, starting from a balanced budget and not compensated for by higher taxes or reductions in other transfer payments, leads to a permanent deficit in the budget because interest has to be paid on the debt. Debt financing raises the interest rate and reduces investment in the short run compared with the effects of money financing.[25]

19-5 THE BURDEN OF THE DEBT

As deficits continue, the national debt piles up. The U.S. (gross) national debt at the end of 1992 exceeded $4 trillion, an amount that is enough to get anyone worried. In per capita terms, the national debt amounts to more than $16,000 per person in the United States. Do we actually have to pay off this debt? It is the notion that every person in the country has a large debt that makes the existence of the debt seem so serious.

However, by and large, we owe the national debt to ourselves. Each individual shares in the obligation to repay the public debt, but many individuals own the national debt. To a first approximation, one could think of the liability that the debt represents as canceling out the asset that the debt represents to the individuals who hold claims on the government. In this case, the debt would not on net be a burden on society.[26]

The only factor ignored so far is that part of the debt is owned by foreigners. In that case, for the U.S. economy as a whole, part of the asset represented by the debt is held by foreigners, while the future tax liability accrues entirely to residents. Then that part of the debt held by foreigners represents a net debt of U.S. residents.

A more important sense in which the debt may be a burden is through the potential long-run effects of the deficit and debt on the capital stock. We saw earlier that debt financing increases the interest rate and reduces investment. Hence the capital stock will be lower with debt financing than otherwise, and thus output will be lower as a result of debt financing of a deficit. This *is* a real burden.

Moreover, the debt can also be a burden because the higher taxes needed for debt servicing could have adverse effects on the economy, for instance, by discouraging investment or work effort. Such effects would also reduce output.

Thus, if the debt is a burden, it is a burden for reasons very different from those suggested by the statement that every person in the United States has a debt of $16,000 as a share of the national debt. The major source of the burden arises from the possible effects of the national debt on the country's net national worth: an increase in the national debt can reduce the capital stock and/or increase the nation's external debt.

---

[25]On the link between deficits and interest rates see the extensive review in George Iden and John Sturrock, "Deficits and Interest Rates: Theoretical Issues and Empirical Evidence," Congressional Budget Office, Staff Working Paper, January 1989. See, too, Preston Miller and William Roberds, "How Little We Know About Deficit Policy Effects," Federal Reserve Bank of Minneapolis *Quarterly Review,* Winter 1992.

[26]We should recognize that we are now dealing again with the issue of Ricardian equivalence.

Intergenerational Accounting

When Ricardian equivalence does not hold, the national debt creates a burden on future generations by reducing their capital stock. This means that deficit financing shifts some of the burden of current government spending to future generations.

There is no hard-and-fast economic principle that describes what is fair and not fair in allocating burdens among generations. Nonetheless, politicians as well as nonpoliticians probably have little trouble reaching a view on how burdens should be shared across generations. Such decisions, of course, have to be based on an accounting of just how much current policies impose burdens on different generations. *Intergenerational accounting* evaluates the costs and benefits of the entire fiscal (tax and spending) system for various age groups in society.

Laurence Kotlikoff of Boston University has made a systematic estimate of the intergenerational redistribution involved in U.S. fiscal policies. He comes up with a stark and controversial finding:[27]

> The average (over males and females) damage done in the 1980s to future generations was only 0.5 percent of the damage done in the 1950s, only 2.7 percent of the damage done in the 1960s, and only 2.5 percent of the damage done in the 1970s. The big winners from fiscal policy in the 1980s were Americans over forty at the time. Americans under forty were hurt by the policies. Young women were particularly hard hit by the decline in real welfare benefits and the rise in excise taxation.

As the last sentence of the quotation suggests, Kotlikoff arrives at his unexpected conclusion by taking into account not only the future tax burdens imposed by the growing debt, but also the burdens and benefits different generations derive from government tax and spending programs.

Government Assets

It is important to recognize that the government has assets as well as debts. Imagine a government that runs a deficit, borrowing from the public, in order to add to the capital stock. For example, the government builds roads, post offices, or universities. The real capital acquired by the government should be treated as an offset against the debt issued. But in public discussions it is often forgotten that government spending is not all consumption or transfers.

Robert Eisner of Northwestern University has strongly emphasized this point in presenting government balance sheets in which both government debts and assets are listed.[28] For example, in 1990 the federal government owned reproducible assets (valued at replacement cost) of $834 billion but had debts of $2,687 billion. Thus the government had a net debt of only $1,853 billion, far less than the size of the debt itself would

---

[27]Laurence Kotlikoff, *Generational Accounting* (New York: Free Press, 1992), p. 184.

[28]See Robert Eisner, *How Real Is the Federal Deficit?* (New York: Free Press, 1986), and "Budget Deficits: Rhetoric and Reality," *Economic Perspectives,* Spring 1989.

suggest. If additional adjustment were made for holdings of land, the net debtor position would be far lower.[29]

The valuation of government assets raises serious issues. Unquestionably, the government can sell a school, the national parks, a post office, a jet fighter, or an offshore oil lease. But if it does not plan to do so, and if—as in the case of a jet fighter—the government will more likely have to continue to spend large amounts to keep the asset operating, it is not entirely clear whether that item should count as a government asset in calculating the government's net worth. Whatever the details, concentrating only on government debt rather than on all the government's potential sources of future income and outlays is misleading.

The Budget Deficits of the 1980s and 1990s

The U.S. budget deficits of the 1980s and 1990s do not correspond to public sector capital formation such as the building of roads and schools and therefore do place a burden on future generations.[30] Moreover, they have been accompanied by very large deficits in the U.S. current account of the balance of payments, and thus by borrowing from foreigners. And on the domestic side, the deficits have not been matched by an increase in private saving. On the contrary, the savings rate declined in the 1980s.

Simplifying somewhat, we can say that the government offered consumers lower present taxes, financing a significant part of the deficit by borrowing abroad. Someone will ultimately have to pay the taxes that finance the interest on those loans from abroad. In this respect the United States is no different from developing countries such as Mexico and Brazil, which have incurred a public debt by borrowing abroad. This is part of the case for deficit correction.

The Size-of-Government Debate

There has been a worldwide trend over the last 30 years toward an increased share of government in GDP. In the United States outlays by all levels of government were 26 percent of GDP in 1960 and 33 percent in 1990. This increase reflects in large measure the broadening of government social programs, especially the growth of transfer programs. Since 1981, growth in spending has been under sharp attack.

How large should the government be? That is, of course, a difficult question to answer. The baseline has to be the existing government programs. Clearly some government programs are widely regarded as desirable; for instance, few dispute the need for an adequate national defense. Other programs, such as the Social Security program,

---

[29]See the data series on the economy's capital stock in *Survey of Current Business,* January 1992.

[30]See Adrian Thorp, "Fiscal Policy in the Reagan Years: A Burden on Future Generations?" Federal Reserve Bank of San Francisco *Economic Review,* Winter 1991, and M. Akhtar and Ethan Harris, "The Supply-Side Consequences of U.S. Fiscal Policy in the 1980s," Federal Reserve Bank of New York *Quarterly Review,* Spring 1992.

box 19-2 **THE U.S. FISCAL DILEMMA**

In 1993, the incoming Clinton administration faced a tough problem. The election had been won because of the economy. President Clinton had promised to create jobs and restore growth in a weak economy. That promise had been decisive. But how was the new administration going to create new jobs with infrastructure investment, funds for the inner cities, and education projects with deficits that had already reached $1 billion a day? Worse, the candidate promised to cut the deficit in half by 1996, and how could that be done while creating more jobs?

The ten-year budget outlook (prepared before the new administration's program) is shown in Table 1. It offers no easy way out—the budget deficit would still be above 5 percent of GDP even by the year 2002, and the debt ratio would have been rising throughout.

TABLE 1

LONG-TERM BUDGET TRENDS (percent of GDP)

	1992	1997	2002
Deficit	5.4	3.8	5.2
Revenues	18.6	18.9	19.0
Outlays	24.0	22.7	24.2
Interest	3.4	3.7	4.2
Health care	3.4	4.4	5.8
Debt	51.3	57.1	65.6

SOURCE: Congressional Budget Office.

The President proposed to combine a short-term stimulus with long-term fiscal tightening. The stimulus would cut taxes and raise spending by about $30 billion—0.5 percent of GDP—in the first year. The fiscal tightening would be phased in over the next four years, largely by raising taxes but also by cutting defense spending. The anticipation of future deficit reductions will probably have favorable effects, not only by instilling confidence but also by reducing long-term interest rates. Indeed, long-term interest rates fell sharply after the President's State of the Union address.

The President did not announce a long-run deficit target. We do not have a good theory of optimal deficits except to say that deficits (at full employment) crowd out investment and, if large and persistent, may lead to financial instability. A plausible target might be to reach by the end of the century a deficit small enough to keep the debt ratio constant. Note from Table 1 that this would take quite some deficit cutting. ∎

also command wide assent, though just how large such programs should be is controversial.[31] To conservatives government is far too large, and hence the deficit—and the pressures it puts on interest rates and financial stability—is desirable. Deficit pressure, in this view, is the best way to get spending cuts.[32]

Although there is no simple test that will tell us whether we get our money's worth from government spending in general, a number of particular government programs have been evaluated. Studies show that many programs are less effective than was originally expected; indeed, some programs should be abandoned, leaving the free market to handle the problem. Even the Social Security system and the food stamp program have received substantial criticism. The approach that looks at individual programs to examine their success and suggest changes is clearly the most careful way to evaluate government spending.

In practice, of course, the issue of how much government spending there should be is handled by the political process. In the 1930s and in the 1960s the rules and traditions of fiscal policy were changed by activist government policy in pursuit of full employment and widening social objectives. In the 1980s there was a widespread sentiment that things had gone too far and needed to be brought under control. We have seen that long-run control of deficits is necessary to ensure macroeconomic stability. The rest of the fiscal revolt reflects a disagreement in society on how best to use resources. At the same time at the start of the Clinton administration in 1993, there was a strand of thinking that calls for a resumption of government activity in areas ranging from infrastructure to education. The debate is not over and the acute fiscal problem is bound to keep the difficult tradeoffs involved at the forefront of the discussion.

19-6 SUMMARY

1. Federal government expenditures are financed through taxes and borrowing. The borrowing takes place directly from the public and can also take place indirectly, from the Fed.

2. Federal Reserve financing of the deficit increases the stock of high-powered money. In the United States, there is no necessary link between Treasury borrowing and changes in the stock of high-powered money. However, when the Fed tries to control the level of interest rates, it creates an automatic link between Treasury borrowing and the creation of high-powered money.

3. Federal government receipts come chiefly from the individual income tax and from social insurance taxes and contributions. The share of the last category has increased rapidly in the postwar period, especially since the 1960s.

4. Federal government expenditures are chiefly for defense and transfer payments to individuals. The share of defense in federal expenditure has fallen over the past 30 years, while the shares of transfers and interest have risen.

---

[31]These issues are debated in all industrial countries. See Howard Oxley and John Martin, "Controlling Government Spending and Deficits: Trends in the 1980s and Prospects for the 1990s," *OECD Economic Studies,* Autumn 1991.

[32]See the essay by Hoover and Sheffrin cited in footnote 11,

5. A temporary increase in government spending or a cut in taxes financed by debt will raise the price level and increase the interest rate.

6. The Barro-Ricardo equivalence proposition notes that debt represents future taxes. It asserts that debt-financed tax cuts will not have any effect on aggregate demand.

7. The debt-income ratio rises if the growth rate of debt—determined by interest payments and the primary deficit—exceeds the growth rate of nominal income.

8. Debt financing of a permanent increase in government spending is not viable if the economy is not growing. The interest payments on the debt would continually increase, making for a rising deficit that has to be funded by ever-increasing borrowing. In a growing economy, small deficits can be run permanently without causing the debt-GDP ratio to rise.

9. The major sense in which the national debt may be a burden is that it may lead to a decline in the capital stock in the long run.

10. Large U.S. deficits over more than a decade had consumption as their primary counterpart, and they were in part financed by external borrowing. This external borrowing increases the net external debt of the United States and gives rise to a debt burden.

KEY TERMS

Public debt	Laffer curve
Debt financing	Primary deficit
Money financing	Noninterest deficit
Entitlement programs	Barro-Ricardo equivalence
Discretionary spending	Burden of the debt
Transfers	Intergenerational accounting
Debt-income ratio	

PROBLEMS

1. What effect does a federal government surplus have on the stock of money and the stock of debt? Explain in detail the mechanics of how the stocks of money and bonds are affected.

2. Suppose the Treasury issues $1 billion in Treasury bills that are bought by the public. Then the Fed carries out an open market purchase of $300 million. Effectively, how has the debt been financed?

3. Under what circumstances are fiscal and monetary policy related rather than existing as two completely independent instruments in the hands of the government?

4. Trace the path the economy follows when there is a permanent increase in government spending that is financed by borrowing from the public. Assume the economy is growing.

5. Analyze the difference in the impact on the interest rate, investment, and the price level of a temporary change in government spending financed by borrowing rather than taxes. State explicitly the assumptions you are making about Ricardian equivalence.

6. Suppose the real interest rate is 3 percent, output growth is 7 percent, the debt-income ratio is 50 percent, and the primary budget shows a deficit of 5 percent of GDP. Is the debt-income ratio rising or falling?

7. Explain in words why a high growth rate of output will tend, other things being equal, to reduce the debt-income ratio. How does your answer help explain Figure 19-5?

8. A government increases spending by building a dam. The spending is financed by issuing debt. Does the debt issue create a debt burden? Would your answer be different if the government had bought a fleet of automobiles for the Pentagon?

9. The Kemp-Roth tax cuts of the early 1980s cut government receipts from an average of 19.7 percent of GDP in 1980–1982 to only 18.6 percent in 1985. Are these tax cuts the main explanation for the budget deficit problem of the 1980s?

10. "The unsustainable deficits of the 1980s and early 1990s urgently call for a new approach to fiscal policy. Budgets need to be balanced year by year so that today's taxpayers pay the full cost of what they want the government to do for them." Comment on this statement.

11. "The United States faces a fiscal crisis because mounting deficits are driving the debt-income ratio far beyond the range that this country has experienced. From these high debt levels there is no return except by 12 years of high taxes to pay off the debt." Comment on this statement.

12. German unification involved massive expenditures for infrastructure in the East and transfer payments. Should such expenditures be financed by (a) money creation because of their transitory, exceptional nature, (b) debt, or (c) taxes?

COMPUTER EXERCISES

1. Experiment with the effect of different assumptions. What happens to the deficit if
   (a) Tax rates are raised 1 percent?
   (b) The interest rate is 1 percent higher than in the base?
   (c) The economy grows more rapidly by 1 percent per year?
   (d) The government spending growth rate is 1 percent higher than in the base?

2. Try some inflation scenarios, recognizing that as inflation rises, interest rates also rise, and so does government spending. What is the effect of inflation on the burden of the debt?

3. Find the tax rate that will balance the budget by 1996. When is the debt eradicated?

4. What kind of growth is needed to eliminate the deficit over five years? Remember that higher growth may be achieved by lowering interest rates by easing monetary policy. But also remember that easy money implies more rapid inflation. What mix do you recommend?

APPENDIX: THE POTENTIAL INSTABILITY OF DEBT FINANCING

In this appendix we develop a framework to assess debt dynamics and potential instability. Instability arises if the debt-income ratio rises year after year without limits.

The derivation uses definitions, addition, and subtraction, and it avoids calculus. The purpose is to see where Table 19-5 comes from and to understand the discussion of explosive debt situations and unsustainable deficits.

B = nominal stock of debt outstanding

i = nominal interest rate

$$r \equiv i - \pi = \text{real interest rate}$$

$$P = \text{price level}$$

$$Y = \text{level of real output}$$

$$z = \text{noninterest, or primary, budget surplus (as a share of GDP)}$$

$$b = \text{debt-income ratio}$$

$$y = \text{growth rate of output}$$

The debt-income ratio is defined as the ratio of debt outstanding to nominal GDP:

$$\text{Debt-income ratio} = b = \frac{B}{PY} \tag{A1}$$

Over time the debt-income ratio changes by Δb. From equation (A1) the change over time can be calculated (we assert rather than derive here the well-known "fraction rule" of calculus) as

$$\Delta b = \frac{\Delta B}{PY} - b\left(\frac{\Delta P}{P} + \frac{\Delta Y}{Y}\right) = \frac{\Delta B}{PY} - b(\pi + y) \tag{A2}$$

We simplify by substituting an expression for the increase in the nominal debt outstanding. The increase in debt from one year to the next is the result of the budget deficit and therefore is equal to interest payments, which are equal to the debt outstanding times the interest rate, iB, less the noninterest budget surplus, z, which we can write as the primary budget share times nominal GDP, zPY:

$$\Delta B \equiv iB - zPY \tag{A3}$$

The final step is to substitute equation (A3) into (A2) to obtain

$$\Delta b = ib - z - b(\pi + y)$$

In this form the increase in the debt ratio has three components: nominal interest payments less the contribution to debt stabilization from noninterest budget surpluses less the contribution from growing nominal income. The former two tell us about the growth of the numerator in equation (A1) and the latter about the growth of the denominator.

A more useful form of this equation is obtained by collecting terms and writing

$$\Delta b = b(r - y) - z$$

where we have used the definition of the real interest rate, $r \equiv i - \pi$. In this form, which is commonly used, we see that the debt ratio rises whenever the real interest rate exceeds the growth rate, or $r > y$, *and* the primary budget is balanced or in deficit. But there are other combinations that could maintain a stable or falling debt ratio, for example, a negative real interest rate (as in the 1970s) combined with noninterest deficits.

Deficits are called unsustainable if on the current path of expected future fiscal policy the debt ratio rises without bounds. "Unsustainable" simply means that at some point fiscal policy must change to avoid a snowballing of the debt ratio. Note, too, that the higher the debt ratio, b, the more important becomes the real interest component. If real interest rates exceed the growth rate, as in the 1980s though not before, debt problems can become worse by themselves, even if the primary surplus is positive.

DATA APPENDIX

All data refer to the federal government and are expressed as fractions of GDP. The full-employment deficit is the series developed by DRI/McGraw-Hill Inc.; *F*1 measures the discretionary *change* in fiscal policy.

year	budget deficit total	deficit excluding social security	net interest	debt	full-employment budget deficit	*F*1
1960	− 0.7	− 0.4	1.3	56.1	− 1.1	0.0
1961	0.5	0.3	1.2	54.8	− 0.3	0.6
1962	0.6	0.7	1.2	52.4	0.4	0.9
1963	− 0.2	0.2	1.2	50.9	− 0.3	− 0.2
1964	0.4	0.8	1.2	48.5	0.8	0.8
1965	− 0.2	0.1	1.2	45.4	0.6	0.4
1966	0.2	1.2	1.2	42.1	1.3	1.5
1967	1.6	2.3	1.2	41.1	2.3	1.2
1968	0.5	1.1	1.3	40.7	1.5	0.3
1969	− 0.9	− 0.1	1.3	39.1	0.0	− 0.7
1970	1.3	1.7	1.4	38.6	1.2	− 0.2
1971	2.0	2.0	1.3	38.1	1.7	− 0.3
1972	1.4	1.6	1.2	36.9	1.5	0.7
1973	0.5	1.2	1.3	35.1	1.0	− 0.5
1974	0.8	1.2	1.4	33.7	0.2	− 0.1
1975	4.4	3.5	1.4	34.9	2.5	0.6
1976	3.0	2.3	1.5	36.1	2.2	0.1
1977	2.1	1.6	1.5	35.5	1.9	0.1
1978	1.3	1.2	1.6	34.5	1.6	0.2
1979	0.6	0.8	1.7	33.2	0.7	0.1
1980	2.2	1.7	1.9	33.3	1.3	0.1
1981	1.9	1.6	2.4	32.9	0.8	− 0.5
1982	4.3	3.3	2.7	35.7	2.0	0.9
1983	5.3	4.3	2.7	39.4	3.4	0.9
1984	4.4	4.5	3.0	41.2	3.7	0.4
1985	4.5	4.8	3.1	45.0	3.9	0.4
1986	4.7	5.1	3.1	49.2	4.1	− 0.0
1987	3.3	3.9	3.0	51.5	2.9	0.2
1988	2.8	3.9	3.0	52.9	2.7	− 0.1
1989	2.3	3.5	3.1	54.5	2.2	− 0.4
1990	3.0	4.2	3.2	58.5	2.6	− 0.2
1991	3.7	4.6	3.3	64.1	2.5	− 0.3
1992	4.9	5.8	3.1	69.2	3.6	− 0.4

SOURCE: DRI/McGraw-Hill Inc., Federal Reserve Board, and Congressional Budget Office.

INTERNATIONAL ADJUSTMENT AND INTERDEPENDENCE

*I*nternational economic issues are playing an increasingly prominent part on the macroeconomic stage. Countries are interdependent: booms or recessions in one country spill over to other countries through trade flows; and changes in interest rates in any major country cause immediate exchange or interest rate movements in other countries.

In 1991–1993, for example, German interest rates were at the center of European and international controversy. As a result of massive government spending to finance German unification, the German economy began to boom, and inflation rose. The German central bank, the Bundesbank, fought the inflation by sharply raising interest rates. Countries such as Britain and France either had to match the German interest rate increase—even though their economies were not booming—or they had to accept a depreciation of their currencies. The British and Italians wanted to do neither, and as a result there was a major European currency crisis in September 1992.

We introduced the basic facts and models of international linkages in Chapter 6. Now we explore the issues of international interdependence further. In the first three sections we discuss aspects of the mechanisms through which a country with a fixed exchange rate adjusts to balance of payments problems. This discussion helps clarify current international economic issues even though exchange rates among the dollar, yen, and other major currencies have been flexible since 1973; the fixed exchange rate mechanisms remain relevant both because some smaller countries still operate with fixed exchange rates and also because exchange rates are fixed among European countries in the European Monetary System (EMS). In addition, an understanding of the adjustment mechanisms that operate under fixed exchange rates helps in grasping the operation of flexible exchange rates.

In the rest of the chapter we take up aspects of the behavior of the current flexible exchange rate system.

20-1 ADJUSTMENT UNDER FIXED EXCHANGE RATES

Adjustment to a balance of payments problem can be achieved in two ways. One is to change economic policy; the second is through *automatic* adjustment mechanisms. The automatic mechanisms are two: payments imbalances affect the money supply and hence spending; and unemployment affects wages and prices and thereby competitiveness. Policy measures by contrast include monetary and fiscal policy, and also changes in tariffs or the exchange rate.

The Role of Prices in the Open Economy

We start the analysis by bringing prices explicitly into our analysis of the open economy. In Chapter 6 we assumed that the price level was constant. With fixed prices and a given exchange rate the *real* exchange rate is also fixed. Recall the definition of the real exchange rate:

$$R = \frac{eP_f}{P} \tag{1}$$

Here e is the nominal exchange rate, P_f the foreign price level, and P the domestic price level. We now abandon the assumption of a fixed domestic price level, but for the time being we take the exchange rate and foreign prices as given.

How does the openness of the economy affect the aggregate demand curve of Chapter 7 and later chapters? In the closed economy version of the model, a higher price level implies lower real balances, higher interest rates, and lower spending. In an open economy with a fixed exchange rate, an increase in the price level reduces demand for an additional reason: an increase in our prices makes our goods less competitive with (more expensive relative to) foreign-produced goods. Given the exchange rate, when the prices of goods produced at home rise, our goods become more expensive for foreigners to buy, and their goods become *relatively* cheaper for us to buy. An increase in our price level thus shifts demand away from our goods toward imports, as well as reducing exports.

In Figure 20-1 we show the downward-sloping demand schedule for our goods, AD. Demand is equal to aggregate spending by domestic residents, plus net exports, or $AD \equiv A + NX$, and now there are two reasons for the aggregate demand curve to slope down.

The demand for domestic goods, AD, is drawn for a given level of foreign prices, a given nominal money supply, given fiscal policy, and an exchange rate that is fixed. An increase in the nominal money stock shifts the schedule upward, as does expansionary fiscal policy. We show, too, the short-run aggregate supply schedule, AS, and the full-employment level of output, Y^*. Initial equilibrium is at point E, at which we have unemployment.

Next we look at the trade balance equilibrium schedule, $NX = 0$. An increase in our income raises imports and worsens the trade balance. To restore trade balance equilibrium, domestic prices would have to be lower. This would make the home country more competitive, raise exports, and reduce imports. Thus, we show the trade

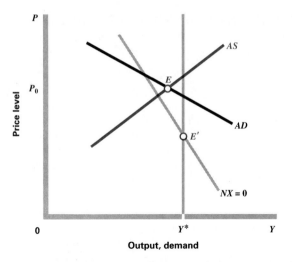

FIGURE 20-1
OPEN ECONOMY EQUILIBRIUM WITH PRICE ADJUSTMENT. *AD* is the
aggregate demand schedule. It is downward-sloping because a
reduction in our prices raises the real money stock, lowering interest
rates, and because lower prices for our goods increase our
international competitiveness. The trade balance equilibrium
schedule (*NX* = 0) is also downward-sloping, reflecting the
increased competitiveness that we derive from a lower relative price
of our goods. Macroeconomic equilibrium obtains at *E*, at which
aggregate demand equals aggregate supply. This need not be a
point of full employment and external balance, which obtain at *E'*.

balance equilibrium schedule as downward-sloping.[1] We assume that it is steeper than
the demand schedule for domestic goods. The schedule is drawn for a given level of
prices abroad.

Financing and Adjustment

At point *E* the home country has a trade deficit. Our prices are too high or our income
is too high to have exports balance imports. To achieve trade balance equilibrium, we
would have to become more competitive, thus exporting more and importing less.
Alternatively, we could reduce our level of income in order to reduce import spending.

---

[1]We assume that a decline in domestic prices improves the trade balance. This requires that exports and
imports be sufficiently responsive to prices. There is a possibility that a reduction in our price level (which
reduces the prices of our exports) lowers our revenue from exports—because the increased sales are not
sufficient to compensate for the lower prices. We assume that this possibility (see also footnote 6, Chap.
6) does not occur. We assume, too, that import spending does not depend on the interest rate.

What does a country with a current account deficit, like that at E, do? In a fixed exchange rate system, it is possible for the central bank to use its reserves to finance temporary imbalances of payments—that is, to meet the excess demand for foreign currency at the existing exchange rate arising from balance of payments deficits. Alternatively, a country experiencing balance of payments difficulties can borrow foreign currencies abroad.

A current account deficit cannot be financed by borrowing from abroad without raising the question of how the borrowing will be repaid. If the foreign lenders are convinced the country can repay—for instance, because the cause of the current account deficit is temporary, or because they believe the borrowings will be used to increase the country's ability to export—the loans will be available. However, problems may well arise in repaying the foreign debt if borrowing is used to finance consumption spending.

But maintaining and financing current account deficits indefinitely or for very long periods of time is impossible. The economy has to find some way of *adjusting* the deficit, that is, of getting rid of or at least reducing it. Again, that can happen automatically or through policy. We examine first the important automatic adjustment mechanisms.

Automatic Adjustment

First we look at the aggregate demand side. When a country runs a balance of payments deficit, the demand for foreign exchange is by definition larger than the amount being supplied by the private markets, and the central bank has to sell the difference. When it sells foreign exchange, it reduces domestic high-powered money and therefore the money stock—unless it *sterilizes* its foreign exchange intervention by buying bonds as it sells foreign exchange. Ruling that possibility out, the deficit at point E implies that the central bank is pegging the exchange rate, selling foreign exchange to keep the exchange rate from depreciating, and reducing the domestic money stock. It follows immediately that over time the aggregate demand schedule (which is drawn for a given money supply) will be shifting downward and to the left.

Turning now to the aggregate supply side: point E in Figure 20-1 is also a point of unemployment. Unemployment leads to declines in wages and costs, which are reflected in a downward-shifting aggregate supply schedule. Over time, therefore, the short-run equilibrium point, E, moves downward as both demand and supply schedules shift (not shown). The points of short-run equilibrium move in the direction of point E', and the process will continue until that point is reached. (The approach may be cyclical, but that is not of major interest here.)

Once point E' is reached, the country has automatically achieved long-run equilibrium. Because the trade balance is in equilibrium, there is no pressure on the exchange rate, therefore no need for exchange market intervention, and therefore no further changes in the money supply. On the supply side, wages and costs are constant, so that the supply schedule is not shifting. Thus at E' the country has successfully and automatically adjusted to the initial balance of payments deficit: it has achieved trade balance equilibrium combined with full employment.

This is the *classical adjustment process*. It relies on price adjustments and an adjustment in the money supply based on the trade balance. The adjustment process "works," *but* it may take a very long time and require a very long recession.[2] The alternative to waiting for the automatic adjustment mechanisms to do the whole job is to make explicit policy changes to move the economy more rapidly toward balance.

Policies to Restore Balance: Expenditure Switching/Reducing

Because of their side effects, policies to restore external balance must generally be combined with policies to achieve full employment: policies to create employment will typically worsen the external balance, and policies to create a trade surplus will affect employment. In general it is necessary to combine *expenditure switching policies*, which shift demand between domestic and imported goods, and *expenditure reducing* (or *expenditure increasing*) *policies* in order to cope with the two targets of internal and external balance. This point is of general importance and continues to apply when we take account of capital flows and other phenomena omitted in this section.

One method of adjusting a current account deficit is by imposing tariffs—taxes on imports. However, tariffs cannot be used freely to adjust the balance of trade, partly because international organizations and agreements such as GATT (General Agreement on Tariffs and Trade) and the IMF (International Monetary Fund) outlaw, or at least frown on, the use of tariffs. Tariffs have fallen in the post–World War II period as the industrialized world has moved to desirably freer trade between countries.

Another way of adjusting a current account deficit is to use policies to reduce aggregate demand. These are expenditure reducing policies. In this regard, it is important to note that a trade deficit reflects an excess of expenditure over income. The identities at the end of Chapter 2 imply that

$$NX \equiv Y - (C + I + G) \tag{2}$$

where *NX* is the trade surplus and *I* is actual investment. Thus, a balance of trade deficit can be reduced by reducing spending $(C + I + G)$ relative to income (Y), through restrictive monetary and/or fiscal policy.

The link between the external deficit and budget deficits is shown in equation $(2a)$:[3]

$$NX \equiv S - I + T - G \tag{2a}$$

where *S* denotes *private* saving and $T - G$ is the budget surplus. Equation $(2a)$ shows an immediate relation between the budget and the external balance. If saving and investment were constant, then changes in the budget would translate, one for one, into changes in the external balance; budget cutting would bring about equal changes

---

[2] Olivier Blanchard and Pierre-Alain Muet, "Competitiveness through Disinflation: An Assessment of French Macro Policy," *Economic Policy*, 16, April 1993, show that it took France almost a decade to achieve such an adjustment starting in 1983.

[3] To derive equation $(2a)$, we combine (2) with the accounting identity $YD = C + S$ and the definition $YD = Y - TA + TR$. For convenience, we assume $TR = 0$ in this discussion.

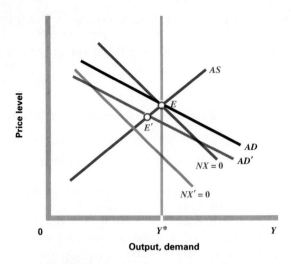

FIGURE 20-2
A LOSS OF EXPORT REVENUE. The economy starts out in full
equilibrium at point E. An export loss shifts the NX = 0 and AD
schedules to the left. The new short-run equilibrium is at point E'
with unemployment and a deficit.

in the external deficit. But budget cutting will affect saving and investment, and
we therefore need a more complete model to explain how budget cuts affect the
external balance.

DEVALUATION

The unemployment that typically accompanies automatic adjustment and the desirability
of free trade, which argues against the use of tariffs, both suggest the need for an
alternative policy for restoring internal and external balance. The major policy instrument for dealing with payments deficits is *devaluation*, which usually has to be combined
with restrictive monetary and/or fiscal policy. A devaluation is an increase in the
domestic currency price of foreign exchange. Given the nominal prices in two countries,
devaluation increases the relative price of imported goods in the devaluing country
and reduces the relative price of exports from the devaluing country. Devaluation is
primarily an expenditure switching policy.

How does a devaluation work? Consider first the special case of a country that
has been in full employment with balance of trade equilibrium and is at point *E*
in Figure 20-2. Now let there be an exogenous decline in export earnings, so that the
$NX = 0$ schedule shifts to the left to $NX' = 0$. With a lower demand for exports, and
with a fixed exchange rate, output would decline. The *AD* schedule moves to the left
as a result of the fall in exports. The lower level of income reduces imports, but not

enough to make up for the loss of export revenue. The net effects are therefore unemployment and a trade deficit.

The automatic adjustment mechanism would work, but slowly, to restore equilibrium. Alternatively, the country can devalue its currency. This has the obvious advantage that it does not require a protracted recession to reduce domestic costs. The adjustment is done by the stroke of a pen—a devaluation of the currency. Why would a devaluation achieve the adjustment? *Given* prices of foreign goods in terms of foreign currency (for example, the mark prices of German goods), a devaluation raises the relative price of foreign goods. Imports fall, and exports rise.

The case we have just considered is special, however, in one important respect. The economy was initially in balance of trade equilibrium at full employment. The disturbance to the economy took place in the trade account. Accordingly, if we could move the $NX' = 0$ locus back to the full-employment level of income—as we could with a devaluation—both internal and external balance would be attained. Put differently, the reason there was unemployment in Figure 20-2 was the reduction in exports and consequent external balance problem. Both problems could thus be solved through devaluation.

In general, though, a country cannot secure both external and internal balance following a disturbance by using just one instrument of policy. A general rule of policy making is that we need to use as many policy instruments as we have policy targets.

Finally, a comment on the role of the exchange rate in a fixed rate system: in a fixed rate system, the exchange rate is an *instrument of policy*. The central bank can change the exchange rate for policy purposes, devaluing when the current account looks as though it will be in for a prolonged deficit. In a system of clean floating, by contrast, the exchange rate moves freely to equilibrate the balance of payments. In a system of dirty floating, the central bank attempts to manipulate the exchange rate while not committing itself to any given rate. The dirty floating system is thus intermediate between a fixed rate system and a clean floating system.

Exchange Rates and Prices

A devaluation that takes place when domestic and foreign prices are constant will succeed in reducing the relative price of a country's goods, and will thus improve the trade balance. However, the price level typically changes along with the exchange rate. The essential issue when a country devalues is whether it can achieve a *real devaluation*. A country achieves a real devaluation when a devaluation reduces the price of the country's own goods relative to the price of foreign goods.

Recalling the definition of the real exchange rate, eP_f/P, and taking the foreign price level, P_f, as given, a real devaluation occurs when e/P rises, or *when the exchange rate increases by more than the price level*.

We use Figure 20-3, and the example of Mexico, to illustrate the problem of securing a real devaluation. Let P_{US} be the price level in the United States, P the Mexican price level, and e Mexico's exchange rate, that is, the number of pesos per dollar. Mexico's competitiveness then is measured by U.S. prices relative to Mexican prices, both measured in dollars: $P_{US}/(P/e)$ ($= eP_{US}/P$). We assume that the U.S. price level is given and show P/e, the Mexican price level measured in dollars, on the verti-

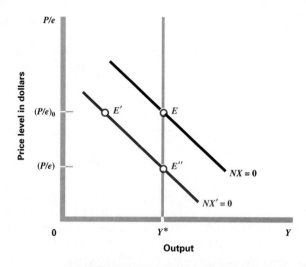

FIGURE 20-3

COMPETITIVENESS AND ADJUSTMENT. When a country faces an
adverse external shock, this can be shown as a leftward shift of the
NX schedule. On the vertical axis we show the price of the country's
output measured in dollars (*P/e*). To achieve internal and external
balance the economy must move to point *E''*. The price in dollars
must decline to achieve an increase in competitiveness. Because it
is often difficult to achieve such a gain in competitiveness, countries
with external constraints will tend to be at a point like *E'*, at which
there is unemployment.

cal axis in Figure 20-3. For a given U.S. price level, a rise in Mexican dollar prices
(*P/e*) worsens Mexico's net exports. Accordingly, points to the right of *NX* = 0
correspond to deficits.

Consider now the problem of adjustment to external shocks. Suppose that an oil
price fall in world markets reduces Mexico's export earnings at each price level and
thus creates a deficit. Initially we were at *E*, with internal and external balance, and
now external balance prevails only along *NX'* = 0.

In the short run a country might absorb an external shock by staying at point *E*,
borrowing abroad to finance the external deficit. But that is not possible forever; the
country has somehow to return to point *E''*. It could do it slowly, through the automatic
mechanisms. Or it can devalue the currency and move directly to point *E''*.

But the devaluation can be frustrated if it is offset by an increase in domestic
prices. What matters is that a country with an external deficit (say Mexico) succeeds
in reducing its prices in dollars, *P/e*. If devaluation leads to a rise in domestic prices,
then there is no gain in competitiveness.

Figure 20-4 shows the U.S. price level and Mexican prices in dollars. Note that
exchange rate devaluations in 1982 and in 1985–1986 sharply reduced the dollar prices
of Mexican goods. But the gains in competitiveness did not last. Inflation in Mexico

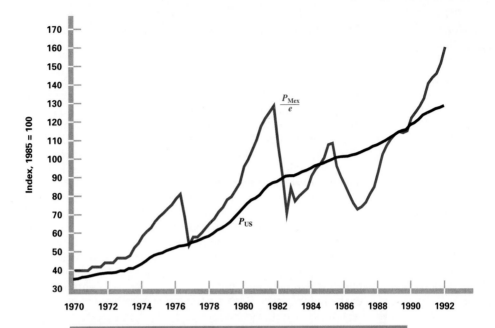

FIGURE 20-4
DOLLAR PRICE LEVELS: THE UNITED STATES AND MEXICO, 1970–1992
(INDEX, 1985 = 100). The U.S. price level is shown as the gradually
rising line P_{US}. The Mexican price level in *dollars* is represented by
the erratic schedule; devaluation by Mexico reduces prices in
dollars, but inflation without offsetting depreciation raises prices in
dollars. By 1992 the Mexican level of competitiveness had
deteriorated strongly because the peso was not deteriorating rapidly
enough to offset the inflation differential.

soon raised prices relative to the exchange rate; by 1992 the *real* exchange rate was
less than it had been in 1987. Failure to keep exchange rates in line with prices—that
is, failure to maintain competitiveness—ultimately results in devaluation crises.[4] In
Box 20-1 we discuss Mexican adjustment.

CRAWLING PEG EXCHANGE RATES

When a country experiences inflation above the rate of its trading partners, holding
the exchange rate fixed would imply a steady loss in competitiveness. In order to avoid

---

[4]See Paul Krugman, *Currencies and Crises* (Cambridge, Mass.: MIT Press, 1992), and Pierre-Richard
Agenor, Jagdeep Bhandari, and Robert Flood, "Speculative Attacks and Models of Balance of Payments
Crises," *IMF Staff Papers*, June 1992. The problem of postponed adjustment is not peculiar to developing
countries, as the European currency crisis of 1992 in countries including Italy, Finland, and the United
Kingdom demonstrates.

box 20-1

MEXICO'S EXTERNAL BALANCE

In the 1980s Mexico went through a deep crisis. The country had borrowed too much in world markets and under the pressure of high world interest rates in the early 1980s found it impossible to service its external debt. Borrowing abroad became impossible from one day to the next. Mexico had to rebuild its economy, starting by depreciating its currency, reducing import tariffs and quotas, privatizing state-owned firms, and reducing government regulation of the economy. By the end of the 1980s these reforms bore fruit; the Mexican economy was growing again.*

With the return of growth and especially with a domestic investment boom, the current account worsened sharply. There was no trouble financing the current account deficit, because foreign firms and investors were investing heavily in Mexico. The question that arose was whether the Mexican government should allow the deficit to continue and even grow, or rather cut the deficit by devaluation and a reduction in domestic spending. Table 1 shows how large the Mexican capital account surplus was. Much of the surplus went to the Mexican private sector. But capital inflows far exceeded the borrowings of Mexican private residents. A large part of the inflow was bought by the Mexican central bank to add to its foreign exchange reserves. Such a situation is possible when, as in the Mexican case, the rest of the world decides that a country has outstanding profit opportunities, and as a result other countries invest in that country's stock market or in high-yield government bonds. Mexico in 1990–1992 offered that attraction and thus had no trouble attracting large capital flows.

The problem, of course, is that when borrowing in world markets is too easy, a country may overborrow—as Mexico certainly did in the 1970s. In the face of a current account deficit of almost $20 billion in 1992 that question emerged once again. Was it not a more prudent policy choice to say no to foreign investors,

---

*On the Mexican experience in the 1980s, see Pedro Aspe, *Economic Transformation: The Mexican Way* (Cambridge, Mass.: MIT Press, 1993). An annual account is given in *The Mexican Economy*, published by Mexico's central bank, Banco de Mexico.

---

the widening deficits, many countries follow a *crawling peg* exchange rate policy. Under a crawling peg exchange rate policy, the exchange rate is depreciated at a rate roughly equal to the inflation differential between the country and its trading partners. The idea of a crawling peg is to maintain the *real* exchange rate, $R = P_f/(P/e)$, constant by raising e at the same rate as (P/P_f) is rising.

It is clear from Figure 20-4 that for lengthy periods, for example, in 1989–1992, Mexico failed to offset the impact of its inflation on competitiveness. The exchange rate was not depreciated fast enough to maintain the real exchange rate. As a result competitiveness fell and foreign exchange problems remained.

Countries are often and easily tempted to use the exchange rate to slow inflation. When the exchange rate is held constant, the prices of imports stay constant (assuming foreign prices are not rising), and therefore the prices of some of the goods that enter the consumer price index are not increasing. This slows inflation. But the reduction in inflation is bought by steadily reducing competitiveness. Often such a strategy ultimately

TABLE 1

MEXICO'S EXTERNAL BALANCE (billions of U.S. dollars)

	1989	1990	1991
Current account	−6,050	−7.114	−13,283
Trade balance	−404	−882	−6,930
Capital account	6.050	7,114	13,283
Private*	5,564	3,881	5,777
Increase in reserves	396	3,233	7,506

*Including errors and omissions.

reduce demand by a tightening of fiscal policy, and perhaps even devalue the peso to make Mexican goods more competitive in world trade and imports more expensive in Mexico?

Countries rarely adjust early because tightening policy before it becomes inevitable is politically difficult. That is what happened in 1982. A crisis emerged when foreign lenders and investors lost confidence in Mexico and were no longer willing to buy Mexican assets and when the Mexican private sector sent its capital abroad. A huge financing gap emerged. For a while the central bank met the financing gap by running down its reserves. Ultimately the process ended in a major devaluation and a deep recession. Many observers in 1992 were conscious of just how destructive it would be to go through the same cycle once more.

The argument against devaluation was that it would be disruptive to confidence in capital markets and to the attempt to reduce inflation. Moreover, it was argued, the deficit in the current account primarily reflected a high level of Mexican investment, which would generate the revenues with which to pay off the borrowing. According to this scheme, in a few years the current account deficit would decline, and in the meantime it could be financed without grave risk. A good story, but for how long? ■

brings about a foreign exchange crisis. In the end, inflation has to be stopped by monetary and fiscal policy; exchange rate policy is at best a supplementary tool—at times a very valuable one,[5] but it cannot do most of the work in disinflation.

20-2 EXCHANGE RATE CHANGES AND TRADE ADJUSTMENT: EMPIRICAL ISSUES

In this section we take up two important empirical issues related to the possibility of adjusting current account imbalances by changes in the exchange rate. The first is whether nominal devaluations do usually succeed in achieving real devaluations or whether, as Figure 20-4 suggests, that may be unusual.

---

[5] For example, as discussed in Chap. 18, when it is necessary to stop an extreme inflation.

The second issue is whether changes in relative prices, if they occur, do improve the current account. We have explicitly assumed here that a decline in a relative price of our goods improves the current account. But a perverse reaction is possible. When import prices rise, import demand may not decline sufficiently to compensate for the higher prices of imports, and thus total import spending (price times quantity) may actually increase. We turn our attention now to these two issues.

Exchange Rates and Relative Price Adjustment

In studying the flexible wage-price model, we assumed that wages and prices adjust to achieve full employment. But in practice prices are based on labor cost or wages. Now suppose that wages are inflexible in real terms, because labor wants to maintain the purchasing power of wages. This may be reflected in the formal indexation of wages to the consumer price index, or it may be the outcome of the bargaining between firms and workers. In such a world, changes in the cost of living triggered by a devaluation would lead to changes in money wages, which would feed back into prices, which could offset the effects of the nominal devaluation.

A process in which changes in prices feed back into wages and from there into prices is one of a *wage-price spiral* that may produce considerable volatility in the price level. Small disturbances can set off quite large changes in the price level. Suppose, first, that the real wage is fixed in terms of the consumer price index, which includes both domestic goods and imports, so that changes in the consumer price index are fully passed on into wages. Assume, second, that changes in wages are fully passed on into increased domestic prices.

Now suppose that the country has to devalue, to try to restore the trade balance. The devaluation raises import prices and thereby raises consumer prices. To maintain the real wage, workers demand higher money wages, which firms grant and pass on by raising prices. Where are we after the process ends? Real wages are constant, which means wages and the price level (a weighted average of the prices of domestic and imported goods) have risen in the same proportion; wage increases have been fully passed on, which means that real wages *in terms of domestic output* are also unchanged. The two results imply that relative prices are unchanged, *and that the nominal devaluation has had no effect on the real exchange rate*.

Of course, this is not the whole story, because we have to ask how the higher price level affects aggregate demand. If the government does not increase the money stock, then the higher prices reduce real balances and aggregate demand; with income down, the current account improves. The spiral will take place only if, when wages rise, the government raises the money stock so as not to create unemployment. Hence in this context, of a devaluation, it is crucial that the Fed not accommodate nominal price increases if it wants to achieve a real devaluation.

A second context in which the idea of *sticky real wages* (wages that are difficult to change) is important is that of real disturbances. Suppose our export demand declines permanently because of, say, the introduction of superior technology abroad. To return to full employment, the relative price of our goods must fall in order to encourage foreign demand. But how can the relative price fall? If we devalue, and workers succeed in restoring their real wages and prices are marked up on wages, there will be no change in the relative price of our goods. Then the only way to reduce the real wage would be protracted unemployment.

The empirical question, then, is, How flexible are real wages? That is, to an important extent, a question of institutional arrangements. In small, open economies with substantial cost-of-living indexation in wage agreements, it may indeed be very difficult to change real wages and relative prices through exchange rate changes. In general, countries that devalue have to use restrictive aggregate demand policies to make sure that induced increases in prices do not simply undo the real effects of the nominal devaluation.

Relative Prices and the Trade Balance: The J Curve

We come now to the second issue, the effect of changes in relative prices on the trade balance and the possibility that a depreciation *worsens* the trade balance. To make this point clear, we write out the trade balance, measured in terms of domestic goods, as

$$NX = X - \frac{eP_f}{P}Q \tag{3}$$

where X denotes the foreign demand for our goods or exports and Q denotes our own import quantity. The term $(eP_f/P)Q$ thus measures the *value* of our imports in terms of domestic goods.

Suppose that we now have an exchange depreciation and that in the first instance, domestic and foreign prices, P and P_f, are unchanged. Then the relative price of imports, eP_f/P, rises. This leads to two effects. First, if the physical *volume* of imports does not change, their *value* measured in domestic currency unambiguously increases because of the higher price. This means higher import spending (measured in terms of the domestic currency) and thus a worsening of the trade balance. This is the source of the potentially perverse response of the trade balance to exchange depreciation.

However, there are two *volume* responses that run in the opposite direction: exports should rise because our goods are now cheaper for foreigners to buy, and the volume of imports should decline because imports are more expensive.

The question, then, is whether the volume effects on imports and exports are sufficiently strong to outweigh the price effect, that is, whether depreciation raises or lowers net exports. The empirical evidence on this question is quite strong and shows the following result:[6] *The short-term volume effects, say, within a year, are quite small and thus do not outweigh the price effect. The long-term volume effects, by contrast, are quite substantial, and certainly enough to make the trade balance respond in the normal fashion to a relative price change.*

Why does this pattern of responses take place? First, the low short-term and high long-term volume effects result from the time consumers and producers take to adjust

---

[6] See Ellen Meade, "Exchange Rate Adjustment and the J Curve," *Federal Reserve Bulletin*, October 1988; and Paul Krugman; "The J-Curve, the Fire Sale and the Hard Landing," *American Economic Review*, May 1989.

to changes in relative prices. Some of these adjustments may be instantaneous, but it is clear that tourism patterns, for example, may take 6 months to a year to adjust and that relocation of production internationally in response to changes in relative costs and prices may take years. A case in point is increased foreign direct investment in the United States—say Toyota moving from Japan to California. In the long term, such direct investment leads to reduced imports by the United States, and thus to an improved trade balance, but such an adjustment takes years, not weeks or months.

The lag in the adjustment of trade flows to changes in relative prices is thus quite plausible. What do these lags imply about the impact of relative price changes on the trade balance? Suppose that at a particular time, starting with a deficit, we have a depreciation that raises the relative price of imports. The short-term effects result primarily from increased import prices with very few offsetting volume effects. Therefore, the trade balance initially worsens. Over time, as trade volume adjusts to the changed relative prices, exports rise and import volume progressively declines. The volume effects come to dominate, and in the long run, the trade balance shows an improvement. This pattern of adjustment is referred to as the *J-curve effect*, because diagrammatically the response of the trade balance looks like a J.

The J-curve effect can be seen in the behavior of the U.S. current account after 1985. Despite a rapid depreciation of the dollar starting in February 1985, the current account continued to worsen for the next year. But the current account began to improve in 1987 and continued improving in 1988.

The medium-term problem of sticky real wages and the J-curve effect provides important clues for the interpretation of macroeconomic experiences across countries, particularly in showing why depreciations typically do not lead to improvements in the current account in the short term.

HYSTERESIS EFFECTS OF OVERVALUATION

A further complication has been suggested in the aftermath of the large and persistent overvaluation of the dollar in 1980–1985, namely, *hysteresis effects*. Such effects are present, in the case of the exchange rate, when a change in the exchange rate that is later exactly reversed nonetheless leaves a long-term impact on the trade account. In the early 1980s, the U.S. dollar was very strong. This put U.S. firms at a sharp disadvantage in world trade and in the U.S. market. The dollar prices of imports declined, and in foreign markets, U.S. firms lost out because their relative prices increased.

These are the normal effects of a currency appreciation. The hysteresis argument is that when exchange rate changes are very large and long lasting, then they will lead to a relatively permanent change in trade patterns.[7] Once foreign firms have become established in the United States, and consumers have become accustomed to their goods, even a reversal of the exchange rate to the initial level will not be enough to enable U.S. firms to recapture their share of the market. Similarly, when U.S. firms have lost foreign market share and even left some foreign markets entirely, going back to the initial exchange rate will not be enough to bring U.S. firms back. To return to

---

[7]See Richard Baldwin and Paul Krugman, "Persistent Trade Effects of Large Exchange Rate Shocks," *Quarterly Journal of Economics*, November 1989.

the initial trade pattern, exchange rates would have to overshoot in the opposite direction, making it profitable to incur the costs of starting up export operations and competing with foreign firms that supply imports.

The evidence on these hysteresis effects remains tentative, but the idea is certainly plausible. The continued higher share of imports into the U.S. market and the failure of the U.S. external balance to correct itself fully, even after the 1985–1988 depreciation brought the real exchange rate back close to its 1980 level, support the idea that the damage of overvaluation may be a lasting one.

20-3   THE MONETARY APPROACH TO THE BALANCE OF PAYMENTS

It is frequently suggested that external balance problems are monetary in nature, and that balance of payments deficits, in particular, are a reflection of an excessive money supply.

There is a simple first answer to this claim. It is obviously true that for any given balance of payments deficit, a sufficient contraction of the money stock will restore external balance. The reason is that a monetary contraction, by raising interest rates and reducing spending, reduces income and therefore imports. It is equally true that this result could be achieved by tight fiscal policy, and so there is nothing especially monetary about this interpretation of remedies for external imbalance.

A more sophisticated interpretation of the problem recognizes the links among the balance of payments deficit, foreign exchange market intervention, and the money supply in a fixed exchange rate system. The automatic mechanism is for a sale of foreign exchange—as arises in the case of a balance of payments deficit—to reduce the stock of high-powered money, and hence the money stock. In a surplus country the central bank increases the outstanding stock of high-powered money when it buys foreign exchange, thereby expanding the money stock. Given this link between the money supply and the external balance, it is obvious that this adjustment process must ultimately lead to the right money stock so that external payments will be in balance. This is the adjustment process discussed in Section 20-1.

Sterilization

The only way the automatic adjustment process can be suspended is through *sterilization operations*. Central banks frequently offset, or sterilize, the impact of foreign exchange market intervention on the money supply through open market operations. Thus, a deficit country that is selling foreign exchange and correspondingly reducing its money supply may offset this reduction by open market purchases of bonds that restore the money supply.[8]

---

[8]Proposals for *currency boards* in Eastern Europe and the former Soviet Union, in which high-powered money can be created only if it is fully backed by holdings of foreign currency, essentially amount to a fixed exchange rate system strictly without sterilization. Because sterilization is ruled out, adjustment is automatic though of course not painless.

TABLE 20-1

BALANCE SHEET OF THE MONETARY AUTHORITIES

assets	liabilities
Net foreign assets (*NFA*)	High-powered money (*H*)
Domestic credit (*DC*)	

With sterilization, persistent external deficits are possible because the link between the external imbalance and the equilibrating changes in the money stock is broken. It is in this sense that persistent external deficits are a monetary phenomenon: by sterilizing, the central bank actively maintains the stock of money too high for external balance.

The Monetary Approach and the IMF

The emphasis on monetary considerations in the interpretation of external balance problems is called the *monetary approach to the balance of payments*.[9] The monetary approach has been used extensively by the IMF in its analysis and design of economic policies for countries in balance of payments trouble. We give the flavor of the approach by describing typically IMF procedure in analyzing a balance of payments problem.

We start with the balance sheet of the monetary authority, usually the central bank, as in Table 20-1. The monetary authority's liabilities are high-powered money. But on the asset side it can hold both foreign assets—including foreign exchange reserves, gold, and claims on other central banks or governments—and domestic assets, or *domestic credit*. Domestic credit consists of the monetary authority's holdings of claims on the public sector—government debt—and on the private sector—usually loans to banks.

From the balance sheet identity, we have

$$\Delta NFA = \Delta H - \Delta DC \tag{4}$$

where ΔNFA denotes the change in net foreign assets, ΔH the change in high-powered money, and ΔDC the change in the central bank's extension of domestic credit. In words, the change in the central bank's holdings of foreign assets is equal to the change in the stock of high-powered money minus the change in domestic credit.

The important point about equation (4) is that ΔNFA is the balance of payments: official reserve transactions, which are all that ΔNFA is, are equal to the balance of payments.

---

[9]For a collection of essays on this topic, see Jacob Frenkel and Harry G. Johnson (eds.), *The Monetary Approach to the Balance of Payments* (London: Allen & Unwin, 1976). See also *The Monetary Approach to the Balance of Payments* (Washington, D.C.: International Monetary Fund, 1977) and Nadeem Haque, Kajal Lahiri, and Peter Montiel, "A Macroeconometric Model for Developing Countries," *IMF Staff Papers*, September 1990.

The first step in developing a monetary approach type of stabilization policy package is to decide on a balance of payments target, ΔNFA^*. The IMF asks how much of a deficit the country can afford and then suggests policies to make the projected deficit no larger. The target is based largely on the availability of loans and credit from abroad and the possibility of drawing down existing reserves.

The next step is to ask how much the demand for money in the country will increase. The planned changes in the stock of high-powered money, ΔH^*, will have to be just sufficient to produce, via the money multiplier process, the right increases in the stock of money to meet the expected increase in demand. Then, given ΔNFA^* and ΔH^*, equation (4) tells the monetary authority how much domestic credit it can extend consistent with its balance of payments target and expected growth in money demand. Typically, a stabilization plan drawn up by the IMF will include a suggested limit on the expansion of domestic credit.

The limit provides a *ceiling on domestic credit expansion*. The adoption of such a ceiling helps the central bank avoid the temptation of expanding its loans to the government or private sector in the face of rising interest rates or government budget deficits.

How Does It Work?

The simplicity of equation (4) raises an obvious question. Since all it takes to improve the balance of payments is a reduction in the rate of domestic credit expansion, why not balance payments immediately and always? To answer this question, we need to understand the channels through which the curtailment of domestic credit improves the balance of payments.

Controlling domestic credit means operating tight monetary policy. Consider an economy that is growing and has some inflation, so that demand for nominal balances is rising. If domestic credit expansion is slowed, an excess demand for money develops. This, in turn, causes interest rates to rise and spending to decline. The increase in interest rates leads to a balance of payments improvement. That is, the monetary approach as used by the IMF relies on restrictive monetary policy to control the balance of payments. There is, though, a subtle difference between domestic credit ceilings and ordinary tight money. In an open economy with fixed exchange rates, the money stock is endogenous. The central bank cannot control the money stock, since it has to meet whatever demand arises for foreign currency. But it can make "money" tight by reducing the growth of domestic credit. That will imply that the only source of money growth becomes an increase in foreign exchange reserves or foreign borrowing. The economy has to go through enough of a recession or rise in interest rates to generate a balance of payments surplus.

The use of domestic credit ceilings is a crude but easy-to-understand policy to improve the balance of payments. Both the simplicity of the conceptual framework, and the apparent definiteness of the policy recommendations to which it leads, frequently make it the best policy tool available, particularly if dramatic action is needed and the credibility of the government's policies needs to be restored.

The Monetary Approach and Depreciation

Proponents of the monetary approach have argued that depreciation of the exchange rate cannot improve the balance of payments except in the short run. The argument is that in the short run the depreciation does improve a country's competitive position and that this very fact gives rise to a trade surplus and therefore to an increase in the money stock. Over the course of time, the rising money supply raises aggregate demand and therefore prices until the economy returns to full employment and external balance. Devaluation thus exerts only a transitory effect on the economy, which lasts as long as prices and the money supply have not yet increased to match fully the higher import prices.

The analysis of the monetary approach is entirely correct in its insistence on a longer-run perspective in which, under fixed exchange rates, prices and the money stock adjust and the economy achieves internal and external balance. It is also correct in arguing that monetary or domestic credit restraint will improve the balance of payments. Typically, the tight money policy produced by slow domestic credit growth produces a recession.

The monetary approach is misdirected when it suggests that exchange rate policy cannot, even in the short run, affect a country's competitive position. More importantly, exchange rate changes frequently arise from a position of deficit and unemployment. In that case, a devaluation can be used to speed the adjustment process.

We return now to the world of flexible exchange rates.[10]

20-4 FLEXIBLE EXCHANGE RATES, MONEY, AND PRICES

In studying flexible exchange rates, we assume as in Chapter 6 that capital is perfectly mobile. The only difference from that earlier treatment is that now prices are allowed to change. We examine how output, the exchange rate, and prices respond to monetary and fiscal policies, and how that response evolves over time. The starting point is a discussion of the adjustment of prices and the exchange rate to the state of the economy.

The Adjustment Process

Figure 20-5 shows the interest rate and output, with full employment at Y^*. The assumption of perfect international capital mobility is reflected in the horizontal BB schedule. Only at an interest rate $i = i_f$ will the balance of payments be in equilibrium. If the interest rate were higher, there would be net inflows of capital. Conversely, with a lower domestic interest rate, capital would flow out and the balance of payments would turn toward a deficit position.

We make two strategic assumptions to describe the adjustment process. First, prices are rising whenever output exceeds the full-employment level. Second, because

---

[10] See Ronald MacDonald and Mark Taylor, "Exchange Rate Economics: A Survey," *IMF Staff Papers*, March 1992, for a broad discussion of models of exchange rate determination and the empirical evidence.

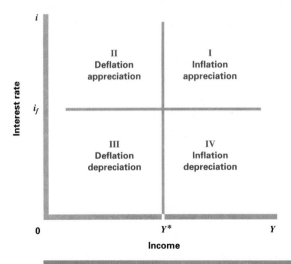

FIGURE 20-5

ADJUSTMENT OF EXCHANGE RATES AND PRICES. Prices move in response to the deviation of the economy from full employment. When output is above potential, prices are rising (regions I and IV), and they are falling at output levels below potential (regions II and III). With capital highly mobile the balance of payments is sensitive to interest rates. If our interest rate falls below the world level, capital tends to flow out, and that leads to a deficit and depreciation of the exchange rate (regions III and IV). Conversely, a rise in interest rates leads to capital inflows, a surplus, and appreciation (regions I and II).

capital is highly mobile, the interest rate in Figure 20-5 is always moving toward the *BB* schedule—our interest rate cannot diverge far from that in the rest of the world.

There is a complicated set of adjustments in the background as the economy moves toward *BB*. For instance, a monetary expansion causes a decline in interest rates. Capital flows out, which means that people try to sell our currency to buy foreign currencies. Our currency depreciates, exports and income increase, money demand rises, and so do interest rates, thus moving us back toward *BB*. This mechanism works in reverse if domestic interest rates tend to rise because of a monetary tightening or fiscal expansion.

With these assumptions we can study the adjustment process using Figure 20-5. Anywhere to the right of Y^* prices are rising, and to the left prices are falling. Points above *BB* lead to capital inflows and appreciation; points below, to capital outflows and depreciation. Moreover, with extremely high capital mobility, the exchange rate will adjust very rapidly, so that we are always close to or on the *BB* schedule.

A Monetary Expansion: Short- and Long-Run Effects

With given prices a monetary expansion under flexible rates and perfect capital mobility leads to depreciation and increased income. We ask how that result is modified once

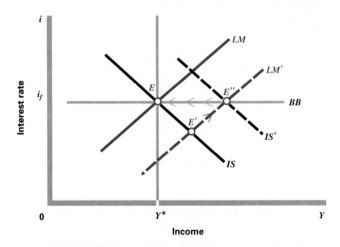

FIGURE 20-6

THE SHORT- AND LONG-RUN EFFECTS OF A MONETARY EXPANSION. The
economy is in initial equilibrium at *E* when a monetary expansion
shifts the *LM* schedule to *LM'*. The goods and money market
equilibrium at *E'* involve an interest rate below the world level.
Capital outflows now lead to immediate exchange depreciation, and
therefore the *IS* schedule shifts to *IS'*. The economy thus moves
rapidly from *E* to *E''*. But at *E''* there is overemployment, and hence
prices are rising. Rising prices reduce real balances and shift the *LM*
schedule back toward *E*. As real balances decline, interest rates tend
to rise, drawing in capital and leading to appreciation, which shifts
the *IS'* schedule back toward *E*. In the long run, output returns to
normal, and money, prices, and the exchange rate all rise in the
same proportion.

we take adjustments in prices into account. The answer is that the output adjustment
is now only transitory. In the long run a monetary expansion leads to an exchange
depreciation and to higher prices with no change in competitiveness.

In Figure 20-6 we start at point *E* with full employment, a payments balance,
monetary equilibrium, and equilibrium in the domestic goods market. Now a monetary
expansion takes place and shifts the *LM* schedule to *LM'*. The new goods and money
market equilibrium at *E'* involves an interest rate below the world level, and therefore
the exchange rate immediately depreciates, raising home competitiveness and thus
shifting the *IS* schedule to *IS'*. The economy moves rapidly from *E* via *E'* to *E''*. Output
has risen, the exchange rate has depreciated, and the economy has thereby gained in
external competitiveness. But that is not the end of the story.

At *E''* output is above the full-employment level. Prices are therefore rising, and
that implies real balances are falling. As the real money stock, *M/P*, declines because
of rising prices, the *LM* schedule starts shifting to the left. Interest rates tend to rise,
capital tends to flow in, and the resulting appreciation leads now to a decline in
competitiveness that also shifts the *IS* schedule back toward the initial equilibrium.

TABLE 20-2

THE SHORT- AND LONG-RUN EFFECTS OF A
MONETARY EXPANSION

	M/P	e	P	eP_f/P	Y
Short run	+	+	0	+	+
Long run	0	+	+	0	0

Both the *IS* and *LM* schedules thus move back toward point *E*. The process continues until point *E* is reached again.

What adjustments have taken place once the economy is back to point *E*? At point *E*, interest rates have returned to their initial level and so have relative prices, eP_f/P. In moving from *E* to *E'* the exchange rate depreciated immediately, ahead of the rise in prices. But when prices increased and real balances fell, some of that depreciation was reversed. Over the whole adjustment process, prices and exchange rates rose in the same proportion, leaving relative prices, eP_f/P, and therefore aggregate demand unchanged. In the long run money was therefore *entirely neutral*. Table 20-2 summarizes these results. By the end of the adjustment process, nominal money, prices, and the exchange rate have all increased in the same proportion, so that the real money stock and relative prices—including the real exchange rate—are unchanged.

Exchange Rate Overshooting

The analysis of monetary policy under flexible exchange rates, given above, leads to an important insight about the adjustment process. The important feature of the adjustment process is that *exchange rates and prices do not move at the same rate*. When a monetary expansion pushes interest rates down, the exchange rate adjusts immediately, but prices adjust only gradually. Monetary expansion therefore leads in the short run to an immediate and abrupt change in relative prices and competitiveness.

Figure 20-7 shows time paths of nominal money, the exchange rate, and the price level implied by the analysis of Figure 20-6. For each of these variables we show an index that is initially equal to 100. The economy starts at long-run equilibrium. Then, at time T_0, the money stock is increased by 50 percent and stays at that higher level, as shown by the solid schedule. The exchange rate immediately depreciates. In fact the exchange rate index rises by more than money, say from the initial level of 100 at point *A* to a new level of 170 at point *A'*. Prices, by contrast, do not move rapidly.

Following the impact effect at time T_0, further adjustments take place. Because the gain in competitiveness at time T_0 has raised output above potential, there is now inflation. Prices are rising, and at the same time the exchange rate is appreciating, thus undoing part of the initial, sharp depreciation. Over time, prices rise to match the increase in money, and the exchange rate will also match the higher level of money and prices. In the long run, real variables are unchanged. The adjustment pattern for

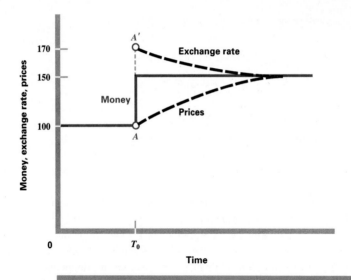

FIGURE 20-7

EXCHANGE RATE OVERSHOOTING. The diagram shows indexes for prices, money, and the exchange rate. Initially the economy is in full equilibrium, and the value of each index is chosen as 100. A permanent increase in the money stock of 50 percent takes place at time T_0, as shown by the solid line. The exchange rate immediately depreciates from A to A', more than the increase in money. Prices adjust only gradually. In the short run, the relative price of imports, eP_f/P, increases sharply. That gain in competitiveness causes a transitory income expansion. But over time prices rise and the exchange rate appreciates somewhat, undoing the initial overshooting. In the long run, nominal money, the exchange rate, and prices all rise in the same proportion (50 percent, from 100 to 150), and real balances and the relative price of imports are therefore unchanged.

the exchange rate seen in Figure 20-7 involves *overshooting*. The exchange rate overshoots its new equilibrium level when, in response to a disturbance, it first moves *beyond* the equilibrium it ultimately will reach and then gradually returns to the long-run equilibrium position. Overshooting means that changes in monetary policy produce large changes in exchange rates.

Those who believe that exchange rate overshooting introduces an undesirable instability into the economy argue that governments should intervene in foreign exchange markets to avoid large, excessive exchange rate fluctuations. The sharp dollar appreciation of 1980–1985 strongly reinforced the call for such intervention. In 1985 the major countries agreed in principle that they would intervene to try to prevent exchange rate instability. The agreement notwithstanding, major exchange rate movements continue to occur and often they are hard to explain. Accordingly, although the current flexible rate system emerged because the Bretton Woods system[11] of fixed rates broke down in 1973, it is not viewed as the last word, and reform of the international monetary system is always on the agenda.

Purchasing Power Parity

In the preceding analysis, the exchange rate rose by precisely the right amount to offset the effects of domestic inflation on the real exchange rate. That is, the exchange depreciation maintained the *purchasing power* of our goods in terms of foreign goods between the initial and the final equilibrium points.

An important view of the determinants of the exchange rate is the theory that exchange rates move primarily as a result of differences in price level behavior between the two countries in such a way as to maintain the terms of trade constant. This is the *purchasing power parity* (PPP) theory. The purchasing power parity theory of the exchange rate argues that exchange rate movements primarily reflect differences in inflation rates between countries. After examining the real exchange rate, eP_f/P, the theory maintains the following: when P_f and/or P changes, e changes in such a way as to maintain eP_f/P constant.

PPP is a plausible description of the trend behavior of exchange rates, especially when inflation differentials between countries are large. In particular, we have seen that the PPP relationship does hold in the case of an increase in the money stock. If price level movements are caused by monetary changes—as they are likely to be if the inflation rate is high—then we should expect PPP relationships to hold in the long term.

But qualifications are necessary. First, even a monetary disturbance affects the real exchange rate in the short run. Exchange rates tend to move quite rapidly relative to prices, and thus in the short term of a quarter or a year, we should not be at all surprised to see substantial deviations of exchange rates from the rates implied by PPP even if the exchange rate change is caused by monetary policy.

The second important qualification concerns the effects of nonmonetary disturbances on exchange rates. For example, we saw that an increase in exports leads to currency appreciation at unchanged domestic prices. This example illustrates that, over time, adjustments to *real* disturbances will affect the *equilibrium* real exchange rate. In the longer run, exchange rates and prices do *not* necessarily move together, as they do in a world where all disturbances are monetary. On the contrary, we may have changes in relative prices, which run counter to the purchasing power parity view of exchange rates.

Consider Figure 20-8 where we see that the real exchange rate between the dollar and the deutsche mark (eP_{Ger}/P_{US}) fluctuates a great deal over time. We also show the nominal exchange rate in Figure 20-8. According to PPP, when the exchange rate index (DM/$) changes, the real exchange rate should not—because according to PPP

---

[11] This is the system of fixed exchange rates that prevailed from the end of World War II to 1973, so-called because it was designed, in 1944, in a major international conference held in Bretton Woods, New Hampshire.

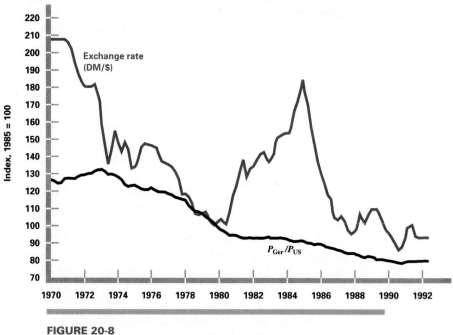

FIGURE 20-8

THE EXCHANGE RATE AND RELATIVE PRICES: GERMANY AND THE UNITED
STATES, 1970–1992 (INDEX, 1985 = 100). (SOURCE: DRI/McGraw-Hill.)

the exchange rate should be moving only because relative price levels change. However,
clearly the real exchange rate moves roughly in parallel with the nominal exchange
rate, showing that PPP does not hold, in the case of Germany and the United States,
over the period since 1979. Nor is PPP a good description of the behavior of exchange
rates among the major currencies over any recent period.

External Competitiveness

PPP measures are closely related to the behavior of a country's competitiveness in
external trade. A decline in a country's relative price level makes the country's goods
relatively cheaper, and thus more competitive. Table 20-3 presents indices of unit labor
costs in manufacturing measured in U.S. dollars for several countries.

The data make it clear that nominal exchange rates affect unit labor costs in
dollars. In 1985, when the dollar peaked, Germany and Japan had very low costs in
dollars compared, say, to 1990, when the dollar had weakened considerably. Thus
nominal exchange rate movements clearly affect competitiveness.

We have now completed the core of this chapter. The remaining sections take
up a number of issues that extend the basic analysis.

TABLE 20-3

UNIT LABOR COSTS IN MANUFACTURING (dollar index, 1982 = 100)

	U.S.	Germany	Japan	Korea
1970	46	34	33	36
1980	87	150	117	83
1985	97	121	103	84
1990	97	176	168	103

SOURCE: U.S. Department of Labor.

20-5 INTEREST DIFFERENTIALS AND EXCHANGE RATE EXPECTATIONS

A cornerstone of our theoretical model of exchange rate determination was international capital mobility. In particular, we argued that with capital markets sufficiently integrated, we would expect interest rates to be equated across countries. How does this assumption stand up to the facts? In Figure 20-9 we show the U.S. federal funds rate and the money market rate in Germany. Obviously, these rates are not equal. How do we square this fact with our theory?

Exchange Rate Expectations

Our theoretical analysis was based on the assumption that capital flows internationally in response to nominal interest differentials. For example, if domestic interest rates were 6 percent and German rates were 10 percent, we would expect a capital outflow.

However, such a theory is incomplete in a world in which exchange rates can, do, and are expected to change.[12] For example, consider a situation in which the deutsche mark is expected to depreciate by 5 percent over the next year relative to the dollar. With a 5 percent DM depreciation, the return *in dollars* of investing in Germany is only 5 percent (= 10 percent − 5 percent). The natural preference will be to invest in American bonds, even though the U.S. interest rate is below that in Germany.

It is clear, therefore, that we must extend our discussion of interest rate equalization to incorporate expectations of exchange rate changes. Anyone who invests in domestic bonds earns the interest rate i. Alternatively, by investing in foreign bonds, the investor earns the interest rate on foreign bonds, i_f, *plus* whatever she earns from the appreciation of the foreign currency. The total return on foreign bonds, measured in our currency, is then

$$\text{Return on foreign bonds (in terms of domestic currency)} = i_f + \Delta e/e \qquad (5)$$

---

[12] On capital mobility see Jeffrey Frankel, "International Capital Mobility: A Review," *American Economic Review*, May 1991.

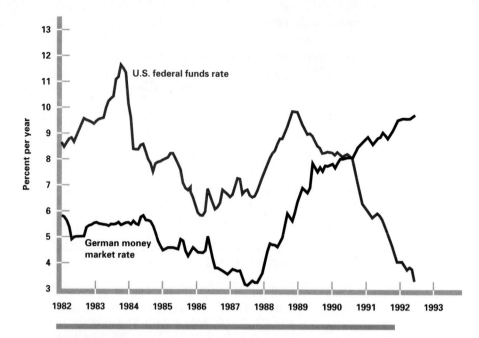

FIGURE 20-9
THE U.S. FEDERAL FUNDS RATE AND GERMAN MONEY MARKET RATES,
1982–1992 (PERCENT). (Source: DRI/McGraw-Hill.)

Of course, since the investor does not know at the time she is making her decision by how much the exchange rate will change, the term $\Delta e/e$ in equation (5) should be interpreted as the *expected* change in the exchange rate.

The introduction of exchange rate expectations modifies our equation for the balance of payments. Now capital flows are governed by the difference between our interest rate and the foreign rate adjusted for expected depreciation: $i - i_f - \Delta e/e$. An increase in foreign interest rates or an expectation of depreciation, given our interest rates, would lead to a capital outflow. Conversely, a rise in our rates or an expectation of appreciation would bring about a capital outflow. We thus write the balance of payments as

$$BP = NX\left(Y, \frac{eP_f}{P}\right) + CF\left(i - i_f - \frac{\Delta e}{e}\right) \tag{6}$$

The adjustment for exchange rate expectations thus accounts for international differences in interest rates that persist even when capital is freely mobile among countries. When capital is completely mobile, interest rates are equalized, after adjusting for expected depreciation:

$$i = i_f + \Delta e/e \tag{6a}$$

Expected depreciation helps account for differences in interest rates among low- and high-inflation countries. When the inflation rate in a country is high, its exchange rate is expected to depreciate. In addition, the Fisher relationship suggests that the nominal interest rate in that country will be high. Thus high-inflation countries tend to have high interest rates and depreciating currencies. This is an international extension of the Fisher equation, which relies on PPP to argue that inflation differentials internationally are matched by depreciation. Our long-term relation then is

$$\text{Inflation differential} \cong \text{interest differential} \cong \text{depreciation rate} \qquad (7)$$

The $\cong$ means "approximately equal to." The relation is approximate because exchange rates can move independently of prices and also because obstacles to capital flows may create long-term interest differentials.

Speculative Capital Flows

Changes in exchange rate expectations can affect the actual exchange rate as well as the domestic interest rate and output. The point is made with the help of Figure 20-10, which assumes perfect capital mobility, as specified in equation (6a). Here the *BB* schedule is drawn for a given foreign interest rate and a given expected rate of change of the exchange rate, say zero.

Suppose that we start in full equilibrium at point *E* and that the market develops the expectation that the home currency will appreciate. This implies that even with a lower home interest rate, domestic assets are attractive, and so the *BB* schedule shifts downward by the amount of expected appreciation.

Point *E* is no longer an equilibrium, given the shift of the *BB* schedule to *BB'*, but rather a position of surplus with large-scale capital inflows motivated by the anticipation of appreciation. The surplus at *E* causes the exchange rate to start appreciating, and we move in a southwesterly direction, as indicated by the arrow. The speculative attack causes appreciation, a loss in competitiveness, and, consequently, falling output and employment. Thus the expectation of an exchange rate appreciation is *self-fulfilling*.

This analysis confirms that exchange rate expectations, through their impact on capital flows and thus on actual exchange rates, are a potential source of disturbance to macroeconomic equilibrium—something which policy makers who try to fix exchange rates when capital is fully mobile keep having to learn.

20-6 EXCHANGE RATE FLUCTUATIONS AND INTERDEPENDENCE

In the 1960s there was growing dissatisfaction with fixed exchange rates. The Bretton Woods system put in place at the end of World War II was called a crisis system because from time to time exchange rates would get out of line and expectations of exchange rate changes would mobilize massive capital flows that often precipitated the exchange rate changes that speculators expected. Is the system of flexible rates among the major currencies of the period since 1973 better? Is it less crisis-prone, and

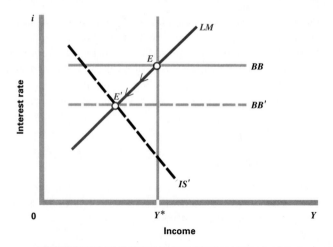

FIGURE 20-10
RESPONSE TO AN EXPECTED APPRECIATION OF THE CURRENCY. The
initial equilibrium at *E* is disturbed by the expectation that the home
currency will appreciate. The *BB* schedule shifts down to *BB'*,
reflecting the fact that people are willing to hold domestic assets at
a reduced interest rate since they expect to be compensated for the
differential by the anticipated appreciation of the currency. At *E*
there is now a capital inflow that leads to exchange appreciation.
The *IS* schedule (not drawn) shifts to *IS'*, and the economy moves
into a recession. The capital inflow has brought about a loss of
trade competitiveness and thus unemployment at point *E'*.

does it provide a better framework for macroeconomic stability? Before providing an
answer, we look briefly at how flexibly the system has, in fact, operated.

Foreign Exchange Market Intervention

When exchange rates are fully flexible, the government takes no action in the foreign
exchange market. It stays out of the foreign exchange market, whatever happens to
the exchange rate. Such a system is almost unheard of, although the United States did
behave that way briefly in 1981–1982. More commonly, governments intervene in
the foreign exchange market to a lesser or greater extent. Foreign exchange market
intervention occurs when a government buys or sells foreign exchange in an attempt
to influence the exchange rate.

The extent to which governments intervene in the foreign exchange markets
varies substantially. They may try only to offset short-term fluctuations and buy or
sell foreign exchange to maintain "orderly markets." But they also may try to keep an
overvalued exchange rate from depreciating or an undervalued exchange rate from

appreciating. *Dirty* (as opposed to clean) *floating* is the practice of using substantial intervention to try to maintain an exchange rate against the pressure of market forces.

For almost the entire period since 1973, exchange rate floating has been of the decidedly dirty variety. Governments have intervened on a very large scale. This leads naturally to the question of why a government should try to resist market forces, to prevent an appreciation or a depreciation of the currency.

Why Governments Intervene

Central banks intervene to affect exchange rates for several reasons.[13] Probably the main reason is the belief that many capital flows represent merely unstable expectations and that the induced movements in exchange rates cause unnecessary changes in domestic output. The second reason for intervention is a central bank's attempt to move the real exchange rate in order to affect trade flows. The third reason arises from the effects of the exchange rate on domestic inflation. Central banks sometimes intervene in the exchange market to prevent the exchange rate from depreciating, with the aim of preventing import prices from rising, and thereby helping slow inflation.

The basic argument for intervention is that the central bank can intervene to smooth out fluctuations in exchange rates. This is the usual rationale for dirty floating. The only—and overwhelming—objection to the argument that the central bank should smooth out fluctuations is that there is no simple way of telling an erratic movement from a trend movement. How can we tell whether a current appreciation in the exchange rate is merely the result of a disturbance that will soon reverse itself, rather than the beginning of a trend movement in the exchange rate? There is no way of telling at the time a change occurs, although with the benefit of hindsight one can see which exchange rate movements were later reversed.

There is one circumstance under which central bank intervention might be desirable. It is clear from our earlier analysis that one of the key determinants of exchange rate behavior is expectations of economic policy. It may sometimes be possible to make it clear that there has been a change in policy only by intervening in the foreign exchange market. This is a case of putting your money where your mouth is.

Sterilized versus Nonsterilized Intervention

In discussing intervention, it is important also to ask whether it works. For instance, does it make any difference to the exchange rate if the Bundesbank sells $1 billion from its foreign currency reserves?

To judge the effectiveness of intervention we must distinguish between *sterilized* and *nonsterilized intervention*, discussed earlier in this chapter. In the case of sterilized

---

[13] Some academic critics oppose intervention. See, for instance, Milton Friedman, "Deja Vu in Currency Markets," *Wall Street Journal*, September 22, 1992. Paul Volcker and Toyoo Gyohten, two prominent practitioners of intervention, discuss the merits in *Changing Fortunes: The World's Money and the Threat to American Leadership* (New York: Random House, 1992).

intervention a central bank, say, buys foreign exchange, issuing domestic money. But then the increase in the money stock is reversed by an open market sale of securities. In the sterilized intervention case, therefore, the home money supply is kept unchanged. In the case of nonsterilization, by contrast, there is a change in the money stock equal to the amount of intervention.

Thus nonsterilized intervention results in a change in the money stock. It is widely agreed that nonsterilized intervention, because it changes the money supply, will affect exchange rates. There is widespread skepticism, however, about the effectiveness of sterilized intervention. In 1978–1979 the U.S. dollar was depreciating in currency markets even though there was intervention on a massive scale. But that intervention was carefully sterilized. Only in late 1979, when the dollar depreciation began to alarm the Fed, did a change in policy take place. Monetary policy was tightened, and immediately the dollar depreciation was stopped and soon massively reversed.

That episode, and other evidence, strongly suggests the effectiveness of nonsterilized intervention and of intervention that is backed by credible policies. The earlier failure of sterilized intervention suggested that only unsterilized intervention could affect the exchange rate. But a more recent episode gives cause for rethinking that issue.

The very large appreciation of the dollar from 1980 to 1985, described in Box 20-2, was a major concern to policy makers in the United States, Europe, and Japan. Many policy makers thought that the markets had pushed the dollar too high, and that only speculative forces were keeping it up. In September 1985 the finance ministers of the Group of Five (the United States, Japan, Germany, France, and the United Kingdom) announced their view that the dollar was too high, and their central banks went into action to sell dollars in order to drive the rate down. The dollar responded quickly, suggesting that concerted action can affect the exchange rate even if there is no obvious change in monetary policy. Such action is certainly not guaranteed to work, but it could work if there is widespread speculation in the markets about the future course of policy and if announcements and intervention suggest that future policy will try to move the exchange rate in a particular direction. By contrast, if policy makers are unwilling to use interest rates to defend their currency, as was the case in the United Kingdom in September 1992, even a $30 billion intervention cannot help the exchange rate.

Interdependence

It used to be argued that under flexible exchange rates countries can pursue their own national economic policies—monetary and fiscal policy and the inflation rate—without having to worry about the balance of payments. That is certainly correct, but it is also misleading. There are important linkages between countries *whatever the exchange rate regime.*[14]

---

[14] On interdependence, see Ralph C. Bryant et al., "Domestic and Cross-Border Consequences of US Macroeconomic Policies," International Finance Discussion Paper 344, Board of Governors of the Federal Reserve System, March 1989; Jeffrey Shaffer, "What the US Current Account Deficit Has Meant for Other OECD Countries," *OECD Studies,* Spring 1988; and Paul Masson et al., *Multimod Mark II: A Revised and Extended Model,* IMF Occasional Paper No. 71, 1990.

TABLE 20-4
MONETARY AND FISCAL POLICY EFFECTS WITH
INTERDEPENDENCE

	U.S. MONETARY CONTRACTION		U.S. FISCAL EXPANSION	
	U.S.	rest of the world	U.S.	rest of the world
Exchange rate	$ appreciates		$ appreciates	
Output	−	+	+	+
Inflation	−	+	−	+

These *spillover*, or *interdependence*, effects have been at the center of the discussion about flexible exchange rates. For instance, suppose the United States tightens monetary policy. As discussed earlier, U.S. interest rates rise and that attracts capital flows from abroad. The dollar appreciates, and foreign currencies depreciate. Table 20-4 shows the effects in other countries.

The U.S. appreciation implies a loss in competitiveness. World demand shifts from U.S. goods to those produced by our competitors. Therefore, at home, output and employment decline. Abroad, our competitors benefit from the depreciation of their currency. They become more competitive, and therefore output and employment abroad expand. Our monetary tightening thus tends to promote employment gains abroad, which come, of course, at the expense of our own employment.

There are also spillover effects through prices. When our currency appreciates, import prices in dollars fall. Therefore our inflation tends to decline quite rapidly when there is a sharp dollar appreciation. But abroad the opposite occurs. Their currency depreciates, and therefore prices in foreign currency tend to increase. Inflation abroad thus rises. Foreigners might welcome an increase in employment as a side effect of our monetary policy, but they certainly can do without the inflation that comes from their currency depreciation.

In the same way, U.S. fiscal policies exert effects abroad. A U.S. fiscal expansion, such as the one in the 1980–1985 period, will lead to dollar appreciation and a loss in competitiveness. The direct increase in our spending and the deterioration in our competitiveness are the channels through which our expansion is shared abroad. When the United States has a fiscal expansion, the rest of the world shares via their increased exports.

Table 20-4 also shows the effects of monetary and fiscal policy on inflation. Because fiscal expansion leads to appreciation, the decline in import prices helps reduce inflation in the expanding country. But abroad import prices will rise, and that means inflation will be increased. These impacts of exchange rate movements on inflation were important factors in changing inflation rates in industrial countries in the 1980–1985 period.

Policy makers abroad therefore must decide whether to accept the higher employment–higher inflation effects of our policies or whether they should change their own policies. If inflation is already a problem abroad, or if the rest of the world is highly

box 20-2

UNSUSTAINABLE DEFICITS AND THE DOLLAR BUBBLE

In the early 1980s there was very little concern about U.S. current account deficits. Following the 1982 world recession, the U.S. economy was growing much faster than others, and a deficit in the current account was seen as a by-product of a strong expansion. But increasingly the strong dollar added to the deficit by eroding U.S. competitiveness (see Figure 1).

By 1985 an ever larger deficit and an ever stronger dollar started raising questions. If the dollar remained at its 1985 level, would the deficit ever go away? And if the deficit did not decline, would the United States soon become a net foreign debtor, and then year after year have to go increasingly into debt? And if debt and the interest that had to be paid on the debt were to grow for a long period, was that consistent with a strong dollar?

THE DOLLAR AS A BUBBLE

The extreme rise of the dollar and the large deficit in 1985 led to the conclusion that the dollar was overvalued. Dollar depreciation on a major scale would have to take place at some time in order to trim the deficit and thus slow down the rate of increase in foreign indebtedness. But if a major dollar depreciation was inevitable, why were the foreign exchange markets still pushing it up? For if the foreign exchange markets anticipated a major dollar decline, traders would be quick to buy other currencies, trying to avoid being caught when the dollar fell. The attempt by everybody to sell would therefore bring about a very rapid alignment of the dollar.

Even as the discussion of an unsustainable dollar emerged, the dollar actually started its post-1985 decline. But that left unanswered the question of why it had risen so much in the first place. Explanations of tight U.S. monetary policy and fiscal expansion went some way in explaining the rise of the dollar, but that could not be the whole story; the timing did not match, since monetary policy had started easing already in the fall of 1982.

Some observers concluded that the dollar peak of 1985 had been a speculative *bubble*, a departure of the dollar from the level justified by the fundamental factors that should determine its value: interest rates, the current account, and expected future current accounts. Once the bubble had burst, in part because of central bank cooperation in intervention, the dollar declined for 2 years to reach more realistic

averse to inflation, then the policy response abroad to this *imported inflation* may well be to tighten money. If the dollar appreciation was caused by a tightening of U.S. monetary policy, then it will also cause a monetary contraction abroad if foreign countries decide to fight imported inflation. That means our monetary tightening touches off worldwide tightening. This was substantially what happened in the worldwide recession of 1981–1982.

Policy Synchronization

The large changes in exchange rates that occur when policies are not fully synchronized between countries pose a major threat to free trade. When import prices fall by 20 or

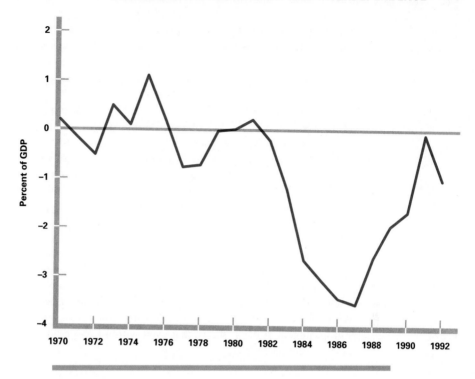

FIGURE 1
THE UNITED STATES CURRENT ACCOUNT, 1970–1992 (PERCENT OF GDP).
(Source: DRI/McGraw-Hill.)

levels. The discussion of whether assets markets and, in particular, the foreign exchange market are or are not rational continues unresolved.* ■

*See Jeffrey Frankel and Ken Froot, "Using Survey Data to Test Standard Propositions Regarding Exchange Rate Expectations," *American Economic Review*, March 1987. Exchange rate expectations, and their rationality, are reviewed in Takatoshi Ito, "Foreign Exchange Rate Expectations: Micro Survey Data," *American Economic Review*, June 1990; Shinji Takagi, "Exchange Rate Expectations," *IMF Staff Papers*, March 1991; and Ken Froot and Richard Thaler, "Anomalies: Foreign Exchange," *Journal of Economic Perspectives*, Summer 1990.

30 percent because of a currency appreciation, large shifts in demand will occur. Domestic workers become unemployed, and they have no trouble seeing that it is foreigners who gain the jobs they just lost. Accordingly, there will be pressure for protection—tariffs or quotas—to keep out imports that are "artificially cheap" due to the currency appreciation. In the United States in the 1980s repeated calls for protection in the automobile industry, in steel, and in many other industries reflected in large part the side effects of a dollar that appreciated sharply in response to tight money and easy fiscal policy.

The experience of the last 20 years offers an unambiguous answer to the question of whether flexible exchange rates isolate countries from shocks that originate abroad.

Under flexible exchange rates there is as much or more interdependence as there is under fixed rates. Moreover, because exchange rates are so flexible and so ready to respond to policies (good or bad), macroeconomic management does not become easier. Further, to the extent that exchange rate overshooting causes sharp changes in competitiveness, it leads to protectionist sentiment.

On all counts then, flexible rates are far from being a perfect system. But there is no better system, for the Bretton Woods system collapsed. Therefore we can ask only whether, through international coordination of interests and policies, we can make the system work better than it has in the recent past. Although the leaders of the major industrial countries have repeatedly recognized their interdependence and agreed to work toward more coordinated policies, there have been no major institutional changes to ensure coordination of economic policies.[15]

One major suggestion calls for establishment of *target zones*. In a target zone arrangement central banks limit the fluctuations of exchange rates to a specified range. Target zones require policy coordination. Specifically, in an effective target zone arrangement, governments must synchronize both their monetary and their fiscal policies.[16] The unwillingness to give up this sovereignty stands in the way of more limited exchange rate fluctuations between the United States, Europe, and Japan. Moreover, discussion concerning the Maastricht Treaty, which envisages the creation of a common European central bank, shows that even within Europe, giving up monetary independence is not an easy step.[17]

20-7   SUMMARY

1. A monetary expansion in the long run increases the price level and the exchange rate, keeping real balances and the real exchange rate constant. In the short run, though, the monetary expansion increases the level of output and reduces the interest rate, depreciating the exchange rate. The exchange rate overshoots its new equilibrium level.

---

[15] See Jacob A. Frenkel, Morris Goldstein, and Paul Masson, *Characteristics of a Successful Exchange Rate System*, IMF Occasional Paper No. 82, July 1991; and Morris Goldstein, Peter Isard, Paul Masson, and Mark Taylor, *Policy Issues in the Evolving International Monetary System*, IMF Occasional Paper No. 96, June 1992.

[16] For a proposal on target zones see John Williamson and Marcus Miller, *Targets and Indicators: A Blueprint for the International Coordination of Economic Policy* (Washington, D.C.: Institute for International Economics, 1987); J. Williamson, "The Case for Roughly Stabilizing the Real Value of the Dollar," *American Economic Review*, May 1989; and Martin Feldstein, "The Case against Trying to Stabilize the Dollar," *American Economic Review*, May 1989. See, too, Jacob Frenkel and Morris Goldstein, "Exchange Rate Volatility and Misalignment: Evaluating Some Proposals for Reforms," in Federal Reserve Bank of Kansas City, *Financial Market Volatility* (Kansas City, 1989).

[17] See Daniel Gros and Niels Thygesen, *European Monetary Integration: From the European Monetary System to European Monetary Union* (London: Longman, 1992); Paul de Grauwe, *The Economics of Monetary Integration* (Oxford: Oxford University Press, 1992); and Horst Ungerer et al., *The European Monetary System: Developments and Perspectives*, IMF Occasional Paper No. 73, 1990.

2. External imbalances can be financed in the short term. In the long run they call for adjustment through expenditure reducing and expenditure switching policies. The former change the level of spending; the latter affect the composition of spending between domestic goods and imports and exports.

3. Under fixed exchange rates, the automatic adjustment mechanism works through prices and money. Unemployment leads to a decline in prices, a gain in competitiveness, increased net exports, and a gain in employment. The money supply responds to trade imbalances, affecting the level of interest rates, spending, and hence the payments deficit.

4. Because trade flows respond only gradually to a change in the real exchange rate, we observe a J- curve: a real depreciation will worsen the trade balance in the short run, but then gradually improve it in later years as volume effects dominate.

5. The monetary approach to the balance of payments draws attention to the fact that a payments deficit is always a reflection of a monetary disequilibrium and is always self-correcting. But the correction mechanism, because it involves unemployment, may be excessively painful compared with policy actions such as devaluation.

6. Exchange rate overshooting results from the rapid response of exchange rates to monetary policy and the sluggish adjustment of prices. A monetary expansion will lead to an immediate depreciation but only a gradual increase in prices. Exchange rate overshooting implies that real exchange rates are highly volatile.

7. Purchasing power parity (PPP) refers to the long-run tendency of exchange rates to offset divergent trends in national price levels. The currency of the country with the higher rate of inflation would tend to be depreciating at a rate equal to the inflation differential. If exchange rates follow PPP, then nominal exchange rate movements have no effects on competitiveness. In the short run, exchange rates certainly do not follow a PPP pattern.

8. Capital moves internationally in response to yield differentials, taking into account anticipated exchange rate movements. Interest rates in a country with a depreciating currency have to be sufficiently high to compensate asset holders for the depreciation of the assets.

9. Changes in nominal exchange rates will affect relative prices only if there are no offsetting changes in wages and prices. The real exchange rate, $R = e_f/P$, can change as a result of nominal exchange rate movements only if P_f/P does not move in a fully offsetting manner. Among industrialized countries stickiness of wages and prices ensures that real exchange rates change when nominal rates do.

10. Governments can intervene in exchange markets to limit the impact on output and prices of exchange rate fluctuations stemming from asset market disturbances. But intervention is problematic when the authorities cannot determine whether the exchange rate is moving on account of fundamentals or for purely speculative reasons.

11. Even under flexible exchange rates economies are closely tied to one another. A monetary expansion at home will lead to unemployment and disinflation abroad. A fiscal expansion will cause an expansion abroad along with inflation. These interdependence effects make a case for coordinating policies.

KEY TERMS

Real exchange rate

Expenditure switching policies

Expenditure reducing policies

J curve

Monetary approach

Sterilization

Competitiveness

Intervention

Dirty floating

Crawling peg

Exchange rate overshooting

Exchange rate expectations

Purchasing power parity (PPP)

Interdependence

Policy coordination

Synchronization

PROBLEMS

1. It is sometimes said that a central bank is a necessary condition for a balance of payments deficit. What is the explanation for this argument?

2. Use the central bank balance sheet to show how a balance of payments deficit affects the stock of high-powered money under fixed exchange rates. Show, too, how sterilization operations are reflected in the central bank's balance sheet.

3. Consider a country that is in a position of full employment and balanced trade. Which of the following types of disturbance can be remedied with standard aggregate demand tools of stabilization? Indicate in each case the impact on external and internal balance as well as the appropriate policy response.
   (a) A loss of export markets
   (b) A reduction in saving and a corresponding increase in demand for domestic goods
   (c) An increase in government spending
   (d) A shift in demand from imports to domestic goods
   (e) A reduction in imports with a corresponding increase in saving

4. Suppose in year 1 we have price levels $P = 100$ and $P_f = 100$. Suppose next that in year 2 the respective price levels are $P_2 = 180$ and $P_{2f} = 130$. Let the exchange rate initially be \$2 per pound and assume the balance of payments is in equilibrium.
   (a) If there were no real disturbances between year 1 and year 2, what would be the equilibrium exchange rate in year 2?
   (b) If the real exchange rate, eP_f/P, had deteriorated between years 1 and 2 by 50 percent, what would the exchange rate be in year 2?

5. Discuss the manner in which income, price adjustments, and money supply adjustments interact in leading the economy ultimately to full employment and external balance. Choose as an example the case in which a country experiences a permanent increase in exports.

6. Explain the purchasing power parity theory of the long-run behavior of the exchange rate. Indicate whether there are any circumstances under which you would not expect the PPP relationship to hold.

7. In relation to external imbalance, a distinction is frequently made between imbalances that should be "adjusted" and those that should be "financed." Give examples of disturbances that give rise, respectively, to imbalances that require adjustment and those that should more appropriately be financed.

8. Consider a world with some capital mobility: the home country's capital account improves as domestic interest rates rise relative to the world rate of interest. Initially, the home country

is in internal and external balance. (Draw the *IS, LM,* and *BB* schedules.) Assume now an increase in the rate of interest abroad.
   (a) Show the effect of the foreign interest rate increase on the *BB* schedule.
   (b) What policy response would immediately restore internal and external balance?
   (c) If the authorities took no action, what would be the adjustment process along the lines described by the "monetary approach to the balance of payments"? (You may refer here to your answer to problem 5.)

9. Explain why an expansionary fiscal policy reduces foreign income less than direct (unsterilized) intervention by the central bank in the foreign exchange markets to depreciate the exchange rate.

10. Assume that there is perfect mobility of capital. How does the imposition of a tariff affect the exchange rate, output, and the current account? (*Hint:* Given the exchange rate, the tariff reduces our demand for imports.)

11. Consult the *Wall Street Journal* or some other newspaper that lists foreign exchange rates on its financial pages. For some countries, such as Britain and Germany, you should find futures prices listed. That is the price to be paid today to receive one unit of the foreign currency in the future. A 30-day futures price for the pound sterling, say, is the price paid today to receive 1 pound 30 days from now. Explain why the futures prices are not generally equal to the spot prices—the price paid today to receive the foreign currency today. See whether you can explain the difference between the relationship of spot and futures prices for the pound and deutsche mark, respectively.

12. Assume you expect the pound to depreciate by 6 percent over the next year. Assume that the U.S. interest rate is 4 percent. What interest rate would be needed on pound securities—such as government bonds—for you to be willing to buy those securities with your dollars today and then sell them in a year in exchange for dollars? Can you relate your answer to this question to problem 11?

13. Should countries intervene to stabilize the exchange rate?

COMPUTER EXERCISES

1. Under the fixed exchange rate regime, increase *e* by 20 percent. Why do the *IS* and *BP* curves shift right while the *LM* curve shifts left? What can you say about the relative magnitudes of these shifts and their effects on the *AD* curve and on equilibrium GDP and *BP*?

2. Under floating exchange rates, how much must $\overline{A}$ increase to get the same increase in GDP as in exercise 1? What happens to *e* and *R* in this case compared with the fixed exchange rates case in exercise 1?

3. Experiment with changing the *cf* parameter which governs the sensitivity of capital flows to differences between the domestic and foreign interest rate ($i - i_f$). How does *cf* affect monetary and fiscal policies under *fixed* versus under *floating* rates?

GUIDE TO OPERATION FOR *PC-MACROECONOMICS,* VERSION 2.0

Self-Instruction Computer Exercises in Macroeconomics
by F. Gerard Adams and Eugene Kroch, with Christopher Geczy

INTRODUCTION

This set of computer-based exercises is designed to accompany the sixth edition of *Macroeconomics* by Rudiger Dornbusch and Stanley Fischer. The computer modules are organized by chapter and operate on IBM-compatible personal computers in the electronic spreadsheet environment of either Lotus 1-2-3 or Quattro.[1] The modules will run on either the professional or student version of these packages. Computer-based spreadsheet programs are ideal instruments for learning macroeconomics. No knowledge of the Lotus or Quattro program is necessary to use these modules, since they are entirely self-explanatory and customized for the textbook. They can be used as supplementary exercises, as preparation for exams, and for self-instruction.

This guide to operation will help the student (and the instructor) use the *PC-Macroeconomics* program. Virtually every chapter in the textbook has a corresponding computer module. Chapters 4 and 5 are combined, as are Chapters 8 and 9 on aggregate supply, Chapters 13 and 14 on money supply and demand, and Chapters 16 to 18 on analyzing the tradeoffs between inflation and unemployment and the consequences of government policy in an inflationary environment. Each module has three distinct modes of operation: (1) a demonstration mode, (2) an interactive mode, and (3) an open mode.

The demonstration mode (or DEMO) takes the student through the main topics in the chapter, illustrating each point with graphs, equations, and numerical examples.

---

[1]Lotus 1-2-3 is a trademark of Lotus Corporation. Quattro is a trademark of Borland Corporation.

All that is required of the user is to press the return key to progress through the presentation. The user can back up to any step in the presentation using the Escape key <Esc> and can break out of the demonstration at any time with <Ctrl>-<Break>.

The interactive mode (or INTERACT) requires more active input from the student. The student will encounter a set of exercises and questions to be answered using the computer module. The exogenous variables and model parameters can be changed; the results are then computed and shown numerically and graphically. These exercises can be printed out as "hard copy." More elaborate versions of these computer exercises are given at the end of the textbook chapters.

Finally, the OPEN mode is provided for those familiar enough with the Lotus or Quattro spreadsheet environment to experiment with the chapter models in more advanced and creative ways. Instructors may want to use this mode to modify models to meet their own teaching objectives.

TO THE INSTRUCTOR

Instructors should consider using these modules in the classroom (with suitable display equipment such as an oversized monitor or a projection display), as well as having students work with them on their own. The DEMO mode can be an effective way to liven up lectures with very little effort, since no user input is required and all explanations come up on the screen. You should, of course, review the DEMO yourself before showing it in class, and you may want to think of how to build part of a lecture around it. (Keep in mind that you can go backward in DEMO mode whenever you need to review a step in class. You can also break out at any time.) The INTERACT mode, too, can be helpful in the classroom, since you can generate examples and graphs to illustrate key concepts, such as how the effectiveness of monetary and fiscal policy depends on the slopes of the *IS* and *LM* curves.

The OPEN mode allows the instructor to explore the inner workings of each model more thoroughly. You can move around the spreadsheet to see how the relationships fit together and how the model is solved—highlighting a cell of the spreadsheet displays (upper left of the screen) the formula that generated the cell's value. If you are familiar with the spreadsheet environment, you can run the model from OPEN mode, making changes in the unprotected cells. If you are a sophisticated Lotus or Quattro user, you can modify the model to suit your particular pedagogical needs and even reprogram the macros to alter the way the program works. Even if you know very little about Lotus or Quattro, you can modify the tolerance limits that restrict changing the exogenous variables and parameter values. To do so simply press <Alt> -T and follow the prompts.

TO THE STUDENT

First, select the chapter you want—details of how to do that are given below. Next, go through the DEMO. Take your time. You may want to back up (using the escape key) at key points and even go through it several times until you fully understand what is being done. Having the textbook in front of you for reference can be a great help, since the DEMO explanations are quite terse and cannot substitute for textbook development of basic concepts. Remember that you can always go backward or break out of the DEMO at any time.

Next, go to the INTERACT mode. Try a few "Change" options in the model and "View" the resulting graphs. Do you understand what is going on? Note that the original model solution is always shown as the "base" along with "current" solution that reflects the changes you have put into the model.

Finally, go to "Exercises." If you have a printer attached to your computer, you may want to print them out, so that you have them in front of you when you do the calculations. Related exercises are also printed at the end of each textbook chapter. You do the calculations suggested by the exercises in the INTERACT mode. In many cases you must decide for yourself what changes you must make to answer the questions. Write up your answers on the basis of the results of your alternative comparisons.

PROGRAM FEATURES

The *PC-Macroeconomics* exercises have the following features:

- They are user friendly, with a readily accessible DEMO mode introducing each exercise. No computer programming and no knowledge of Lotus or Quattro is required—just press the return key to go forward and the escape key to back up.
- They have broad coverage—there are exercises for virtually every chapter of the Dornbusch and Fischer text.
- They are closely coordinated in content and notation with the text.
- They allow active student interaction with the computer in the INTERACT mode.
- They allow full access to modify the program in the OPEN mode.
- They combine display of the equations with numerical examples and graphical presentation in a consistent manner.
- They include questions and exercises for student analysis and practice.
- They include an up-to-date marcoeconomic data base, whose variables can be transformed and plotted in a variety of ways, including scatter plots with regression lines (Chapter 1).
- They include a macro computer game model which allows the student to experience the challenge of true-to-life economic policy making.
- They operate on any IBM PC, PS/2, or IBM compatible (with at least 256K of memory).
- They run on student editions of Lotus 1-2-3 or Quattro electronic spreadsheets.

GETTING STARTED

Equipment Required

These modules will run on all IBM personal computers (PC, XT, AT, PS/2, Portable, or Convertible) and on IBM-compatible PCs with at least 256K of random access memory (RAM). Although the modules will work with all monochrome as well as color displays, a graphics board and a monitor capable of displaying color graphics are highly recommended. If your computer is not capable of displaying graphics, the graphics functions of the program will be automatically disabled, but you will still be able to read the text displays and the tabulated results.

Software Required

To run the program you must have DOS 2.0 or higher and either Lotus 1-2-3 or Quattro in either the standard edition or the student edition. Note that when this *Guide to Operation* refers to Lotus, you should understand that the statements apply equally to Quattro users, except as noted in the section "To Quattro Users."

Be sure that your version of Lotus (or Quattro) is properly configured to display graphics on your computer. For example, if you have the standard color graphics adapter (CGA), you should check that your spreadsheet is installed with the CGA option; if you have enhanced color graphics (EGA or VGA), Lotus should be installed with the EGA or VGA option; if you have a monochrome monitor with a Hercules display adapter, your Lotus must have the HERCULES option. If you are uncertain about how Lotus has been installed on your machine, check the manual. You can rerun the install procedure to verify which installation options have been selected. At the same time you can change these options to conform to the requirements of your computer system.

To Quattro Users

Quattro users can install *PC-Macroeconomics* just as you would for Lotus, except that you must first run Quattro's "123 menu" installation program as well. [The Quattro manual tells you to type 123 menu on the DOS command line and respond to the displayed questions.] To use the program, type Q123 to start *PC-Macroeconomics* from Quattro. If you want *PC-Macroeconomics* to start automatically on a hard-disk system, be sure to copy the program modules to your hard disk and follow the steps described below for installing the program. [Quattro will not start *PC-Macroeconomics* automatically from a floppy diskette, even if you set the default drive to the floppy.] If you want to start *PC-Macroeconomics* from a floppy diskette, set the default drive to A or B (wherever you have placed the *PC-Macroeconomics* diskette), as described on page A-5. Then type "/fr" followed by the <Enter> key to start the program. Since the program was not originally designed for Quattro, occasionally text on the main screen will be obscured by a pop-up menu. In most cases this is a minor annoyance and the information can be seen as you proceed through the menu choices. To clear away the offending menu, however, you can always go to OPEN mode and then return to the program by pressing <Alt>-A.

Installing the Program

The program modules come standard on one $3\frac{1}{2}''$ diskette, but can be special ordered on two $5\frac{1}{4}''$ diskettes for users who do not have a $3\frac{1}{2}''$ disk drive. They can be used as is, but you should make identical copies of each diskette, using the DOS DISKCOPY[2] command; then run the program from the copy to keep anything from happening to your original diskette(s).

If you have a hard disk, you may want to put *PC-Macroeconomics* on the disk. Use the following procedure:

(1) Turn on your computer and wait for the c> prompt.
(2) Type
      md c:\pcmacro
followed by pressing the <Enter> key.
(3) Put the distribution diskette into the A drive and type
      copy a:*.* c:\pcmacro
and press the <Enter> key.
(4) If you have the $5\frac{1}{4}''$ diskettes, repeat step (3) for the second diskette.

Remember that in order to have the program start automatically upon entering Lotus, you must set the default drive and directory to "c:\pcmacro" for hard-disk operation and to "a:\" or "b:\" for floppy-diskette operation, as described below.

Setting the Default Drive for Lotus

To set the default drive for Lotus (or Quattro), you must start Lotus (or Quattro) and follow its menu options. You will enter the following key strokes:

    \wgdd

You will then see the prompt "Directory at startup:" If anything follows this prompt, you must press the Escape key <Esc> or backspace to the beginning of the prompt to erase the current default directory. Then type in

    c:\pcmacro

followed by the <Enter> key. To run *PC-Macroeconomics* from a floppy diskette, instead of typing "c:\pcmacro," type

    a:\   <Enter>   (to use the A drive)

or   b:\   <Enter>   (to use the B drive)

But be sure to put the diskette in the drive that you are using when you do this.

---

[2]See DOS manual for specific instructions.

You are still in a Lotus menu. You must now type.

uq

to update Lotus to use this directory when it starts up in the future. Now *PC-Macroeconomics* will start automatically when you start Lotus.

You can now start *PC-Macroeconomics* by leaving Lotus (/qy) and then starting Lotus again; the program will start up automatically. Alternatively, rather than leaving Lotus, you can just type

\fr

followed by the <Enter> key to start the program.

Starting the Program

This program runs under Lotus 1-2-3 or Quattro, so to start the program you must first start Lotus (or Quattro). How you start depends on whether or not you have a fixed disk with Lotus (or Quattro) installed on it.

- *For two floppy-diskette drives:* Put your Lotus system diskette in drive A (with DOS installed on it as instructed in the Lotus manual) and put one of the program diskettes in drive B. Then turn on the computer. Lotus should start up on its own and read the program diskette you placed in drive B to start up *PC-Macroeconomics.*

- *For hard-disk system:* Start Lotus in the usual way. If you have not copied the program modules onto the fixed disk, make sure that the default drive for Lotus is A (or B, in some cases). If you have copied the program diskettes onto the hard disk, make sure that the default drive is "c:\pcmacro," as indicated above under "Installing the Program."

If *PC-Macroeconomics* does not start up automatically, it is because Lotus is reading from a drive and directory that does not contain the *PC-Macroeconomics* program modules. Go back to the section on "Setting the Default Drive for Lotus" and follow the instructions. Lotus is a very friendly environment in that it guides the user with its menus, but you may want to consult the Lotus manual, if you have trouble setting up the default drive.

USING *PC-MACROECONOMICS*

Menu Operation

The operation of the computer program is through a series of nested menus. The first screen identifies the program and displays the MAIN MENU, which will prompt you to choose a chapter from one of the four main divisions of the textbook or the policy "GAME." Figure 1 shows the "tree" structure of the MAIN MENU. To choose Chapter 3 (Ch 3), for example, you must first select PART I (which is the part of the textbook that contains this chapter) and then select Ch 3. Once you are in Chapter 3, you will work through the nested menu options, as illustrated in Figure 2; selecting an option either executes it or generates a new menu from whose options you can again make selections. These options vary somewhat from chapter to chapter, but the basic structure does not change, and all chapters have the three modes of operation described in the "Introduction": DEMO, INTERACT, and OPEN.[3]

You select items from the menu by using the arrow keys (→ and ←), which control the cursor or highlighter. When the option you want is highlighted, press the <Enter> key to select it. You will notice that as you highlight a given menu option, a brief explanation will appear below the menu items. For example, when Ch 3 is highlighted, underneath will appear the chapter title, "Income and Spending." So if you are not sure which chapter you want, you can find out by moving across the menu options with the arrow keys until you find the right title. Once you are in the chapter, you will notice that highlighting the menu choices generates explanations of what they do.

Once you have become familiar with the program menus, you can select options using a short-cut method: Just press the first letter of the menu option to select it; for example, press "v" for "View." But be careful using this method. In a few places more than one option begins with the same letter; for example, in the MAIN MENU all the chapter options begin with "c." In such cases you must use the arrow keys to make a selection (otherwise you will get the first item that begins with the letter pressed, whether or not you want it).

Loading a Chapter

Once you have chosen a chapter by highlighting it in the menu and pressing <Enter>, the program will ask you to be sure the diskette is in the active drive. The screen will display the chapter that you have selected to verify your choice. If the chapter you have chosen is not on the diskette that you put into the drive, or if you are using a hard-disk system but have not set up the proper default directory (see "Getting Started" above), *PC-Macroeconomics* will give you an error message and allow you to check your diskette and/or drive designation.

After you select and load the chapter you want, you will be asked to wait while the chapter module is being loaded into memory. When the program is ready, the "WAIT" message in the upper right-hand corner will change to "MENU" to indicate that a new menu is in place. You will see a screen with a brief introduction to the chapter material. The menu appears above this introduction with the prompt "Choose a menu heading."

---

[3]Chapters 2, 11, and 20 each contain two parts. You must choose which part of the chapter to work on before you choose the mode of operation, as explained on the introductory screens for these chapters.

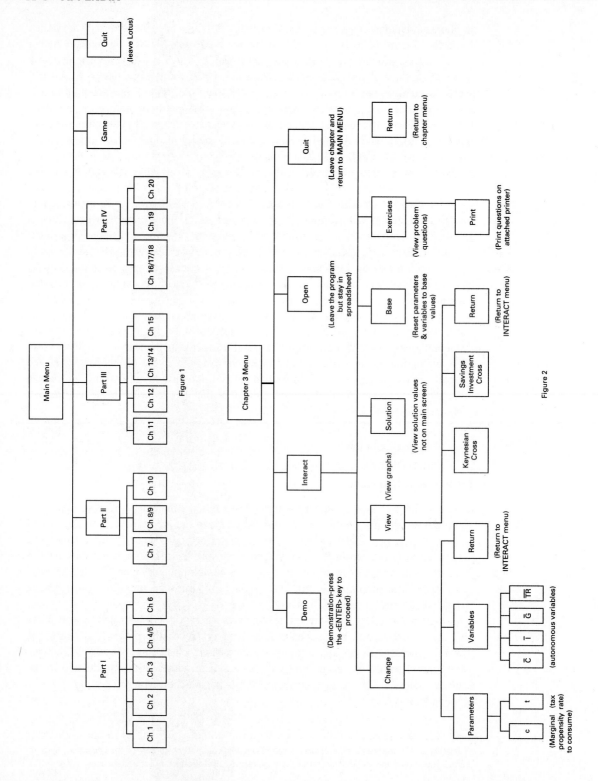

Figure 1

Figure 2

Running the Chapter

Once again refer to Figure 2 to see how the nested menus are organized for a typical chapter, such as Chapter 3. Use the arrow keys (➔ and ←) to select items from the menu—as you highlight each item, a brief explanation will appear on the line below the options—and choose an option by highlighting it and pressing the <Enter> key.

You should begin by choosing the DEMO option. This will give you a chapter orientation and introduce you to the capabilities of the module; you will be prompted to press <Enter> to proceed through the demonstration until the original chapter menu appears again. Every time a graph appears, you must press <Enter> (or any key) to clear the graph from the screen and proceed. You can go backward at any time to see a previous screen by pressing <Esc> (but not when a graph is on the screen—you must clear it first by pressing any key). Each time you press <Esc> you will back up one panel in the DEMO. If at any time you want to break out of the DEMO, press <Ctrl>-<Break> (hold down the <Ctrl> key and press the <Break> key.

If you choose the OPEN mode, you will leave the menus altogether and will be free to operate in the Lotus spreadsheet and even change the model (see "To the Instructor" above). This mode is also useful for printing out graphs. To return to the program, press <Alt>-A (hold down the <Alt> key and press A).

Choosing INTERACT will bring you to the second level of the menu, as shown in Figure 2. You will then be offered the following options:

- **CHANGE** asks which variable or parameter in the model the student would like to change and then calls for a numerical entry.

- **VIEW** presents graphs contrasting the base (original) solution with the current (changed) solution.

- **SOLUTION** displays solution values not on the main screen.

- **BASE** resets all current values to the original base values.

- **EXERCISES** brings the appropriate exercises to the screen and allows them to be printed out.

- **RETURN** returns to the chapter menu.

INTERACT menus differ somewhat by chapter to allow for the special aspects of each chapter presentation. For example, the model in the GAME module does not solve automatically, so it has a SOLVE option.

Chapter 1 is quite different from the other chapters in that it contains an up-to-date macroeconomic data base that can be used to illustrate basic macroeconomic trends and relationships. This module allows you to plot up to three time series on the same graph or to plot one series against another in a scatter plot. The decades are color coded in the scatter plot and you can even ask the program to fit a regression line through the points and display its equation. Finally this module allows you to perform eight different kinds of data transformations that include the four basic arithmetic operations, the natural logarithm, first differences, percentage changes, and index creation based on 1987. Any combination of these operations can be performed and the resulting series can be named and stored for use in the graphs.

CONVENTIONS

- \<Alt\>-A restarts the program (from OPEN mode).

- \<Enter\> key advances the program. When in doubt, press \<Enter\>.

- All input must end by pressing \<Enter\>, since the computer cannot know that you have finished without that signal.

- If you press a key that is not valid, the computer will beep and wait for you to press a valid key. For example, if you are typing in a number and press the letter o rather than a zero (0), the computer will beep.

- The \<Esc\> key ("Escape") backs up the DEMO and also backs you out through the nested menus of the INTERACT mode. Pressing \<Esc\> is an alternative to using the "Return" option.

- In the DEMO mode, you use the \<Enter\> key to proceed and the \<Esc\> key to back up; to stop in the middle press \<Ctrl\>-\<Break\>.

- Pressing any key will remove a displayed graph from the screen and restore the text and the menus.

- Occasionally you will be asked to wait while the computer sets up the screen or resets the model or creates a data series or a graph. You will know that you can proceed when READY or MENU is displayed in the upper right-hand corner of the screen.

PC-MACROECONOMICS CONTENTS

Following the organization of *Macroeconomics*, Sixth Edition, by R. Dornbusch and S. Fischer, *PC-Macroeconomics* is organized into four main parts:

Part I—Introducing the Economy: Facts and First Models
Chapter 1 Introduction
Presentation of basic macroeconomic relationships; access to the data base; graphing variables over time; scatter plots to illustrate relationships between variables.
Chapter 2 National Income Accounting
Presentation of the National Income and Product Accounts; sectoral income statements; finding and correcting accounting errors; constructing price indexes.
Chapter 3 Income and Spending
Income determination and equilibrium in the goods market; presentation of the Keynesian cross and the multiplier; experimenting with a simple macroeconomic model.
Chapter 4 Money, Interest, and Income
Chapter 5 Monetary and Fiscal Policy
Extension of the Keynesian model to include equilibrium in money markets as well as in goods markets; the IS/LM diagram; the role of interest rates in determining equilibrium; using IS/LM to understand the effects of fiscal and monetary policies; the fiscal-policy multiplier.

Chapter 6 International Linkages
  Extension of the IS/LM model to account for the effects of foreign trade; imports and exports and the trade balance; international capital flows and balance of payments.

Part II—Aggregate Demand, Supply, and Growth

Chapter 7 Aggregate Demand and Supply: An Introduction
  Derivation of the aggregate demand curve from IS/LM; the effects of changes in the price level; the aggregate supply curve under a variety of assumptions.

Chapter 8 Aggregate Supply: Wages, Prices, and Employment

Chapter 9 The Rational Expectations Equilibrium Approach
  Developing the aggregate supply relation; linkages between aggregate supply and the labor market; the shifting aggregate supply curve; the evolution of prices and output over time; the Lucas supply curve.

Chapter 10 Long-Term Growth and Productivity
  Determinants of the long-run growth potential of the economy; the neoclassical growth model; attaining a steady-state growth path; capital deepening and worker productivity.

PART III—Behavioral Foundations

Chapter 11 Consumption and Saving
  Foundations of consumption analysis; refinements to the Keynesian consumption function; the life-cycle model of consumption; the permanent income model of consumption.

Chapter 12 Investment Spending
  Foundations for investment spending; the desired level of the capital stock; accelerator models and business cycles; the simple accelerator versus the flexible accelerator.

Chapter 13 The Demand for Money

Chapter 14 The Fed, Money, and Credit
  Foundations for the demand for real money balances; bank reserves and the determinants of the money supply; the money multiplier; interest rates and equilibrium in the market for money.

Chapter 15 Stabilization Policy: Prospects and Problems
  Problems of policy making; lags in the effects of fiscal and monetary policy on the economy; tracking the economic performance over time.

PART IV—Inflation, Unemployment, Budget Deficits, and International Adjustment

Chapter 16 Inflation and Unemployment

Chapter 17 The Tradeoffs between Inflation and Unemployment

Chapter 18 Money, Deficits, and Inflation: Evidence and Policy Issues
  Effects of expectations on inflation and unemployment; dynamic aggregate supply and the expectations-augmented Phillips curve; dynamic aggregate demand; monetary growth and long-run inflation; fiscal expansion; dynamic adjustment and cycles.

Chapter 19 Budget Deficits and the Public Debt
  Assessing the burden of the debt; deficits and the public debt over time; the effects of inflation and of interest rate variation on the debt burden; growing out of deficits.

Chapter 20 International Adjustment and Interdependence
Representing the open economy under price variation; the real effective exchange rate; fixed exchange rate regimes versus floating exchange rates; combining balance-of-payments equilibrium with aggregate demand and supply equilibrium.

POLICY GAME
Policy modeling computer game using a complete macroeconomic system; meeting multiple objectives with a variety of policy options; dynamic adjustments with lags; assessing economic performance and comparing alternative policy scenarios.

POLICY GAME EXERCISES

1. Look closely at the equation structure of the model. Identify the following feedback linkages:
   a. the effect of changes in government spending on investment;
   b. the effect of the exchange rate on inflation;
   c. the impact of money policy on the balance of payments;
   d. the effect of inflation on the interest rate.
2. Compare the timing of the impact of changes in fiscal and monetary policy. Compare their implication on the balance of payments.
3. A threat from abroad causes the administration to increase defense spending to push the economy beyond its potential output. What are the appropriate policy responses?
4. The economy suffers from a "supply shock." Foreign prices go up by 5 percent from 1991 to 1995. What is the impact on economic activity and inflation. What is the welfare loss?
5. A challenge: How close can you come to the targets? Try to reduce the welfare loss as closely to zero as you can.

TROUBLE SHOOTING

Problems you may encounter can usually be solved by consulting the Lotus 1-2-3 manual. Here is some guidance.

Problem	Cause	Remedy
Graphs do not appear	using a computer without graphics capability	none
	Lotus 1-2-3 not configured for computer being used Example: Lotus is configured for color and used on mono computer	reconfigure Lotus 1-2-3 using the Lotus "Install" program

(continued on next page)

Problem	Cause	Remedy
Program does not start	DOS not loaded	start the computer with the DOS system diskette or Lotus system diskette that has DOS installed on it
	Lotus 1-2-3 not running	start up Lotus 1-2-3 version 2, student or regular version
	Lotus 1-2-3 Version 1 being used	substitute Lotus version 2
	computer is defective	check plug, start entire process over
		press <Alt>-<Ctrl>-<Del> to start over
Program hangs up	unlikely, but possible from inadvertently hitting inappropriate keys	press <Alt>-A
		turn off computer and start over
		press <Alt>-<Ctrl>-<Del> to start over
Critical part of graph appears outside of graph range	combinations of changes that lead to extreme model responses	try other values
INTERACT program says "the number you have entered is out of reasonable range for . . ."	you have picked an extreme value, one which will not show on the graphs	try another value
	you have forgotten the sign	put in the sign followed by the value
	you have put in the level of the variable when the program called for the change or vice versa	put in an acceptable value as prompted
Nothing happens	program is processing	sign says "wait" so be patient
	program is waiting for you to do something	press <Enter>
Program beeps	you have pressed the wrong key	try another key
Program skips ahead	you pressed the key more than once or held down the key too long	press the key without holding it down and wait for the program to respond

INDEX

SELECTED HISTORICAL SERIES ON GROSS DOMESTIC PRODUCT AND RELATED SERIES, 1929–1958 (billions of dollars; except as noted)

| | gross domestic product | | | | | | constant 1987 dollars | | | | | | | |
| | | | | PERCENT CHANGE FROM PRECEDING PERIOD | | | per-sonal con-sump-tion ex-pendi-tures | gross private domestic invest-ment | net exports | gov-ern-ment pur-chases | DISPOSABLE PERSONAL INCOME | | saving as per-cent of dispos-able per-sonal income[a] | popula-tion (thou-sands)[b] |
year	cur-rent dol-lars	1987 dollars	im-plicit price deflator (1987 = 100)	current dollars	1987 dollars	implicit price de-flator					total	per cap-ita (dol-lars)		
1929	103.1	821.8	12.5				554.5	152.8	1.9	112.6	585.8	4,807	3.0	121,878
1930	90.4	748.9	12.1	−12.4	−8.9	−3.2	520.0	107.2	−.3	122.0	542.2	4,402	2.5	123,188
1931	75.8	691.3	11.0	−16.2	−7.7	−9.1	501.0	67.2	−2.3	125.5	519.7	4,186	2.1	124,149
1932	58.0	599.7	9.7	−23.5	−13.3	−11.8	456.6	25.0	−2.4	120.5	449.8	3,600	−3.1	124,949
1933	55.6	587.1	9.5	−4.1	−2.1	−2.1	447.4	26.6	−3.0	116.1	437.0	3,477	−3.9	125,690
1934	65.1	632.6	10.3	17.1	7.7	8.4	461.1	41.1	−1.0	131.4	462.0	3,652	−1.1	126,485
1935	72.3	681.3	10.6	11.1	7.7	2.9	487.6	65.2	−7.2	135.7	505.2	3,967	2.3	127,362
1936	82.7	777.9	10.6	14.4	14.2	.0	534.4	89.9	−5.1	158.6	565.9	4,415	4.4	128,181
1937	90.8	811.4	11.2	9.8	4.3	5.7	554.6	106.4	−1.9	152.2	585.5	4,540	4.0	128,961
1938	84.9	778.9	10.9	−6.5	−4.0	−2.7	542.2	69.9	4.2	162.5	547.6	4,213	−.3	129,969
1939	90.8	840.7	10.8	7.0	7.9	−.9	568.7	93.4	4.6	174.0	590.3	4,505	2.4	131,028
1940	100.0	906.0	11.0	10.2	7.8	1.9	595.2	121.8	8.2	180.7	627.2	4,747	3.8	132,122
1941	125.0	1,070.6	11.7	25.0	18.2	6.4	629.3	149.4	2.8	289.1	713.9	5,352	10.7	133,402
1942	158.5	1,284.9	12.3	26.8	20.0	5.1	628.7	81.4	−11.1	586.0	824.7	6,115	23.1	134,860
1943	192.4	1,540.5	12.5	21.3	19.9	1.6	647.3	53.5	−28.1	867.7	863.8	6,317	24.5	136,739
1944	211.0	1,670.0	12.6	9.7	8.4	.8	671.2	59.8	−29.0	968.0	901.8	6,516	25.0	138,397
1945	213.1	1,602.6	13.3	1.0	−4.0	5.6	714.6	82.6	−23.9	829.4	890.9	6,367	19.2	139,928
1946	211.9	1,272.1	16.7	−.6	−20.6	25.6	779.1	195.5	26.5	271.0	860.0	6,083	8.5	141,389
1947	234.3	1,252.8	18.7	10.6	−1.5	12.0	793.3	198.8	41.9	218.8	826.1	5,732	3.0	144,126
1948	260.3	1,300.0	20.0	11.1	3.8	7.0	813.0	229.8	16.6	240.6	872.9	5,953	5.8	146,631
1949	259.3	1,305.5	19.9	−.4	.4	−.5	831.4	187.4	17.3	269.3	874.5	5,862	3.7	149,188
1950	287.0	1,418.5	20.2	10.7	8.7	1.5	874.3	256.4	3.2	284.5	942.5	6,214	5.9	151,684
1951	331.6	1,558.4	21.3	15.5	9.9	5.4	894.7	255.6	11.1	397.0	978.2	6,340	7.3	154,287
1952	349.7	1,624.9	21.5	5.4	4.3	.9	923.4	231.6	2.3	467.6	1,009.7	6,433	7.2	156,954
1953	370.0	1,685.5	22.0	5.8	3.7	2.3	962.5	240.3	−7.1	489.8	1,053.5	6,603	7.0	159,565
1954	370.9	1,673.8	22.2	.2	−.7	.9	987.3	234.1	−2.3	454.7	1,071.5	6,598	6.2	162,391
1955	404.3	1,768.3	22.9	9.0	5.6	3.2	1,047.0	284.8	−5.2	441.7	1,130.8	6,842	5.7	165,275
1956	426.2	1,803.6	23.6	5.4	2.0	3.1	1,078.7	282.2	−1.2	444.0	1,185.2	7,046	7.1	168,221
1957	448.6	1,838.2	24.4	5.2	1.9	3.4	1,104.4	266.9	1.6	465.3	1,214.6	7,091	7.2	171,274
1958	454.7	1,829.1	24.9	1.4	−.5	2.0	1,122.2	245.7	−14.9	476.0	1,236.0	7,098	7.4	174,141

[a] Percents based on data in millions of dollars.

[b] Population of the United States including Armed Forces overseas; includes Alaska and Hawaii beginning 1960.

SOURCE: Department of Commerce, Bureau of Economic Analysis.

NATIONAL WEALTH IN 1987 DOLLARS, 1960–1992 (billions of 1987 dollars)

| | | private net worth[b] | | | | | | government net financial assets | | |
| | | TANGIBLE WEALTH[c] | | | FINANCIAL WEALTH | | | | | |
end of year	total net worth[a]	total	total[d]	owner-occupied real estate	con-sumer durables	total[e]	corpo-rate equity[f]	non-corpo-rate equity	total[g]	federal	state and local
1960	6,049.8	7,025.3	2,796.9	1,870.5	742.1	4,228.4	1,514.9	1,330.3	−975.5	−818.4	−160.5
1961	6,525.9	7,513.5	2,861.7	1,926.7	739.8	4,651.9	1,882.7	1,336.8	−987.6	−819.5	−171.8
1962	6,369.7	7,361.3	2,931.7	1,977.5	746.5	4,429.5	1,612.9	1,346.9	−991.5	−815.1	−180.1
1963	6,801.5	7,792.4	3,029.1	2,033.5	773.8	4,763.3	1,867.3	1,363.3	−990.9	−807.6	−187.3
1964	7,121.7	8,114.9	3,113.5	2,080.4	796.1	5,001.4	2,007.5	1,380.1	−993.2	−803.6	−194.0
1965	7,506.9	8,475.8	3,180.6	2,109.3	817.0	5,295.2	2,196.9	1,415.2	−968.9	−776.1	−197.2
1966	7,449.3	8,402.7	3,306.0	2,173.0	861.7	5,096.7	1,916.0	1,443.3	−953.3	−755.0	−203.0
1967	8,109.0	9,065.5	3,417.4	2,220.0	913.5	5,648.1	2,320.3	1,460.0	−956.5	−748.7	−212.9
1968	8,731.3	9,673.0	3,625.8	2,358.0	963.8	6,047.2	2,627.0	1,495.7	−941.7	−731.0	−216.3
1969	8,458.0	9,361.8	3,751.6	2,421.9	1,002.0	5,610.2	2,171.1	1,500.6	−903.8	−681.9	−228.0
1970	8,392.0	9,302.5	3,790.6	2,415.5	1,031.6	5,511.9	2,014.4	1,490.3	−910.5	−675.6	−241.8
1971	8,784.7	9,724.2	3,903.7	2,502.4	1,036.1	5,820.5	2,186.8	1,537.1	−939.5	−693.9	−253.2
1972	9,416.8	10,346.9	4,194.2	2,735.3	1,064.4	6,152.6	2,301.8	1,644.4	−930.1	−699.7	−238.3
1973	9,172.6	10,037.0	4,405.3	2,887.2	1,094.2	5,631.6	1,644.9	1,833.5	−864.4	−664.0	−210.7
1974	8,723.9	9,536.2	4,553.9	2,964.9	1,150.5	4,982.2	1,040.2	1,832.3	−812.3	−626.8	−199.4
1975	9,197.6	10,110.4	4,713.4	3,104.5	1,170.3	5,397.1	1,255.8	1,863.3	−912.8	−733.2	−196.1
1976	9,750.2	10,722.8	4,986.1	3,331.9	1,208.9	5,736.7	1,403.9	1,964.4	−972.6	−802.2	−188.9
1977	9,990.3	10,972.1	5,359.9	3,640.8	1,255.2	5,612.3	1,226.5	2,042.9	−981.8	−844.6	−155.2
1978	10,495.1	11,447.7	5,742.9	3,957.6	1,296.0	5,704.8	1,120.8	2,224.5	−952.6	−836.1	−134.8
1979	11,287.9	12,185.4	6,127.2	4,253.7	1,351.5	6,058.2	1,252.9	2,387.6	−897.5	−800.1	−115.9
1980	11,878.9	12,773.9	6,250.9	4,378.1	1,343.4	6,523.0	1,540.9	2,470.2	−895.0	−804.6	−108.1
1981	11,692.4	12,621.9	6,246.5	4,386.0	1,326.3	6,375.3	1,347.7	2,463.9	−929.4	−834.6	−112.7
1982	11,922.8	12,985.3	6,290.9	4,419.4	1,326.0	6,694.4	1,397.8	2,360.9	−1,062.5	−969.6	−111.8
1983	12,241.3	13,469.7	6,390.3	4,494.8	1,339.8	7,079.3	1,532.9	2,318.1	−1,228.4	−1,147.5	−100.3
1984	12,428.1	13,795.5	6,660.9	4,709.7	1,380.9	7,134.6	1,489.4	2,191.1	−1,367.3	−1,298.1	−90.5
1985	13,165.6	14,689.2	6,916.3	4,877.5	1,452.1	7,773.0	1,898.0	2,149.6	−1,523.7	−1,472.3	−71.4
1986	13,766.6	15,479.3	7,237.6	5,080.9	1,552.3	8,241.7	2,141.9	2,156.3	−1,712.7	−1,671.1	−61.7
1987	13,979.0	15,830.6	7,549.4	5,300.4	1,631.8	8,281.2	1,973.1	2,215.4	−1,851.6	−1,795.9	−77.0
1988	14,237.9	16,195.0	7,652.0	5,313.7	1,702.8	8,543.0	2,012.1	2,234.6	−1,957.2	−1,901.2	−79.2
1989	15,024.3	17,088.7	7,887.9	5,494.0	1,743.1	9,200.8	2,254.5	2,280.8	−2,064.4	−1,981.8	−107.5
1990	14,093.8	16,268.8	7,553.9	5,185.8	1,753.6	8,714.9	2,034.5	2,115.2	−2,175.0	−2,061.1	−140.5
1991	14,766.2	17,109.0	7,752.3	5,417.6	1,777.8	9,356.8	2,563.6	1,987.1	−2,342.8	−2,200.7	−170.4
1992	14,910.2	17,537.8	7,772.6	5,485.3	1,794.4	9,745.2	2,811.4	1,853.8	−2,627.4	−2,462.8	−196.1

[a] Sum of private net worth and government net financial assets.

[b] Referred to as household net worth in the *Balance Sheets*.

[c] Held by households and nonprofit institutions.

[d] Also includes nonprofit institutions' real estate.

[e] Also includes credit market instruments, life insurance and pension reserves, security credit, and miscellaneous assets, and is net of liabilities.

[f] Includes households and nonprofit institutions' direct (or through mutual funds) holdings of corporate equity. Equity held through pension and life insurance reserves is not included.

[g] Also includes sponsored credit agencies and the Federal Reserve. Some tangible wealth is included for these agencies.

NOTE: Data are from *Balance Sheets for the U.S. Economy, 1960–91*, September 1992; deflated by the GDP implicit deflator. (The deflator was averaged for fourth quarter of year shown and first quarter of following year.)
Data are measured at market value where available. For example, corporate equity and land are measured at market value, but bonds are measured at par value.

SOURCE: *Economic Report of the President*, 1993. Updated by the author from *Balance Sheets for the U.S. Economy, 1945–92*.